DATE DUE

MAR 0 1 2001			
6-12-01 Ⅱ:8257026			
9-10-04 IL: 7071634			

Demco, Inc. 38-293

Emergencies in
Mental Health Practice

EMERGENCIES IN MENTAL HEALTH PRACTICE

Evaluation and Management

Edited by
PHILLIP M. KLEESPIES

THE GUILFORD PRESS
New York   London

Emergencies in mental
health practice :

*To my parents, Tillie and Philipp;
my wife, Penelope; and my children,
Ingrid and Gavin*

©1998 The Guilford Press
A Division of Guilford Publications, Inc.
72 Spring Street, New York, NY 10012
http://www.guilford.com

Printed in the United States of America

This book is printed on acid-free paper.

Last digit is print number: 9 8 7 6 5 4 3 2 1

Library of Congress Cataloging-in-Publication Data
Emergencies in mental health practice : evaluation and
   management / Phillip M. Kleespies, editor
      p.   cm.
   Includes bibliographical references and index.
   ISBN 1-57230-255-0
   1. Psychiatric emergencies.   I. Kleespies, Phillip M.
   [DNLM: 1. Crisis Intervention.   2. Emergencies.   3. Suicide—
prevention & control.   4. Violence—prevention & control.
5. Self-Injurious Behavior—prevention & control.
6. Substance Abuse—prevention & control.   WM 401 M2669 1998]
RC480.6.M33   1998
616.89'025—dc21
DNLM/DLC
for Library of Congress   97-33643
                                                              CIP

CONTRIBUTORS

Esme J. Blackburn, MSW, MA, Emergency Services Clinician, South Shore Mental Health Center, Quincy, MA; Doctoral Candidate in Clinical Psychology, University of Massachusetts at Boston, Boston, MA

Bruce Bongar, PhD, ABPP, Professor, Pacific Graduate School of Psychology, Palo Alto, CA; Consulting Professor of Psychiatry and the Behavioral Sciences, Stanford University School of Medicine, Stanford, CA; Diplomate in Family Psychology, American Board of Professional Psychology

Joan Laidig Brady, PhD, Assistant Professor of Psychology, Wheaton College, Wheaton, IL

Jay Callahan, PhD, Assistant Professor of Social Work, University of Illinois at Chicago, Chicago, IL

Amy Ehrlich Charney, PhD, Licensed Psychologist, Traumatic Stress Institute/Center for Adult and Adolescent Psychotherapy, South Windsor, CT

Catherine Chase, DO, Clinical Assistant Professor, Department of Psychiatry and Human Behavior, Brown University School of Medicine and The Miriam Hospital, Providence, RI

David C. Clark, PhD, Director, Center for Suicide Research and Prevention, and Director of Research, Rush Institute for Mental Well-Being, Rush–Presbyterian-St. Luke's Medical Center, Chicago, IL; Stanley G. Harris Family Professor of Psychiatry and Psychology, Rush Medical College, Chicago, IL

Matthew M. Clark, PhD, Assistant Professor, Department of Psychiatry and Human Behavior, Brown University School of Medicine and The Miriam Hospital, Providence, RI

Ronald Cohen, PhD, Associate Professor, Department of Psychiatry and Human Behavior, Brown University School of Medicine and The Miriam Hospital, Providence, RI

Pamela J. Deiter, PhD, Licensed Psychologist and Postdoctoral Fellow, Traumatic Stress Institute/Center for Adult and Adolescent Psychotherapy, South Windsor, CT

James D. Deleppo, EdD, Clinical Psychologist, Acute Inpatient Psychiatry, Boston Department of Veterans Affairs (VA) Medical Center, Boston, MA; Clinical Instructor of Psychiatry, Tufts University School of Medicine, Boston, MA

Sara Eddy, EdD, JD, Counseling Psychologist and Attorney, Law and Psychiatry Service, Massachusetts General Hospital, Boston, MA; Faculty member, Harvard Medical School, Boston, MA; Fellow, Massachusetts Psychological Association

Sheila Greaney, PhD, Clinical Psychologist, U.S. Armed Forces and Walter Reed Army Medical Center, Washington, DC

James D. Guy, PhD, ABPP, Dean and Professor of Psychology, Graduate School of Psychology, Fuller Theological Seminary, Pasadena, CA; Diplomate in Clinical Psychology, American Board of Professional Psychology; Fellow, American Psychological Association

Eric Harris, JD, EdD, Attorney and Psychologist in Private Practice, Risk Management Consultant to the American Psychological Association Insurance Trust; Counsel, Choate Health Management, Inc.; Faculty member, Massachusetts School of Professional Psychology, Newton, MA

Mary R. Harvey, PhD, Director, Victims of Violence Program, The Cambridge Hospital, Cambridge, MA; Assistant Clinical Professor of Psychology, Department of Psychiatry, Harvard Medical School, Boston, MA

Phillip M. Kleespies, PhD, ABPP, Coordinator of Emergency Room Services for Psychology and Clinical Psychologist, Acute Inpatient Psychiatry, Boston VA Medical Center, Boston, MA; Assistant Clinical Professor of Psychiatry, Boston University School of Medicine, Boston, MA; Assistant Clinical Professor of Psychiatry, Tufts University School of Medicine, Boston, MA; Diplomate in Clinical Psychology, American Board of Professional Psychology

Maxine Krengel, PhD, Clinical Neuropsychologist, Boston VA Medical Center and Boston Environmental Hazards Center, Boston, MA; Clinical Instructor of Neurology, Boston University School of Medicine, Boston, MA; Assistant Clinical Professor of Psychiatry, Tufts University School of Medicine, Boston, MA

Robert M. Levin, MD, Chief, Endocrine Clinic, Boston Medical Center, Boston, MA; Associate Professor of Medicine, Boston University School of Medicine, Boston, MA

Karen S. Marans, PhD, Clinical Neuropsychologist, Boston VA Medical Center and Boston Medical Center, Boston, MA; Clinical Instructor of Neurology, Boston University School of Medicine, Boston, MA

Dale E. McNiel, PhD, Director of Psychological Services, Langley Porter Psychiatric Institute, San Francisco, CA; Adjunct Professor of Psychology, Department of Psychiatry, School of Medicine, University of California at San Francisco, San Francisco, CA

DeAnna L. Mori, PhD, Director of Medical Psychology, Boston VA Medical Center, Boston, MA; Assistant Clinical Professor of Psychiatry, Tufts University School of Medicine, Boston, MA

Justin M. Nash, PhD, Clinical Assistant Professor, Department of Psychiatry and Human Behavior, Brown University School of Medicine and The Miriam Hospital, Providence, RI

Raymond Niaura, PhD, Associate Professor, Department of Psychiatry and Human Behavior, Brown University School of Medicine and The Miriam Hospital, Providence, RI

Barbara L. Niles, PhD, Clinical Psychologist, National Center for Posttraumatic Stress Disorder, Boston VA Medical Center, Boston, MA; Clinical Instructor of Psychiatry, Tufts University School of Medicine, Boston, MA

Laurie Anne Pearlman, PhD, Research Director, Traumatic Stress Institute/Center for Adult and Adolescent Psychotherapy, South Windsor, CT; President, Trauma, Research, Education, and Training Institute, South Windsor, CT; Adjunct faculty member, Department of Psychology, University of Connecticut, Storrs, CT

Nico Peruzzi, BA, Doctoral Student, Pacific Graduate School of Psychology, Palo Alto, CA

Sabrina M. Popp, MD, Staff Psychiatrist, Substance Abuse Treatment Program, Boston VA Medical Center, Boston, MA; Assistant Professor of Psychiatry, Tufts University School of Medicine, Boston, MA

Gary S. Richardson, MD, Associate Physician, Division of Endocrinology, Brigham and Women's Hospital, Boston, MA; Instructor of Medicine, Harvard Medical School, Boston, MA

Jacqueline A. Samson, PhD, Associate Psychologist, McLean Hospital, Boston, MA; Assistant Professor of Psychology, Department of Psychiatry, Harvard Medical School, Boston, MA

Glenn R. Trezza, PhD, Staff Psychologist, Substance Abuse Treatment Program, Boston VA Medical Center, Boston, MA; Assistant Clinical Professor of Psychiatry, Tufts University School of Medicine, Boston, MA

Roberta F. White, PhD, ABPP, Director of Neuropsychology, Boston VA Medical Center, Boston, MA; Research Director, Boston Environmental Hazards Center, Boston, MA; Professor of Neurology (Neuropsychology) and Environmental Health, Boston University Schools of Medicine and Public Health, Boston, MA; Diplomate in Clinical Neuropsychology, American Board of Professional Psychology

Janet Yassen, LICSW, Coordinator of Crisis Services, Victims of Violence Program, Department of Psychiatry, The Cambridge Hospital, Cambridge, MA; Cofounder, Boston Area Rape Crisis Center, Boston, MA

ACKNOWLEDGMENTS

There are few complicated endeavors that one undertakes entirely alone—certainly not a book such as this. Clearly, there are a number of people whom I wish to acknowledge and thank.

First, I would like to express my gratitude to the excellent group of authors who agreed to contribute chapters to this volume. Many of them are already experts in their fields, and others are well on their way to becoming so. Their efforts have enriched this work. I would also like to thank Sharon Panulla, Senior Editor at The Guilford Press, who skillfully and courteously guided me through the publication process.

The inspiration for this book came from my clinical and supervisory work with psychology interns in Admissions and Dispositions and in the Emergency Department (ED) at the Boston Department of Veterans Affairs (VA) Medical Center. I consider myself fortunate to have had the opportunity to instruct so many fine young professionals in emergency psychological services. They have kept me thinking about the needs of psychologists and other mental health professionals for training in this area. I hope that they had some fun along the way; I know that I have.

I could not have done the training in emergency services at the Boston VA without the support of several staff colleagues. In this regard, I am indebted to Drs. James D. Deleppo, DeAnna L. Mori, and Barbara L. Niles for their assistance and support. They have also contributed their ideas and skills as coauthors to several chapters in this book. Dr. Mori and Dr. Niles were very generous in contributing their word-processing skills where mine (all too quickly) failed. Thanks also to Drs. Dudley Blake, Patricia Gallagher, and Stephen Quinn, all of whom have assisted with the training in emergency services at different times. Margo Turrentine, Kimberly McNulty, MA, and Dr. Stephen Lancey also deserve my acknowledgment for their help with a variety of word processing problems.

As noted above, the clinical work that was the source of the conceptualization of this book occurred in the ED at the Boston VA Medical Center. The work there was made much easier by the collaborative efforts of Dr. David Holmes, Dr. Douglas Hughes, and Dr. Glenn Saxe, and by consultations with Dr. Robert Mayer, all of whom have taught me a great deal. The charge nurse in the ED, Judy Ledwith, RN, and the rest of the ED nursing staff also deserve my thanks for their consistent support of our efforts. In addition, I have learned many things about managing emergencies from the Acute Inpatient Psychiatry staff at the Boston VA, especially the day and evening staff on Ward 13C, who have helped to make "Thursday" a special day of the week and who have never been reluctant to share their good-humored observations about the handling of admissions. My thanks as well to those who have helped to educate me and the psychology interns by giving lectures on emergency-related topics: John Bergen, RN, Richard Daunais, RN, Geraldine McCabe, RN, Dr. Sabrina M. Popp, Dr. Nancy Pratt, and Dr. Roberta F. White.

PHILLIP M. KLEESPIES, PhD
Cambridge, Massachusetts

CONTENTS

Part VI. The Impact of Emergency Service on the Clinician

INTRODUCTION

PHILLIP M. KLEESPIES

Assume that a male patient whom you have treated for several months comes to his regular therapy appointment. He has had problems with alcohol misuse in the past but has struggled and attained sobriety while in treatment. His marriage with a woman who is still actively drinking is troubled. She becomes verbally abusive to him when he refuses to go drinking with her. At times, she has thrown things and become assaultive. He has a history of being physically abusive to her, but thus far has not responded in kind to her recent violence. Now he has heard that she may be having an affair. He is outraged and states that if this proves true, he has thoughts of shooting her and himself. He plans to confront her about the issue tonight.

Although this exact scenario may not occur in your clinical practice, psychological emergencies such as patients' suicidal states and violent states are events that nearly all mental health practitioners will need to deal with at some point in their professional lives. During their training years alone, nearly 97% of the psychologists in one survey (Kleespies, Penk, & Forsyth, 1993) worked with patients who had either an episode of suicidal ideation, a suicide attempt, or a suicide completion. More than one in four had a patient make a suicide attempt, and one in nine had an actual patient suicide. In a national survey of patient violence, Pope and Tabachnick (1993) found that 83% of their sample of psychologists had had episodes in which they felt afraid that a patient might attack them, and 89% had had episodes in which they felt afraid that a patient might attack a third party. Guy, Brown, and Poelstra (1990) reported that nearly 50% of their sample of psychologists (with a mean of 16.8 years of practice) had been threatened with physical attack by a patient, and 40% indicated that they had actually been attacked. These same authors as well as others (e.g., Bernstein, 1981) also found a significant negative relationship between level of professional experience and the likelihood of being attacked (i.e., the greatest number of attacks occurred during the training years; more generally, the less the experience, the greater the likelihood of being assaulted).

In spite of the findings noted above we (Kleespies et al., 1993), in our study of the stress of patient suicidal behavior during clinical training, reported that only an estimated 55% of our sample of former graduate students in clinical or counseling psychology had some form of didactic instruction on suicide in their graduate school years. The instruction (when given) was typically minimal (i.e., one or two lectures). In a similar vein, Bongar and Harmatz (1991) conducted national surveys of the Council of University Directors of Clinical Psychology Programs and the National Council of Schools of Professional Psychology; they found that when all the efforts of these groups were combined, only 40% of all graduate programs in clinical psychology offered any formal training in the study of suicide. In their survey of patient violence, Guy et al. (1990) reported that the psychologists in their sample had a mean of 1 hour of clinical training on the management of patient violence during their predoctoral training years. In the field of psychiatric social work, Star (1984) and Walsh (1985) have both observed that skills in assessing and managing dangerous patients are needed in practice, yet professional training in these skills has been lacking.

Not only do mental health practitioners such as psychologists and clinical social workers need more systematic training in the management of patient suicidal or violent states, but they also need better preparation for handling the affects that are aroused by work with such conditions (Pope & Tabachnick, 1993) and for dealing with the psychological aftermath of such events as patient suicide or patient violence (Kleespies et al., 1993; Guy et al., 1990). The same, of course, can be said in terms of assisting those patients who run the risk of becoming victims of domestic violence, or who have been acutely victimized and may be revictimized. Education and training in psychological emergency work can provide the forum in which this sort of "affective education" can occur. Research has provided support to the notion that anxiety associated with working with dying patients is reduced by increased educational preparation (Benoliel, 1988; Dickinson & Pearson, 1980; Miles, 1980). Increased preparation for working with suicidal patients, violent patients, or victims of violence would seem to be parallel cases.

Several authors (e.g., Bongar, Lomax, & Harmatz, 1992; Chemtob, Bauer, Hamada, Pelowski, & Muraoka, 1989; Kleespies, 1993) have pointed out that graduate and professional schools of psychology, as well as clinical sites, have a responsibility to make training in the study of suicide and effective suicide risk management a more routine part of the educational process. Bongar et al. (1992) have gone so far as to recommend that all psychology training programs require trainees to receive formal didactic and supervised experience in the management of suicidal states. In the case of patient violence, Whitman, Armao, and Dent (1976) and Guy et al. (1990) have recommended that all practitioners obtain the training necessary to manage patient threats and violence. Immediate response to and management of both suicidal and violent states, however, fall within the larger domain of emergency psychological services. It is a thesis of this book that those mental health disciplines that have not already done so need to incorporate training in the management of emergencies as a professional requirement.

In the 1970s, several authors attempted to draw the attention of the field of psychology to the benefits and importance of training psychologists who are mental health care providers in emergency services (Barlow, 1974; Pederson & Weiner, 1970; Zimet & Weissberg, 1979). Similar attempts seem to have been made in the field of psychiatric social work (Groner, 1978; Grumet & Trachtman, 1976). Perhaps the efforts of these clinicians have had some impact, but it seems to have been limited. Thus, for example, in a sample of American Psychological Association (APA)-accredited predoctoral internships in psychology, Covino (1989) found that approximately one-third of the internship agencies made their medical emergency area and/or psychiatric emergency area available as a training site for psychology interns. The majority of the remaining internships provided some limited experience in handling patients in crisis on an outpatient basis, or often no such experience at all. At least among psychology internship sites, there still does not appear to be routine and systematic training in emergency psychological services.

Kranz (1985) and Covino (1989) further suggest that graduate and professional school programs themselves are often deficient in teaching the skills needed for emergency services. This suggestion seems very likely to be the case, given the results of a survey of after-hours coverage in psychology training clinics in which Bernstein, Feldberg, and Brown (1991) concluded that "the current standard for training clinics in emergency coverage appears to be less than adequate" (p. 207). Twenty-five percent of the clinics in their sample provided no emergency coverage. Among those that did, there were reports of disarray in the emergency policies and procedures; concern that the services would not be sufficiently responsive; and uncertainty about continuity of student and supervisor availability, particularly during vacations and semester breaks. The authors have suggested that this state of affairs reflects a general inattention to emergency services in the field of professional psychology. Yet, if psychologists wish to provide the full range of services to patients with serious psychopathology, they must be prepared to meet the ethical responsibility of emergency intervention when such patients are in acute crises.

Zimet and Weissberg (1979) have taken this argument one step further and asserted that training in emergency services should not be limited only to those who work with seriously disturbed patients, but in fact should be part of the training of any psychologist who does psychotherapy. They have pointed out that even if patients are screened for degree of psychopathology, there is no absolute guarantee that a patient may not regress and/or become a risk to self or others. In the event of such an emergency, the therapist or clinician must be prepared to manage it effectively. This sort of skill, however, does not simply come with customary training in psychotherapy; it is obtained through specific training in the delivery of emergency services.

As Bongar and Harmatz (1991) have noted, the importance of training in dealing with emergency situations has been acknowledged in the APA's "Casebook for Providers of Psychological Services" (APA, Board of Professional Affairs, Committee on Professional Standards, 1987). This publication presents the case of a suicidal patient seen by a counseling psychologist, and, in reference to it, states that all counseling psychologists should have training that will prepare them to meet the demands of psychological emergencies. It goes on to say that if such training is not obtained at the graduate level, it will need to be obtained through postdoctoral training or continuing education.

Our mental health colleagues in psychiatry have made training in emergency services a required component of the psychiatric residency (Weissberg, 1988). This is not to say that emergency psychiatric training is without its problems, as Weissberg (1988) points out; nonetheless, it is recognized as an essential component of preparation for functioning as a professional in psychiatry. Psychology and the other mental health disciplines (e.g., clinical social work) seem to have been slower to come to the realization of this need, probably because of differences in their history and development as professions. Psychology's roots, for example, have been academic and scientific, and although there are now different models for practitioners (e.g., the professional model), one of the predominant models remains the Boulder or scientist–practitioner model. The "scientist" component of this model, and the academic roots of the profession more generally, would seem to make psychologists more likely to approach problems in a contemplative manner than in the more action-oriented manner that is often needed in emergency situations.

Kingsbury (1987), in a discussion of cognitive differences between clinical psychologists and psychiatrists, has spoken to this issue. He has noted that even in regard to something as fundamental as the nature of science, psychology and psychiatry enculturate new members quite differently. Thus, psychology graduate students are taught that science is a method of inquiry in which hypotheses are generated and empirically tested. Psychiatric residents, on the other hand, first receive a medical school education, in which science tends to be viewed as a body of facts and procedures that one must know in order to treat individuals with illnesses. As Kingsbury (1987) has stated:

> In emergencies such as cardiac arrests or the appearance of acutely psychotic, destructive individuals in the emergency room, one must act immediately, contemplating and critiquing performance later. Although physicians do not act only in emergencies, the tasks of preparing for them and of learning treatment algorithms shape one's view of the nature of science. (p. 153)

Generally speaking, it seems safe to say that at present, training programs in the mental health disciplines (and particularly those that are not medical in their orientation) do not prepare graduate students to respond to emergencies to the degree noted above for physicians. To place more emphasis on such training, however, does not require the sacrifice of any fundamental principle. Rather, as Zimet and Weissberg (1979) have pointed out, it will extend practitioners' competence as psychotherapists and as auyonomous professionals. Regardless of what training model they adhere to, if clinicians hold themselves out as independent practitioners, it is imperative that they be prepared to assist patients in the event of life-threatening behavior or a psychological emergency. The structure of this book is intended as a curriculum for teaching a knowledge base in such emergency services.

REFERENCES

American Psychological Association (APA), Board of Professional Affairs, Committee on Professional Standards. (1987). Casebook for providers of psychological services. *American Psychologist, 42*, 704–711.

Barlow, D. H. (1974). Psychologists in the emergency room. *Professional Psychology, 5*, 251–256.

Benoliel, J. (1988). Health care providers and dying patients: Critical issues in terminal care. *Omega, 18*, 341–363.

Bernstein, H. A. (1981). Survey of threats and assaults directed toward psychotherapists. *American Journal of Psychotherapy, 35*, 542–549.

Bernstein, R. M., Feldberg, C., & Brown, R. (1991). After-hours coverage in psychology training clinics. *Professional Psychology: Research and Practice, 22*, 204–208.

Bongar, B., & Harmatz, M. (1991). Clinical psychology graduate education in the study of suicide: Availability, resources, and importance. *Suicide and Life-Threatening Behavior, 21*, 231–244.

Bongar, B., Lomax, J. W., & Harmatz, M. (1992). Training and supervisory issues in the assessment and management of the suicidal patient. In B. Bongar (Ed.), *Suicide: Guidelines for assessment, management, and treatment* (pp. 253–267). New York: Oxford University Press.

Chemtob, C. M., Bauer, G., Hamada, R. S., Pelowski, S. R., & Muraoka, M. Y. (1989). Patient suicide: Occupational hazard for psychologists and psychiatrists. *Professional Psychology: Research and Practice, 20*, 294–300.

Covino, N. A. (1989). The general hospital emergency ward as a training opportunity for clinical psychologists. *Journal of Training and Practice in Professional Psychology, 3*, 17–32.

Dickinson, G., & Pearson, A. (1980). Death education and physicians' attitudes toward dying patients. *Omega, 11*, 167–174.

Groner, E. (1978). Delivery of clinical social work services in the emergency room: A description of an existing program. *Social Work in Health Care, 4*, 19–29.

Grumet, G., & Trachtman, D. (1976). Psychiatric social workers in the emergency department. *Health and Social Work, 1*, 113–131.

Guy, J. D., Brown, C. K., & Poelstra, P. L. (1990). Who gets attacked? A national survey of patient violence directed at psychologists in clinical practice. *Professional Psychology: Research and Practice, 21,* 493–495.

Kingsbury, S. J. (1987). Cognitive differences between clinical psychologists and psychiatrists. *American Psychologist, 42,* 152–156.

Kleespies, P. M. (1993). The stress of patient suicidal behavior: Implications for interns and training programs in psychology. Professional *Psychology: Research and Practice, 24,* 477–482.

Kleespies, P. M., Penk, W. E., & Forsyth, J. P. (1993). The stress of patient suicidal behavior during clinical training: Incidence, impact, and recovery. *Professional Psychology: Research and Practice, 24,* 293–303.

Kranz, P. L. (1985). Crisis intervention: A new training approach to crisis intervention: A mentor training mode. *Crisis Intervention, 14,* 107–114.

Miles, M. (1980). The effects of a course on death and grief on nurses' attitudes toward dying patients and death. *Death Education, 4,* 245–260.

Pederson, A. M., & Weiner, I. B. (1970). Psychology training in emergency services. *American Psychologist, 25,* 474–476.

Pope, K. S., & Tabachnick, B. G. (1993). Therapists' anger, hate, fear, and sexual feelings: National survey of therapist responses, client characteristics, critical events, formal complaints, and training. *Professional Psychology: Research and Practice, 24,* 142–152.

Star, B. (1984). Patient violence/therapist safety. *Social Work, 29,* 225–230.

Walsh, S. (1985). The psychiatric emergency service as a setting for social work training. *Social Work in Health Care, 11,* 21–31.

Weissberg, M. P. (1988). Weaknesses in emergency psychiatric education: A solution. *Journal of Psychiatric Education, 12,* 134–137.

Whitman, R. M., Armao, B. B., & Dent, O. B. (1976). Assault on the therapist. *American Journal of Psychiatry, 133,* 426–429.

Zimet, C. N., & Weissberg, M. P. (1979). The emergency service: A setting for internship training. *Psychotherapy: Theory, Research, and Practice, 16,* 336.

PART I

FOUNDATIONS

CHAPTER 1

THE DOMAIN
OF PSYCHOLOGICAL
EMERGENCIES

An Overview

PHILLIP M. KLEESPIES

Some might take the position that psychological emergencies are in the eye of the beholder; in other words, if a person asking for help says that the situation is an emergency, then it is an emergency (Everstine & Everstine, 1983). Although this approach has some truth and wisdom to it, most of those who provide emergency services do not make an emergency response to every patient-defined emergency. For example, let us say that you are called by a male patient who reports that he routinely misused cocaine until 3 days ago. He tells you that he is experiencing depressive feelings now, and it sounds very likely that his depression is secondary to cocaine withdrawal. He denies that he is suicidal or homicidal, but says that this is an emergency and he wants you to send an ambulance to bring him to the hospital. Although you might empathize with this man's sense of crisis (or perhaps understand his sense of entitlement), you would very probably not be likely to see this situation as one requiring such immediate action as providing an ambulance. Generally, clinicians make some judgments of their own about what circumstances and events are emergencies and require an emergent response.

In a review of the international literature on emergency psychiatry, the authors (Munizza et al., 1993) make the point that one of the first problems they encountered in conducting their review had to do with the uncertainty of concepts and the lack of agreement about definitions. Although they offer little by way of resolving this lack of agreement, one concept that they discuss at some length seems most pertinent to defining the domain of psychological emergencies. This is the concept of *"urgenza"* from the Italian literature. *"Urgenza"* is defined as "a serious, acute situation requiring immediate treatment" (Munizza et al., 1993, p. 7). It has three key elements: (1) acuteness or intensity; (2) seriousness or a high level of danger; and (3) need for immediate treatment (without which irreversible harm or death might occur).

The notion of *"urgenza"* seems closest to what is meant in the present treatise by "emergency"—that is, an acute clinical situation in which there is an imminent risk of serious harm or death to self or others unless there is some immediate intervention. Fortunately, there are relatively few situations in clinical practice that meet this definition. Such situations include serious suicidal states, serious violent states, and states in which a known and relatively defenseless victim is at risk of being reexposed to serious harm (e.g., a physically or sexually abused child who remains in the custody of an abusing parent).

As Callahan (1994) has pointed out, the concepts of psychological "emergency" and psychological "crisis" have been "frequently confused, or erroneously used interchangeably" (p. 165). He further notes that it is important to understand the distinction between these concepts because it drives our thinking, our decision making, and our interventions when dealing with potential emergencies. A "crisis" is a serious disruption of the individual's baseline level of functioning, such that his or her usual coping mechanisms are inadequate to restore equilibrium. It is an emotionally significant event in which there may be a turning point for better or worse. It does not necessarily imply danger of serious physical harm or life-threatening danger (as in an emergency). Working for an emergency service or in an emergency room, however, one is asked to assess a variety of psychological crises, and an important part of the work is attempting to distinguish between crises that may also be emergencies and those that are not.

The first step in learning to make such a distinction is to learn about the knowledge base available for assessing such things as the risk of suicide or violence. The next step is to learn under what conditions risk or dangerousness might be considered imminent. Then one must learn how best to elicit information from the patient that is needed for such an assessment. Finally, one must learn what can be done to manage and resolve situations in which a patient is assessed as imminently in danger or at risk.

There are clearly different skills involved in making this sort of assessment of and response to emergency situations. As Bongar, Lomax, and Harmatz (1992) have pointed out with respect to the assessment of suicidality, "There is research to support the contention that knowledge of risk factors and the capacity to respond in an effective way to those patients who present as an imminent risk of suicide may be independent areas of clinical competence" (pp. 262–263). The same can undoubtedly be said of the assessment of potentially violent patients or of potential victims of violence. It is important that psychologists, clinical social workers, and other mental health practitioners develop these differing areas of competence.

It has been said that most psychological emergencies are treated in a service located in or adjacent to the emergency room (ER) of a general hospital (Dubin & Weiss, 1991). Although emergency cases may frequently be referred or transported to a hospital ER, the need for initial assessment and management can arise in a wide variety of settings—for example, even in psychology training clinics, which traditionally deal with a lower-risk population. Bernstein, Feldberg, and Brown (1991) reported that 35% of the psychology training clinics in their national sample did not exclude clients who were considered a potential danger to others, and 41% did not exclude those considered a potential danger to themselves. Clearly, the need to assess and manage the emergency nature of a client's condition can arise in such settings. As noted in the Introduction to this book, there is no absolute guarantee that a patient in any clinical setting may not regress and/or become a risk to self or others (Zimet & Weissberg, 1979), and the therapist or clinician must be prepared to deal with this effectively.

TRAINING IN EMERGENCY PSYCHOLOGICAL SERVICES

Bongar et al. (1992) have suggested that a model curriculum needs to be developed for the study of suicide; indeed, they cite a curriculum proposed by Lomax (1984, 1986) for psychiatry residency programs. Although the recommendation of Bongar et al. (1992) is clearly a good one, it would seem that it does not go far enough if one considers the need for training among mental health practitioners in assessing and managing emergencies, more broadly speaking (see the Introduction). Thus, it seems that the field needs a model curriculum and a required training sequence on dealing with psychological emergencies, including those involving suicidal patients, violent patients, and those who are the potentially helpless victims of violence.

The training in each type of emergency might parallel the broad categories suggested by Lomax (1986) for training in the care of the suicidal patient. These categories include (1) knowledge, (2) skill, and (3) attitudes. First, a knowledge base should be taught early in the training sequence as part of a graduate seminar on clinical practice or clinical methods. Lomax (1986) has suggested that this didactic component should include such topics as epidemiology; methods of assessment (including the mental status examination); management and treatment (including forensic considerations); and personal reactions the clinician may experience when dealing with these difficult clinical situations. Other relevant emergency-related topics that could also be included in this component might be differentiating delirium, dementia, and depression; signs and symptoms of alcohol/drug intoxication and withdrawal; and signs and symptoms of pertinent neurological, endocrine, and cardiac disorders.

Second, skill development occurs with clinical assignments and supervision. It would seem wise for there to be close supervision and a graduated approach to actual work with high-risk patients and the clinical responsibility that this entails. Thus, known high-risk cases might not be assigned until the latter phases of training, perhaps in the internship year rather than during preinternship practica. In this regard, it is important to remember that one survey (Guy, Brown, & Poelstra, 1990) found that the greatest number of patient attacks on therapists occurred during the training years, and that another (Kleespies, Penk, & Forsyth, 1993) found that 40% of patient suicides during training years occurred when the trainees were at a preinternship level. The latter survey also found a negative relationship between the emotional impact on the trainee and the year of training in which a patient suicide was experienced (i.e., the earlier in training that a patient suicide occurred, the greater the perceived acute impact on the trainee).

Third, the development of constructive attitudes about work with emergency cases takes root in good program support and case supervision. As Weissberg (1988) has pointed out in regard to emergency psychiatry training, service pressures can pervert training objectives; as a result, the least experienced trainees may be placed on the front lines with little support, and emergency work may be poorly integrated into the larger framework of training. In such an event, emergency work is inevitably seen as anxiety-arousing and burdensome. Good support and supervision, however, can go a long way toward preventing such a scenario and toward aiding in the development of a sense of competence in dealing with these emotionally charged cases.

A PROPOSED CURRICULUM
FOR THE KNOWLEDGE BASE

As noted in the Introduction, the structure of the present book is intended as a curriculum for teaching the knowledge base of emergency psychological services (see Table 1.1). This curriculum would begin with an overview of the definition and domain of psychological emergencies (Chapter 1), then proceed to instruction in crisis theory and crisis intervention as applied in emergencies (Chapter 2). Although I have noted earlier that not all crises are emergencies, in fact many emergencies develop from or involve personal or interpersonal crises. It is helpful to have a framework within which to conceptualize and manage such events, as well as some strategies for immediate crisis resolution. Likewise, it is important to offer a method by which one can systematically evaluate someone in an emergency or crisis condition. Thus, teaching a psychodiagnostic interview format (Chapter 3), including a mental status examination, is fundamental. Teaching a psychodiagnostic interview also involves showing how provisional diagnoses are

TABLE 1.1. Proposed Curriculum for a Knowledge Base in Emergency
Psychological Services

I. Foundations
   1. The domain of psychological emergencies
   2. Crisis theory and crisis intervention in emergencies
   3. The emergency interview
II. The evaluation and management of life-threatening behavior
   4. The evaluation and management of the suicidal patient
   5. The evaluation and management of the violent patient
   6. The evaluation and management of the victim of violence
   7. The evaluation and management of the patient who wishes to refuse
      life-sustaining treatment
   8. The emergency telephone contact
III. Risk management in a clinical emergency
   9. Risk management with the suicidal patient
   10. Risk management with the violent patient
IV. Emergency-related crises and conditions
   11. The evaluation and management of the self-mutilating patient
   12. The evaluation and management of alcohol- and drug-related crises
V. Medical conditions presenting as psychological crises
   13. Side effects of and reactions to psychotropic drugs
   14. Psychological/behavioral symptoms in neurological disorders
   15. Psychological/behavioral symptoms in endocrine disorders
   16. Psychological/behavioral symptoms in cardiac conditions
VI. The impact of emergency service on the clinician
   17. The stress of patient suicidal behavior for the clinician
   18. The stress of patient violent behavior for the clinician
   19. "Vicarious traumatization" in working with victims

derived from the interview data, and discussing the importance as well as limitations of diagnosis in risk assessment.

Once the fundamental skills noted above have been taught, the next step in the proposed curriculum is to teach more specific knowledge related to the most frequent emergencies that the clinician is likely to encounter. These emergency situations include the evaluation and management of the following types of patients: the suicidal patient (Chapter 4), the violent patient (Chapter 5), the victim of violence (Chapter 6), and the patient who wishes to refuse life-sustaining treatment (Chapter 7). In addition, telephone contacts with potentially suicidal or violent patients can be difficult and complicated. Some guidelines and strategies for dealing with such emergency calls can be helpful (Chapter 8). Depending on the particular type of emergency, the syllabus might also include the teaching of information about assessing for a variety of risk factors (e.g., epidemiological factors, diagnostic factors, empirically derived factors, etc.); information about assessing for suicidal or violent ideation; information about estimating the imminence of risk; information about assessing for impaired judgment and competence to refuse treatment; and the integration of such factors and issues in a comprehensive estimate of risk. The teaching of management strategies would include discussions of the risks and benefits of outpatient versus inpatient care, indications for close observation or precautions, the duty to protect, community resources for the potentially suicidal or violent patient, and the like.

Given that the evaluation and management of life-threatening behavior inevitably involve legal risks for the clinician, it seems crucial to have a component of the curriculum that examines the risk management issues frequently confronted in emergency services (Chapters 9 and 10). Thus, some of the more frequently occurring dilemmas—such as the obligation to maintain confidentiality versus the duty to protect, and the right to self-determination versus involuntary commitment or restraint—need to be studied and discussed. Case examples are helpful in clarifying standards of care for these differing situations and circumstances.

Those who work in emergency services or with a difficult patient population will encounter certain crises or conditions that are not (technically speaking) emergencies, but that nonetheless can make for trying situations. Knowledge of such frequently encountered crises and conditions can help in discriminating a true emergency situation from a nonemergency. The patient in a crisis who mutilates himself or herself, but has no suicidal intent, needs to be distinguished from and treated differently from the suicidal patient (Chapter 11). Alcohol- and drug-related crises are also common in emergency settings, and they are often associated with and complicate the evaluation and management of life-threatening behavior (Chapter 12). In addition, it is important to recognize the possible side effects of and reactions to psychotropic drugs, so that appropriate medical consultation or treatment can be sought (Chapter 13). Moreover, there are many neurological disorders (Chapter 14), endocrine disorders (Chapter 15), and cardiac conditions (Chapter 16) whose presenting symptoms may seem psychological in nature. Being alert to signs and symptoms of possible neurological, endocrine, or cardiac disease, and seeking appropriate consultation, can be invaluable in sorting out a crisis situation.

Working with emergencies and crises can be very stressful for the clinician (Chemtob, Bauer, Hamada, Pelowski, & Muraoka, 1989; Guy et al., 1990; Kleespies et al., 1993; Kleespies, Smith, & Becker, 1990; McCann & Pearlman, 1990; Pope & Tabachnick, 1993; Rodolfa, Kraft, & Reilley, 1988). It is important that those learning to manage emergency situations also learn about the stresses that they themselves may experience, and begin to consider how they might handle such stress. The stress of patient suicidal behavior (Chapter 17), the stress of patient violent behavior (Chapter 18), and the "vicarious traumatization" that clinicians can develop when seeing patients who have endured serious trauma (Chapter 19) are all topics that should be part of the educative process. This sort of background can make the "affective education" that occurs with actual clinical experience more tolerable and meaningful.

A SUPERVISORY MODEL
FOR SKILL/ATTITUDE DEVELOPMENT

Some time ago, Barlow (1974) observed that psychology interns responded initially to emergency room duty with moderate to severe anxiety. He further observed that within approximately 3 months, a second response—one of increased clinical confidence and mastery—began to emerge. This sense of mastery was described by interns as one of the more important developments in their training.

It is important to note that work with patients in crisis or in a state of emergency can be anxiety-arousing for seasoned professionals, let alone for those who are in training and less confident of their clinical abilities and status. When it comes to stressful clinical events, some have felt that clinicians-in-training have a "protective advantage" over professionals, in that they work under the direction of a supervisor, have the support of a supervisory relationship, and can process events in an organized program (cf. Brown, 1987). Rodolfa et al. (1988), however, found that patient suicidal statements, patient suicide attempts, and patient attacks on the therapist were all rated as moderately to highly stressful by both professional psychologists and psychologists-in-training; similarly, we (Kleespies et al., 1993) found that the negative emotional impact of patient suicidal behavior on psychologists-in-training was as great as or greater than that on professional-level psychologists. It seems clear that those who are first learning to cope with such difficult emergency situations need considerable instruction and support to reduce their level of stress and make learning more feasible.

The "mentor model" of training and supervision proposed by Kranz (1985) for crisis intervention seems well suited for training in the high-stress context of emergency services. My colleagues and I at the Boston Department of Veterans Affairs (VA) Medical Center have used this model very successfully. In this model, an experienced clinician and an intern are paired. The intern has the opportunity to observe and work closely with a seasoned professional who has been successfully engaged in this type of clinical work. The pressure of more complete clinical responsibility is only gradually assumed by the trainee, and anxiety is kept at more acceptable levels. Cases can be processed subsequently in a supervisory session. In this sort of model, it is important for the supervisor to be aware of the balance between support and intern responsibility, and to shift the balance appropriately over time to promote the more independent functioning of the clinician-in-training.

THE SETTING FOR TRAINING
IN EMERGENCY PSYCHOLOGICAL SERVICES

The hospital ER is probably the best setting in which to obtain systematic training and clinical experience in assessing and managing psychological emergencies. Zimet and Weissberg (1979) have suggested that one of the reasons why psychologists seem to have avoided work in an ER is that it is a very medical setting, and medical factors can complicate the psychological presentation. Covino (1989), however, found that the majority of psychiatric patients seen in a hospital ER had complaints that fell well within the competence of psychologists to manage. Moreover, with good collaboration and backup from the nursing and medical staff, complications can be minimized. Several authors (Covino, 1989; Gerson & Bassuk, 1980; Zimet & Weissberg, 1979) have commented on the unique nature of the ER setting and the training opportunities that it affords. A clinician who works in the ER must learn to deal with the pressure of time, the intensity of affect, the disruptiveness of certain behaviors, the need for rapid assessment, the press for a decision, the legal and ethical aspects of decisions about dangerousness, and the need for interdisciplinary consultation—all of which can be part and parcel of the work in this setting. If a clinician-in-training can gain mastery of such conditions, then he or she will have developed the algorithms that can be applied in future clinical emergency situations.

However, it is also important to note that the hospital ER is not the only setting in which training in emergency services can occur. Thus, for example, Asnis, Kaplan, van Praag, and Sanderson (1994) recently reported that 26% of a sample of patients seeking treatment at the outpatient psychiatry department of a private medical center in New York had a history of homicidal ideation or of homicide attempts. Nearly a third (32%) of the group with past homicidal ideation reported having had such ideation within the past week. Eighty-six percent of the group with homicidal ideation or homicide attempts also had a history of suicide ideation, and 39% had a history of suicide attempts. Clearly, such an outpatient department is dealing with a subpopulation that is at risk and will present with emergencies with some regularity. Moreover, and as noted earlier, Bernstein et al. (1991) reported that a significant number of the psychology training clinics in their sample did not exclude clients who were considered a potential danger to others or to themselves. These authors called for training clinics to become more rigorous in defining responsibility for emergency coverage for clients at risk.

A MODEL TRAINING PROGRAM
FOR EMERGENCY PSYCHOLOGICAL SERVICES

Psychology interns at the Boston VA Medical Center[1] have received training in emergency psychological services for approximately 20 years; however, the emergency services component of the VA internship program has only

---

[1]Since 1989, the psychology internship at the Boston VA Medical Center has been part of the Tufts University School of Medicine/Boston VA Internship Consortium.

taken its present form since 1987. The internship year consists of three 4-month rotations in different clinical areas. During one of their 4-month rotations, each intern is required to participate in consulting to the Emergency Department (ED) of the Medical Center on patients who present with psychiatric problems or crises and who are often seeking psychiatric hospitalization. Given that there have been 12–14 interns in the program per year, there are 45 interns available for this clinical experience on each rotation. The interns are on call to the ED 1 day per week, and only during the daytime hours. Thus, two interns cover the morning shift, and another two or three interns cover the afternoon shift.

As noted earlier, the evaluation of patients in crisis or in a state of emergency can be stressful and difficult even for seasoned professionals; it follows that those at a training level need good instruction and support to reduce their stress and to make learning feasible. At the Boston VA, this is accomplished by a thorough orientation, a lecture series on emergency-related topics, the use of the "mentor model" of training, and group supervision. The interns begin their rotation with an introductory lecture on emergency services by the psychology staff member who has been designated as the Coordinator of Emergency Room Services for Psychology. This lecture includes a brief tour of the admitting and ED area. At this initial meeting, they are given a folder containing a variety of useful materials—for example, a written description of the procedural steps taken in responding to and carrying out a consultation request (called a "Mental Walk Thru A&D [Admissions and Dispositions]"), a semistructured interview form that includes a mental status checklist, a listing of useful phone numbers and extensions, an article on emergency psychiatric services, and so forth. In keeping with the mentor model, they then begin their experience by accompanying and observing a staff psychologist over the course of two or three weekly shifts. The rule of thumb is to have each intern observe at least two interviews conducted by staff psychologists.

During these initial weeks, weekly orientation sessions are held in which the "Mental Walk" is used as a guide; these sessions continue until all of the procedural steps have been clarified. Meanwhile, a separate, weekly group supervision and wrap-up session is held at which all ED evaluations are reviewed and discussed. This group supervision continues for the duration of the rotation.

Once the interns have observed at least two evaluations, they are asked to begin doing evaluations themselves, but with either the Coordinator or another staff psychologist present to assist them. This close staff supervision continues for two or three evaluations, at which point the interns become more autonomous in their interviewing, but always have the Coordinator present in the ED for consultation or assistance with difficult situations or decisions. The weekly orientation sessions mentioned above are transitioned into a brief lecture series covering such emergency-related topics as assessment of the suicidal patient; assessment of the potentially violent patient; signs and symptoms of alcohol and drug intoxication and withdrawal; procedures for restraint; and neurological, endocrine, and cardiac disorders that present with psychological symptoms.

Complementing the training in emergency psychological services, the psychology training program sponsors a monthly case conference for all of the interns called the "Risk Assessment and Management Rounds," or "Risk Rounds" for short. This conference is chaired by the Coordinator of Emergency Room Services for Psychology. Each month, an intern presents a case in which there is a question of the patient's presenting acute or longer-term risk to self or others. The conference examines the assessment and management of risk with some of the interns' more anxiety-arousing and difficult patients. It can also serve as a consultation on the standard of care observed in the management of the case.

Interns from the Boston VA who have completed this training sequence have reported that it was at times intense and anxiety-arousing. The vast majority, however, have also reported that with the instruction, close supervision, and support built into the program, they achieved greater clinical competence and confidence in managing psychological emergencies and crises.

CONCLUSION

It would seem that routine and systematic training in the assessment and management of psychological emergencies or patients at risk can only make for more complete and competent professional practitioners. It would also seem that the standards and status of the mental health disciplines can only be enhanced when their practitioners are more formally trained to respond to and deal with those sometimes frightening, often difficult, and usually trying instances when patients are at risk. In psychology and clinical social work, it seems clear that there have been some efforts to provide such training (Covino, 1989; Walsh, 1985), but it seems equally clear that these respective disciplines have lacked strong direction in this regard (Bongar & Harmatz, 1991; Guy et al., 1990; Kleespies et al., 1993).

It is promising that the Committee on Professional Standards of the American Psychological Association (APA) Board of Professional Affairs (1987) has seen fit to publish a case that illustrates the need to be prepared to handle psychological emergencies. The Committee's "Casebook for Providers of Psychological Services," however, was intended to provide clarification of the professional standards or guidelines stated in the "Specialty Guidelines for the Delivery of Services" (APA, 1981a, 1981b), and these documents offer no guidelines specific to such preparation. Likewise, the APA Committee on Accreditation (1986) has made no requirement that graduate or internship training programs train students and interns in the assessment and management of emergencies. Yet it would seem that clear direction from such levels is needed if the discipline of psychology is to become more fully capable in this very important area of clinical practice.

Work with the patient at risk can be a life-and-death issue. With regard to patient suicide, Chemtob, Hamada, Bauer, Kinney, and Torigoe (1988) found that more than one in five psychologists in their national sample had a patient who committed suicide at some point in their careers. As noted earlier, we (Kleespies et al., 1993), found that one in nine psychology graduate students had a patient suicide at some time during their training years alone.

When patient violence, patient suicide, or even a serious patient suicide attempt occurs, it is typically very distressing to the therapist. We (Kleespies et al., 1993) found a graduated increase in the acute negative emotional impact on therapists-in-training with increasing severity of patient suicidal behavior (i.e., from suicide ideation to suicide attempt to suicide completion). Trainees who had a patient suicide completion were distinguished from those who experienced patient suicide ideation by significantly greater feelings of shock, disbelief, failure, sadness, self-blame, guilt, shame, and depression. In addition, there was evidence of longer-term effects, in that those who had a patient suicide completion were reportedly more likely to experience anxiety when subsequently evaluating suicidal patients. With respect to patient homicide, one need only mention the *Tarasoff* case to raise most therapists' anxiety level. Moreover, Rodolfa et al. (1988) found that physical assault on the therapist was ranked as the most stressful event faced by therapists.

As mentioned earlier, several recent authors (Bongar et al., 1992; Chemtob et al., 1989; Guy et al., 1990; Kleespies, 1993; Star, 1984; Walsh, 1985; Whitman, Armao, & Dent, 1976) have independently called for increased training in the areas of patient violence and patient suicidality. Increased emphasis by the mental health disciplines on training in emergency psychological services would be a significant step toward accomplishing both, and could inherently include preparation for dealing with both the risk management and the emotional impact of these twin "occupational hazards."

REFERENCES

American Psychological Association (APA). (1981a). Specialty guidelines for the delivery of services by clinical psychologists. *American Psychologist, 36,* 640–651.

American Psychological Association (APA). (1981b). Specialty guidelines for the delivery of services by counseling psychologists. *American Psychologist, 36,* 652–663.

American Psychological Association (APA), Board of Professional Affairs, Committee on Professional Standards. (1987). Casebook for providers of psychological services. *American Psychologist, 42,* 704–711.

American Psychological Association (APA), Committee on Accreditation and Accreditation Office. (1986). *Accreditation handbook* (rev.). Washington, DC: APA.

Asnis, G. M., Kaplan, M. L., van Praag, H. M., & Sanderson, W. C. (1994). Homicidal behaviors among psychiatric outpatients. *Hospital and Community Psychiatry, 45,* 127–132.

Barlow, D. H. (1974). Psychologists in the emergency room. *Professional Psychology, 5*, 251–256.

Bernstein, R. M., Feldberg, C., & Brown, R. (1991). After-hours coverage in psychology training clinics. *Professional Psychology: Research and Practice, 22,* 204–208.

Bongar, B., & Harmatz, M. (1991). Clinical psychology graduate education in the study of suicide: Availability, resources, and importance. *Suicide and Life-Threatening Behavior, 21,* 231–244.

Bongar, B., Lomax, J. W., & Harmatz, M. (1992). Training and supervisory issues in the assessment and management of the suicidal patient. In B. Bongar (Ed.), *Suicide: Guidelines for assessment, management, and treatment* (pp. 253–267). New York: Oxford University Press.

Brown, H. N. (1987). Patient suicide during residency training: 1. Incidence, implications, and program response. *Journal of Psychiatric Education, 11,* 201–206.

Callahan, J. (1994). Defining crisis and emergency. *Crisis, 15,* 164–171.

Chemtob, C. M., Bauer, G., Hamada, R. S., Pelowski, S. R., & Muraoka, M. Y. (1989). Patient suicide: Occupational hazard for psychologists and psychiatrists. *Professional Psychology: Research and Practice, 20,* 294–300.

Chemtob, C. M., Hamada, R. S., Bauer, G., Kinney, B., & Torigoe, R. Y. (1988). Patient suicide: Frequency and impact on psychologists. *Professional Psychology: Research and Practice, 19,* 416–420.

Covino, N. A. (1989). The general hospital emergency ward as a training opportunity for clinical psychologists. *Journal of Training and Practice in Professional Psychology, 3,* 17–32.

Dubin, W. R., & Weiss, K. J. (1991). *Handbook of psychiatric emergencies.* Springhouse, PA: Springhouse.

Everstine, D. S., & Everstine, L. (1983). *People In crisis: Strategic therapeutic interventions.* New York: Brunner/Mazel.

Gerson, S., & Bassuk, E. (1980). Psychiatric emergencies: An overview. *American Journal of Psychiatry, 137,* 19.

Guy, J. D., Brown, C. K., & Poelstra, P. L. (1990). Who gets attacked? A national survey of patient violence directed at psychologists in clinical practice. *Professional Psychology: Research and Practice, 21,* 493–495.

Kleespies, P. M. (1993). The stress of patient suicidal behavior: Implications for interns and training programs in psychology. Professional *Psychology: Research and Practice, 24,* 477–482.

Kleespies, P. M., Penk, W. E., & Forsyth, J. P. (1993). The stress of patient suicidal behavior during clinical training: Incidence, impact, and recovery. *Professional Psychology: Research and Practice, 24,* 293–303.

Kleespies, P. M., Smith, M. R., & Becker, B. R. (1990). Psychology interns as patient suicide survivors: Incidence, impact, and recovery. *Professional Psychology: Research and Practice, 21,* 257–263.

Kranz, P. L. (1985). Crisis intervention: A new training approach to crisis intervention: A mentor training mode. *Crisis Intervention, 14,* 107–114.

Lomax, J. W. (1984). Suicide. In M. Sacks, W. Sledge, & P. Rubinton (Eds.), *Core readings in psychiatry: An annotated guide to the literature* (pp. 218–224). New York: Praeger.

Lomax, J. W. (1986). A proposed curriculum on suicide for psychiatric residency. *Suicide and Life-Threatening Behavior, 16,* 56–64.

McCann, I. L., & Pearlman, L. A. (1990). Vicarious traumatization: A framework for understanding the psychological effects of working with victims. *Journal of Traumatic Stress, 3,* 131–149.

Munizza, C., Furlan, P. M., d'Elia, A., D'Onofrio, M. R., Leggero, P., Punzo, F., Vidini, N., & Villari, V. (1993). Emergency psychiatry: A review of the literature. *Acta Psychiatrica Scandinavica, 88*(Suppl. 374), 1–51.

Pope, K., & Tabachnick, B. (1993). Therapists' anger, hate, fear, and sexual feelings: National survey of therapist responses, client characteristics, critical events, formal complaints, and training. *Professional Psychology: Research and Practice, 24,* 142–152.

Rodolfa, E. R., Kraft, W. A., & Reilley, R. R. (1988). Stressors of professionals and trainees at APA-approved counseling and VA Medical Center internship sites. *Professional Psychology: Research and Practice, 19,* 43–49.

Star, B. (1984). Patient violence/therapist safety. *Social Work, 29,* 225–230.

Walsh, S. (1985). The psychiatric emergency service as a setting for social work training. *Social Work in Health Care, 11,* 21–31.

Weissberg, M. P. (1988). Weaknesses in emergency psychiatric education: A solution. *Journal of Psychiatric Education, 12,* 134–137.

Whitman, R. M., Armao, B. B., & Dent, O. B. (1976). Assault on the therapist. *American Journal of Psychiatry, 133,* 426–429.

Zimet, C. N., & Weissberg, M. P. (1979). The emergency service: A setting for internship training. *Psychotherapy: Theory, Research, and Practice, 16,* 334–336.

CHAPTER 2

CRISIS THEORY
AND CRISIS INTERVENTION
IN EMERGENCIES

JAY CALLAHAN

This chapter defines, explores, and discusses psychological crises, psychological emergencies, and the interactions between these two phenomena. Because most—but not all—psychological emergencies arise in the context of crises, the overlap and interactions between them constitute an especially important area of concern. The chapter offers a brief history of crisis intervention, followed by a discussion of the important components of crisis intervention as a form of brief treatment. The techniques of crisis intervention are outlined, using a model based on work by Aguilera (1994) and Puryear (1979), and this model is applied to psychological emergencies as well. Finally, this chapter presents the limitations and contraindications of crisis intervention.

DEFINITIONS

Clinicians and therapists frequently use the words "crisis" and "emergency" interchangeably. Although in certain contexts one or the other of these terms seems most appropriate, many in-between and ambiguous situations exist. Not only are these terms used in ill-defined and unclear ways in clinical practice, many articles and books on crisis intervention and emergency psychiatry also omit specific definitions or blur the important distinctions between a crisis and an emergency (Callahan, 1994; Munizza et al., 1993). The literature on crisis intervention, for example, tends to be found in the disciplines of psychology, social work, and nursing, and tends to emphasize disruptions in living experienced by relatively normal individuals who are treated in outpatient settings (Aguilera, 1994; Cohen, Claiborn, & Specter, 1983; Duggan, 1984; Everstine & Everstine, 1983; Golan, 1974, 1978; Hoff, 1989; Parad & Parad, 1990; Roberts, 1996a; Slaikeu, 1990). Writing that focuseson emergencies tends to be conceptualized from the perspective of emergency psychiatry, and emphasizes the acute reactions of individuals with diagnosed psychopathology (Comstock, Fann, Pokorny, & Williams, 1984; Gorton & Partridge, 1982; Rund & Hutzler, 1983; Slaby, Lieb, & Tancredi, 1986; Urbaitis, 1983; Walker, 1983). Work that focuses on crisis intervention rarely defines or discusses emergencies, and work that focuses on psychiatric or psychological emergencies rarely defines or discusses crises. One recent book makes an attempt to distinguish between these two concepts, but does so only by offering examples (Janosik, 1994).

Definitions are needed. As described by Kleepsies in Chapter 1 of this book, the distinctions between "crisis" and "emergency" emphasize the presence or lack of presence of danger, as well as the nature of the response that is needed. A psychological emergency is a relatively abrupt, sudden situation in which there is an imminent risk of harm. Such circumstances are limited, and include only four situations: (1) risk of suicide, (2) risk of physical harm to others, (3) states of seriously impaired judgment in which an individual is endangered (delirium, dementia, acute psychotic episode, severe dissociative state, etc.), and (4) situations of risk to a defenseless victim (abused child or elder). In summary, a psychological emergency is an unpredictable, acute situation that requires an immediate response to avoid possible harm (Callahan, 1994).

A psychological crisis, on the other hand, is generally nonspecific, is longer-lasting, and does not include the risk of danger. A crisis is a loss of psychological equilibrium (Caplan, 1961; Cohen & Nelson, 1983; Golan, 1978; Slaikeu, 1990). People function in a state of psychological homeostasis or balance, in which they respond to and resolve the normal problems of living through a variety of strategies. Such strategies vary from person to person and may change over time. Sometimes, however, exposure to environmental stressors (alone or in combination with certain vulnerable states) may overwhelm this homeostasis. At such a time, an individual's normal coping responses are insufficient to resolve the situation, a marked increase in anxiety or tension occurs, and the individual searches for alternative methods of coping. If these other, secondary attempts to cope are also unsuccessful, the individual enters a state of crisis. A crisis state includes high levels of anxiety and agitation, or of depression and defeat; the individual is unable to carry out his or her normal activities of daily living in an efficient and productive manner, or sometimes at all ("functional impairment").

In summary, a crisis is a self-limiting period of a few days to 6 weeks in which environmental stress leads to a state of psychological disequilibrium. Crisis intervention is a form of brief therapy (approximately one to six sessions) initiated during a crisis, and designed to return an individual to his or her previous level of adaptive functioning as soon as possible.

Many clinicians and laypeople use the term "crisis intervention" in a casual or ambiguous way that does not fulfill this definition. For example, crisis intervention is not reassuring an upset individual after a family member has been hurt in an auto accident, or calming an angry mentally ill resident of a group home, or talking a frustrated adolescent into returning to class and not walking out of school. In many cases, the professionals carrying out these activities describe them as crisis intervention, but they do not meet the present definition. All of these activities are important, of course, but they are not crisis intervention.

A psychological emergency, by contrast, is an acute situation that requires an immediate response to avoid possible harm. Emergency intervention is a single session, designed to lessen or eliminate this possibility of danger. It consists of three overlapping components: (1) an evaluation of the emergency, including an explicit assessment of the risk of harm; (2) an intervention, designed to try to reduce the risk during the interview by the use of standard psychotherapeutic techniques (empathy, confrontation, interpretation, suggestion); and (3) a disposition for further assistance. Often this disposition is a concrete environmental manipulation, such as voluntary or involuntary hospitalization, warning a possible victim (Monahan, 1993), or removing at-risk children from the home of abusive caretakers.

Perhaps some of the confusion between crises and emergencies comes from clinicians' perceptions that crisis intervention as defined here is needed when an individual is suicidal or potentially violent (e.g., is experiencing a psychological emergency). It is true that the large majority of emergencies occur in the context of a crisis. For example, a middle-aged man who is in crisis because of an unwanted marital separation may very well consider killing himself, and may experience one or more psychological emergencies when he is most acutely suicidal. Similarly, recent years have seen an increase in workplace violence, almost always in the context of an individual who is in crisis because of a real or threatened job loss. These are examples of psychological emergencies that occur in the context of crises. Crisis intervention is certainly appropriate in these instances, because the individuals in question are in crisis, not simply because of the potential suicide or violence.

The appropriate response to a psychological emergency, however, is not crisis intervention, but emergency intervention. Since most emergencies take place in the context of a crisis, it is understandable that confusion has arisen regarding these overlapping phenomena. Occasionally, however, emergencies arise that are not in the context of a crisis. In these instances an emergency intervention is indicated, but crisis intervention is not appropriate. This distinction is discussed below.

HISTORY AND THEORY OF CRISIS INTERVENTION

Many writers have documented the relatively brief history of the concepts of crisis and crisis intervention (e.g., Aguilera, 1994; Gilliland & James, 1993; Hoff, 1989; Slaikeu, 1990). An especially detailed chronology is offered by Golan (1974). Although the concepts of crisis and crisis intervention can be traced back to numerous theories, practices, and models throughout the 20th century, a few major influences can be identified. One such major influence is that of military psychiatry during World War II and the Korean War. In contrast to previous wars, soldiers with "shell shock" or "traumatic neurosis" were treated in medical units close to the front lines, as opposed to being sent home to psychiatric hospitals (Golan, 1974; Hoff, 1989). The success of this practice has been attributed in part to the expectation verbalized by medical staff members that such soldiers were having understandable difficulties, and that they would soon overcome these and return to active duty; this contrasted sharply with a perception of the difficulties as evidence of major mental illness that would require lengthy inpatient treatment and rehabilitation (Amada, 1977).

Another significant influence on crisis theory was provided by the work of Erich Lindemann (1944). Lindemann's description of the bereavement reactions of survivors of the 1942 Cocoanut Grove nightclub fire in Boston, in which almost 500 people died, was one of the original works on the now familiar "stages of grief."

The concept of crisis as a "turning point," and as providing both danger and opportunity, derives largely from the work of Erik Erikson (1950). His classic work outlines the normative developmental crises throughout life, and has had a major impact on the field of crisis intervention.

Perhaps the most central influence is Gerald Caplan (1961, 1964). Caplan's work on preventive psychiatry and on community mental health is the foundation of crisis intervention.

One other major influence on the field of crisis intervention has been the suicide prevention "movement" (Hoff, 1989). Beginning in the late 1950s, a group of suicidologists in Los Angeles began working with the medical examiner's office. In these instances, "psychological autopsies" were conducted as part of an effort to establish whether equivocal deaths were suicide or not (Litman, Curphey, Shneidman, Farberow, & Tabachnick, 1963). Interestingly, the publicity surrounding the death of Marilyn Monroe, and the subsequent attention given to these suicidologists, led to the founding of the Los Angeles Suicide Prevention Center (S. M. Heilig, cofounder, personal communication, April 1994).

Given such a complex historical background, it is no surprise that theoretical conceptions of crisis intervention are equally multifaceted. Different authors emphasize different theories and models. The early work in the 1940s and 1950s was almost all psychodynamic. However, by the 1960s other perspectives began to emerge. For example, Caplan's seminal work was based on both psychodynamic and public health disease prevention models, and grew into what he called "preventive psychiatry." General systems theory and family systems models have been important (Gilliland & James, 1993; Hoff, 1989), along with sociological and psychological studies of stress (Lazarus, 1980; Selye, 1976). More recently, cognitive-behavioral viewpoints have arisen (Dattilio & Freeman, 1994).

CURRENT CONCEPTS OF CRISIS

In recent years, a consensus appears to have emerged about the broad outlines of what constitutes a "crisis" and the general framework for crisis intervention. As described above, a crisis is a loss of psychological equilibrium. Exposure to environmental stressors under certain circumstances may sometimes overwhelm this homeostasis. If an individual's normal coping responses are insufficient to resolve the situation, functional capabilities are impaired. During a crisis, individuals are almost always uncharacteristically open to novel or seldom-used coping methods (Puryear, 1979; Rapoport, 1965). Some of these new coping methods may be constructive and adaptive in the long run, whereas others may be quite destructive. For example, individuals who tend to be characterologically closed may find that talking over their difficulties with friends or professionals helps them to cope, and may integrate this new method of coping into their daily lives. On the other hand, the use of drugs or alcohol may be thought of as possibly adaptive or perhaps neutral during a crisis, but clearly maladaptive and destructive if adopted as a coping technique.

Because individuals cannot maintain the high levels of arousal and tension inherent in a crisis, the duration of a crisis is limited. Traditionally, it has been thought that a crisis either ends with appropriate treatment or terminates spontaneously after approximately 4–6 weeks, at which time the individual attains a new level of adaptive functioning. In most cases, this new level will be roughly equivalent to the precrisis state. In other cases, depending upon the assistance and support received, an individual may find a new psychological equilibrium at either a higher or a lower level than previously. Formerly isolated individuals who learn to reach out to others may achieve a higher level of adaptive functioning, whereas a person who has coped during a crisis by using alcohol frequently may end up with a heightened vulnerability to alcoholism, and thus a lower level of functioning (Gilliland & James, 1993; Golan, 1974; Slaikeu, 1990).

In some conceptions of crisis, the precipitating event is only the last in a series of stressors to which an individual has been subjected. Earlier stressors have produced a "hazardous situation," in which the individual is at risk for entering a state of crisis if further stressors occur (Janosik, 1994; Parad & Parad, 1990; Smith, 1990). A developmental transition, such as marriage or the birth of a child, may also be defined as a hazardous situation producing a heightened risk of crisis. Other conceptions blur the distinction between the hazardous situation and the precipitating event, and use both terms to refer to the "last straw" that apparently initiates the crisis (Golan, 1974, 1978; Hoff, 1989). When the precipitating event is a disaster or other catastrophic occurrence, no particular hazardous situation or vulnerable state is necessary; most people will experience a state of crisis simply because of the magnitude of the traumatic event.

Another important aspect of a crisis is the subjective nature of the situation. Some theorists have used the word "appraisal" to denote the making of meaning that occurs with all events in people's lives, including normally stressful and even catastrophically stressful events (Lazarus, 1980). For example, even with comparable financial situations, two workers may make entirely different appraisals of a potential layoff (Slaikeu, 1990). One person may feel terrified of the loss of income and overwhelmed at the prospect of a job search, whereas another may feel relieved and energized about the possibility of finding another position. The nature of the meaning that an individual draws from events has a great deal to do with whether he or she experiences a crisis or not. As one author has stated, "one man's crisis may be another man's ordinary train of events" (Slaikeu, 1990, p. 19). Although there appears to be more homogeneity in how people view highly traumatic or catastrophic events—a natural disaster, or the sudden death of a family member, appears to cause a crisis for most people—much variation in the subjective meaning of events is still apparent.

Crises have been classified in a variety of ways. Caplan (1964), for example, conceived of two primary types of crises: (1) "developmental" or "maturational," growing out of the normal stages and changes in an individual's or family's life; and (2) "situational," unpredictable accidents or stressful incidents that can happen to anyone at any time. Developmental crises are best understood within the framework of Erikson's (1950) theory of adult development. In this perspective, development takes place via a series of transitions from one stage to the next; each transition can be characterized by certain tasks. Any of these normative transitions can become a crisis if an individual's attempts to cope are maladaptive or inadequate, if too many aspects of such a transition occur all at once, or if the transition is viewed as inherently repugnant or negative. Other theories of life development that focus on normal events (e.g., finishing high school, graduating from college, leaving home, getting married, having children, etc.) also predict that crises are more likely to occur during these stressful transitions than in times of relative stability. Most theorists acknowledge, however, that the vast majority of people accomplish these transitions without experiencing a crisis.

Situational crises, on the other hand, are those that are precipitated by unpredictable stressful events. An auto accident, a job loss, the death of a friend, or a move from one home to another are life events that may be thought of as situational, not developmental. Again, most people cope with and adapt to these stressful events in a more or less straightforward way. However, for some people whose internal and/or external resources are limited, these stressful events may precipitate a crisis. A crisis may also take place when several stressful events, each of manageable proportions taken singly, occur together or within a brief time period ("cumulative stress").

Another method of classifying crises is by the nature of the stressors. One type of crisis is precipitated by so-called normative stressors, such as those described above. As discussed, these normative stressors may be either part of a developmental or maturational transition, or may be entirely situational. Examples include a job loss, a divorce, a new job in a new city, an illness in a family member, and the like; these are "normal" aspects of life that precipitate a crisis only in certain vulnerable individuals.

The other type of crisis is precipitated by overwhelming, traumatic events that involve the threat of death or injury. These stressors correspond to the definition of a "traumatic event" (Criterion A) in the diagnostic criteria for posttraumatic stress disorder (PTSD) and acute stress disorder (ASD) in the fourth edition of the *Diagnostic and Statistical Manual of Mental Disorders* (DSM-IV):

> The person has been exposed to a traumatic event in which both of the following were present:
>
> (1) the person experienced, witnessed, or was confronted with an event or events that involved actual or threatened death or serious injury, or a threat to the physical integrity of self or others
> (2) the person's response involved intense fear, helplessness, or horror. (American Psychiatric Association [APA], 1994, pp. 427–428)

These stressors include such events as experiencing combat, being a captive in a concentration camp or a prisoner of war, having a family member or friend die by suicide or homicide, sexual assault, childhood sexual abuse/incest, and the like. Natural and human-caused disasters, such as plane crashes, terrorist bombings, and hurricanes and tornadoes, also constitute traumatic stressors. The distinction between normative and traumatic stressors is that the former cause crises only in at-risk individuals during vulnerable times in their lives, whereas the latter usually cause crises in almost everyone who experiences them. Indeed, much controversy has arisen regarding the DSM's conception of PTSD as a psychiatric disorder, as opposed to a normal syndrome of adaptation that takes place in a large majority of people after exposure to an especially traumatic event (Yehuda & McFarlane, 1995).

Another aspect of crisis that has been controversial is its time-limited quality. Caplan (1964) has written that individuals cannot remain in a state of active crisis indefinitely, and that crises tend to be resolved within 4–6 weeks.

Resolution, however, does not mean that the psychological distress is over, or that the need for further adjustment has ended. It simply means that individuals reach a new equilibrium—a new state of relative stability. As noted above, this new equilibrium may represent a higher or lower level of functioning than, or the same level of functioning as, the precrisis state (Golan, 1974; Hoff, 1989; Puryear, 1979; Slaikeu, 1990). In many cases, especially crises precipitated by traumatic stress, the period of distress and the need for psychological assistance in adapting to the new situation that the traumatic event has created may go on for years. In the first few weeks after a traumatic stressor, an individual may experience a crisis, exhibit functional impairment, and undergo many symptoms of stress. However, because of the overwhelming nature of the stress, lack of appropriate support or professional assistance, maladaptive cognitive appraisal of the event, or other factors, many individuals settle into a relatively stable, chronic state that represents a lower level of functioning. They are no longer in crisis, but have developed PTSD. In fact, according to DSM-IV, PTSD cannot be diagnosed until the symptoms have persisted for at least a month. This minimum duration reflects the understanding that symptoms of PTSD may exist in the immediate aftermath of a traumatic event for many people, but then diminish and gradually disappear over the subsequent few weeks (APA, 1994).

Indeed, DSM-IV has introduced a new disorder, ASD, which essentially represents a PTSD-type reaction with a duration of 2 days to 1 month. This new disorder has been introduced in order to identify posttraumatic reactions over the short run, with the understanding that most people who go on to develop PTSD have ASD first. (Delayed onset of PTSD does occur, but it is much more rare than an immediate onset of symptoms; APA, 1994.) However, many people experience ASD and do *not* go on to develop PTSD. ASD, then, may be thought of as representing a state of crisis, although many crises (especially those precipitated by "normative" stressors) do not fulfill the diagnostic criteria for ASD.

This discussion raises the issues of disorder/illness/disease and of diagnosis. Traditionally, even though the concept of crisis developed in part from a psychodynamic framework, a medical model has not been emphasized. In most writings, crisis has been conceptualized as a normal or normative response to ordinary or extraordinary stress, with its subsequent threats to adaptation, demand for constructive coping, and implications for future functioning (Dixon, 1979; Golan, 1974; Hoff, 1989; Rapoport, 1965; Slaikeu, 990). This nonmedical perspective appears to have been an instrumental factor in the development of separate literatures for crisis intervention and emergency psychiatry. Books and articles on crisis intervention have prim-arily been written by nonmedical professionals who prefer social-psychological and other nonmedical perspectives.

However, this professional separation appears to be disappearing. Historically, crisis intervention programs were free-standing office-based clinics, usually staffed by psychologists and social workers, and in some cases large cadres of volunteers. Crises were handled well, but psychological emergencies required referral to a hospital. Emergency psychiatry programs, by contrast, were consultation/liaison programs staffed by psychiatric residents and attending psychiatrists, located in hospital emergency rooms. The emphasis was on treating emergencies, and individuals in need of crisis intervention usually had to be referred to the hospital outpatient program (where a waiting list was likely) or to an outside program.

Increasingly, integrated services that provide both crisis intervention and emergency intervention are replacing these separate programs. These programs are usually administratively part of and physically housed in emergency rooms of general hospitals, and are staffed by combinations of professionals. Volunteers, however, seem to be less and less part of the picture, and many freestanding telephone crisis intervention and suicide prevention centers that were formerly staffed by volunteers are increasingly being operated by paid professional staffs (P. Couto, Chief Certification Examiner, American Association of Suicidology, personal communication, April 1994).

This integration of services has led to an attempt to integrate theoretical frameworks as well. For example, crisis intervention programs have traditionally criticized psychiatry and medicine for providing tranquilizers to individuals in acute grief reactions or other forms of crisis (Hoff, 1989). In recent years, however, a compromise position has arisen: Professionals on both sides of the former controversy agree that medication should not be provided automatically or reflexively, but can be useful when individuals in crisis are too overwhelmed to function, too distraught to sleep, or otherwise unable to engage in verbal treatment.

This new integration of viewpoints has led to some innovative conceptions of crisis. With few exceptions (e.g., Langsley & Kaplan, 1968; Reding& Raphelson, 1995), crisis intervention has not been applied to individuals exhibiting major psychiatric disorders such as schizophrenia. However, an acute psychotic episode in an individual with schizophrenia, an episode of major depression, a period of time in which an individual experiences frequent panic attacks, and a manic episode are all time-limited losses of psychological equilibrium. Typically these have not been considered psychological crises, because of biologically based conceptions of etiology and the frequent need for somatic treatment. However, it is increasingly clear that a biopsychosocial perspective on major mental disorders is necessary. Despite the increased attention paid to biological factors in recent years, psychosocial stress is an underappreciated but important aspect of these disorders (e.g., Kendler, Kessler, Neale, Heath, & Eaves, 1993; Post, 1992). As such, a crisis perspective and the use of crisis intervention have advantages. Such a perception underscores the extremely frequent presence of a psychosocial stressor in the initiation of an episode; highlights the need to address stress as a factor in preventing future episodes; and reminds clinicians that during such times, symptomatic individuals are more open to receiving professional assistance than during times of stability. In these instances crisis intervention is an appropriate treatment, although it should be supplemented by medication or other somatic treatment. It must again be understood that the 4- to 6-week limitation on active crisis does not necessarily mean that all symptoms will be resolved in that time, or that an individual will necessarily return to full premorbid functioning, but rather that a new equilibrium will be established. In some cases, this new equilibrium will be at a lower level of functioning. In diagnostic terms, this new equilibrium may be described as chronic schizophrenia, or as major depression, panic disorder, or bipolar I disorder in partial remission.

On the other hand, other psychiatric or biopsychosocial disorders are often referred to as crises, but do not fit this model. For example, a number of crisis intervention books include chapters on alcoholism and drug dependence (Gilliland & James, 1993; Wambach, 1996), and discuss these disorders as if they were crises. However, as Puryear (1979) points out, alcoholism and drug dependence are relatively stable, long-term disorders that do not represent crises. A crisis, it will be recalled, is a temporary state of disequilibrium. The equilibrium that individuals with drug and alcohol problems possess is often "a backdrop against which a crisis can develop" (Puryear, 1979, p. 182), but the substance dependence itself is not the crisis. Crises related to the substance dependence do develop, of course (e.g., missing work, irresponsible family behavior, and drunken driving); however, *these* are the crises, not the drinking or drug taking.

Other significant problematic situations are also frequently thought of as crises, yet represent dysfunctional equilibriums of their own. Domestic violence is a good example. Some books on crisis intervention include chapters on spouse abuse as if it automatically constituted a crisis (Brekke, 1990; Dziegielewski & Resnick, 1996; Gilliland & James, 1993; Janosik, 1994). Unfortunately, it is clear that in most cases of domestic violence, the situation is chronic and constitutes a malignant equilibrium; this is not a crisis.

A MODEL OF CRISIS INTERVENTION

Many different models of crisis intervention exist. For example, Dixon (1979), Gilliland and James (1993), Golan (1978), Hoff (1989), Janosik (1994) Roberts (1996b), and Slaikeu (1990) all offer models. For our purposes, however, the basis of an effective model was developed at the Benjamin Rush Center for Problems of Living in Los Angeles; Aguilera (1994) has elaborated on this model in some detail. It posits crisis intervention as treatment consisting of one to six sessions, initiated during a crisis, and taking place during the crisis period of a few days to 4–6 weeks.

A crisis situation is seen as developing because of difficulties in as many as three areas of the individual's functioning: (1) meaning, (2) coping, and (3) support. That is, a stressful situation may be handled constructively and may not lead to disequilibrium if the individual perceives the stressor in a realistic fashion, utilizes constructive coping mechanisms, and has adequate social support. If any of these three aspects are not present, or are problematic in some way, a crisis may result. Crisis intervention, then, targets these same three areas for therapeutic work.

The first aspect, "meaning," refers to the individual's subjective perception of the event. This has been referred to earlier as the appraisal of the stressor. As Aguilera (1994) writes, " . . . what does the event mean to the individual? How is it going to affect his [sic] future? Can he look at it realistically or does he distort the meaning?" (p. 35). At a basic level, it is important that the individual realize the connection between the event(s) and his or her tension, depression, or other symptoms of crisis. In addition, the meaning that a person draws from an event is both individually subjective and culturally based. For example, a job layoff is a very different event for a young woman just embarking on a career who is unsure whether the job was right for her anyway, and a middle-age man with a family to support and no reasonable prospects for another job at comparable pay. Cultural aspects also strongly influence the meaning that events have (Gilliland & James, 1993; Parson, 1985). For example, inappropriate social behavior in many Asian cultures is shameful because of its negative reflection on one's family, whereas in mainstream Western society, such behavior is much less significant.

Disasters and other traumatic events tend to have more universal meaning, although individual variations are also important. Generally, traumatic events caused by human malevolence are perceived as more stressful than those caused by human error or accident, and these are in turn generally seen as more stressful than natural disasters (Bolin, 1986; Wilkinson & Vera, 1989). Some traumatic events appear to be particularly difficult to cope with because of their apparent meaninglessness (Janoff-Bulman, 1985). Family survivors of suicide and homicide, for example, frequently report struggling with a "search for explanation," looking for clues and reasons why their family members died (Dunne, 1987; Wertheimer, 1991). Family survivors of people who die in transportation disasters (large plane or train accidents), possibly because of the rarity of such accidents, report a meaninglessness about their family members' death that seems to add to their crisis state.

The second aspect of crisis is coping. "Coping" refers primarily to conscious and/or habitual ways of problem solving, although psychodynamic defense mechanisms can be included as well. Researchers have suggested that coping can be categorized as "active problem-focused," "passive problem-focused," or "passive avoidant" (Koopman, Classen, & Spiegel, 1996). For example, active problem-focused coping in the case of job loss includes all activities that focus on obtaining a new job, handling financial issues, and so on. Passive problem-focused coping includes talking with others (a source of support), reading about job prospects, and related activities. Passive avoidant coping includes activities that the individual carries out in an attempt not to think about the situation, including "escapes" such as alcohol and drug use. Passive avoidant coping is not necessarily destructive per se, but can be maladaptive if it dominates an individual's repertoire. In general, a wide range of coping responses, including some active problem-focused activities, is most adaptive.

Social support is the third aspect of crisis. Aguilera (1994) notes that "meaningful relationships with others provide a person with nurturance and support, resources vital for coping with a wide variety of stressors" (p. 35). Individuals can handle a great deal of stress given appropriate support, but the lack of a support system can cause a moderately stressful event to plunge an individual into crisis.

The main focus of crisis intervention from this perspective consists of evaluating and carrying out active work in the three areas: meaning, coping, and support.

AN INTEGRATED MODEL OF CRISIS AND EMERGENCY INTERVENTION

An overall model of crisis intervention is described below. It is based on the work of Aguilera (1994) and Puryear (1979), but adds elements of emergency intervention, which take precedence over crisis intervention. The crisis intervention itself consists of one to six sessions over a period of a few daysto 4–6 weeks, with intersession phone calls if needed, beginning within 24 hours of the initial call. Note that crisis intervention need not begin immediately—within 24 hours or so is sufficient. Puryear (1979) suggests not letting more than one night go by. Emergency intervention, in contrast (because of the potential danger), should occur immediately (Callahan, 1994).

All sessions of crisis intervention consist of both evaluation and treatment. Obviously, with time at a premium, it is impossible to engage in leisurely history taking. However, it is desirable to address several content and process issues in the first session. First, the client tells his or her story. The clinician's questions should be open-ended and designed to elicit pertinent details. A helpful perspective is to understand what has motivated the client to come for help *now* (Smith, 1990). Ideally, sufficient time will be available to allow the client to tell the story in as much detail as he or she wants or is able to do. There is no need to confine a crisis intervention session to 45 or 50 minutes; 75–80 minutes is often ideal, at least for the first one or two sessions. In the case of a particularly traumatic stressor, an individual in crisis may be unable or unwilling to tell the entire story because of the need for purposeful avoidance of overwhelming material, or because of dissociative amnesia for part or all of the event (Koopman, Classen, Cardeña, & Spiegel, 1995).

Second, the clinician should obtain some preliminary understanding of the meaning of the situation to the individual, as well as his or her attempts at coping, and the availability of support systems (utilized or not) (Aguilera, 1994).

Third, the clinician must assess the presence of any psychological emergencies. When a psychological emergency does exist, crisis intervention is temporarily delayed until the emergency is resolved one way or the other. As noted above, a psychological emergency is an immediate situation of potential harm, including only four possibilities: (1) risk of suicide; (2) risk of physical harm to others; (3) states of seriously impaired judgment in which an individual is endangered (delirium, dementia, acute psychotic episode, manic episode, or severe dissociative state); and (4) situations of risk to a defenseless victim (abused child or elder).

Therefore, an explicit inquiry concerning suicidal or homicidal ideation must be included; when a significant positive response is obtained, a specific risk assessment needs to be conducted. The details of this procedure are beyond the scope of this chapter; the reader is referred to Chapters 3, 4, and 5 of this volume. A mental status exam should also be part of this assessment (see Chapter 3). This will enable the clinician to determine whether psychosis, dissociation, delirium, dementia, mania, or any other disturbed mental state impairs the individual's judgment to such an extent that he or she is at risk of being harmed. Finally, an assessment of the individual's social situation is necessary, particularly if arrangements for the protection of a defenseless child or elder may need to be carried out (see Chapter 6).

Whenever any of these situations appears to exist, the emergency intervention takes precedence over crisis intervention. As noted above, emergency intervention consists of three stages, the first of which is the evaluation of the emergency. Second, an in-session intervention to try to reduce the risk should also be carried out. In some instances, little can be done to alter the probability of an individual's attempting suicide or trying to harm someone else. In other cases, standard therapeutic techniques such as active listening, explicit empathizing, negotiating conflicts with significant others, offering hope, and pointing out the realistic consequences of fantasized actions can significantly reduce the risk. When the probability of danger is judged by the end of the session to be low or moderate, no substantive disposition is necessary, and crisis intervention can continue. On the other hand, when the risk is judged to be high, a concrete disposition such as hospitalization, referral to the legal system, warning a potential victim and the police, or contacting the local child protective services is necessary. This disposition is the third stage of the emergency intervention.

To summarize, an emergency intervention is conducted whenever there is any evidence of potential danger. It precludes crisis intervention until the risk is judged to be low or moderate. If the risk is high, an alternative plan is needed.

Two other aspects of crisis intervention should be conducted during the first session, if time permits. (When insufficient time exists, these other aspects can be delayed until the second session.) The first of these two additional topics is a more detailed evaluation of the degree of functional impairment, along with some assessment of the individual's ego functions of impulse control, quality of relationships, and integrity of ego boundaries (Dixon, 1979; Gerhart, 1990; Gilliland & James, 1993).

Second, although time is limited, it is important to get at least a basic sense of the individual's personal history. Questions such as "Has this ever happened to you before?," "Have you ever felt this way before?," and "How did you cope?" will generate useful information about the individual's characteristic ways of coping (Janosik, 1994; Rhine & Weissberg, 1982). In addition, the emotional burden of previously unresolved crises can add to the current crisis (Rapoport, 1965). Thus, in reviewing recent history, the clinician needs to assess whether the situation is actually a crisis or not. Many individuals present with problematic situations and emotional upset, but a crisis is only a crisis if it is a state of disequilibrium, distinct from that individual's baseline. Some clients with borderline personality disorder, alcohol dependence, or drug dependence present to crisis facilities in very emotional states, with much urgency; however, a review of their histories reveals that their chaotic lifestyles are chronic conditions and therefore not crises. The provision of crisis intervention for these individuals who are not in crisis will not be helpful, and may even be destructive because it promotes regression (Callahan, 1996; Golan, 1974).

In addition to these content areas, certain process issues are important in beginning crisis intervention. The clinician must approach the situation with certain attitudes and behaviors that are often contrary to his or her previous training, especially if that training was primarily psychodynamic. An active style is essential. The clinician must take charge of the situation and project an attitude of calm optimism. Indeed, the provision of hope may be one of the most important components of effective crisis intervention. It is best described by Puryear (1979):

> You are attempting to convey by your entire approach your attitude that the client is a capable, decent person who has been temporarily overwhelmed by extreme stresses, and who will use your help to cope with these stresses and get back on the track. (p. 49)

It is important to pay careful attention to building communication and rapport, to be empathic and nonjudgmental, and to strive for a moderate level of emotional discharge. Too much emotional ventilation can lead to later embarrassment and a decrease in motivation (Puryear, 1979).

Subsequent sessions of crisis intervention build on these beginnings. The primary focus in the second through fifth sessions is active work on the three areas of meaning, support, and coping. Work on meaning includes confronting grossly inaccurate depictions of reality and suggesting other ways to view the situation. In other, less extreme cases, the clinician and client should discuss the implications of the meaning of the event, and the clinician can often point out other possible implications. Frequently the provision of psychoeducation about particular issues (e.g., job loss, divorce, and illness) or about medical or psychiatric disorders is helpful.

Attention to coping includes supporting adaptive coping activities and confronting or undermining negative coping activities. Adaptive coping can be supported by helping the client to process and clarify feelings.

In the area of support, it is important to encourage the client to identify and make use of support systems. Many individuals have supportive individuals in their lives whom they have not contacted, for a variety of reasons. Encouragement to do so is appropriate. In addition, support groups are available in most communities for a wide variety of life situations and generic stressful events.

Throughout the sessions, the clinician should keep in mind the "golden rule" of crisis intervention: "Do for others that which they cannot do for themselves, and no more!" (Rusk, 1971, p. 251).

PSYCHOLOGICAL EMERGENCIES THAT ARE NOT PART OF CRISES

Finally, an important consideration is that of psychological emergencies that are *not* part of crises. As discussed above, most emergencies (e.g., suicide or interpersonal violence) take place during a time of psychological disequilibrium. In some uncommon situations, however, emergencies can rise in states of psychological equilibrium. Individuals with borderline personality disorder, for example, are known to make suicide attempts of relatively low lethality. Increasingly, it is being recognized that responding to these individuals in the traditional manner—aggressively intervening with hospitalization, even on an involuntary basis—is inappropriate. That is, the traditional crisis intervention approach focuses on acute suicide risk, and this approach may be unproductive or even contraindicated in chronic suicidality (Callahan, 1996; Fine & Sansone, 1990; Lewin, 1992; Maltsberger, 1994; Pulakos, 1993; Rosenbluth, Kleinman, & Lowy, 1995).

Similarly, acts of violence may in some cases be carried out by individuals not in crisis, but in times of psychological equilibrium. People with antisocial personality disorder and some individuals (a large proportion of whom are men) who are wife or partner batterers may threaten or carry out violence during "stable" and relatively routine parts of their lives.

These acts of actual or potential suicide or violence are psychological emergencies without crises. As such, the appropriate therapeutic approach is to conduct emergency intervention, as described above, but not crisis intervention. This approach avoids the regression that frequently comes about through crisis intervention's intense, rapid involvement—an intensity that is temporary and helpful for people genuinely in crisis, but that fosters significant regression among many clients with personality disorders or substance dependence.

At times, the outcome of the emergency intervention is a disposition such as hospitalization or referral to the legal system. When the assessment of the emergency yields an estimate of low or moderate risk, routine, ongoing treatment is initiated or continued. The nature of this treatment depends, of course, on the diagnosis of the individual and the problems in the specific situation.

The point is that it is routine, ongoing outpatient treatment, not crisis intervention.

SUMMARY

The distinctions between crises and emergencies, and between crisis intervention and emergency intervention, lead us to new conceptualizations. Ideally, the implications of these new conceptualizations will lead to more efficient use of resources and more effective interventions.

REFERENCES

Aguilera, D. C. (1994). *Crisis intervention: Theory and methodology* (7th ed.). St. Louis: Mosby.

Amada, G. (1977). Crisis-oriented psychotherapy: Some theoretical and practical considerations. *Journal of Contemporary Psychotherapy, 9*, 104–111.

American Psychiatric Association (APA). (1994). *Diagnostic and statistical manual of mental disorders* (4th ed.). Washington, DC: Author.

Bolin, R. (1986). Disaster characteristics and psychosocial impacts. In National Institute of Mental Health (Ed.), *Disasters and mental health* (pp. 11–35). Washington, DC: American Psychiatric Press.

Brekke, J. (1990). Crisis intervention with victims and perpetrators of spouse abuse. In H. J. Parad & L. G. Parad (Eds.), *Crisis intervention: Book 2. The practitioner's sourcebook for brief therapy* (pp. 161–178). Milwaukee: Family Service America.

Callahan, J. (1994). Defining crisis and emergency. *Crisis, 15*, 164–171.

Callahan, J. (1996). A specific therapeutic approach to suicide risk in borderline clients. *Clinical Social Work Journal, 24*, 443–459.

Caplan, G. (1961). *An approach to community mental health.* New York: Grune & Stratton.

Caplan, G. (1964). *Principles of preventive psychiatry.* New York: Basic Books.

Cohen, L. H., Claiborn, W. L., & Specter, G. A. (Eds.). (1983). *Crisis intervention* (2nd ed.). New York: Human Sciences Press.

Cohen, L. H., & Nelson, D. W. (1983). Crisis intervention: An overview of theory and technique. In L. H. Cohen, W. L. Claiborn, & G. A. Specter (Eds.), *Crisis intervention* (2nd ed., pp. 13–26). New York: Human Sciences Press.

Comstock, B. S., Fann, W. E., Pokorny, A. D., & Williams, R. L. (Eds.). (1984). *Phenomenology and treatment of psychiatric emergencies.* New York: SP Medical & Scientific Books.

Dattilio, F. M., & Freeman, A. (Eds.). (1994). *Cognitive-behavioral strategies in crisis intervention.* New York: Guilford Press.

Dixon, S. L. (1979). *Working with people in crisis.* St. Louis: Mosby.

Duggan, H. A. (1984). *Crisis intervention: Helping individuals at risk.* Lexington, LA: Lexington Books.

Dunne, E. J. (1987). Special needs of suicide survivors in therapy. In E. J. Dunne, J. L. McIntosh, & K. Dunne-Maxim (Eds.), *Suicide and its aftermath: Understanding and counseling the survivors* (pp. 193–207). New York: Norton.

Dziegielewski, S. F., & Resnick, C. (1996). Crisis assessment and intervention: Abused women in the shelter setting. In A. L. Roberts (Ed.), *Crisis management and brief treatment: Theory, technique, and applications* (pp. 123–141). Chicago:Nelson-Hall.

Erikson, E. (1950). *Childhood and society*. New York: Norton.

Everstine, D. S., & Everstine, L. (1983). *People in crisis: Strategic therapeutic interventions*. New York: Brunner/Mazel.

Fine, M. A., & Sansone, R. A. (1990). Dilemmas in the management of suicidal behavior in individuals with borderline personality disorder. *American Journal of Psychotherapy, 44,* 160–171.

Gerhart, U. C. (1990). *Caring for the chronic mentally ill*. Itasca, IL: Peacock.

Gilliland, B. E., & James, R. K. (1993). *Crisis intervention strategies* (2nd ed.). Pacific Grove, CA: Brooks/Cole.

Golan, N. (1974). Crisis theory. In F. J. Turner (Ed.), *Social work treatment: Interlocking theoretical approaches* (pp. 420–456). New York: Free Press.

Golan, N. (1978). *Treatment in crisis situations*. New York: Free Press.

Gorton, J. G., & Partridge, R. (Eds.). (1982). *Practice and management of psychiatric emergency care*. St. Louis: Mosby.

Hoff, L. A. (1989). *People in crisis: Understanding and helping* (3rd ed.). Redwood City, CA: Addison-Wesley.

Janoff-Bulman, R. (1985). The aftermath of victimization: Rebuilding shattered assumptions. In C. R. Figley (Ed.), *Trauma and its wake* (Vol. 1, pp. 15–35). New York: Brunner/Mazel.

Janosik, E. H. (1994). *Crisis counseling: A contemporary approach* (2nd ed.). Boston: Jones & Bartlett.

Kendler, K. S., Kessler, R. C., Neale, M. C., Heath, A. C., & Eaves, L. J. (1993). The prediction of major depression in women: Toward an integrated etiologic model. *American Journal of Psychiatry, 150,* 1139–1148.

Koopman, C., Classen, C., Cardeña, E., & Spiegel, D. (1995). When disaster strikes, acute stress disorder may follow. *Journal of Traumatic Stress, 8,* 29–46.

Koopman, C., Classen, C., & Spiegel, D. (1996). Dissociative responses in the immediate aftermath of the Oakland/Berkeley firestorm. *Journal of Traumatic Stress, 9,* 521–540.

Langsley, D., & Kaplan, D. (1968). *Treatment of families in crisis*. New York: Grune & Stratton.

Lazarus, R. S. (1980). The stress and coping paradigm. In L. A. Bond & R. C. Rosen (Eds.), *Competence and coping during adulthood* (pp. 28–74). Hanover, NH: University Press of New England.

Lewin, R. A. (1992). On chronic suicidality. *Psychiatry, 55,* 16–27.

Lindemann, E. (1944). Symptomatology and management of acute grief. *American Journal of Psychiatry, 101,* 141–148.

Litman, R. E., Curphey, T. J., Shneidman, E. S., Farberow, N. L., & Tabachnick, N. D. (1963). Investigations of equivocal suicides. *Journal of the American Medical Association, 184,* 924–930.

Maltsberger, J. T. (1994). Calculated risks in the treatment of intractably suicidal patients. *Psychiatry, 57,* 199–212.

Monahan, J. (1993). Limiting therapist exposure to *Tarasoff* liability: Guidelines for risk containment. *American Psychologist, 48,* 242–250.

Munizza, C., Furlan, P. M., d'Elia, A., D'Onofrio, M. R., Leggero, P., Punzo, F.,Vidini, N., & Villari, V. (1993). Emergency psychiatry: A review of the literature. *Acta Psychiatrica Scandinavica, 88*(Suppl. 374), 1–51.

Parad, H. J., & Parad, L. G. (1990). Crisis intervention: An introductory overview. In H. J. Parad & L. G. Parad (Eds.), *Crisis intervention: Book 2. The practitioner's sourcebook for brief therapy* (pp. 3–66). Milwaukee: Family Service America.

Parson, E. R. (1985). Ethnicity and traumatic stress: The intersecting point in psychotherapy. In C. R. Figley (Ed.), *Trauma and its wake* (Vol. 1, pp. 314–337). New York: Brunner/Mazel.

Post, R. M. (1992). Transduction of psychosocial stress into the neurobiology of recurrent affective disorder. *American Journal of Psychiatry, 149,* 999–1010.

Pulakos, J. (1993). Two models of suicide treatment: Evaluation and recommendations. *American Journal of Psychotherapy, 47,* 603–612.

Puryear, D. A. (1979). *Helping people in crisis.* San Francisco: Jossey-Bass.

Rapoport, L. (1965). The state of crisis: Some theoretical considerations. In H. J. Parad (Ed.), *Crisis intervention: Selected readings* (pp. 22–31). New York: Family Service Association of America.

Reding, G. R., & Raphelson, M. (1995). Around-the-clock mobile psychiatric crisis intervention: Another effective alternative to psychiatric hospitalization. *Community Mental Health Journal, 31,* 179–187.

Rhine, M. W., & Weissberg, M. P. (1982). Crisis intervention. In J. G. Gorton & R. Partridge (Eds.), *Practice and management of psychiatric emergency care* (pp.3–12). St. Louis: Mosby.

Roberts, A. R. (Ed.). (1996a). *Crisis management and brief treatment: Theory, technique, and applications.* Chicago: Nelson-Hall.

Roberts, A. R. (1996b). Epidemiology and definitions of acute crisis in American society. In A. R. Roberts (Ed.), *Crisis management and brief treatment: Theory, technique, and applications* (pp. 16–33). Chicago: Nelson-Hall.

Rosenbluth, M., Kleinman, I., & Lowy, F. (1995). Suicide: The interaction of clinical and ethical issues. *Psychiatric Services, 46,* 919–921.

Rund, D. A., & Hutzler, G. G. (1983). *Emergency psychiatry.* St. Louis: Mosby.

Rusk, T. N. (1971). Opportunity and technique in crisis psychiatry. *Comprehensive Psychiatry, 12,* 249–263.

Selye, H. (1976). *The stress of life.* New York: McGraw-Hill.

Slaby, A. E., Lieb, J., & Tancredi, L. R. (1986). *Handbook of psychiatric emergencies* (3rd ed.). New York: Elsevier.

Slaikeu, K. A. (1990). *Crisis intervention: A handbook for practice and research* (2nded.). Boston: Allyn & Bacon.

Smith, L. L. (1990). Crisis-intervention: Theory and practice. In J. E. Mezzich & B. Zimmer (Eds.), *Emergency psychiatry* (pp. 305–331). Madison, CT: International Universities Press.

Urbaitis, J. C. (1983). *Psychiatric emergencies.* Norwalk, CT: Appleton-Century-Crofts.

Walker, J. I. (1983). *Psychiatric emergencies: Intervention and resolution.* Philadelphia: Lippincott.

Wambach, K. G. (1996). Crisis assessment and intervention with the alcoholic client: The dilemma of involuntariness. In A. R. Roberts (Ed.), *Crisis manage-*

ment and brief treatment: Theory, technique, and applications (pp. 195–219). Chicago:Nelson-Hall.

Wertheimer, A. (1991). *A special scar: The experiences of people bereaved by suicide.* New York: Routledge.

Wilkinson, C. B., & Vera, E. (1989). Clinical responses to disaster: Assessment, management, and treatment. In R. Gist & B. Lubin (Eds.), *Psychosocial aspects of disaster* (pp. 229–267). New York: Wiley.

Yehuda, R., & McFarlane, A. C. (1995). Conflict between current knowledge about posttraumatic stress disorder and its original conceptual basis. *American Journal of Psychiatry, 152,* 1705–1713.

CHAPTER 3

THE EMERGENCY INTERVIEW

PHILLIP M. KLEESPIES
JAMES D. DELEPPO
DEANNA L. MORI
BARBARA L. NILES

The interview is often considered the very foundation of all clinical endeavors. It has been said that one cannot be a good clinician without having developed good interviewing skills (Turner & Hersen, 1994). Such a statement is probably never more true than when the clinician is faced with a patient who is presenting as acutely suicidal or potentially violent. When the patient is filled with self-loathing and says "I'm a coward and I don't deserve to live," or is rageful and says "I feel like putting a bullet in that s.o.b.'s head," it is obviously not the time to reach for standardized tests or even a structured interview schedule. Emergency conditions demand a more immediate, personal, and flexible type of interview and assessment if a tragedy is to be averted.

In the Introduction to the present volume, the point is made that any mental health clinician with an active practice may be confronted with a patient who is having an emergency such as that noted above. More often than not, however, practitioners have received little formal training in the evaluation and management of such emergencies. In addition, some have contended that training programs give far too little attention in general to teaching the interviewing process (Turner & Hersen, 1994).

Shea and Mezzich (1988) have pointed out that the structure of a clinical interview is, in no small measure, determined by the immediate task facing the mental health clinician. Thus, an interview with a patient who may be on the verge of life-threatening behavior will be different in many respects from an interview with a patient who is seeking psychotherapy for a nonemergent problem. In the case of the former, the clinician will be preoccupied with assessing the degree of risk and formulating an appropriate response; in the case of the latter, the clinician may be far more interested in the patient's personal and family history and its relationship to the patient's presenting problem.

The interview presented in this chapter is intended for use in assessing and managing the patient who presents with what may be a psychological emergency (i.e., with potentially life-threatening behavior). In addition to determining the degree of risk, the major tasks in such an interview (as noted by Gerson & Bassuk, 1980) are to contain and define the emotional turmoil of the patient, and then to direct him or her to appropriate care and treatment.

In the sections that follow, these major tasks are explored in greater depth. The initial focus is on methods of containing the patient's emotional turmoil in an emergency interview. Although such an interview necessarily requires more of an evaluative than a therapeutic approach, the interviewer who ignores the need to establish a working alliance does so at his or her own risk. The patient may react quite negatively, and little will be accomplished.

On the other hand, it is not best to approach an emergency interview in quite the same manner as one would approach forming a therapy relationship. In a crisis or emergency situation, there is usually an expectation that the role of the interviewer is a helping one, and that part and parcel of this role is doing an evaluation of the problem (Echterling & Hartsough, 1989). In other words, the inexperienced interviewer working from a therapy model may also run the risk of dwelling too long on establishing what is already assumed by the patient. In such a case, the patient may begin to feel that his or her presenting problems are not being addressed. Thus, it is important to be aware of the need to titrate the therapeutic and evaluative aspects of an emergency interview.

CONTAINMENT OF EMOTIONAL TURMOIL

General Principles in the Engagement Process

Engaging a patient in a working alliance for the purpose of conducting a clinical interview under crisis/emergency conditions can be a formidable task. Regardless of where the interview takes place, certain elements must be present for the patient to develop a sense of trust and safety. A major element is the ability of the clinician to convey empathy. Hersh (1985) has found that both verbal and nonverbal methods of expressing empathy are effective when interviewing college students in a crisis. Extending one's hand, making appropriate eye contact, head nodding, and demonstrating concern and interest with facial and body gestures and movements are all helpful ways to engage the patient. The use of empathic statements complements the nonverbal expression of empathy. Timely words and phrases that capture the emotional meaning of the patient's communication require patience, concentration, and skill. As the patient senses he or she is being understood and accepted, his or her anxiety and guardedness diminish.

Shea (1988) emphasizes the use of basic to complex empathic statements, whereby the clinician possesses and reflects degrees of certainty regarding what the patient is experiencing; the more certainty, the more incisive the empathic comment. Basic empathic statements are usually made in the earlier part of the interview, when rapport is developing and the clinician is less knowledgeable about the patient's presenting issues and mental status. A basic empathic comment, such as "It sounds like things have gotten more difficult to manage since the loss of your wife," is more general and open and less likely to be threatening to the patient. On the other hand, when the clinician feels more confident about the rapport with the patient and has a better understanding about the issues and corresponding affect, a complex empathic comment, such as "You are feeling quite sad and are having more difficulty managing since the loss of your wife," can be quite timely and may facilitate more verbal material and emotional expression (Shea, 1988).

Authenticity, like empathy, comes from the capacity of the interviewer to be "real" and "genuine" in his or her interaction with the patient. If the patient shows humor, a clinician's smile may allay some of the patient's anxiety, while also conveying the message that the clinician appreciates the levity. The interviewer who is spontaneous, nondefensive, and flexible is role-modeling that it is acceptable to be responsive and expressive about one's feelings and problems. Rapport between the clinician and patient comes from the patient's identification with the clinician in relation to the clinician's caring, availability, and skill in pursuing the issues. When the clinician allows the person in him or her to come through the professional role, a common ground is established for the patient.

Increased Structure for Managing Increased Emotional Turmoil

The more disturbed and decompensated the patient, the more difficult and challenging it is for the clinician to establish rapport. An increase in structure is therefore necessary for the interview to proceed and the work to be accomplished. Patients who are too disorganized, confused, and preoccupied require more direction and prompting. Clear and gentle reminders about the purpose of the interview and the ways the information will be used can help maintain a focus. A patient who is fearful of losing control can be further contained by reassurance that he or she is in a protective environment, and that it is acceptable to express feelings and thoughts with words but not with actions. The clinician's consistent use of both verbal and nonverbal empathic interventions communicates to the patient that his or her inner turmoil is being acknowledged and efforts are being made to help him or her manage it.

Involvement of Family and Friends in the Interview

If family members or friends accompany the patient to the interview setting, the clinician must decide whether they should participate. Advantages to their inclusion are that they may provide critical information regarding precipitants to the crisis, as well as relevant past medical, psychological, and family history. Those close to the patient can speak to his or her baseline functioning and compliance with treatment and medication. Also, the patient's sense of safety may be enhanced when a familiar face is present in the room. In most cases the patient can be asked whether he or she wants a family member present, and, if so, at what point during the interview. This can give the patient some control over the process in which he or she will be the main focus. There are circumstances when the clinician may want to speak with family members separately from the patient. This may be necessary when information critical to diagnosis and disposition is not forthcoming from the patient. At times family involvement may be contraindicated, because confidentiality and/or the patient's cooperation may be compromised; examples include situations where there may be intimidation or abuse (Perlmutter & Jones, 1985). The guiding question the clinician may use when deciding whether family and friends are to be an active part of the interview is this: How will it benefit the interview process and facilitate the work to be done?

In sum, the major initial task of the clinician is to provide for safety within the context of the relationship, as well as within the setting. With this accomplished, the goals of the interview can usually be realized. The patient senses that his or her emotional turmoil is containable because of the availability of support and structure.

Special Issues in Engagement

Many different factors can affect the development of a working alliance with the patient. These issues include the impact of specific settings, as well as patient demographic variables (e.g., ethnicity, race, socioeconomic factors, and gender). In addition, issues the clinician brings to the interaction are discussed, and special attention is given to the management of specific patient problems.

Issues in Specific Settings

The setting in which the emergency interview is conducted can have a major impact on both the patient and the clinician. As Turner and Hersen (1994) point out, the clinical approach used often varies with the setting, and different contexts bring about a different set of expectations on the part of both clinician and patient.

Emergency or Crisis Settings. The ideal setting in which to conduct an emergency interview would be a spacious, well-lit, and comfortably furnished private room. Emergency rooms or crisis clinic environments, however, are often chaotic and can be less than ideal. Interview rooms or areas are often not quiet, private, or comfortable, and multiple interruptions may occur. Time pressure and a demand for rapid assessments often exist (Gerson & Bassuk, 1980). A broad spectrum of mental disorders may be seen in this setting, and patients often present with severe psychopathology (e.g., schizophrenia, bipolar disorders, major depression, organic brain syndrome, and anxiety disorders) (Turner & Hersen, 1994). As a result, patients who are seen in these environments are often frightened and intimidated—by their own feelings, by other patients, and by their surroundings. The goal in such a situation is to obtain enough information to form a reasonable diagnostic impression that will allow the clinician to arrange a safe disposition for the patient (Turner & Hersen, 1994). Given the constraints noted above, this can be a challenging task.

Outpatient Settings. Although the types of cases seen in outpatient settings are typically less acute and severe, emergencies do arise. These emergencies may occur in the context of an ongoing therapeutic relationship. When an emergency arises in the context of an ongoing relationship, the shift to conducting a more structured emergency interview can be a difficult transition for both the clinician and the patient. Although there is often more established rapport, and a more detailed interview can be conducted than in crisis settings, there needs to be a heightened focus on evaluating mental status and developing a treatment plan to address the immediate emergency. It may be useful for the clinician to address this issue and to assure the patient that the questions being asked will help the clinician understand more fully the nature of the emergency and devise the most appropriate treatment plan.

Medical Settings. Providing psychological services to patients in medical settings can be quite challenging, since it is not unusual to receive a consultation to see someone who has not asked for mental health services and may not even know that such a consultation has been requested (Turner & Hersen, 1994). Some patients can feel threatened by such a consultation and feel that the medical staff is disregarding the medical nature of their problem. Patients in this position may fear that they are being viewed as psychosomatic and can be extremely resistant to psychological intervention. For a patient who feels like this to be successfully engaged, it is critical that the clinician approach the situation with great sensitivity. Validating the medical aspects of the patient's problems while highlighting the relationship between physical and mental stress can be an effective way to engage the patient in a dialogue about his or her psychological status.

Demographic Factors

Ethnicity and Race. Being sensitive to and aware of how ethnicity and race affect one's perceptions, beliefs, values, and norms is critical. These factors can affect the manner in which a patient presents and his or her attitude toward seeking treatment. Communication can also be affected, since words or phrases can have very different connotations across cultures (Garrison & Podell, 1981). If not sensitive to such issues, the interviewer can misunderstand or misinterpret culture- or race-specific behavior patterns (Turner & Hersen, 1994). This lack of understanding may be a contributing factor to the finding that minority populations are often overpathologized and misdiagnosed (Jones & Gray, 1986; Lopez & Hernandez, 1986). It appears that race also plays a role in treatment and disposition decisions (Adebimpe, 1982; Gross, Herbert, Knatterud, & Donner, 1969; Hanson & Babigian, 1974; Rosenfield, 1984). Furthermore, Segal, Bola, and Watson (1996) found that emergency service clinicians, most of whom were European-Americans, "prescribed more psychiatric medications to African Americans than to other patients and devoted less time to their evaluation" (p. 282). These authors suggested that a greater degree of interpersonal distance may occur between a clinician and a minority patient, which can result in overpathologizing and therefore in heavier use of antipsychotic medication.

Socioeconomic Factors. There is evidence that people of lower socioeconomic status (SES) receive different diagnostic and treatment recommendations than those of higher SES. Studies have shown that lower-SES individuals are hospitalized more frequently, regardless of diagnosis, and that higher-SES individuals are more frequently offered psychotherapy (Hollingshead & Redlich, 1958; Shader, Binstock, Ohly, & Scott, 1969). Horwitz (1987) found that the courts were more likely to refer lower-SES than higher-SES people to treatment. Much as coming from a minority ethnic or racial background may do, coming from a lower-SES background may result in patients' feeling disempowered or feeling that they have little control as they seek help. Turner and Hersen (1994) suggest that it may be wise to devote additional time to cultivating trust when interviewing people of lower SES, as they may feel less confident about their ability to negotiate their needs in a system they perceive as unresponsive.

Gender. There is evidence to suggest that the sex of the patient influences diagnostic decisions and disposition outcomes (Loring & Powell, 1988). For example, it has been shown that men are more likely to be hospitalized than women, and at a younger age (Errera, Wyshak, & Jarecki, 1963; Gross et al., 1969; Tudor, Tudor, & Gove, 1977). There are also studies indicating that women are more likely to be diagnosed with histrionic personality disorder when they are seen by male clinicians (Loring & Powell, 1988).

This is just a brief discussion of some of the types of influences that occur as a result of patient demographic features. In order to be sensitive to these factors, it is imperative that the clinician be aware of possible group differences so as to minimize the potential negative impact of misinterpretation. In some instances, it may be helpful to consult with or bring into the interview a clinician of the same race, ethnic group, or gender as the patient.

Clinician Variables That Affect the Interaction

Issues that the clinician brings to the evaluation are particularly relevant. Emergency work can be challenging, high-pressure work; it can expose clinicians to many difficult, hostile patients who are not cooperative. Adding to the challenge of this work is the fact that it is often unappreciated by other staff members. In fact, in emergency settings, psychiatric staffers and patients are often perceived as being less important and as having lower status than those who are part of the more emphasized medical agenda of the emergency setting (Barton, 1974; Blais & Georges, 1969).

Hanke (1984) reports that clinicians may respond to the pressure of emergency work with a range of feelings, including anger, anxiety, and despair. Although these feelings are very common in clinicians, they can be difficult to acknowledge (Pope & Tabachnick, 1993). If not adequately addressed, there can be negative treatment consequences, and clinical judgment and decision making can be affected (Dubin, 1990; Pope & Tabachnick, 1993). Although it is difficult to eliminate negative feelings, Dubin (1990) points out the importance of neutralizing them so that they do not distort clinical judgment in a way that impedes care. One way to neutralize negative feelings is to remind oneself of the clinical context of the behavior. Pope and Tabachnick (1993) suggest that such negative feelings can actually be a "therapeutic resource" when acknowledged and appropriately addressed (p. 142).

Specific Patient Problems and Techniques for Managing Them

As discussed above, a number of patient factors can make an emergency evaluation challenging. Knowing how to approach these obstacles is critical; it can help a clinician feel more confident and achieve a more optimal outcome for the patient.

The Agitated/Hostile Patient. When interviewing an acutely disturbed, agitated patient, the clinician is advised to provide structure and to ask straightforward questions (Dubin, 1990; Jessee & Anderson, 1990). Such patients often act out angrily when feeling disempowered and out of control. Setting firm limits while acknowledging a patient's anger is an effective way to diffuse the tension (e.g., "I can see that you are angry and upset, but you need to stop hitting the wall and tell me about your anger, or we'll need to stop the interview."). It is important that the clinician not respond defensively or harshly. To do this, it is crucial to maintain a clinical perspective and not to take the patient's reaction personally. It can be helpful to remind oneself that the patient is behaving in a difficult way because of his or her pathology.

The Paranoid Patient. Patients who are paranoid are particularly challenging because they are often defensive, secretive, irritable, and angry, and
quick to react in a hostile fashion if they perceive a threat. As Dubin (1990)
suggests, these patients are often reassured if clinicians remain professionally
confident and in control. Interviewers should maintain a professional demeanor
and distance, treating such patients respectfully without being overly familiar
or friendly. In fact, Shea (1988) found that overly empathic statements can
serve to disengage guarded or paranoid patients. By acknowledging such a
patient's anger, an interviewer can sometimes engage the uncooperative patient
enough to have him or her participate to some degree with the evaluation (Jessee
& Anderson, 1990). Perry (1976) suggests that it may be useful for the clinician
to acknowledge his or her discomfort directly to the patient, and to provide the
patient with an opportunity to identify ways to help him or her feel in greater
control.

More Structured Containment

Despite the best of efforts, there are times when a patient is unable to form a
working alliance and his or her emotional turmoil exceeds the bounds of verbal
interaction. When a clinician is doing an emergency interview, it is very important to be alert to signals of potential impulsivity, and to take the opportunity
to estimate the patient's level of agitation and/or degree of self-control. A major
objective is to gauge the type of response that will be needed to keep the interaction safe, and to make this response appropriate to the patient's behavior. This
approach is outlined below; it attempts to allow the patient as much autonomy as
he or she can manage, and respects his or her civil right to the least restrictive
treatment alternative (Kaplan & Sadock, 1993).

In an emergency, the importance of observing the patient's behavior cannot be overemphasized. Sometimes warnings of increasing tension will be heard
in verbal expressions of impatience, frustration, and anger, or statements made
in a loud and aggressive manner; often, however, behavioral manifestations of
tension speak louder than words. If the patient paces, has difficulty sitting still,
maintains a rigid posture, clenches and unclenches his or her fists, or shows
other signs of psychomotor agitation, it may be a sign that his or her control is
tenuous (Hilliard, 1990; Kaplan & Sadock, 1993). Some patients will be dis-
trustful or fearful, or will show a startle response. These patients may act impulsively. Still others may demonstrate more subtle signs of anger with a sullen
and defiant demeanor. Psychotic patients may show signs of responding to internal stimuli (e.g., hallucinated voices).

If the clinician has observed some of the behavioral or emotional cues noted
above, or has a "gut" feeling that there is danger, he or she should not be
isolated in a room with the patient. It is recommended that the interview room
be arranged so that, in the event of a serious threat to safety, the clinician will
have easy access to an exit and can obtain help. The clinician should begin the
interview by acknowledging what has been observed and by testing the patient's

ability to respond to verbal intervention (e.g., "You seem tense and upset. Is there some way in which I can be of help?"). If this empathic approach fails and the patient's tension only escalates, an effort at seeing whether the patient can respond to direction or limit setting seems indicated. If the patient is pacing, for example, the clinician should ask him or her to sit down, and then observe whether he or she can remain seated or must quickly get up and pace again.

If the patient cannot respond to empathic efforts at limit setting, it is time to consider that the situation may be getting beyond the control of a single interviewer. One approach is to involve another person in the interview. The presence of additional help can reassure some patients that control will be maintained even if they are struggling with self-control. In a hospital, other staff members are usually nearby and can be enlisted. In a private practice or outpatient setting, however, it is useful to have previously considered how one can obtain help if it is needed. Some clinicians simply excuse themselves from the interview by saying, "I think I need to consult with someone about working with your problem; I'll be right back." Others have prearranged statements or codes that can be given to a clerk or receptionist, who in turn can request the assistance of a nearby professional colleague.

If the patient persists in or escalates his or her agitated or threatening behavior, those working in a private practice or counseling center setting may wish to consider the options of terminating the interview (if it is safe to do so), summoning security officers, or if necessary calling the local police and an ambulance to take the patient to a more secure setting (e.g., a hospital emergency room) for further evaluation. It is in instances like this that it is helpful to be working with a colleague, who can assist either by calling or by staying with the patient while the clinician calls.

Those working in an emergency room, hospital, or clinic setting usually have more options than those in less secure environments; in particular, they can consider a "show of force" and/or tranquilizing medication as alternatives. With some patients, the presence of a single police officer at the door of the interview room can help to restore self-control, and the evaluation can move forward. With those who are angrier or more disturbed, the presence of a clinical staff team and/or a police team may be needed. Independent of or in conjunction with a show of force, the clinician may wish to involve medical staffers or a psychiatrist and to request that the patient be offered psychopharmacological intervention.

For the short-term control of agitated or potentially violent behavior, benzodiazepines and antipsychotics have been the medications of choice (Hilliard, 1990; Kaplan & Sadock, 1993; Tardiff, 1989). If a patient is already on an antipsychotic, usually more of the same medication can be offered. Otherwise, either haloperidol (Haldol; 5 mg by mouth) or lorazepam (Ativan; 1–2 mg by mouth) is customary for an initial trial. If the patient's agitation has not decreased in 30–60 minutes, a second dose is suggested. Benztropine (Cogentin; 1–2 mg) may also be added if there is a risk of extrapyramidal side effects from the antipsychotic. If the patient is psychotic and agitated, both Haldol and Ativan may be used (Kaplan & Sadock, 1993).

In recent times, risperidone (Risperdal), one of the newer neuroleptics, has been used as an alternative to Haldol with agitated patients. It is less sedating and has less risk of extrapyramidal side effects. The initial dose is 1–2 mg and can be repeated in 1–2 hours.

Benzodiazepines such as Ativan are considered less effective for those who have developed a tolerance for them—for example, through excessive use of the medication or through excessive use of alcohol. Although it is a rare finding, benzodiazepines are believed also to disinhibit violent behavior in some patients. Haldol is said to be preferred in patients who have been known to have adverse reactions to benzodiazepines, as well as in patients who are intoxicated on alcohol or sedatives/hypnotics (and could suffer respiratory depression) (Hilliard, 1990). Antipsychotics are generally the treatment of choice for elderly or medically complicated patients; typically, one-half to one-third the usual dose should be employed in these patients. Also, since antipsychotics can lower the seizure threshold, Haldol is usually avoided in patients who are at significant risk for seizures (i.e., unless they are on anticonvulsant medication and stable).

If a show of force has no impact and a patient refuses to take medication voluntarily, yet remains at serious risk or actually loses control, physical restraint may be necessary as an effective and humane response to a dangerous situation. As Kaplan and Sadock (1993) point out, the frustration and confusion of being restrained is a temporary stressor for the patient, but the consequences of uncontained violence can be irreversible. Indications for restraint include preventing imminent harm to the patient or to other persons, as well as preventing damage to the treatment environment or significant disruption of the treatment program (Tardiff, 1989).

The restraint procedure itself involves risks of injury for both patient and staff members, and should be undertaken with a clear plan for maintaining the safety of all concerned. This objective is obviously most effectively carried out by those who have specific training in the safe physical management of violent patients. In hospital settings, restraint procedures are typically considered the province of trained nursing personnel and police or security staff. In cases of extreme violence (e.g., if a patient has a weapon), it is generally regarded as a police matter.

It is beyond the scope of this chapter to go into great detail about the procedures for restraint or seclusion. Suffice it to say that there should be a restraining team consisting of a minimum of five members (i.e., one to control each limb, and one to be the team leader who directs the process and assists others). There should be a plan and a backup plan. Having come to the decision that restraint is necessary, the clinician may be involved in formulating the approach of the team and in helping to calm the patient. The team leader should inform the patient of the reason for the restraint and request that the patient cooperate voluntarily with being restrained. Often patients will do so. To help alleviate feelings of helplessness, the team leader should explain each step of the restraint process to the patient; however, there should be no negotiation. Negotiation at such times can result in confused messages to the team and increased risk (see Hilliard, 1990; Tardiff, 1989).

Many patients become calmer once they are in restraints and control has been instituted. Others, however, may continue to be agitated or may even become more so. In such cases, it may be necessary to request that a medical staff member or a psychiatrist prescribe medication to ease the distress and turmoil of the patient. If feasible, the patient should again be offered oral medication as noted above. If the patient refuses and continues to be very agitated, he or she may need to have an injection of an antipsychotic (e.g., Haldol, 5 mg, i.m.) administered as an emergency measure. This dosage can be repeated in 30–60 minutes if the patient's agitation has not decreased. Again, Cogentin may be added to decrease side effects as long as there is no contraindication to anticholinergic medications. A benzodiazepine (e.g., Ativan, 2 mg, i.m.) may be given if needed to augment the antipsychotic (Kaplan & Sadock, 1993). The patient's physical and emotional condition should be closely monitored while he or she is in restraints and/or receiving emergency medication.

DEFINING OR FORMULATING
THE PROBLEM

As the patient's turmoil is attenuated, the clinician needs to address the task of defining the presenting problem. Although at times in an emergency setting the presenting problem is clearly stated, a patient is often unable to present his or her difficulties in an organized, coherent manner; in some cases the patient is not even cognizant that there is a problem. In order to distill the potentially vast amounts of data into a formulated problem, the clinician must be guided by a theoretical framework that will provide structure to the interview. It is recommended that clinicians (1) use a biopsychosocial model to generate different ideas about the multidimensional nature of the presenting problems, and (2) utilize a hypothesis-testing strategy to determine how best to understand the data gathered during the interviewing process.

The Biopsychosocial Model

A myriad of intricate theories of human behavior have been developed as efforts to account for mental disorders and functional difficulties; these theories are often based on biological, psychological, or social principles. In an emergency room interview, however, these complex theories are often too cumbersome or not adequately inclusive to organize the many pieces of information confronting the clinician (Lazare, 1976). The biopsychosocial model is a multidimensional approach to problem formulation that utilizes principles from each of these three general frameworks. In this approach, biological influences such as medications, physical illness, and family history of mental illness are considered. Psychological factors, such as expression of unresolved conflict, the psychodynamic meaning of the problem, and the patterns of reinforcement of the problem behaviors, are also included in conceptualization. The patient's social environment, which includes such aspects as interpersonal functioning, occupational functioning, family system influences, and the current living situation, is evaluated.

Hypothesis Testing

In an emergency interview, the clinician is confronted with innumerable bits of information about the patient's biological state, psychological functioning, and social milieu, both past and present. Many details are presented by the patient, family members, other staff members, and medical records. Mental status tests and focused questioning provide additional information to flesh out the picture. Finally, clinicians' observations of patients' behaviors, reactions to the interviewing process, and interactions with family members and clinic staff are valuable sources of information. Lazare (1976) articulates a hypothesis-testing approach to help organize the interview and evaluation process, and to prevent the clinician from being overloaded by large numbers of disconnected facts.

Early in the interview, the clinician uses the first few bits of data collected (e.g., the nurse's note, the referral form, etc.) to generate several hypotheses, based on biopsychosocial theories, about how the presenting problem may be formulated. For example, a clinician receives a nurse's note on a consultation form indicating that a patient, Mr. B, has presented to the emergency room feeling depressed and having suicidal ideation. Mr. B's chart indicates that he presented to the emergency room 1 year ago, that he was hospitalized at that time and diagnosed with major depression and posttraumatic stress disorder (PTSD), and that he responded well to the antidepressant medication that was prescribed. From these few bits of information, the clinician then generates some hypotheses about the precipitant of the current episode of depression and suicidality. A recent psychosocial stressor, noncompliance with medications, drug or alcohol use, and/or an anniversary reaction to a previous traumatic stressor are all to be considered as possible precipitants or factors to be weighed.

The various hypotheses are then simultaneously considered and investigated as the clinician proceeds through the interview. Thus, the clinician questions Mr. B about recent stressors; his use of prescribed medication, other drugs, and alcohol; and whether he has run into problems during this time of year in the past.

Each new piece of data about the patient is used either to support and develop or to refute each hypothesis. As the interview progresses, some hypotheses appear more likely than others, and particular attention is given to information pertaining to those hypotheses. For example, Mr. B denies any recent psychosocial stressors, but reports that he often has difficulty with depression this time of year. He describes that he has stopped taking his medication because he does not like the side effects, and that he has been drinking more alcohol recently to help him sleep. The clinician then questions him in more detail about his anniversary reactions, the quantity and frequency of his alcohol use, and his specific negative reactions he had to the medication.

At the end of the interviewing process, the clinician can present a formulation based on one or more biopsychosocial hypotheses that have been tested during the interview. In Mr. B's case, the clinician may determine that this patient has been experiencing more severe PTSD symptoms near the anniversary of his original traumatic stressor, and that he has been using alcohol to self-medicate because the side effects of his prescribed medication outweigh the relief he obtains with it.

The Interview

Interview Stages

At the first stage of the interview (as noted above), the clinician's task is to generate several viable hypotheses about the nature of the presenting problem. Thus, open-ended questions such as "What brings you here today?" or "What seems to be the problem?" are most appropriate at this point. Once the initial hypotheses have been identified, the clinician then proceeds to test these hypotheses by asking more focused questions about certain issues, such as "Did you begin feeling depressed after your aunt died, or before?" At this second stage in the interview, existing ideas about the nature and scope of the presenting problems are developed. In addition, new hypotheses based on new information may be generated. Questioning at this point is very specific, such as "Do you have any medication at home?" At the termination of the interview, the clinician may determine that several complementary formulations best describe the problem. For example, a patient may have a prolonged history of depression, resulting in a biological conceptualization of the current depression; in addition, a recent psychosocial stressor (e.g., the loss of a job or the death of a friend) may provide further explanation for the patient's current state. "Yes–no" questions or closed-ended questions to confirm the hypotheses are most useful at this stage.

Validity

It is crucial to consider how valid the patient's information is in an emergency assessment. Validity in the clinical interview has to do with the accuracy of data elicited from the patient. Shea (1988) has suggested two ways to test the validity of the patient's information. One method is to ask the patient to describe specific details of events, rather than asking for opinions about these events. For example, the interviewer might ask a woman what sort of things her husband actually did to give her emotional support, rather than whether she felt satisfied with her husband's support. A second method of establishing validity is to seek verification of information from family and friends—provided, of course, that they are available and that the patient gives the clinician permission to seek their input.

Gathering of Information

Individuals may differ immensely in terms of the information they present to clinicians. Likewise, clinicians may vary greatly in terms of the information they seek in an interview as they tailor their questions to test specific hypotheses. Despite these variations, there are several topics that should be covered in all emergency interviews, except perhaps when a patient's condition will not allow it. Identifying information, the chief complaint, factors precipitating the current problem, current functional status, mental health and substance use history, and assessment of lethality are all essential components of a thorough emergency interview.

Chief Complaint. Interviews typically begin with elicitation of the chief complaint. This can often be assessed simply with a question such as "What seems to be troubling you today?" It can be useful to record verbatim parts of the patient's response to this question for use in the written report. In such a case, however, as Siassi (1984) points out, the patient may be unaware of or deny that there are any problems. In these cases the patient's family or mental health care professional may provide the chief complaint. Here it can be useful to record both the patient's statement (e.g., "Nothing is troubling me; I'm feeling great!") and a description of the behavior that has led to the current evaluation (e.g., the patient's brother reports that the patient has been making plans to hijack a space ship to fly to Venus).

Precipitating Factors. After the chief complaint has been determined, the next task for the clinician is to identify the factors leading to the current crisis. It is useful to know how long the patient has been in the current state, and to understand the course of the present illness. Questions such as "Have you felt this way before, or is this the first time?" can be useful in this context. The interviewer should also inquire about any recent stressors, losses, or changes in circumstances that may have contributed to the current problem.

Current Functioning. Information about the patient's current social and occupational functioning is necessary for the formulation of the problem and the plan of action. Clinicians should assess how well the patient is able to work or go to school; interact with family, friends, and/or coworkers; and perform tasks of daily living (e.g., grooming, eating). The quality of the patient's social network may be particularly important in treatment planning. If the patient has friends or relatives who will monitor his or her status and assist the patient in seeking further help when necessary, hospitalization can sometimes be avoided. Perlmutter and Jones (1985) stress the importance of utilizing the rich information that family members can often provide in an emergency assessment. The patient's presenting problem may well be a family issue; the family often both contributes to and is affected by the patient's ability to function.

Mental Health and Substance Use History. Because past behavior is one of the best predictors of future problems in the area of emergency mental health, the patient's history of suicide attempts and aggressive acting out is vital in treatment planning. A brief history of previous inpatient and outpatient therapy, diagnoses conferred during previous therapeutic encounters, and assessment of current psychotropic medication are all useful pieces of information in formulating the problem and the plan of action. Assessment of substance use problems is particularly important in the formulation of the case and in managing the interview.

Lethality Assessment. Patients often present for emergency assessments because they are at risk for harming either themselves or others. It is, in fact, the risk of lethality that causes the interview to be an "emergency." Thus, assessment of risk of suicidality, violent acting out, or inability to protect oneself adequately is often a major focus in the emergency interview. Clinical issues in the assessment and management of the suicidal patient, the violent patient, and the victim of violence are covered in detail elsewhere in this volume (see Chapters 4, 5, and 6) and cannot be adequately covered in this chapter; however, a few guidelines for assessment are offered here.

In a lethality assessment, the clinician should ask about suicidal or homicidal ideation in a straightforward manner. Both clinicians and patients often wish to skirt these difficult topics. Less experienced interviewers may hesitate to ask such questions; they may be influenced by the myth that asking them can give patients ideas and increase the chances of such behavior. In fact, examination of a patient's ideation will allow a clinician to take the steps necessary to ensure safety. Patients may be hesitant to reveal their suicidal or violent ideation for various reasons: They may want to avoid appearing "crazy" or to avoid being hospitalized, or they may feel it is inappropriate to burden someone else (even a mental health clinician) with their troubles. In such cases, the clinician needs to be sensitive to subtle expressions of despair or frustration, and to follow up on indirect indications. For example, a patient may simply report, "I'm just so tired of all the hassles." Further questioning of this patient may reveal a wish to die or to commit suicide.

Once it is determined that a patient has ideation about suicide or violent acting out, the clinician should inquire about the plan to determine (1) the level of intent (2) the viability of the plan, and (3) the likelihood that the patient will act impulsively. The level of intent might be assessed by asking the patient,

"Can you tell me on a 1-to-10 scale—where 1 means that you definitely would not carry out your plan, and 10 means that you definitely would carry out your plan—where you are on that scale now?" How viable the plan is should be determined from all the information the patient presents. In particular, access to weapons, pills, or other means of harming self or others should be evaluated. The patient's impulsivity might be ascertained by asking about similar situations in the past and how the patient handled them, such as "Have you ever been this angry at your neighbor before? What did you do then?" In addition, the clinician should evaluate how likely it is that the patient will use psychoactive substances, especially those that have disinhibiting effects, such as alcohol or cocaine. Use of such substances may cloud all judgment.

The patient's ongoing mental health treatment (or lack thereof) will also influence the clinician in determining current lethality. Even in the midst of an emergency, it is generally well worth the effort to track down and speak to the patient's outpatient treater to determine how far from "baseline" the patient's current state is.

Assessment of Current Functioning/Mental Status Testing

The mental status examination (MSE) is the portion of the assessment that provides many of the objective observations the clinician gathers while interviewing the patient. Whereas the data obtained during the information-gathering portion of the interview are focused on the recent history of the problem, the MSE is more of a cross-section of data reflecting the patient's functioning at the current time. Some of the observations made during the information-gathering portion of the interview can be used to generate hypotheses that help to guide the questioning during the MSE.

In emergency evaluations, the MSE is at the very heart of the assessment. This is the information that allows the clinician to attend to the immediate goal of forming a diagnostic opinion and treatment disposition. In fact, there are times when a clinician may have to rely solely on the information from the MSE to make his or her diagnostic and disposition decision. For example, when patients are resistant and uncooperative, they may not be interested or willing to give a more open-ended account of their presenting problems. Patients who are highly disorganized may be very willing to elaborate on their problems, but may be so tangential or unreliable in their accounts that clinicians might benefit from moving quickly to the MSE, where more objective data are gathered in a more directive manner. Clinicians should be careful, however, not to make the critical mistake of moving too quickly to this portion of the interview before establishing a comfortable rapport with patients.

In its most comprehensive form, the MSE should cover all areas of mental and behavioral functioning that are involved in diagnostic classification (Kaplan, Freedman, & Sadock, 1980). An MSE that is so inclusive may be rather unwieldy, however, and is usually unnecessary. A skilled clinician can glean a lot

of information from his or her observations or from deductive reasoning throughout the interview. Clinicians, however, should be aware of all the components
of the MSE, and should be sufficiently comprehensive in their interviews that
all the major bases are covered. There are also structured MSEs that are relatively short and can be used fairly reliably as brief screening tools. One particularly well-known test is the Mini-Mental State (Folstein, Folstein, & McHugh,
1976).

The purpose of the present discussion is to familiarize clinicians with the
basic components of the MSE. Exhaustive descriptions of these components are
not provided, since excellent overviews and examples of questions and tests
exist in the literature (e.g., Akiskal & Akiskal, 1994; Kaplan et al., 1980; Siassi,
1984; Zuckerman, 1995). In addition, a sample MSE form is provided in Figure 3.1.

General Appearance. The patient's overall appearance in the interview is
described. In this section, observations can be made about clothing, grooming,
hygiene, or anything that strikes the clinician as being particularly outstanding
or unusual. The clinician should be as specific or objective as possible, and
should minimize vague or subjective comments.

Behavior and Psychomotor Activity. Observations about the patient's
behavioral presentation are made. Tics, gestures, posturing, or other unusual behavior is noted; in addition, the level of activity is commented upon.
For example, patients who are highly restless or agitated might be described
as "psychomotor-accelerated." Patients who appear sedated, exhibit poor
eye contact, and move slowly could be described as "psychomotor-retarded."

Attitude toward Examiner. The manner in which the patient engages with
the clinician can provide very important diagnostic information, and can also
help the clinician interpret the information obtained during the interview. For
example, if the patient is overly friendly or appears to be seeking approval, the
clinican needs to be alerted to the possibility that this patient may underreport
or distort certain information in order to make sure the clinician maintains a
favorable impression of him or her.

Orientation. Disturbances in orientation tend to predominate in individuals who are delirious, although they can also be seen in people who are severely
demented or psychotic (Akiskal & Akiskal, 1994, Siassi, 1984). To be described
as fully oriented, a person must demonstrate that he or she is oriented to person, place, time/date, and situation. It is within normative limits for people to
miss the date by a day or so. When this occurs, it is not necessarily an indication
of disorientation to time, but instead may result from distraction secondary to
other problems (Kaplan et al., 1980).

MENTAL STATUS EXAM FORM

ORIENTATION: Person _____ Place _____ Time/date _____ Situation _____
MOOD: (How would you describe your mood/spirit today?) Depressed _____
       Elated ___ Anxious ___ Agitated ___ Irritable ___ Euthymic ___ Angry ___
APPEARANCE: Neat ___ Disheveled ___ Obese ___ Emaciated ___ Average ___
PSYCHOMOTOR ACTIVITY: Normal ___ Accelerated ___ Retarded ___
SPEECH: Tone _____ Rate _____ Variability _____ Articulation _____
AFFECT: Flat ___ Blunted ___ Constricted ___ Labile ___ Appropriate ___
CONGRUENCE: Appropriate ___ Incongruent ___ (mild/moderate/profound?)

IMMEDIATE RECALL: Baby   Pen   Tree
        (or)   295 Oxford Street   *Gone with the Wind*   Purple

CONCENTRATION: Serial 7's _____
        (or)   Spell WORLD: _____   Spell WORLD backwards:_____
FUND OF INFORMATION: Presidents C__ B__ R__ C__ F__ N__ J__ K__
        (or)   Name five large U.S. cities _____
RECENT MEMORY: Recent major news event _____
ABSTRACTION: Similarities—Apple and banana_____
                     Table and chair _____
        Proverbs—Don't judge a book by its cover _____
                   Too many cooks spoil the broth _____
                   People who live in glass houses shouldn't throw stones _____

DELAYED RECALL: Baby   Pen   Tree
        (or)   295 Oxford Street   *Gone with the Wind*   Purple

THOUGHT PROCESSES: Logical + -, Coherent + -, Tangential/circumstantial + -, Looseness of association (LOA) + -, Flight of ideas (FOI) + -, Ideas of reference (IOR—Are people talking about you?) + -, Obsessions + -
THOUGHT CONTENT: Paranoia + -, Suicidal + -, Homicidal + -, Self-esteem + -, Somatization + -, Nihilistic + -
HALLUCINATIONS: Auditory (AH—Have you heard voices or sounds others have not?
        Content?) _____, Visual (VH) _____, Olfactory (OH) _____,
   Gustatory (GH) _____, Tactile (TH) _____
DELUSIONS: Persecutory (Have you felt as if someone is out to get you?) + -, Thought broadcasting (Are you able to put your thoughts into other people's minds and influence them?) + -, Mind control (Have you felt that someone can control your mind?) + -, Thought insertion (Have you ever had thoughts put in your mind which were not your own? Source?) + -, Mind reading (Have you felt that someone can read your mind?) + -, Grandiosity (Are you an especially gifted or important person?) + -, Reference (Do things happen which only you really understand? e.g., get special messages from TV or radio) + -
PERCEPTUAL ILLUSIONS (Perceiving actual stimuli incorrectly): + - _____
PANIC ATTACKS: (Have your ever experienced times of great fear or anxiety?) + - ____
PHOBIAS: (Are you afraid of things/places/activities that don't frighten most people?) + - ___
SLEEP DISTURBANCES: + - ___ hrs/nt. ___ ENERGY LEVEL: Up down _____
APPETITE: + - Weight loss or gain ___ lbs. (over what period of time?) _____
ALCOHOL MISUSE: + - Last use: ___ Hx. of DTs? ___ Hx. of withdrawal szs.? _____
DRUG ABUSE: + - Last use: ___ Type of drug(s): _____
JUDGMENT: (What would you do if while in the movies you are the first person to see smoke and fire? Or use an example relevant to the patient's real-life experience.)
INSIGHT: (Why are you here?) _____

FIGURE 3.1. Sample mental status examination (MSE) form.

Attention and Concentration. The patient's level of attention and concentration can sometimes be inferred from behavior during the interview. For example, the attention and concentration of a patient must be questioned if he or she is easily distractible or is constantly asking the clinician to repeat questions. In terms of more objective tests, the serial subtraction of 7's from 100 is a traditional way of measuring concentration.

Memory. Memory deficits are often classified according to the span of time involved in the loss of function (Akiskal & Akiskal, 1994). "Immediate memory" is memory for events or things that just took place; this can be tested by asking a patient to repeat numerical digits immediately after the clinician says them first. Short-term retention can be measured by asking the patient to repeat three items after 5 minutes have elapsed. "Long-term memory" can be tested by asking patients to recall events that occurred in the past several months or years, and "remote memory" can be assessed by asking about events that occurred many years ago. In order to get an accurate and reliable test of memory, it is important for the patient to concentrate and attend to the task at hand. These are obviously very basic tests of memory, and more extensive neuropsychological testing should be considered for patients who show significant deficits.

Mood and Affect. "Mood" can be defined as the pervasive and sustained emotion that affects the patient's view of the world (Kaplan et al., 1980). Information about the patient's mood can be obtained both by observing the patient and by asking him or her direct questions about subjective symptoms and vegetative symptoms (e.g., significant change in appetite and sleep, or decrease in energy and libido). Whereas "mood" refers to the more pervasive emotion that a patient experiences over time, "affect" refers to the prevailing emotional expression during the interview (Akiskal & Akiskal, 1994). The consistency, intensity, depth, and duration of the patient's affect should be noted (Siassi, 1984).

Intelligence. An estimate of intellectual ability is made from information obtained through the interview, from the patient's educational level and fund of information, and from the patient's demonstrated ability to conceptualize and reason. Abstract reasoning is often measured by using similarities (e.g., "In what way are a table and chair alike?") or asking patients to provide meanings for proverbs. Fund of information can be measured by asking whether a patient is aware of any major news stories, or by asking him or her to name the last several U.S. Presidents (or, in other nations, the last several heads of state).

Speech and Thought. A tremendous amount of information can be obtained by paying attention to the quality of a patient's speech, which reflects the integrity of his or her thoughts. "Thought form" or "thought process" refers to how thoughts are put together and communicated (Akiskal & Akiskal, 1994). An individual's thought process can be described in terms of both quantity and quality. Quantity indicates how productive the thought process is (e.g., paucity of ideas, flight of ideas), and quality is reflected by the flow and organization of thoughts (e.g., goal-directed, loosely associated, circumstantial, tangential). "Thought content" refers to *what* the patient is communicating. This can include suicidal or homicidal thoughts, obsessions, compulsions, phobias, delusions (e.g., grandiose or persecutory), and ideas of reference (e.g., the patient thinks he or she is the focus of negative attention).

Perceptual Disturbances. Disorders of perception include both hallucinations and illusions. "Hallucinations" are perceptions without an external stimulus (Akiskal & Akiskal, 1994), and can involve any of the senses (e.g., auditory, visual, olfactory, gustatory, or tactile). "Illusions" are misperceptions of actual stimuli (Akiskal & Akiskal, 1994). Perceptual distortions are often seen in psychotic or organic disorders, but can also be brought about by affective disturbances, anxiety disorders, and substance use disorders.

Judgment and Insight. The social judgment of an individual often becomes clear through the interviewing process, and as the patient reports his or her life events. Judgment questions can also be posed by using classic examples (e.g., "What should you do if while in the movies you are the first person to see smoke and fire?") or making up a scenario that requires a level of social judgment in order to respond appropriately. The patient's attitude and understanding of the problem reflect his or her level of insight.

Psychodiagnostic Impressions

An important function of the clinician conducting a crisis/emergency interview is to establish a working diagnosis and formulation of the patient's presenting problem and complaints (Lazare, 1976; Siassi, 1984). When these goals are achieved, the clinician is able to determine which therapeutic interventions would be most helpful to the patient. During the early phase of the interview, the clinician considers probable diagnoses that fit the data—including all relevant information from the MSE and clinical records, as well as observations from those who are familiar with the patient. A multidimensional approach to the testing of hypotheses provides a comprehensive model that facilitates the examination of the biopsychosocial aspects of the patient's current and past functioning. Diagnoses are ruled out by sifting through the available information and discerning how it corresponds with the DSM-IV diagnostic categories. Shea and Mezzich (1988) emphasize the value of arriving at a differential diagnosis as early in the diagnostic and formulation phase as possible. These authors support the concept of diagnostic-specific treatments (Siassi, 1984), in which the clinician's diagnostic assessment and formulation determine the particular therapeutic intervention. For example, a patient who is manic with auditory hallucinations and paranoid delusions would be started on a neuroleptic and a mood stabilizer to alleviate the symptoms associated with the diagnosis of bipolar I disorder with psychotic features, whereas a patient who presents with recent psychological trauma would be referred for further evaluation for PTSD.

With the advent of managed care and its focused, time-limited orientation throughout the mental health system, the diagnostic-specific treatment approach has been attractive and heavily utilized. Preauthorization is often required before inpatient or outpatient mental health services can be provided to a patient. Most times the clinician must provide a diagnosis, formulation, and treatment plan before the services are approved, while the patient waits in the emergency room or in other settings where the evaluation is being conducted. When there are safety issues involved, such as suicidality and homicidality, the diagnosis-specific approach takes on more urgency because an immediate disposition has to be made. A working or preliminary diagnosis should be acceptable under these emergency conditions until a more definitive diagnosis can be made and the most appropriate treatment can be recommended and begun.

Case Formulation

As mentioned above, arriving at a diagnosis or a set of diagnoses is a very important and necessary step in organizing and making sense of the data gathered in the interview. It is typically not sufficient, however, for a more complete understanding of the patient. A "case formulation" is a more encompassing organization that takes into account not only clinical syndromes (or Axis I diagnoses), but also precipitating events, predisposing vulnerabilities, personality styles and/or disorders, family system and social network factors, coping resources, and so forth.

As Lazare (1976) has pointed out, the clinician who uses the hypothesis-testing approach generates hypotheses not only about possible diagnoses, but also about a more inclusive case formulation. When the interview is completed, the clinician must examine the biopsychosocial data to see not only which hypothesized diagnoses are supported and which are refuted, but also which hypothesized case formulation makes most sense of the data. Thus, for example, the interviewer may have found that a male patient's thinking is loose and tangential; that for the past month he has been having auditory hallucinations of voices telling him not to trust anyone; and that during that same time frame he has had the delusional belief that his neighbor is attempting to poison him. These data are consistent with the interviewer's diagnostic hypothesis that the patient is having an acute episode of paranoid schizophrenia. The interviewer, however, has also learned that the patient's family recently moved out of the area and sees him less frequently; that the patient has become increasingly isolated; and that he stopped taking his neuroleptic medication approximately 6 weeks ago, shortly after the family's move. The interviewer's hypothesized formulation is thus that the patient is having an acute psychotic episode precipitated by feeling abandoned by those whom he trusted, losing a crucial part of his support system, feeling more vulnerable, and discontinuing his medication in protest.

A critical component of the formulation following an emergency interview is arriving at a clinical estimate of the risk of suicide or violence to others. In this regard, it is important to understand that a clinician cannot predict with accuracy events such as completed suicide or homicide, which are statistically rare even in patient populations (Murphy, 1984; Monahan, 1993). This statement should not be taken as meaning that practitioners do not need to make every effort to try to detect those who are suicidal or homicidal. Rather, as Motto, Heilbron, and Juster (1985) have pointed out, the clinician's efforts should be directed at making a carefully reasoned estimate of the degree of risk, not at the improbable task of actual prediction.

As noted earlier in the "Lethality Assessment" subsection, the knowledge base needed to formulate an estimate of risk is discussed in detail elsewhere in this volume (see Chapters 4, 5, and 6). What is offered here is a synopsis of some factors to consider in attempting to estimate the level of risk.

A knowledge of the demographics of suicide and violence can be helpful, but it is best not to become too reliant on statistics. Thus, although widowed men have a higher rate of suicide, it does not follow that married men are not vulnerable. It is also important to consider diagnosis, since some diagnostic categories (e.g., depression, substance abuse/dependence, schizophrenia) have much higher rates of suicide (Tanney, 1992), and some (e.g., antisocial personality disorder, bipolar I disorder, schizophrenia) have much higher rates of violence (McNiel & Binder, 1994). Diagnosis alone, however, is of limited use, and it may be more fruitful to consider high-risk factors within specific diagnostic categories. Thus, McNiel and Binder (1994) found that a hostile, suspicious mood state in a manic patient greatly heightened the risk of violence.

A history of suicidal and/or violent behavior is suggestive of higher risk. However, clinicians can become too reliant on the presence or absence of previous suicide attempts in making decisions about suicide risk. Maris (1992), for example, has estimated that more than 50% of suicides are completed with no prior attempts. Thus, an absence of prior attempts cannot be taken as necessarily lessening risk. A family history of completed suicide heightens risk. It is possible that there is a biological or genetic influence (Asberg, Nordstrom, & Traskman-Bendz, 1986; Kety, 1986), or that the family history provides a model of suicide as a solution to problems. With respect to violence, a history of childhood or adolescent violence or cruelty, or a history of having been a childhood victim of violence, can be a warning sign of possible future violent behavior (Tardiff, 1989). Some families condone violence as a method of conflict resolution, and a patient who comes from such a family may see violence as an accepted part of life.

In terms of the data gathered about the patient's current state, it is crucial to have obtained an estimate of his or her emotional pain, despair, or anger (as the case may be). In the information-gathering phase of the interview, the clinician will have obtained data about such precipitating factors as losses, reversals in status, or changes in circumstance or health. The clinician should also consider the interview findings not only about the patient's suicidal or violent ideation, but about his or her apparent intent to act. One measure of intent can be the degree of planfulness or premeditation. An effort must be made to understand what intrapersonal problem suicide or violence might solve for the patient (e.g., some patients might see violence as the only way to restore a sense of control or self-worth). The clinician should factor in the patient's coping resources, as manifested in his or her current functioning (e.g., frustration tolerance, ability to form and sustain relationships, ability to tolerate emotion, etc.). Personal beliefs or values that may inhibit action should be weighed in the balance as well. If substance misuse is a part of the patient's condition, it can, as noted earlier, be disinhibiting and cloud judgment. Imminence of action can at times be detected through psychomotor restlessness or agitation, as well as through verbal indicators of pain or anger. Finally, access to the means of self-destruction or violence should be given serious consideration.

The practitioner must use his or her clinical judgment in weighing the many possible contributing factors and risk indicators. Whether his or her clinical opinion suggests mild, moderate, or severe risk, it is seldom a matter of a single "cause" but involves the consideration of multiple possible determinants on several different levels—including the biological, psychological, and social.

DISPOSITION PLANNING

Response to Risk

While the clinician is evaluating the viability of various hypotheses and formulating the presenting problems, he or she is simultaneously considering various disposition options. Three general categories of possible disposition plans are as follows: (1) intervention and problem solving with the patient to allay the current crisis; (2) referral for outpatient services; and (3) inpatient hospitalization. The risk that the patient will do harm to self or others is the factor that generally has the greatest bearing on which of these three options should be pursued. Thus estimation of risk is integrally involved in disposition planning. The level of risk should be appraised by means of a risk–benefit analysis (Bongar, 1992), whereby the clinician reviews the patient's risk factors (e.g., impulsivity, substance use, etc.) and the factors that mediate risk (e.g., stabilizing influence of a friend). When conducting a risk–benefit analysis, a clinician is generally well advised to verify the patient's self-report by talking directly with the patient's sources of support—family, friends, and/or mental health care professionals who are significant in the patient's life. Information obtained from these sources can be crucial; the patient's self-report may be verified, or new information may come to light that may have a considerable impact on the risk–benefit analysis.

The patient's ability to enter into a contract for safety can also dramatically influence the risk–benefit analysis. Stanford, Goetz, and Bloom (1994) have suggested that the process of making a therapeutic contract concerning issues of safety can enhance the therapeutic alliance, provide the clinician with important pieces of information about the patient's plan to harm self or others, and indicate the patient's ability to enter into such a contract. Although these authors indicate that such contracts do not protect the clinician legally, they have found that contracting can reduce anxiety for both clinicians and patients.

The clinician uses all information provided in the risk–benefit analysis to determine which one of the three general disposition plans to pursue. If the patient appears to be at no risk for harm to self or others, and he or she is noticeably calmed by the interview process, the clinician may decide that crisis intervention during the interview is a sufficient disposition plan. Depending on the setting, the clinician may wish to make referrals for other resources to encourage the patient to use nonemergency services for problem-solving purposes.

When a decision is made to release the patient with a referral for outpatient services, it is necessary to provide the patient with specific names and phone numbers of clinics or clinicians who will be able to help; calling ahead to verify that the patient can be seen is advised. Another important part of this disposition plan is a contract with the patient that he or she will return to the emergency setting for reevaluation if the level of risk increases. If a mental health care professional is already involved in treating the patient, the evaluating clinician should call this professional to discuss the treatment plan.

If the outpatient treatment provider has a role in the disposition plan, it is vital that he or she agree to perform that role. If a decision is made that inpatient treatment is necessary for a patient, that decision and the reasoning behind it should be explained to the patient. In most cases, when given sufficient explanation, patients will endorse the plan and agree to voluntary hospitalization. In some cases, however, patients must be involuntarily hospitalized if they do not agree with the plan. Regulations and procedures for involuntary hospitalization vary from state to state. Clinicians should be well aware of the procedures for involuntary hospitalization in their state.

Problems in Disposition Planning

Deciding on the most appropriate disposition is one thing, but securing such a disposition is another. The clinician may have to contend with such factors as the patient's access to health insurance and ability to pay for treatment, availability of community resources (including hospital beds), and patient and/or staff resistance to the disposition plan.

The evaluating clinician is often thrust into the role of trying to convince a hospital intake worker or an outpatient mental health provider to accept a patient for treatment when the patient lacks mental health insurance and has limited financial resources. If the patient's health care is managed, then the clinician must receive approval from the case reviewer of the managed care company, especially if full or partial hospitalization is sought (Appelbaum, 1993). Although this process is time-consuming and frustrating for both the clinician and the patient, it is necessary.

It is common knowledge that the success of a disposition depends upon the social and community support system available to the patient (Gerson & Bassuk, 1980). It has been found that less psychiatric hospitalization is required as more community resources are available (Mendel & Rapport, 1969); however, the accessibility of mental health services varies significantly from state to state and community to community (Brown, 1985). The state hospital system, which has historically provided for the indigent, is undergoing massive changes in its provision of mental health services. At times a clinician will not be able to effect the optimal disposition because of a lack of community resources. In such a case, medication can be offered with a referral to outpatient treatment, if the patient agrees. This may be an appropriate disposition if it meets the patient's immediate clinical needs, and if its purpose is not to avoid the issues in making a more complete and thorough disposition.

Aside from external factors that affect the disposition of a case, issues such as patient and/or staff resistance must be managed by the clinician for the outcome to be successful. There are times when the working alliance between a patient and clinician is not sufficient to allay the patient's fear and anxiety about being admitted to a psychiatric unit or to a less intensive treatment program. It is important that the clinician maintain an empathic stance and explore the resistance with the patient. As the decision regarding disposition gets closer, the patient may experience stronger feelings of paranoia and abandonment, and may become help-rejecting. If the clinician cannot work through the resistance with the patient, it may be helpful (if possible) to bring in family and friends who are supportive of the treatment recommendations, and to reassure the patient that he or she will not be abandoned. If the patient is to be treated in the same facility where the interview is taking place, it can be helpful to have a staff member from the treatment location (e.g., ward, day hospital, outpatient clinic) participate during the latter part of the interview. For some patients, a familiar face will make the transition from the emergency room to the treatment location less intimidating, and may decrease the amount of anxiety and fear. In cases where the resistance cannot be worked through, the clinician, as mentioned earlier, must determine whether the patient has the decision-making capacity to refuse treatment.

A problem that presents itself during the disposition and referral process is the difficulty treatment staff members have in working with certain types of problems and patients. As a group, mental health professionals would prefer to treat patients who are cooperative, compliant, and interesting, and who possess motivation and psychological-mindedness. Tischler (1966) found that when patients being seen in an emergency room had good psychotherapy potential, they were often referred to outpatient treatment even though hospitalization could have been justified. On the other hand, patients who present as being dangerous to themselves or others, who are manipulative and difficult to manage, or who are passive and clinging can generate negative feelings of helplessness and anger in their mental health care providers (Gerson & Bassuk, 1980; Pope & Tabachnick, 1993). Some diagnoses can be "red flags" for some clinicians. For example, when some clinicians hear that a patient carries a diagnosis of borderline or antisocial personality disorder and has a history of alcoholism or drug addiction, many negative stereotypes emerge before the actual patient is seen. The person behind the diagnosis may not be considered unless the referring clinician provides a more complete understanding of the patient and his or her problems.

THE WRITTEN REPORT

A tremendous amount of information is often obtained during the emergency interview, and it can be a challenge to prioritize and organize this information quickly into a concise and informative report. This is an important skill, however, since it is essential to document an accurate account of how the patient presented during the acute crisis. Often the report is the sole vehicle for communicating this critical information to other treatment providers. Furthermore, the report becomes a part of the patient's medical or mental health record, and future treatment and diagnostic decisions may be based in part on the information presented there.

The emergency evaluation report is a concisely written summary of the interview data and culminates in a diagnostic formulation and disposition plan. The information should be organized and presented in a manner that emphasizes the logic of the clinician's decision-making process and supports the formulation and plan. The report is generally organized into several sections. It is helpful to start with demographic and descriptive features of the patient, followed by a brief description of the patient's presenting problem. Recent history that is directly relevant to the presenting problem can also be reported here. A more detailed history of the patient is often unnecessary for the purposes of this type of report. Information about the patient's mental health history and most recent treatment or crisis should be reported, along with information about his or her history of substance use and most recent substance use. The mental status portion of the report is often a substantial section where both subjective and objective observations are reported, and examples of the patient's performance are provided to substantiate the hypotheses that are made. Finally, the clinician should provide a diagnostic impression that is clearly derived from the reported information, and a disposition plan should be formulated.

The Intoxicated Patient. Patients who misuse substances appear frequently in emergency rooms, and on occasion in outpatient settings. If an intoxicated patient appears agitated, it may be important to place him or her in an environment where he or she can be observed and have minimal stimulation. It is best to delay the clinical interview until the patient is sober. Given the potential for medical problems that can occur with intoxication, a medical evaluation is critical. Clinicians should be familiar with the symptoms of withdrawal and delirium tremens (DTs); the latter can be a potentially lethal condition that requires immediate medical attention (Dubin, 1990).

It is particularly challenging to manage intoxicated patients in an outpatient setting, where one's access to additional medical and psychological support is limited. Many clinicians feel that it is unwise to meet with a patient in this condition because it reinforces maladaptive behavior. Although conducting therapy with an intoxicated patient is unproductive, it is important to evaluate the patient's safety carefully before turning the patient away. This is particularly important, given the potential for medical complications and the fact that intoxication is a risk factor for suicidality. If a patient appears too intoxicated to manage his or her immediate needs (e.g., driving home), it may be advisable to call a family member or friend who can assist the patient. If the patient is in imminent danger because of his or her psychological state (e.g., suicidal or homicidal), or appears to be experiencing symptoms of withdrawal, DTs, or other medical problems, it is important to seek emergency assistance. In an outpatient setting, this may mean calling the police or a nearby hospital.

The Disorganized/Psychotic Patient. When a clinician is working with a disorganized or psychotic patient, it is helpful to provide him or her with more interpersonal structure. For example, the clinician can guide the patient back to the more pertinent line of thought when he or she becomes tangential or loose. This will increase the clinician's ability to obtain more useful information while helping to contain the patient. When interviewing psychotic patients, clinicians should assess the symptoms without attempting to use logic to challenge them or convince them that their perceptions are wrong (Dubin, 1990; Jessee & Anderson, 1990).

The Resistant/Unresponsive Patient. When a patient does not respond to questioning at all, Dubin (1990) suggests that the interviewer obtain data through the patient's behaviors, expressions, and appearance, and attend to his or her own subjective' experience of the patient. If the patient withdraws when threatened by the more formal cognitive aspects of the mental status portion of the evaluation, it is sometimes possible to weave the mental status questions creatively into dialogue that the patient can tolerate, or to ask the more challenging questions toward the end of the interview (after a rapport has become established). It is also wise to present questions that may feel threatening or evaluative in a very casual manner.

The disposition plan is a crucial part of the report, because this is where the clinician indicates how he or she has chosen to resolve and/or treat the crisis situation. From both an ethical and a legal standpoint, it is important that the clinician provide a reasonable and thorough rationale for the disposition plan. This is always necessary, but particularly critical in situations where the disposition is inconsistent with the patient's wishes (e.g., when the patient is being admitted against his or her will) or when, after weighing the risks and benefits, the clinician has decided not to hospitalize a patient who has some risk potential. In such cases, Bongar (1992) suggests that the clinician document both the risk factors and the patient's strengths and coping resources, and note how this information, along with the patient's history, has contributed to the rationale for the disposition plan. It is also wise to consult with and document the input from other professionals (e.g., the patient's outpatient therapist), as well as from the patient's friends or family members. Not providing adequate reasoning for a disposition could potentially be viewed as negligence on the part of the clinician.

TRAINING AND SUPERVISION ISSUES

As noted in Chapter 1 of this volume, learning to manage patients who are at acute risk can be anxiety-arousing. The "mentor model" of training proposed by Kranz (1985) seems well suited for providing the support and close supervision needed in such a high-stress context. In this model, a less experienced clinician is paired with a more experienced clinician and initially observes the more experienced practitioner doing emergency interviews. After several opportunities to observe, the clinician new to emergency work can assume interviewing responsibility, with the senior clinician there to offer assistance and support. In this way, quality of care is maintained through a training period, and the anxieties of those in a training capacity are kept at levels where learning can occur. In addition, this affords the supervisor with direct experience of the clinician's interviewing style and gives the clinician-in-training the opportunity for immediate supervisory feedback.

Shea and Mezzich (1988) have suggested that the interviewer who is less experienced in emergency evaluations may tend to err in one of two ways: "performing the interview in an overly rigid manner or allowing the patient to ramble unproductively" (p. 393). The rigid interviewer is likely to be anxious about his or her performance and unable to respond to the changing needs of the patient. The interviewer who allows the patient to ramble may have trouble being directive or setting limits, or may be functioning more in the role of an empathic therapist than in that of an evaluator. Such difficulties may not be immediately apparent in the reconstructed interview that is presented in a traditional supervisory session, but can be more readily seen and worked with when direct observation and supervision are taking place.

There are clearly many things for clinicians to learn from doing emergency evaluations. Shea and Mezzich (1988) have noted a number of them: for example, basic engagement skills, structuring techniques, skills for handling resistance, skills for inquiring into sensitive material, diagnostic skills, and so forth. As mentioned in Chapter 1, good support and supervision (as in the "mentor model" of Kranz [1985]) are critical to the development of these skills, but they are also critical to the development of a positive attitude about dealing with psychological emergencies. Without this support and structure, the stress of dealing with high-risk situations can quickly become overwhelming and onerous to one who is new to this type of interviewing. With it, the clinician will gradually acquire the competence needed to evaluate and manage patients who are at risk, and will attain a sense of mastery of this difficult area of clinical practice.

ACKNOWLEDGMENTS

We wish to thank Lisa Fisher, PhD, for her thoughtful review of this chapter. We also wish to thank Sabrina M. Popp, MD, for her review of and helpful comments on the use of psychotropic medication as described in the "More Structured Containment" section.

REFERENCES

Adebimpe, V. (1982). Psychiatric symptoms in black patients. In S. M. Turner & R. T. Jones (Eds.), *Behavior modification in black populations: Psychological issues and empirical findings* (pp. 57–69). New York: Plenum Press.

Akiskal, H. S., & Akiskal, K. (1994). Mental status examination: The art and science of the clinical interview. In M. Hersen & S. M. Turner (Eds.), *Diagnostic interviewing* (2nd ed., pp. 21–51). New York: Plenum Press.

Appelbaum, P. S. (1993). Legal liability and managed care. *American Psychologist, 48*(3), 251–257.

Asberg, M., Nordstrom, P., & Traskman-Bendz, L. (1986). Biological factors in suicide. In A. Roy (Ed.), *Suicide* (pp. 47–71). Baltimore: Williams & Wilkins.

Barton, G. M. (1974). A hospital's political environment and its effect on the patient's admission. *Hospital and Community Psychiatry, 25,* 156–169.

Blais, A., & Georges, J. (1969). Psychiatric emergencies in a general hospital outpatient department. *Canadian Psychiatric Association Journal, 14,* 123–133.

Bongar, B. (1992). Guidelines for risk management in the care of the suicidal patient. In B. Bongar (Ed.), *Suicide: Guidelines for assessment, management, and treatment* (pp. 268–282). New York: Oxford University Press.

Brown, P. (1985). *The transfer of care: Psychiatric deinstitutionalization and its aftermath.* Boston: Routledge & Kegan Paul.

Dubin, W. R. (1990). Psychiatric emergencies: Recognition and management. In A. Stoudemire (Ed.), *Clinical psychiatry for medical students* (pp. 497–526). Philadelphia: J. B. Lippincott.

Echterling, L., & Hartsough, D. (1989). Phases of helping in successful crisis telephone calls. *Journal of Community Psychology, 17,* 249–257.

Errera, P., Wyshak, G., & Jarecki, H. (1963). Psychiatric care in a general hospital emergency room. *Archives of General Psychiatry, 9,* 105–112.

Folstein, M. H., Folstein, S. E., & McHugh, P. R. (1976). Mini-mental state: A practical method for grading the cognitive state of patients for the clinician. *Journal of Psychiatric Research, 12,* 189–198.

Garrison, V., & Podell, J. (1981). *Community support systems assessment* for use in clinical interview. *Schizophrenia Bulletin, 7*(1), 101–108.

Gerson, S., & Bassuk, E. (1980). Psychiatric emergencies: An overview. *American Journal of Psychiatry, 137,* 1–11.

Gross, H., Herbert, M., Knatterud, G., & Donner, L. (1969). The effect of race and sex on the variation of diagnosis and disposition in a psychiatric emergency room. *Journal of Nervous and Mental Disease, 148,* 638–642.

Hanke, N. (1984). *Handbook of emergency psychiatry.* Lexington, MA: Collamore Press.

Hanson, G., & Babigian, H. (1974). Reasons for hospitalization from a psychiatric emergency service. *Psychiatric Quarterly, 3,* 336–351.

Hersh, J. B. (1985). Interviewing college students in crisis. *Journal of Counseling and Development, 63*(5), 286–289.

Hilliard, J. (1990). *Manual of clinical emergency psychiatry.* Washington, DC: American Psychiatric Press.

Hollingshead, A., & Redlich, F. (1958). *Social class and mental illness.* New York: Wiley.

Horwitz, A. V. (1987). Help-seeking processes and mental health services. *New Directions for Mental Health Services, 36,* 33–45.

Jessee, S. S., & Anderson, G. (1990). Emergency services. In S. T. Levy & P. T. Ninan (Eds.), *Schizophrenia: Treatment of acute psychotic episodes* (pp. 27–43). Washington, DC: American Psychiatric Press.

Jones, B. E., & Gray, B. A. (1986). Problems in diagnosing schizophrenia and affective disorders among blacks. *Hospital and Community Psychiatry, 37,* 61–65.

Kaplan, H., Freedman, A., & Sadock, B. (Eds.). (1980). *Comprehensive textbook of psychiatry.* Baltimore: Williams & Wilkins.

Kaplan, H., & Sadock, B. (1993). *Pocket handbook of emergency psychiatric medicine.* Baltimore: Williams & Wilkins.

Kety, S. (1986). Genetic factors in suicide. In A. Roy (Ed.), *Suicide* (pp. 41–45). Baltimore: Williams & Wilkins.

Kranz, P. (1985). Crisis intervention: A new training approach to crisis intervention: A mentor training mode. *Crisis Intervention, 14,* 107–114.

Lazare, A. (1976). The psychiatric examination in the walk-in clinic: Hypothesis generation and hypothesis testing. *Archives of General Psychiatry, 33,* 96–102.

Lopez, S. R., & Hernandez, P. (1986). How culture is considered in evaluations of psychopathology. *Journal of Nervous and Mental Disease, 176,* 598–606.

Loring, M., & Powell, B. (1988). Gender, race, and DSM-III: A study of the objectivity of psychiatric diagnostic behavior. *Journal of Health and Social Behavior, 29,* 1–22.

Maris, R. (1992). The relationship of nonfatal suicide attempts to completed suicides. In R. Maris, A. Berman, J. Maltsberger, & R. Yufit (Eds.), *Assessment and prediction of suicide* (pp. 362–380). New York: Guilford Press.

McNiel, D., & Binder, R. (1994). The relationship between acute psychiatric symptoms, diagnosis, and short-term risk of violence. *Hospital and Community Psychiatry, 45,* 133–137.

Mendel, W. & Rapport, S. (1969). Determinants of the decision for psychiatric hospitalization. *Archives of General Psychiatry, 20,* 321–328.

Monahan, J. (1993). Limiting therapist exposure to *Tarasoff* liability: Guidelines for risk commitment. *American Psychologist, 48,* 242–250.

Motto, J., Heilbron, D., & Juster, R. (1985). Development of a clinical instrument to estimate suicide risk. *American Journal of Psychiatry, 142,* 680–686.

Murphy, G. (1984). The prediction of suicide: Why is it so difficult? *American Journal of Psychotherapy, 38,* 341–349.

Perlmutter, A., & Jones, J. E. (1985). Assessment of families in psychiatric emergencies. *American Journal of Orthopsychiatry, 55*(1), 130–139.

Perry, S. (1976). Acute psychotic states. In R. T. Glick, A. T. Meyerson, E. Robbins, & J. A. Talbott (Eds.), *Psychiatric emergencies* (pp. 51–88). New York: Grune & Stratton.

Pope, K. S., & Tabachnick, B. G. (1993). Therapists' anger, hate, fear, and sexual feelings: National survey of therapist responses, client characteristics, critical events, formal complaints, and training. *Professional Psychology: Research and Practice, 24*(2), 142–152.

Rosenfield, S. (1984). Race differences in involuntary hospitalization: Psychiatric vs. labeling perspectives. *Journal of Health and Social Behavior, 25,* 14–23.

Segal, S. P., Bola, J. R., & Watson, M. A. (1996). Race, quality of care, and antipsychotic prescribing practices in psychiatric emergency services. *Psychiatric Services, 47*(3), 282–286.

Shader, R., Binstock, W., Ohly, J., & Scott, D. (1969). Biasing factors in diagnosis and disposition. *Comprehensive Psychiatry, 10*(2), 81–89.

Shea, S. (1988). *Psychiatric interviewing: The art of understanding.* Philadephia: Saunders.

Shea, S., & Mezzich, J. (1988). Contemporary psychiatric interviewing: New directions for training. *Psychiatry, 51,* 385–397.

Siassi, I. (1984). Psychiatric interview and mental status examination. In G. Goldstein & M. Hersen (Eds.), *Handbook of psychological assessment* (pp. 259–275). Elmsford, NY: Pergamon Press.

Stanford, E. J., Goetz, R. R., & Bloom, J. D. (1994). The no harm contract in the emergency assessment of suicidal risk. *Journal of Clinical Psychiatry, 55,* 344–348.

Tanney, B. (1992). Mental disorders, psychiatric patients, and suicide. In R. Maris, A. Berman, J. Maltsberger, & R. Yufit (Eds.), *Assessment and prediction of suicide* (pp. 277–320). New York: Guilford Press.

Tardiff, K. (1989). *Concise guide to assessment and management of violent patients.* Washington, DC: American Psychiatric Press.

Tischler, G. L. (1996). Decision-making process in the emergency room. *Archives of General Psychiatry, 14,* 69–78.

Tudor, W., Tudor, J., & Gove, W. (1977). The effect of sex role differences on the social control of mental illness. *Journal of Health and Social Behavior, 18,* 98–112.

Turner, S., & Hersen, M. (1994). The interviewing process. In M. Hersen & S. M. Turner (Eds.), *Diagnostic interviewing* (2nd ed., pp. 3–24). New York: Plenum Press.

Zuckerman, E. L. (1995). *The clinician's thesaurus* (4th ed.). New York: Guilford Press.

PART II

THE EVALUATION AND MANAGEMENT OF LIFE-THREATENING BEHAVIOR

THE EVALUATION AND MANAGEMENT OF THE SUICIDAL PATIENT

DAVID C. CLARK

The emotional storm of a suicidal crisis draws on all the different facets of the mental health clinician's training and experience simultaneously: empathic skills, diagnostic acumen, grasp of developmental and social history, ability to obtain and integrate corroborative data, ability to build a therapeutic alliance, ability to construct a well-orchestrated treatment plan, and creative use of mental health resources. In this chapter, the problem of evaluating and managing acute suicide risk is discussed as follows:

- Crisis, emergency, and suicide risk
- Background influences on suicide risk assessments
- Resources for a good emergency evaluation
- The evaluation itself: The first five objectives
- Exploring suicidal thoughts and behavior
- Psychological dimensions of suicide risk
- Management issues
- Legal considerations

CRISIS, EMERGENCY, AND SUICIDE RISK

Suicide risk is not always a crisis for the patient or an emergency for the clinician. From a statistical point of view, all patients seeking treatment are at greater risk for suicide than a matching sample of the general population because the most common psychiatric disorders—major affective disorder and substance abuse/dependence—are associated with a markedly elevated risk for suicide. It is fundamental to good clinical practice to assume that all patients are at non-trivial risk for suicide until the clinician completes a thorough evaluation and to continue to revisit the question of suicidal tendencies periodically throughout therapy, even with patients who exhibited no suicidal tendencies at initial assessment.

When suicidal thoughts do surface, the clinician does well to remember that crises do not always bespeak emergencies, and emergencies do not always bespeak crises. Thus, some severely suicidal patients may not appear dysphoric and may not complain about the impulse to suicide. The patient's subjective *experience* of crisis, the clinician's *judgment* that a state requiring some emergency action pertains, and the clinician's *estimation* of suicide risk should be considered as three independent but overlapping domains, as in Figure 4.1.

The sector where all three domains overlap (labeled "1" in Figure 4.1) is the stereotypical suicidal emergency. In this situation, the patient is distraught and in some tension state, the therapist is aware that he or she must take steps promptly to help or protect the patient, and the therapist has integrated all available observations and information to conclude that there is a significant danger that the patient will kill or harm himself or herself.

There are, however, many crisis/emergency situations ("2" in Figure 4.1) where the patient is in distress and the therapist feels compelled to take emergency action but where suicide risk is estimated to be low or absent. For example, a full-blown manic state often warrants emergency intervention. Likewise, a young adolescent intent on running away from home following a bitter quarrel with parents may require prompt and decisive intervention by the therapist to forestall greater problems, but sometimes the runaway crisis implicates little or no suicide risk.

Other persons in acute turmoil and *not* posing any clinical emergency give

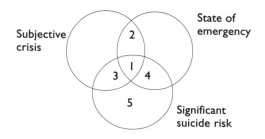

FIGURE 4.1. Three domains of perception.

serious thought to the possibility of suicide (sector "3"). These can be tough judgment calls. When the patient describes continuing suicidal thoughts in the context of a major mental disorder and/or destabilizing alcohol/drug use, suicide risk must always be taken seriously—even when there are no convincing grounds for emergency measures (e.g., elaborate plans for suicide, clear-cut intent to die, or acute perturbation).

The experienced clinician is aware too that not all suicidal thoughts or impulses are strong enough in their own right, or supported by enough risk factors, to warrant direct intervention for suicide risk. A man upset and disturbed about a marital separation unilaterally imposed by his spouse, for instance, may develop suicidal thoughts. But if the thoughts are fleeting, not associated with much planning, not amplified by alcohol use or a supervening episode of major depression, the patient may pose a relatively low level of suicide risk.

Some persons in acute distress run through their mental repertoire of "how desperate persons behave" and experiment with the idea of suicide in an effort to communicate or assimilate the desperation they feel. In this way, the suicidal ideation of some low-risk patients is little more than a costume or a role tried on and studied for effect in the mirror of others' reactions.

The most difficult assessment situations for mental health practitioners arise in sectors "4" and "5," when the patient does not self-identify any crisis or lacks insight into his or her unfolding crisis. Here the clinician may not be alerted to the gravity of the problem by a crisis call, an emergency room visit, visible consternation on the part of the patient, or alarm on the part of a concerned family member. Yet the patient may be plotting his or her own demise with quiet efficiency and composure. In the "emergency" scenario (sector "4"), the clinician may need to hospitalize the patient on an emergency basis to prevent a suicide already in motion. In the "non-emergency" scenario (sector "5"), the clinician may be dealing with a patient suffering from intractable depression and chronically high levels of suicide risk. In this case, ongoing therapy may revolve around nothing more than the tenuous balance between reasons for living and reasons for dying, the strength of the therapeutic alliance, and the slim rays of hope engendered by that relationship.

The lesson behind scenarios "4" and "5" is that the clinician should always entertain the possibility that suicide risk will appear unexpectedly in a noncrisis context. The clinician must not fail to conduct a thorough suicide risk evaluation when it is warranted simply because the patient does not appear sufficiently despondent, hopeless, angry, or apathetic.

Until now, I referred to Figure 4.1 as though perceptions of crisis, emergency, and suicide risk were monolithic—as though the patient and clinician think alike, evolve a common understanding in the course of conversation, or as though it is fair to expect that the patient would invariably defer to the mental health practitioner's training and experience. Of course, life is rarely so simple.

More often than not, the patient and clinician assess the same situation differently. When differences are small, differences can be appreciated or overlooked. When differences are great, the clinician may find, for example, that he or she pegged the situation in sector "1" whereas the patient sees only an ordinary "neither-1-nor-2-nor-3" crisis. If the clinician is unable to convince or persuade the patient that an emergency and significant suicide risk pertain, what possibilities remain available to the clinician?

1. The clinician may invoke his or her "professional stature" to engender trust by arguing that "the professional knows best."
2. The clinician may obtain authorization from someone other than the patient (family members, court) to supersede the patient's wishes and judgments.
3. The clinician is unable to act or is barred from taking emergency action, knowing emergency action is required, and thus must leave the patient to make all clinical decisions for himself or herself.

It should be clear, therefore, that the mental health practitioner dealing with a psychological emergency has to construct and continuously update a cognitive map of both the patient's and the clinician's perspectives of the central situation—and accomplish these feats as the emergency unfolds. Figure 4.2 illustrates the essential task.

The creation of two distinct mental maps allows the clinician to compare and contrast the two perspectives so as to pinpoint areas where the patient and the clinician see eye-to-eye and where the two diverge. If the clinician is to convince or persuade a disbelieving patient that an emergency exists or that the clinician must act to prevent a suicide, it is particularly important for the clinician to build a dispassionate case for his or her analysis based on explainable observations, symptoms, impairment, and direct quotations. If the patient cannot understand the clinician's observations,

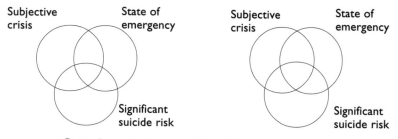

FIGURE 4.2. Mental maps of patient/clinician perceptions.

conclusions, recommendations, or thinking, the patient is less likely to be swayed. This amounts to a lost opportunity to build the therapeutic alliance, recruit the patient's cooperation, and teach the patient to act in his or her own self-interest.

Two common obstacles to the successful management of a psychological emergency are the clinician's failure to involve the patient—by educating the patient and recruiting his or her collaboration—and the clinician's failure to involve the patient's significant others in exactly the same way. When the patient does not evidence an ability to cooperate with the clinician in a given emergency situation, intervention may still be possible—but it remains important for the clinician to consider the patient's long-term welfare by continuing to try to teach the patient the essence of a cooperative working relationship.

BACKGROUND INFLUENCES ON SUICIDE RISK ASSESSMENTS

Personal Beliefs

Long before mental health practitioners are faced with a crisis, emergency, or suicidal patient, graduate school and practicum training should have provided them with a series of in-depth opportunities to explore personal feelings about: (1) human capacity for suffering; (2) the role of free will and personal choice in suicide decisions; (3) philosophical, religious, and/or spiritual beliefs about suicide, life, and afterlife; and (4) the clinician's capacity to endure the death of a patient by suicide.

Clinicians who have not worked out their own beliefs about each of these important issues are not likely to be prepared to listen calmly and dispassionately when a patient in the throes of acute suicidal crisis struggles out loud with these vexing questions. The clinician who feels unprepared for the responsibility of a full-blown suicidal crisis is likely to signal his or her fright or panic to the patient. The clinician whose professional or personal self-esteem is not prepared to absorb a patient death by suicide is likely to resort to arbitrary or dogmatic treatment measures in desperation or else flee from the patient by transferring or dumping the patient in an untimely and countertherapeutic manner.

Few mental health professionals think of themselves as surgeons, yet the metaphor is apt. The well-trained surgeon is acutely aware that only some patients are good candidates for surgery, and the surgeon is skillful at picking out the better candidates. The well-trained surgeon is aware that the prognosis is different for each patient: some patients are more likely to survive the surgery than others. The well-trained surgeon understands that despite the best surgical team efforts, some patients will die in the operating or recovery room.

Persons in crisis who qualify for a diagnosis of "major mental disorder" on Axis I of the *Diagnostic and Statistical Manual of Mental Disorders,* fourth edition (DSM-IV; American Psychiatric Association, 1994) are 10 times more likely to die by suicide than those who do not qualify for a diagnosis. Longterm follow-up mortality studies of psychiatric patients consistently show that more than 15% of patients with major affective disorder eventually die by suicide, as opposed to a base rate of 1.4% in the U.S. general population. Ten percent of patients with schizophrenia eventually die by suicide. Some 2% to 3% of hospitalized alcoholics eventually die by suicide. Thus, it should be clear that all mental health practitioners working in crisis-response settings are dealing with persons at greatly elevated risk for suicide. In 1997, it is still fair to say that experts still do not know enough to recognize, treat, or prevent suicide risk with success on a consistent basis.

Those clinicians who "believe in" suicide, to the extent that they believe that suicide may sometimes be a good or best option for the patient, or to the extent that they believe that patients are the best judges of what is best even in the case of suicide, have simply failed to keep abreast of replicated research in the field. It is a dangerous thing to harbor permissive thoughts about suicide, or to believe that certain repugnant life situations usually engender suicide in human beings, when one has responsibilities for suicidal persons in emergency situations.

Even if the clinician tries to keep his or her private beliefs separate from his or her clinical work, even if the clinician scrupulously avoids discussing his or her private beliefs and reactions with a suicidal patient, the private (conscious and unconscious) beliefs of the clinician will have a palpable impact on the intervention. This is usually apparent in the form of a perceived tolerance or permissiveness about suicidal impulses, as distinct from empathic concern for the patient's experience; it is also apparent in the form of a perceived agreement with the patient's own rationale for suicide. Clinicians often find it difficult to discern these biases or their effects in their emergency work, regardless of level of experience. This is one strong reason why clinicians who respond to suicidal emergencies and who treat suicidal patients over time should make regular use of supervision and consultation.

Personal Experience

Some persons are initially attracted to the mental health professions in part because of prior personal experience with symptoms, impairment, mental disorders, relationship problems, and/or therapy. If mental health professionals and their family members have more than an average amount of experience with psychological symptoms and disorders, it follows that they also might have more than an average amount of firsthand experience with suicidal communications and suicidal behavior.

The experience of living with a suicidal family member is searing; the experience of losing a family member by suicide is unforgettable. Clinicians whose sensibilities have been shaped by these kinds of experiences rarely find it easy to acquire objectivity and maintain a clear-cut separation between their personal and professional experiences. Sometimes a course of psychotherapy provides the clinician with sufficient insight and equanimity to maintain appropriate boundaries; sometimes it is better for a therapist colored by these experiences to forego evaluating and treating suicidal patients. For some, good emergency management consists of knowing which emergency cases to transfer in a safe and timely manner to a capable colleague.

RESOURCES FOR A GOOD EMERGENCY ASSESSMENT

Place and Time

Readers who do a large volume of emergency assessments in the emergency room or in the community may wonder how this "place and time" discussion can offer any practical assistance because emergency suicidal patients are almost always evaluated at a place and time of the patient's choosing.

Yet the clinician has considerable leeway about the physical setting and duration of the evaluation, even in the emergency room. It is imperative that the clinician find a space, preferably an enclosed room, that has no visual or auditory distractions, and where the two will not be interrupted. It is difficult to overemphasize the damage that interruptions can inflict on an time-limited emergency evaluation. The therapeutic alliance is so tenuous and scrutiny of the patient's thought processes is necessarily so limited in an hourlong emergency evaluation, even when the patient is fully cooperative, that "ordinary" disruptions have the potential to compromise the entire value of the findings.

More time devoted to an evaluation is better than less time, up to a point. It is difficult to imagine any adequate emergency evaluation lasting less than 60 to 90 minutes—although one must hasten to admit that sometimes the emergency context requires decisions to be reached in a briefer span of time. Two of many reasons for drawing out the emergency evaluation are to observe the patient's alterations in status over time and to extend the opportunities to collect information from a collateral informant, present in the emergency room or accessible by telephone.

The clinician may project a sense of hurry or timelessness, largely a function of his or her own psychic state. It is possible to make a patient feel rushed throughout the course of a 3-hour interview. Similarly, it is possible to help the patient feel as though the clinician has all the time in the world while a 30-minute interview unfolds. The quality of observations made and information elicited always vary as a function of the relationship the clinician establishes with the patient, even in a brief emergency evaluation.

Supporting Clinical Resources

Suicidal emergencies come in all sorts of shapes and sizes. The clinician who maintains a well-stocked toolbox of supporting resources will be in the best position to produce "the right tool for the job."

Some suicidal patients require hospitalization, and a subset of those may require involuntary commitment according to policies and procedures legislated by the state government. The clinician must be knowledgeable and prepared to coordinate a hospital admission, voluntary or involuntary. A clinician who does not have hospital privileges or does not have a partner who can hospitalize must cultivate a relationship with several other professionals who specialize in inpatient work and work out mutually agreed on procedures for emergency consultations.

Some suicidal patients require psychopharmacotherapy in the emergency situation—for example, for extreme anxiety or agitation or for the hallucinations and delusions that define psychotic features. If the clinician does not have prescribing privileges and does not have a partner who can prescribe, it is likewise necessary to cultivate a relationship with several other professionals who specialize in psychopharmacotherapy and work out mutually agreed on procedures for emergency consultations.

Some suicidal patients require specialized substance abuse treatment services. Some suicidal patients do not require hospitalization and cannot be kept in an emergency room but require more intensive watching and more support than family members and friends can provide. Most suicidal patients should be seen again within a short period of time following the emergency evaluation for follow-up reassessment and continuing care. The emergency responder who is not prepared to match services to the individual patient's needs in the emergency situation is akin to the runner who makes a good start and gets over the first hurdle quickly in a race but then trips over a second or third hurdle and fails to finish.

THE EVALUATION ITSELF: THE FIRST FIVE OBJECTIVES

In a crisis, the patient may be anxious, flustered, or confused and may not know where to start. Faced with an unfamiliar patient in a likely suicidal crisis, the clinician may find it difficult to know where to start. Thus the clinician's purposeful poise, sense of calm unflappability, and orderliness in pursuing the assessment may have value beyond the obvious goal of efficient information processing. It helps the patient to perceive that the clinician is solid and unlikely to be frightened by the thoughts and feelings frightening the patient. It helps the patient to perceive that another person can make sense of the inchoate crisis experience.

Presenting Complaint

First, the clinician should listen attentively without interrupting the patient for at least 5 minutes, to try to understand (1) what is bothering the patient most and (2) the sense that the patient has made of his or her problems. This listening period creates an initial information base from which the clinician can work, provides the clinician with a "mental map" of the patient's perspective as described earlier (see Figure 4.2), gives the clinician some clues about the intelligence and interpersonal style of the patient, and ideally helps the patient believe that the clinician is truly interested in him or her as a person. As a practical matter, it is easier to make the switch to interview format and begin to limit or control overtalkative patients after the patient has had a chance to tell his or her own story without interruption.

Mental Status Examination

The traditional mental status examination of psychiatry should be pursued and revised throughout the course of the entire emergency evaluation. But it is a priority second only to that of listening to the patient. It is difficult to gauge how best to conduct a thorough interview and impossible to formulate diagnoses and treatment plans without pinpointing the patient's cognitive, affective, and behavioral status in a systematic fashion.

Systematic Evaluation for Psychopathology

Many patients acutely ill with mental disorders are unaware that they are ill and actively resist the notion. Their ignorance may stem from naivet%pge, inexperience, or lack of education or may be related to the subtle, complex presentation of their own illness. Their resistance may stem from pride, intolerance for "psychological stuff," fear of stigma, or fear that they are indeed more insane or crazy than anyone has ever realized.

Clinicians may be slow to pick up on the role that mental disorders play in an individual case if they are is too attentive to the patient's or the family's formulation of the core problem, or if they focus so intently on single aspects of the patient (e.g., financial, interpersonal, and intrapsychic) that they miss the bigger picture. This classical mistake is most likely to occur when clinicians believe that a precipitant for the patient's dysphoria or crisis is so obvious/understandable that applicable diagnoses are irrelevant or that they need not bother to evaluate for mental disorders. In this regard Fawcett's (1972) aphorism is extremely valuable: "The presence of a *reason* for depression does not constitute a reason for ignoring its presence" (p. 1305) (i.e., does not constitute a reason for failing to make the diagnosis of depression or for weighing the impact of a depressive disorder on the patient's functioning).

In an emergency situation it is important to screen for the most common mental disorders (mood disorders, anxiety disorders, posttraumatic stress disorders, alcohol and drug abuse/dependence, psychotic disorders, eating disorders, personality disorders). This portion of the interview should be semistructured to be efficient and thorough but should not be so formal that patients feel as though they are talking to a computer. I recommend that the clinician draw on, for example, the Structured Clinical Interview for DSM-III-R (SCID; Spitzer, Williams, Gibbons, & First, 1992), a good semistructured clinical interview for psychopathology that zeros in on the details of specific disorders only in response to positive answers to carefully wrought screening questions. The SCID can be administered with the spontaneous and positive affective tone of a pleasant conversation by a skilled interviewer, assuming that the interviewer has learned, practiced, and memorized the gist of the interview well in advance.

Characterological Features

Beyond collecting evidence for the diagnosis of any personality disorders that may contribute to the clinician's formulation about the emergency and may begin to shape the clinician's treatment strategy, the evaluator should undertake as much of a "personality study" of the patient as time allows. It goes without saying that patients are a great deal more than their emergencies and their diagnoses. It is useful to develop preliminary impressions about (1) what the patient is like when he or she is well, (2) what personality features might constitute coping abilities or advantages, and (3) what personality features might constitute coping liabilities.

Some patients in crisis are chronically ill persons who spend significant portions of their life struggling with suicidal impulses. For them, suicidal tendencies may wax and wane but rarely remit. These patients pose a different type of problem than the patient who was relatively well not so many weeks or months ago. Maltsberger (1986) made invaluable contributions to our understanding of these chronically suicidal patients with his emphasis on their problematic experiences of perpetual aloneness, rage, and perturbation. He also chronicled the kind of "countertransference hate" suicidal patients are prone to engender in the clinician who devotes any time and energy to their care (Maltsberger & Buie, 1974). The qualities emphasized by Maltsberger cut across traditional personality disorder nomenclature (e.g., these patients may qualify for a diagnosis of schizoid personality disorder, narcissistic personality disorder, or borderline personality disorder).

Collateral Informants

The clinician would be wise to interview at least one and preferably several family members or significant others at the time of the emergency suicide evaluation. These collateral informants should be interviewed individually, outside the hearing of the patient. Those who can be reached by telephone should be called. If the clinician asks each of the informants, "Who is the family member or friend who can help me the most with this problem?," the informants may steer the clinician to a particularly knowledgeable and there-fore useful source.

There are several reasons to make strenuous efforts to interview family members and/or friends in the course of an emergency suicide evaluation. Usually they can supply additional information. Moreover, they can some-times be more objective about the patient's experiences. Often, they can provide a chronology with longitudinal observations of the patient. In addi-tion, direct contact with family members and friends allows the clinician to contrast the patient's account of his or her social support network with the clinician's firsthand impression. Finally, close family members and spouses should routinely be notified when the patient is judged to be at risk for suicide. They should be educated about the nature of suicide risk, and the clinician should outline the treatment plan for them, as well as any role they might play in terms of treatment compliance, vigilance, or reporting obser-vations regularly to the clinician.

EXPLORING SUICIDAL THOUGHTS AND BEHAVIOR

If the world were simple, we could assume without penalty that lots of suici-dal thinking is a more ominous sign than a little suicidal thinking, that sui-cidal behavior is more ominous than suicidal thoughts, and that a medically serious suicide attempt (e.g., near death) is more ominous than a medically trivial attempt (e.g., scratching one's wrist). But the world is not simple, and clinical research and experience do not support such glib generalizations. Sometimes it is precisely those persons with few suicidal thoughts and no history of attempts who kill themselves next. What is the clinician to think?

This unsettling observation has two implications, which may seem con-tradictory at first blush. Considered together, these implications are meant to engender a tension in the clinician that is necessary for optimal open-mindedness in a context where firm decisions must be made with limited amounts of information in a short amount of time.

Ascending Inquiry about Suicidal Ideation

An "ascending" strategy for inquiring about suicidal thoughts and behavior (Clark & Fawcett, 1992) is most appropriately timed once the clinician devel-ops a good preliminary understanding of (1) the patient's experiential sense of the crisis, (2) the patient's mental status, (3) the contribution of any concurrent psychopathology, (4) the patient's intrinsic personality, and (5) the quality of the alliance or relationship that links patient and therapist at that moment. The strategy for inquiry is called ascending because the idea is to probe for some nonspecific suicidal thinking the patient will freely admit to, then to explore the extent to which that thinking has become engrossed with details and plans.

I recommend that the clinician—by pinpointing the exact word for dysphoric feeling the patient uses and the extent of hopelessness already voiced—ask two questions, one soon after the other: (1) "When people feel this [*torn up inside*] and [*have trouble thinking that things could ever get any better*] it is not unusual for them to think that they would be better off dead. Have you had thoughts like that?" and (2) "It is not unusual for such people to have thoughts about killing themselves. Have you?" Without exception, the clinician must inquire directly about suicidal thoughts and behavior in the course of each and every crisis or emergency evaluation.

The clinician should determine how frequently the patient is having passive and active suicidal thoughts and how intense or compelling they are. As a next step, the clinician can ask patients to name all the different ways they thought to kill themselves. It is best to press patients to name as many different ways as they can without inciting them to produce new ways, and it is best to avoid digressions into a discussion of one particular method before the patient completes the entire list.

Then, working from the list of suicide methods generated by the patient, the therapist should explore each method one at a time, in the same order as produced by the patient. The idea here is to explore how much time the patient has spent working out the details of a suicide by that method. When a patient seems engrossed or preoccupied with a mental script pertaining to one particular method, and particularly when the patient has begun to schedule or rehearse suicide according to that script, the therapist must consider the risk of imminent suicide to be a strong possibility.

The clinician should be on the lookout for examples of "experimental action." Many suicidal patients are ambivalent and struggle mightily from moment to moment with their suicidal tendencies—one moment backing away from the idea of killing themselves, the next moment changing their minds. Some of these patients try to work up their own courage by "dipping a toe in the water to test the temperature" (e.g., standing where the suicide might occur, holding the pills, lifting a gun to their heads, or tying something around their necks).

For this reason I think it is dangerously misleading to categorize suicidal behavior by outward appearance or by medical consequences. Some of the strongest clues that a suicide is about to happen come in the form of tentative, benign-appearing experimental actions. If questioned about their experimental actions, many patients are quick to voice the side of their thinking that struggles against suicide (suppressing the countervailing voice in their mind) or quick to deny that the action meant anything at all. Those clinicians not so attentive to the ominous possibilities of experimental actions and those who accept the patient's explanations for their motives and intentions at face value are especially prone to dismiss an important clue about suicide risk as nothing more than a "gesture," a "cry for help," or a "manipulation."

Formulate Suicide Risk without Regard to Explicit Suicidal Communications

Although the most direct way to estimate suicide risk is to probe the patient's suicidal thoughts and behavior in the context of a more comprehensive interview, the clinician cannot dismiss the possibility of high suicide risk when the patient evidences no suicidal thoughts or behavior. In the only study of completed suicide among psychiatric patients for whom standardized face-to-face assessments were completed beforehand for all patients (Fawcett et al., 1987, 1990), depressed patients who died by suicide within a year of assessment were judged at baseline to be less suicidal than depressed patients who continued to live for the next 5 years on a number of standard clinical indices: suicidal thinking, recent attempts, medical seriousness of recent attempts, intention to die in recent attempts. The persons who rendered these judgments were senior clinicians at major university medical centers trained to a high degree of reliability; their ratings integrated all available information from patient interviews, from current treatment records, from observations on an inpatient psychiatric unit, and from interviews with significant others. Nor did any dimension of previous suicidal behavior or family history of suicidal behavior help identify the patients who died soon after.

It is not clear whether these results mean that the suicidal crisis state is short-lived, evanescent, and as difficult to capture as it is to bottle lightning; that the most imminently suicidal patients tend to conceal their intentions with skill; or that suicide is much harder to predict than we like to admit. In any case, the results do show that it is a mistake to dismiss the issue of suicide risk based on a narrow finding of "not much suicidal ideation or behavior." Clinicians who undertake emergency evaluations must therefore school themselves in the clinical research pertaining to suicide risk in the absence of frank suicidal thoughts or behavior, and they must constantly apply this knowledge to estimate suicide risk independently of available information about frank suicidal thoughts and behavior.

Elsewhere I presented reasons for conceptualizing the final behavioral outcome of suicide as the product of a complex equation with many contributing variables and for assuming that one necessary variable in this equation is a major mental disorder. The remainder of the equation may take different forms, depending on whether the critical diagnostic variable is major depression, alcoholism, schizophrenia, or some other disorder. The implication is that suicide risk prediction criteria should vary according to the principal psychiatric diagnosis implicated (Clark, 1990; Clark & Fawcett, 1992). A diagnostically organized set of reference criteria for suicide risk has the potential to refine clinical thinking and improve our ability to predict suicide.

From this perspective, the prognostic significance of one clinical feature may differ from patient to patient, depending on the underlying diagnosis or diagnoses. For example, Murphy, Armstrong Hermele, and Clendenin (1979) and Murphy and Wetzel (1990) have shown that the experience of a significant interpersonal loss within the last 6 weeks is a contributing variable for about for a quarter all patients who die by suicide, but the same clinical feature does not help identify which depressed patients die by suicide.

The emergency responder should be expected to have sound training and considerable prior experience working with patients at all levels of major psychopathology and all levels of functional impairment. For example, sometimes an emergency situation demands that the responder address the acute severity of a depressive disorder or an acute cocaine intoxication for a patient whose suicide risk is relatively easier to estimate and manage. Those lacking a thorough grasp of the effectiveness research for different mental disorders and conditions by age, taking into account both psychosocial and biological therapies, are severely handicapped as emergency responders.

PSYCHOLOGICAL DIMENSIONS OF SUICIDE RISK

Reasons for Living

It is generally safe to make three assumptions about more severely suicidal patients, and the clinician is often right: (1) an acute episode of mental disorder (often undiagnosed and untreated) is influencing their thinking; (2) their despair and wish to kill themselves are waxing and waning from minute to minute and hour to hour; and (3) they have some "reasonable," near-unassailable justifications for their wish to die, firm in the belief that their own objectivity has not been corrupted by the current crisis or by their flagrant emotionality. "Loss of insight" is a common feature of depressive episodes that escapes clinical attention.

Therefore, probing for a suicidal patient's "reasons for living" is a little like sitting down to play craps when you know your opponent is playing with loaded dice. Expect that the discussion will take crooked turns, with patients showing stubborn prejudice against themselves. The patient's faulty cognitions will bias arguments in favor of conclusions consistent with the patient's pathological despair and morbidity.

A positive consequence of reviewing reasons for living is that the exercise sometimes exposes the patient's faulty cognitions and prejudice against self in a way that the patient can assimilate. In the emergency management situation, it is at this point that evaluation and trial therapy overlap. For purposes of a good suicide risk evaluation, the clinician would like to know whether the patient can produce any reasons for living, whether the patient has the objectivity to distinguish between his or her healthy and morbid selves, and whether the patient can make the stretch to side with the healthy self against distortions, pessimism, and death wishes.

Clinicians also have the opportunity to launch an important intervention if they can coax the patient to embellish his or her reasons for living, help the patient become more aware and more concerned about cognitive distortions, or facilitate the patient's decision to oppose the internal suicidal force. Generally, only those reasons for living produced spontaneously by the patient pack any punch—experience shows that perfectly sensible reasons produced by the clinician fail to shift the life balance.

Pernicious Affects

There are affective states that are too painful to bear and affective storms that are too powerful to endure. Shneidman (1985, 1993) wrote evocatively about "perturbation" and "psychache" as precipitants for suicide. Maltsberger (1986) took pains to illustrate the states of "aloneness" and rage that tend to make suicide seem like a refuge and a respite to vulnerable patients. Our own work sifting for clues about which depressed patients die by suicide soon after evaluation (Fawcett et al., 1987, 1990) suggests that those with concurrent panic attacks and the most severe concurrent anxiety symptoms (e.g., nervousness, fearfulness, jumpiness, or apprehensiveness) are most prone to suicide.

The lesson in this is that clinicians evaluating suicidal patients in emergency situations should be familiar with the clinical and experiential definitions for these overlapping concepts. All other things being equal, the presence of one of these states should contribute to a rating of greater suicide risk. Similarly, longer durations of time spent in one of these states for a patient should contribute to a rating of greater suicide risk.

Siren Song

Previously I theorized that there is a point far along the continuum of suicidal preoccupations where patients become absolutely convinced that suicide is an intelligent choice for themselves (Clark & Fawcett, 1992). At this point the patient may continue to respond to questioning and may be able to debate the pros and cons of suicide with the clinician, but if the clinician listens carefully he or she detects that the "suicide option" has begun to take on a glow of cleverness, esthetic beauty, comfort, and conviction that was not present earlier.

"Siren song" (as in the enrapturing mermaids' song that lured sailors to their death on hidden rocks in the tale *Ulysses*) is simply a metaphor designed to help the clinician and the patient alike recognize and attack this ominous phenomenon when the patient's thinking begins to sound so overheated—although the shift is usually quite subtle. Verbal therapies may no longer be effective when patients reach this point, although it may not be entirely obvious from conversation with the patient. At this stage of suicidal preoccupation, and for as long as it lasts, the patient requires constant observation (e.g., while sleeping and even going to the bathroom) and prompt institution of those therapies that might be expected to hasten remission (e.g., biological therapies) to prevent a suicide.

Destabilizing Influences

Any patient in the middle of a true-life situational crisis, laboring under the influence of a mental disorder, and/or having suicidal ideation is likely to be fairly destabilized. Beyond the average expectable symptoms and impairments that accompany crisis, the clinician should anticipate other possible transient or chronic destabilizing influences likely to have an impact on the already suicidal patient on a particularly bad night. Possibilities that should be considered include alcohol use, even at low levels; drug use, even at low levels; dementia; physical illness; sleep deprivation; characterological impulsivity or aggressivity; responses to hallucinations or delusions; and reactions to exceptionally excitable or critical family members.

MANAGEMENT ISSUES

Decisions to Hospitalize and Hospital Alternatives

Although each patient is unique and there is no magic formula for calculating suicide risk, the clinician must integrate his or her knowledge and observations to estimate suicide risk in the course of every emergency evaluation. The clinician should have worked out his or her own thresholds defining when to recommend hospitalization and when to require hospitalization. Otherwise there is a danger that the clinician will rely too much on the patient's own thoughts and feelings to make a decision—allowing the patient's inexperience, lack of insight, anxiety, or denial to have too much of a say for a sound clinical decision.

If the clinician feels that hospitalization is necessary, he or she should act decisively and do everything within his or her power—prevailing on the patient, notifying and involving family members, and/or initiating commitment proceedings—before capitulating. When the patient cannot be convinced to enter the hospital and involuntary admission is not feasible, it is wise for the clinician to arrange for some form of follow-up care to help the patient as best he or she can under the circumstances, with the hope that perhaps the patient can be gradually interested in the practical value of inpatient care.

Biological Therapies

Clinicians with strong biases against biological or psychosocial therapies do their patients a great disservice. The short- and long-term effectiveness of the various therapies as determined by random-assignment, controlled clinical trials is an empirical matter. Those therapies likely to reduce suicidal behavior and/or reduce the severity of the contributing mental disorder(s) should be considered evenhandedly. Quick-acting therapies have particular value when the patient is acutely or imminently suicidal. Any therapy that might reduce depression severity, curb alcohol or drug intake, reduce hallucinations and delusions, help the patient return to normal sleep patterns, or quell acute anxiety and agitation in afflicted suicidal patients has potential value. One of the safest and most effective biological therapies for severe depression—electroconvulsive therapy (ECT)—tends to act quicker than antidepressant therapy and thus has real value for some of the most extremely suicidal patients. But public misperceptions have led many to (incorrectly) think of ECT as a primitive or barbaric therapy.

Short-Term Psychotherapy

Few psychotherapies have been tailored specifically for suicidal behavior and fewer still have demonstrated any empirical evidence for effectiveness in reducing suicidal behavior, with two notable exceptions (Linehan, Armstrong, Suarez, Allmon, & Heard, 1991; Linehan, Tutek, Heard, & Armstrong, 1994; Salkovksis, Atha, & Storer, 1990). These two therapy models are tailored to chronically suicidal patients with borderline personality disorder.

For most disorders, the clinician managing a suicidal emergency must fall back on his or her grasp of the clinical literature testing the effectiveness of different psychotherapies for specific mental disorders in random-assignment, controlled clinical trials. In general, Beck's cognitive therapy (Hollon, Shelton, & Davis, 1993), Weissman's interpersonal therapy (Weissman & Markowitz, 1994), and several of the cognitive-behavioral therapy models (Linehan et al., 1991, 1994) have shown the most consistently positive results.

It is often useful to make a small-scale, trial psychotherapy intervention with the acutely suicidal patient in the course of an emergency evaluation to test the patient's ability to participate collaboratively in the therapy and obtain some relief. This strategy yields the biggest dividends when the emergency responder continues to see the patient for outpatient therapy in the following weeks.

"Suicide Contracts"

Drye, Goulding, and Goulding (1973) were the first to describe a "no-suicide decision" process, intended as an intervention more than an evaluation, wherein suicidal patients were asked whether they could "make a decision" not to attempt suicide until the next outpatient appointment. Today few clinicians are acquainted with the details of Drye's intervention model.

But a truncated version of Drye's model persists in the form of the "suicide contract." Typically, the clinician or mental health worker asks the patient whether he or she agrees to abstain from any suicidal behavior for a fixed period, and the patient is under an obligation to notify or contact the staff first if a suicidal urge becomes strong. In some circles staff members are taught that this kind of "contract" provides some legal protection if a suicide should occur, because clearly the onus is on the patient who broke the contract.

There is in fact no empirical evidence that patients who agree to "suicide contracts" are less likely to injure or kill themselves than patients who do not agree. The contract may reassure the clinician and help him or her to sleep better at night, but its value for the patient remains uncertain. Certainly one does no harm by teaching the patient that the clinician is interested in hearing promptly about changes or surges in suicidal thinking, but the clinician should not bank on the contract as a sole or primary intervention.

LEGAL CONSIDERATIONS

"Defensive medicine" is driven by fear of legal reprisals, rather than by sound patient care and good clinical decisions. Too much fear of punitive malpractice actions drives clinicians to make excessively conservative judgment calls, to the detriment of some patients, or else to avoid patients who manifest any serious suicidal tendencies, to the detriment of their patients who develop suicidal tendencies at unpredictable points in time.

For those clinicians not subject to excessive anxiety about legal action, the best course is to simply provide good care, make the best decisions possible, and document these activities to the best of one's ability. Suicidal thoughts and behavior should be evaluated with every new patient, and the findings should be recorded. Legible clinical notes should chart the waxing and waning of suicidal tendencies over time. Whenever judgment calls or decisions about suicide risk have to be made, the clinician should record his or her rationale in writing, weighing the factors on both sides of the question as well as the reasons for the course chosen.

Earlier I stated that clinicians who conduct a large number of emergency evaluations and those who treat suicidal patients should access consultations or participate in supervision on some regular schedule. It is wise to develop the habit of asking for a brief, formal consultation from a trusted colleague whenever a difficult decision about a suicidal patient must be rendered. This habit provides the opportunity for the clinician to review his or her formulation and planning aloud and to solicit some independent thoughts about what constitutes the "community standard of care" in like situations. This second opinion should always be recorded and preserved with the clinician's own treatment records.

Finally, there are a host of reasons for establishing contact with family members and close friends when the clinician is evaluating a suicidal patient in crisis. The clinician benefits from access to more complete information, and access to observations made of the patient by persons familiar with the patient. The clinician benefits by learning firsthand about the quality of social support available to the patient and by learning what family members and friends understand about the suicidal crisis. The clinician benefits when he or she can marshal support for the treatment from family members and friends by showing them how to encourage compliance and report observations over time directly to the clinician. The patient benefits when family members and friends understand something about the nature of the suicidal crisis, understand appropriate roles they can play in the course of treatment, and have an opportunity to develop confidence in the treatment itself. There need not be any conflict between patient confidentiality and contact with family members as long as everyone understands the ground rules for protecting confidentiality about patient–therapist discussions.

SUMMARY

The patient slipping deeper into the clutches of a death tug inspires aversion and terror in many clinicians. To be a good and effective responder to suicidal crises and emergencies, the clinician should be fully aware of his or her own tendencies to respond to some patients with these kinds of feelings—overtly or privately. Those who maintain unawareness are the ones most vulnerable to the troublesome kinds of countertransference reactions described eloquently by Maltsberger and Buie (1974), reactions that have the capacity to compromise the intervention.

In this chapter I propose a handful of tasks that the clinician responding to a suicidal emergency has to juggle seamlessly during the interview: absorbing the patient's subject sense of the crisis, conducting a semistructured mental status exam and screening interview for psychopathology, cross-checking information with collateral family informants, exploring suicidal thoughts and behavior by "ascending" strategy, weighing risk factors by diagnosis independently of documented suicidal tendencies, and always listening for such ominous features as perturbation, panicky agitation, or the "siren song." I propose that one of the best evaluation tools available to the clinician in an emergency situation is to try out an indicated therapy, once he or she has sufficient data to make a formulation.

The job requirements for those who undertake competent suicide evaluations include vast relevant knowledge at one's fingertips, the ability to integrate fragments of data to shape and test a parsimonious formulation, the ability to seamlessly integrate the half dozen tasks described earlier, keen therapy skills for a variety of common mental disorders, all in the context of a knack for remaining clearheaded, focused, and calm. Clearly the job is not for the fainthearted, those with less than considerable experience and training, or those soft on details.

REFERENCES

American Psychiatric Association. (1994). *Diagnostic and statistical manual of mental disorders* (4th ed.). Washington, DC: Author.

Clark, D. C. (1990). Suicide risk assessment and prediction in the 1990s. *Crisis, 11,* 104–112.

Clark, D. C., & Fawcett, J. (1992). Review of empirical risk factors for evaluation of the suicidal patient. In B. Bongar (Ed.), *Suicide: Guidelines for assessment, management, and treatment* (pp. 16–48). New York: Oxford University Press.

Drye, R., Goulding, R., & Goulding, M. (1973). The no-suicide decision: Patient monitoring of suicidal risk. *American Journal of Psychiatry, 130,* 171–174.

Fawcett, J. (1972). Suicidal depression and physical illness. *Journal of the American Medical Association, 219,* 1303–1306.

Fawcett, J., Scheftner, W. A., Clark, D. C., Hedeker, D., Gibbons, R. D., & Coryell, W. (1987). Clinical predictors of suicide in patients with major affective disorders: A controlled prospective study. *American Journal of Psychiatry, 144,* 35–40.

Fawcett, J., Scheftner, W. A., Fogg, L., Clark, D. C., Young, M. A., Hedeker, D., & Gibbons, R. (1990). Time-related predictors of suicide in major affective disorder. *American Journal of Psychiatry, 147,* 1189–1194.

Hollon, S. D., Shelton, R. C., & Davis, D. D. (1993). Cognitive therapy for depression: conceptual issues and clinical efficacy. *Journal of Consulting and Clinical Psychology, 61,* 270–275.

Linehan, M. M., Armstrong, H. E., Suarez, A., Allmon, D., & Heard, H. L. (1991). Cognitive-behavioral treatment of chronically parasuicidal borderline patients. *Archives of General Psychiatry, 48,* 1060–1064.

Linehan, M. M., Tutek, D. A., Heard, H. L., & Armstrong, H. E. (1994). Interpersonal outcome of cognitive behavioral treatment for chronically suicidal borderline patients. *American Journal of Psychiatry, 151,* 1771–1776.

Maltsberger, J. T. (1986). *Suicide risk: The formulation of clinical judgement.* New York: New York University Press.

Maltsberger, J. T., & Buie, D. H. (1974). Countertransference hate in the treatment of suicidal patients. *Archives of General Psychiatry, 30,* 625–633.

Murphy, G. E., Armstrong, J. W., Hermele, S. L., Fischer, J. R., & Clendenin, W. W. (1979). Suicide and alcoholism: Interpersonal loss confirmed as a predictor. *Archives of General Psychiatry, 36,* 65–69.

Murphy, G. E., & Wetzel, R. D. (1990). The lifetime risk of suicide in alcoholism. *Archives of General Psychiatry, 47,* 383–392.

Salkovskis, P.M., Atha, C., & Storer, D. (1990). Cognitive-behavioral problem solving in the treatment of patients who repeatedly attempt suicide: A controlled trial. *British Journal of Psychiatry, 157,* 871–876.

Shneidman, E. (1985). *Definitions of suicide.* New York: Wiley.

Shneidman, E. (1993). *Suicide as psychache: A clinical approach to self-destructive behavior.* Northvale, NJ: Jason Aronson.

Spitzer, R. L., Williams, J. B. W., Gibbon, M., & First, M. B. (1992). The Structured Clinical Interview for DSM-III-R (SCID): I. History, rationale, and description. *Archives of General Psychiatry, 49,* 624–629.

Weissman, M. M., & Markowitz, J. C. (1994). Interpersonal psychotherapy: Current status. *Archives of General Psychiatry, 51,* 599–606.

CHAPTER 5

EMPIRICALLY BASED CLINICAL EVALUATION AND MANAGEMENT OF THE POTENTIALLY VIOLENT PATIENT

DALE E. McNIEL

Clinical assessment of violence potential and management of aggressive behavior are routine components of contemporary practice in psychiatric emergency rooms and inpatient units. Even in the outpatient context, psychological emergencies involving violence arise on occasion. Most past research on assessing violence potential has emphasized long-term predictions of dangerousness (Monahan, 1981). However, over the last decade, substantial data have accrued concerning the correlates of short-term violence risk. This chapter reviews the practical implications of this research for the clinical assessment and management of violence risk in emergency settings.

The chapter considers four classes of variables: demographic/personal history variables, clinical variables, situational variables, and clinician variables. In each domain, readers are encouraged to pay special attention to acute and state-dependent variables while concurrently considering background variables. Following this, I present a strategy for systematically integrating these variables in assessment of patients' violence potential, and translating this assessment into a plan to manage patients' short-term risk of violence.

Before reviewing the pertinent risk factors, a few comments are warranted about the scope of the problem. This chapter concerns evaluation and management of short-term risk (i.e., within the next few hours, days, or weeks). Short-term risk assessment is relevant to decisions such as whether to admit patients to the hospital or treat them on an outpatient basis, whether to implement a duty to protect others, whether to discharge patients from hospitals, and so on. Similarly, this information is relevant to assessment of the risk of violence by an outpatient until the patient is seen at the next session. Detailed descriptions of approaches to more extended evaluation and treatment of violent patients have been published elsewhere (e.g., Eichelman & Hartwig, 1995; Mulvey & Lidz, 1984; Roth, 1987; Tardiff, 1989).

RISK ASSESSMENT

Demographic/Personal History Variables

History of Violence

A history of violence has been consistently shown to be the best single predictor of future violent behavior (Monahan, 1981; McNiel, Binder, & Greenfield, 1988).

It is useful to evaluate how recently any aggressive behavior has occurred, as this may provide clues to whether the patient is in an ongoing crisis of which violence is a manifestation. Inquiry about whether anyone was harmed during previous violent episodes may provide useful information about the severity of risk in the current situation. Evaluation of the frequency of past violence is useful, as studies of both inpatients and outpatients have shown that a disproportionate amount of violent behavior is perpetrated by a small number of repeatedly violent individuals (Convit, Isay, Otis, & Volavka, 1990; Gardner, Lidz, Mulvey, & Shaw, 1996). Similarly, it is useful to be alert to patterns of escalation (e.g., in domestic violence situations), which may provide information regarding whether the patient is repeating a cycle of violence (Binder & McNiel, 1986). It is also useful to evaluate whether particular symptoms were associated with previous violent episodes. Inquiry about the circumstances of previous violence (e.g., in the community or during hospitalization) is also important. Inquiry about whether a weapon was involved in previous violence may provide information about the lethality potential posed by a patient's aggression.

Neurobiological studies suggest the utility of inquiring about other impulsive behavior in addition to physical attacks on persons, such as property damage, reckless driving, criminal behavior, and potentially reckless spending or sexual acting out. Several neurobiological studies have linked repetitive impulsive aggression to low concentrations of the major serotonin metabolite 5-hydroxyindoleacetic acid (5-HIAA) in the cerebrospinal fluid (Linnoila & Virkkunen, 1992). Although it is not practically feasible to directly evaluate patients' serotonin levels, people who act without thinking and have difficulty controlling certain behaviors despite vowing to do so frequently have impulsive traits that extend to impulsive aggression (Barratt, 1994).

The significance of a history of violence has several clinical implications:

1. Obtaining a violence history is an essential part of assessing a patient's risk of violence. Recent studies have shown a willingness of patients to self-report a history of violence that is rather remarkable in view of the socially undesirable nature of the behavior. Several authors have obtained rates of self-reported violence by mental patients that were similar to other sources, such as collateral informants (e.g., family and friends) and institutional records, although these separate sources often did not agree with each other regarding specific instances of violence (e.g., Mulvey, Shaw, & Lidz, 1994; Steadman et al., 1994).

One approach to facilitating patients' self-disclosure about their violent behavior is to precede such questions by inquiry about whether the patient has been the victim of such behavior (Monahan, 1994). (Parenthetically, information about victimization is clinically useful in its own right.)

2. Because of the importance of a history of violence in evaluating risk of future violence, it is useful to obtain records from previous health care providers. In many situations, it is also possible to obtain such information from other collateral persons, such as family, friends, or others who were involved in the patient's coming to clinical attention. For example, if the patient was brought to a psychiatric emergency service by police, the police may have relevant information about recent violence that would be otherwise unavailable (McNiel, Hatcher, Zeiner, Wolfe, & Myers, 1991).

3. Clinicians working in an institutional setting may wish to develop an organized system to make information about history of violence immediately available for decision making. Drummond, Sparr, and Gordon (1989) described such an intervention at the Portland Veterans Administration Medical Center. A flag was entered in the computerized database for any patient with a history of a violent incident at the facility. When the patient returned to the facility, the flag alerted staff to the patient's potential for violence and security was called immediately, who then sat with the patient throughout his or her visit. The number of violent incidents decreased by 91.6% in the first year of the program compared with the preceding year.

Violent Threats/Fantasies

The *Tarasoff* decision (*Tarasoff v. Regents of University of California*, 1974, 1976) and subsequent judicial rulings and legislation established in many jurisdictions that when a patient makes a serious threat of violence, the therapist has a duty to protect the intended victim of the threat (Beck, 1985; Binder & McNiel, 1996). Relevant variables to consider in assessing the seriousness of the threat include how specific the threat is, the extent of planning, and any preparations that have been undertaken.

Research with acutely mentally ill patients suggests that there is not a perfect correlation between threats and violence. For example, McNiel and Binder (1989) found that patients who made threats, especially those with schizophrenic diagnoses, were more likely to become violent. However, the victim was not necessarily limited to the target of the threats. For example, some patients made threats against outpatient therapists and family members and yet actually attacked staff on an inpatient unit. The authors concluded that when acutely psychotic patients threaten violence, the danger extends beyond the victim of the threat.

In general, the clinician must consider that some patients who make threats do not pose a serious risk of violence, and some patients who do pose a risk do not make threats. Consequently, the presence or absence of a threat should be evaluated in the context of other risk factors for violent behavior.

Age

Numerous studies have found that violence is most common among younger people (Klassen & O'Connor, 1994). However, age appears to interact with other risk factors in terms of risk of violence. For example, among younger patients, diagnoses such as acute schizophrenia or acute mania are associated with increased risk of violence (McNiel & Binder, 1994a; Tardiff, 1992). Among elderly patients, there is an increased representation of organic mental disorders such as dementia among the patients who become violent (Haller, Binder, & McNiel, 1989; Kalunian, Binder, & McNiel, 1990). The predictive value of age as an indicator of violence risk also appears to vary as a function of phase of illness. Among community samples, younger people are consistently found to be at greater risk of violence (Swanson, Holzer, Ganju, & Jono, 1990). However, among acutely mentally ill patients who are sufficiently impaired to warrant hospitalization, clinical factors such as diagnosis and symptoms appear to overshadow demographic factors such as age in influencing risk of violence (Beck, White, & Gage, 1991; McNiel et al., 1988; Rossi et al., 1986).

Gender

Traditionally, males have been considered much more likely to be violent than females (Monahan, 1981). However, recent research with psychiatric patients has suggested that more violence is perpetrated by females than was previously thought. For example, in a study of psychiatric inpatients, females were actually more physically assaultive than males, although males engaged in more fear-inducing behavior (e.g., threats, property damage, and verbal assaults) than females (Binder & McNiel, 1990). This relationship held up when controlling for other correlates of violence. Similarly, a recent study of patients seen in a psychiatric emergency service who were followed in the community found comparable rates of violence among female and male patients, although males tended to engage in more severe forms of violence than women (Newhill, Mulvey, & Lidz, 1995).

History of Child Abuse

Numerous studies have shown that having been a victim of child abuse or having grown up in a violent home increases a patient's risk of violence later in life. This relationship has been obtained in both hospitalized (Yesavage et al., 1983) and ambulatory samples (Klassen & O'Connor, 1994). Consequently, routine inquiry about child abuse is a useful component of violence risk assessment.

Culture

Among mentally ill persons, race/ethnicity has not been shown to be reliably associated with risk of violence when other correlates of violence such as diagnosis, social class, and so on, are taken into account (McNiel et al., 1988; Swanson et al., 1990; Tardiff & Sweillam, 1980). However, culture may be a relevant factor, as some cultural groups (e.g., some gangs) view violence as an acceptable way of getting things.

Social Class

Data from epidemiological studies (Swanson et al., 1990) suggest that lower socioeconomic status is associated with increased risk of violence in the community. However, among acutely mentally ill patients, the predictive significance of social class is attenuated (McNiel et al., 1988; Rossi et al., 1986).

Intelligence

Low intelligence has been associated with crime in general (Volavka, 1995), and mental retardation has been linked to aggressive behavior in institutionalized populations (Tardiff, 1992).

Clinical Variables

Diagnosis

The relationship between psychiatric diagnosis and violence is controversial. The research literature contains many inconsistent findings. One reason for this is that many studies have used samples containing a mixture of acute and nonacute patients. Since many major mental disorders are *episodic*, their influence on violence risk may only occur when the patient is in an exacerbation of the disorder. Mixing symptomatic patients with those in remission solely on the basis of diagnosis (e.g., schizophrenia or bipolar disorder) may have contributed to the contradictions in the literature. Another factor that may complicate interpretation of the level of risk associated with particular diagnoses concerns the comparison group. For example, compared with other acute civil psychiatric patients, schizophrenic patients have a higher risk of violence (McNiel & Binder, 1994a). However, compared with a group of patients incarcerated in a maximum security psychiatric hospital with a documented history of serious violence, current criminal charges, and a high rate of personality disorders, persons with schizophrenia may have a somewhat lower risk of violence (Harris, Rice, & Quinsey, 1993). (Of course, in the case of studies such as Harris et al. (1993), the lower risk may have nothing to do specifically with schizophrenia but with a greater proportion of other risk factors in the comparison group.)

Acute Schizophrenia, Mania, and Mental Disorders Due to General Medical Conditions. Among acutely ill patients seen in a civil (i.e., nonforensic) context, diagnoses of schizophrenia; bipolar disorder, manic episode; and organic psychotic conditions are associated with elevated short-term risk of violence (McNiel & Binder, 1994a; Tardiff, 1992).

Some research suggests that there can be an interaction between diagnosis and context (Binder & McNiel, 1988). For example, both schizophrenic and manic patients are at elevated risk of assaultive behavior during the interval preceding psychiatric hospital admission. During the period shortly following hospital admission, manic patients are at greater relative risk of physical aggression, possibly due to differential response to the containment and limits associated with hospitalization or differential response to psychotropic medication.

Many studies have shown that organic brain disease can result in violence. Head injuries have been linked to aggressive behavior, in the context of agitation and confusion during the first few days following the injury (Mysiew, Jackson, & Corrigan, 1988) and, subsequently, in the context of the irritability associated with posttraumatic personality change (Brooks, Campsie, Symington, Beattie, & McKinlay, 1986). Lesions of the brain, particularly in the temporal lobe and orbitomedial part of the frontal lobe may elicit aggression (Volavka, 1995). Diffuse brain dysfunction, identified by neuropsychological test batteries, neurological examinations, and surface electroencephelograms, has been linked to aggressive behavior, particularly among institutionalized populations (Krakowski, Convit, Jaeger, Lin, & Volavka, 1989; Volavka, 1990). Descriptively, organic mental disorders such as delirium and dementia have been associated with violence in psychiatric settings; these disorders can be caused by multiple etiologies. Numerous diseases of the brain can be associated with violence, including viral encephalitis, acquired immunodeficiency syndrome, tuberculosis, syphilis, herpes simplex, fungal meningitis, normal pressure hydrocephalus, cerebrovascular disease, tumors, Huntington's chorea, multiple sclerosis, Pick's disease, multi-infarct dementia, Alzheimer's disease, Parkinson's disease, Wilson's disease, and postanoxic or posthypoglycemic states associated with brain damage, as can various medical illnesses such as hypoxia, electrolyte imbalances, vitamin deficiencies (e.g., B_{12}, and folate), hepatic disease, renal disease, Cushing's disease, hyperthyroidism, hypothyroidism, systemic lupus erythematosus, poisoning by heavy metals and insecticides, and porphyria (Tardiff, 1992). Many of these disorders are reversible with treatment. The violence that is associated with organic impairment of the brain can be related to generalized dyscontrol or psychotic symptoms such as delusions.

Substance-Related Disorders. Substance-related disorders clearly are associated with elevated risk of violence. For example, Swanson (1994) analyzed data from the Epidemiologic Catchment Area (ECA) project, which consisted of a representative sample of 10,000 people from five cities. Each respondent had been given a structured diagnostic interview, the Diagnostic Interview Schedule (DIS), which includes questions about violence. The authors found that (1) 3.5% of the total sample had completed some type of violence during the previous year, (2) mental illness alone was twice as prevalent in the violent subjects than in the nonviolent subjects, and (3) substance abuse alone and comorbidly was five times as prevalent in the violent group than in the nonviolent group.

Research to date has shown a strong association between substance abuse and community violence. The mechanism of the association appears to be complex. For example, the disinhibiting effect of alcohol intoxication increases violence potential. Similarly the agitation, grandiosity, suspiciousness, and delusional beliefs that can accompany intoxication with amphetamines, cocaine, and phenylcyclidine (PCP) may increase violence risk, as may the disorganization associated with inhalant intoxication and the agitation and disorganization associated with withdrawal delirium (e.g., from alcohol). In addition, some substance-related violence is associated with crimes committed to obtain the substance and with the violent subcultures associated with the drug distribution network (e.g., for crack cocaine).

A practical implication of the association between substance abuse and violence is the importance inquiring about substance use when evaluating a patient's violence risk. Furthermore, it is important to observe for acute signs of intoxication or withdrawal. Although the specific syndrome varies depending on the substance, some common indicators of intoxication include slurred speech, incoordination, unsteady gait, flushed face, dilated pupils, tremors, fluctuating level of consciousness, and disorientation. Common indicators of withdrawal include elevated vital signs including pulse, blood pressure, and heart rate, sweating, tremors, hypervigilance, anxiety, and hallucinations.

Personality Disorders. A variety of personality disorders have been associated with violence, particularly antisocial personality disorder and borderline personality disorder (Volavka, 1995; Widiger & Trull, 1994). Quantitative research has demonstrated a strong relationship between *psychopathy* and risk of violence. Psychopathy represents a subset of people generally diagnosed with antisocial personality disorder who manifest traits measured by the Psychopathy Checklist—Revised (PCL-R; Hare, 1991). These traits comprise two main factors: (1) selfish, callous, and remorseless use of others (manifest by glibness/superficial charm, grandiose sense of self-worth, pathological lying, conning/manipulative, lack of remorse or guilt, shallow affect, callous/lack of empathy, and failure to accept responsibility for own actions); and (2) a chronically unstable, antisocial, and socially deviant lifestyle (manifest by a need for stimulation, parasitic lifestyle, poor behavioral controls, early behavioral problems, lack of realistic goals, impulsivity, irresponsibility, juvenile delinquency, and, in a criminal setting, revocation of conditioned release). In forensic samples, people who score above the threshold for classification as a psychopath based on the PCL-R are much more likely to show violence than are controls (see Hare, 1991, for a review). Preliminary findings suggest that the construct of psychopathy may have similar utility among nonforensic patients seen in the civil context (Hart, Hare, & Forth, 1994).

Personality disorders appear to be more relevant to assessing long-term risk rather than short-term risk of violence in emergency settings. The reason for this is the difficulty in obtaining a valid personality disorder diagnosis of a patient who is in the midst of an acute symptomatic clinical (i.e., Axis I) disorder. However, if sufficient background information is available to substantiate a personality disorder, evidence of psychopathy is likely pertinent.

Symptoms

There is consistent empirical support for the utility of acute symptoms as indicators of the short-term risk of violence (Krakowski, Volavka, & Brizer, 1986; Convit et al., 1990; Lowenstein, Binder, & McNiel, 1990; Link, Andrews, & Cullen, 1992). These include hostile–suspiciousness (hostility, suspiciousness, uncooperativeness) agitation–excitement (tension and excitement), and thinking disturbance (conceptual disorganization, hallucinations, and unusual thought content) (Lowenstein et al., 1990; McNiel & Binder, 1994a). Clinical lore suggests that command hallucinations (e.g., of a voice telling the patient to harm others) increase the risk of violence, although the empirical literature has not uniformly supported the hypothesis that the presence of command hallucinations increases the risk more than the presence of other hallucinations (see McNiel, 1994, for a review). The co-occurrence of command hallucinations with associated delusions appears to increase the danger (e.g., a patient who hears a voice telling him to kill his sister who also has the delusional belief that his sister is the devil).

Link et al. (1992) identified a subset of psychotic symptoms, labeled "threat-control override" symptoms, that substantially increased the risk of violence. This symptom pattern refers to the patient's feeling threatened and not being under his or her own control. The symptoms are elicited by asking patients whether they feel their mind is dominated by forces beyond their control, whether they feel that thoughts are being put into their head that are not their own, and whether they feel that there are people who wish to do them harm. Clinically, it can be useful to ask patients experiencing such symptoms what they would do if they came in contact with those they perceive as tormenting or persecuting them.

The association between symptoms and short-term violence risk that has been identified in recent studies underscores the usefulness of a thorough mental status examination in evaluating a patient's violence potential. For example, a patient may not threaten violence but may still have symptoms that increase the risk of violence (e.g., a guarded, paranoid patient). Similarly, symptoms of decreased orientation and memory raise the possibility of an organic mental disorder that may constitute a reversible risk factor. More generally, the association that research has documented between psychopathology and violence underscores the importance of careful diagnosis, including assessment of the history of present illness, medical and psychiatric history, and mental status examination.

Treatment Adherence

Treatment of psychopathology that is associated with violence potential can reduce patients' risk of violence. For example, Yesavage (1984) showed an inverse relationship between the serum neuroleptic levels in a group of hospitalized schizophrenic patients and their level of assaultiveness. It is possible that some differences between community violence and hospital violence are due to the extent to which patients adhere to their treatment. For example, some patients are not assaultive in hospital settings while receiving appropriate pharmacological treatment, yet discontinue their medications in the community, and then become violent in the community when their symptoms relapse (Johnson, Pasterski, Ludlow, Street, & Taylor, 1983).

Situational Variables

Even very aggressive patients are typically violent only for a small proportion of the time. Conceptually, a person with a propensity for violence is likely to actually exhibit violent behavior in the context of certain situational precipitants. Several of these have practical implications for risk assessment.

Relationship with Potential Victim

Research suggests that more than half of the victims of violence that is perpetrated by mentally ill people are family members (Estroff, Zimmer, Lachicotte, & Benoit, 1994; Straznickas, McNiel, & Binder, 1993). In the family, the person at greatest risk is the primary caregiver (e.g., the mother of a young adult chronic patient or the spouse or adult child of a demented psychotic patient) (Straznickas et al., 1993).

Clinically, it is useful to assess the extent of family conflict. For instance, the identified patient may not be the only violent individual in the family. It is also useful to evaluate the topic of frequent conflict. For instance, the conflict may pertain to caretaking relationships, to a chronic pattern of family communication, or to a repeated sequence of escalating interchanges (e.g., one spouse criticizes the other, who gets drunk, then becomes violent) (cf. Binder & McNiel, 1986). Finally, it is useful to assess whether a patient with a history of violence restricts the aggression to certain targets (e.g., family) or is more generally violent across types of potential victims (e.g., strangers and family).

Availability of Potential Victim

The risk of violence can be influenced by the availability of and accessibility to potential victims (Binder & McNiel, 1986). For example, an individual with the same propensity for violence would have varying degrees of likelihood of carrying out the violence if the aggressive impulses were focused on a public figure, on a spouse with a restraining order who continued to initiate contact with the patient, or on people who wear red clothing.

Social Support

Existing research suggests that an individual's social network can increase or decrease the risk of violence depending on the nature of the network. For example, Estroff et al. (1994) found that patients who were married made fewer threats than single patients, and that the risk of violence was lowered by having a mental health professional in the patient's social network. On the other hand, Steadman (1982) found that some social networks can actually raise a person's potential for violence and act as instigators.

Availability of Weapons

The presence of a weapon increases the lethality potential in someone with a propensity for violence. Therefore, inquiry into a patient's history of weapon use, interest in weapons, and possession of weapons is useful.

The issue of weapons has gained particular attention in psychiatric emergency rooms. Surveys of clinicians have shown that the most common settings in which they are the targets of violence by patients are psychiatric emergency rooms and inpatient units (American Psychiatric Association, 1992). Past research suggests that about 4% to 8% of patients bring weapons with them to the psychiatric emergency room (Anderson, Ghali, & Bansil, 1989; McNiel & Binder, 1987; McCulloch, McNiel, Binder, & Hatcher, 1986). Furthermore, weapon-carrying patients are difficult to distinguish from other patients other than that they are more likely to be male and substance abusers (McNiel & Binder, 1987). One intervention that has addressed this problem has been to conduct routine screening of all patients for weapons when they enter the psychiatric emergency room. Evaluation of such programs indicates that most patients feel safer with a policy of routine weapon screening, and that a substantial number of weapons are identified (McCulloch et al., 1986).

Clinician Variables

Knowledge of Relevant Base Rates

In evaluating an individual's risk of violence, probably the most useful single piece of information is the base rate of violence among similar patients. Recent research has provided preliminary data about base rates of violence among groups where risk assessment is commonly required. For example, among patients seen in civil (as opposed to criminal) contexts, approximately 10% to 20% are physically assaultive during the few weeks preceding hospitalization, and an additional 20% to 30% engage in fear-inducing behavior such as threats, property damage, and verbal aggression (McNiel & Binder, 1986; Rossi et al., 1986; Tardiff & Sweillam, 1980). During short-term hospitalization, about 15% of civilly committed patients are physically assaultive, while another 30% to 35% engage in fear-inducing behavior (McNiel et al., 1988). During the first several months following hospital discharge, about 25% to 30% of patients become physically assaultive in the community (Klassen & O'Connor, 1988; Klassen & O'Connor, 1989; Steadman et al., 1994). (See Borum, 1996; Brizer & Crowner, 1989; Otto, 1992, for reviews of studies on base rates.)

Actuarial Aids

Several authors have recently developed actuarial aids that may assist the clinician in screening for the risk of violence. In this approach, items are included based on their empirical association with violence, not necessarily their relevance to any clinical formulation. Such tools have been developed for assessing the risk of violence by psychiatric inpatients (McNiel & Binder, 1994b), psychiatric emergency room patients (Gardner et al., 1996), maximum security forensic psychiatric patients (Webster, Harris, Rice, Cormier, & Quinsey, 1994), potential spousal batterers (Kropp, Hart, Webster, & Eaves, 1994), and others (Webster, Eaves, Douglas, & Wintrup, 1995; Quinsey, Rice, & Harris, 1995). In general, those measures are still in the early stages of development, but offer considerable potential in anchoring clinical judgment by allowing the clinician access to an actuarial estimate of risk.

Therapeutic Alliance

The therapeutic alliance represents the extent to which the patient is actively collaborating with treatment as a resource for change (Clarkin, Hurt, & Crilly, 1987).

Recent findings suggest that, among groups of patients with a high base rate of violence (e.g., inpatients), patients with a poor initial alliance are at increased risk of violence (Beauford, McNiel, & Binder, 1997). The quality of the alliance is a potentially changeable risk factor. Moreover, the quality of the therapeutic alliance may be useful to consider when evaluating the significance of other risk factors (Truscott, Evans, & Marsell, 1995). For example, the quality of the therapeutic alliance is a useful indicator of treatment adherence, which can predict relapse of symptoms associated with violence.

Cognitive Biases

The experimental literature on human judgment suggests that people are prone to a variety of cognitive biases when making decisions under conditions of uncertainty, such as neglecting base rate information, selectively attending to information that confirms one's initial assumptions, ignoring disconfirming evidence, and so on (Kahnemann & Tversky, 1996). Naturalistic research has suggested that when evaluating patients' risk of violence, clinicians tend to overestimate the risk among nonwhite minority patients and underestimate the risk among female patients (McNiel & Binder, 1995; Lidz, Mulvey, & Gardner, 1993). Several authors have suggested strategies that clinicians can use to counter these types of cognitive errors (e.g., Borum, Otto, & Golding, 1993). For example, when evaluating a female patient, the clinician would do well to not discount the individual's potential for violence solely based on her gender.

Consultation

In situations in which the decisions have a high cost and/or the clinician has limited confidence in the accuracy of his/her evaluation of violence potential, consultation with colleagues can be helpful. Some research suggests that assessments when two clinicians concur have higher predictive validity than individual assessments, especially if there are discordant opinions (McNiel & Binder, 1993). Furthermore, obtaining consultation has distinct advantages from a risk-management perspective. That is, if there is a negative outcome, the clinician will be held accountable to community standards of care. Obtaining consultation at the time of the decision provides useful documentation that the clinician's assessment is in accord with prevailing community practices of other clinicians.

Integration

Models for the clinical assessment of risk of violence have been proposed by several authors (Gutheil, Bursztajn, & Brodsky, 1986; Monahan, 1993; Tardiff, 1989). The general process involves four steps:

1. The clinician gathers information about pertinent risk factors and rationally weighs this information to formulate an evaluation of the level of risk.

2. Based on the assessed risk, the clinician develops a plan of intervention to reduce the risk.
3. The clinician implements the plan.
4. The clinician documents this process.

RISK MANAGEMENT

Initial Encounter with Acutely Violent Patients

Because of clinical issues involving the evaluation of possible biological causes of violent behavior and legal issues pertaining to coercive interventions that may be required to contain acute violence, multidisciplinary teamwork including physician involvement is usually desirable when evaluating and managing acutely violent patients.

Various texts have articulated in detail principles of the initial management of acutely violent patients (e.g., American Psychiatric Association, 1992; Rund & Helzer, 1983; Tardiff, 1989; Thackery, 1987). The next sections briefly outline some of the major issues.

Rapid Differential Diagnosis

The clinician should immediately form an opinion of whether the patient is suffering from an organic mental disorder, functional psychosis, or a nonpsychotic, nonorganic disorder. If the patient is suffering from an organic mental disorder, verbal intervention is likely to be fruitless, and diagnosis and treatment of the underlying medical condition are essential. If the patient is suffering from a functional psychosis (e.g., schizophrenia or mania), verbal intervention will have limited utility, and rapid administration of medication (e.g., neuroleptic and/or anxiolytic drugs) is often most effective, although the patient may have to be secluded or restrained until the medication takes effect. If the patient has a nonpsychotic, nonorganic disorder, verbal intervention may be effective, although offering the option of medication (e.g., an anxiolytic drug) may give the patient a sense of control.

Verbal Intervention

This intervention primarily involves limit setting. The therapist clearly points out the behavior that is unacceptable and maladaptive and explains why it is not acceptable. The clinician then explains the consequences if the behavior continues. At this point, it is often helpful either to ask the patient what he or she thinks the consequences of the behavior should be, or to offer the patient two choices when limits are imposed (e.g., "you can have a time out in your room or in the seclusion room," or "you can take the medication by mouth or by injection").

The safety of the process of verbal intervention in emergencies is likely to be enhanced if the clinician presents a calm appearance and speaks softly in a neutral, concrete, nonjudgmental and nonprovocative way. Putting space between the clinician and the patient, avoiding intense eye contact, and showing respect for the patient are useful. It is helpful to facilitate the patient's talking and not to make promises that cannot be kept.

The clinician should select the setting in which the interview is conducted based on safety considerations, as interviewing the patient in an office with the door closed may be unsafe with potentially violent patients. Other options include interviewing the patient alone in an office with the door open while staff wait outside or interviewing the patient in an office with staff present. If the patient is interviewed in the office with the door closed, there should be a prearranged method for the clinician to indicate that he or she is in danger, such as with a "panic button" or in a predetermined message to a receptionist. Similarly, there should be some method for a person outside the office to indicate a dangerous situation to the clinician before the patient enters the office.

The clinician should select the decoration and furniture of the office with consideration of the types of patients who will be treated there. For instance, chairs, pictures, ashtrays, and other small objects can be used as weapons. Similarly, when interviewing potentially violent patients, clinicians should attend to their own dress (e.g., remove eyeglasses, remove jewelry such as necklaces and dangling earrings, and remove neckties).

Finally, Thackery (1987) has described various physical defense moves that are useful in reacting to attacks by patients. Many people feel that such maneuvers should be learned not only by reading about them but also by practicing them.

Pharmacotherapy

The management of an acute emergency in which an agitated, threatening, and possibly psychotic patient poses an immediate risk of harming others can often be accomplished by rapid tranquilization (Dubin, 1988). In this procedure, standard to low doses of neuroleptic medication are administered over 30- to 60-minute intervals, with the goal of reducing extreme agitation, hyperactivity, excitement, and combativeness. Recently, benzodiazepines, particularly lorazepam, have been used for this purpose, usually in addition to neuroleptic medication.

After resolving the emergency situation, a variety of pharmacological treatments can be beneficial in reducing aggressive behavior—the specific treatment varying according to the diagnosis. For example, neuroleptic medications have been used to reduce aggression associated with delusions and hallucinations in schizophrenic patients, lithium has been used to treat aggression and irritability related to mania, beta blockers have been used with violent head-injured patients, and lithium and anticonvulsants have been used in aggressive patients with personality disorders or those with intermittent explosive disorder (Corrigan, Yudofsky, & Silver, 1993; Eichelman, 1988).

Seclusion and Restraint

Seclusion and restraint may also be needed to control violent behaviors in the emergency situation. The American Psychiatric Association has developed guidelines for the appropriate and safe use of these procedures (American Psychiatric Association, 1985). Decision making about the use of seclusion and restraint requires reasonable clinical judgment depending on the individual case and situation. For example, with a manic patient, less medication may be needed while the patient is in seclusion because of the decrease in stimulation. Conversely, seclusion may be contraindicated in a patient with unstable medical status due to cardiac illness, infection, metabolic illness, or disorders of thermoregulation, which require close monitoring and close proximity of staff.

The management of acutely violent patients should be accomplished with adequate force, which may include hospital security, police, or a coordinated team of hospital staff. Singlehanded attempts to subdue obviously violent patients carry a high risk of injury and should be avoided. Agitated patients who are confronted with ample force often are less assaultive. Acting in a prompt and decisive fashion, while showing respect for the patient, is important. The process of seclusion and restraint should be an organized team effort.

Outcome research has shown that staff who receive regular, systematic continuing education about management of assaultive behavior are at lower risk of injury (Carmel & Hunter, 1990; Infantino & Musingo, 1985). Hence, many facilities serving acutely mentally ill patients include such training in their staffing practices, in a manner analogous to inclusion of regular training in cardiopulmonary resuscitation (CPR) in staff recertification processes.

Other Interventions

Hospitalization

If the clinician believes that a patient poses an imminent danger to others due to a mental disorder, psychiatric hospitalization is frequently the best course of action. This may need to include involuntary civil commitment in accord with relevant local statutes. Hospitalization accomplishes the goal of containment of the acute risk and can permit more thorough diagnostic evaluation and rapid initiation of treatment. If the patient's imminent danger is not due to a mental disorder, the clinician may need to consider alternative dispositions, including substance abuse treatment, involvement of the criminal justice system, or other approaches (McNiel, Myers, Zeiner, Wolfe, & Hatcher, 1992).

Family Intervention

A number of family interventions can be helpful in addressing patient violence. These interventions can include education about early warning signs of psychiatric decompensation and referral to peer support groups (e.g., the National Alliance for the Mentally Ill) to learn ways other families have responded to escalation. When a patient's violence is related to difficulty in family communication or problem solving, family therapy may be beneficial. Such therapy can include clarifying and intervening in cycles or patterns of violence. The establishment of impulse-delay procedures such as no-harm contracts and planned timeouts if conflicts escalate to higher levels may be useful. The family can be educated about the benefits of removing weapons from easy accessability. For patients with substance abuse problems, the concomitant referral of family members to pertinent support groups (e.g., Al-Anon) may complement the patient's treatment. Finally, the family may be educated about the role of the criminal justice system in managing violence.

Psychological Intervention

Because of the important role of treatment compliance in ameliorating the risk of violence, establishment of a therapeutic alliance is an important goal. This may be facilitated by education, increased efforts to make contact (e.g., follow-up calls), demonstrating to the patient that what he or she says is heard and taken seriously, and so on. Many people feel that the treatment of repetitively violent patients is better provided in clinic settings rather than solo practice contexts. The focus of ongoing treatment of potentially violent patients varies as a function of the source of the violence risk, although the development of anger management strategies is a common component (Roth, 1987).

Increased Intensity of Treatment

Depending on the clinician's evaluation of the patient's level of risk and therapeutic alliance, intensification of treatment short of hospitalization may be effective. This may include increased frequency of therapy sessions, increased doses of psychoactive medication, partial hospitalization or day treatment, and so on. With chronically mentally ill people who have erratic treatment adherence, assertive case management may be helpful in diminishing violence potential (Dvoskin & Steadman, 1994).

Duty to Protect

In many jurisdictions, the therapist has a duty to protect the intended victim of a patient's threat (Beck, 1985). This may be accomplished by various interventions, such as those mentioned in the preceding paragraphs. In addition, the therapist may need to warn the potential victim and the police (see Eddy &

Harris, Chapter 10, this volume, for the pertinent legal issues). Clinically, this process can be facilitated by informing the patient of the necessity of the warning prior to carrying it out (Binder & McNiel, 1996).

SUMMARY

The perspective of this chapter is that the clinical evaluation and management of short-term risk of violence by mentally ill patients can be informed by recent research, which has identified pertinent variables in the areas of demographic/ personal history factors, clinical factors, situational factors, and clinician factors. Based on an evaluation of these factors, the clinician has an array of interventions available depending on the patient's level of risk. As the level of risk increases, the clinician may have to take more coercive actions to contain the patient's violence potential. While such interventions are necessary at certain risk levels, the gains in short-term safety must also be weighed against the potential negative effects on longer-term therapeutic objectives that may result from more coercive interventions.

ACKNOWLEDGMENT

Portions of this chapter were presented at the annual convention of the American Psychological Association, August 9–13, 1996, Toronto.

REFERENCES

American Psychiatric Association. (1985). *Seclusion and restraint: The psychiatric uses* (Task Force Report No. 22). Washington, DC: Author.

American Psychiatric Association. (1992). *Clinician safety* (Task Force Report No. 33). Washington, DC: Author.

Anderson, A. A., Ghali, A. Y., & Bansil, R. K. (1989). Weapon carrying among patients in a psychiatric emergency room. *Hospital and Community Psychiatry, 40,* 845–847.

Barratt, E. S. (1994). Impulsiveness and aggression. In J. Monahan & H. J. Steadman (Eds.), *Violence and mental disorder: Developments in risk assessment* (pp. 61–79). Chicago: University of Chicago Press.

Beauford, J. E., McNiel, D. E., & Binder, R. L. (1997). Utility of the initial therapeutic alliance in evaluating psychiatric patients' risk of violence. *American Journal of Psychiatry, 154,* 1272–1276.

Beck, J. C. (Ed.). (1985). *The potentially violent patient and the* Tarasoff *decision in clinical practice.* Washington, DC: American Psychiatric Press.

Beck, J. C., White, K. A., & Gage, B. (1991). Emergency psychiatric assessment of violence. *American Journal of Psychiatry, 148,* 1562–1565.

Binder, R. L., & McNiel, D. E. (1986). Victims and families of violent psychiatric patients. *Bulletin of the American Academy of Psychiatry and the Law, 14,* 131–139.

Binder, R. L., & McNiel, D. E. (1988). Effects of diagnosis and context on danger-ousness. *American Journal of Psychiatry, 145,* 728–732.

Binder, R. L., & McNiel, D. E. (1990). The relationship of gender to violent behavior in acutely disturbed psychiatric patients. *Journal of Clinical Psychiatry, 51,* 110–114.

Binder, R. L., & McNiel, D. E. (1996). Application of the *Tarasoff* ruling and its effect on the therapeutic relationship. *Psychiatric Services, 47,* 1212–1215.

Borum, R. (1996). Improving the clinical practice of violence risk assessment: Technology, guidelines and training. *American Psychologist, 51,* 945–956.

Borum, R., Otto, R., & Golding, S. (1993). Improving clinical judgment and decision making in forensic evaluation. *Journal of Psychiatry and the Law, 21,* 35–76.

Brizer, D. A., & Crowner, M. C. (Eds.). (1989). *Current approaches to the prediction of violence.* Washington, DC: American Psychiatric Press.

Brooks, N., Campsie, L., Symington, C., Beattie, A., & McKinlay, W. (1986). The five year outcome of severe blunt head injury: A relatives' view. *Journal of Neurology, Neurosurgery and Psychiatry, 49,* 764–770.

Carmel, H., & Hunter, M. (1990). Compliance with training in managing assaultive behavior and injuries from inpatient violence. *Hospital and Community Psychiatry, 41,* 558–560.

Clarkin, J. F., Hurt, S. W., & Crilly, J. L. (1987). Therapeutic alliance and hospital treatment outcome. *Hospital and Community Psychiatry, 38,* 871–875.

Convit, A., Isay, D., Otis, D., & Volavka, J. (1990). Characteristics of repeatedly violent psychiatric inpatients. *Hospital and Community Psychiatry, 41,* 1112–1115.

Corrigan, P. W., Yudofsky, S. C., & Silver, J. M. (1993). Pharmacological and behavioral treatments for aggressive inpatients. *Hospital and Community Psychiatry, 44,* 125–133.

Drummond, D. J., Sparr, L. F., & Gordon, G. H. (1989). Hospital violence reduction among high risk patients. *Journal of the American Medical Association, 261,* 2531–2534.

Dubin, W. R. (1988). Rapid tranquilization: Antipsychotics or benzodiazepines. *Journal of Clinical Psychiatry, 49*(Suppl.), 5–11.

Dvoskin, J. A., & Steadman, H. J., (1994). Using intensive case management to reduce violence by mentally ill persons in the community. *Hospital and Community Psychiatry, 45,* 679–684.

Eichelman, B. S. (1988). Toward a rational pharmacotherapy for aggressive and violent behavior. *Hospital and Community Psychiatry, 39,* 31–39.

Eichelman, B. S., & Hartwig, A. C. (Eds.). (1995). *Patient violence and the clinician.* Washington, DC: American Psychiatric Press.

Estroff, S. E., Zimmer, C., Lachicotte, W. S., & Benoit, J. (1994). The influence of social networks and social support on violence by persons with serious mental illness. *Hospital and Community Psychiatry, 45,* 669–679.

Gardner, W., Lidz, C. W., Mulvey, E. P., & Shaw, E. C. (1996). A comparison of actuarial methods for identifying repetitively violent patients. *Law and Human Behavior, 20,* 35–48.

Gutheil, T. G., Bursztajn, H., & Brodsky, A. (1986). The multidimensional assessment of dangerousness: Competence assessment in patient care and liability prevention. *Bulletin of the American Academy of Psychiatry and the Law, 14,* 123–129.

Haller, E., Binder, R. L., & McNiel, D. E. (1989). Violence in geriatric patients with dementia. *Bulletin of the American Academy of Psychiatry and the Law, 17,* 183–188.

Hare, R. D. (1991). *The Hare Psychopathy Checklist—Revised.* Toronto: Multi-Health Systems.

Harris, G. T., Rice, M. E., & Quinsey, V. L. (1993). Violent recidivism of mentally disordered offenders: The development of a statistical prediction instrument. *Criminal Justice and Behavior, 20,* 315–335.

Hart, S. D., Hare, R. D., & Forth, A. E. (1994). Psychopathy as a risk marker for violence: Development and validation of a screening version of the Revised Psychopathy Checklist. In J. Monahan & H. J. Steadman (Eds.), *Violence and mental disorder: Developments in risk assessment* (pp. 81–98). Chicago: University of Chicago Press.

Infantino, J. A., & Musingo, S. Y. (1985). Assaults and injuries among staff with and without training in aggression control techniques. *Hospital and Community Psychiatry, 36,* 1312–1314.

Johnson, D. A. W., Pasterski, G., Ludlow, I. M., Street, K., & Taylor, R. D. W. (1983). The discontinuance of maintenance neuroleptic therapy in chronic schizophrenic patients: Drug and social consequences. *Acta Psychiatrica Scandinavia, 67,* 339–352.

Kahnemann, D., & Tversky, A. (1996). On the reality of cognitive illusions: A reply to Gigrenzer's critique. *Psychological Review, 103,* 582–591.

Kalunian, D. A., Binder, R. L., & McNiel, D. E. (1990). Violence by geriatric patients who need psychiatric hospitalization. *Journal of Clinical Psychiatry, 51,* 340–343.

Klassen, D., & O'Connor, W. A. (1988). A prospective study of predictors of violence in adult male mental health admissions. *Law and Human Behavior, 12,* 143–158.

Klassen, D., & O'Connor, W. A. (1989). Assessing the risk of violence in released mental patients: A cross-validation study. *Psychological Assessment: A Journal of Consulting and Clinical Psychology, 1,* 75–81.

Klassen, D., & O'Connor, W. A. (1994). Demographic and case history variables in risk assessment. In J. Monahan & H. J. Steadman (Eds.), *Violence and mental disorder: Developments in risk assessment* (pp. 229–257). Chicago: University of Chicago Press.

Krakowski, M. I., Convit, A., Jaeger, J., Lin, S., & Volavka, J. (1989). Neurological impairment in violent schizophrenic inpatients. *American Journal of Psychiatry, 146,* 849–853.

Krakowski, M. I., Volavka, J., & Brizer, D. (1986). Psychopathology and violence: A review of the literature. *Comprehensive Psychiatry, 27,* 131–148.

Kropp, P. R., Hart, S. D., Webster, C. D., & Eaves, D. (1994). *Manual for the Spousal Assault Risk Assessment Guide.* Vancouver: British Columbia Institute on Family Violence.

Lidz, C. W., Mulvey, E. P., & Gardner, W. (1993). The accuracy of predictions of violence to others. *Journal of the American Medical Association, 269,* 1007–1011.

Link, B. G., Andrews, H., & Cullen, F. T. (1992). The violent and illegal behavior of mental patients reconsidered. *American Sociological Review, 57,* 275–292.

Linnoila, V. M. I., & Virkkunen, M. (1992). Aggression, suicidality, and serotonin. *Journal of Clinical Psychiatry, 53*(Suppl.), 46–51.

Lowenstein, M., Binder, R. L., & McNiel, D. E. (1990). The relationship between admission symptoms and hospital assaults. *Hospital and Community Psychiatry, 41,* 311–313.

McCulloch, L. E., McNiel, D. E., Binder, R. L., & Hatcher, C. (1986). Effects of a weapon screening procedure in a psychiatric emergency room. *Hospital and Community Psychiatry, 37,* 837–838.

McNiel, D. E. (1994). Hallucinations and violence. In J. Monahan & H. J. Steadman (Eds.), *Violence and mental disorder: Developments in risk assessment* (pp. 183–202). Chicago: University of Chicago Press.

McNiel, D. E., & Binder, R. L. (1986). Violence, civil commitment, and hospitalization. *Journal of Nervous and Mental Disease, 174,* 107–111.

McNiel, D.E., & Binder, R. L. (1987). Patients who bring weapons to the psychiatric emergency room. *Journal of Clinical Psychiatry, 48,* 230–233.

McNiel, D. E., & Binder, R. L. (1989). Relationship between threats and later violent behavior by acute psychiatric inpatients. *Hospital and Community Psychiatry, 40,* 605–608.

McNiel, D. E., & Binder, R. L. (1993, August). *Inter-rater agreement: A strategy for improving violence risk assessment.* Paper presented at the annual convention of the American Psychological Association, Toronto.

McNiel, D. E., & Binder, R. L. (1994a). The relationship between psychiatric symptoms, diagnosis, and imminent risk of violence. *Hospital and Community Psychiatry, 45,* 133–137.

McNiel, D. E., & Binder, R. L. (1994b). Screening for risk of inpatient violence: Validation of an actuarial tool. *Law and Human Behavior, 18,* 579–586.

McNiel, D. E., & Binder, R. L. (1995). Correlates of accuracy in the assessment of psychiatric inpatients' risk of violence. *American Journal of Psychiatry, 152,* 901–906.

McNiel, D. E., Binder, R. L., & Greenfield, T. K. (1988). Predictors of violence in civilly committed acute psychiatric patients. *American Journal of Psychiatry, 145,* 965–970.

McNiel, D. E., Hatcher, C., Zeiner, H., Wolfe, H. L., & Myers, R. S. (1991). Characteristics of persons referred by police to the psychiatric emergency room. *Hospital and Community Psychiatry, 42,* 425–427.

McNiel, D. E., Myers, R. S., Zeiner, H. S., Wolfe, H. L., & Hatcher, C. (1992). The role of violence in decisions about hospitalization from the psychiatric emergency room. *American Journal of Psychiatry, 148,* 1317–1321.

Monahan, J. (1981). *The clinical prediction of violent behavior.* Rockville, MD: National Institute of Mental Health.

Monahan, J. (1993). Limiting therapist exposure to *Tarasoff* liability: Guidelines for risk containment. *American Psychologist, 48,* 242–250.

Monahan, J. (1994). *MacArthur Community Violence Instrument.* Charlottesville, VA: University of Virginia.

Mulvey, E. P., & Lidz, C. W. (1984). Clinical considerations in the prediction of dangerousness in mental patients. *Clinical Psychology Review, 4,* 379–401.

Mulvey, E. P., Shaw, E., & Lidz, C. W. (1994). Editorial: Why use multiple sources in research on patient violence in the community? *Criminal Justice and Mental Health, 4,* 253–258.

Mysiew, W. J., Jackson, R. D., & Corrigan, J. D. (1988). Amitriptyline for post-<

traumatic agitation. *American Journal of Physical Medicine and Rehabilitation, 67,* 29–33.

Newhill, C. E., Mulvey, E. P., & Lidz, C. W. (1995) Characteristics of violence in the community by female patients seen in a psychiatric emergency service, *Psychiatric Services, 46,* 785–789.

Otto, R. (1992). The prediction of dangerous behavior: A review and analysis of "second generation" research. *Forensic Reports, 5,* 103–133.

Quinsey, V. L., Rice, M. E., & Harris, G. T. (1995). Actuarial prediction of sexual recidivism. *Journal of Interpersonal Violence, 10,* 85–105.

Rossi, A. M., Jacobs, M., Monteleone, J., Olsen, R., Surber, R. W., Winkler, E. L., & Wommack, A. (1986). Characteristics of psychiatric patients who engage in assaultive or other fear-inducing behaviors. *Journal of Nervous and Mental Disease, 174,* 154–160.

Roth, L. H. (Ed.). (1987). *Clinical treatment of the violent person.* New York: Guilford Press.

Rund, D. A., & Helzer, J. C. (1983). *Emergency psychiatry.* St. Louis: Mosby.

Steadman, H. J. (1982). A situational approach to violence. *International Journal of Law and Psychiatry, 5,* 171–186.

Steadman, H. J., Monahan, J., Appelbaum, P. S., Grisso, T., Mulvey, E. P., Roth, L. H., Robbins, P. C., & Klassen, D. (1994). Designing a new generation of risk assessment research. In J. Monahan & H. J. Steadman (Eds.), *Violence and mental disorder: Developments in risk assessment* (pp. 297–318). Chicago: University of Chicago Press.

Straznickas, K. A., McNiel, D. E., & Binder, R. L. (1993). Violence toward fam-%m%mily caregivers of the mentally ill. *Hospital and Community Psychiatry, 44,* 385–387.

Swanson, J. W. (1994). Mental disorder, substance abuse, and community violence: An epidemiological approach. In J. Monahan & H. J. Steadman (Eds.), *Violence and mental disorder: Developments in risk assessment* (pp. 101–136). Chicago: University of Chicago Press.

Swanson, J. W., Holzer, C. E., Ganju, V. K., & Jono, R. T. (1990). Violence and psychiatric disorder in the community: Evidence from the Epidemiologic Catchment Area surveys. *Hospital and Community Psychiatry, 41,* 761–770.

Tarasoff v. Regents of University of California. (1974). 529 P. 2d 553, 118 Cal. Rptr. 129.

Tarasoff v. Regents of University of California. (1976). 17 Cal. 3d 425, 551 P. 2d 334, 131 Cal. Rptr. 14.

Tardiff, K. (1989). *Concise guide to assessment and management of violent patients.* Washington, DC: American Psychiatric Press.

Tardiff, K. (1992). The current state of psychiatry in the treatment of violent patients. *Archives of General Psychiatry, 49,* 493–499.

Tardiff, K., & Sweillam, A. (1980). Assault, suicide, and mental illness. *Archives of General Psychiatry, 37,* 164–169.

Thackery, M. (1987). *Therapeutics for aggression: Psychological and physical crisis intervention.* New York: Human Sciences Press.

Truscott, D., Evans, J., & Marsell, S. (1995). Outpatient psychotherapy with dangerous clients: A model for clinical decision making. *Professional Psychology: Research and Practice, 26,* 484–490.

Volavka, J. (1990). Aggression, electroencephalography, and evoked potentials: A critical review. *Neuropsychiatry, Neuropsychology, and Behavioral Neurology, 3,* 249–259.

Volavka, J. (1995). *Neurobiology of violence.* Washington, DC: American Psychiatric Press.

Webster, C. D., Eaves, D., Douglas, K., & Wintrup, A. (1995). *The HCR-20 scheme: The assessment of dangerousness and risk.* Burnaby, B.C., Canada: Simon Fraser University and Forensic Psychiatric Services Commission of British Columbia.

Webster, C. D., Harris, G. T., Rice, M. E., Cormier, C., & Quincy, V. L. (1994). *The violence prediction scheme: Assessing dangerousness in high risk men.* Toronto: Centre of Criminology, University of Toronto.

Widiger, T. A., & Trull, T. J. (1994). Personality disorders and violence. In J. Monahan & H. J. Steadman (Eds.), *Violence and mental disorder: Developments in risk assessment* (pp. 203–226). Chicago: University of Chicago Press.

Yesavage, J. A. (1984). Correlates of dangerous behavior by schizophrenics in hospital. *Journal of Psychiatric Research, 18,* 225–231.

Yesavage, J. A., Becker, J. M. T., Werner, P. D., Patton, K., Seeman, D. W., Brunstig, D. W., & Mills, M. J. (1983). Family conflict, psychopathology, and dangerous behavior by schizophrenic patients. *Psychiatry Research, 8,* 271–280.

CHAPTER 6

CRISIS ASSESSMENT
AND INTERVENTIONS
WITH VICTIMS OF VIOLENCE

JANET YASSEN
MARY R. HARVEY

Victimization resulting from interpersonal violence has become commonplace in the United States. Investigations document the widespread prevalence of child physical and sexual abuse and domestic violence, as well as adult rape, murder, muggings, and so on (e.g., Boney-McCoy & Finkelhor, 1995; Koss, Gidcyz, & Wisniewski, 1987; Russell, 1984; National Center on Child Abuse and Neglect, 1988). In some parts of the country, interpersonal violence in epidemic proportions is considered a major public health issue. There is also documentation regarding the acute and potentially devastating consequences of victimization (e.g., Burgess & Holmstrom, 1979; Figley, 1985; Koss & Harvey, 1991; Green, Wilson, & Lindy, 1985; Wilson, 1987; Herman, 1992; Hoff, 1995; Janoff-Bulman, 1992; McCombie, 1983; Ochberg, 1988). Clearly, clinicians, especially those in emergency settings, are increasingly being called on to provide psychological care to people victimized by current or prior violence, such as the consequences of war or political torture.

This chapter is based on the work of the Victims of Violence (VOV) program. VOV is an adult outpatient specialty clinic of the Cambridge Hospital's Harvard-affiliated Department of Psychiatry. Since its inception in 1985, VOV has pioneered innovative and theory-informed approaches to the treatment of psychological trauma at individual, group, and community levels. Its clinical services include crisis response (emergency room liaison, crisis assessment, and crisis counseling) to acutely traumatized crime victims and their families, longer-term clinical care for adult survivors of childhood trauma and chronic victimization, and a wide array of groups. In addition, VOV has a community crisis response team (CCRT) which provides consultation to assist local agencies in their crisis response planning, traumatic stress debriefings, community meetings, and training. VOV receives referrals from both public and private sources. They include men and women of diverse ethnicity and economic status. It is supported in part by the Massachusetts Office of Victims Assistance.

Unifying VOV's diverse interventions are a shared set of program values and a common understanding of psychological trauma, treatment, and recovery. VOV recognizes the prevalence of violence and crime victimization, the value of community-based social action, and the importance of competence-building, empowering care. Its services assume that life-threatening and violent events can have a traumatic impact on individuals, families and loved ones, and communities. We also assume that individuals who were victimized by physical or sexual violence differ in their responses to violence and in their need for and responses to psychotherapeutic intervention. Not all victims develop posttraumatic stress disorder and not all require or desire the assistance of mental health professionals. Some may experience significant distress but manage to cope by drawing on their own internal resources and those of a supportive environment (Harvey, 1996). VOV values and makes use of nonpsychiatric community-based services while also striving to make positive use of the psychiatric setting.

This chapter presents the theoretically informed approach to crisis intervention developed and implemented at VOV. It describes the principles of crisis intervention based on an ecological understanding of violence combined with the understanding of the stages of response in the aftermath of crime victimization. The chapter also offers effective clinical intervention strategies to manage responses to crime victimization. A case example illustrates this approach.

ECOLOGICAL FRAMEWORK

First and foremost, the model of crisis intervention at VOV is based on an ecological understanding of violence, its impact, and its implications on service delivery. Ecology is the science concerned with the interrelationship of organisms and their environments (*Webster 's Ninth New Collegiate Dictionary,* 1985). Within the field of community psychology, there is an interest in the ecological context of human community and the interrelationship of individuals and the communities from which they draw identity, belongingness, and meaning (Kelly, 1968; Koss & Harvey, 1991). The ecological analogy understands violent and traumatic events as ecological threats not only to the adaptive capacities of individuals but also to the ability of human communities to foster health and resiliency among affected community members (Koss & Harvey, 1991; Harvey, 1996; Norris & Thompson, 1995). Thus, violence, racism, sexism, homophobia, poverty, and so on, can be thought of as environmental pollutants.

While the etiology of traumatic events can be thought of as occurring from the environment, the ecological analogy can also assist us in understanding the complex attributes and variables that affect the crisis responses of victims to these external, environmental events.

An ecological view of trauma (Harvey, 1996; Koss & Harvey, 1991) attends to the environmental context of victimization and attributes responses to trauma and recovery to a complex interaction among the person, event, and environmental factors. Table 6.1 (Harvey, 1996) lists some of the dimensions of these variables.

An ecologically informed trauma assessment and plan take into consideration the dynamic interaction among the person x event x environment variables. For instance, a victim of a hit-and-run accident who is also a non-English-speaking refugee from a country where her family experienced political torture may face many personal obstacles in trusting institutional help, as well as in recovering in a society that is showing a rise in anti-immigrant sentiments and hostilities.

An ecological view of recovery (Harvey, 1996) acknowledges the many

TABLE 6.1. Factors Affecting Responses to Trauma and Trauma Recovery

Person	Age/development stage
	Relationship to offender(s)
	Pretrauma personality, functioning, and coping capabilities
	Ability to utilize social support and to perceive help as helpful
	Immediate response/subsequent response
	Perceptions of and meaning ascribed to trauma
	Qualities assigned to self and others posttrauma
	Cultural, ethnic, religious, racial, sexual orientation variables
Event	Severity, duration, frequency
	Degree if physical violence/personal violation
	Shared with others of suffered alone
	"Power politics"
Environment	Quality and continuity of social supports
	Responses of the "recovery environment"
	Community attitudes and values
	Quality, availability and diversity of community resources
	Measure of physical and emotional safety ensured posttrauma

Note. Adapted from Harvey (1996, p. 6).

ways in which trauma survivors and communities may demonstrate resiliency and offers to clinicians and survivors a set of criteria by which to understand various domains of the recovery process over time. (Lebowitz, Harvey, & Herman, 1993). This view of trauma recovery emphasizes the importance of assessing domains of strength as well as domains of impairment. It assists both the clinician and the survivor to build on the individual and community health and the adaptive nature of the survivors. This theoretically directed model assists clinicians in developing interventions that are timed appropriately, in using a variety of modalities, and in returning the locus of control to the survivors. These guiding principles are the foundation of the crisis intervention model of VOV.

PRINCIPLES OF CRISIS INTERVENTION IN THE AFTERMATH OF CRIME

Callahan (Chapter 2, this volume) describes crisis theory and crisis intervention in general, but it is important to note that a crisis resulting from crime victimization differs from a crisis resulting from internal psychological causes. Its etiology is derived from external causes. The external events can be either a single incident of crime or ongoing/chronic crime victimization (domestic violence, urban violence, war, etc.). The offenders can be strangers, acquaintances, or those known well by the victims. Keeping in mind the ecological model, the definition of crisis from crime victimization includes a context that goes beyond the individual; it involves a *personal* and *interpersonal* violation and it means the rules/laws that *society* has developed to mediate human behavior have also been violated. It is characterized by violation and loss of control of one's own individual and physical safety as well as loss of safety in one's environment. The principles of crisis intervention focus on restoring power and control to the victim's internal and external environments.

IMPACT OF CRIME VICTIMIZATION

Our understanding of the impact of crime victimization comes from combining what we know about reactions to other traumas such as disaster and loss (Lindemann, 1944; Kubler-Ross, 1975; Caplan, 1964) with what we have begun to document since the post-Vietnam War era. We draw our understanding from those who helped war veterans (Wilson, 1988; Green et al., 1985), survivors of the Holocaust of World War II (Danieli, 1988), victims of rape (Koss & Harvey, 1991; McCombie, 1983; Ledray, 1994; Scherl & Sutherland, 1970; Yassen & Glass, 1984; Burgess & Holmstrom, 1979; Roth & Lebowitz, 1988), survivors of domestic violence (Stark & Flitcraft, 1988; Schechter, 1982) and other various kinds of crime victimization (Herman, 1992; Wilson, 1987; Janoff-

Bulman, 1992; van der Kolk, 1987; Figley, 1985; Ochberg, 1988; Hoff, 1995; Bard & Sangrey, 1986; Young, 1987; Harvey, Tobey, & Aldrich, 1996; Comas-Díaz & Padilla, 1990; McCann & Pearlman, 1990).

From these various sources, we learn that reactions to crime, although individual and unique, have a multilevel effect on people. They affect people physically (and biologically), cognitively, psychologically, behaviorally, interpersonally, and spiritually. Table 6.2 summarizes some of the reactions reported and observed through the VOV program.

The following case example, based on a vignette developed by Shorin and Greenwald (1995), illustrates the levels of impact. It is developed throughout as we discuss stages of recovery and treatment interventions. However, it is a composite of clinical intervention—an overview. It does not give justice to the complex texture of individuals and community described in the ecological model. The vignette highlights only a few dimensions and is to be used only as a guide.

Henry Jackson, age 24, is a very involved white youth leader in an after-school peer leadership program at the community center. Leaving the center after work, Henry sees a group of adolescent males (of various cultural and racial backgrounds) surrounding a female in the corner of the playground. They are taunting and harassing her and pulling at her clothes. Henry yells into the building for help and then attempts to intervene with the youths. In the process of trying to break up the group, Henry is cut by one boy who pulls out a knife. The boys become scared and flee. The police and the ambulance arrive on the scene and Henry and the young woman, Catherine (age 15 and white) are taken to the emergency room. They identify the perpetrators who are not immediately arrested. At the emergency room, Henry and Catherine are treated for their injuries. The nurse discusses the impact of the trauma. *Henry* reports feeling calm and angry. He just finished the working day and is very tired. He spent the afternoon trying to get bus transportation for the community center to transport some kids to a basketball game. The last thing he wants to do is to "deal with more aggravation." His arm is aching and he just wants to sleep. He says he will deal with it tomorrow.

Catherine is quite shaken. She is upset that her blouse is ripped because she borrowed it from her sister. She is worried that her sister will be angry. She is also worried that she is going to be late getting home and that her mother will wonder where she is. She is confused about how she will get home. She wants to know where her book bag is because she has a lot of homework to do. Catherine reports seeing a whirl of faces among whom were some of her friends. She keeps saying, "How could they do this to me, I never did anything to them. I thought they were going to kill me."

In the *community,* the *community center,* and in the *neighborhood,* people begin to react. The information being spread is that Henry was stabbed and needs surgery and that Catherine was raped. Fear sets in as other kids begin to worry that they are in danger, too. Night falls and staff,

TABLE 6.2. Common Reactions to Violence and Trauma

Following is a partial list of common reactions to violence and other traumatic events. Each person reacts differently and may have some or many of these reactions.

Physical

Reactions to injuries
Fatigue
Somatic complaints
Stomach problems
Vomiting/diarrhea
Sweating, rapid pulse
Chest/head pains
Dizziness, trouble breathing
Startle reactions
Shock
Heightened senses
Numbness

Psychological

Feeling helpless, powerless, hopeless
Grief over losses
Sense of injustice
Guilt
Overwhelmed, vulnerable
Feeling not yourself
Reminders of prior losses or traumas
Emotional roller coaster
Anger, feelings of revenge
Depression, sadness
Fear, terror
Nervousness, frustration
Disbelief, denial
Shame, embarrassment
Loss of pride, dignity, security

Relational

Withdrawing/clinging to others
Alienation from friends, coworkers,
    family
Breakdown in trust
Changes in sexual activity
False or distorted generalizations about
    others
Doubts about relationships
Being demanding of others
Suspiciousness, fear of others
Differences in perception of your
    situation or healing process
Inability of others to meet your needs

Cognitive

Confusion
Difficulty concentrating
Too many thoughts at once
Hard time making decisions
Distortion of time
Difficulty remembering things
Threatened assumptions (that the
    world is not safe)
Intrusive imagery, flashbacks
Replaying the event
Thinking about suicide/homicide
Disorientation, spaciness
Euphoria or guilt about being alive

Behavioral

Irritability, moodiness
Regression to more youthful or
    harmful coping strategies
Disturbances of sleep or appetite
Substance abuse—alcohol, food, drugs,
    etc.
Engaging in dangerous behaviors
    toward oneself or others
Changes in how you usually act
Dissociation
Crying, calmness, hysteria
Silence/talkativeness

Spiritual

Loss of/clinging to faith
Spiritual doubts
Withdrawal from one's spiritual
    community
Lapses in spiritual practice
Despair, hopelessness
Questioning old beliefs
Sense of world being changed
Out of kilter
Questioning the meaning of life

kids, and parents worry about the emotional and physical status of Henry and Catherine.

As we can see, the reactions of Henry, Catherine, and the community are quite varied, ranging from numbness, anger, fear, physical pain, worry, confusion, betrayal of trust, fear, frustration, loss, concern about other's reactions, questioning of individual behavior, and exaggeration of the facts. They are, in fact, among the various responses described in Table 6.2. Clusters of these responses also appear in the *Diagnostic and Statistical Manual of Mental Disorders,* fourth edition (DSM IV; American Pspychiatric Association, 1994) in the sections that describe acute reactions to stress and /or posttraumatic stress disorder. These reactions result from the disruption of physical, relational, and environmental autonomy and loss of safety and physical integrity. Victims of crime may experience their reactions in different ways at different times subsequent to their victimization. Understanding these stages assists clinicians in planning interventions that meet the needs of the survivors. From an ecological perspective, victims, their loved ones, and their various communities are affected. Their ages, prior experiences, and reactions of those in their environment, for example, will affect their reactions and how they may change over time. To understand Henry and Catherine's reactions we must understand the concept of stages of response.

STAGES OF RESPONSE

Victims of violence experience reactions that may differ over time and are affected by their own person x event x environment variables. In studying crime victims, various researchers identify several stages of response (Horowitz, 1986; Forman, 1980; Burgess & Holstrom, 1979; Herman, 1992; Bard & Sangrey, 1986; Koss & Harvey, 1991; Bassuk, 1980; Yassen & Glass, 1984). At VOV, our experience is empirically consistent with the earliest research by Scherl and Sutherland (1970). We adapted our model from their initial and ground-breaking data.

Acute Crisis

This stage begins with the immediate impact in the aftermath of crime victimization. Victims are suddenly propelled into a whirlwind of physiological and emotional reactions. They are faced with decisions regarding medical care, criminal justice involvement, and sudden changes in safety and routine, as well as whether and how to disclose the events to family, friends, coworkers, and so on. Victims have to deal with not only the reality of what has occurred to them but their own and others' reactions toward them. Symptoms such as those described in Table 6.2 begin to appear. They often occur in clusters of either intrusiveness or constriction (numbing, shut down), sometimes alternating suddenly between the two. When symptoms are extreme, victims can feel like they are "going crazy." Survivors report experiencing a physical or emotional regression to earlier coping strategies. As an attempt to gain mastery over their feelings of powerlessness, survivors can transfer their fears to a complet focus on their symptoms. This initial stage occurs in two parts: the first 24–48 hours, when the most intense involvement with other institutions occurs (e.g., police, hospitals, family), and then 48 hours to 12 weeks, when the victim begins to develop coping strategies for his or her various reactions. The therapeutic tasks for the patient in this first stage are to understand and manage symptoms, to begin to reestablish control and trust, and to develop safety plans.

Outward Adjustment

This stage can begin within 24 hours and last for many months or years. Commonly, it lasts through the first year after the end of the violence and/or the termination of the prosecution process. Because crime victims often feel a sense of internal disorganization, many individuals assume an external sense of control by returning to a routine of activities they followed before the victimization. Reclaiming one's own life events offers opportunities for mastery over one's environment again and provides the chance, too, to be with people who have the potential to be safe, caring, and supportive. Thus, victims achieve the possibility of rebuilding some interpersonal trust.

Integration

Once the violence ends, victims often go through a process of integrating the experience of the violence into their views of themselves, others, and the world. Survivors report a process similar to the experience of those who are grieving the death/loss of a loved one. In the case of single-incident crime victimization, survivors go through all the seasons, holidays, and events posttrauma with this new view of themselves as victims of crime. The integration process means developing and incorporating new aspects to their personal identity and having enough distance from the actual danger to reflect on its meaning in their life on both a personal and interpersonal level. This process of integration can only occur when symptom management has been achieved and when the survivor is physically and emotionally in a safe situation. If this level of safety is not achieved, the survivor cannot integrate the experience. This stage can occur spontaneously at an anniversary time or can be activated by other events such as another life crisis or even a newspaper article or television show about crime. The process of integration can occur over time and can also be reworked over time. Other life crises may also remind the individual of the powerlessness of his or her criminal victimization. This does not mean that the individual has "unresolved issues." It actually may mean that the individual is reacting "normally" to this new crisis. It is in the nature of crisis to be reminded of times in our life when we experienced other emotional or life-threatening events. It is not uncommon to get calls from people after the death of a parent to help them work through an additional level of grief regarding a prior assault, or from people who are now seeking counseling for physical or sexual trauma as a result of confronting another life-threatening situation (e.g., a car accident).

As with all stage theories, the stages can go in cycles or sometimes spirals. For crime victims, prosecution of the crimes can reactivate symptoms of the initial crisis stage. It is important to remember that symptoms occur at various stages and in various ways. Emergency room clinicians most often see victims of crime in the acute stage. The focus in the section on clinical interventions emphasizes the acute stage. However, emergency room clinicians may also see individuals who, as a result of some other psychiatric crisis, have reactions stemming from a prior crime victimization that they have not yet integrated or are working through in a different way, or patients with psychiatric illness who have become prey to crime due to their vulnerabilities.

Let's return to Henry and Catherine and their community to explore their initial stage of response. Both Henry and Catherine have very different reactions as well as different concerns. Their reactions continue over the next few days.

> *Henry:* That same evening, Henry returns home and talks with anger about what happened on the playground. His roommates tell him that he is crazy to continue to work there, that he is lucky to be alive. Henry does not feel that way. He is not thinking of his own emotional reactions but rather feels more committed than ever to return to his job and to help to develop better violence prevention programs. That night he sleeps fitfully, awakening often with aching pains in his arm. He returns to work the next day continuing to keep his emotions at bay and rebuffing any suggestions that he take any time off from work to let himself heal. Being at work and continuing his mission give Henry a sense of power and control in his crisis response.

> *Catherine:* With the assistance of the nurse, Catherine calls a trusted aunt to come to pick her up. Catherine remains tearful but does not want to talk about the details of what happened to her. When they hear from the aunt about what happened, Catherine's mother and sister are supportive but want to know why Catherine did not leave the community center with the other girls. Catherine remains quiet for the rest of the evening and does not want to go to school the next day. She is afraid to be by herself and to see her assailants. Her guidance counselor calls and arranges to meet with Catherine to discuss Catherine's safety at school. Catherine returns to school and to the community center with the encouragement of her friends.

> *The community:* At the community center, the activities inside go on as usual because many of the people inside have not heard about the

incident. The director is concerned that there may be rumors or that kids may hear about what happened and either get scared or try to seek revenge. Over the course of the evening, he consults with staff members and board members. He is worried about Catherine and Henry and calls them later that night. He decides to have a staff meeting the next morning to plan some meetings with the kids. Someone mentions the CCRT, which he calls. Team members send him some information to discuss with his management team. The CCRT also encourages him to give the information about the CCRT to anyone in the community whom he thinks could benefit from it.

As this illustration demonstrates, all the parties involved have different kinds of reactions, from experiencing physical symptoms to being action oriented. The range is quite varied. In planning clinical interventions to treat victims of violence, the first thing to keep in mind is the ecological perspective. That implies that interventions are most effective when they take into consideration the individual as well as his or her environment. A second fundamental principle has to do with the clinician's view of psychological interventions. Many clinicians are trained in psychodynamic methodology. Ochberg (1988) suggests that the type of treatment that focuses on the preexisting personality and symptom formation (which has more to do with weaknesses, limitations, and unresolved antebellum issues) is not advisable in the aftermath of violent crime. Treatment interventions must be formulated with the supposition that recent events can and do have catastrophic emotional consequences and that the focus of the intervention may be on the coping skills and strengths of the victims. Even if there is evidence of prior psychopathology, the presenting problem of crime victimization is a separate as well as concurrent problem. Hoff (1995) reminds us that we should be mindful of not "medicalizing" the needs of crime victims. Even though they are being seen in a medical setting and may have medical injuries, the etiology of the conditions have social/cultural origins.

INTERVENTIONS

The goal of psychological intervention in the aftermath of crime victimization is to prevent further psychological harm and to empower both the individual and his or her environment to proceed on the path of healing. This goal can be complicated to achieve because of the potential of secondary victimization caused by the setting (Symonds, 1975). Effective interventions are timed appropriately, incorporate various modalities, and show an understanding of both the setting and the use of the therapeutic relationship. The clinician must simultaneously assess the psychological situation and provide treatment interventions. The general structure of the interview should include slowly building a connection, then eliciting emotionally evocative material, and finally returning to a more cognitive frame of mind at the end of the session. This structure enables the client to leave the interview psychologically capable of managing the world. The following overview offers guidelines for providing psychological care to crime victims.

Establishing an Initial Alliance

Because crime victimization represents a breach of human attachment, the rebuilding of interpersonal trust must begin immediately. Clinicians must be always mindful of this goal and pay particular attention to the details of creating a safe, private, confidential space in which to provide care. Involving and informing the patients about what the clinician is doing and what they can expect creates an environment of safety and starts them on the road to taking back control of their lives. It is important to help restore a sense of choice, control, and predictability to the victim/survivor's environment. In the hectic pace of an emergency setting, it is easy for the clinician to forget basics such as making a proper introduction, offering a glass of water, or expressing the human reaction of sympathy for the individual having experienced an event that brought him or her to the emergency room. If the individual is accompanied by someone, the clinician should introduce him- or herself to that person as well. The clinician should try to arrange for a quiet, private place for the interview. If that is not possible, he or she should explain the limitations of the setting. If there will be a need for interruptions, the clinician should be sure to let the patient know and be sure that the staff knows to knock. Sudden interruptions can add to the patient's sense of powerlessness.

Assessment

Before Seeing the Patient

It is important for the clinician to know some of the basics about the nature of the crime before they see the patient (e.g., what happened, when, where, by whom, and how). Also, the clinician should keep in mind what the patient has already experienced in the hospital setting and how long the patient has already been there. A contextual understanding of the patient allows a clinician to better understand the patient and to plan his or her interventions. In Henry's case, for instance, he was exhausted and in physical pain, factors that clearly have an impact on how the clinician should structure the interview and how Henry could make use of it.

Identify Patient Concerns

From the beginning it is important to identify the concerns of the patient. This gives the patient the immediate message that it is his or her needs about which the clinician is concerned. This is in direct contradiction to how the perpetrator of the crime saw the situation. The clinician should ask the patient to describe what he or she is experiencing in order to get a symptom picture. In addition, the clinician cannot anticipate what the patient's own particular concerns may be. For Catherine, her family, rather than the actual impact of the assault, was foremost in her mind at that time. Many survivors often have immediate and/or practical concerns that may require attention (e.g. housing, child care, and clothing). While the clinician must maintain a nonjudgemental and neutral stance toward his or her clinical interventions, he or she must also be clear that violence is never an acceptable behavior.

Ongoing Mental Status Assessment

The psychological assessment of someone in acute crisis can be compromised by possible psychological regression. This is a common occurrence in crime victims. The mental status examination (MSE) in this context is different from an MSE in other types of psychiatric crisis. It is usually done in a less formalized way. The clinician can learn a great deal about the patient's mental status by discussing his or her prior crises, coping strategies, psychological strengths, social and community supports, levels of impact, and individual, social, and community vulnerabilities. For example, the clinician might ask Henry and Catherine if they ever experienced other crises, illnesses, accidents, and so on, in their lives and how they managed them. Such questions may help them to begin to figure out how they can manage this crisis. The clinician can learn the patient's crisis history as well as other possible vulnerabilities without having the patient experience the questioning as overly intrusive or overly pathologizing. Similarly, the clinician might ask if things ever got so bad in their lives that patients felt like harming or killing themselves or anyone else. It may also help for the clinician to explain that sometimes, in times of crisis, people try to cope in the best way they know how, even if they know their coping strategy is not so great. For example, some people try to cope by physically hurting themselves or by drinking or drugging to forget. In asking in this way, the clinician does an MSE in a more indirect way and provides information for the client about crisis reactions at the same time. Again, these questions are interspersed throughout the interview so that the clinician is not bombarding the patient. It is always important to be mindful not to ask emotionally evocative questions too close to the end. Table 6.1 can be a guide for developing categories in assessing the person factors of an ecological assessment. Let's return to the vignette that has been used as an example:

> In assessing *Henry,* the clinician finds out that while Henry was at college, there was a murder on campus and the perpetrators were caught. Henry's parents encouraged him to transfer schools, which he did not want to do. Henry says that he did not receive or "need" any counseling at the time and he found that team sports helped him to work it out. Sometimes he and his friends got drunk on weekends. He has a couple of good friends and a girlfriend to whom he talks. Thinking of the person x event x envi-

ronment foundation of an ecological assessment, we see Henry as a young adult who was exposed to a one-time incident by strangers at his job. He experienced a prior trauma which may or may not have been integrated. He has not had any prior counseling experiences to draw on as positive, but he does indicate that he has a support system which, in fact, he says he uses. The MSE formulation does not lead the clinician to worry about Henry's isolation or self-harm, but the clinician might be able to predict that Henry would not see counseling or therapy as a resource. He is part of an environment in his past and present that has been supportive.

Catherine talks about her father dying when she was 4 years old, so she would never hurt herself because it would "kill her mother." She was in family counseling for a while when she was 10 and enjoyed talking. The clinician learns that Catherine has had a positive experience with counseling in the past so she may know how to make use of it. The clinician feels reassured that although Catherine has suffered a severe loss, she does not seem at risk for self-harm and may be able to make use of the counseling resources offered. Although this is a one-time incident, the ecological framework reminds us that Catherine's environment has had many exposures to violence so, in fact, Catherine may continue to be further exposed.

Legal/Criminal Justice Involvement

It is important to have such information as described previously to be able to assess what kind of safety planning is needed, to know what emotional preparation the patient will need, and to structure the timing of the interview itself. If the police were waiting to interview Henry and Catherine, an abbreviated session might be necessary so they could conserve their energy and also receive some reassurance that steps were being taken to arrest the assailants. If criminal justice involvement had not occurred, the clinician would want to include information about legal/criminal justice involvement in his or her interview. Some patients may worry about how their medical bills will be paid or what will happen if they have to miss work. Many states have victim compensation programs which can assist with financial support.

Intervention Strategies

Physical and Emotional Safety

The foundation of healing from criminal victimization is dealing with basic needs for physical and emotional safety. These needs include safety from the perpetrators, control over one's physical and emotional self, and the basic needs of shelter, food, and so on. The clinician must assist the patient in tending to the immediacy and urgency of these issues. Different crime victims have different needs in these areas. Henry and Catherine both had safe, supportive living situations away from the perpetrators. They both, however, need assurances and practical suggestions regarding their fears of future harm. Because the perpetrators have not yet been arrested, both Catherine and Henry may feel particularly vulnerable and need to develop concrete plans regarding their own physical safety. The clinician will collaborate on this issue with the police involved with the case as well as victim/witness offices that are affiliated with many district attorneys' offices. If the patient is a victim of domestic violence, clinicians should be familiar with how to do safety/risk planning. Although physical safety is not always possible if the perpetrator(s) have not been apprehended, if the abuse is ongoing, or if the community is chronically traumatized, the patient may have to identify times or places when and where he or she feels safer.

Planning for emotional safety is also included in safety planning. This can mean identifying who in one's environment is safe to tell and how much one chooses to disclose about what happened or what one is experiencing. When a crime occurs in a public place, as was the case with Henry and Catherine, others may have witnessed or heard about what happened. In such cases, it is important to prepare patients for emotional safety in situations in which people may ask questions or make comments. At times such people may include the media. The client must know that he or she has choices about whom to speak with. Part of crime victimization includes having your privacy violated and having people know things about you that you did not choose to tell them. This is another loss of control, so choices are particularly important.

Ventilation and Validation

It is often the telling and retelling of an event that assists in the healing process. It is helpful for the patient to tell what happened in his or her own words and to be able to tell what parts are important to him or her. Telling another human being also begins the process of reconnecting the patient to humanity in the face of the inhuman things that he or she may have experienced. In the immediate crisis, there is often a window of opportunity for the victim to tell what happened to them before a rigid defense structure sets in. It is not necessarily recommended or considered mandatory for patients to tell every detail of what happened. They may have already told some of the narrative to the medical or police personnel. It may be important to the patient that the clinician already knows some of the horrors of what happened. Being overly disclosative to a stranger may not be in the patient's best interest in the long run. Conversely, the clinician is a safe, anonymous person whom the patient may experience as someone who can listen without being burdened or judgmental. Because it is hard to assess the extent to which the telling may contribute to shame or to feelings of being out of control, it is important for the clinician to periodically check in with patients about their level of comfort in sharing. This checking-in also teaches patients how to check in with themselves periodically and monitor their own feeling states.

Telling the narrative of what happened can offer a sense of relief and give the clinician assistance in assessing the impact of the crime on the patient. For example, the clinician might observe that Catherine was worried about her family, which may be related to what she brought up earlier about her father's death. During the telling of the narrative, clinicians will have the opportunity to validate the range of feelings that the patients may express. Even if patients have been victimized more than once, they may feel out of control of their feelings or feel like they are the only ones who have ever felt like this or that they may be going crazy. Catherine felt reassured when the nurse nodded attentively and told her that it was common for victims of crime to experience the kinds of feelings that she was describing. Catherine said that this validation helped her to feel more normal and to understand her reactions.

If patients are reluctant to tell what has happened, it may be for a variety of reasons including (but not limited to) cultural factors, the nature of the setting, or concern that in the telling they would have to "relive what happened to them." They may also feel that the clinicians may judge them in their behavior or reactions. Frequently, clinicians believe they must decide whether this was a "real" crime or whether the reactions are "appropriate" to the events before they can provide good clinical care. Although a clinical assessment is not detective work, clinicians may feel a pull to use diagnosis to judge and manage their own reactions or lack of control over their own powerlessness or feelings of inadequacy. Patients must feel supported and assured of the nonjudgmental nature of the setting to feel safe to tell their narrative. The clinician may need to clarify to patients that they have a choice in what and how much they tell and that sometimes in telling what happened they might give the clinician a better sense of what they might need. Patients may need to know that the therapeutic setting will give them an opportunity to express their thoughts and feelings in a way that they were not able to do during their violent experience. (Many victims want validation, reassurance, and understanding that what they are experiencing is normal.)

Education/Information

Many people do not have basic information about common reactions to crime or what their options are. Providing information to patients also helps them to gain a sense of control over their lives as they begin to understand what is happening. The tool to feeling more power in one's life is information. Providing a framework of understanding can help to contain what feels completely overwhelming. This may also be another time to discuss the vulnerabilities that people experience in the aftermath of violence, such as the urge to use drugs or alcohol or to do other high-risk behaviors to cope with overwhelming feelings.

Henry was especially appreciative because although he did not want to talk about his reactions at the time, the clinician in the emergency room gave him a pamphlet describing common reactions. He took this pamphlet with him and read it at another time when he felt more able to let it in, was less distracted by physical pain, and felt more emotionally safe than he did at the hospital.

Patients might have questions about medical procedures, police involvement, and so on, which the clinician may or may not be able to answer; however, the clinician will be a resource for information that assists them in their healing process.

Mobilization of Internal and External Resources

The ongoing mental status assessment will assist both the patient and the clinician to evaluate the victim's internal resources to cope with this overwhelming set of circumstances. These internal resources enable patients to cope with the various reactions that they may experience, to problem-solve effectively, and to reach out for help should they need it. Identifying coping mechanisms can help patients to recognize their own strengths and adaptive capabilities, qualities that are sometimes diminished in the course of the violent experience. The clinician may refer to the chart of common reactions (see Table 6.2) to plan strategies to address the set of reactions the patient may be experiencing. For instance, cognitively based skills may be needed to alleviate racing thoughts or sleep disturbance.

This may also be another time for education. It is important that patients identify resource people in their own environment with whom they feel safe and from whom they can get support. In the aftermath of violence, it can be easy to isolate oneself so it is important for the patient to plan for connections with others. This is also the time that the clinician should review safety plans.

> *Catherine's* concern for her mother's reaction makes it even more important for the nurse to identify Catherine's aunt as a support person. Her aunt can be available in Catherine's own environment to help and support her. Catherine also decides to tell two girlfriends who can accompany her in the hall between classes on the first day back, and she reports feeling comfortable using her counselor if she has a hard time during the day. Catherine says that she is not at risk for self-harm. She does not, however, feel safe in her community because the police told her that the boys who assaulted her have not been arrested. They are from another town so she feels somewhat reassured. She made plans not to be alone. Her sense of security is tenuous. Catherine is an athlete and is looking forward to returning to track and field as a way to distract herself. She also finds music a comfort.
>
> *Henry* also mentions that he has people in his life to whom he can turn. He, however, is too tired to be more specific about his plans but assures us that he will reach out for help if he needs it. He is more angry

than anything else, but not to the point of having plans for revenge or other violence. If homicidality were an actual concern, we would have to consider *Tarasoff* warnings.

It is important to offer psychological care to the patient's significant other network so that they get support as well and do not have the sole burden of sharing the impact. The clinician's job is to offer support to the immediate ecological support system in the patient's life. It is for this reason, too, that both Catherine and Henry were given brochures about common reactions to violence and strategies for self-care and about the CCRT of the VOV program, which provides crisis consultation and interventions with communities that have been affected by violence. In this case, other people in the Community such as; the community center, other teenagers, parents, or the neighborhood may be additional groups that have been affected by the violence.

It may also be important to mobilize additional external resources for the victim(s). For instance, in the case of domestic violence, the clinician may need to assist in making shelter arrangements or inform the survivor of the availability of victim/witness advocates from the district attorney's office or of the availability of a rape crisis center hotline. The role of the psychiatric emergency room is quite focused and limited. The availability and the utilization of additional resources can provide a comprehensive array of services for the victim. If symptomotolgy may be alleviated through medication, the clinician could make those arrangements.

Preparation and Planning

Because criminal victimization disrupts their life on many levels, it is important to assist patients in planning to address all these levels (but not necessarily all at the same time). Of particular concern during this acute phase are the more daily functions, symptom management, self-care, and reorientation with these new events as part of the patient's life. For some patients, the clinician may have to assist in decision making due to their level of cognitive disorganization and confusion. For others, their defenses and adrenaline have propelled them into a state of calmness and organization. Both of these reactions are common.

On the physical level, reviewing and planning for such basic self-care activities as eating and sleeping and, if there are physical injuries, managing the care of the injuries (including making follow-up medical appointments) are crucial. Thinking through the activities for the next day or two helps patients to prepare for and plan for changes that they need or would like to make. For some people, returning to routine daily activities provides a sense of control over their life, whereas others prefer to take a break from their routines to sort things out. Sorting out priorities for the next few days and keeping things simple often minimize the cognitive disruptions. Anticipating with the patient that he or she may or may not experience additional symptoms can prevent the shock and fear of increased disruptions. Although the clinician does not want to overwhelm the patient with too much information, awareness of the possibility of increased symptomotolgy can prepare the patient to better manage symptoms should they arise. In addition to symptom management, the clinician should focus his or her time on self-care strategies, reminding the patient that he or she has experienced a traumatic event and needs to plan for ways to get comfort during this time. The patient can be referred to the pamphlet should he or she want to be reminded of common reactions and suggestions for self-care. There is a lot to remember and to organize (especially if there is a death involved) during this initial phase, so in addition to informational pamphlets the clinician can help the patient to figure out ways to stay organized. This can help to minimize confusion. If the patient requests follow-up counseling, the clinician might also prepare him or her for other possible milestones which may be discussed in counseling and can evoke a return of symptoms.

The final step in planning is arranging for follow-up mental health care, whether it be with the clinician or a referral to some other setting. Although not everyone will need or want additional professional help, each patient can be given some choices. Victims should also leave with phone numbers of help providers who are available in case of emergency or in case they feel an urgent need to talk. If they are not going to see the clinician again, the clinican may offer to check in with them to be sure that the referral connection was successful. Attentiveness to follow-up helps the patient to feel more grounded at a time when he or she may be feeling disoriented, powerless, and disconnected. Sometimes, patients are not able to plan ahead for follow-up so making arrangements with the emergency service to follow up with either an appointment or a phone call is recommended.

Closure

When closing, the structure of the interview begins to refocus the content and process to more cognitive areas of functioning. It provides a transition to enter the world outside the emergency room setting and to have some boundaries around the interview. At VOV, clinicians keep in mind the following diagram (Figure 6.1) to remind themselves of the structure of the interview.

Spending the last part of the interview on planning initiates the process of cognitive reorientation. If there is a time limit, the person should be made aware of how much time is left. In the acute phase, time can take on a different feeling. It is important to have some time boundaries. Although flexibility is important, it is not true that quantity of time is equal to quality of intervention. Before completing the interview, it is important to ask if the patient has any other concerns or questions so he or she is not left with a feeling of incompleteness (of course, additional concerns will arise in the

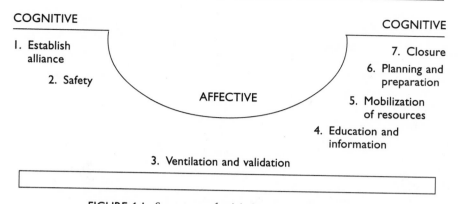

FIGURE 6.1. Structure of crisis intervention interview.

moments and days that follow the interview). Once all questions have been answered, patients should be asked what they think will be helpful for them to remember from the time spent together. This affords an opportunity to review, to think more clearly, and to reflect on some of the additional practical ways patients can use to cope during this time. If follow-up appointments are made, the patient should write them down. The end of the interview should include an acknowledgment, again, of the regret that this event ever happened and a reminder of the next therapeutic contact.

> Both Henry and Catherine indicated that it was important for them to be able to talk about what happened to them. They indicated that it made them feel supported that all the medical personnel with whom they came into contact expressed concern and support for their reactions. This tone of respect and nonjudgmentalness created a strong foundation from which to start the journey toward healing. The interventions themselves were competence-based as well as timely, important components of the ecological model of crisis intervention.

In the midst of the chaos of acute trauma, it is easy to forget one's own knowledge base or the model of crisis intervention. Table 6.3 provides a summary of the tasks and interventions in the acute stage of the aftermath of crime victimization.

FOLLOW-UP TREATMENT

Although clinicians in emergency settings usually do not do the follow-up counseling, it is important for them to understand the full recovery process because (1) survivors may want to know some of what they can anticipate and (2) it is

TABLE 6.3. Principles of Crisis Intervention in the Acute Stage

Therpeutic tasks of the patient	Tasks of the therapist	Helpful techniques

1. Understand and manage symptoms
 	
2. Reestablish control, trust
 	
3. Develop satety plans
	1. Establish alliance
	
	2. Conduct ongoing assessment
	  a. Person (MSE, his or her concerns)
	  b. Event (nature, legal involvement)
	  c. Environment (support system)
	  d. Suspend judgments
	
	3. Intervention strategies
	  a. Physical and emotional safety
	  b. Ventilation and validation
	  c. Education and information
	  d. Mobilization of internal and external resources
	  e. Preparation and planning
	
	4. Closure
		1. Focus on the current situation
		2. Listen carefully
		3. Respond honestly, humanly
		4. Be calm, attentive, concerned, empathic
		5. Avoid being controlling or patronizing
		6. Offer decision-making control when possible
		7. Explain the system
		8. Offer help to family and friends
		9. Know community resources
		10. Be flexible
		11. Get help and support for yourself

important to hold on to hope and the larger picture of the recovery process as you witness and assist survivors through some of the raw beginning stages.

The acute stage usually lasts from 6 to 12 weeks. The focus of the care continues to be mobilization of internal and external resources, symptom management, regaining control over one's life, interfacing with daily life activities, possible criminal justice involvement, and beginning to face the various levels of impact of the victimization. This stage can overlap with the outward adjustment stage in which the survivor is reclaiming a sense of a daily routine.

Catherine, for instance, really found it helpful and enjoyable to talk. She came in for periodic appointments but mostly called to check in and to ask questions about her reactions. Her hypervigilance continued until there was an arrest. Safety planning continued to be an important focus. *Henry* chose not to come back immediately afterward but subquently called when he was contacted by the victim/witness office about coming to court.

As court appearances approach or the "anniversary" time of the assault comes near, survivors and their communities can reexperience some of the same symptomatology as in the acute stage. If the trauma involved publicity in the media, newspapers frequently choose these times to rewrite about the trauma, often in great detail. This publicity adds to the traumatic nature of the events for the individuals involved as well as their communities because the private nature of their recovery process is often exposed publicly. This publicity can be experienced as further victimization and an invasion of privacy. Treatment during this period often involves the domains of symptom management as well as mastery over affect-laden memory. Once the court proceedings are complete and the first anniversary has passed, survivors often feel freed to begin the process of integrating the experience into their lives and their identities. While working through all of the multidimensional domains at the various stages, the process of reflection takes on a different level of meaning and integration. This is often a time that group treatment can be very useful.

Catherine returns to school and does average in her studies. From time to time she feels herself withdrawing from social activities that involve groups of kids from the community center. As the trial approaches, she is reluctant to testify. She is afraid of retribution and also wants to move on with her life. She has many meetings with the victim/witness advocate and her therapist about her concerns. She feels reassured that she was not the only victim in the case, and that she shares the burden of her testimony with Henry. She is on call during the 2-day trial so her daily activities are not disrupted. The attorneys for the boys involved appeal to the judge for leniency because it is their first offense. The judge wants to send a strong message to the boys and places them on strictly supervised probation as well as weekly community service for 1 year. Catherine feels that writing her victim/witness impact statement enables her to make more public the various ways she feels hurt by what has happened to her and the fears that she still has.

After the trial is over, Catherine sees her therapist for a few more sessions. She continues through her high school years without further incidence. However, several of her friends experience date rapes or have a relative physically assaulted or murdered. Her community continues to be traumatized. Whenever she assists a friend, she recalls her own assault and the help she received. Helping others helps her to feel validated in her own experience. Eventually Catherine goes to college. During that time, she decides to join a group for women who have experienced physical/sexual trauma. She is concerned that she is not able to have dating relationships and wonders about the connection between the assault and her mistrust of men. Catherine enters another stage in her recovery process—another dimension of healing. She still has additional domains of impact to explore.

Henry returns to work at the community center and works until after the trial. He, too, is reluctant to testify, not for fear of retribution but because in his cultural context he does not think that the criminal justice system is going to help the boys who are involved. He is very confused. He knows he wants them punished but his value system is being shaken. He continues to feel powerless and withdraws socially from his friends. He is haunted by nightmares and plagued by feelings of shame and embarrassment. He finally blurts out to his girlfriend that if he were a "real man" he would not be so upset. Clearly, gender and class issues are affecting Henry's ability to get help to deal with the multidimensional level of his pain. After the trial, Henry decides to take some time off to travel. Before he leaves his job at the community center, Henry and Catherine meet to say good-bye, to acknowledge the crisis they shared, and to wish each other well.

Henry and his girlfriend break up. The next year, Henry decides to go to graduate school. Unable to sleep or to concentrate, he seeks services at the counseling center. His immediate symptoms are helped by medication, and individual treatment helps him to face the levels of impact from the assault that he did not face in the initial aftermath. Treatment also helps him to face the unresolved reactions of the prior murder in his college community. He later joins a therapy group where he can better explore the interpersonal dimensions not only of the assault but of the other ways he has been interpersonally limited even prior to the assault. The experience of the victimization is a catalyst for further personal growth. In the course of treatment, the therapist helps Henry to regain his interest in fighting for social causes and Henry begins to volunteer for an organization combating domestic violence.

The community center benefits a great deal from the CCRT intervention, and in fact, when the trial approaches the community center invites the CCRT members back for another meeting. In the meantime, the director of the community center feels better prepared for subsequent instances of violence should they occur. He also feels better prepared to assist kids and their families who now approach him after violent incidents. In addition, the community center decides to be more proactive in its approach to violence prevention and holds workshops by kids for kids and for parents about alternatives to violence and how to treat people more humanely. The kids have a lot of fun preparing the events and a real sense of community spirit evolves.

Both on the individual and the community level, there are various stages of responses and reactions. Fortunately, on all levels individuals are able to make use of internal and external resources to heal from the impact of the violence. Each individual is able to make personal meaning of the event and to translate his or her meaning into social actions for others—the true antidote to the powerlessness of crime victimization.

THE ECOLOGICAL CONTEXT OF THE THERAPIST IN THE ACUTE AFTERMATH OF VIOLENCE

The role of the therapist in the aftermath of violence is as multidimensional as the reactions of the victims. The quality that has been reported by survivors as most important is being human. They appreciate a sense of professionalism without coldness or formality. They appreciate being given information regarding the process of their care. They appreciate empathy without sympathy or patronization. In cases of domestic violence, the victims appreciate nonjudgmentalness.

Clinicians find themselves functioning as evaluators, planners, educators, resource accessors, and sometimes the interface between the client and other institutions (police, child welfare, etc.). It is important to develop flexibility. Many emergency room clinicians are trained to assist individuals suffering from mental illness and may feel initial discomfort or lack of confidence in treating victims of violence. When in doubt, it is helpful to ask ourselves what we would need or find helpful in a similar situation, or to consult with a colleague before proceeding. In cases of rape or domestic violence, there may be a 24-hour hotline that could provide the clinician with assistance.

The context in which the clinician practices will enhance or detract from his or her ability to practice effective crisis intervention. The environment of the clinician is an important ecological variable for the delivery of successful crisis intervention. Because VOV is also a training sight, staff members give particular attention to providing a training model for crisis intervention. This model not only holds the work for the patient but also for the clinician. The clinicians attend a crisis seminar which is the setting for the supervision of the crisis cases. To do this work effectively, clinicians must have a setting in which to brainstorm ideas for interventions as well as to discuss or to debrief in the aftermath of being exposed to the trauma of violence. This setting not only offers the sharing of ideas but decreases the sense of personal and professional isolation. Attending to the ecological context of the clinician is in fact the final stage of the approach to crisis intervention as practiced at VOV.

SPECIAL CONSIDERATIONS

Recordkeeping

In short, records should be clear, direct, concise, and symptom focused. If there is criminal justice involvement, records may be subject to subpoena. What is relevant to clinical care may not be relevant to forensic inquiry. The local district attorney's office can provide training in recordkeeping. Clinicians do not want to compromise good clinical care or their client's well-being. At VOV, clinicians document symptoms and danger to self or others as well as treatment plans and objectives.

Patients with Ongoing Psychiatric Illness

Such clients may be more vulnerable to crime victimization and often are not believed. If a patient has been victimized by violence, the impact of that particular event or series of events is his or her presenting problem and that is what he or she should be treated for. His or her psychiatric illness will be one of the components in the ecological assessment of the situation. Patients with ongoing alcoholism may also be victimized by crime. Even if the environment made them more vulnerable to crime victimization, they deserve treatment without being judged. Unfortunately, in both these situations, the crime victim's credibility in the criminal justice system is severely compromised and the victim may not have ready access to the societal process of prosecuting his or her attackers.

Ongoing Danger

Victims of domestic violence need to focus on safety planning. They may be accompanied to the emergency room by their perpetrators. They should be interviewed separately. Those involved in intimate partner violence usually know how safe they are. They can be directed to resources. Clinicians should know how to access safety and security. They should not judge someone's potential for harming his or her partner by the way he or she looks. Batterers come in all sizes, shapes, colors, professions, and sexual orientations.

When their are children in the family, they may have been directly victimized or have witnessed domestic violence. Their psychological and physical care needs to be attended to and planned for. Check with your localities regarding your professional obligations to report family violence to child protection agencies. Many agencies have programs geared especially for these children.

History of Prior Victimization

Clients may present in a mental health crisis resulting from earlier childhood abuse or war experiences. This may be compounded by mental illness. Survivors of earlier violence need to be validated for their ongoing struggle to cope with their recurring symptomatology. They can be reassured that remembering prior traumas is a normal part of a crisis response. Their trauma history must be validated (and not minimized) as part of the ecological assessment. However, it should not be explored during the acute phase but should be used to understand the impact of the current victimization.

Secondary Traumatic Stress

A comprehensive discussion of countertransference and vicarious traumatization can be found in Chapters 11 and 19. A few points are worth emphasizing specifically in relation to treating victims of current violence. At VOV, clinicians have found that they are more vulnerable when treating recently traumatized survivors. First, the level of safety and boundaries is decreased. Clinicians realize that we are all susceptible to being victims of adult crime. The people in our lives whom we love are also possible victims. Not acknowledging this vulnerability can lead to victim blaming. Each of us can feel powerless in the face of crime victimization. This powerlessness can result in questioning our own clinical competency. Second, in situations of ongoing danger, such as in domestic violence, there is the perceived as well as the real possibility of being confronted by the perpetrator. Another area of vulnerability is treating children who have been victimized by violence. The unfairness of the situation and our own powerlessness, as well as our own anger and aggression, can surface when treating children. Clinicians may have acute posttraumatic stress disorder symptoms or may hide behind the work of the emergency setting. They may think that it is unprofessional to have such reactions or that it is severe countertransference. They may feel that they had better get into therapy. However, secondary traumatic stress is a normal part of doing this work. It is important to have individual and environmental self-care plans to manage its effects (Yassen, 1995).

Further Training

One way to manage feelings of incompetence is to acknowledge those areas in which we may need further training or awareness. These areas may include but are not limited to how to do a safety plan and knowledge of the resources in our own community, as well as understanding the different ways people may be affected by different kinds of crimes (e.g., Bard & Sangrey, 1986). Expanding one's knowledge may include learning about different modalities of intervention or being engaged in research activities. The parameters of one's own professional training may actually limit one's knowledge. Networking, collaborating, and learning different points of view from the diverse groups in the community working to eliminate violence are suggested. The effect of collaboration can be energizing, as well as another important antidote to the powerlessness evoked by violence.

SUMMARY

This chapter presented an ecological approach to crisis intervention in the aftermath of violent crime. It stresses the importance for the victims, the community, and the clinicians of understanding the person, the impact of events, and the environment. The focus of clinical training is often on the first part of the ecological framework (i.e., the person) and mostly the intrapsychic or psychopathological dimensions. This chapter provides some challenges to the appropriateness of these views in the treatment of victims of violence. It offers a concrete guide for providing treatment. It also suggests that clinicians get to know their own local resources (rape crisis centers, domestic violence shelters, veterans groups, those who serve refugees, victim witness offices). Without an ecological awareness and collaboration with community groups, the risk is that of providing limited and uninformed care to victims of violence. The world is changing in many ways. The incidence of violence is not. It is incumbent upon clinicians to provide comprehensive care for those who present with emergencies. In doing so, they assist in the foundation of the patients' healing and the healing of their communities.

REFERENCES

American Psychiatric Association. (1994). *Diagnostic and statistical manual of mental disorders* (4th ed.). Washington DC: American Psychiatric Press.

Bard, M., & Sangrey, D. (1986). *The crime victim's book* (2nd ed.). Secaucus, NJ: Citadel Press.

Bassuk, E. (1980). A crisis theory perspective on rape. In S. Mccombie (Ed.), *The rape crisis intervention handbook*. New York: Plenum Press.

Boney-McCoy, S., & Finkelhor, D. (1995). Psychosocial sequelae of violent victimization in a national youth sample. *Journal of Clinical and Counseling Psychology, 63*(5), 726–736.

Burgess, A., & Holmstrom, L. L. (1979). *Rape: Crisis and recovery.* Bowie, MD: Brady.

Caplan. G. (1964). *Principles of preventive psychiatry.* New York: Basic Books.

Comas-Díaz, L., & Padilla, A. (1990). Countertranseference in working with victims of political repression. *American Journal of Orthopsychiatry, 60*(1), 125–134.

Danieli, Y. (1988). Treating survivors and children of survivors of the Nazi holocaust. In F. M. Ochberg (Ed.), *Post-traumatic therapy and victims of violence* (pp. 278–294). New York: Brunner/Mazel.

Figley, C. (Ed.). (1985). *Trauma and its wake.* New York: Brunner/Mazel.

Forman, B. (1980). Psychotherapy with rape victims. *Psychotherapy: Theory, Research and Practice, 17*(Fall), 304–312.

Green, B. L., Wilson, J. P., & Lindy, J. D. (1985). Conceptualizing posttraumatic stress disorder: A psychosocial framework. In Figley, C. (Ed.), *Trauma and its wake, Vol. I: The study and treatment of post-traumatic stress disorder* (pp. 53–69). New York: Brunner/Mazel.

Harvey, M. (1996). An ecological view of psychological trauma and trauma recovery. *Journal of Traumatic Stress, 9*(1), 3–23.

Harvey, M., Tobey, A., & Aldrich, H., (1996). *Responding to community violence: A community empowerment model and its application.* Unpublished manuscript.

Herman, J. L. (1992). *Trauma and recovery.* New York: Basic Books.

Hoff, L. A. (1995). *People in crisis: Understanding and helping* (4th ed.). San Francisco: Jossey-Bass.

Horowitz, M. (1986). *Stress response syndromes* (2nd ed.). Northvale, NJ: Jason Aronson.

Janoff-Bulman, R. (1992). *Shattered assumptions: Towards a new psychology of trauma.* New York: Free Press.

Kelly, J. G. (1968). Towards an ecological conception of prevention interventions. In J. W. Carter (Ed.), *Research contributions from psychology to community mental health* (pp. 3–57). New York: Behavioral Publications.

Koss, M. P., & Harvey, M. R. (1991). *The rape victim: Clinical and community interventions* (2nd ed.). Newbury Park, CA: Sage.

Koss, M. P., Gidcyz, C. A., & Wisniewski, N. (1987). The scope of rape: Incidence and prevalence of sexual aggression and victimization in a national sample of higher education students. *Journal of Counseling and Clinical Psychology, 55,* 162–170.

Kübler-Ross, E. (1975). *Death, the final stage of growth.* Englewood Cliffs, NJ: Prentice-Hall.

Lebowitz, L., Harvey, M. R., & Herman, J. L. (1993). A stage by dimension model of recovery from sexual trauma. *Journal of Interpersonal Violence, 8*(3), 378–391.

Ledray, L. (1994). *Recovering from rape* (2nd ed.). New York: Holt.

Lindemann, E. (1944). Symptomatology and management of acute grief. *American Journal of Psychiatry, 101,* 141–148.

McCann, L., & Pearlman, L. (1990). *Psychological trauma and the adult survivor: Theory, therapy and transformation.* New York: Brunner/Mazel.

McCombie, S. L. (Ed.). (1983). *The rape crisis intervention handbook.* New York and London: Plenum Press.

National Center on Child Abuse and Neglect. (1988). *National incidence and prevalence of child abuse and neglect.* Washington, DC: Author.

Norris, F., & Thompson, M. P. (1995). Applying community psychology to the prevention of trauma and traumatic life events. In J. Freedy & S. Hobfoll (Eds.), *Traumatic stress: From theory to practice.* New York: Plenum Press.

Ochberg, F. M. (Ed.). (1988). *Post-traumatic therapy and victims of violence.* New York: Brunner/Mazel.

Roth, S., & Lebowitz, L. (1988). The experience of sexual trauma. *Journal of Traumatic Stress, 1*(1), 79–107.

Russell, D. E. H. (1984). *Sexual exploitation: Rape, child sexual abuse and workplace harassment.* Beverly Hills, CA: Sage.

Schechter, S. (1982). *Women and male violence.* Boston: South End Press.

Scherl, D., & Sutherland, S. (1970). Patterns of response among victims of rape. *American Journal of Orthopsychiatry, 40,* 503–511.

Shorin, J., & Greenwald, J. (1995). *Crisis response at individual and community levels: Illustrations of empowerment.* Paper presented at Conference, "Responding to Violence," The Cambridge Hospital/Harvard Medical School Continuing Education, Boston.

Stark, E., & Flitcraft, A. (1988). Personal power and institutional victimization: Treating the dual trauma of woman battering. In F. Ochberg (Ed.), *Post-traumatic therapy and victims of violence* (pp. 115–152). New York: Brunner/Mazel.

Symonds, M. (1975). The rape victim: Psychological patterns of response. *American Journal of Psychoanalysis, 35,* 19–25.

Webster's ninth new collegiate dictionary. (1985). Springfield, MA: Merriam-Webster.

Wilson, J. P. (Ed.). (1987). *Trauma, transformation, and healing.* New York: Brunner/Mazel.

Wilson, J. (1988). Treating the Vietnam veteran. In F. Ochberg (Ed.), *Post-traumatic therapy and victims of violence* (pp. 254–278). New York: Brunner/Mazel.

van der Kolk, B. (1987). *Psychological trauma.* Washington, DC: American Psychiatric Association.

Yassen, J. (1995). Preventing secondary traumatic stress disorder. In C. Figley (Ed.),

Compassion fatigue: Coping with secondary traumatic stress disorder in those who treat the traumatized (pp. 178–209). New York: Brunner/Mazel.

Yassen, J., & Glass, L. (1984). Sexual assault survivors groups: A feminist practice perspective. *Social Work, 29*(3), 252–257.

Young, M. (1987). *Crisis and stress.* Washington, DC: National Organization for Victim Assistance.

CHAPTER 7

LIFE-AND-DEATH DECISIONS
Refusing Life-Sustaining Treatment

PHILLIP M. KLEESPIES
DEANNA L. MORI

Technological advances in medicine make it possible to sustain life beyond the point where it is meaningful. The widely publicized case of Karen Ann Quinlan graphically brought this state of affairs to national attention. At the age of 20, Quinlan suffered irreversible brain damage with no hope of recovery and was kept alive in a comatose state on a respirator. In the words of Maddi (1990), cases such these "are forcing us to consider a range of existential issues concerning the meaning of life and death and our responsibility to each other" (p. 155).

Advances in medicine and other health-related disciplines have had another related effect that bears on this issue. Improvements in the treatment of diseases have extended life expectancy to the point where 70% to 80% of people now die later in life but slowly and essentially of degenerative rather than acute disease (Battin, 1994). The prospect of prolonged and, in some cases, agonizing death alarms many. The AIDS epidemic, which has aroused the concerns of a younger segment of the population, further highlights this alarm.

Prolonged deaths often become "medicalized" in that they occur in hospitals and nursing homes with attendant medical procedures that can deprive the individual of privacy and dignity. Concerns about loss of control over the final stages of life result in concerted efforts to establish some degree of self-determination. Thus, we have seen the emergence of the hospice movement and the formation of organizations such as Compassion in Dying and the Hemlock Society, not to speak of the more extreme activities of Dr. Jack Kevorkian.

Since the *Quinlan* case in 1976 and others (e.g., Nancy Beth Cruzan), the right of the terminally ill to refuse life-sustaining treatment under certain conditions has become widely accepted. It is now not uncommon to have Do Not Resuscitate (DNR) or Do Not Intubate (DNI) orders in hospitals. These changes occurred relatively rapidly as have changes in how we view and use medical technologies. In the not very distant past, life-sustaining treatments were referred to as "heroic measures" because they were seen as relatively new and technologically advanced, as an extraordinary departure from conventional treatment, as requiring special knowledge and skill, and as expensive and limited in availability (Maddi, 1990). Although many of the previous statements still characterize such measures, their use is more widespread and reference to them is more commonplace. Included among these technologically assisted treatments is the use of respirators and endotracheal intubation for breathing difficulties, intravenous feeding for hydration and nutrition problems, hemodialysis for kidney failure, radiation and chemotherapy to impede the growth of cancer, cardiopulmonary resuscitation, the implantation of a defibrillator and/or a pacemaker for cardiac problems, and so on. Thus, life-sustaining treatment can be taken to mean any medical intervention that would have little or no effect on the underlying disease, injury, or condition but is administered to forestall the time of death or to reinstate life when death can be regarded as having occurred (Hafemeister, Keilitz, & Banks, 1991; McKnight & Bellis, 1992; Maddi, 1990).

As noted earlier, refusing life-sustaining treatment is regarded as a right of those with a terminal illness. Powell and Cohen (1994) indicate, however, that there is no real consensus on a medical definition of "terminal." One definition found with some frequency is that an illness is taken to be terminal when it has a predictably fatal outcome and there is no known cure. Often this definition is set within a time frame and limited to cases in which death is expected within either 6 months or a year. Yet, Maddi (1990) points out that medicine is not an exact science and it is often quite difficult to predict with accuracy when a patient will die. Complicating matters still more, there are those rare instances when illnesses remit for no known reason. Such issues suggest that it might be best to keep predictions of death to a time that it indeed appears to be close. When death is near, however, and suffering is great, the prolongation of life by continued treatment in the hope of a "miraculous" remission may become irresponsible unless there is good reason to believe that there is real hope of recovery (Battin, 1994).

THE ROLE OF THE MENTAL HEALTH PRACTITIONER IN DECISIONS TO REFUSE LIFE-SUSTAINING TREATMENT

A tremendous amount of complexity and emotion surrounds decisions about ending life-sustaining treatment. Professionals in the mental health arena possess training and expertise that can be used to provide some guidance and assistance in this difficult process. Most significantly, mental health professionals can facilitate communication during a time that effective communication can be difficult. For example, some patients are reluctant to burden family and staff with the weighty issues they are considering. Clinicians can help patients, families, and professionals tease apart the emotional, legal, professional, and ethical issues that complicate decisions that may not have one clear and easy answer. Clinicians can help the parties involved obtain, sort through, and prioritize information so that the best possible treatment decision for the patient and for all concerned is identified. This is no small task, however, and clinicians involved in this type of work must prepare themselves by being knowledgeable about all the dimensions involved in such cases (i.e., not only the emotional issues but also the medical, legal, and ethical issues). This task can be challenging given that legal and ethical precedents are constantly changing as landmark legislative and court decisions around the country are being made.

In addition, mental health practitioners can also work with patients to enhance the quality of their remaining life. For example, clinicians can help patients cope with pain or with difficult and invasive treatments. With such help, the option of continued treatment might feel more tolerable. Counseling or providing stress management skills can strengthen a patient's ability to maintain hope and a positive attitude. Providing compassion and support can also help sustain patients who are not yet ready to give up or, alternatively, help patients in their conviction to stop treatment (Maddi, 1990).

Helping patients and their families to face death and cope with their grief can be emotionally demanding work. Rando (1984) speaks of how caring for the dying and the bereaved elicits a grief response in the professional care‹ givers as well. The rewards, however, can be great. As Maddi (1990) points out, the mental health professional should not overlook the fact that "the patient may actually improve his or her psychosocial quality of life through the confrontation of death" (p. 175). For example, patients and their families are sometimes able to work through or accept major issues that plagued them for years, or to be emotionally expressive in a manner not previously achieved. This type of experience can provide dying patients with inner peace and give their loved ones tremendous strength as they begin to cope with their loss and sense of grief.

Helping patients and their families make decisions about life-sustaining treatment can be complicated by the fact that patients do not always have the capacity to participate in this type of decision making. Cognitive deficits, psychological factors, or physical illness can affect a patient's ability to partake in the process meaningfully, and when this is the case, these problems can render the patient incapacitated to make decisions about his or her own health care. Mental health professionals are often called on to provide an opinion about the mental capacity of individuals to make medical treatment decisions (Auerbach & Banja, 1993). Although laws vary by state, many states recognize that nonmedical professionals, such as psychologists, have the training and expertise to evaluate cognitive abilities and functional capacity (Mishkin, 1989), and that given their background in psychometrics, they may be equipped to make a special contribution to the development of more standardized methods of assessing decisional capacity. The complexities of actually determining an individual's competency are discussed in much greater detail later in this chapter.

WITHDRAWING AND WITHHOLDING LIFE-SUSTAINING TREATMENT

Withdrawing or withholding life-sustaining treatment is a legally protected means for those who are considered terminally ill and wish to exercise some choice in the time and circumstances of their death. (This, of course, does not address the issues of those who are suffering and terminally ill and not in need of life-support systems.) To many people, refusing life-sustaining treatment means choosing a "natural" death or "death with dignity" and without invasive medical procedures. Some may envision an easy, peaceful farewell. As Battin (1994) indicates, however, there is no guarantee that this will be the case, and, in fact, many natural deaths can be very painful and far from peaceful. She describes various possibilities including, for example, an untreated respiratory death that can leave a patient gasping with air hunger and panic-stricken for hours.

What few people seem to realize, however, is that withdrawing or withholding treatment does not need to be absolute but can be done selectively and humanely. It is here that the patient and the physician can work cooperatively to produce what Battin (1994) refers to as "the least worst death" (p. 36). Thus, the patient with a terminal respiratory condition can choose to have ventilatory support gradually decreased rather than suddenly stopped and can die more slowly but without quite the same intense panic and agony (Faber-Langendoen & Bartels, 1992).

Although ethicists have long equated withholding and withdrawing life-sustaining treatment, some evidence suggests that physicians may have a preference for withholding treatment as opposed to withdrawing it (Committee on Bioethics, 1994; Singer, 1992; Snyder & Swartz, 1993). In this regard, one hypothesis is that it may be easier psychologically if the physician maintains a more passive role in "allowing the patient to die" rather than stopping a treatment that will result in the patient's death (McCamish & Crocker, 1993). A potential risk of preferentially withholding rather than withdrawing treatment, however, is that some patients may be subtly influenced not to try a treatment they might find acceptable.

One of the most emotionally charged and debated issues related to refusing life-sustaining treatment is withholding or withdrawing artificial nutrition and hydration (Boisaubin, 1993). Having adequate food and water is a very basic need and providing food and drink to others is closely linked to caring and nurturance. It should come as no surprise that withholding or withdrawing nutrition and hydration is a difficult issue to decide. The argument revolves around whether nutrition and hydration are basic needs or, when artificially given, a medical treatment indistinguishable in any morally relevant way from other life-sustaining treatments (McCamish & Crocker, 1993). In this regard, the case of Nancy Beth Cruzan was argued before the U.S. Supreme Court in 1989. Cruzan was a young woman in a persistent vegetative state following a motor vehicle accident and her parents requested the removal of her feeding tube. The Court adopted the consensus opinion that considers artificial nutrition and hydration as a medical treatment. This judicial opinion has not totally resolved the issue, however, because a few states still have laws which do not permit the refusal of artificial nutrition and hydration (Snyder & Swartz, 1993). With respect to children, a 1985 congressional amendment, commonly referred to as the "Baby Doe Rules," attempted to require that artificial feeding be continued for children even in terminal conditions (Boisaubin, 1993).

ETHICAL PRINCIPLES UNDERLYING THE RIGHT TO REFUSE LIFE-SUSTAINING TREATMENT

Given the enormity of decisions to withdraw or withhold life-sustaining treatment, people struggle with the question of whether it is "right" or moral to do so. Ethicists who have examined these issues have put forth various principles to guide these decisions and, in some instances, to support the right to refuse. Mercy, beneficence, and autonomy are principles frequently discussed in this context.

Mercy has two major components: the duty not to cause further pain or suffering (sometimes referred to as "nonmaleficence") and the duty to act to end pain or suffering already occurring (Battin, 1994). Under the first component, a caretaker would be acting mercifully by preventing invasive or painful interventions that do not provide the patient with relief of pain or hope of improvement. For example, cardiac resuscitation can be a harsh procedure resulting in substantial physical pain and injury. The principle of mercy justifies using this procedure when there is some hope of survival but not when there is little hope of improvement or survival. The second component of mercy, the duty to end suffering that is already occurring, also provides justification for the practice of withholding or withdrawing treatment. For example, though a treatment may allow an individual to live a longer life, the patient might choose to withdraw the treatment because the disease progression itself is causing pain and the treatment would only result in a prolongation of misery.

The principle of beneficence speaks to the duty of promoting the best interest of the patient (Kloezen, Fitten, & Steinberg, 1988). Beneficence guides individuals to make treatment decisions based on the benefits that treatment can provide and not to employ treatment merely because there is an ability to do so

(Committee on Bioethics, 1994). Some researchers suggest that the principle of beneficence can be applied in a paternalistic manner if it prevents the wishes of a patient from being carried out because a caretaker determines that the patient's wishes do not represent the "best" decision (Headley, 1991; Kloezen et al., 1988). Grant and Steel (1990) point out, however, that the patient's values can be emphasized and incorporated into the meaning of this principle. For example, a caretaker can determine the best interest of the patient and act in a beneficent manner by including the values of the patient in the treatment decision-making process.

Although the principles discussed above are critical to the issue of limiting medical treatment and providing guidelines for medical and family caretakers, the principle of autonomy is viewed by some as the very foundation of the right to refuse life-sustaining treatment (Wachter & Lo, 1993). The principle of autonomy, or the right of self-determination, states that "one ought to respect a competent person's choices, where one can do so without undue cost to oneself, where doing so will not violate other moral obligations, and where these choices do not threaten harm to other persons or parties" (Battin, 1994, p. 107). When applied to the right to refuse treatment, this principle asserts that competent individuals should have the right to make their own medical decisions, whether it means life or death, provided that it is a thoughtful choice and does not create harm for others. Furthermore, autonomy should not be restricted by the limitations that others establish through their own personal values or normative standards (Fulbrook, 1994).

THE LEGAL BASIS FOR THE RIGHT TO REFUSE LIFE-SUSTAINING TREATMENT

As noted earlier, the right to refuse life-sustaining treatment is grounded in the concept of individual autonomy, a concept and value that has deep roots in U.S. culture and law. United States Supreme Court Justice Benjamin Cardozo is widely credited with the ruling in 1914 that "every human being of adult years of sound mind has a right to determine what shall be done with his own body" (Nicholson & Matross, 1989, p. 234). This ruling laid the legal foundation for the doctrine of informed consent/refusal. Yet, even earlier, in a case in 1891, the U.S. Supreme Court stated that "no right is held more sacred, or is more carefully guarded by the common law, than the right of every individual to the possession and control of his own person, free from all restraint or interference of others, unless by clear and unquestionable authority of law" (Powell & Cohen, 1994, p. 170). In more recent times, the case of Karen Ann Quinlan (discussed earlier) is cited as the landmark case on legal issues on the right to refuse life-sustaining treatment (Overman, 1993). When Quinlan's father sought court authority to disconnect all life-support systems, the court granted him that authority based on a constitutional right to privacy which it saw as including the right to refuse unwanted medical treatment. It ruled that Quinlan could exercise this right through her father as guardian.

Still more recently, in the case of Nancy Beth Cruzan, the Supreme Court recognized a "liberty interest" (under the Fourteenth Amendment) in refusing unwanted medical treatment, including artificial nutrition and hydration. Cruzan was also a young woman in a persistent state of unconsciousness following an automobile accident and for whom there was no hope of recovery. Based on her statements (prior to the accident) that she would not wish to live in her current condition, her parents sought to have the feeding tube that sustained her life removed. Eventually, the court granted this request and she died 12 days later.

The case law in these situations presents the three major arguments on which the right to die or the right to refuse life-sustaining treatment is based— that is, the right to control one's own body (the basis for the doctrine of informed consent), the right to privacy, and the liberty interest in refusing unwanted medical treatment. The existence of these individual rights, however, should not be taken as indicating that society or the state has no interest in these decisions. As Flarey (1991) pointed out, several legitimate state interests are commonly weighed against a patient's right to refuse treatment. Among these are the state's interest in preserving the life of its citizens, in protecting innocent third parties (such as a fetus), and in the protection of the ethical integrity of the medical profession. In terms of the protection of third parties, the courts have recognized "the overriding right of the state to treat certain infectious or contagious diseases to safeguard its citizens, even in the setting of a patient's refusal of treatment" (Siegel, 1993, p. 838).

Be this as it may, Powell and Cohen (1994) have noted that U.S. law revolves around individual autonomy to a greater extent than it does around concepts of connectedness or community. Greater weight tends to be given to protecting individual rights than to state interests. Powell and Cohen (1994) hold that society's interest in preserving human life should be manifested in establishing appropriate guidelines for the exercise of the right to die. In this way, the state would ensure that the right to die is only exercised by those who want to end their lives and are not coerced in making that decision.

ESSENTIAL ELEMENTS
OF INFORMED CONSENT/REFUSAL

Informed consent is a legal theory founded on the principles described previously. An informed consent procedure ensures patients' rights to be educated adequately about the nature and consequences of the medical treatments for which they are being considered (Simon, 1994). The three major components to informed consent are information, voluntariness, and competency.

The first component supports the patient's right to have adequate information about his or her treatment so that he or she can make a reasonable decision. Although standards for what defines a legally sufficient disclosure vary from state to state, the standard most commonly applied in the past has been measured from the professional's standpoint or "what a reasonable physician would disclose under the circumstances or the customary disclosure practices of physicians in a particularly community" (Simon, 1994, p. 1306). Over time, an increasing number of courts have been shifting toward a patient-oriented standard that instead focuses on information that would "materially affect" a patient's decision or "information that a reasonable person in the patient's position would want to know in order to make a reasonably informed decision" (Simon, 1994, p. 1306). In general, the patient should be made aware of the risks and benefits of the various treatment options, the risks and benefits of refusing treatment, and, if known, the probable outcome with or without treatment.

The next component to informed consent is that it must be voluntary. Circumstances surrounding the consent process must be free of coercion, threats, or fraud, and the patient should not be experiencing duress that is affecting his or her decision-making ability (Simon, 1994).

Competency, the third element of informed consent, has been the component most discussed and debated in the literature. "Competence" is a legal term that, in this context, refers to one's decision-making ability with regard to medical treatment. In our legal system, an individual is presumed competent unless shown to be otherwise (Mishkin, 1989). Although there is some ambiguity and inconsistency in the legal standards that determine one's competency, four standards currently appear regularly in court decisions (Grisso & Appelbaum, 1995a). These standards and the complex issues that surround them are discussed in much greater detail in the next section of this chapter.

Although it is legally imperative to obtain an informed consent before providing or withholding treatment, there are four exceptions to this requirement. The first exception can occur in emergency situations when immediate treatment is necessary and consent cannot be obtained because the patient is unable to provide it (e.g., patient is in a coma) or there is not sufficient time to obtain it. The emergency must be serious and imminent, and the emergency must be determined by the patient's condition and not the environmental or surrounding situation (e.g., a lack of resources) (Simon, 1994).

The second exception to informed consent occurs when a patient has been found to be legally incompetent to make treatment decisions. When this occurs, a substitute decision maker needs to be identified to make decisions for the patient.

Therapeutic privilege provides another exception to informed consent and is applicable when it has been determined that full disclosure about the treatment options and the associated risks might have a negative impact on the patient (Simon, 1994). As one might expect, the necessary conditions for this exception to be applied are vague, and as the emphasis on patient autonomy expands in our society, there may be fewer justifiable instances when this more paternalistic action can be condoned.

The final condition when treatment providers would be exempt from obtaining informed consent occurs when a patient waives his or her right to be fully informed. To waive his or her right, a patient must be fully aware of the nature of the request, be competent to make this decision, and be making it in a voluntary manner.

DECISION-MAKING CAPACITY AND COMPETENCY

Auerbach and Banja (1993) pointed out that although mental health professionals are routinely involved in decisions about competency, most of them are poorly versed in the significant issues related to this process. As noted previously, practitioners need to understand that a person is considered competent under the law unless a court has ruled that he or she is incompetent. Until recently, incompetence was associated with mental illness or mental retardation. Moreover, people were thought to be either universally competent or universally incompetent; that is, competency was considered an all-or-none affair. Court decisions and legislation, however, have moved competency proceedings in the direction of an approach that emphasizes functional abilities with regard to discrete domains of behavior (competence to refuse treatment or competence to stand trial, etc.) rather than attempting to say that a person is either competent or incompetent for all functions.

Given the legal status of the terms "competence" and "incompetence," mental health practitioners must also understand that they may express their opinions about the functional abilities of an individual, but they cannot determine the competency of that individual. Such a determination is, again, a legal matter. Thus, in the field of mental health, the language of "competency" has been replaced by the language of decision-making capacity (Auerbach & Banja, 1993).

Standards or "Tests" of Competency

Over the past 20 years, there has been a heightened interest in attempting to define the so-called tests or criteria for competency to consent to or refuse treatment. Initially, there was some hope that the field might agree on a single acceptable criterion, but, in the words of Roth, Meisel, and Lidz (1977), this quest was eventually abandoned as "a search for a Holy Grail" (p. 283). It was gradually recognized in the field that judgments of competence or incompetence reflect not only medical and legal issues but also complex psychosocial issues and societal mores, values, and biases.

Roth et al. (1977) discussed five categories of tests for competency: (1) evidencing a choice, (2) "reasonable" outcome of choice, (3) choice based on "rational" reasons, (4) ability to understand, and (5) actual understanding. Albeit in modified form, four of these seem to have survived the scrutiny of the courts and forensic experts in the field. One of the five, "reasonable" outcome of choice, has generally been questioned as contrary to the value that our society places on personal autonomy. It entails making a decision that is roughly equivalent to a decision that a "reasonable" person in similar circumstances would make. Frequently, the decision of a reasonable person was defined as that of the physician or of the treatment staff; hence, the criterion has been found to be biased in favor of accepting treatment.

In attempting to resolve the complicated issue of standards of competency for the widely varying medical decisions that people must make, Drane (1984) proposed a sliding standard: "The more dangerous the medical decision, the more stringent the standards of competency" (p. 926). Thus, if a patient is critically ill with a life-threatening illness and there is a low-risk effective treatment with few alternatives, a simple choice for treatment would be considered rational with little questioning. On the other hand, if this patient wishes to refuse treatment and death is likely to result from his or her refusal, the patient must satisfy what Drane conceptualized as the most demanding standard of competency: the capacity to appreciate the nature and consequences of the decision to be made as it applies to him or her.

The sliding-standard approach has been seriously criticized in recent years. Sullivan and Youngner (1994) objected to the fact that Drane's proposal links the criteria to outcome. They argue that this linkage erodes the independence of the competence determination from the treatment decision in question. In other words, a potential refusal of treatment should not be the basis for altering the criteria for competence/incompetence and certainly should not be the basis for a determination of incompetence. As McCrary and Walman (1990) indicated, competency evaluation should be based on an assessment of the patient's processes of understanding and reasoning, not on the content of his or her decisions. To this criticism, Venesy (1994) has added that a sliding standard would make it more likely that a patient's views could be outweighed by a physician's views insofar as the physician has control over shifts in what standard is applied.

Despite the fact that the field seems to have worked through issues such as those noted earlier, Grisso and Applebaum (1995a) pointed out that considerable confusion remains about what standard or standards to apply and how to assess a patient's functioning on any given standard. They indicate that there are four standards currently found in the law: (1) the ability to express a choice, (2) the ability to understand information relevant to the decision about treatment, (3) the ability to appreciate the significance of the information disclosed for one's own illness and possible treatment, and (4) the ability to manipulate the information in a rational way or in a manner that permits one to make comparisons and consider options.

To date, it has not been clarified, either clinically or legally, whether one is to apply one standard, all four standards, or some combination of two or three.

Of course, it could have implications for patients if one standard or one set of standards was applied and was either more or less demanding than other standards. Overly demanding criteria might have the effect of ruling out people who should be allowed to make decisions about discontinuing treatment; criteria that demand too little might fail to protect people who are incapacitated and make poor judgments (Grisso & Applebaum, 1995a).

The first standard seems like a sine qua non to us (P.M.K. and D.L.M.) Thus, if patients are totally incapable of making their wishes known or of coming to a choice (and have made no prior communications about their wishes), they can make no decision even if understanding, appreciation, and rationality can be assessed. The other question, of course, is whether expressing a choice is sufficient in and of itself as a standard. It seems doubtful that this could be the case because someone who was incapable of thinking rationally about his or her condition, incapable of understanding the relevant information, and incapable of appreciating its implications could still express a choice, but it would be a very hollow and uninformed choice.

The ability to express or communicate a choice, then, is a necessary but not a sufficient criterion for competency. It must be taken in conjunction with one or more of the other three criteria, the first of which is the ability to understand information relevant to the decision about treatment. According to Grisso and Appelbaum (1992), this criterion refers to the patient's capacity to comprehend the meaning and intent of the following information: (1) the nature of the disorder, (2) the nature of the recommended treatment, (3) the likely benefits of the treatment, (4) the likely risks and discomforts of the treatment, and (5) any alternative treatments and their relevant risks and benefits.

The next criterion goes beyond the understanding of information and requires an ability to appreciate the significance of the information for one's own illness and possible treatment. Appelbaum and Grisso (1992) noted that legal incompetence under this standard means that there is a failure to recognize that one has a particular illness or to accept the relevance of an appropriate treatment for one's condition. Beyond this, however, this standard also requires that such failures of recognition stem from some mental or organic disorder or disturbance. Thus, if a patient rigidly denies symptoms or the potential efficacy of appropriate treatment to avoid painful emotions or thoughts, it would be considered indicative of a "defense-based" lack of appreciation. Likewise, if a patient had neurological impairment that led to a denial of illness, it would be considered indicative of an "organic based" lack of appreciation.

On the other hand, Appelbaum and Grisso (1992) pointed out that there can also be "reality-based" and "value-based" disavowals. These disavowals occur when, for example, a patient has had personal experience with similar but unsuccessful treatments in the past (reality-based) and therefore doubts that the proposed treatment will have any greater success, or when a patient's religious or cultural beliefs (value-based) are in conflict with a proposed medical intervention. Disavowals such as these could not be considered consistent with a determination of incompetence.

The final criterion is that the patient shows the ability to manipulate the relevant information in a rational way. According to Grisso and Appelbaum (1993), this refers to the quality of the patient's mental operations, not to the quality or reasonableness of his or her actual choice. It is distinct from understanding and appreciation insofar as one can, for example, engage in a logical reasoning process even though information is misunderstood or engage in illogical thinking with accurately understood information. Grisso and Appelbaum (1993) indicate that the courts have not defined the specific abilities that comprise rational thinking or rational manipulation of information. They suggest that there are a wide range of cognitive abilities that contribute to the rational processing of information during decision making (e.g., attention, memory, abstract thinking, and higher-level functions associated with problem solving). They also note that there are several models of decision making and problem solving in the literature, and, based on commonalities in these models, they propose the following elements as most relevant to a determination of a rational thought process in decision making.

First, there is evidence that the patient seeks information about alternatives and their possible consequences. Second, the patient demonstrates an ability to generate future consequences of the different possible treatment choices. Third, there is evidence that the patient can weigh the potential consequences of different choices based on their value to him or her. Fourth, the patient shows the ability to understand the meaning of probability and apply it to the probability that different consequences will occur if a particular alternative is taken. Fifth, the patient is found to be able to compare alternatives and their respective consequences in reaching a decision.

Grisso and Appelbaum (1995a) studied two related questions pertinent to the use of the three standards discussed previously. First is whether patients impaired on one standard tend to be impaired on the other two standards as well; second is whether there is a hierarchy of rigorousness among the three standards such that some standards are more difficult to meet than others. They used data from a large, multisite controlled study of decision-making capacities. Three groups of patients (schizophrenic patients, depressive patients, and patients with ischemic heart disease) were rated with three instruments developed specifically to assess the abilities associated with the standards of understanding, appreciation, and reasoning. They also had three comparison groups matched to the study groups for age, gender, race, and socioeconomic status.

The proportion of subjects who scored in the impaired range was not significantly different across instruments and standards; however, a substantial number of subjects who performed adequately on one measure were found to have impaired performance on another. This finding suggests that those who do poorly on one standard will not necessarily do poorly on another, and choosing to use a single standard may not be warranted. Nor does the data support the notion of a hierarchy of stringency among the standards.

Given that the study suggests that there may be partially distinct populations identified by each standard, using a combination of standards would produce a greater proportion of patients considered impaired in their decision-making capabilities. Thus, Grisso and Appelbaum (1995a) reported that about one-fourth of their subjects with schizophrenia showed impaired judgment on any one measure, whereas more than 50% of them would be considered impaired if they were required to meet all three standards. The study, therefore, does not provide an answer to the question of where to fix the threshold of competence or incompetence. This question may be clarified by further research or by court decisions. In the meantime, the investigators suggest that clinicians proceed cautiously on a case-by-case basis and use their best clinical judgment.

Clinical Factors Affecting the Assessment of Decision-Making Capacity

Bursztajn, Harding, Gutheil, and Brodsky (1991) highlighted the fact that there is a heavy emphasis on cognition in the existing criteria for competency but only slight emphasis on the influence of affect or affective states. They pointed out that such affective states as unresolved grief, depression, or hypomanic denial can impair or distort the cognitive processes involved in decision making. Both Bursztajn et al. (1991) and Appelbaum and Roth (1981) indicated that competency has too often been viewed as a fixed state but in fact, it may fluctuate with changes in the more basic mental and emotional attributes that underlie it. As a result, they recommend approaching competency assessment as a dynamic process rather than a mere "test." This means understanding that intrapersonal and interpersonal issues as well as affective states can lead an individual to undervalue the positive outcomes of potential treatment, and if these issues can be investigated and resolved, the patient may view his or her prospects in a different light.

Sullivan and Youngner (1994), however, pointed out that it seems inappropriate to assume that the mere presence of depression or any other psychological factor or conflict distorts a patient's decision-making capacity. As noted previously, these assessments must be made on a case-by-case basis, and, in fact, the courts have not held that the simple presence of a mental or emotional disorder is sufficient to assume incompetence. The mental health clinician, then, must assess the patient's cognitive abilities to make decisions as well as weigh the influence exerted by affective and dynamic factors on the decision-making process. This is a challenging task and, as Bursztjan et al. (1991) stated, should be "linked to an overall process designed to enhance the patient's autonomy" (p. 387) while attempting to ensure that reversible issues that distort judgment have been addressed and treated.

Methods of Assessing Decision-Making Capacity

Assessment by Interview

Traditionally, the clinical assessment of decision-making capacity has started with careful history taking and a thorough mental status examination (MSE). The MSE is considered useful in evaluating some of the cognitive functions that underlie decision making as well as in determining whether there is a psychiatric disorder that might seriously affect decision-making capability (Kaplan & Price, 1989; Farnsworth, 1990; Searight, 1992). Some have advocated for the inclusion of psychometric instruments (e.g., the Wechsler Adult Intelligence Scale—Revised) to test such functions as reasoning, memory, and judgment in a more standardized way (Bentivegna & Garvey, 1990).

This more traditional approach is questioned by those who hold that the capacity to make health care decisions requires different functional abilities than those tested by the MSE or by psychological testing (Mishkin, 1989; Venesy, 1994). They stress the importance of direct questioning about the patient's understanding and appreciation of the nature of his or her disorder, of the recommended treatment for that disorder, of the risks and benefits involved, and of the alternatives and their consequences.

Logically enough, still others (e.g., Auerbach & Banja, 1993) argue for a more comprehensive approach that might include history taking, mental status testing, psychological and/or neuropsychological assessment, and direct questioning about understanding and appreciation, as well as the use of some vignettes that simulate actual health care decision-making situations. The use of clinical vignettes has been viewed as innovative and promising in terms of the development of competency assessment instruments. As Marson, Schmitt, Ingram, and Harrell (1994) noted, the clinical vignette is hypothetical but can be made to closely approximate real-life situations. They presented some preliminary findings that suggest that vignettes with an operationalized scoring system could be very helpful in reliably and validly assessing the capacity to consent to treatment. These same investigators highlighted the relative absence of standardized measures for competency assessment and proposed that the development of such standardized instruments be viewed as a priority in the domain of competency research.

Assessment by Standardized Instruments

In recent years, standardized measures of decision-making capacity are being developed. The Hopkins Competency Assessment Test (HCAT; Janofsky, McCarthy, & Folstein, 1992) was conceived as a tool for rapidly screening large numbers of patients for their competency to make treatment decisions and to write advance directives; the Competency Interview Schedule (CIS; Bean, Nishisato, Rector, & Glancey, 1994) was devised to assess the decision-making ability of patients exploring the treatment option of electroconvulsive therapy.

These two instruments are brief and easy to administer but suffer from psychometric limitations. The HCAT tends to focus almost exclusively on only one of the standards used in determining competency: the ability to understand the relevant information involved in informed consent. The CIS is somewhat more comprehensive in that it incorporates items related to the five standards of competency discussed by Roth et al. (1977), but it and the HCAT were both validated by comparing subjects' results with the global opinion of a clinician about competence/incompetence. Moreover, the authors (Janofsky et al., 1992; Bean et al., 1994) provide little information about the standard or standards of legal competency employed by the clinicians in their studies.

A far more complex and sophisticated effort at developing standardized and objectively scored measures of competence/incompetence was undertaken in the MacArthur Treatment Competence Study (Applebaum & Grisso, 1995; Grisso, Applebaum, Mulvey, & Fletcher, 1995; Grisso & Applebaum, 1995b). The investigators in this study initially worked on developing reliable and valid measures of decision-making abilities that were conceptually related to the major legal standards for competence to consent to treatment. Three research instruments were constructed, and each instrument had a different form for use with three different diagnostic groups: schizophrenia, depression, and ischemic heart disease.

First, Grisso and Appelbaum (1992) constructed an instrument called Understanding Treatment Disclosures (UTD). It consists of the standardized presentation of five paragraphs of information corresponding to all five content elements for informed consent. It has objective scoring criteria with different scoring versions for the different forms of disclosure (Grisso et al., 1995).

Next, Applebaum and Grisso (1992) developed an instrument called Perceptions of Disorder (POD). The POD provides a standardized interview procedure that consists of two subtests: a Nonacknowledgement of Disorder (NOD) subtest and a Nonacknowledgement of Treatment Potential (NOT) subtest. The NOD interview assesses the patient's acknowledgement of his or her symptoms, his or her beliefs about the severity of the symptoms, and his or her acknowledgement of the diagnosis; the NOT interview assesses the patient's acknowledgement of the relevance of obtaining any treatment for his or her condition, the potential benefit of the proposed treatment, and the likelihood of improvement without treatment. Again, each subtest has objective scoring criteria. The score for each subtest is summed separately because a patient might acknowledge one content area but not the other.

Finally, Grisso and Applebaum (1993) designed an instrument called Thinking Rationally about Treatment (TRAT). It has two standardized procedures, the TRAT Vignette and the TRAT Tasks, which assess eight functions involved in the rational processing of information. The TRAT Vignette consists of the presentation of a brief story describing a hypothetical patient's mental or medical illness. It ends with a description of three treatment alternatives as well as their benefits and risks. The patient is asked to pretend that he or she is assisting the hypothetical patient by recommending one of the three treatment alternatives; a series of standardized questions elicits the patient's explanation of his or her choice. There are detailed procedures for recording responses and specific criteria and decision rules for identifying evidence of functions such as consequential thinking and comparative thinking. The TRAT Tasks present patients with problems in which they must perform functions such as weighing different consequences or distinguishing the relative values of different probabilities. The total TRAT score is the sum of the scores for the two procedures: TRAT Vignette and TRAT Tasks (Grisso et al., 1995).

Data on these three instruments were collected in a large, multisite study using samples of hospitalized patients with schizophrenia, major depression, and ischemic heart disease as well as matched non-ill community samples. In a psychometrically sound manner, the authors examined scoring reliability, internal consistency, intertest correlations, test–retest correlations, and construct validity. They discussed and documented psychometric strengths, weaknesses, and limitations of each instrument (Grisso et al., 1995; Grisso & Appelbaum, 1995b).

Because research demands required that the instruments be more lengthy and complex than desirable for clinical purposes, the principal authors are developing and validating an instrument designed for standardized clinical assessments of competence to consent to treatment. The MacArthur Competence Assessment Tool for Treatment Decisions (MacCAT-T) is based on the three instruments developed for the MacArthur Treatment Competence Study. The MacCat-T is described as assessing abilities related to each of the four legal standards for competence, as requiring brief administration time, and as allowing the assessment of abilities in the context of the patient's own specific symptoms and treatment options.

Grisso and Appelbaum (1995b) caution that the measures that they developed should not be interpreted as though the measures, in themselves, can provide determinations of legal competence. As the investigators say, no numerical criterion can give this sort of judgment across cases. Too many individual factors specific to each case need to be weighed in making a determination. As a result, they suggest that those who score low on these standardized measures be considered as "at greater risk" (p. 170) of not meeting the legal criteria for competency.

Special Populations and Decision-Making Capacity

Several special populations of patients can present particular challenges in terms of determining their decision-making capacity. These include patients who are mentally ill, patients who have dementia, patients who are children or adolescents, and patients who are developmentally disabled.

As noted earlier in this section, it was common practice to consider the mentally ill incompetent. In more recent years, however, forensic experts and the courts maintain that there is little substantial support for the position that psychiatric patients need protections from making incompetent decisions that differ from the protections given to medical patients when they consent to or refuse treatment (Cournos, 1993).

Yet, in the MacArthur Treatment Competence Study noted earlier, Grisso and Appelbaum (1995b) found that the schizophrenia group had much higher proportions in the impaired categories on all three measures of competency (UTD, POD, and TRAT) than either the depressive group or the ischemic heart disease group. Approximately one-quarter of the schizophrenia sample was found to be impaired on each measure, and, when all three measures were utilized, 52% of the schizophrenia sample scored in the impaired range. Likewise, when combining all three measures, a greater proportion of the depressive sample scored in the impaired range than did the angina sample. Thus, as a group, patients with mental illness could be said to manifest decision-making deficits more often than medically ill patients and their non-ill controls.

Grisso and Applebaum pointed out, however, that there was considerable variability within and across the schizophrenia and depression groups. In fact, on any given measure, the majority of patients with schizophrenia did not do worse than other patients and nonpatients. The poorer mean performance of the schizophrenia group was attributable to a minority within that group, and the minority tended to be those who manifested more severe psychopathology (especially those with an acute thought disorder). The investigators concluded that significant differences exist in decision-making abilities between persons with and without mental illness, but one cannot maintain that all persons with mental illness lack decision-making capability. Each case must be evaluated on an individual basis.

Much the same can be said for patients with dementia. Both Stanley (1983) and Marson et al. (1994) stated that a diagnosis of dementia should not be taken as presumptive evidence of incompetence. Dementia can be caused by various diseases, Alzheimer's disease being the most common. With Alzheimer's dementia, the onset of the illness is typically slow and there is a gradual decline in memory and cognitive functioning. In the earlier stages of the disease, deficits may be mild and considerable cognitive ability may be retained. With multi-infarct dementia, the onset is typically more abrupt and there may be more of a stepwise decline. Initially, however, many of the person's cognitive functions may be relatively unimpaired and there can be recovery of function not seen in a dementia of the Alzheimer type (Stanley, 1983).

Because there can be such variation in the cognitive capacities of dementia patients, Marson et al. (1994) argued that a determination of decisional capacity should always involve a "functional" analysis of the patient. Neuropsychological and mental status test measures are clearly important in gauging the level of cognitive impairment, but the findings from such testing must be linked to the kinds of capacities with which the law is concerned (i.e., understanding, appreciation, and rational thinking).

An important concern with the dementia patient has to do with his or her ability to retain information over time. Stanley (1983) argued that it is not necessary to retain all consent information, but if retention is a serious concern, the patient should be reevaluated on repeated occasions.

Given that dementia of the Alzheimer's type can have a rather insidious progression, there are frequently cases in which the patient's decisional capacity seems to be in the borderline range. In the interest of promoting autonomous decision making for as long as possible in such cases, Stanley (1983) advocated that the process of informed consent be altered to accommodate the patient's needs. Thus, she suggested such things as making the consent material more readable, allowing the patient more time to review the consent material, using teaching and review methods, involving family members who may be able to use language that is more familiar to the patient, and so on. In these ways, the dementing patient's ability to exercise autonomous decision making can be respected and optimized until the disease becomes too debilitating.

The general rule of law with regard to children or minors is that they are legally incompetent to make medical decisions on their own behalf (Sigman & O'Connor, 1991). Parental consent is required for either treatment or the refusal of treatment, and parents are to be guided by the ethical principle of promoting their child's best interests. The American Academy of Pediatrics, however, emphasized that "physicians and parents should give great weight to clearly expressed views of child patients regarding LSMT (life sustaining medical treatment), regardless of the legal particulars" (Committee on Bioethics, 1994, p. 532). Moreover, with adolescents, there can be two exceptions to the parental consent requirement.

The first exception is for "emancipated minors." Emancipation means that the parents have relinquished control and authority over an adolescent who usually is living apart and is financially independent. Other circumstances that may be interpreted as indicating emancipation are marriage, military service, pregnancy, and parenthood. According to Sigman and O'Connor (1991), the emancipated-minor exception has long been recognized as a common-law rule, and there are statutes in approximately half the states that define circumstances under which a minor may be partially or wholly emancipated from his or her parents.

The second possible exception to the parental consent requirement has to do with the so-called mature-minor doctrine. According to many courts, some state legislatures, and common law, adolescents 14 years of age or older can be assessed as sufficiently mature to make medical decisions for themselves (Sigman & O'Connor, 1991; Committee on Bioethics, 1994). "Mature" in this case means able to understand the nature of the illness and the nature and consequences of the proposed medical treatment. Traditionally, the courts view the age of 14 as the cutoff for the application of this doctrine. There is some empirical evidence supporting this point of view. Weithorn and Campbell (1982) presented 9-, 14-, 18-, and 21-year-olds with hypothetical treatment dilemmas and found that although 9-year-olds appeared to be less competent according to legal standards, 14-year-olds did not differ from the 18- and 21-year-olds.

Nonetheless, the mature-minor doctrine remains shrouded in legal uncertainty. According to Sigman and O'Connor (1991), the courts have allowedphysicians to act with impunity on the decisions of minors when the intervention entailed small risk (e.g., a tonsillectomy). When a major medical intervention or a refusal of life-sustaining treatment was at issue, however, either a court order has been required or the assent of a parent to the minor's decision.

Some have argued that mild mental retardation does not preclude good judgment and decision making with regard to specific decisions about treatment (Kaplan, Strang, & Ahmed, 1988). Clearly, all efforts should be made to respect the autonomy of such patients in the informed consent process. Patients who are considered more seriously developmentally disabled or suffer from moderate to severe mental retardation, however, have never had and have no hope of attaining decision-making capacity or competency. Some of these individuals live with parents or their legal guardians; others are wards of the state and live in public facilities. The state has a special interest in and responsibility for the protection of these vulnerable people.

A few courts have argued for the extension of the right to refuse life-sustaining treatment even to those patients such as the developmentally disabled who never attained competency to express treatment preferences. They typically proposed that the patient may exercise this right through a surrogate who utilizes substituted judgment. With the realization, however, that it would be impossible for a surrogate to formulate a substituted judgment for someone who was never competent to express treatment preferences, the best interests standard began to replace substituted judgment in court proceedings.

McKnight and Bellis (1992) asserted that developmentally disabled patients do not have the right to refuse life-sustaining treatment but do have a right to have appropriate medical decisions made on their behalf. They proposed that a legally appointed primary decision maker may choose to forgo life-sustaining treatment for a developmentally disabled person in such situations as a persistent vegetative state for 12 months or a terminal illness with uncontrollable pain. In each situation, they hold that the best interests standard is to be applied and is to focus on the value of continuing life to the individual patient. They caution that there is a need to protect this population against societal and financial pressures and propose prohibiting the consideration of the cost of life-sustaining treatment.

DECISION MAKING AND THE INCOMPETENT TERMINALLY ILL PATIENT

The need to make decisions about life-sustaining medical treatment often occurs after patients no longer have the capacity to participate meaningfully in these decisions. Although competent and informed individuals can exercise their rights of autonomy and self-determination, this right is only realized for incompetent individuals who expressed their wishes in advance, while still competent. Advanced directives are legal documents that allow competent individuals to extend their autonomy into the future by allowing them to document their treatment preferences and/or to designate a health care proxy to make their health care decisions in the event that they are not able to do so for themselves.

By preserving the autonomy of the individual, advance directives can help to address the ethical and legal complications that arise when incompetent individuals are faced with treatment decisions. This is an issue that has become increasingly salient to our society since the *Quinlan* case, and it was most dramatically highlighted in the previously noted Supreme Court decision in the *Cruzan* case. In the *Cruzan* case, it was established that incompetent individuals could forgo treatment if there is "clear and convincing evidence" that this would be what the incompetent individual would have wanted for himself or herself. Related to this decision, the Supreme Court strongly advocated the use of advance directives to protect the autonomy of individuals (Wachter & Lo, 1993).

Concurrent with this case, the U.S. Congress enacted the Patient Self-Determination Act (PSDA) on December 1, 1991, in an attempt to promote more extensive use of advance directives. This legislation applies to all health care facilities, including hospitals, nursing homes, hospices, managed care organizations, and home health care agencies, that participate in Medicare or Medicaid and receive federal funds. The PSDA requires these institutions to provide written information to patients about their rights to accept or refuse medical treatment and to complete advance directives. The goal of this statute was to both encourage the use of advance directives and to prompt health care institutions to honor these documents (Wolf et al., 1991).

Despite widespread support for this legislation and anticipation that it would lead to a significant increase in the number of people who complete advance directives, evidence suggests that the PSDA has been minimally effective in promoting greater use. Although there is variation between studies, the most generous estimates suggest that only one in five people have completed advance directives, reflecting, at best, a slight increase in the use of advanced directives (Gallup & Newport, 1991). Even with educational efforts, it has been speculated that this disappointing outcome may be as a result of insufficient medical information and discussion time with medical care professionals. Discomfort in contemplating one's own mortality may also prevent people from completing advance directives.

A number of studies addressed the shortcomings that surround the use of these instruments and may contribute to the fact that they have not become more widely used (Emanuel, Barry, Emanuel, & Stoeckle, 1994; Wolf et al., 1991). For example, Peterson (1992) discussed the ethical complications that arise when advance directives allow surgery but not the use of other interventions that could enhance the outcome of surgery (e.g., resuscitation, ventilators, and artificial feeding). In addition, significant discrepancies often occur regarding treatment decisions between patients and their potential health care proxies. One study found only 70% agreement on health care decisions between patients and their self-selected surrogate decision makers, even though the surrogates were asked to base their decision on what they thought the patient would choose for himself or herself (Hare, Pratt, & Nelson, 1992). There is always the risk of misinterpretation or difficulty in applying specific directives to unique situations, but an individual can do several things to minimize the likelihood that this could happen. Probably the most important thing is to have a thorough discussion with the patient's identified health care proxy. Although this appears obvious, some studies show that a large proportion of people never discuss their beliefs and desires about life-Sustaining treatment with their health care proxies (Emanuel & Emanuel, 1992; Gamble, McDonald, & Lichstein, 1991). Some studies also suggest that in addition to specific instructions on advance directives, a general statement regarding the patient's beliefs about life-sustaining treatment can enhance the proxy's understanding of the patient's wishes (Wachter & Lo, 1993).

These issues highlight the fact that advance directives do not provide easy answers to the questions surrounding the provision of life-sustaining treatment to people who have become incompetent. Instead, these issues raise a number of complex questions that deserve scholarly reflection and discussion. In the absence of an easy answer, families and loved ones continue to struggle with decisions regarding life-sustaining medical treatment for incompetent friends and relatives. The goal for proxies that has been most strongly supported is to be guided by the principle of substituted judgment: to make the decision that the patient would make if he or she had the capacity to do so for himself or herself (Dresser & Whitehouse, 1994). This can be a stressful task for the proxy, particularly if the decision that the patient would make runs counter to the decision that the proxy would want for himself or herself. If the patient did not express his or her desires either verbally or in advance directives, it is incumbent upon the health care proxy to make medical decisions for the patient that are based on the best interests principle. This principle guides decision makers to carefully identify and weigh the risks and benefits associated with the decision and then make a thoughtful decision that reflects what is believed to be in the best interest of the patient. This standard is considered by many to be paternalistic because the decision reflects the values and desires of the decision maker rather than the patient. It is for this reason that the principle of substituted judgment is preferred.

Dresser and Whitehouse (1994) provide an alternative perspective on this issue. They believe that our societal preoccupation with the autonomy of competent patients has contributed to the inadequate development of the best interests standard. As a result, proxy decision makers are left with little moral guidance about how to make decisions in the very common scenario where the incompetent family member or friend has not provided any indication of his or her treatment preferences, or the treatment preferences provided by the incompetent individual are vague and/or ambiguous.

Dresser and Whitehouse (1994) also feel that the substituted judgment principle is limited in that it does not take into account the likelihood that an individual could have a substantial shift in interest with the onset of incompetence. In other words, what may seem like an intolerable situation from the viewpoint of a competent individual may be experienced very differently by someone whose capacity is more limited. These patients continue to have an experiential world, unlike patients who are permanently comatose, and they have a subjective experience of the treatment process. Dresser and Whitehouse therefore advocate for objective treatment standards where the goal is to determine which treatment option is most preferable from the patient's point of view, but where the focus is on the incompetent patient's current condition rather than prior preferences. To measure or discern the actual experience of the incompetent individual is tremendously difficult, and much of the work that has been done on assessment has been limited to physical sensations, primarily pain. Dresser and Whitehouse (1994) stress the importance of learning to identify and measure other dimensions that give meaning to the life of one who is conscious though incompetent because it is "a necessary element in morally defensible decision making about life-sustaining treatment" (p. 8).

"ALLOWING TO DIE"
VERSUS "EUTHANASIA" OR "SUICIDE"

Those who oppose a right to refuse life-sustaining treatment at times refer to it as "killing" or "suicide." Many clinicians and bioethicists who support such a right have struggled to counter such claims by establishing a distinction between letting someone die and killing or suicide (McCamish & Crocker, 1993; Parry, 1990). The gist of their argument is that withdrawing or withholding a life-sustaining treatment does not cause death; it is the underlying disease or condition that takes over and causes death. Thus, for those with this perspective, removing a respirator may seem to be killing but it is actually letting the patient die because his or her lung function can no longer support life. In a corollary argument, it is not seen as killing when a physician gives an agonized, terminally ill patient morphine in large doses to reduce pain but, as a result, shortens his or her life. This action is justified under the principle of the "double effect": The physician foresees the patient's death, but does not intend it. The intent is to reduce pain and suffering.

In terms of a distinction between allowing to die and suicide, the argument has been that refusing life-sustaining treatment is a decision on the part of the patient to forgo an intrusion into his or her body which results in death. Suicide, on the other hand, is seen as the initiation of an action that harms the person and ends his or her life (Parry, 1990).

Whether or not these distinctions between letting someone die and killing or suicide can be sustained is questioned not only by those who oppose a right to refuse life-sustaining treatment but also by some who favor a right to die (Battin, 1994; Mayo, 1992; Sullivan & Youngner, 1994). These authors have argued that there can be killing and/or suicide by inaction as surely as by action. Thus, for example, it was considered homicide when a woman left her infant daughter completely unattended for 2 weeks while she flew to another state to be with her boyfriend (Mayo, 1992). Likewise, one could commit suicide by deciding not to get out of the way of an oncoming vehicle. From this perspective, "allowing someone to die" could be viewed as so-called passive euthanasia and/or suicide by inaction. What is germane is not the activity or lack of it but the intention behind the action or inaction. On the other hand, Finucane and Harper (1996) have argued that the use of the term "passive euthanasia" is troubling and misleading. If euthanasia means an action or inaction that brings about death before it would naturally occur, allowing someone to die a natural death by withholding or withdrawing treatments that make for no change in the underlying condition or disease could hardly be considered euthanasia.

The "double effect" argument noted above is likewise complicated. It is held that although death results, the intent is not to kill but to relieve suffering. On the one hand Battin (1994) has been extremely skeptical about such a position and considered it implausible that a physician could know that such a central effect as death would result and yet be said not to intend it. On the other hand, Annas (1996) has argued that "there is a difference between an intended result and an unintended but accepted consequence" (p. 685).

Battin (1994) and Mayo (1992) further argued, however, that not all killing or suicide is immoral; that is, although in most instances there is an ethical obligation to preserve life and prevent killing or suicide, there can be instances of both that, in fact, promote human dignity rather than destroy it. Thus, Battin (1994) noted that the "coup de grace granted a mortally wounded soldier who cannot be saved on the battlefield" (p. 17) is not seen as an immoral act but an act of mercy. Similarly, the Israelite soldiers who killed themselves at Masada rather than be taken by the Romans are not seen as acting in an immoral way. Thus, it becomes hard to maintain that all killing and/or suicide is wrong.

These are complicated and controversial issues and are likely to be the subject matter of debate well into the foreseeable future. For clinicians who work with the terminally ill, it would seem that the effort should always be to make the necessity of decisions about ending life as infrequent as possible. Such an effort requires that great attention be given to pain management and palliative care, to the recognition of treatable anxiety and depression, to assisting the patient in bringing closure to previously unresolved issues with family and friends, to supporting the patient in grieving and saying farewell, to bringing about the good death or, perhaps, in Battin's terms, "the least worst death" (Battin, 1994, p. 36). With clinical assistance, some patients are able to avoid what could be a

fear-driven or despair-driven, impulsive and premature decision to terminate treatment. It must also be borne in mind, however, that there will always be some cases when it is more merciful to allow the patient to die now
rather than having him or her endure a more prolonged but horrible death
later.

THE OTHER SIDE
OF THE EXISTENTIAL COIN

As is evident from the preceding sections of this chapter, our society places a
tremendous value on protecting life and on providing individuals with the autonomy to make their own decisions regarding life-sustaining medical treatment. When these rights are discussed, there is often an implicit assumption
that medical resources would be available should the individual choose to utilize them. Ethical principles that guide decision making, such as that of mercy,
often rest on the assumption that "each person . . . has a claim on whatever
medical resources might be effective in the full treatment of his or her condition" (Battin, 1994, p. 113). Furthermore, our society has demonstrated its
commitment to provide life-sustaining treatment through various health care
policies that have been passed through the years. For example, Congress voted
in 1972 to provide funding for dialysis and renal transplantation for any citizen
of the United States with end-stage renal disease. At the time, these treatments
were considered fairly extreme medical procedures and many people would
have died had they not been granted access to these expensive, chronic treatments.

More currently, there has been a greater awareness of the tremendous expense of such programs and the limited availability of medical resources. Health
care reform has become a major political issue that focuses on providing care
more economically. Despite the reality of this situation, the implications of such
cutbacks are often ignored by academics and ethicists who explore the questions surrounding life-sustaining treatment. Battin (1994), however, directly
addressed the issue by applying the ethical principle of justice or the "fairer
distribution of medical resources in a society that lacks sufficient resources to
provide maximum care for all" (p. 113). This, of course, leaves us with the
question of what is meant by "fairer distribution"? Some believe that it is fairer
to provide a treatment to an individual who can benefit from that treatment
rather than one who cannot benefit. Andereck (1992) and Normand (1994)
point out that the futility of treatment is determined by looking not only at
medical outcome but at quality-of-life issues as well. Andereck further speaks
of how health care ethics are shifting from the protection of patient autonomy,
"the hallmark of healthcare ethics in the United States," to the question of how
medical futility is defined and "what are the rights of individuals in our society
to insist on expensive, invasive, and possibly even nonproductive care?" (pp.

49–50). This issue often becomes salient when family members make health care decisions for their loved ones who have lost the capacity to make health care decisions on their own. Family members often have a difficult time terminating treatment for their loved ones and may want more aggressive treatment even when the treatment is futile. This is an issue of great controversy. For example, in discussing resuscitation, Fields and McKenna (1988) said that the competent patient's wishes must be respected and "followed despite a determination by the physician that the patient may not benefit" (p. 324). This stands in contrast to the viewpoint held by Levenson and Pettrey (1994) that the "healthcare team is not required to undertake interventions that cannot help" (p. 88).

The issue of withholding health care from those who request treatment becomes increasingly complex when the treatment in question may not be futile and could potentially enhance longevity and quality of life but the resources to provide the treatment are scarce. How best to allocate finite health care resources has become a major focus of public health policy, and the controversial issues that surround this question are highlighted in the field of organ transplantation (Levenson & Olbrisch, 1993; Olbrisch & Levenson, 1995). As medical technology has advanced, the proportion of appropriate transplant candidates has increased but there has been a persistent shortage of donated organs. Out of necessity, the allocation of organs has occurred in medical practice for years. Although the medical community is looking to the organ allocation process for insight into this decision-making process, it is apparent that many serious problems exist. For example, no standardized format is used to determine the appropriateness of a transplant candidate, and so many sites have different criteria to determine who makes an appropriate candidate (Beresford et al., 1990; Levenson & Olbrisch, 1993). There is also an indication that decisions are skewed by social class and income, age, race and gender (Kutner, 1994; Normand, 1994).

Psychologists and other mental health professionals can play a major role in helping to address and tease apart the complex bioethical questions and dilemmas that our society is facing with increasing urgency. Many patients wish to have their life prolonged, even against all odds. The health care system is increasingly faced with the inability to extend resources to all patients and there are those within the system who see it as unjustifiable to use the resources when treatment is futile or could be utilized more beneficially by another recipient. Psychologists have been at the forefront in developing standardized research protocols that will facilitate the health care professionals' ability to engage in the more ethical distribution of medical resources (Hecker, Norvell, & Hills, 1989; Olbrisch, 1996; Olbrisch & Levenson, 1995). Although we are achieving a greater understanding about the quality of life individuals experience in the face of medical illness and treatment, we have much more to learn before medical resources can be allocated with greater moral confidence.

ACKNOWLEDGMENTS

We wish to thank Glenn Trezza, PhD, for his thoughtful review of this chapter. The views and opinions expressed in this chapter are those of the authors and do not represent the views and opinions of the Veterans Health Administration.

REFERENCES

Andereck, W. (1992). Development of a hospital ethics committee: Lessons from five years of case consultations. *Cambridge Quarterly of Healthcare Ethics, 1,* 41–50.

Annas, G. (1991). The promised-end-Constitutional aspects of physician-assisted suicide. *New England Journal of Medicine, 335,* 683–687.

Appelbaum, P., & Grisso, T. (1992). *Manual for perceptions of disorder (POD).* Worcester, MA: University of Massachusetts Medical School.

Appelbaum, P., & Grisso, T. (1995). The MacArthur Treatment Competence Study. I: Mental illness and competence to consent to treatment. *Law and Human Behavior, 19,* 105–126.

Appelbaum, P., & Roth, L. (1981). Clinical issues in the assessment of competency. *American Journal of Psychiatry, 138,* 1462–1467.

Auerbach, V., & Banja, J. (1993). Competency determinations. In A. Stoudemire & B. Fogel (Eds.), *Medical–psychiatric practice* (Vol. 2, pp. 515–535). Washington, DC: American Psychiatric Press.

Battin, M. (1994). *The least worst death: Essays in bioethics on the end of life.* New York: Oxford University Press.

Bean, G., Nishisato, S., Rector, N., & Glancy, G. (1994). The psychometric properties of the competency interview schedule. *Canadian Journal of Psychiatry, 39,* 368–376.

Bentivegna, S., & Garvey, K. (1990). Applications of Hartman's competency to consent and right to refuse treatment concepts. *American Journal of Forensic Psychology, 8,* 25–34.

Beresford, T., Turcotte, J., Merion, R., Burtch, G., Blow, F., Campbell, D., Brower, K., Coffman, K., & Lucey, M. (1990). A rational approach to liver transplantation for the alcoholic patient. *Psychosomatics, 31*(3), 241–254.

Boisaubin, E. (1993). Legal decisions affecting the limitation of nutritional support. *The Hospice Journal, 9,* 131–147.

Bursztajn, H., Harding, Jr., H., Gutheil, T., & Brodsky, A. (1991). Beyond cognition: The role of disordered affective states in impairing competence to consent to treatment. *Bulletin of the American Academy of Psychiatry and Law, 19,* 383–388.

Committee on Bioethics, American Academy of Pediatrics. (1994). Guidelines on forgoing life-sustaining medical treatment. *Pediatrics, 93,* 532–536.

Cournos, F. (1993). Do psychiatric patients need greater protection than medical patients when they consent to treatment? *Psychiatric Quarterly, 64,* 319–329.

Drane, J. (1984). Competency to give an informed consent: A model for making clinical assessments. *Journal of the American Medical Association, 252,* 925–927.

Dresser, R., & Whitehouse, P. J. (1994). The incompetent patient on the slippery slope. *Hastings Center Report, 24,* 6–12.

Emanuel, L. L., Barry, M. J., Emanuel, E. J., & Stoeckle, J. D. (1994). Advance directives: Can patients' stated treatment choices be used to infer unstated choices? *Medical Care, 32*(2), 95–105.

Emanuel, E. J., & Emanuel, L. L. (1992). Proxy decision making for incompetent patients: An ethical and empirical analysis. *Journal of the American Medical Association, 267*(15), 2067–2071.

Faber-Langendoen, K., & Bartels, D. (1992). Process of forgoing life-sustaining treatment in a university hospital: An empirical study. *Critical Care Medicine, 20,* 570–577.

Farnsworth, M. (1990). Competency evaluations in a general hospital. *Psychosomatics, 31,* 60–66.

Fields, F, & McKenna, J. (1988). Practical guidelines for action regarding application of CPR/DNR. *Death Studies, 12,* 319–328.

Finucane, T., & Harper, M. (1996). Ethical decision-making near the end of life. *Clinics in Geriatric Medicine, 12,* 369–377.

Flarey, D. (1991). Advanced directives: In search of self-determination. *Journal of Nursing Administration, 21*(11), 16–22.

Fulbrook, P. (1994). Assessing mental competence of patients and relatives. *Journal of Advanced Nursing, 20,* 457–461.

Gallup, G., & Newport, F. (1991). Mirror of America: Fear of dying. *Gallup Poll News Service, 5,* 1.

Gamble, E., McDonald, P., & Lichstein, P. (1991). Knowledge, attitudes, and behavior of elderly persons regarding living wills. *Archives of Internal Medicine, 151,* 277–280.

Grant, R., & Steel, E. (1990). Decision-making with psychiatrically impaired patients. *Psychiatric Clinics of North America, 13,* 149–156.

Grisso, T., & Appelbaum, P. (1992). *Manual for understanding treatment disclosures.* Worcester, MA: University of Massachusetts Medical School.

Grisso, T., & Appelbaum, P. (1993). *Manual for thinking rationally about treatment.* Worcester, MA: University of Massachusetts Medical School.

Grisso, T., & Appelbaum, P. (1995a). Comparison of standards for assessing patients' capacities to make treatment decisions. *American Journal of Psychiatry, 152,* 1033–1037.

Grisso, T., & Applebaum, P. (1995b). The MacArthur Treatment Competence Study. III: Abilities of patients to consent to psychiatric and medical treatments. *Law and Human Behavior, 19,* 149–174.

Grisso, T., Appelbaum, P., Mulvey, E., & Fletcher, K. (1995). The MacArthur Treatment Competence Study. II: Measures of abilities related to competence to consent to treatment. *Law and Human Behavior, 19,* 127–114.

Hafemeister, T., Keilitz, I., & Banks, S. (1991). The judicial role in life-sustaining medical treatment decisions. *Issues in Law and Medicine, 7,* 53–72.

Hare, J., Pratt, C., & Nelson, D. (1992). Agreement between patients and their self-selected surrogates on difficult medical decisions. *Archives of Internal Medicine, 152,* 1049–1054.

Headley, J. A. (1991). The DNR decision—Part II. Ethical principles and application. *Dimensions in Oncology Nursing, 5*(2), 34–37.

Hecker, J., Norvell, N., & Hills, H. (1989). Psychologic assessment of candidates for heart transplantation: Toward a normative data base. *Journal of Heart Transplant, 8,* 171–176.

Janofsky, J., McCarthy, R., & Folstein, M. (1992). The Hopkins Competency Assessment Test: A brief method for evaluating patients' capacity to give informed consent. *Hospital and Community Psychiatry, 43,* 132–136.

Kaplan, K., & Price, M. (1989). The clinician's role in competency evaluations. *General Hospital Psychiatry, 11,* 397–403.

Kaplan, K., Strang, J. P., & Ahmed, I. (1988). Dementia, mental retardation, and competency to make decisions. *General Hospital Psychiatry, 10,* 385–388.

Kloezen, S., Fitten, L. J., & Steinberg, A. (1988). Assessment of treatment decision-making capacity in a medically ill patient. *Journal of the American Geriatrics Society, 36,* 1055–1058.

Kutner, N. (1994). Is there bias in the allocation of treatment for renal failure? In H. McGee & C. Bradley (Eds.), *Quality of life following renal failure* (pp. 153–168). Langhorne, PA: Harwood.

Levenson, J., & Olbrisch, M. (1993). Psychosocial evaluation of organ transplant candidates: A comparative survey of process, criteria, and outcomes in heart, liver, and kidney transplantation. *Psychosomatics, 34*(4), 314–323.

Levenson, J., & Pettrey, L. (1994). Controversial decisions regarding treatment and DNR: An algorithmic guide for the uncertain in decision making ethics (GUIDE). *American Journal of Critical Care, 3*(2), 87–91.

Maddi, S. (1990). Prolonging life by heroic measures: A humanistic existential perspective. In P. T. Costa, Jr. & G. R. VandenBos (Eds.), *Psychological aspects of serious illness: Chronic conditions, fatal diseases, and clinical care* (pp. 155–184). Washington, DC: American Psychological Association.

Marson, D., Schmitt, F., Ingram, K., & Harrell, L. (1994). Determining the competency of Alzheimer patients to consent to treatment and research. *Alzheimer Disease and Associated Disorders, 8,* 5–18.

Mayo, D. (1992). What is being predicted? The definition of "suicide." In R. Maris, A. Berman, J. Maltsberger, & R. Yufit (Eds.), *Assessment and prediction of suicide* (pp. 88–101). New York: Guilford Press.

McCamish, M., & Crocker, N. (1993). Enteral and parenteral nutrition support of terminally ill patients: Practical and ethical perspectives. *The Hospice Journal, 9,* 107–129.

McCrary, S., & Walman, A. (1990). Procedural paternalism in competency determination. *Law, Medicine, and Health Care, 18,* 108–113.

McKnight, D., & Bellis, M. (1992). Forgoing life-sustaining treatment for adult, developmentally disabled, public wards: A proposed statue. *American Journal of Law and Medicine, 18*(3), 203–232.

Mishkin, B. (1989). Determining the capacity for making health care decisions. In N. Billig & P. Rabins (Eds.), *Issues in geriatric psychiatry: Advances in psychosomatic medicine* (Vol. 19, pp. 151–166). Basil, Switzerland: Karger.

Nicholson, B., & Matross, G. (1989, May). Facing reduced decision-making capacity in health care: Methods for maintaining client self-determination. *Social Work,* 234–238.

Normand, C. (1994). Health care resource allocation and the management of renal failure. In H. McGee & C. Bradley (Eds.), *Quality of life following renal failure* (pp. 145–152). Langhorne, PA: Harwood.

Olbrisch, M. (1996). Picking winners and grooming the dark horse: Psychologists evaluate and treat organ transplant patients. *The Health Psychologist, 18*(1), 10–11.

Olbrisch, M., & Levenson, J. L. (1995). Psychological assessment of organ transplant candidates: Current status of methodological and philosophical issues. *Psychosomatics, 36*(3), 236–243.

Overman, W. (1993). Living wills and advance medical treatment directives. In A. Stoudemire & B. Fogel (Eds.), *Medical psychiatric practice* (Vol. 2, pp. 537–560). Washington, DC: American Psychiatric Press.

Parry, J. (1990). The court's role in decision making involving incompetent refusals of life-sustaining care and psychiatric medications. *Mental and Physical Disability Law Reporter, 14*(6), 468–476.

Peterson, L. M. (1992). Advance directives, proxies, and the practice of surgery. *American Journal of Surgery, 163,* 277–282.

Powell, J., & Cohen, A. (1994). The right to die. *Issues in Law and Medicine, 10,* 169–182.

Rando, T. A. (1984). *Grief, dying, and death: Clinical interventions for caregivers.* Champaign, IL: Research Press.

Roth, L., Meisel, A., & Lidz, C. (1977). Tests of competency to consent to treatment. *American Journal of Psychiatry, 134,* 279–284.

Searight, H. (1992). Assessing patient competence for medical decision making. *American Family Physician, 45,* 751–759.

Siegel, D. (1993). Consent and refusal of treatment. *Emergency Medicine Clinics of North America, 11,* 833–840.

Sigman, G., & O'Connor, C. (1991). Exploration for physicians of the mature minor doctrine. *Journal of Pediatrics, 119,* 520–525.

Simon, R. I. (1994). The law and psychiatry. In R. Hales, S. Yudofsky, & J. Talbott (Eds.), *The American Psychiatric Press textbook of psychiatry* (2nd ed., pp. 1297–1335). Washington, DC: American Psychiatric Press.

Singer, P. (1992). Nephrologists' experience with and attitudes towards decisions to forego dialysis. *Journal of the American Society of Nephrology, 7,* 1235–1240.

Snyder, J., & Swartz, M. (1993). Deciding to terminate treatment: A practical guide for physicians. *Journal of Critical Care, 8,* 177–185.

Stanley, B. (1983). Senile dementia and informed consent. *Behavioral Sciences and the Law, 1,* 57–71.

Sullivan, M., & Youngner, S. (1994). Depression, competence, and the right to refuse lifesaving medical treatment. *American Journal of Psychiatry, 151,* 971–978.

Venesy, B. (1994). A clinician's guide to decision making capacity and ethically sound medical decisions. *American Journal of Physical Medicine and Rehabilitation, 73,* 219–226.

Wachter, R. M., & Lo, B. (1993). Advanced directives for patients with human immunodeficiency virus infection. *Critical Care Clinics, 9*(1), 125–136.

Weithorn, L., & Campbell, S. (1982). The competency of children and adolescents to make informed treatment decisions. *Child Development, 53,* 1589–1598.

Wolf, S. M., Boyle, P., Callahan, D., Fins, J. J., Jennings, B., Nelson, J. L., Barondess, J. A., Brock, D. W., Dresser, J. D., Emanuel, L., Johnson, S., Lantos, J., Mason, D. R., Mezey, M., Orentlicher, D., & Rouse, F. (1991). Special report: Sources of concern about the patient self-determination act. *New England Journal of Medicine, 325*(23), 1666–1671.

CHAPTER 8

THE EMERGENCY
TELEPHONE CALL

PHILLIP M. KLEESPIES
ESME J. BLACKBURN

> A patient about whom you have been worried calls you. His speech is slightly slurred as if he has been drinking. He says that his wife asked him to get out, but to him marriage is "until death do us part." He has a loaded gun and he says that he is planning to shoot his wife and then himself.

Most clinicians would agree that such a scenario constitutes a high-stress call. Fortunately, calls that sound as serious as this one do not occur too often. Nonetheless, it is not unusual for a clinician with an active case load to receive calls from patients who are in a crisis or an emergency of one sort or another, and attempting to deal with them can be stressful. As Gilmore (1984) pointed out, telephone calls from patients in crisis must be handled differently from an in-person interview. The caller is in control in the sense that he or she can unilaterally decide to terminate the contact at will. The fact that the phone allows only auditory information limits the available data and makes the clinician's task all the more difficult. Thus, the patient can conceal aspects of his or her situation more easily (the weapon or pills on the table, the dejected look, etc.). In spite of such issues, the clinical and legal management of emergency calls has not been a focus for clinical training programs or for those in clinical practice. Thus, in the literature of the past 25 years, only one model of the process of telephone crisis intervention was articulated in some detail and empirically tested (Echterling, Hartsough, & Zarle, 1980; Echterling & Hartsough, 1989). As discussed later in this chapter, the potential professional and legal risks inherent in the mismanagement of such phone contacts suggest that they warrant greater attention from researchers and practitioners.

Emergency calls from patients who are at risk are received by 24-hour telephone counseling services, mental health agencies, private practitioners, and emergency care facilities. Mental health centers, and emergency care facilities (e.g., hospital emergency rooms) are generally staffed by trained professionals in contrast to hotlines or 24-hour telephone counseling services whose staff are trained volunteers or paraprofessionals who function with professional consultation. The goals of hotlines are generally to provide empathic listening, help the caller mobilize personal resources, effectively problem-solve, provide support, and offer appropriate referrals (Gilmore, 1984). In contrast to mental health professionals, staff at hotlines are not trained to initiate the rescue of callers who are at risk.

A second difference between professionally staffed sites (e.g., mental health clinics, private practice offices, and emergency care facilities) and volunteer staffed hotlines is their ability to assess people in person rather than just on the phone. The goal of the professional is to establish an alliance and then move toward determining whether or not an in-person assessment is needed. If such an assessment is needed, the person is encouraged to come into the clinic or emergency room on his or her own. If the person is not able to do this, however, the professional initiates rescue efforts. Mental health professionals generally do not provide in-depth crisis counseling on the telephone. The focus of this chapter is on the emergency telephone call that reaches the professional.

BRIEF HISTORY OF THE USE OF THE TELEPHONE IN THE MENTAL HEALTH DELIVERY SYSTEM

In our present day and age, the telephone is ubiquitous, but such was not always the case. In 1940, less than 40% of households in the United States had a phone. By the 1980s, however, an estimated 97% of households had telephones (Wellin, Slesinger, & Hollister, 1987). The expanding availability of the telephone formed the backdrop for its increased use in mental health services. The telephone call actually became a more significant form of communication in the delivery of mental health services beginning in the 1950s. The first Samaritan service was started in London in 1953. It offered empathic listening and "befriending" by phone to persons who were struggling with suicidal ideation. The Samaritans now have branches in many parts of the world including the United States (Singh & Brown, 1973).

In 1958, two psychologists, Edwin Shneidman and Norman Farberow, were instrumental in opening the Los Angeles Suicide Prevention Center, an agency dedicated to preventing suicide that used a 24-hour phone service as a major component of its operation. Using Shneidman and Farberow's center as a prototype, many suicide prevention and crisis intervention centers sprang up in the major cities of the United States as well as in other parts of the world (Singh & Brown, 1973; Tekavcic-Grad, Farberow, Zavasnik, Mocnik, & Korenjak, 1988).

In the 1960s, deinstitutionalization, the community mental health movement, and the Community Mental Health Centers Act led to the establishment of community mental health centers that offered 24-hour emergency services (Gerson & Bassuk, 1980; Wellin et al., 1987). The act mandated that a basic component of these emergency services would be a telephone service (Resnik, 1971). The telephone provided the patient with immediate and direct communication with sources of help. Thus, phone services became part of the network set up to replace much of the extensive hospital-based care that previously existed. To some degree, the phone services seem to serve this function to the present day.

Interest in the development of 24-hour telephone crisis intervention services was fostered when the National Institute of Mental Health established a committee to set forth criteria for defining community mental health center emergency services (Resnik, 1971). In addition to recommending that emergency telephone services be available "seven days a week, twenty-four hours a day" (p. 4), the committee recommended that all workers on the emergency service acquire basic instruction in crisis intervention techniques and learn "by direct exposure to crisis situations (both telephone calls and face-to-face), first under supervision, then under observation, and finally with consultative support" (p. 5).

The 1990s have seen an intensified focus on cost containment in health services. The pressure to reduce the use of high-cost inpatient services has, if anything, increased in the current managed care environment. In this context, the point has been reached where commercial vendors offer relatively inexpensive, pay-per-call telephone therapy, something the American Psychological Association's Board of Professional Affairs and Ethics Committee have found questionable except as an adjunct to conventional, in-person psychotherapy (Haas, Benedict, & Kobos, 1996). Be this as it may, the present emphasis on more economical outpatient treatment is only likely to increase the use of the telephone as a means of managing crises and as a source of help in an emergency.

THE "DUTY OF CARE" AND ITS RELEVANCE TO EMERGENCY PHONE CONTACTS

Perhaps because the telephone call does not involve visual contact between the clinician and the patient, it seems easier to regard it as rather ephemeral and of less significance. If a clinician adopts such an attitude with an emergency phone call, however, he or she may do so at some peril. Willett (1977) reports a $1.2 million verdict against a physician who had a single telephone contact with a patient whom he never saw in person. Simon (1987) also pointed out that in a court case in New York (*O'Neill v. Montefiore Hospital*), the court ruled that a telephone conversation alone was sufficient to create a "duty of care" on the part of the clinician. In that particular case, the patient called a doctor from an emergency room and the doctor offered advice. The patient died, and, in a subsequent malpractice action, the doctor, who had never even met the patient, was held potentially liable (Goldstein, 1986).

There can be no professional duty of care unless a clinician–patient relationship exists. According to Simon (1987), there are two bases on which courts may hold that there is such a relationship. First, if the clinician and the patient have a specific agreement as to the terms of treatment, or if the clinician accepts or expects a fee in exchange for treatment, a contract is assumed to exist. Second, if a clinician by his or her statements or actions "undertakes to treat a patient" (p. 8), he or she creates a professional relationship with a consequent duty of care. Thus, giving advice about treatment, attempting to make a diagnosis, or offering psychological interpretations of patient comments or behaviors could be viewed as creating a clinician–patient relationship with associated duties and liabilities. These sorts of activities need not occur in person but could occur by mail or by phone as in *O'Neill v. Montefiore Hospital,* cited previously (Goldstein, 1986).

Once a clinician–patient relationship is established, the mental health practitioner has a legal duty of ordinary and reasonable care to his or her patient (Robertson, 1988). This does not mean that there is a guarantee of positive results but only that there is an obligation to provide an acceptable standard of care. The standard of care for patients who are at risk of suicide or violence is typically determined by expert testimony about the degree of care practiced by other qualified clinicians in the same field and under similar circumstances as well as by examining decisions rendered in prior malpractice cases (Berman & Cohen-Sandler, 1982).

Whether on the phone or in person, if a clinician does not wish to establish a professional relationship and a duty of care, he or she must avoid giving advice, making interpretations, or offering any other interventions beyond recommending that the patient find other appropriate professional assistance. The clinician may wish to clearly state that he or she is not entering into treatment with the patient. However, it is also clear that the ethical mental health clinician, when confronted with a caller who appears to be at risk, will attempt to render what Wheeler (1989) has referred to as "interim first aid" to prevent injury or death. There may also be a legal issue in that gross negligence could potentially be found were the clinician to ignore efforts to assist a patient who is in clear and present danger. Once the decision has been made to try to assist the patient, Simon (1987) notes that there is "a duty not to abandon the rescue and to use whatever reasonable means available to continue the rescue effort without jeopardizing one's self" (p. 10). For the person assessed as a serious risk of suicide, this may entail sending a crisis team or the police and an ambulance to move the individual to an emergency room or other safe setting. For the mentally ill person who is assessed as potentially violent, it might entail warning the identified victim, voluntarily hospitalizing the caller, and/or sending the police to involuntarily hospitalize the caller and prevent injury or death to the intended victim. How a clinician is to meet his or her "duty to protect" under such *Tarasoff*-like conditions may vary from state to state and it behooves each practitioner to be aware of the legal obligations in his or her state or locality.

Given the preceding discussion of ethical and legal issues, it is important also to provide a cautionary note about defensive practice. Defensive practice refers to a clinician's act or omission that is not done for the benefit of the patient but solely to provide a good legal defense against any potential claims of malpractice. Simon (1987) suggests that defensive practice comes in two forms; positive and negative. Positive defensive practice entails taking actions simply to prevent or limit liability. Thus, the overly defensive practitioner might have an automatic response to send the police and have a caller involuntarily taken to an emergency room at the first mention of suicidal or homicidal ideation. Further evaluation might have led to a reduced estimate of risk and/or to less drastic and coercive action. Negative defensive practice, on the other hand, entails avoiding engagement with the patient at risk, again in an effort to prevent becoming the object of a liability claim. Thus, the clinician might immediately disengage with the caller who mentions suicidal or homicidal ideation. This course of action is questionable from an ethical perspective and could backfire legally if the patient or his surviving relatives bring a claim of substandard care against the clinician.

THE IMPORTANCE OF A STANDARD POLICY AND PROCEDURE FOR EMERGENCY PHONE CALLS

As suggested earlier, the emergency phone call is an area of practice for which there are few standards and guidelines. Dale (1995) reports that the Clinical Services Committee of the British Association for Accident and Emergency Medicine has proposed a set of guidelines on managing emergency phone calls. These guidelines include statements about the experience level required of those taking calls, the need for formal training, and the need for documentation. Yet, in a survey also reported by Dale (1995), not one of 34 emergency departments in the survey had a formal policy on telephone inquiries, and only three of them reported documenting calls.

Interest in good clinical practice and concern for risk management suggests that it is important for mental health clinicians and clinical sites to develop policies and guidelines for dealing with emergency phone calls: to become proactive in setting a standard of care for such situations. If a reasonable policy exists and is followed, it should lead to a more consistent level of good care and to decreased risk from claims of negligence or of significant deviation from a standard of good practice. Table 8.1 provides

TABLE 8.1. Sample Policy for Managing Psychological Crisis Phone Calls in an Emergency Department

Policy

1. Staff answering crisis phone calls will have had in-service training on the management of such calls. They are to forward these calls to a clinician designated as responsible for their disposition.
2. The clinician responsible for the final disposition of such calls will be the mental health clinician on duty in the emergency room. The focus of this clinician is to engage the patient in defining the problem, determine whether an emergency evaluation is needed, and, if so, encourage an in-person evaluation or arrange for the patient to be taken on a temporary involuntary commitment to an emergency room for evaluation (should that prove necessary).
3. The emergency room does not offer a more extensive telephone counseling or hot line service.
4. There is an established procedure for routing crisis calls to the responsible clinician.
5. Staff will not discourage patients from coming to the emergency room, but, when appropriate, may suggest alternative solutions.
6. Staff will document all crisis calls, including identifying information, presenting complaint, and plan of action.

an example of a possible policy for an emergency service. Of course, any actual policy must be individualized to the requirements of the particular clinical site.

Berman (1991) raised the issue of such new telephone technologies as Caller Identification and Call Trace and their implications for the policy and mission of hotlines. Caller Identification provides a visual display of the number of each incoming call; Call Trace, instantly traces the current call. Such capabilities greatly facilitate rescue efforts, but they also can be a new level of intrusion on confidentiality and autonomy. Hotlines are dedicated to allowing the caller to preserve his or her anonymity. They attempt to foster self-direction and usually do not initiate rescue efforts unless the caller specifically requests them to do so. Hence, hotlines are likely to be, at the least, ambivalent if not opposed to using such technology.

Emergency departments and crisis centers, on the other hand, typically feel an obligation to engage in more active rescue efforts when needed. Call Trace or Caller Identification may seem quite appealing. The question arises, however, whether having this enhanced rescue capability for the few outweighs the potential breach of confidentiality for nonemergency callers or for callers who, for clinical reasons (paranoia, shame, etc.), are reluctant to share information about themselves until they have established some rapport with the clinician. Although not ideal, one partial solution to this dilemma would be for the clinical site to inform callers in their introductory message that Caller Identification or Call Trace is in use. The caller could then choose to continue or to seek an alternative source of assistance. A second possible solution is to have the phone system allow the use of Call Trace or Caller Identification only on a selective basis; that is, only in the event of an emergency and only by a clinician who has a need to know in responding to the situation.

STUDIES OF THE EFFECTIVENESS
OF EMERGENCY PHONE SERVICES

Most of the research on the effectiveness of emergency phone services focused on telephone counseling services and/or hotlines staffed by lay volunteers. Stein and Lambert (1984) reviewed the research on the effectiveness of lay or non-professional telephone counselors and concluded that there was some limited evidence for their effectiveness based on client and counselor reported measures of efficacy and on follow through on referrals; however, external evaluations or ratings of effectiveness were less supportive of this conclusion.

One classic study of the effects of suicide prevention centers or crisis centers on suicide rates seems pertinent to the general topic of the effectiveness of emergency phone services. Miller, Coombs, Leeper, and Barton (1984) painstakingly identified 25 central city counties in the United States where no crisis centers existed in 1968–1969 but one or more were initiated in 1970 and continued in operation through 1971–1972. As a comparison group, they found 50 counties that already had crisis centers and maintained the same number of centers from 1968 to 1972. The investigators found a significant reduction in suicides for young white females (under age 25) in those counties that initiated crisis centers. This finding was then replicated with a second set of target and comparison counties during the 1969–1973 period.

Young white females are the most frequent callers to crisis centers or suicide prevention centers. Miller et al. (1984) estimated that 637 lives per year in this group were saved. Although these centers did not seem to reach other segments of the population (e.g., elderly white males, the highest-risk group), the estimated saving in lives is not inconsiderable. Although a review of several studies in this area (Frankish, 1994) concludes that there is a mixed picture with regard to changes in suicide rates, the findings of Miller et al. (1984) suggest that if a segment of the population can be convinced to access such phone services, it may have an impact on their suicide rate.

Mishara and Daigle (1992) pointed out that decreasing the suicide rate is only one of several ways in which telephone intervention at suicide prevention centers can help people. They did a study in which trained investigators listened to live calls at two suicide prevention centers in Quebec and evaluated the calls on three outcome measures: (1) changes in level of depression from beginning to end of the call, (2) decreases or increases of suicidal urgency from beginning to end of the call, and (3) whether or not a contract or agreement was reached concerning steps to take to resolve the suicidal crisis. The data reported from this study are preliminary but seem to indicate that a significant number of callers reported feeling less depressed at the end of the call, had a reduction in suicidal urgency, and agreed to engage in constructive steps to resolve the suicidal crisis.

An extensive computer-assisted literature search for this chapter revealed no studies of effectiveness in managing emergency calls that come to professionally staffed emergency rooms, community mental health agencies, or other such sites. Typically, these are agencies that do not offer telephone counseling services but, rather, attempt to assess the urgency of the crisis and the imminence of risk and then either encourage the person to come for an in-person evaluation or, if necessary, send police and/or a crisis team to the individual. Clearly, there is a need for research on the efficacy of such services; however, the findings of Miller et al. (1984) and Mishara and Daigle (1992) support the importance of such emergency phone contacts.

MODELS FOR THE EMERGENCY TELEPHONE INTERACTION

There are at least two models for telephone crisis intervention in the literature. Slaikeu and Leff-Simon (1990) offer the "psychological first aid" model. In this model, the first step is conceptualized as making psychological contact. It involves listening closely for significant events and feelings and making use of reflective and empathic statements to let the caller know that he or she is understood or accepted. The second step has to do with examining the dimensions of the problem. It entails questioning the caller in a nonthreatening manner with regard to his or her immediate past, current functioning, lethality, strengths and weaknesses, resources, and impending decisions. In the third step, the clinician explores possible solutions that may meet the caller's immediate needs. He or she may ask about solutions already attempted and obstacles encountered. The caller may be encouraged to reconsider solutions that seem to have been rejected prematurely, and the caller and the clinician may generate other, new solutions. Finally, the clinician attempts to assist the caller in taking concrete action. If the risk of lethality is low, this attempt may involve encouraging the caller to initiate actions that will be helpful. If the risk of lethality is high, however, and the caller is not able to safely act on his or her own behalf, the clinician needs to take more directive action. Such action might range from getting the caller's permission to contact and involve a family member to having a crisis or rescue team go to the caller's location.

Echterling et al. (1980) presented a second, somewhat more developed model of telephone crisis intervention. They also took the further step of empirically testing whether the specific four phases of their model actually occur during telephone crisis calls (Echterling & Hartsough, 1989). The first phase in this model is viewed as one in which the clinician is concerned with creating the climate or developing the rapport needed for intervention. Climate-creating

actions are conceptualized as actions that develop a helpful relationship, establish helper and caller roles, and sustain the telephone contact. The second phase
has to do with assessment of the crisis and involves gathering information and
identifying the problem. The third phase is termed "affect integration." In this
phase, the clinician "assists the caller in recognizing, understanding, and expressing
feelings about the crisis" (Echterling & Hartsough, 1989, p. 249). The fourth and
final phase is the problem-solving phase, in which clinician and caller identify
goals and alternatives and make proposals for action to achieve those goals.

This second model was tested at a 24-hour telephone and walk-in crisis
intervention service where crisis calls were monitored by observers who utilized the Crisis Call Interaction Form (Echterling et al., 1980) to classify 19
helper behaviors and the Crisis Call Outcome Form (Dixon & Burns, 1974) to
rate whether there was a successful affective, cognitive, or behavioral outcome
to the call. Calls were divided into beginning, middle, and final thirds, and the
investigators hypothesized that successful outcome would be related to decreasing
levels of climate behavior and assessment behavior over time, increasing and
finally decreasing levels of affect integration over time, and increasing levels of
problem-solving behavior over time.

Using analyses of covariance with stepwise multiple regression procedures, Echterling and Hartsough (1989) found that there was strong support for the hypotheses about changes in assessment and problem-solving
behaviors over time and some support for the hypothesis about changes in
affect integration over time. There was little support, however, for the hypothesis about climate-setting behaviors, and, in fact, high proportions of
behavior intended to develop rapport were a predictor of negative affective
and behavioral outcome. The investigators concluded that for crisis phone
calls, the importance of spending time on rapport building may be overesti-
mated and can be counterproductive. In most calls, a working relationship
was easily established and the roles of helper and caller were readily understood. Assessment through the first two-thirds of a call led to success, but in
the final third it was associated with failure. Affect integration or affective
responding during the middle phase rather than at the end of the call was
most effective; some problem solving done throughout the call was useful
but was most effective when done near the end of the call. The authors
indicated that their findings support the portrayal of the crisis call clinician
"as a directive helper who assesses quickly, intervenes decisively, and generally takes a task orientation to the situation" (p. 256).

SKILLS AND ATTRIBUTES
OF THE EMERGENCY PHONE CLINICIAN

The skills and attributes that make for an effective emergency phone clinician
have not been extensively studied. In the literature on hotlines and telephone
counseling services, the evaluation of phone workers has been divided into two

broad categories: technical effectiveness and clinical effectiveness (Gray, Nida, & Coonfield, 1976; Rosenbaum & Calhoun, 1977). Technical effectiveness seems to refer to a number of abilities: (1) the ability to acquire pertinent data, (2) the ability to evaluate the caller's condition and potential lethality, and (3) the ability to formulate a plan of action with the caller. Clinical effectiveness, on the other hand, seems to refer to the ability of the phone worker to create a positive relationship with the caller through the attributes and qualities of empathy, positive regard, authenticity, and so forth.

With hotlines and telephone counseling services, there is a heavy emphasis on empathic listening and clinical effectiveness. With emergency telephone services in professionally staffed settings, clinical effectiveness is obviously valued, but the heavier emphasis tends to be on so-called technical effectiveness. This emphasis is likely to be in keeping with the professional clinician's obligation and interest in getting the caller to a safe environment where a more complete in-person evaluation can occur (Gilmore, 1984; Hilliard, 1990). It is also consistent with the characterization of the crisis call clinician by Echterling and Hartsough (1989) as one who is directive and task oriented and who assesses quickly and intervenes to provide safety.

In the one published study of the skills and attributes considered important for emergency telephone consulting, Dale (1995) surveyed staff at a major hospital emergency department in London. The skills rated most highly were (1) an ability to extract essential information from the caller's description of the problem, (2) good communication skills, and (3) good listening skills. Attributes rated most highly were (1) confidence in what one says and (2) patience in dealing with the caller. This study suggests that the effective crisis call clinician is seen as one who, first and foremost, can obtain information and evaluate the problem quickly. This ability, however, is blended with the more clinically oriented qualities of good communication skills and patience in listening to the caller.

EMERGENCY CALLS FROM PERPETRATORS AND VICTIMS OF VIOLENCE

The rape and battery of women and the abuse of children, the elderly, and the disabled are all, sadly, quite prevalent. These forms of violence lead to psychological crises for both the victims and the perpetrators and to reaching out through the most immediate means, often the phone, to a mental health professional. Therefore, it is important to be knowledgeable about how to best handle such calls and to know the risk factors for abuse, the mandated reporting laws, and referral sources.

Calls from Potential Abusers of Children, the Disabled, and Elders

Emergency calls from abusers may be especially difficult for the mental health professional as they generate unique questions around confidentiality and advocacy. The clinician must listen both as an ally to the overwhelmed caller and as a potential rescuer to the child, the disabled, or the elderly person. Complicating these calls further are the feelings they generate in the mental health professional (e.g., disgust, anger, and sympathy or empathy for the caller's "victim").

It is very important for the private practitioner or emergency room mental health clinician to keep these negative feelings from interfering with forming an alliance with the caller. Talking with coworkers and supervisors about the types of feelings these calls generate may help to diffuse their potentially deleterious effects. A second strategy for facilitating an alliance with a potentially abusive caller is to elicit positive aspects of the caller's personality (Tapp, Ryken, & Kaltwasser, 1974).

Once a rapport has been established with the potentially abusive caller, it is important to move from talking about generalities to talking about more specifics (Tapp et al., 1974). Abusive callers are likely to have multiple problems and may be feeling very overwhelmed. Discussion of their stressors may lead, for example, into a more natural discussion of their abilities to cope with being a parent or caretaker. Here it is helpful to get a sense of how realistic their ideas are about their child's behavior. Questions they should consider are: Do they see their child as a miniature adult? Do they personalize their child's bad behavior, feeling, for example, that it is intentional? If the caller appears to set unrealistic standards for the child, educating the caller about reasonable expectations may be useful.

Feelings of shame, fear of being stigmatized, or fear of losing one's children make it very difficult to admit to and disclose abusive behavior. The caller's often disguised presentation makes it important to be aware of risk factors and the "profile" of a potential abuser. Child abuse risk factors include a history of having been abused or neglected, high levels of family stress, limited financial resources, and few social supports (Burrell, Thompson, & Sexton, 1994). Risk factors associated with caretakers of the elderly and handicapped who become abusive are substance abuse or mental illness, dependence on the victim, shared living arrangements, social isolation, and a history of violence (Lachs & Pillemer, 1995; Vida, 1994; Coyne, Reichman, & Berbig, 1993). If these risk factors are present it is important to assess for potential abuse.

Asking callers if they are abusing a child or elderly person should be done directly but in as nonjudgmental a way as possible. Kempe and Helfer (1972) suggest that it is best to ask something like, "Have you been thinking about hurting your child?" rather than "Are you a child abuser?" Callers are likely to fear being judged and/or having unwanted social services forced on them, or, worse, having their children removed from their care.

Callers have some reason to be concerned about revealing abuse. Although it requires breaking confidentiality, mental health professionals are mandated in all states to report suspected child abuse and in 42 states to report elder abuse (Lachs & Pillemer, 1995). Child and elder abuse are defined in similar ways with one important exception: An elderly person, in contrast to a child, can refuse intervention in cases of substantiated abuse as long as he or she is considered competent and cognitively intact.

A serious difficulty with mandated reporting laws involves the vagueness of the abuse statutes. Elder and child abuse laws usually define abuse as including the following forms: physical, psychological, and neglect. People's definitions of these types of abuse, however, are by no means uniform. For example, when does unkindness become psychological abuse? When does family poverty and the resulting inability to provide food and shelter translate into neglect? These are questions with which mental health professionals frequently have to struggle to determine whether or not they need to file a report. Once the professional "suspects abuse" and files a report with a protection agency, it becomes the agency's job to more thoroughly investigate the potential abuse, which may or may not be substantiated.

When abuse is clearly occurring, immediate problem solving is necessary. It is important to assess whether the child or elderly person needs medical care. Then, it is important to find out whether someone else is available to temporarily care for the abused person. The Department of Social Services or Services for Elder Abuse will need to be notified. It is always best to give the caller, if he or she appears to be reliable and interested in receiving help, a chance to voluntarily report the abuse and request services. After the client has called the protection agency, the mental health professional should also call protective services to make certain that important information has been relayed and that services will be rendered.

Calls from Potentially Abused Children, Adolescents, and Elders

The increased public attention to problems of violence in the home is likely to generate more crisis calls from victims of violence. It is also likely that, given the complex nature of the relationship of the victim to the perpetrator, such calls will come with a "disguised" presentation. The abused child or adolescent caller, for example, may report failing grades, truancy, enuresis, and acting-out behaviors as these may be easier to reveal than familial abuse (Teare, Garrett, Coughlin, Shanahan, & Daly, 1995). The report of these types of symptoms should prompt the clinician to ask specifically whether abuse is going on in the home.

It is often difficult for the victim of abuse to "tell" on a parent or caretaker. This is because the caretaker provides for the basic needs of the victim. It can be frightening to think of the consequences of revealing abuse. The child or adolescent may wonder whether revealing will result in being forced to stay with a foster family. Similarly, the elderly victim may fear placement in a nursing home.

A second obstacle to revealing abuse is the strong bond formed with the caretaker, even if he or she is at times mean and violent. Some researchers have referred to this as the "Stockholm syndrome," whereas others refer to it as a process of "traumatic bonding" (Graham et al., 1995). The Stockholm syndrome refers to the paradoxical reaction of hostages to their captors. Studies of nine groups of hostages revealed a paradoxical reaction to the captors in which victims blamed themselves and professed love and kindness to their abusers even after severe beatings. This type of bonding is observed in abusive families when victims begin to fear for their lives, see no escape, and rely on the abuser for nurturance and support (Graham et al., 1995). It is important to be aware of this process and understand what high stakes the victim has in staying connected to the abuser. Awareness of the complexities of this type of relationship helps clinicians to manage the frustrations they may feel with abused clients who use denial or minimization.

Tomita (1990), who has written a theoretical paper on the process of denial among victims of elder abuse, advocates challenging the distortions of abuse whenever possible while still maintaining an alliance. She suggests that the clinician may need to tell the elderly person over and over that no matter how much he or she loves his or her adult child, the elderly person does not deserve to be abused. She goes on to write, "The practitioner as an outsider can also reinterpret as inappropriate or illegal those acts to which the victim has become accustomed" (Tomita, 1990, p. 181).

Calls from potentially abused children can generate special issues. Children are totally dependent on their caregivers and have few life experiences with which to compare their current situation. If they are young children or the abuse began when they were young, events and consequences are likely to be understood from an entirely egocentric position in which the child believes that he or she is the cause of all events and behaviors. It is important to challenge this notion and let the child know that no behavior justifies a beating and that he or she cannot cause the abuse.

If there is serious reason to suspect that a child or adolescent is being abused, clinicians are mandated to report it to the proper authorities. If the parent or caretaker is available, the clinician might consider attempting to speak to him or her; however, clinicians should not do anything that would further endanger the child. A report can be filed without notifying the parents and the child protective services can evaluate the situation in person. In cases of elder abuse and abuse of physically disabled persons, most states also mandate reporting. The issues are somewhat more complicated, however, because, as noted earlier, the competent elderly or disabled person may choose to remain in the abusive environment and refuse all forms of intervention. In such cases, the clinician can, at least, inform the victim of available resources that can be accessed should he or she decide to do so at a later time.

Calls from Battered Women

It has been estimated that as many as one in three women will be battered at some time in their lives (Straus, Gelles, & Steinmetz, 1980). The consequences of battering are often severe or deadly, and crime statistics reveal that two-thirds of deaths from domestic violence are women killed by their male partners and more than one-half of all murders of women are committed by current or former partners (Walker, 1989).

Given the frequency of this phenomenon, it is likely that clinicians will at some time or another receive a call from a battered woman in crisis. Upon receiving a call from a battered woman, the clinician must make an assessment of her safety. If she is in danger or unsure of her current safety, she should be encouraged to call the police. If there are no immediate threats to the caller, the question arises as to how to be of help. This is an important question to ask because it has often been erroneously assumed that when a battered woman makes a call for help, she wants to leave the relationship. Rather, it may be a very complicated relationship that has elements of the traumatic bonding discussed in the previous section. The woman as the victim may have taken on the shame and responsibility for the abuse to protect the relationship with the abuser.

Battered women are frequently not ready to leave an abusive relationship even when they place calls directly to shelters. Loseke and Fenstermaker-Berk (1983) found in a study of 114 calls to a battered women's shelter that less than half desired immediate shelter entry, but, rather, most wanted information and support. Giving information and support can feel inadequate to the clinician who is aware of the potential danger to the caller. The face value of this information and support may seem slight; however, its full value may not be seen in the moment and may not manifest for months or years. Loseke and Fenstermaker-Berk (1983) quote one shelter staff worker as saying of callers, "Some women call and we hear from them four months later. They're just starting to formulate stuff in their minds. We encourage them." Another worker in this same study is quoted as saying, "She may not be ready . . . as difficult as that may be for me to accept. Maybe she has to be beaten one more time" (p. 42). Having appropriate referral information and affirming the caller's basic right to life without violence is important even if it creates no immediate change.

Calls from Rape Victims

Statistics suggest that as many as one in five women will be raped over the course of their lifetime. Thus, it seems likely that many clinicians will be presented, at some time or other, with a crisis call from a rape victim (Koss, 1990). The needs of rape victims change with time. If the rape has just occurred, a supportive, practical, problem-solving approach is recommended. It is important to address questions of safety: Is the rapist gone? Is he likely to return? Is the victim injured? Does she want to be medically examined? Does she want to speak with the police?

The victim may have difficulty labeling her experience as rape if the perpetrator was her husband or a date; so, the beginning phase of helping during such a crisis phone call may be to listen carefully and to discourage minimization and self-blaming. Self-blaming can be especially insidious as cultural scripts encourage this in women (e.g., the rape victim may think such things as I "'must have wanted it' if I wore that dress or if I accepted that ride home"). The issues of self-blame and betrayal associated with date rape seem almost certainly part of the explanation for why there is more psychological distress reported with this type of rape than with acquaintance, stranger, or husband rape (Roth, Wayland, & Woolsey, 1990).

Rape is a trauma that frequently evokes terror, helplessness, and fear for one's physical safety. Like other trauma, it often leads to the development of a posttraumatic stress reaction (Roth, Dye, & Lebowitz, 1988). This stress reaction may manifest as persistent fear, anxiety, depression, diminished self-esteem, intrusive memories, and emotional numbing. These symptoms are often quite severe and, unfortunately, may last for years without intervention. Supportive of these observations is Koss and Burkhart's (1989) study with rape victims, which found that 26% of the victims did not feel recovered even 4 to 6 years after the rape. In fact, only 37% of the rape victims reported feeling psychologically "recovered" several months after the rape. It is important for clinicians to be aware of this research so that when the rape survivor calls in crisis, months or even years after the rape, she can be reassured that she is not alone in her continued struggles toward psychological recovery.

Frazier and Burnett (1994) found that the following coping strategies often work best at facilitating recovery from rape: expressing feelings, seeking social support, and keeping busy. In contrast, withdrawing and staying home are associated with slower recovery. Such information may legitimize the rape victim's need for more formal and informal supports.

Managing the Difficult Caller

Beyond or in addition to being at risk, some callers in crisis may be very difficult to engage due to interfering issues and conflicts. Hotlines whose function it is to counsel callers over the phone are probably more likely to persist with the "difficult" caller than the professional in the emergency room or in private practice when there are no immediate issues of risk to self or other. For one group of difficult-to-manage patients, however, telephone contact may become part of a working treatment plan.

Linehan (1993) has incorporated the use of the telephone into her treatment with patients diagnosed with borderline personality disorder. Treatment plans utilizing the phone for those with borderline personality disorder are important as these patients tend to be in crisis more frequently, have difficulty managing their affect, and use parasuicidal behaviors as a primary (albeit maladaptive) coping mechanism. Parasuicidal behaviors are self-injurious behaviors without suicidal intent. Linehan writes that these behaviors have often been reinforced for the borderline patient by (1) the therapist giving extra time and attention following a self injurious gesture and (2) the behaviors often providing temporary relief from overwhelming affective states.

It is often difficult for the patient to resist these powerful reinforcers of parasuicidal behaviors and therefore the contingencies must be changed. For the patient with a well-established pattern of engaging in parasuicidal behaviors, Linehan (1993) proposes that the therapist not reinforce these behaviors but rather be available and encouraging to patients to increase their distress tolerance and help them to implement the skills they have been learning in therapy. In fact, as a way of discouraging such a pattern, the patient is asked to contract not to call the therapist for 24 hours after making a gesture. If medical attention and hospitalization are necessary, these, of course, are arranged.

Linehan (1993) acknowledges that encouraging patients to use the skills of her dialectical behavior therapy (DBT) is not always easy, especially if they are new to therapy. She writes, "The trap is to avoid conducting (DBT) individual psychotherapy over the phone. This can be difficult because the patient often presents a crisis as irreparable or may be so emotionally aroused that their problem-solving skills are compromised. Rigid thinking and inability to see new solutions are common" (Linehan, 1993, p. 500). She goes on to suggest that the clinician should be careful to interweave empathy and validation of the patient's distress while focusing on practical problem solving.

Borderline patients often have difficulty being direct about their needs and affective states, which creates interpersonal problems. Two of the primary defenses that may obfuscate their real needs are "splitting" and "projective identification." Splitting occurs when all the patient's negative affect is centered on one individual while all his or her good affect is centered on another. Splitting might manifest itself by patients calling an emergency room or crisis clinic if they are angry or hurt by their therapist. The emergency clinician may then be the "good guy" who rescues the patient from his or her crisis through hospitalization or other means. It is important not to get caught up in this conflict and instead to consult with the patient's treatment provider whenever possible. A second defensive maneuver which often creates antagonism between helper and patient is the process of "projective identification." This maneuver may occur when the caller gets the helper in the interaction to feel as powerless and angry as the caller may be. The focus of distress is thus removed from the patient. In a later section, strategies for managing the stresses invoked by these types of callers are explored, as are the stresses involved with other types of difficult callers.

Several authors (King, 1977; Hinson, 1982) catalogued a variety of other difficult-to-engage clients and strategies for working with them, including the "secondhand caller," the "intoxicated caller," the "angry and abusive caller," the "chronic caller," and the "obscene caller."

The *secondhand caller* is one who calls on behalf of someone else. These types of calls can range from a person calling for a friend who is anxious and needs contact with a professional to a boyfriend who calls and states that his girlfriend has overdosed across town in her apartment (King, 1977). In the first situation it is easy enough for the mental health professional to let the individual know that it is a violation of the "anxious" person's privacy to receive an unsolicited call from a mental health professional and that the person himself or herself should be encouraged to initiate the call. The second call is obviously much more difficult and the credibility of the caller needs to be fully explored. The best solution, if possible, is to have the secondhand caller take action on his or her own. This solution may involve having him or her call the police or check on the person he or she is concerned about. The clinician can act as a "coach" and ensure that the needed steps are taken. If it is not possible for the secondhand caller to take action on his or her own, the clinician should, if time permits, get as many other credible sources involved before taking action. In the case of the alleged overdose noted in the previous example, King (1977) reported that the police were sent out only to find a surprised, worried woman reading a book. Had they been more forceful in invading her privacy, it could have been the basis for a suit against the police as well as against the clinician.

Intoxicated callers can be very frustrating for the clinician as they may be unpredictable, impulsive, and have problems listening to and remembering what is being said. It is important not to dismiss suicidal or homicidal statements as just "drunk, empty, talk" as these callers may indeed be at even higher risk for self-injury or injury to others while under the influence (Murphy, 1992). It is often helpful to talk to sober individuals involved with the caller as they may be able to provide more information and if necessary transport the caller to an emergency room.

An especially difficult type of caller is one who is *abusive or sadistic*. These callers may be verbally abusive or provocative presenting with contradictory help-seeking behaviors and help-rejecting behaviors. An example of this type of caller is one who states that he or she is suicidal with a plan but then refuses to talk more about it or give an address. One of the authors (E.J.B.) talked with an intoxicated abusive caller who stated that he was in the process of cutting himself and then proceeded to give a vivid description of the blood "going everywhere, splattering the walls." During this time, he refused to give his address so that help could be sent to his location. Eventually, a trace was put on the call and police and an ambulance were sent to his home. Once they arrived, they found him very intoxicated, with superficial lacerations to his wrist that required no medical attention.

It is important with these types of callers to remain calm and not to engage in an angry struggle for information. It is also sometimes helpful to make explicit the message they are communicating through their behaviors. For example, the clinician might say something such as, "Your behavior is making me feel very powerless and frightened for your safety. I am wondering if that is how you are feeling or have felt at different times in your life." Making their behaviors explicit may help such callers to talk out rather than act out their conflicts.

Other patients talk out their feelings too much and become "chronic callers." A subgroup of chronic callers are lonely and without well-developed social skills. For callers such as these (who just want to "talk"), referral to a hotline or encouragement to find a therapist may be the best solutions. Another subgroup of chronic callers are the seriously mentally ill. Seriously mentally ill callers may be quite delusional, tangential, and difficult to follow. It is important to establish whether this is the caller's baseline of functioning or if, in fact, his or her mental state is decompensating. If there is considerable concern about impaired judgment and ability to care for self, the clinician needs to initiate action to have the individual seen in person. Decisions around whether an in-person evaluation is needed in part depends on the individual's living situation. For example, does he or she live alone or in a staffed group home? If possible, it is always best to get as much information as possible from other sources.

The *obscene caller* is also difficult to manage. These callers may frequently persist in making calls if they feel they are getting a reaction from a mental health professional, even if this reaction is just in the form of hanging up loudly. As a result, it is especially important to remain calm and neutral. Matek (1988) writes, "to engage with the telephone masturbator, who certainly needs help for his deviancy, is to become involved in his sexual scenario" (p. 125). He recommends a brief response that reflects the caller's problem and suggests therapy: "It's so sad that you are confusing sex by yourself with your inability to feel right unless you are intimidating a woman. Please get professional help" (p. 126).

Matek (1988) found that obscene callers may initially present with more legitimate issues. He cautions, however, that even if it is "the kind of question commonly asked by many callers . . . this caller is interested in the woman's voice and her response to him, more than the 'answers' she may provide" (p. 117). As an example, a seemingly distressed male caller asked one of the authors (E.J.B.) for advice on how to respond to his young child who had walked into the bedroom and discovered him having sex with a strange woman. Initially, this call was taken very seriously with the assumption that he was genuinely concerned about his child. It soon became apparent, however, that it was, in fact, an obscene phone call as his breathing became heavy and he alluded to masturbating.

THE STRESS OF MANAGING EMERGENCY PHONE CALLS AND STRATEGIES FOR COPING WITH IT

Emergency phone calls and other difficult calls, as described above, can be very stressful for the clinician. In a survey of crisis telephone counselors, Walfish (1983) presented 58 counselors with 100 clinical telephone interactions and asked them to rate their comfort/discomfort with each. Thirty-two situations were rated as being associated with high levels of discomfort, and Walfish rationally grouped them into seven types of calls. These seven types of calls had to do with the following caller content areas: suicidal ideation, anger toward others (including homicidal ideation), obscenity, physical and sexual abuse, anger toward the counselor, positive feelings toward the counselor, and unresponsiveness on the part of the caller. Although this survey was done with paraprofessional counselors, it seems likely that professional clinicians would also have discomfort with calls of this nature.

In another study with paraprofessional phone workers at a suicide prevention center, Mishara and Giroux (1993) had the participants rate their stress level before, during, and after their shifts. As might be expected, the level of stress during a shift was found to vary with the urgency of the calls received. Adding to the stress during the most urgent call was the total duration of the calls received during the shift and the absence of colleagues in the intervention room during the call. The authors suggested that it would be of interest to compare their results with those of professionals who work with suicidal patients. They recommended limiting the number and total length of calls taken by a single worker and making sure that there are coworkers present who can provide advice and support.

Often, one of the biggest challenges in coping with emergency phone calls (as with any emergency) is dealing with one's own feelings. Tapp et al. (1974) made this point graphically in regard to the caller who has hurt or abused a child, but, of course, it applies more generally to feelings aroused by callers who are suicidal or homicidal, obscene, and so on. Pope and Tabachnick (1993) indicated how such patients can elicit feelings of anxiety, fear, anger, hatred, as well as other feelings in their treating clinicians. It is clearly important for the clinician to acknowledge these feelings and to use them to inform his or her response.

As noted in the section on the management of difficult callers, to have some established guidelines for responding to particular types of callers (e.g., the abusive or obscene caller) can be helpful. Preparation can reduce feelings of helplessness. Beyond this, Mishara and Giroux (1993) found that those study subjects who were able to manage the stress of crisis calls better were able to attain a level of detachment which limited their sense of personal involvement and personal responsibility. Having coworkers available during calls and/or processing the calls afterwards can help one attain this sort of objectivity.

As stated at the outset of this chapter, emergency phone calls can be emotion-laden and time-consuming. The stress of managing them has been underappreciated in the literature that relates to the professional clinician. For the reasons articulated throughout this chapter, there seems to be a need for further study and research in this area of clinical practice.

ACKNOWLEDGMENTS

We wish to thank Christine Pierce for a computer-assisted literature search for this chapter and Lisa Fisher, PhD, for her thoughtful review of this chapter.

REFERENCES

Berman, A. (Ed.). (1991). Case consultation: New technologies and telephone hotlines. *Suicide and Life-Threatening Behavior, 21,* 407–413.

Berman, A., & Cohen-Sandler, R. (1982). Suicide and the standard of care: Optimal vs. acceptable. *Suicide and Life-Threatening Behavior, 12,* 114–122.

Burrell, B., Thompson, B., & Sexton, D. (1994). Predicting child abuse potential across family types. *Child Abuse and Neglect, 18,* 1039–1049.

Coyne, A., Reichman, W., & Berbig, L. (1993). The relationship between dementia and elder abuse. *American Journal of Psychiatry, 150*(4), 643–646.

Dale, J. (1995). Development of telephone advice in A&E: Establishing the views of staff. *Nursing Standard, 9,* 28–31.

Dixon, M., & Burns, J. (1974). Crisis theory, active learning and the training of telephone crisis volunteers. *Journal of Community Psychology, 2,* 120–125.

Echterling, L., & Hartsough, D. (1989). Phases of helping in successful crisis telephone calls. *Journal of Community Psychology, 17,* 249–257.

Echterling, L., Hartsough, D., & Zarle, T. (1980). Testing a model for the process of telephone crisis intervention. *American Journal of Community Psychology, 8,* 715–725.

Frankish, C. J. (1994). Crisis centers and their role in treatment: Suicide prevention versus health promotion. *Death Studies, 18,* 327–339.

Frazier, P., & Burnett, J. (1994). Immediate coping strategies among rape victims. *Journal of Counseling and Development, 72,* 633–639.

Gerson, S., & Bassuk, E. (1980). Psychiatric emergencies: An overview. *American Journal of Psychiatry, 137,* 1–11.

Gilmore, B. (1984). The telephone in psychiatric emergencies. In E. Bassuk & A. Birk (Eds.), *Emergency psychiatry: Concepts, methods, and practices* (pp. 407–415). New York: Plenum Press.

Goldstein, R. (1986). Legal liabilities of long-distance intervention. *American Journal of Psychiatry, 143,* 1202.

Graham, D., Rawlings, E., Ihms, K., Latimer, D., Foliano, J., Thompson, A., Suttman, K., Farrington, M., & Hacker, R. (1995). A scale for identifying "Stockholm Syndrome" reactions in young dating women: Factor structure, reliability, and validity. *Violence and Victims, 10,* 3–22.

Gray, B., Nida, R., & Coonfield, T. (1976). Empathic listening test: An instrument for the selection and training of telephone crisis workers. *Journal of Community Psychology, 4,* 199–205.

Haas, L., Benedict, J., & Kobos, J. (1996). Psychotherapy by telephone: Risks and benefits for psychologists and consumers. *Professional Psychology: Research and Practice, 27,* 154–160.

Hilliard, J. (1990). *Manual of clinical emergency psychiatry.* Washington, DC: American Psychiatric Press.

Hinson, J. (1982). Strategies for suicide intervention by telephone. *Suicide and Life-Threatening Behavior, 12*(3), 176–184.

Kempe, C., & Helfer, R. (1972). *Helping the battered child and his family.* Philadelphia: J.B. Lippincott.

King, G. (1977). An evaluation of the effectiveness of a telephone counseling center. *American Journal of Community Psychology, 5*(1), 75–83.

Koss, M. (1990). The women's mental health research agenda: Violence against women. *American Psychologist, 45,* 374–380.

Koss, M., & Burkhart, B. (1989). A conceptual analysis of rape victimization. *Psychology of Women Quarterly, 9,* 193–212.

Lachs, M., & Pillemer, K. (1995). Abuse and neglect of elderly persons. *New England Journal of Medicine, 332*(7), 437–443.

Linehan, M. (1993). *Cognitive-behavioral treatment of borderline personality disorder.* New York: Guilford Press.

Loseke, D., & Fenstermaker-Berk, S. (1983). The work of shelters: Battered women and initial calls for help. *Victimology: An International Journal, 7,* 35–48.

Matek, O. (1988). Obscene phone callers. Special Issue: The sexually unusual: Guide to understanding and helping. *Journal of Social Work and Human Sexuality, 7*(1), 113–130.

Miller, H., Coombs, D., Leeper, J., & Barton, S. (1984). An analysis of the effects of suicide prevention facilities on suicide rates in the United States. *American Journal of Public Health, 74,* 340–343.

Mishara, B., & Daigle, M. (1992, September). The effectiveness of telephone interventions by suicide prevention centres. *Canada's Mental Health,* 24–29.

Mishara, B., & Giroux, G. (1993). The relationship between coping strategies and perceived stress in telephone volunteers at a suicide prevention center. *Suicide and Life-Threatening Behavior, 23*(3), 221–229.

Murphy, G. (1992). *Suicide in alcoholism.* New York: Oxford University Press.

Pope, K., & Tabachnick, B. (1993). Therapists' anger, hate, fear, and sexual feelings: National survey of therapist responses, client characteristics, critical events, formal complaints, and training. *Professional Psychology: Research and Practice, 24*(2), 142–152.

Resnik, H. L. P. (1971). Criteria for defining community mental health centers' emergency services. *Bulletin of Suicidology, 8,* 4–6.

Robertson, J. (1988). *Psychiatric malpractice: Liability of mental health professionals.* New York: Wiley.

Rosenbaum, A., & Calhoun, J. (1977). The use of the telephone hotline in crisis intervention: A review. *Journal of Community Psychology, 5,* 325–339.

Roth, S., Dye, E., & Lebowitz, L. (1988). Group therapy for sexual assault victims. *Psychotherapy, 25,* 82–93.

Roth, S., Wayland, K., & Woolsey, M. (1990). Victimization, history, and victim-assailant relationships as factors in recovery from sexual assault. *Journal of Traumatic Stress, 3*(1), 169–180.

Simon, R. (1987). *Clinical psychiatry and the law.* Washington, DC: American Psychiatric Press.

Singh, A., & Brown, J. (1973). Suicide prevention: Review and evaluation. *Canadian Psychiatric Association Journal, 18,* 117–121.

Slaikeu, K., & Leff-Simon, S. (1990). Crisis intervention by telephone. In K. Slaikeu (Ed.), *Crisis intervention: A handbook for practice and research.* Boston: Allyn & Bacon.

Stein, D., & Lambert, M. (1984). Telephone counseling and crisis intervention: A review. *American Journal of Community Psychology, 12,* 101–126.

Straus, M., Gelles, R., & Steinmetz, S. (1980). Societal change in family violence from 1975 to 1985 as revealed by two national surveys. *Journal of Marriage and the Family, 48,* 465–479.

Tapp, J., Ryken, V., & Kaltwasser, C. (1974). Counseling the abusing parent by telephone. *Crisis Intervention, 5,* 27–37.

Teare, J., Garrett, C., Coughlin, D., Shanahan, D., & Daly, D. (1995). America's children in crisis: Adolescents' requests for support from a national telephone hotline. *Journal of Applied Developmental Psychology, 16,* 21–33.

Tekavcic-Grad, O., Farberow, N., Zavasnik, A., Mocnik, M., & Korenjak, R. (1988). Comparison of the two telephone crisis lines in Los Angeles (USA) and in Ljubljana (Yugoslavia). *Crisis, 9,* 146–157.

Tomita, S. (1990). The denial of elder mistreatment by victims and abusers: The application of neutralization theory. *Violence and Victims, 5,* 171–184.

Vida, S. (1994). An update on elder abuse and neglect. *Canadian Journal of Psychiatry, 39*(Suppl. 1), 534–540.

Walfish, S. (1983). Crisis telephone counselors' views of clinical interaction situations. *Community Mental Health Journal, 19*(3), 219–226.

Walker, L. (1989). Psychology and violence against women. *American Psychologist, 44,* 695–702.

Wellin, E., Slesinger, D., & Hollister, C. (1987). Psychiatric emergency services: Evolution, adaptation, and proliferation. *Social Science and Medicine, 24,* 475–482.

Wheeler, S. (1989). ED telephone triage: Lessons learned from unusual calls. *Journal of Emergency Nursing, 15*(6), 481–487.

Willett, D. (1977). Medicine by telephone, continued: A legal opinion. *Modern Medicine, 45,* 73, 77.

PART III

RISK MANAGEMENT IN PSYCHOLOGICAL EMERGENCIES

CHAPTER 9

RISK MANAGEMENT WITH THE SUICIDAL PATIENT

BRUCE BONGAR
SHEILA GREANEY
NICO PERUZZI

The average professional psychologist involved in direct patient care has a better than 20% chance of losing a patient to suicide at some time during his or her professional career (Chemtob, Hamada, Bauer, Torigoe, & Kinney, 1988). More than 50% of psychiatrists will lose a patient to suicide (Chemtob, Hamada, Bauer, Kinney, & Torigoe, 1988). As the possibility of a patient's suicide is not a rare event in psychological practice, it must be seen as a real occupational hazard for those clinicians involved in direct patient care (Chemtob, Hamada, Bauer, Torigoe, & Kinney, 1988). The hazard not only involves the threat of a malpractice action but also includes the intense emotional toll that a patient's suicide can wreak on the survivors (including the patient's clinician).

Currently, malpractice actions against clinicians for the death of a patient are relatively rare, though they are increasing in frequency. The American Psychological Association's Insurance Trust (APAIT) provided summary data that indicate that malpractice related to the suicide of a patient was the sixth most frequent claim brought against psychologists but ranked second in the percentage of total costs (5.4% of the claims and 10% of the costs) (APAIT Claims Frequency, personal communication, May 1, 1990). However, as clinicians (e.g., psychologists and social workers) seek expanded professional privileges, such as hospital staff membership and admission and discharge privileges, they find themselves exposed to many of the same malpractice liabilities as our colleagues in psychiatry (Gutheil & Appelbaum, 1982). In malpractice actions for the death of a patient, two fundamental criteria are used in the evaluation of negligence in the standard of care, namely the ability to foresee and issue of causation. Given that current case law provides a limited view of the total malpractice picture, it is difficult to discern clear legal guidelines for what constitutes an adequate standard of care for the suicidal patient (Harris, 1988). Hence, clinicians should anticipate that there may be a conflict between the clinical and legal standards of care (Bongar, 1991). We believe that the best response to this dilemma is a sound risk management approach, as the assessment and management of a suicidal patient is one of the most complex and challenging clinical tasks.

To develop a professionally sound risk management approach when working with the suicidal patient, the clinician must understand legal perspectives of suicide, must know how the law defines negligence and what are the common causes of malpractice actions, and must be knowledgeable about and practice the duty to prevent suicide through the use of reasonable care and skill. This chapter begins with a review of the first two tasks, and expands on the third by explaining the utility of documentation and consultation as key activities supporting all risk-management activities.

LEGAL PERSPECTIVES OF SUICIDE

Simon (1988) reported that the law most commonly interjects into health care practice when a patient sues a practitioner for malpractice. Hence, we believe that effective risk management and high-quality clinical care in professional practice must demonstrate a basic working knowledge of the legal system and an understanding of contemporary legal views on standards of care. As recently as the 1970s the incidence of lawsuits against mental health professionals was quite low, especially when compared to what the courts regard as other medical specialties (Robertson, 1988). Although a review of case law (cases that go to trial and to appeal) indicates that the majority of cases that go to trial deal with issues of inpatient management and treatment (Bongar, 1991; Litman, 1982), outpatient therapists today may also be the likely targets of a suit (Bongar, Maris, Berman, & Litman, 1992).

Lawsuits over suicide usually fall into one of three legal fact patterns: (1) psychotherapists or institutions may be sued when an inpatient commits suicide, with survivors claiming that the facility failed to provide adequate care and supervision; (2) a recently released patient commits suicide; or (3) an outpatient commits suicide (VandeCreek, Knapp, & Herzog, 1987). Both Perr (1979) and Meyer, Landis, and Hays (1988) pointed out that mental health clinicians carry a tremendous legal burden when it comes to a patient's suicide becasue, simply stated, the clinician is asked to be responsible for someone else's behavior. Although generally the law does not hold any person responsible for acts of another, suicidal and other self-destructive acts represent a clear exception.

The duty of therapists to exercise adequate care and skill in diagnosing suicidality is well established (e.g., *Meier v. Ross General Hospital,* 1968). When the risk of self-injurious behavior is identified, an additional duty to take adequate precautions arises (*Abille v. United States,* 1980; *Pisel v. Stamford Hospital,* 1980). When clinicians fail to meet these responsibilities, they may be held liable for injuries that result (Meyer et al., 1988).

Further obscuring the issue is a discrepancy in clinical and legal philosophies: Psychotherapists "on the one hand are told . . . not to hospitalize unless the need is blatantly clear; on the other, they are threatened with legal liability if they do not do so and thus minimize a patient's ability to kill himself" (Perr, 1979, p. 91).

Thus, many mental health practitioners are reluctant to work with suicidal patients for fear of being sued if the patient takes his or her own life. In fact, Bernstein, Feldberg, and Brown (1991) reported that 59% of psychology training clinics do not provide service to suicidal clients, though decisions by courts have usually maintained that the clinician is not liable if he or she has maintained adequate care of his or her patient (Kermani, 1982). In both inpatient and outpatient settings, legal liability for a patient's suicide clusters into three general categories: (1) failure to properly assess the potential and severity of suicide risk, (2) failure to use reasonable treatment interventions and precautions, and (3) failure to reasonably carry out treatment (Simon, 1992). Also, Simon (1992) noted, "In all three, liability is fundamentally based on a clinician's failure to act reasonably to provide appropriate care to the patient. What is reasonable treatment depends on what is likely to happen with the patient. Foreseeability of suicide is often a central issue in patient suicides that lead to wrongful death or personal injury lawsuits. Was there sufficient evidence to suggest to a reasonable clinician, making a reasonable assessment, that suicide was foreseeable?" (pp. 40–41).

A review of case law indicates that a number of legal theories are brought into play in imposing liability on mental health professionals (Robertson, 1988).

Failure to Properly Diagnose

If the clinician had taken ordinary and accepted care in making a diagnosis, he or she would have ascertained that the patient was suicidal (see *Dillman v. Hellman,* 1973).

At the present time, much of the case law on suicide is based on claims that allege liability for a misdiagnosis or lack of prediction of the risk of suicide (Swenson, 1986; VandeCreek et al., 1987). Most suits brought on this basis are directed against hospitals and institutions for clinical care and involve either inpatients or recently discharged patients (Rachlin, 1984). However, the potential certainly exists for an increase in suits involving outpatient care. Perr (1985), in his review of suicide litigation and risk management, pointed to a study of completed suicide in Veterans Administration patients. This study found that 65% of the suicides occurred outside the hospital (Farberow, 1981).

Failure to Take Adequate Protective Measures

The clinician must take adequate precautions against patient suicide, consistent with accepted psychotherapeutic practices and based on his or her knowledge and assessment of the patient (see *Bellah v. Greenson*, 1978; *Dimitrijevic v. Chicago Wesley Memorial Hospital*, 1968; *Meier v. Ross General Hospital*, 1968; *Topel v. Long Island Jewish Medical Center*, 1981).

Both Swenson (1986) and VandeCreek and Knapp (1989) cited *Dinnerstein v. United States* (1973). In this case, clinicians were held liable when a treatment plan overlooked or neglected the patient's suicidal tendencies. VandeCreek and Knapp (1989) also pointed out that courts will generally not find a psychotherapist liable when the patient's suicide attempt was not foreseeable.

The courts tend to be less stringent in evaluating cases of outpatient suicide in the absence of clear signs of foreseeability because of to the obvious increased difficulty in controlling the patient's behavior (Fremouw, de Perczel, & Ellis, 1990; Simon, 1988). The case law seems to put forward the basic rule that the clinician needs to recognize the risk of suicide and to balance appropriately the risk of suicide with the benefits of greater control through hospitalization (Simon, 1987, 1988, 1992). In addition, VandeCreek and Knapp (1983) noted that although only a few cases deal with outpatient suicide, the principles are the same as for inpatient cases. Thus, in both venues, clinicians must use reasonable care in the comprehensive assessment of suicidal intent and in the development and implementation of the treatment plan. Although the courts have not imposed a *Tarasoff*-type duty to warn relatives of potential suicide risk (see *Bellah v. Greenson*, 1978), it remains one of the options for action clinicians should consider seriously when a patient presents as at risk (Fremouw et al., 1990). Finally, when a suicide attempt is foreseeable, the treatment provided must be consistent with professional standards (VandeCreek & Knapp, 1983).

Early Release of Patient

A clinician may be found liable for the death of a patient if the release from the hospital is negligent and not a valid exercise in professional judgment (Robertson, 1988). Fremouw et al. (1990) pointed out that when a clinician makes a reasonable assessment of danger and believes that there is no longer a risk, he or she will not usually be held liable for the postdischarge death of a patient.

Failure to Commit

One must ask whether the clinician took a complete history and made a thorough examination of the patient's status, then exercised sound judgment in the decision to commit or not to commit the patient (Robertson, 1988). The more "obvious the suicidal intent, the greater will be the practitioner's liability" for his or her failure to account for this elevated risk in the treatment plan (VandeCreek & Knapp, 1983, p. 276).

Liability of Hospitals

The malpractice law regarding hospitals is a complex and ever-changing field and a review of the liability of hospitals is beyond the scope of this chapter (for more information, see Bongar, Maris, Berman, Litman, & Silverman, 1993; Silverman, Berman, Bongar, Litman, & Maris, 1994). However, as VandeCreek and Knapp (1983) underscored, psychotherapists should know that malpractice actions for inpatient suicides can be directed against the therapist, the hospital, or both. A wide net of legal liability is often cast, holding anyone and everyone involved responsible. An important point here is that malpractice actions can be brought against psychiatrists or psychologists within the hospital setting, provided they have staff or hospital privileges.

The duty of a hospital can best be defined as the generally accepted standard of using reasonable care in the treatment of the patient (Robertson, 1988). "If however, the hospital is on notice that a patient has suicidal tendencies, then the hospital also assumes the duty of safe guarding the patient from self-inflicted injury or death" (p. 193). Thus, as is the case for judging the behavior of the practitioner, the issue of foreseeability is crucial. Even when the patient is under the care of a private clinician, the hospital staff must still perform the proper evaluation and observation (and must take affirmative action if necessary).

Robertson (1988) stated that hospitals generally have not been held liable when a physician has determined that the patient was under adequate surveillance. Nor have hospitals been found liable when proper procedures were followed. Robertson (1988) further noted that "psychiatric hospitals can be found liable when adequate standards for the protection of patients were not followed" (p. 197?, referring practitioners on the point to the Joint Commission on Accreditation of Hospitals guidelines for nursing and safety standards.

The courts, in considering malpractice actions against hospitals, have slowly moved the standard of liability away from an earlier "custodial model" to more of an "open door" model (VandeCreek & Knapp, 1983). In the earlier custodial model, the hospital was to correctly diagnose suicidal intentions and then to observe the patient so closely that an attempt could not be made. Yet, in recent years, hospitals have implemented so-called open-door policies, which decrease the level of restrictions and encourage patients to assume more responsibility for their own behavior. The courts have observed such changes in psychotherapeutic policies, recognizing that "some of the traditional policies harmed patients because they engendered feelings of helplessness" (VandeCreek & Knapp, 1983, p. 277).

Indeed, VandeCreek and Knapp (1983) noted that courts no longer require strict observation in all suicide cases: "The law and modern psychiatry have now both come to the conclusion that an overly restrictive environment can be as destructive as an overly permissive one. . . . Now the courts recognized that the therapist must balance the benefits of treatment against the risks of freedom." (p. 277).

Yet, as Gutheil (1990) noted, hospitalization also has its drawbacks. Although laypersons may perceive it (and plaintiffs attorneys may present it) as a panacea, experienced clinicians are aware that a psychiatric hospitalization presents some clear risks, including regression, fostering dependency, loss of time from work or studies, and severe stigma.

In summary, clinicians mindful of maintaining a coherent treatment philosophy with their suicidal patients are protected to the extent that they demonstrate their best professional judgment in assessing the therapeutic risks of freedom. They also must carefully assess decisions (their own and those of others) to reduce the level of supervision of suicidal patients, whether those decisions involve discharge, transfer, decision to commit, or other actions (VandeCreek & Knapp, 1983). However, it is critical to remember that when a "patient is dangerously suicidal, hospitalization and close supervision are clearly indicated—an 'open door' policy does not mean an open window policy for highly suicidal patients" (p. 77).

Abandonment

Once a professional relationship is established, a clinician must provide treatment until the relationship is properly terminated. Abandonment can be overt or implied, for example, by a failure to be available, or to monitor the patient adequately. VandeCreek and Knapp (1983) noted that the therapeutic relationship may not be terminated by the therapist unless treatment is no longer necessary, or the relationship is terminated by the patient, or suitable notice is given by the therapist that gives the patient adequate time to engage another therapist. Typically, abandonment is based on two theories:

1. If a therapist errs in his judgment that treatment is no longer needed, he may be liable for negligence under the criteria for malpractice. Usually this is decided by expert witnesses after the fact.
2. If a therapist willfully terminates or withholds treatment knowing that further care is needed or that a referral is indicated, he may be held liable for intentional abandonment.

The circumstances under which liability could be determined are fairly explicit, especially if a crisis occurs or is foreseeable. Clinicians face charges of abandonment when they fail to provide patients with a way of contacting them after hours, between sessions, when on vacation, on leave, and so forth (with being on vacation or leave requiring that the therapist provide adequate coverage). Also, reasonable contact must be maintained with hospitalized patients (Simon, 1988; VandeCreek & Knapp, 1983).

Only if there is not an emergency or threatened crisis (e.g., threatened suicide or danger to the public) may a therapist safely terminate a patient by "giving reasonable notice, assisting the patient in finding another therapist, insuring that appropriate records are transferred to the new therapist, as requested by the patient" (Simon, 1988, pp. 11–12).

NEGLIGENCE AND MALPRACTICE

The key issue underlying malpractice actions against mental health professionals is the concept of negligence (Bongar, 1991; Robertson, 1988; Simon, 1988). Simon (1988) pointed out that negligence on the part of a mental health professional can be "described as doing something which he or she should not have done [commission] or omitting something which he or she should have done [omission]" (p. 3). The fact that a mental health professional's act is a consequence of carelessness or ignorance, rather than willfully committed, does not excuse the clinician from liability (Robertson, 1988; Simon, 1988). The law "presumes and holds all practitioners and psychotherapists to a standard of reasonable care when dealing with patients" (Robertson, 1988, p. 7).

Sadoff (cited in Rachlin, 1984) described four essential legal elements to establish negligence. These elements "may be remembered by the 4D mnemonic: Dereliction of—Duty—Directly causing—Damages" (p. 303). To prevail against a clinician in a malpractice action, the plaintiff must prove by a preponderance of evidence that:

1. There was a clinician–patient relationship that created a duty of care.
2. The clinician breached the duty of care that was owed to the patient.
3. The patient was damaged.
4. The damage was proximately caused by the clinician's negligence (Simon, 1992, p. 41).

The simple fact that the patient was receiving any psychological treatment creates a relation between the two parties and therefore a legal duty of care. In determining whether or not a patient was damaged, a key issue is whether, and with what degree of medical certainty, the suicide or suicide attempt could have been foreseen or predicted (Maris, Berman, Maltsberger, & Yufit, 1992). However, because suicide is a rare event, the accurate prediction of suicide is extremely difficult and results most often in false, not true, positives (Pokorny, 1983). At issue is the relative benefit of a standard of care that necessitates great health care expense and yet provides a large number of false positives. Because suicide is a multifaceted, multicausal product (Shneidman, 1985), it is extremely difficult to determine whether a therapist's actions or failures to act, decisions, and so forth, actually caused a suicide.

Bongar et al. (1992) noted that "suicide prevention is an ideal, that the responsibility of the clinician or institution is to follow acceptable standards of care, and that these standards of care are dynamic and ever changing. Clinicians must understand that there is no magical 'right' way to act in every clinical situation and that for every decision in clinical practice there are always potential risks and benefits" (pp. 459–460).

The threat of litigation exacerbates the burden that a patient's death creates for the clinician (Rachlin, 1984). In a general clinical practice setting, the threat of patient suicide is always a possibility. Berman (1986) reported that one in six completers are in therapy, and close to 50% of all completers have a history of psychotherapeutic treatment. In addition, a recent review of risk assessment and treatment procedures for suicidal patients estimates that 10% to 15% of patients with major psychiatric disorders (i.e., affective disorder, substance abuse, and schizophrenia) will die by suicide. This review asserted unequivocally that the assessment and diminution of suicide potential among psychiatric patients should be a task of the highest priority for mental health professions (Brent, Kupfer, Bromet, & Dew, 1988).

Malpractice actions against mental health professionals are also "plagued by such issues as what constitutes an acceptable level of care in suicide treatment and who is qualified as an expert witness to testify to the reasonableness of deviations from that standard" (Berman & Cohen-Sandler, 1983, p. 6). Furthermore, mental health and legal professionals have not yet been able to resolve such basic issues as "who legitimately may decide what constitutes standard or acceptable care in the treatment of suicidal patients, and what level of quality should be considered standard; that is, ought we to demand some minimum degree of care or, instead, more optimal care?" (Berman & Cohen-Sandler, 1982, p. 115).

Moreover, the pivotal elements in most cases of malpractice and suicide are the twin issues of the ability to foresee and causation (Bongar, Peterson, Harris, & Aissis, 1989; Perr, 1979, 1988; Rachlin, 1984; Simon, 1988; VandeCreek & Knapp, 1989; VandeCreek et al., 1987). Generally, as the courts have grappled with these two important issues in cases of suicide (Simon, 1988), their deliberations have focused specifically on whether the clinician should have predicted the suicide and whether there was sufficient evidence for an identifiable risk of harm. Ultimately, the clinician and/or the institution will be judged according to whether enough was done to protect the patient (VandeCreek et al., 1987). Negligence is typically indicated only when, based on expert testimony, the treatment or assessment of the patient was found to be unreasonable (Berman & Cohen-Sandler, 1982). Berman and Cohen-Sander (1982) noted that although failures in treatment are often blamed on the patient, mental health professionals often play a significant role in the suicidal deaths of their patients.

Demonstrated negligence requires evidence that the patient was clearly iden-tifiable as suicidal, based on the recognized criteria used by most clinicians of the same training (Meyer et al., 1988).

THE STANDARD OF THE "REASONABLE AND PRUDENT PRACTITIONER"

Up to the present, the courts have not been consistent in defining a standard of care for the suicidal patient (Bongar, 1991). What then are some options for care that are available to the reasonable and prudent clinician who assesses and treats suicidal patients?

Rachlin (1984) made several recommendations designed to minimize the risk of being found negligent as a result of a patient's suicide. These included careful documentation of decisions to grant patients increased freedom, detail-ing the specifics of suicide precautions, consultation from supervisors or col-leagues, and outreach to survivors. There will always be areas of indecision— "gray" areas where clinicians will disagree, resulting in differences of opinion among both treating clinicians and expert witnesses (Sadoff, 1985). "A key element (in the context of the legal system that provides confusing or even con-tradictory rules) has been attributing to professional people the capacity to pre-dict and control the behavior of the mentally ill" (Perr, 1988, p. 4). Although a patient's suicide is not always preventable, the only course for clinicians is to integrate appropriate guidelines within our treatment plans, in good faith that we will prevail in convincing the court that no liability need be attached to the patient's demise.

Bongar et al. (1992), in accord with Berman and Cohen-Sandler (1982), asserted that it is the duty of a clinician or institution to prevent suicide through the use of reasonable care and skill.

> "Reasonable" is considered by law to be the "average standard of the profession"—"the degree of learning, skill, and experience which ordi-narily is possessed by others of the same profession" (American Jurispru-dence, 1981) . . .the average standard is essentially defined by the legal system through decisions rendered in malpractice cases, which, in turn, determine completely the liability of the clinician who treats suicidal pa-tients. (p. 116)

Thus, the suicidal patient presents great challenges for the clinician who hopes to provide quality care while maintaining a sound risk management approach. Various authors have provided more recent guidelines for achieving this bal-ance. Jobes and Berman (1993) discussed clinical risk management in outpa-tient settings, Bongar et al. (1992) reviewed outpatient standards of care, Bongar et al. (1993) and Silverman et al. (1994) provided inpatient standards of care, and Maltsberger (1994) presented important forensic questions to be asked before the discharge of a patient with a chronically suicidal personality disorder. Cantor and McDermott (1994) approached the problem of the chronically suicidal patient from a legally defensive position. Common to these approaches is an emphasis on the use of documentation and consultation. In the sections that follow, we focus our discussion on these twin "pillars of liability prevention" (Appelbaum & Gutheil, 1991, p. 201).

Documentation

Jobes and Berman (1993) cogently operationalized an approach to providing adequate documentation. These authors advocated that beyond the ongoing use of progress notes, structured forms that track suicide status should be used. Their "Suicide Status Form (SSF) can be used to provide detailed and specific assessment and treatment plan data relevant to suicide as well as key information should there be an emergency" (p. 94). These authors added a Suicide Assessment Slip, filled out after each session, "which addresses whether the patient continues to have suicidal thoughts and feelings and is able to agree to maintain his or her safety" (p. 94). These procedures provide ongoing tracking, help maintain clinical responsibility and accountability, and lend structural guidance to risk assessments (Jobes & Berman, 1993).

Cantor and McDermott (1994) emphasized the importance of documenting the patient's competency to consent to treatment. In the event of a patient's suicide, as long as the clinician followed all proper standards of care, this documentation places proximate cause of death on the independent action of the patient.

Whereas many authors have put forth guidelines for adequate documentation, little empirical research exists showing whether or not clinicians have read and are implementing these guidelines. Malone, Szanto, Corbitt, and Mann (1995) examined the clinical management of patients at high risk for suicide (those patients with a diagnosis of major depressive episode). Documentation in clinical assessments was compared to a concurrently and independently completed research assessment. In general, the documentation of clinicians was inferior to research assessments. Clinicians "failed to document adequately the presence of a lifetime history of a suicide attempt in 24% of cases on admission and in 28% of cases in the discharge summary" (p. 1604). Clinicians also reported fewer lifetime attempts than the research assessment and often forgot to document a family history of suicidal behavior. Malone et al. (1995) found that the adequacy of assessment increased under the following circumstances: higher lethality attempts, low number of attempts, no Axis II borderline personality disorder diagnosis, higher level of suicidal ideation in the week before admission, more recent suicide attempt, higher number of previous depressive episodes, and longer hospital stay. In conclusion, these authors advocated the use of semistructured clinical interviews relevant to suicidal behavior (such as the Scale for Suicidal Ideation and the Suicidal Intent Scale), emphasized that documentation must occur before intervention and management are possible, and specified that the discharge summary should include "a comprehensive assessment of long- and short-term indicators of risk of suicide, and . . . past and recent suicidal behavior and ideation" (Malone et al., 1995, pp. 1604–1605).

Consultation

Shneidman (1981) noted that there is almost no instance in the clinician's professional life when consultation with a colleague is more important than when dealing with the suicidal patient. Appelbaum and Gutheil (1991) noted that even a brief and informal consultation with a senior clinician when at a treatment impasse represents a "biopsy of the standard of care" (p. 201). In the discussion that follows, we provide guidelines for consultation when working with the suicidal patient.

Various authors suggest that clinicians are reluctant to obtain second opinions because of a lack of clear, professional guidelines in the area regarding confidentiality and informed consent procedures (Applebaum & Gutheil, 1991; Bongar, 1991; Kapp, 1987). A study by Jobes, Eyman, and Yufit (1991) confirmed this theory, finding that only 27% of clinicians surveyed routinely sought consultation to assist in their assessment of suicidality.

In a review of this area, Clayton and Bongar (1994) discovered that "for both psychologists and physicians, informal peer or peer group consultation, when available, is the most widely valued and used method of consultation" (p. 46). Yet, other authors have found that, among psychologists, this informal consultation is often less useful or effective than formal consultation for managing risky therapeutic situations (Bongar, 1991; Stromberg et al., 1988). Thus, although clinicians may find informal peer consultation to be convenient, "they must be aware that it does not necessarily ensure better decisions, more effective practice, or protection from legal or ethical complaints" (Clayton & Bongar, 1994, p. 46).

Bongar (1991) believed that, for psychologists to ensure legal protection in situations of risk or serious clinical uncertainty, the clinician's consultations should always be formal in nature (as indicated by a written agreement of service, signed by both parties, and formal documentation in the chart). The action of documenting an appropriate consultation in the chart is vital in providing quality care, and in providing evidence of clinical standards upon which legal findings may turn (Applebaum & Gutheil, 1991; Bongar, 1991; Simon, 1992; Stromberg et al., 1988).

Bongar (1991) operationalized a consultation model that seeks to maximize clinical, legal, and ethical standards of care for suicidal patients. The model suggested first emphasizes the importance of developing a strong therapeutic alliance, facilitated via informed consent procedures at treatment initiation. Bongar (1991) stated that the informed consent procedure should begin an "ongoing process of information-giving and collaboration" with the client (p. 177). By involving patients and their families, when appropriate, as "collaborative risk management partners" (Bongar, 1991, p. 177), cooperation with treatment is improved, the protective net is widened, responses to treatment are more closely monitored, and the quality and quantity of available data are improved.

In addition, the model emphasizes the importance of retaining appropriate consultants. These consultants should be senior or expert in the field, have forensic experience, or both. They should be retained on a regular basis for formal (as opposed to informal) consultation. That is, "In order for the consultation to be more forensically effective it must be a formal one, one where the psychologist and the consultant provide notes for the written record and where both consultant and psychologist of record formally acknowledge that a consultant relationship is in effect" (Bongar, 1991, p. 185). This written record is necessary for the consultation to be legally recognized and unquestioned (Applebaum & Gutheil, 1991; Bongar, 1991). Finally, consultants should be given sufficient information to provide reasonable advice.

Bongar (1991) further provided a detailed list of questions the consultant should be asked to cover when the clinical situation is one of risk, uncertainty, or danger. These include reviewing:

1. the overall management of the case, specific treatment issues, uncertainties in the assessment of elevated risk or in diagnosis. This can include a review of the mental status examination, history, information from significant others, the results of any psychological tests and data from risk estimators, suicide lethality scales, and so forth. The psychologist's formulation of the patient's [DSM-IV] diagnosis, together with any other specific psychotherapeutic formulations, clinical assessments, and evaluation of any special treatment and management issues (e.g., comorbidity of alcohol/substance abuse, physical illness, etc.) should also be reviewed.

2. issues of managing the patient with chronically suicidal behavior, violent behavior, patient dependency, patient hostility and manipulation, toxic interpersonal matrices, lack of psychosocial supports, and the patient's competency to participate in treatment decisions. An assessment of the quality of the therapeutic alliance and the patient's particular response to the psychologist and to the course of treatment (e.g., intense negative or positive transference, etc.) should also be discussed.

3. the psychologist's own feelings about the progress of treatment and feelings toward the patient (e.g., the psychologist's own feelings of fear, incompetency, anxiety, helplessness, or even anger) and any negative therapeutic reactions such as countertransference, and therapist burnout.

4. the advisability of using medication, the need for additional medical evaluation (e.g., any uncertainties as to organicity or neurological complications), or both. Reevaluation of any current medications that the patient is taking (e.g., effectiveness, compliance in taking medication, side-effects, polypharmacy) should be included in this review of medication options.

5. the indications and contraindications for hospitalization. Some considerations should be what community crisis intervention resources are available for the patient with few psychosocial supports, day treatment options, emergency and backup arrangements and resources, and planning for the psychologist's absences.

6. indications and contraindications for family and group treatment. This discussion should include the possible use of other types of psychotherapy and somatic interventions, and questions on the status of and progress in the integration of multiple therapeutic techniques.

7. the psychologist's assessment criteria for evaluating dangerousness and imminence (i.e., whether the consultant agrees with the clinician's assessment of the level of perturbation and lethality). The specifics of the patient's feelings of despair, depression, hopelessness, impulsivity, cognitive constriction, and impulses toward cessation should also be discussed.

8. the issues of informed consent and confidentiality, and the adequacy of all current documentation on the case (e.g., intake notes, progress notes, utilization reviews, family meetings, supervisor notes, telephone contacts, etc.).

9. whether the consultant agrees with the psychologist's current risk-benefit analysis and management plan. Does the consultant agree that the dual issues of foreseeability and the need to take affirmative precautions have been adequately addressed? (pp. 183–184)

GUIDELINES

Bongar (1991) noted the following:

1. For each patient seen as part of a [clinician's] professional practice activities, there must be an initial evaluation and assessment, regular ongoing clinical evaluations and case reviews, consultation reports and supervision reports (where indicated), and a formal treatment plan. All of these activities need to demonstrate specifically a solid understanding of the significant factors used to assess elevated risk of suicide and how to manage such risk—with a documented understanding of the prognosis for the success (or possible paths to failure) of subsequent outpatient (or inpatient) treatment or case disposition.

2. [Clinicians] must be aware of the vital importance of documentation. In cases of malpractice, courts and juries often have been observed to operate on the simplistic principle that "if it isn't written down, it didn't happen" (no matter what the subsequent testimony or elaboration of the defendant maintains). Defensive clinical notes, written after the fact, may help somewhat in damage control, but there is no substitute for a timely, thoughtful, and complete chart record that demonstrates (through clear and well-written assessment, review, and treatment notes) a knowledge of the epidemiology, risk factors, and treatment literature for the suicidal patient. Such a case record should also include (where possible) a formal informed consent for treatment, formal assessment of competence, and a documentation of confidentiality considerations (e.g., that limits were explained at the start of any treatment).

3. [Clinicians] must obtain, whenever possible, all previous treatment records, and consult with previous psychotherapists. When appropriate, mental health practitioners should involve the family and significant others in the management or disposition plan. The family and significant others are good sources of information (both current and background) and can serve as an integral and effective part of the support system.

4. [Clinicians] should routinely obtain consultation and/or supervision (or make referrals) on any case where suicide risk is determined to be even moderate, and after a patient suicide or serious suicide attempt. They also should obtain consultation on and/or supervision on (or refer) cases that are outside their documented training, education, or experience, as well as when they are unsure of the best avenue for initiating or continuing treatment. A guiding principle in moments of clinical uncertainty is that two perspectives are better than one.

5. [Clinicians] should be knowledgeable about the effects of psychotropic medication and make appropriate referrals for a medication evaluation. If the clinician decides that medication is not indicated in the present instance, he should thoroughly document the reasoning for this decision in the written case record. Where appropriate, the patient (and, when it is indicated, the patient's family or significant others) should be included in this decision-making process. [Clinicians] need to know the possible organic etiologies for suicidality and seek immediate appropriate medical consultation for the patient when they detect any signs of an organic condition.

6. [Clinicians] who see suicidal patients should have access to the full armamentarium of resources for voluntary and involuntary hospital admissions, day treatment, 24-hour emergency backup, and crisis centers. This access can be direct or indirect (through an ongoing collaborative relationship with a psychologist or psychiatrist colleague).

7. If a patient succeeds in committing suicide (or makes a serious suicide attempt), [clinicians] should be aware not only of their legal responsibilities (e.g., they must notify their insurance carrier in a timely fashion), but, more important, of the immediate clinical necessity of attending to both the postvention needs of the bereaved survivors and to the clinician's own emotional needs. (The [clinician] must acknowledge that it is both normal and difficult to work through feelings about a patient's death or near-death and that he or she, having lost a patient to suicide, is also a suicide survivor.) The concern should be for the living. After consultation with a knowledgeable colleague and an attorney, immediate clinical outreach to the survivors is not only sensitive and concerned clinical care, but in helping the survivors to deal with the catastrophic aftermath via an effective clinical postvention effort, the clinician is also practicing effective risk management.

8. Most important, [clinicians] must be cognizant of all of the standards above and take affirmative steps to ensure that they have the requisite knowledge, training, experience, and clinical resources prior to accepting high-risk patients into their professional care. This requires that all of these mechanisms be in place before the onset of any suicidal crisis. (pp. 202–204)

SUMMARY

The fear of mental health litigation should not lead to clinicians' responding to suicidal patients with trepidation, defensive practice, or other adversarial reactions (Gutheil, 1992). Although there is no specific set of clinical practices that can absolutely guarantee a psychologist that he or she will be immune from either losing a patient to suicide or being sued (and being held liable), good clinical care as reviewed earlier should provide a solid foundation for reducing the clinician's exposure to malpractice action.

Clinicians are less likely to be sued successfully when they can demonstrate that their decision-making process and management efforts were coherent and appropriate and fell within the guidelines of the profession's standard of care (Bongar, 1991). However, readers should remember that the information contained in this chapter is no substitute for a timely and formal consultation with a knowledgeable attorney and with one's professional colleagues. In particular, clinicians with specific questions or those who are threatened with a suit should follow the suggestion of Wright (1991) and VandeCreek and Knapp (1983) that the first step (when one has specific legal concerns or has reason to believe that a malpractice suit is imminent) is quite straightforward: Consult an attorney who is expert in matters of mental health and the law (Bongar, 1991).

ACKNOWLEDGMENTS

Portions of this chapter are adapted from Bongar and Greaney (1994). Copyright 1994 by Taylor & Francis. Reproduced by permission.

The views of Sheila Greaney do not represent the views of the United States Armed Forces or of the Walter Reed Medical Center.

Portions of the section on "Consultation" are adapted from Clayton and Bongar (1994). Copyright 1994 by Lawrence Erlbaum. Reproduced by permission.

Portions of the section on "Guidelines" are adapted from Bongar (1991). Copyright 1991 by the American Psychological Association. Reproduced by permission. The questions a consultant should be asked to cover, in the "Consultation" section, are reprinted from the same source.

REFERENCES

Abille v. United States, 482 F. Supp. 703 (N.D. Cal. 1980).
American jurisprudence 2d(rev.) (1981). §61. New York: Lawyer's Cooperative.
Appelbaum, P. S., & Gutheil, T. G. (1991). *Clinical handbook of psychiatry and the law* (2nd ed.). Baltimore: Williams & Wilkins.
Bellah v. Greenson, 146 Cal. Rptr. 535 (1978).
Berman, A. L. (1986). Notes on turning 18 (and 75): A critical look at our adolescence. *Suicide and Life-Threatening Behavior, 16*, 1–12.

Berman, A. L., & Cohen-Sandler, R. (1982). Suicide and the standard of care: Optimal vs. acceptable. *Suicide and Life-Threatening Behavior, 12*(2), 114–122.

Berman, A. L., & Cohen-Sandler, R. (1983). Suicide and malpractice: Expert testimony and the standard of care. *Professional Psychology: Research and Practice, 14*(1), 6–19.

Bernstein, R. M., Feldbberg, C., & Brown, R. (1991). After-hours coverage in psychology training clinics. *Professional Psychology: Research and Practice, 22,* 204–208.

Bongar, B. (1991). *The suicidal patient: Clinical and legal standards of care.* Washington, DC: American Psychological Association.

Bongar, B., & Greaney, S. (1994). Essential clinical and legal issues when working with the suicidal patient. *Death Studies, 18,* 528–548.

Bongar, B., Maris, R. W., Berman, A. L., & Litman, R. E. (1992). Outpatient standards of care and the suicidal patient. *Suicide and Life-Threatening Behavior, 22*(4), 453–478.

Bongar, B., Maris, R. W., Berman, A. L., Litman, R. E., & Silverman, M. M. (1993). Inpatient standards of care and the suicidal patient: Part I. General clinical formulations and legal considerations. *Suicide and Life-Threatening Behavior, 23*(3), 245–256.

Bongar, B., Peterson, L. G., Harris, E. A., & Aissis, J. (1989). Clinical and legal considerations in the management of suicidal patients: An integrative overview. *Journal of Integrative and Eclectic Psychotherapy, 8*(1), 53–67.

Brent, D. A., Kupfer, D. J., Bromet, E. J., & Dew, M.A. (1988). The assessment and treatment of patients at risk for suicide. In A. J. Frances & R .E. Hales (Eds.), *American Psychiatric Press review of psychiatry* (Vol. 7, pp. 353–385). Washington, DC: American Psychiatric Press.

Cantor, C. H., & McDermott, P. T. (1994). Suicide litigation: From legal to clinical wisdom. *Australian and New Zealand Journal of Psychiatry, 28,* 431–437.

Chemtob, C. M., Hamada, R. S., Bauer, G. B., Kinney, B. & Torigoe, R. Y. (1988). Patient suicide: Frequency and impact on psychiatrists. *American Journal of Psychiatry, 145,* 224–228.

Chemtob, C. M., Hamada, R. S., Bauer, G. B., Torigoe, R. Y. & Kinney, B. (1988). Patient suicide: Frequency and impact on psychologists. *Professional Psychology: Research and Practice, 19*(4), 416–420.

Clayton, S., & Bongar, B. (1994). The use of consultation in psychological practice: Ethical, legal, and clinical considerations. *Ethics and Behavior, 4*(1), 43–57.

Dillman v. Hellman, 283 So. 2d 388 (Fla. Dist. Ct. App. 1973).

Dimitrijevic v. Chicago Wesley Memorial Hospital, 92 Ill. App. 2d 251, 236 N.E.2d 309 (1968).

Dinnerstein v. State, 486 F.2d 34 (CT, 1973).

Farberow, N. L. (1981). Suicide prevention in the hospital. *Hospital and Community Psychiatry, 32,* 99–104.

Fremouw, W. J., de Perczel, M., & Ellis, T. E. (1990). *Suicide risk: Assessment and response guidelines.* New York: Pergamon Press.

Gutheil, T. G. (1990). Argument for the defendant-expert opinion: Death in hindsight. In R. I. Simon (Ed.), *Review of clinical psychiatry and the law* (pp. 335–339). Washington, DC: American Psychiatric Association.

Gutheil, T. G. (1992). Suicide and suit: Liability after self-destruction. In D. Jacobs

(Ed.), *Suicide and clinical practice* (pp. 147–167). Washington, DC: American Psychiatric Press.

Gutheil, T. G., & Appelbaum, P. S. (1982). *Clinical handbook of psychiatry and the law.* New York: McGraw Hill.

Harris, E. A. (1988, October). *Legal issues in professional practice.* Workshop materials for the Massachusetts Psychological Association, Northampton, MA.

Jobes, D. A., & Berman, A. L. (1993). Suicide and malpractice liability: Assessing and revising policies, procedures, and practice in outpatient settings. *Professional Psychology: Research and Practice, 24*(1), 91–99.

Jobes, D. A., Eyman, J. R., & Yufit, R. I. (1991, April). *How clinicians assess suicide risk in adolescents and adults.* Paper presented at the annual conference of the American Association of Suicidology, New Orleans.

Kapp, M. B. (1987). Interprofessional relationships in geriatrics: Ethical and legal considerations. *Gerontologist, 27,* 547–552.

Kermani, E. J. (1982). Court rulings on psychotherapists. *American Journal of Psychotherapy, 36*(2), 248–254.

Litman, R. E. (1982). Hospital suicides: Lawsuits and standards. *Suicide and Life-Threatening Behavior, 12,* 212–220.

Malone, K. M., Szanto, K., Corbitt, E. M., & Mann, J. J. (1995). Clinical assessment versus research methods in the assessment of suicidal behavior. *American Journal of Psychiatry, 152*(11), 1601–1607.

Maltsberger, J. T. (1994). Calculated risk taking in the treatment of suicidal patients: Ethical and legal problems. *Death Studies, 18,* 439–452.

Maris, R. W., Berman, A. L., Maltsberger, J. T., & Yufit, R. (Eds.). (1992). *Assessment and prediction of suicide.* New York: Guilford Press.

Meier v. Ross General Hospital, 69 Cal. 2d 420, 445 P.2d 519 71 Cal. Rptr. 903 (1968).

Meyer, R. G., Landis, E. R., & Hays, J. R. (1988). *Law for the psychotherapist.* New York: Norton.

Perr, I. N. (1979). Legal aspects of suicide. In L. D. Hankoff & B. Einsidler (Eds.), *Suicide: Theory and clinical aspects* (pp. 91–100). Littleton, MA: PSG.

Perr, I. N. (1985). Suicide litigation and risk management: A review of 32 cases. *Bulletin of American Academy of Psychiatry and the Law, 13*(3), 209–219.

Perr, I. N. (1988). The practice of psychiatry and suicide litigation. *New Developments in Mental Health Law, 8*(1), 4–19.

Pisel v. Stamford Hospital, 180 Conn. 314, 430 A.2d 1 (1980).

Pokorny, A. D. (1983). Prediction of suicide in psychiatric patients. *Archives of General Psychiatry, 40,* 249–257.

Rachlin, S. (1984). Double jeopardy: Suicide and malpractice. *General Hospital Psychiatry, 6,* 302–307.

Robertson, J. D. (1988). *Psychiatric malpractice: Liability of mental health professionals.* New York: Wiley.

Sadoff, R. L. (1985). Malpractice in psychiatry: Standards of care and the expert witness. *Psychiatric Medicine, 2*(3), 235–243.

Shneidman, E. S. (1981). Psychotherapy with suicidal patients. *Suicide and Life-Threatening Behavior, 11*(4), 341–348.

Shneidman, E. S. (1985). *Definition of suicide.* New York: Wiley.

Silverman, M. M., Berman, A. L., Bongar, B., Litman, R. E., & Maris, R. W. (1994).

Inpatient standards of care and the suicidal patient part II: An integration of clinical risk management. *Suicide and Life-Threatening Behavior, 24*(2), 152–169.

Simon, R. I. (1987). *Clinical psychiatry and the law.* Washington, DC: American Psychiatric Press.

Simon, R. I. (1988). *Concise guide to clinical psychiatry and the law.* Washington, DC: American Psychiatric Press.

Simon, R. I. (1992). *Concise guide to psychiatry and the law for clinicians.* Washington, DC: American Psychiatric Press.

Stromberg, C.D., Haggarty, D. J., Leibenluft, R. F., McMillan, M. H., Mishkin, B., Rubin, B. L., & Trilling, H.R. (1988). *The psychologist's legal handbook.* Washington, DC: The Council for the National Register of Health Service Providers in Psychology.

Swenson, E. V. (1986). Legal liability for a patient's suicide. *Journal of Psychiatry and the Law, 14,* 409–434.

Topel v. Long Island Jewish Medical Center, 431, NE.2d. 293 (1981).

VandeCreek, L., & Knapp, S. (1983). Malpractice risks with suicidal patients. *Psychotherapy: Theory, Research and Practice, 20*(3), 274–280.

VandeCreek, L., & Knapp, S. (1989). Tarasoff *and beyond: Legal and clinical considerations in the treatment of life-endangering patients.* Sarasota, FL: Professional Resource Exchange.

VandeCreek, L., Knapp, S., & Herzog, C. (1987). Malpractice risks in the treatment of dangerous patients. *Psychotherapy: Theory, Research, and Practice, 24*(2), 145–153.

Wright, R. H. (1981). Psychologists and professional liability (malpractice) insurance. *American Psychologist, 36,* 1485–1493.

CHAPTER 10

RISK MANAGEMENT
WITH THE VIOLENT PATIENT

SARA EDDY
ERIC HARRIS

Mental health practitioners, whether in office or hospital practice, are under increasing pressure to assess, manage, and treat individuals who threaten violent behavior. Also, courts and statutes have imposed on practitioners the duty to take reasonable steps to protect identifiable intended victims of such violence. To comply with ethical and statutory responsibilities, mental health professionals need to understand the factors associated with violence, develop measures for assessing and managing violence in their patients, educate themselves with respect to their responsibilities to persons other than their patients who might be at risk for harm, and craft strategies for minimizing their potential liability in the event that someone under their care harms another.

Although some general rules apply, the setting in which the clinician works greatly influences clinical and risk management strategies for managing the violent patient. Some strategies are more appropriate in hospital emergency rooms, others apply to a psychiatric service or hospital, and still others apply to the outpatient office. Often, given the prevalence of managed care, dangerousness to self or others is the only basis for admission to an inpatient service. The hospital is then on notice that the patient may present a risk of harm. In such inpatient settings, the clinician has more control over the patient and his environment, allowing more effective management of potentially violent patients. Frequently clinicians have more time in which to evaluate potential dangerousness and can avail themselves of a variety of resources in the hospital and/or the criminal justice system, thus spreading the decision-making risk. However, with additional control comes additional responsibility. A hospital and a hospital staff member are usually held to a higher standard of care than is an outpatient clinician. Many courts have held hospitals and hospital staff members liable because they failed to adequately foresee an about-to-be-released patient's dangerousness.

In contrast, most individuals who voluntarily consult a mental health professional on an outpatient basis are not at risk for harming others. The base rate for dangerous conduct is so low in outpatient practice that even the most experienced clinicians cannot predict dangerousness with an acceptable level of accuracy. Further, outpatient clinicians have much less information about patients and much less control over their activities. As a result, the outpatient practitioner has a lower risk for liability. In fact, as discussed more fully below, in most jurisdictions, outpatient clinicians are not required to predict dangerousness; they are only required to take protective action when the patient makes a threat.

The rapid development of services that offer care on a continuum between the hospital and an outpatient setting (e.g., partial hospitalization, day treatment, evening treatment, respite care, and managed residential care) creates a whole new area of risk management concerns. Clinicians in these arenas have less control over patients than in a hospital but more than in outpatient practice. It is unclear how court decisions will define professional responsibilities in these settings; however, it seems likely that the analysis will be closer to that applied to hospitals than that applied to outpatient practice if only because most of these programs are connected to hospitals or other large institutions.

The aim of this chapter is to outline general guidelines for assessing and managing dangerous behavior in a variety of settings. It is also intended to describe the liability risks to practitioners presented by dangerous patients and provide some techniques to minimize these risks.

FACTORS ASSOCIATED
WITH VIOLENCE

Some social scientists, in an attempt to more accurately predict violence, developed "profiles" of the likely-to-be-violent individual, based on a variety of demographic and clinical elements shown to be correlated with violence. Such a profile might look like the following:

White male, 30–50 years old
History of poor interpersonal relationships, usually a "loner"
Difficulty with authority
Poor job performance
History of substance abuse

History as victim of abuse
Interest in weapons

The use of such profiles is ill-advised because they give predictors a false sense of confidence about their ability to predict low base rate, but high-risk, human behavior. The use of profiles can lead to both false positives and false negatives and, depending on action taken or not taken as a result of the prediction, liability for the predictor.

Clinicians should, however, educate themselves about various factors that are thought to bear some relation to violent acts: (1) demographic (e.g., males from violent subcultures with limited educational and employment opportunities), (2) historical (e.g., history of or current substance abuse, history of violent acts, history as victim of physical or sexual abuse), (3) environmental (e.g., relationship or family instability and/or loss, available weapons, environment in which violence is an accepted means of dispute resolution, job difficulties or economic struggles), and (4) clinical (e.g., violent ideation, a "grudge" list, verbal indications of a wish to punish or harm someone accompanied by the means by which to accomplish the act, antisocial tendencies, paranoid ideation, and a felt need to protect oneself) (Monahan, 1981).

As a general rule, mental illness is not an accurate predictor of violence. Earlier studies indicated that the mentally ill were as likely or less likely than the general population to engage in violent behavior (Monahan, 1981). Further, absent psychotic symptoms, the risk of violence for mentally ill individuals was no higher than for demographically similar members of the same community who were never treated (Link, Cullen, & Andrews, 1992). Recent evidence from epidemiological studies indicates that "mental disorder may be a consistent, albeit modest, risk factor for the occurrence of violence" (Monahan, 1992). However, this correlation should not encourage providers to predict violence based on the presence of mental illness. Considerably more research is required to identify what aspects of mental disorder have predictive value. In our opinion, this correlation may have more to do with the changing definitions of mental illness and the changing criteria for hospitalization of the mentally ill.

Although no clear information is available about what elements produce an association between mental health and violence, and no reliable tools exist with which to predict violent behavior on the part of an individual, mentally ill or not, mental health professionals should combine actuarial information with clinical judgment to begin to distinguish potentially violent individuals from others. If an individual makes a threat to harm another and meets several of the criteria outlined previously, even if the mental health professional's clinical judgment indicates that the threat is not a serious one, he or she would be prudent to consult with a colleague to obtain another opinion and minimize the risk of underestimating the seriousness of the situation. Even though the actual incidence of violence from patients is low, the consequences of failing to predict and warn are extremely high.

PREPARATION FOR DEALING WITH THE VIOLENT PATIENT

Mental health professionals must assess their own experience and training with respect to the task of predicting dangerousness. Prudent professionals who have had little or no experience and training should avail themselves of continuing education and/or supervisory opportunities to develop these skills before agreeing to evaluate or treat individuals with a known history of violence. As a general rule, the best (albeit imperfect) predictor of future violence is a history of violence. Although some statutes suggest that mental health professionals only have a duty to warn when a patient's history of violence is known to them, it may be negligent not to make every effort to ascertain and document an individual's history of violence. Professionals should, as a part of their initial interview with an individual, ask specific questions with respect to a history of violence, much as they ask about other important events comprising a social history. Many clinicians are uncomfortable asking about such matters, thinking that to do so may interfere with the development of a therapeutic relationship; however, not to ask and document is, in most cases, poor clinical practice. It is also possible to develop an interview format in which the clinician asks direct questions about a history of violence but in a neutral, information-gathering fashion. We provide a sample of such an interview later.

In addition to gathering clinical information from the individual, the clinician should pay careful attention to the reasons for which the patient is seeking assistance. Has she been referred by her divorce lawyer because she is having marital difficulties and her spouse has taken out a restraining order? Is psychotherapy a condition of probation? A more complicated, but increasingly common referral source is an employee assistance program (EAP). The number of violent incidents in the workplace, generally occurring between employees, has increased significantly. The perpetrator(s) of these incidents are frequently referred to the EAP staff, who often recommend counseling and/or psychotherapy as a condition of continued employment.

Another source for important information with respect to violent activity or ideation is the individual's records. Careful clinicians ask for details with respect to violence upon referral and should obtain the patient's permission to request verbal or written information, or both, from previous therapists and/or hospitals. Instead of first entering into a treatment relationship and subsequently requesting information, clinicians should request and obtain such data about a history of violence before entering into a treatment contract with a patient.

WHEN TO ENTER INTO A TREATMENT RELATIONSHIP

If the patient refuses to consent to this request for information, and in the absence of a compelling explanation for the refusal, the therapist should decline to consult further with the patient. It is important to note that failure to secure past treatment records has been held to be negligence in a number of cases (*Peck v. The Counseling Service of Addison County Inc.,* 1983).

Mental health professionals should remember that, as a general rule, they have no duty to treat a patient unless they agree to do so. Once entering into such an agreement, however, the clinician has both a legal and an ethical obligation to continue with the patient until he or she can properly terminate the relationship. Not to take care in this regard can be seen as abandonment. Consequently, a mental health professional who notices a number of the demographic warning signals cited previously should be cautious about entering into a therapeutic relationship with an individual unless the professional is prepared to remain responsible for the patient's care. Clinicians with little experience treating violent individuals should, in the absence of adequate information, consultation, and/or supervision, be especially careful about entering into what the individual may perceive as a therapeutic relationship. Persons may be tempted to extend themselves beyond their experience and training to maintain good relations with their referral sources (the probation officer, the EAP); however, ethical principles require that therapists only practice in areas within their expertise.

Mental health professionals who must decline to enter into a treatment relationship with an individual with a propensity for violence should explain their lack of experience and offer to refer the individual to another who possesses the requisite skills. As a general rule, at this stage the contact between the patient and the proposed therapist has been brief, usually not more than one or two meetings, and the patient will have little difficulty making a transition to another. It would be prudent, however, for the mental health professional to set forth the reasons for and terms of the referral in a letter to the patient, offering always to do what he or she can to facilitate the referral to a professional more particularly qualified to be of assistance with the problems for which the patient has consulted the therapist.

TREATING THE VIOLENT PATIENT

When the professional and the patient have an established therapeutic relationship, the same caveats with respect to abandonment apply; however, in this situation the therapist is obligated to continue treatment until a referral can be effected. When the therapist is inexperienced and the patient is becoming increasingly difficult to manage, the therapist may regret having entered into the relationship in the first place. At this point, it is crucial that the therapist seek consultation and/or supervision for help in controlling a volatile situation. Mental health professionals should expect that a consultant will meet with the patient, if appropriate; review available records; offer guidance and support to the therapist; and, when necessary, intervene directly to warn a potential victim or hospitalize the patient.

If the therapist feels that he or she has both sufficient information and expertise to enter into an evaluation or treatment relationship with a potentially violent individual, the therapist should satisfy himself or herself that he or she understands as much as is reasonably possible about the patient's past predilection for violence. Each professional should develop his or her own clinical interview to assess the potential for violence in the individual patient; the following is one such format, to be shaped to suit the therapist's personal style and circumstances:

1. *Interview behavior.* Is the individual tense, irritable, menacing, or verbally or physically threatening? Does she make you apprehensive?

2. *Recent (past 6 months) history of violence toward self or others, threats of violence, or arrests.* What was said or done, and what were the consequences? Has anyone ever taken out a restraining order against the individual?

3. *Past history of violence toward self or others, threats of violence, or arrests.* What happened, and what were the consequences? Did the individual act violently as a juvenile, an adult, or both?

4. *Family history of violence.* How was discipline administered in the family? Were parents or others ever assaultive toward each other or toward the children? Were children assaultive toward each other or toward others? Have family members been arrested or incarcerated?

5. *Current violent ideation.* Does the individual think about harming others, getting even, paying back? What are the thoughts, and toward whom are they directed? Is there a grudge list?

6. *Substance abuse.* What substances does the individual use, in what amounts, and with what frequency? Have substances been involved in recent or past violent acts?

7. *Medical condition.* Are there medical and/or neurological problems that cause the individual to lose control or to act in an unpredictable fashion?

8. *Weapons.* Is the individual trained in the use of firearms? If she has been in the military, has she been in combat? Was his an honorable discharge? Does he have current access to firearms?

9. *Social/environmental factors.* Does the individual have a stable living situation? Does he have other people in his life, or is he a loner? Is she performing well at her job, or does she have a history of discipline and/or suspension? Is his financial condition precarious?

10. *Response to intervention.* Has the individual sought help in the past, and with what result?

11. *Mental status.* Are there antisocial/paranoid/narcissistic features? Is there an Axis I clinical disorder?

ASPECTS OF THE DUTY TO PROTECT

When a mental health professional's conduct falls below the appropriate standard of care and a patient is damaged as a result, the patient can bring a malpractice action against the mental health provider to recover damages created by that negligent conduct. One of the principles of malpractice law is that a mental health professional can only be held responsible for damages incurred by those to whom he or she owes a "legal duty." Generally, one can only owe a legal duty to those to whom one provides professional service. Until the *Tarasoff* case was decided (*Tarasoff v. Regents of the University of California*, 1974; *Tarasoff v. Regents of the University of California*, 1976), only hospital-based providers could be held liable to individuals other than their patients when they failed to exercise the legal duty to control hospitalized patients who subsequently damaged others. These cases were generally labeled "premature release" cases because the damage was usually inflicted by a patient who had been "'inappropriately released" from a hospital setting. In *Tarasoff*, the California Supreme Court decided that outpatient therapists owed a legal duty to those whom their patients threatened with serious harm. If the therapist did not take reasonable steps to protect such a potential victim, the therapist could be held liable for any damage to the victim caused by the patient.

Maintaining the confidentiality of professionally obtained patient information is one of the most important responsibilities imposed upon mental health practitioners. However, in a number of situations social policy considerations override therapeutic confidentiality. The responsibility to take reasonable steps to protect an identifiable, potential victim from threatened violent behavior by one's patient is one such situation. The Codes of Ethics of all the major mental health professions always provide practitioners with discretion to breach confidentiality "to protect the patient . . . or others from harm" (American Psychological Association, 1992). *Tarasoff* was the first instance in which the appropriate exercise of this discretion was identified as a professional responsibility or duty in an outpatient setting. The *Tarasoff* principle spread eastward like a great wave, and now almost every state imposes some protective responsibilities on providers. In many states, the *Tarasoff* doctrine was first adopted by the courts on a case-by-case basis. A case-by-case approach is neither efficient nor predictable, so mental health provider groups have joined together to support legislation clearly defining the parameters of professional responsibility. In addition, these statutes usually limit professional liability to a breach of the duty defined by the statute. A majority of states now have these statutes, and readers should inform themselves about those in their particular jurisdictions.

Most practitioners think they are required to evaluate the dangerousness potential of their patients and to warn intended victims when the dangerousness is present. In fact, in the vast majority of states, the duty is only triggered by a specific threat, and warning a potential victim is only one of several actions that can discharge the duty. Most states require that there be a threat to kill or inflict serious bodily injury, although some states include threats to property. Further, many states do not require protective action unless the professional, in the exercise of his or her professional judgment, determines that the patient has the intent and ability to carry out the threat (Arizona, Massachusetts, Florida). Some states require that the threatened harm be imminent (Arizona, Colorado, the District of Columbia, and Indiana), and some states require that the threat be explicit (Massachusetts).

Two basic statutory approaches define the responsibility to protect. Many states follow the Massachusetts example of requiring a mental health professional to take "one or more" of the following protective actions:

1. Communicate the threat to the reasonably identified person;
2. Notify an appropriate law enforcement agency;
3. Arrange for the patient to be hospitalized voluntarily; and
4. Take appropriate steps to initiate proceedings for involuntary hospitalization pursuant to law.

The second line of statutes follows the example of California, where the duty to protect is discharged by calling the police and warning the victim. The Massachusetts approach allows the practitioner to exercise more discretion in determining which course of action is most clinically appropriate but means a higher risk if the practitioner's choice does not protect the intended victim from harm. Although the California approach provides more certainty, there are situations in which informing the potential victim may eliminate risk but have adverse clinical consequences. Although the *Tarasoff* doctrine also applies to hospital-based providers, there is a broader legal responsibility that comes from the duty to control the conduct of hospitalized patients. Whereas all providers are required to take protective action when there is a threat to an identified victim, hospitals may be required to do more. Liability was imposed when there was no threat or the threat was very vague and the potential victim was not clearly identified (e.g., *Lipari v. Sears Roebuck & Co.*, 1980; *Durflinger v. Artiles*, 1983; *Petersen v. State*, 1983; *Naidu v. Laird*, 1988).

OUTPATIENT RISK MANAGEMENT

When a potentially dangerous patient confronts a mental health professional, the professional may experience a conflict over his or her dual responsibilities to the patient and to others. When a therapist has to breach confidentiality to warn a potential victim, it may not necessarily sabotage the treatment relationship. One of the ways to protect the therapist–patient relationship is to provide full information to the patient about the potential exceptions to confidentiality at the beginning of therapy, as part of the process of securing informed consent. The therapist should reinforce that patient's prior understanding by raising the issue in the treatment as soon as the therapist recognizes that there is a potential for violence. This action should both minimize the possibility that the patient will feel betrayed by the therapist's responsibilities to protect potential victims and maximize the possibility that the therapeutic alliance can be preserved after the smoke has cleared and the crisis has been resolved.

Further, there is good evidence that keeping the patient fully informed about the therapist's activities to meet the duty to protect and even involving the patient in the communication process with the potential victim can help to decrease the risk to the victim and ensure that the therapeutic relationship can survive the crisis. The therapist should remind the patient of his or her legal obligation to protect the victim and his or her intent to carry out that responsibility. The therapist may then be able to enlist the patient's help in fashioning an appropriate communication so as to present all facts correctly. The patient can help to draft the warning letter, or might even listen in on the warning telephone call. Although unusual, this procedure can reduce risk if the patient's frustration or sense of powerless rage contribute to the threatening behavior. The patient's ability to have some control over the therapist's duties may help the patient regain self-control. If the patient has been properly alerted to these legal limits on confidentiality early in the therapeutic process, even if he or she only vaguely remembers the initial interchange, the patient is less likely to be surprised or feel betrayed by the breach of confidentiality necessary to take protective action.

Beck (1987) referred to data that indicate there is a much better chance of a favorable clinical outcome if the patient is informed, both early in the relationship and at the time of the threat, that the therapist is going to make the warning and is either involved and/or kept informed during the decision-making process and implementation of the protective activities.

Of course, if this kind of patient involvement would endanger the therapist or the potential victim, it is not indicated. For all but the most experienced clinicians, it is probably wise to consult with a more experienced colleague before implementing this strategy.

Professionals can take a number of additional steps to minimize liability when working with a potentially violent patient. It is important to remember that successful *Tarasoff* cases are rare events, particularly in an outpatient practice. Having a patient express violent thoughts or ideation should not cause the therapist to react hastily. Careful detailed questioning about the situation is important to determine the immediacy and seriousness of the risk of violence. Earlier we addressed the value of consultation to the provider who is inexperienced with the violent patient. However, consultation with another professional is an important risk management technique even for the most experienced. In addition to providing a different perspective, which may lead to a more effective clinical approach, a consultation provides corroboration that the clinician's approach to the case meets and exceeds the appropriate professional standard of care. If violence occurs, despite one's best efforts to prevent it, a jury is likely to equate the unfortunate result with a determination that the practitioner was negligent in his or her approach. Having consulted with a colleague who concurred with one's approach is one of the best ways to counter such an assumption.

EVALUATION OF THREATS

Most states only require protective action when there is a threat to kill or inflict serious bodily injury and the apparent intent and ability to carry out the threat. One must look at both the threat and the likelihood that the patient will carry it out. When the probability of action is low, one is not required to take protective action. Mental health professionals should take seriously a specific threatening statement. A therapist should, through careful questioning of the patient, thoroughly evaluate whether or not it is likely to be carried out, examine the patient's history, and assess the context in which the threat is made. Good clinical judgment is called for. Given the extraordinarily low rate of actual patient violence, even when threats are made, a conservative, legally based automatic warning when there is any potential for future liability may produce negative clinical results. In these situations, it is always wise to seek consultation and write a detailed explanation in the record, including all relevant details about the threat and the subsequent actions taken and not taken.

THE REASONABLY IDENTIFIED PERSON

State statutes may impose a duty to warn only when a threat has been made to a reasonably identified person, but case law often does not draw a bright line for the mental health professional as to who is a reasonably foreseeable and readily identifiable potential victim of a patient and as to the duties imposed under ambiguous circumstances. It appears likely, however, that if the patient threatens an individual by name or by category (e.g., "my wife"), the individual so threatened is a readily identifiable potential victim. In this case, the mental health professional would almost certainly have a duty to reach the individual to communicate the threat. Even if the mental health professional believes that the individual is not in immediate danger (e.g., is out of the country), he or she would still have a duty to warn the individual so that the individual could take appropriate protective measures. If the patient threatens someone not as easily identifiable (e.g., "a guy at work"), the mental health professional, we believe, still has a duty to make reasonable efforts to identify that individual. Perhaps he or she should call a security officer, attorney, or human resources manager at the patient's place of employment or, failing the availability of such persons, the police. The mental health professional does not have a duty to warn someone who is not reasonably identifiable (e.g., "a Kansan" or "a homeless person").

WARNING POTENTIAL VICTIMS

If the mental health professional has learned of a threat to an identifiable individual and the harm is reasonably foreseeable, he or she then may have a subsequent duty to take protective action, both to alert the potential victim and to contain the patient. The standard of care that the professional will be required to meet when taking protective action will be that taken by a reasonably prudent member of her or his profession under the same or similar circumstances. Frequently the mental health professional has a duty to communicate the threat, usually to the potential victim, and sometimes to law enforcement officials as well.

In determining how to communicate with potential victims when a warning is required, the clinician should always remember that the primary purpose is protection, with a secondary objective of creating the least harm to the patient and the therapeutic relationship. When the patient leaves the office waving a handgun saying, "I'm going home to shoot my wife," it is not sufficient to send the wife a registered letter. When a real threat exists, it is always advisable to warn the potential victim by a method that could reasonably be anticipated to provide notice of the danger.

Although there are no hard and fast rules, frequently the best method of communication is to contact the victim by telephone. This gives the therapist a chance to talk to an actual person about the risk and ask questions to assist the person in planning a protective strategy. Whatever the content of the conversation, the warning must be sufficient to make the potential victim aware that he or she is in real danger. Regardless of how much sympathy the professional may feel for the potential victim, it is important to remember that he or she is not the patient. The therapist's primary obligation remains to the potential perpetrator. The therapist must provide sufficient information to put the potential victim on notice that he or she is in danger and any data that would help to take protective action, simultaneously minimizing the interference with the patient's privacy. The therapist should disclose only essential information. Courts, however, are far less likely to penalize a clinician for providing too much information than they are for providing too little. If the professional provides more information than is necessary, the person complaining will be the patient. The therapist's defense will be that he or she was doing his or her best to protect someone the patient threatened to endanger. If the therapist provides too little information, the person complaining might be the attorney for the victim's estate, alleging that more information would have prevented a tragedy.

The therapist should avoid even the appearance of a therapeutic stance with a potential victim and take care to avoid the temptation to address the emotional issues and demands the warning is likely to generate. It may be helpful to have a witness to the telephone conversation and, although probably in violation of state wiretap statutes, some therapists choose to tape-record such conversations.

How much effort a clinician must expend in attempting to contact a potential victim depends on the facts and circumstances of the situation. The clinician would not be expected to call every 5 minutes for 24 hours; however, abandoning the effort after failing to reach a potential victim on the first or second telephone call would not be considered a sufficient effort. It is important to remember that the therapist will be held responsible for taking those steps that a prudent member of his or her profession would have taken, and a jury, in retrospect, is more likely to favor extensive efforts.

If telephone contact is not possible and the danger is not imminent, the professional can communicate in writing. Any letter should be sent by registered mail or overnight mail, return receipt requested. In making a decision to use the mail, it is instructive to remember the *Berwick* case[1]: The hospital communicated its warning by mailgram. The mailgram arrived at the home of the estranged wife and potential victim the day after she had been murdered by the patient.

If the victim is already on notice that the patient is dangerous to him or her, the therapist is still responsible for communicating a warning or taking other protective action. It is clear that a change in the clinical situation which substantially increases risk to the victim, such as increased substance abuse, would probably require that the clinician communicate with the potential victim. In fact, it is in these situations that the therapist has a more crucial protective responsibility, because, over a long period, even individuals who know they are in real danger become accustomed to their situation, thus decreasing their vigilance.

Given the current statutes and evolving case law, combined with the difficulty in predicting dangerous behavior, the therapist is likely to be safer with overreaction and overprediction. Although the therapist may be sued by a patient for breach of confidentiality, if a warning was given in good faith, ethical sanctions or legal liability would be unlikely to result. Conservative legal advisers suggest that a therapist should attempt all the protective actions included in the statute of his or her jurisdiction to guard against a successful lawsuit. However, this may be clinically contraindicated. Again, it is important to note that cases in which a patient makes a serious attempt to harm another, even when there has been a threat, are quite rare. *The Psychologist's Legal Handbook* (Stromberg et al., 1988) quotes Mills, Sullivan, and Eth's (1987) summary of court rulings in *Tarasoff* cases and points out the following:

---

[1]This case was a New York case that was presented on the CBS television show *60 Minutes*. We are not aware of any citation or whether the case ever reached an appellate court. The date of the show is unknown.

When the courts have imposed liability, the identity of the subsequently injured party was known to the psychotherapist, or the victim would have reasonably been expected to be in close proximity to the target of violence, as in the case of a young child, or a home in the vicinity of a building burned by arson. In addition, threats were specific, the patient's history was overwhelming, and there were breaches of conventional practice, such as failure to obtain the patient's prior medical record, or to examine closely the patient and his medical record. . . . Liability has not been imposed [where] the patient has, at the time of evaluation, been perceived as not being a threat to any individual or group, even when the patient had a history of violent behavior and alcoholism. (Stromberg et al., p. 532)

HOSPITALIZATION

Because in many instances hospitalization may offer greater protection for the potential victim, as well as being less damaging to the patient and the patient–therapist relationship, mental health professionals should consider its utility. The mental health professional should discuss alternatives with the patient, whenever possible, and encourage the patient to voluntarily enter a hospital. It is also advisable to telephone hospital admissions officials to determine whether the patient is committable before proceeding with more formal procedures. When an outpatient therapist hospitalizes a patient, usually the liability risk shifts to the institution, which will have a responsibility to assess dangerousness before releasing a patient. This, of course, can make the hospital reluctant to take a potentially violent patient on a voluntary basis.

RECORDKEEPING

In addition to obtaining informed consent, and consultation when appropriate, good recordkeeping is one of the most important techniques for managing risk. The rule of thumb in a court proceeding will be, "If you didn't write it down, you didn't do it." This is particularly true when the therapist's conduct is the main issue in contention; even the most convincing presentations from memory will rightly be seen as self-serving.

When clinicians are confronted with a potential *Tarasoff* situation, their records should include a complete, highly detailed report of what actually happened. The records should also include a risk–benefit analysis, detailing all the actions the therapist considered and the reasoning process leading him or her to take some actions but reject others. In fact, the description of the actions considered and rejected and the clinical justifications supporting rejection may be far more important than the actions the therapist took and the justifications therefor. What is in the records will only become important if the actions chosen by the therapist prove unsuccessful in protecting the victim. In that case, the therapist must show that he or she considered and sensibly rejected other actions.

In a jurisdiction in which the duty to protect follows the Massachusetts model, the records should show consideration of all protective actions which, if taken, could satisfy the therapist's obligations. It is important, for example, to discuss why hospitalization might not be a viable option. Often it is desirable to call a hospital admissions officer to discuss commitment, even when the provider does not think it possible. This action documents that hospitalization was considered but deemed inappropriate and prevents second-guessing later by a hostile plaintiff's attorney. This same guidance applies to calling the police, even when one is certain that there is nothing the police can do.

A model record would include an assessment of the threat, including what information alerted the therapist to the risk, what high-risk and low-risk factors were present, the patient's background and history, what questions the therapist asked, and what answers the patient gave. Further, the therapist should analyze how information, combined with the history and his or her own clinical judgment, led the therapist to elect certain actions and reject others. This analysis should include specific pros and cons of each action from both a clinical and a legal perspective. The therapist should also describe any consultations, giving details of what information he or she provided to the consultant, what actions the consultant recommended, and the rationale for them. If the therapist had more than one consultation, his or her notes should describe their agreement or disagreement. Finally, the therapist should describe in detail the action taken, the results, future actions planned, potential victim response, patient reaction, the date and time of all calls made, and copies of all written communications. Upon reviewing the record after the incident has been resolved, the therapist may add any facts that he or she neglected to include at the time of creating the record; however, the therapist should not alter or add to the record after learning that there is some legal or ethical question with respect to his or her handling of the situation. The aim of such detailed recordkeeping is to demonstrate that even though there might have been an unfortunate result, the practitioner behaved in a reasonable, professional manner, given the information he or she had at the time. The extra time and effort required to draft records as if a lawyer were perched on the professional's shoulder will pay high dividends if the professional ever has a patient who commits suicide or attempts to harm another.

Even with good records, it is hard enough to demonstrate that the unfortunate result was not caused by the professional's negligence and to persuade the jury to resist the temptation to decide to compensate a plaintiff for a tragic loss. Professionals who have sparse, unreadable, or disorganized records run the risk of having a jury believe them to be insubstantial, careless practitioners, regardless of their testimony about their behavior. In the alternative, providers with good records will be seen as competent and thoughtful individuals who, when confronted with a difficult clinical situation, behaved in a highly professional manner. Finally, complete and detailed records may act to discourage plaintiff attorneys from pursuing further legal action or encourage them to settle the matter before going to trial.

SUMMARY

Although never entirely free from the risk of liability created by patients with respect to third parties, a practitioner can manage the risk satisfactorily by taking steps that generally characterize good clinical practice: (1) educate himself or herself about violence, its diagnosis, and its management; (2) understand fully his or her duties to third parties required by applicable state statutes; and (3) document the reasoning behind any protective actions taken and other alternatives considered but rejected.

REFERENCES

American Psychological Association. (1992). Ethical principles of psychologists and code of conduct. *American Psychologist, 47*(12), 1597–1611.

Beck, J. (1987). The potentially violent patient: Legal duties, clinical practice, and risk management. *Psychiatric Annals, 17,* 10.

Durflinger v. Artiles, 234 Kan. 484, 673 P.2d 86 (1983).

Link, B., Cullen, F., & Andrews, H. (1992). The violent and illegal behavior of mental patients reconsidered. *American Sociological Review, 57,* 275–292.

Lipari v. Sears Roebuck & Co., 497 F. Supp. 185 (D. Neb. 1980).

Mills, M., Sullivan, G, & Eth, S. (1987). Protecting third parties from harm: A decade after *Tarasoff. American Journal of Psychiatry, 144*(1), 68–74.

Monahan, J. (1981). *The clinical prediction of violent behavior* (DHHS Publication No. ADM 81–921). Washington, DC: U.S. Government Printing Office.

Monahan, J. (1992). Mental disorder and violent behavior. *American Psychologist, 47*(4), 511–524.

Naidu v. Laird, 539 A.2d. 1064 (Del. 1988).

Peck v. The Counseling Service of Addison County, Inc. 146 Vt 61, 499 A.2d 442 (Vt Sup Ct 1985).

Petersen v. State, 100 Wash. 2d 421 (1983).

Stromberg, C., Clifford, D., Haggerty, D., Leibenluft, R. F., McMillian, M. H., Mishkin, B., Rubin, B., & Trilling, H. R. (1988). *The psychologist's legal handbook.* Washington, DC: National Register of Health Service Providers in Psychology.

Tarasoff v. Regents of the University of California, 13 Cal. 3d 177, 529 P.2d 533 (1974), *vacated,* 17 Cal 3d 425, 551 P.2d 334 (1976).

Tarasoff v. Regents of the University of California, 3d 425, 551 P.2d 334 (Cal. 1976).

PART IV

EMERGENCY-RELATED
CRISES AND CONDITIONS

CHAPTER 11

RESPONDING TO
SELF-INJURIOUS BEHAVIOR

PAMELA J. DEITER
LAURIE ANNE PEARLMAN

Many individuals seen in emergency and other care settings have deliberately harmed their bodies. These clients are among the most difficult for emergency personnel to encounter. If treatment providers understand the meanings and functions of self-injury, they are less prone to anger, judgmental responses, and frustration and are better able to help. They can help by gently exploring the meanings or purposes of an episode of self-injury and working with the client to develop short-term strategies for managing distress. Often, the distress that underlies self-injury is around interpersonal connection, affect, and self-esteem. In this chapter, we review some of the psychological literature on self-injury, then provide a theoretical framework for understanding and addressing self-injury in emergency settings. We address the impact on the treatment provider through a brief discussion of countertransference and vicarious traumatization and suggest some resources for helping professionals and their clients.

Self-injury is neither rare nor particularly bizarre. It exists in various forms in cultures around the world. A frequently cited estimate of self-injury among U.S. psychiatric patents is 7–10% (Briere, 1995a; Favazza & Contiero, 1988). This estimate is likely modest. Self-injury is difficult to study for several reasons: Definitions have changed markedly over time, self-injury often evokes great shame in individuals who practice it and so they are unlikely to disclose it, and self-injury evokes strong reactions from treatment providers so they do not ask about it, do not acknowledge it, or misdiagnose it as a suicide attempt. Treatment providers, especially those in medical settings who are trained to help people who were hurt by others, by accident, or by illness, are often non-plussed when they encounter self-inflicted injuries.

Self-injury is one of a number of common sequelae of childhood sexual abuse (Neumann, 1994; Polusny & Follette, 1995). Self-destructive acts are not uncommon among abused children and adolescents (Green, 1978; Simpson & Porter, 1981; van der Kolk, 1991). In the general adult population, Favazza and Rosenthal (1993) estimate that self-injury occurs in about 4% of people, and Walsh and Rosen (1988) estimate the number of individuals self-injuring in the United States at approximately 1.4 million per year. Walsh and Rosen (1988) report that since 1965, epidemiological researchers from the United States, Canada, England, and Denmark consistently cite an increased incidence of self-harm behaviors.

In a study of two clinical samples currently underway by the authors of this chapter, 68% of 135 psychiatric partial hospital patients report a history of active self-injury (e.g., cutting), and 86% of those who report active self-injury also report childhood abuse. Forty-two percent of 100 outpatient psychotherapy clients report active self-injury, and 74% of those clients also report childhood abuse.

Although self-injury is neither uncommon nor bizarre, it presents a number of clinical challenges. Intervention can be time-consuming and complicated and may meet with limited or only gradual success. Level of risk for the self-injuring individual may be difficult to assess at any given time, and it may be difficult or impossible to protect the individual from danger. In addition, providing services to clients who self-injure can provoke reactions including anxiety, confusion, anger, helplessness, pity, and desire to control the situation from treatment providers both at the individual level and the institutional level.

Working with self-injury can be especially challenging in emergency settings, where issues of time and legal liability are pressing. In a study of patients seen in a psychiatric emergency room, Bongar, Peterson, Golann, and Hardiman (1990) concluded that almost 80% of the patients they saw repeatedly and treated as "chronically suicidal" could actually be considered deliberate self-harmers. The group of patients identified as chronically suicidal in that study comprised 1% of patients seen in the psychiatric emergency service in the year studied but accounted for 12% of the visits to the service that year. Describing this type of emergency service patient, Fennig and Fennig (1992) wrote, "While their number is small in comparison to other disorders, they consume a disproportionate amount of energy in terms of time and emotional involvement" (p. 318).

When it is viewed within constructivist self development theory (McCann & Pearlman, 1990a; Pearlman & Saakvitne, 1995), the theoretical framework presented in this chapter, self-injury can be understood as distinct from suicide attempts and laden with meaning and purpose. This perspective allows treatment providers to take a position of respect and collaboration with self-injuring individuals, facilitating better understanding and more effective interventions.

TERMINOLOGY

In this chapter, the term "self-injury" refers to deliberate acts resulting in damage to one's own body when these acts are not intended to bring about death. Familiar forms of self-injury are cutting, burning or scratching at one's skin, especially on wrists and forearms. Tissue self-injury may take many other forms, including destruction of oral tissues, nails, cuticles and other tissue through biting, self-hitting, hair pulling, swallowing and insertion of objects, injurious masturbation, head banging, scalding, and aggravation of chronic wounds. The frequency data reported so far in this chapter reflect this class of self-injury.

Self-injury may also take such forms as tattooing, branding, and piercing. These behaviors are within cultural norms for beautifying oneself or demonstrating identity and affiliation. If they are repeated, severe, unusually damaging, practiced in a painful, humiliating or punitive manner, or experienced by the subject as reducing distress or serving another purpose consistent with self-injury, the behaviors may have clinical significance as self-injury. Similarly, the handling of guns and knives, although not uncommon or deviant in our culture, may serve purposes such as those of self-injurious behaviors.

Authors and researchers express varying opinions about whether another class of behaviors constitutes self-injury. For example, ingestion of dangerous substances (poisoning), drug abuse, alcohol abuse, eating and evacuation practices (starvation, vomiting, enemas), excessive exercise, unprotected or overtly risky sex, and frequent elective surgeries are excluded from most, although not all, self-injury research (Pattison & Kahan, 1983; Favazza & Rosenthal, 1993). They are more often included by current trauma researchers and authors who link self-injury to psychological trauma (Calof, 1995a, 1995b; Miller, 1994).

Similarly, passively self-injurious behaviors, such as neglecting a medical condition; withholding medication, warm clothing, or other necessities; spending time in dangerous places or with dangerous people; or provoking injury by others may serve self-injurious purposes and place individuals at risk of serious harm.

Considering types or categories of self-injury may be useful in understanding a client's behavior. Trautmann and Conners (1994) caution that "behavior alone does not constitute self injury . . . any particular behavior can be viewed in different lights, depending on the social and personal context within which it occurs" (p. 59). They provide a "broad continuum of self harm" that includes all the types described previously. Sakheim (1993) breaks self-injurious behaviors into three types, based on hypothesized motivations and influences. He identifies Type I behaviors as motivated by defenses against the effects of trauma, and includes such behaviors as cutting, burning, head banging, and high-risk activities. Type II behaviors are the result of psychotic influences and include eye enucleation, removal of body parts, and self-surgery. Type III behaviors are attributable at least in part to cultural influences and include cosmetic surgery, body piercing, tattooing, and handling guns and knives.

All categorization offered here is speculative. Categorization is ultimately an empirical question, and individuals often defy categorization. Clinically, it is the internal meaning and purpose of behavior that should guide intervention.

HISTORICAL PERSPECTIVES

Self-injury exists throughout human history. Favazza (1987) reports on cave markings suggesting finger amputations that likely occurred during religious rituals some 20,000 years ago. Private and public rituals of self-torture were practiced for centuries across many cultures for purposes of purification, induction to a state of enlightenment, religious worship, group indoctrination, and identification. Mortification of the flesh and self-torment are common themes in the lives of saints and martyrs, as well as in classical mythology (consider St. Lucy and Oedipus, who each put out eyes in symbolic acts, as noted by Favazza, 1987; Feldman, 1988). Cutting, in particular, is described in the Bible (as Feldman, 1988, noted, the priests of Baal gashed themselves with knives and lances in a rainmaking ceremony). "Self-cutting as homage to God or to cure others has been described among the Chinese, Semites, Tartars, and the Flagellants in America" (Feldman, 1988, p. 254). Starvation is also practiced as a religious or sacred act.

Self-injury first appeared in the psychological literature in the psychoanalytical case of Miss A., a young woman who had experienced childhood abuse (Emerson, 1914). Personal meaning and adaptive function of self-injury were the focus of early theorists. Many older articles offer descriptions of symptoms that are now considered characteristic of borderline personality disorder (American Psychiatric Association, 1994), which remains the most frequent diagnosis for self-injuring women (Feldman, 1988). The literature was quiet about self-injury through the 1940s and the 1950s, addressing it as "suicidal gestures." In the 1960s and the 1970s, a different look at cutting began to emerge in the literature. "Wrist-cutting syndrome," "wrist scratching," "delicate self-cutting," and "coarse cutting" began to be examined as separate from suicide attempts (e.g., Graff & Mullin, 1967).

Despite many publications on self-injury from 1973 through 1993, little consensus emerged about the meaning or function of self-injury. Various theoretical explanations were offered. The possible role of depersonalization, a number of common antecedent events, and the self-injurer's experience of increasing tension relieved by self-injury were addressed. Discriminating self-injury from suicide remains an area of controversy, as do reasons for selfinjury.

UNDERSTANDING SELF-INJURY

The Link to Trauma

Several predisposing factors are identified in the literature. These include childhood physical or sexual abuse, chaotic and neglectful homes in childhood, childhood separation from caregivers, parental alcoholism, early surgical or medical trauma, and childhood and adolescent or adult residence in a full-care institutional setting.

In 1991, van der Kolk, Perry, and Herman found that 79% of individuals who reported self-cutting also reported a history of childhood physical abuse; 89% reported traumatic disruption of parental care leading to neglect. In the same sample, childhood sexual abuse before the age of 13 was more strongly related to adult self-injury than were other forms of childhood trauma.

People who are abused often, severely, and early may injure themselves more severely, more persistently, and in more ways than other people (Calof, 1995a). It appears that earlier abuse leads to more self-directed aggression. van der Kolk (1996) reports that in one sample, "Abuse during early childhood and latency was strongly correlated with suicide attempts, self-mutilation and other self-injurious behavior," with sexual abuse, separation and neglect predicting increased severity and chronicity over a 4-year follow-up period (p. 190). Research indicates that self-injury usually begins during early adolescence and waxes and wanes through adulthood (Favazza & Rosenthal, 1993), although first occurrence has been reported following adult traumas, including war (Pitman, 1990) and rape (Greenspan & Samuel, 1992).

Eating disorders and self-injury are moderately to highly correlated across a number of recent studies (Favazza, 1989; Farber, 1995; van der Kolk et al., 1991). van der Kolk (1996) found abuse during adolescence was associated with anorexia in adulthood in one outpatient sample. Furthermore, atypical purging, including extreme laxative abuse, was highly correlated with other self-injurious behaviors in some samples (Farber, 1995; Mitchell, Boutacoff, & Hatsukami, 1986).

Because "the body keeps the score" of traumatic events (van der Kolk, 1994), action on and by the body can be seen as powerful symbolic and physiological interventions by the survivor. It was speculated that self-injury serves to stimulate endorphins, creating a mood change in the victim (van der Kolk, 1988). In one study, the use of serotonin agonists appeared to provide some relief from compulsive self-injury in psychiatric patients (Markovitz, Calabrese,

& Schutz, 1991). Childhood abuse has profound and lasting physiological effects, leading to depression, hyperarousal, and other highly aversive physical and affective states (Briere, 1995a, 1995b; Davies & Frawley, 1994), which individuals may attempt to manage in many ways, including through self-injury.

Sakheim and Stanek (1994), after interviewing clients who self-injure, described a variety of defensive motivations that self-injury can serve. These include distraction from painful affects, showing others the pain inside, achieving a trance state (thereby regulating dissociative experiences like flashbacks), a way to see blood or feel pain to feel real, part of an internal communication process or part of interpersonal communication, a way to express anger or to self-soothe, and part of a confusion of feeling states (e.g., interweaving sexuality and aggression, see Davies & Frawley, 1994).

For many self-injurers, harming the body has its roots in childhood efforts to adapt to and manage the overwhelming affects and physical pain associated with trauma, including sexual abuse and profound neglect. Over time, self-injurious behavior may become more severe and varied and may eventually become part of the psychological and physical identity of the adult survivor.

Constructivist Self Development Theory Framework

A psychological theory of the impact of trauma can provide a framework for treatment providers and survivors in their work together, making self-injury understandable and guiding treatment of survivors who self-injure. Constructivist self development theory (CSDT; McCann & Pearlman, 1990a; Pearlman & Saakvitne, 1995) views the impact of trauma as unique to every individual. The impact is determined by an interaction of aspects of the event that are psychologically meaningful to the individual with aspects of the individual, including psychological resources, defenses, and needs. The impact of trauma is further shaped by the cultural and social context within which it occurs.

CSDT further delineates aspects of the self that are impacted by trauma. These include frame of reference, psychological needs, ego resources, the memory system, and self capacities.

This chapter focuses on the self capacities because of their hypothesized connection to self-injurious behaviors. CSDT describes three self capacities, or inner abilities people require to maintain a sense of self and to maintain a state of internal balance. They are the ability to maintain a sense of connection with others; the ability to experience, tolerate, and integrate strong affect; and the ability to maintain a sense of self as viable, benign, and positive. The capacity to maintain a sense of connection with others is the basis from which affect regulation and self-worth develop.

The development of self capacities is a concept central to work with self-injurers who are trauma survivors. In emergency interventions, interviewing for self capacities allows the treatment provider to identify areas of need and strength. In addition, the provider and client can develop temporary measures to shore up or increase self capacities to help the client through a crisis.

Self capacities are not fully developed in abusive or neglectful homes (Pearlman, 1998). The ability to maintain a sense of connection cannot fully develop when empathic attunement, affection, and nurturance (the context of Bowlby's [1988] "secure base"), are lacking. When children experience shaming and punitive rhetoric or physical blows rather than responsive words, there can be no effective internalization of loving others. Instead, the images and voices the individual internalizes are challenging, harsh, and mocking.

The ability to experience, tolerate, and integrate strong affect cannot fully develop when strong feelings are met with punishment or derision and need and longing are met with neglect or humiliation. The child learns not to want and not to need. To accomplish this, the child must also learn not to feel. Thus, numbing, dissociation, or self-punishment (through words of reprobation or through actions of self-harm) may become natural responses to, or substitutes for, feelings.

Finally, the ability to maintain a sense of self as viable, benign, and positive cannot fully develop when a child's existence and accomplishments are met with silence or abusive words or actions. The child does not learn that he or she is a person of value. Rather, the lesson is existential self-doubt and self-loathing.

Without strong self capacities and stable external supports, self-injurers cannot afford to let go of the adaptations that have helped them survive the original abusive environment or the current inner life that has resulted. When self capacities are undeveloped, self-injury can act as a substitute for their essential regulatory functions. So-called symptoms such as self-injurious behavior, then, may be viewed as adaptations to powerful psychological circumstances rooted in otherwise impossible developmental conditions. In the next section we review some functions of self-injury for individuals lacking full development of the self capacities.

Self Capacities in Self-Injury

Connection

When the capacity to maintain an inner sense of connection with others is impaired, self-injury can manage the work of connection. Self-injury can be a way for a client to internally manage conflict with the therapist, because interpersonal conflict might feel too dangerous. Loyalty to perpetrators and identification with the aggressor can be demonstrated, preserving a sense of connection to abusive childhood caregivers by denying or joining with their sadism and inadequacy. Self-injury can also be a way of taking control of victimization—being the one to decide when, how, and how much one will be injured. Through this process, the individual may be attempting to master the roles of victim, aggressor, and helpless witness which the child may have internalized over the course of the abuse; Miller (1994) termed the inner experience of self as victim, perpetrator, and bystander the "tripartite self." Self-injury may at times be an effort to obtain recognition, attention, or other forms of interpersonal connection that are sometimes identified as secondary gain. Such efforts demonstrate the level of desperation a trauma survivor may experience in the effort to connect.

Affect Regulation

If the capacity to experience and tolerate strong affect is impaired, self-injury may serve as a solution. The rituals and sensations around it are generally experienced as reducing unbearable tension, that is, self-soothing for individuals who have never had the opportunity to internalize a soothing other. Self-injury can serve as punishment for affect that is forbidden or split off. It can be a way to deal with sexual feelings, especially if sexual abuse linked terror, pain, and sexual feeling together (Davies & Frawley, 1994). Self-injury is also commonly used to manage depersonalization and more extreme levels of dissociation. Some clients report that it is useful to induce dissociation or trance; others report that it brings them back to their bodies and to physical sensation, reducing the dysphoria or the terror of prolonged dissociation. Finally, self-injury can be used to invoke a sense of safety and relief. If abuse is inevitable, its occurrence removes dread and terror. If the safest times of a child's life are the hours following an abusive episode, the aftermath of abuse may feel comforting and safe (Calof, 1994; Sakheim, 1996).

Expression, or externalizing of affective states, is a primary function of self-injury, and developing new ways of expressing is central to the treatment. Calof (1996) wrote in detail about the difficulty childhood abuse survivors experience in feeling, naming, and comprehending anger. The ability to feel and name affects is impaired (termed "alexithymia" by Krystal in 1978). The individual moves from arousal to action without mediating stages of feeling awareness, feeling identification, feeling expression, and self-soothing. This rapid and unmediated movement from arousal to action is demonstrated in the rising sense of tension that self-injurers describe, the preoccupation with achieving self-injury, and the sense of relief that follows the act.

Self-Worth

When the capacity to maintain a sense of self as viable, benign, and positive is impaired, self-injury serves a host of functions. It may be used for purification, transcendence, or penance, as in many mystical practices. It may provide punishment and degradation of the unworthy self. It may reassure the survivor that he or she is a human being—flesh and blood—much like others. It may threaten or remind the individual of his or her unworthiness, intrinsic vileness, and fragile hold on the world of other people. It may also reassure the individual that he or she is, indeed, tough, resilient, and able to take abuse and carry on.

RESPONDING TO SELF-INJURY IN EMERGENCY SITUATIONS

Principles for Assisting in Crisis

A theory provides a way to understand self-injury and a framework for action. This is particularly important in emergency settings, where contact may be brief and clinical information minimal. CSDT allows the treatment provider to act with respect and purpose. Within this framework, four organizing principles guide intervention: (1) return control to the individual in crisis, (2) interview for self capacities, (3) develop short-term strategies to shore up self capacities, and (4) link self-injury to an external or internal antecedent event. The treatment provider should first assess the context of the encounter and the possibility that the self-injuring individual may have a history of childhood abuse. The intervention process we describe here applies to all persons who present with self-inflicted injuries, including those who are not childhood trauma survivors.

There are numerous and significant pressures on clinicians in emergency settings. Sometimes these pressures contradict the recommendations made here. In this chapter the focus is on the client's best interest and the optimal emergency treatment experience. Clinicians in emergency settings struggle to balance organizational and fiscal demands and procedures with respectful treatment of complex cases. These recommendations support the policies of client-focused emergency intervention.

Context

The circumstances of the individual's appearance in the emergency room are significant to the process of addressing his or her safety. Someone who is dragged against his or her will to an emergency room responds differently than someone who has entered the treatment setting independently. The goal under any circumstances is to help the individual regain control and reconstruct a modicum of safety.

In the often rushed and impersonal climate of emergency settings, attention to the interpersonal context is an essential beginning in responding effectively to the self-injuring patient. The encounter should begin with introductions in which the provider states his or her name and role and the purpose of this contact. Many trauma survivors had traumatic encounters with medical providers and developed a suspicious attitude toward powerful others whose formal role is to help. The provider should elicit questions and feedback throughout the course of the interview. It is essential that the provider be direct, honest, and respectful of the patient, behaving in a trustworthy way without expecting unearned trust. Childhood abuse survivors are exquisitely attuned to manipulation and deception, and the encounter cannot succeed if the provider is behaving in an authoritarian, indirect, or otherwise disrespectful manner. If others accompanied the patient, the provider should check with the patient about whether he or she wants the others to stay or to leave and should respect the patient's stated wishes. If other treatment providers are present, the main provider should introduce them and explain their roles, remaining sensitive to the meanings of being observed and objectified to a childhood abuse survivor. If the client has a psychotherapist, the therapist should be contacted, with the client's permission. The therapist may be able to provide understanding of the client, opinions about the severity of this crisis, and extremely valuable information about what helps and what should be avoided. This contact also demonstrates respect for the client and may increase the client's perceived safety by demonstrating alliance with the client's chosen helper and by widening the client's support network to include both regular therapy and emergency services working together.

Return Control

Returning control to the individual may be counterintuitive when the client appears to be out of control. In CSDT, however, the treatment provider's job is not to take control but to hand control back and help the person move toward safety. The provider expects and requests the individual's collaboration in figuring out what is needed to reach this goal. Together the provider and the individual in crisis can determine what level and type of assistance will help. This approach minimizes the possibility of retraumatizing events in the crisis setting, including affect-driven escalation on the part of the client and reenactments of such past abuses as restraint, labeling, rejection, or abandonment. Clients who are accustomed to surrendering control may be ambivalent about collaboration. Even if invited by the client to take over the interview and disposition, the treatment provider should state a commitment to the client's self-control and responsibility and should encourage collaboration.

The provider must assess the impact of the emergency setting on his or her own behavior and approach to the client. It is enormously challenging to impart calm, safety, and confidence and to manage professional liability concerns and countertransferential reactions in a setting that is crowded, noisy, and rushed. These difficulties are intensified by self-injury, an issue associated with affect, intensity, and danger. It is useful to accept that work with a self-injuring individual in crisis may require more time than with another type of patient and to try to arrange for a somewhat slower pace. Although this can be a strain, it is likely to save significant time and trouble overall by facilitating a more effective encounter. Physical surroundings have meaning to trauma survivors. Being placed in a waiting room, cubicle, or interview room may be perceived as restraint, exposure, or isolation. Persons in audible pain in nearby spaces may evoke memories, such as witnessing abuse of others. It is therefore useful to check out a client's comfort level with the surroundings, including levels of noise, privacy, and perceived safety to minimize stimuli that would increase distress.

Providers should interview the client briefly about any pressing fears or concerns that might be stimulated by the crisis situation or emergency services setting. The person may be coping with distressing fears or expectations. For example, the client may feel at risk for "flashing back," being restrained, experiencing violence or other abuse by staff, or becoming violent or otherwise out of control. The provider should explore what could help if these fears become more pressing or if it seems as if feared events are going to take place. The provider should discuss what would make the situation better or worse. The real limits, procedures, and risks of the setting should be reviewed so that the client has the information that is needed to make informed decisions about behavior and to influence the outcome of the intervention. (E.g., clients in a hospital emergency room need to be informed of the criteria for release and for hospital admission so that both parties can operate in an above board and respectful fashion with reduced fears of being manipulated, trapped, or, in the client's case, abandoned.)

As in all interviews, an even, firm, and quiet voice can help to convey the treatment provider's sense of calm and respect. The treatment provider should avoid debate or lecturing even if he or she feels provoked in those directions. A report of trauma history should not be challenged in an emergency setting even if there is reason to doubt it. This is the story that the client believes provides the best context for understanding his or her current needs and the story that providers are being asked to witness and integrate into a treatment plan.

If evidence of escalation appears, a first step is to remain calm and to communicate the expectation that the client also can and will remain calm. Keep in mind the possibility that the person is managing flashbacks, panic, or dissociative experiences. Taking a break, "grounding" techniques or "talking down" techniques may help (e.g., asking the client to review with the provider the date and place, the client's age and name, the current time and time since arrival; to look around and name some objects in the room; and to look at and handle his or her own driver's license or other familiar objects). Suggestions for deep breathing or visualizing a calm scene may be helpful, but only if the client is feeling sufficiently safe in the current setting. The treatment provider should remind the client of what was learned together in the first few minutes of the interview about what can help in this setting. The client should be called on to join with the provider in what helps. Providers should make every attempt to avoid restraint or seclusion, which have retraumatizing effects on survivors.

If treatment providers must advocate for the humane use of external control for purposes of saving a client's life, clearly they should connect their actions to their motivations. For example, the provider might explain that he or she is temporarily acting as an advocate for the safety of the client's body. The provider should communicate the wish that the client will soon feel for himself or herself the hope and respect that he or she feels for the client. The provider should explain that it is hope and respect that motivate him or her to advocate for the client's safety. If the provider must make the decision for the client, he or she should carefully explain the dilemma of balancing control and safety and invite the client to help solve the problem in some way on which they can both agree. The provider should identify every decision that remains under the client's control and work together to make those decisions. With survivors of childhood abuse, forcing unwanted treatment will undoubtedly have some damaging effects. If such a course must be pursued, it is important for the provider to acknowledge that he or she knows of the potential harm but that there may not be another, better way to solve the immediate problem. Failure to acknowledge the hurtful parts of an intervention can be experienced as a repetition of the denial accompanying childhood abuse and so may increase the client's distress. Unless the matter is life and death, or freedom is limited by liability concerns or organizational the policy, the client should remain in the position of decision maker about treatment disposition.

Interview for Self Capacities, and Develop Short-Term Strategies to Shore Up Self Capacities

Assessing self capacities helps make meaning of the incident of self-injury and plan for increased safety. The development of self capacities is a long-term therapy goal. However, deficits in self capacities can be addressed in small ways to help stabilize a crisis and guide disposition. Planned efforts to build self capacities can have strong benefits as short-term interventions and can focus a client's behavior and attention on self-care in the aftermath of a crisis.

The capacity to maintain an inner sense of connection is marked by a belief that some people are benevolent, are interested in and care about the client, and are available to the client through the client's internal processes and, ideally, in the interpersonal world. The person in whom this self capacity is undeveloped experiences a sense of profound alienation and emptiness and may feel exiled to the outside, looking in at life. Attachment difficulties are a hallmark of such impairment, and this individual may live essentially alone in the world, or may function in a social system built on exploitation of the individual and neglect of the individual's needs.

To assess this self capacity, the treatment provider might ask whether the client can think of any person in the world who cares for the client. Ask the client if it is possible to imagine or recall that person's caring now. If the client can tune into messages or voices from important others from the past, ask him or her to identify what they say. Are they caring or hateful, supportive or threatening? How about messages or voices from people in the present?

The capacity to maintain an inner sense of connection can be shored up by invoking a benevolent other or a temporary surrogate for a benevolent other in fantasy. If the client can imagine or remember a caring other, ask the client to call on that caring other for inner support and reminders that the client is not alone. Individuals who cannot achieve this sometimes benefit from physically holding an object. If objects associated with human beings (photographs, letters, clothing) are too threatening or inspire too much pain, objects from the natural world can be considered. A "friendly" object such as a rock or a sea shell can be relied on to be unchanging, real, and present when the client needs it. Music, books or poems that created a sense of connection with others (authors, others who love music, the characters described in literature) can be useful during times of alienation and abandonment. A business card, brochure, or other object from the emergency setting or local hotline might be useful as evidence of caring others. Plants and animals can be valuable aids in addressing this area of need. The goal is to identify an object or being that can be contacted or held in the client's mind—or the client's hand—and can be viewed as benevolent. In long-term psychotherapy this becomes the role of the therapist. Guiding the client to therapy referrals or back to therapy is the central goal of crisis intervention with self-injuring individuals who cannot hold an inner sense of connection with others.

The capacity to tolerate strong affect is marked by experiencing strong feelings, either positive or negative, and expressing them without harm to self or others. The person for whom this capacity is extremely undeveloped may be desperately afraid of or numb to strong feelings and may appear depressed, emotionally detached, or anxiously avoidant. The person may be involved in substance use or other analgesic or tension-reducing practices, and may overreact when strong feelings are aroused and behave in an out-of-control fashion. On the other hand, the person may remain numbed and vigilant to the risk of feeling stimulation and may avoid losing control by experiencing no feelings at all.

The capacity to manage strong affect can be assessed by observing the client's reactions to the present situation as well as to questions that invite an emotional response. The treatment provider can ask whether the client is aware of having feelings in daily life. If so, what kind? How does the client feel right now? How does he or she experience and respond to strong feelings (anger, loneliness, sadness)? What is soothing when the client feels upset? Has the client ever felt happiness? When?

Difficulties in managing strong affect are almost certain to be found in self-injury. Strategies for managing strong affect are many, but most individuals can make use of only one or two early in the therapy process. If the client can collaborate in brainstorming, try to put together a list of possible ways to deal with feelings. Clients in crisis typically need to soothe themselves through quiet activities or to reduce tension through tension-reducing activities (Briere, 1995a)—the list can include strategies for both kinds of coping. Soothing activities might include making tea, taking a bath, listening to music, working in a garden, doing an art activity, looking at a beautiful scene, imagining a safe and pleasant place, petting or grooming an animal, and so on. Activities to reduce tension might include walking fast, tearing up paper, throwing something in a safe place (a soft ball in the house, a tennis ball against a wall), hitting golf balls or going to a batting cage to hit softballs, working with clay, yelling, crying, beating on pillows, and so forth.

Because these activities are not inherently curative, suggesting them as solutions to deep internal pain can seem superficial. It is important to recognize, however, that the client feels as if things are unbearable inside. In this type of crisis intervention, the goal is to find some way to feel even a little bit better, even for just a little while. This is a familiar goal for self-injuring individuals. What is unfamiliar is using multiple self-care strategies to achieve it, instead of achieving it through self-injury. In long-term therapy, the client will discover other ways to feel better and will begin to feel better more of the time, with less effort. Strategies developed in times of crisis are intended to support the individual while working toward long-term therapy arrangements.

The capacity to maintain a sense of self as benign and viable is marked by the belief that one's life has meaning and value, and that one is essentially decent, deserving, and worthy of living. The person in whom this capacity is extremely undeveloped perceives criticism, loss, or failure as evidence of a toxic, damaged, or repulsive nature and as evidence that abuse was or is deserved. This person may believe that he or she is inherently flawed or irreparably damaged and therefore does not belong in the world. This person may believe that he or she has no right to live and should or will be degraded, rejected, and abused by self and others.

Assessment might include asking about how the client sees himself or herself. What words does the client use to describe himself or herself? How is suicide viewed by the client? How does the client make sense of unfair or unkind treatment by others? Can the client think of anything positive or valuable about himself or herself? Can the client even imagine having such a thought?

If the capacity to experience the self as viable and benign is not developed, short-term interventions are intended to direct the client's attention to status as a member of the human race, as an individual who is not toxic and who deserves to be in the world. If the client can tolerate exploration, search openly together for any evidence that the client is a person more or less like other people yet unique. Does the client have a political or philosophical perspective that prescribes tolerance or appreciation for others? If so, is there any room for himself or herself in that perspective? Does the client value any aspect of himself or herself, any talents, abilities? Is there anyone else who values the client? Has the client ever done a nice thing? In other words, look, with the client, for any existing schema, no matter how narrow or fragile, that includes caring and that could be expanded and nurtured to begin to include the client. Bring the client's attention to the interaction at hand, and note the ways that the client is behaving like a viable and benign individual here. Self-help, political, and volunteer activities can foster development of the self capacity, but once again, development is long-term work, and direction to long-term therapy is critical.

Link Self-Injury to External or Internal Antecedent Events

Linking self-injury to an event promotes self-understanding and can provide a view of one's experience as making sense and of oneself as coping, as opposed to being out of control and "crazy." Linking can be approached by asking the client to think about the minutes, hours, and day before the injury took place. What was going on? Was anything important changing? Was anyone important missing or acting different? Was there any interpersonal event, anniversary, television show, or therapy session that served as a memory trigger or otherwise stirred things up? Was tension building? When did the tension become noticeable? When did the idea of self-injury come to mind? How did the person move from thinking about it to doing it? Work together to put words to the wish behind self-injury. Did it seem like the injury would help? Did it help? How did the emergency service get involved?

If the person is a repetitive, ritualized, or frequent self-injurer, there might be a sense, from the client or from others around the client, that this behavior has no meaning and that efforts to understand are futile. It is important to note that this episode is somehow different, because this episode led to the interview. The provider and client must take it seriously and examine it together, avoiding the temptation to dismiss it as only part of an ongoing pattern. The client has created a new interpersonal reality, one that allows for the possibility of change. This time the injury can be known and discussed.

Once an antecedent is identified, alternatives can be explored. The key issue is learning what might help the client cope with the antecedent. If that goal is too big, focus on the behaviors involved. What is the first clue or "red flag" that self-injury will follow the antecedent? Is it possible to do anything different at that point? What is the smallest effective change that could be imagined or instituted? The provider should be aware that this discussion will not necessarily lead to change and should not involve asking the client to promise never to use self-injury to cope in the future.

Treatment providers should bear in mind that self-injury has powerful hidden, individual, and unspoken meanings. Communicating a perspective of curiosity, openness, patience, and respect is critical when the meaning of the behavior is not understood. Calof (1995b) notes that much of the logic that governs self-injury is "trance logic," governed by memories, elements of primary process, magical thinking, and affect-driven problem solving. Miller (1994) describes trauma reenactment syndrome, in which individuals who persistently injure or abuse their bodies unconsciously reenact elements of past abuses they have endured. Walsh and Rosen (1988) identify a series of events, feelings, and behaviors that individuals experience in both an episode of child abuse and in an episode of self-injury, pointing out the ways in which self-injury is an expression of that which became familiar to the abused child. Given the possible complexities of self-injury, the work of linking it to an antecedent should be limited in crisis. The purpose of this discussion is to gently challenge the view that self-injury is out of the client's control, is "crazy" or inexplicable behavior, or is the only alternative available. Further work on this idea must take place in longer-term therapy.

Differentiating Self-Injury from Suicide Attempts

In emergency situations, self-injury should be viewed as distinct from a suicide attempt. Although self-injury does not necessarily indicate a need for inpatient or other protective care, a suicide attempt or ideation clearly indicates elevated needs for intensive assistance and protection. Individuals who self-injure do not typically kill themselves using the same methods that they use for self-injury; that is, the intentions are different, and the behaviors of suicide attempts are distinct from the rituals of self-injury (Allen, 1995). Self-injury may have lethal potential, however. Overdose, infection following deep cutting, or other severe injuries could lead to death without the explicit intention of suicide. Self-injurers, especially those who are childhood abuse survivors, are at some risk for planned or unplanned suicide, as are other individuals who manage chronic dysphoria, a sense of alienation, and impulsive behavior. The literature on suicide and its assessment offers valuable perspectives and directions to clinicians seeking to understand more about this area of practice (e.g., see Buie & Maltsberger, 1983; Shneidman, 1985).

Straightforward discussion of suicide risk is often possible and is most desirable in the context of self-injury. The self-injuring individual may be practiced and thoughtful in self-injuring and able to discriminate between impulses toward injury and suicide. A standard suicide assessment is called for (assessing level of depression, perceived helplessness and hopelessness, suicidal intent, plan, preparations, access to means, previous attempts, social supports, history of suicide in family members, recent bereavement or job loss, etc.) (Fauman & Fauman, 1981). Using the principles described in this chapter sets the stage for a frank and supportive discussion between two adults about the behavior, its meaning, and the individual's needs. Suicide assessment is a natural extension of the discussion. Assessing suicidality or lethal potential and making corresponding decisions about protection and treatment should take place in a dialogue. If communication about risk cannot be achieved, especially with an individual who indicates poorly developed self capacities, suicidal risk should be evaluated with additional reason for concern. The role of two self capacities (maintaining a sense of self-worth and an inner sense of connection to benevolent others) in suicide was acknowledged by Buie and Maltsberger (1983). They stressed the critical role of dynamic formulation in the assessment of suicide risk and cautioned against overreliance on empathy or standard assessment to determine the risk of suicide.

Self-injury is essentially a survival technique. It is a reaction to almost unendurable circumstances or internal experiences. It is intended to allow the individual to endure and to carry on. Self-injury is not typically an expression of hopelessness and helplessness; it is not typically an expression of the wish or decision to die. Rather, it can be seen as Menninger (1938) saw it, a victory of life instinct over death instinct.

Walsh and Rosen (1988) contrasted self-injury with suicide, adapting Shneidman's (1985) work on suicide. They examined the following 10 dimensions: stimulus, stressor, purpose, goal, emotion, internal attitude, cognitive state, interpersonal act, action, and consistency. Especially relevant to this chapter are their contrasts between the suicide stimulus (unendurable psychological pain) and the self-injury stimulus (intermittent, escalating psychological pain), the suicide purpose (seeking a solution to an overbearing problem) and the self-injury purpose (achieving short-term alleviation), the suicide goal (cessation of consciousness) and the self-injury goal (alteration of consciousness), the suicide emotion (hopelessness/helplessness) and the self-injury emotion (alienation), and the suicide internal attitude (ambivalence) as opposed to the self-injury attitude (resignation). (See Walsh & Rosen, 1988, for an interesting treatment of the topic.)

THE TREATMENT PROVIDER AND SELF-INJURY

Countertransference

Understanding and managing countertransference are essential to the effective treatment of self-injuring individuals. The literature on self-injury frequently addresses this topic, and authors comment on the time and emotional investment required in dealing with self-injury, the unusually strong reactions of therapists and other mental health professionals, and the limits these reactions place on our ability to work with the clients. In data gathered from 117 licensed psychologists, self-injury was rated the most distressing and stressful client behavior and the client behavior that psychologists found to be most traumatizing to encounter professionally (Gamble, Pearlman, Lucca, & Allen, 1994). Other studies confirm the challenge of working with self-injury. Simpson (1973) reported that physicians tend to speak pejoratively about self-injuring patients, and Simpson and Porter (1981) described the interpersonal challenges that self-injuring adolescents can pose to caregivers. Feldman (1988) addressed common and complex staff responses to self-injuring inpatient adults.

In emergency situations, clinicians encountering self-injury can be surprised by the complexity and unusual depth of personal feeling they confront. They may feel overwhelmed and may experience urges to punish or control the client. It can be very difficult to manage one's own reactions while making oneself available to the client. This may be especially true if one works in a setting in which self-injury has been understood as an attempt to manipulate treatment providers, a conceptualization that only indirectly acknowledges the survivor's historical lack of access to legitimate means of control. Such settings may endorse the use of management strategies that ignore the individuality or humanity of the client. The provider can be drawn directly into an excruciating drama: the dynamic shifts among internalized roles of victim, perpetrator, and helpless witness (Davies & Frawley, 1994; Miller, 1994; Pearlman & Saakvitne, 1995). We each must understand and monitor our reactions to this work both to protect our own resources and to remain respectful, curious, and open to the client. This can best be accomplished through self-awareness on the part of the treatment provider and ongoing supervision or consultation.

Vicarious Traumatization

Vicarious traumatization is the experience of a transformation in the self of a treatment provider as a result of empathic engagement with trauma survivors and their material (McCann & Pearlman, 1990b; Pearlman & Saakvitne, 1995). It differs from countertransference in that it does not refer to a single therapy relationship but rather to the cumulative impact across time of working with trauma survivors. Encountering and managing self-injury is extremely demanding work. In parallel to the impact of trauma on the survivor, we posit that treatment providers experience the impact of trauma work in the same psychological realms as survivors. Thus, we may feel the impact of working with many self-injurious trauma survivor clients over time, or we may be surprised by a strong reaction to a particular client. We may find ourselves having greater difficulty holding on to our internal connection with caring others, specifically our mentors, our teachers, our supervisors. We may find our own affect tolerance diminished, as evidenced by heightened sensitivity to violence, a new startle response, a numbing of feelings, or feelings of lessened self-worth.

In addition, the treatment provider's frame of reference, or overarching ways of experiencing self and world, may shift. Emergency work is often done without cues of context; the therapist does not know the individual, the individual's resources or history, or the stressors that led to this crisis. The provider may not see the person afterward to enjoy the reassurance that the individual survived and benefited from the emergency intervention. The lack of context for the work can feel like an assault on identity, leading treatment providers to question why they do this work or to question their effectiveness. The provider may be aware of affective states that are not familiar (e.g., living in a state of heightened awareness of the possibilities of loss or harm, rather than a more familiar state of peacefulness). Working with self-injuring clients can raise spiritual issues for the treatment provider, including profound questions about meaning and hope (Neumann & Pearlman, 1997). In doing this work, it is easy to lose a sense of connection with whatever it is beyond oneself that has previously provided spiritual sustenance. Finally, one's world view or understanding of causality, life philosophy, and moral principles can be challenged deeply as a result of working with people who self-injure. We inevitably struggle with questions of why people self-injure, who should decide whether those who self-injure retain control over their freedom, and whether our responses are right or wrong in a moral rather than a clinical sense as we do this work.

Additional issues relating to control may arise for the therapists. They may be facing a life-and-death crisis and, paradoxically, be aware both of their limited ability to influence the outcome and the enormous responsibility they feel (and the legal liability they may indeed hold) in these situations. In hospital settings and in many emergency settings, there is an invitation, even an instruction, to take control. Yet it is the contention of the authors that taking control is often antithetical to the survivor's best interest. In many emergency treatment settings, time is of the essence, yet working with a self-injuring individual in crises is likely to require time and an unrushed demeanor. The provider may be left with complicated feelings about his or her own sense of control, whether they are feelings of frustration related to limitations or anger about the imposition of unwanted control or responsibility.

To remain effective clinically and connected to our own humanity, therapists must address and transform these deleterious effects of working with people who self-injure. To do so requires that they attend to their professional needs in the work, their needs for continuing education and ongoing supervision and consultation from trauma-sensitive colleagues, regardless of their level of experience. They must also attend to their personal needs, by balancing this work with other work and with play and rest. Finally, to transform vicarious traumatization, therapists must remain aware of or create meaning in the work and in their lives (Charney & Pearlman, Chapter 19, this volume; Saakvitne, Pearlman, and the Staff of the Traumatic Stress Institute, 1996). Only through these means can they hope to remain vital, alert, and attuned to the complex needs of self-injuring trauma survivor clients.

SUMMARY

By acknowledging the importance of childhood trauma in the life of the self-injuring survivor and working toward collaboration in the goal of increased safety, treatment providers offer clients an opportunity to explore self-injury in a compassionate, respectful, and nonjudgmental way that holds the promise of resolution. Attention to issues of control, self capacities, and the treatment provider's own reactions can allow for a productive intervention, thereby gently challenging the client's sense of alienation and lack of alternatives to self-injury.

Self-injurious behavior has many meanings and functions. It represents desperate attempts to cope with that which feels unendurable, especially in the wake of childhood abuse. Effective treatment, in emergency settings and in longer-term relationships, takes into account the important functions served by self-injury. Resolution will come about in the context of a respectful therapeutic relationship, through the combined efforts of the client and a therapist, over time. The role of treatment providers in emergency settings is to provide a respectful human encounter, to help begin the process of understanding self-injury, to collaborate on strategies that can help to temporarily shore up self capacities, and to offer hope that such work, approached over time with a trustworthy helper, can lessen the internal pain being experienced. This can be achieved only through a model that views the client as a fellow human being who is resourceful, comprehensible, and able to move toward safety.

ACKNOWLEDGMENTS

We wish to thank Dusty Miller, EdD, and David Sakheim, PhD, for their thoughtful readings of this chapter.

REFERENCES

Allen, J. G. (1995). *Coping with trauma*. Washington, DC: American Psychiatric Press.

American Psychiatric Association. (1994). *Diagnostic and statistical manual of mental disorders* (4th ed.). Washington, DC: Author.

Bongar, B., Peterson, L. G., Golann, S., Hardiman, J. (1990) Self mutilation and the chronically suicidal patient: An examination of the frequent visitor to the emergency room. *Annals of Clinical Psychiatry, 2,* 217–222.

Bowlby, J. (1988). *A secure base*. New York: Basic Books.

Buie, D., & Maltsberger, J. (1983). *The practical formulation of suicide risk*. Somerville, MA: Firefly Press.

Briere, J. (1995a). *Attacks on the body: Meaning and management of self-mutilation in trauma therapy*. Paper presented at the 11th annual meeting of the International Society for Traumatic Stress Studies, Boston.

Briere, J. (1995b). *Trauma Symptom Inventory professional manual*. Odessa, FL: Psychological Assessment Resources.

Calof, D. L. (1994, November). *Self-injury and self mutilation in trauma survivors*. Paper presented at the sponsored seminar, "Healing the Heart," Madison, CT.

Calof, D. L. (1995a). Chronic self-injury in adult survivors of childhood abuse: Sources, motivations and functions of self-injury (part I). *Treating Abuse Today, 5*(3), 11–16.

Calof, D. L. (1995b). Chronic self-injury in adult survivors of childhood abuse: Sources, motivations and functions of self-injury (part II). *Treating Abuse Today, 5*(4/5), 31–36.

Calof, D. L. (1996). Chronic self-injury in adult survivors of childhood abuse: Developmental processes of anger in relation to self-injury (part I). *Treating Abuse Today: Survivorship, Treatment and Trends, 5*(6/1), 61–62, 64–67.

Davies, J. M., & Frawley, M. G. (1994). *Treating the adult survivor of childhood sexual abuse: A psychoanalytic perspective*. New York: Basic Books.

Emerson, L. E. (1914). A preliminary report of psychoanalytic study and treatment of a case of self mutilation. *Psychoanalytic Review, 1,* 41–52.

Farber, S. K. (1995). *Summary of research findings. A psychoanalytically informed understanding of the association between binge–purge behavior and self-mutilating behavior: A study comparing binge–purgers who self-mutilate severely with binge–purgers who self-mutilate mildly or not at all*. Unpublished doctoral dissertation, New York University.

Fauman, B. S., & Fauman, M. A. (1981). *Emergency psychiatry for the house officer.* Baltimore: Williams & Wilkins.

Favazza, A. R. (1987). *Bodies under siege: Self mutilation in culture and psychiatry.* Baltimore: Johns Hopkins University Press.

Favazza, A. R., & Conterio, K. (1988). The plight of chronic self mutilators. *Community Mental Health Journal, 24,* 22–30.

Favazza, A. R., & Rosenthal, R. J. (1993). Diagnostic issues in self mutilation. *Hospital and Community Psychiatry, 44*(2), 134–140.

Feldman, M. D. (1988). The challenge of self-mutilation: A review. *Comprehensive Psychiatry, 29*(3), 252–269.

Fennig, S., & Fennig, S. N. (1992). The interpersonal aspect of the decisionmaking process in the psychiatric emergency room; Correspondence. *International Journal of Social Behavior, 38*(4), 318.

Gamble, S. J., Pearlman, L. A., Lucca, A. M., & Allen, G. J. (1994, October). *Vicarious traumatization and burnout among Connecticut psychologists: Empirical findings.* Paper presented at the annual meeting of the Connecticut Psychological Association, Waterbury, CT.

Graff, H., & Mullin, R. (1967). The syndrome of the wrist cutter. *American Journal of Psychiatry, 124,* 36–42.

Green, A. H. (1978). Self destructive behavior in battered children. *American Journal of Psychiatry, 135*(5), 579–582.

Greenspan, G. S., & Samuel, S. E. (1992). Self-cutting after rape. *American Journal of Psychiatry, 146*(6), 789–790.

Krystal, H. (1978). Trauma and affects. *Psychoanalytic Study of the Child, 33,* 81–117.

Markovitz, P. J., Calabrese, J. R., & Schulz, C. C. (1991). Fluoxetine in the treatment of borderline and schizotypal disorders. *American Journal of Psychiatry, 148,* 1064–1067.

McCann, L., & Pearlman, L. A. (1990a). *Psychological trauma and the adult survivor: Theory, therapy, and transformation.* New York: Brunner/Mazel.

McCann, L., & Pearlman, L. A. (1990b). Vicarious traumatization: A contextual model for understanding the effects of trauma on helpers. *Journal of Traumatic Stress, 3*(1), 131–149.

Menninger, K. (1938). *Man against himself.* New York: Harcourt Brace World.

Miller, D. (1994). *Women who hurt themselves: A book of hope and understanding.* New York: Basic Books.

Mitchell, J. E., Boutacoff, L. I., & Hatsukami, O. (1986). Laxative abuse as a variant of bulimia. *Journal of Nervous and Mental Disease, 174,* 174–176.

Neumann, D. A. (1995). The long-term correlates of childhood sexual abuse in adult survivors. In J. Briere (Ed.), *Assessing and treating victims of violence* (pp. 29–38). San Francisco: Jossey-Bass.

Neumann, D. A., & Pearlman, L. A. (1997). *Toward a psychological language for spirituality.* Manuscript submitted for publication.

Pattison, E. M., & Kahan, J. (1983). The deliberate self-harm syndrome. *American Journal of Psychiatry, 140,* 867–872.

Pearlman, L. A. (1998). Trauma and the self: A theoretical/clinical perspective. *Journal of Emotional Abuse, 1,* 7–25.

Pearlman, L. A., & Saakvitne, K. W. (1995). *Trauma and the therapist: Counter-*

transference and vicarious traumatization in psychotherapy with incest survivors. New York: Norton.

Pitman, R. K. (1990). Self-mutilation in combat-related PTSD. *American Journal of Psychiatry, 147,* 123–124.

Polusny, M. A., & Follette, V. M. (1995). Long term correlates of child sexual abuse: Theory and review of the empirical literature. *Applied and Preventive Psychology, 4*(3), 113–166.

Saakvitne, K. W., Pearlman, L. A., & the Staff of the Traumatic Stress Institute. (1996). *Transforming the pain: A workbook on vicarious traumatization*. New York: Norton.

Sakheim, D. K. (1993, October). *Motivations for self-injurious behavior: A trauma model*. Paper presented at the 10th annual conference of the Albany County Rape Crisis Center, Albany, NY.

Sakheim, D. K. (1996). Clinical aspects of sadistic ritual abuse. In L. Michelson & W. J. Ray (Eds.), *Handbook of dissociation: Theoretical, empirical and clinical perspectives* (pp. 569–592). New York: Plenum Press.

Sakheim, D. K., & Stanek, L. J. (1994, Fall). Assessment of self-injurious behavior [Special issue]. *Raising Issue*.

Shneidman, E. S. (1985). *Definition of suicide*. New York: Wiley.

Simpson, M. A. (1973). Female genital self-mutilation. *Archives of General Psychiatry, 29,* 808–810.

Simpson, M. A., & Porter, S. (1981). Self mutilation in children and adolescents. *Bulletin of the Menninger Clinic, 45*(5), 428–438.

Trautmann, K., & Connors, R. (1994). *Understanding self injury: A workbook for adults*. Pittsburgh: Pittsburgh Action Against Rape.

van der Kolk, B. A. (1988). The trauma spectrum: The interaction of biological and social events in the genesis of the trauma response. *Journal of Traumatic Stress, 1,* 273–290.

van der Kolk, B. A. (1994). The body keeps the score: Memory and the evolving psychobiology of posttraumatic stress. *Harvard Review of Psychiatry, 1,* 253–265.

van der Kolk, B. A., McFarlane, A. C., & Weisarth, L. (Eds.). (1996). *Traumatic stress: The effects of overwhelming experience on mind, body, and society*. New York: Guilford Press.

van der Kolk, B. A., Perry, C., & Herman, J. L. (1991). Childhood origins of self-destructive behavior. *American Journal of Psychiatry, 148*(12), 1665–1671.

Walsh, B., & Rosen, P. (1988). *Self-mutilation: Theory, research and treatment*. New York: Guilford Press.

RESOURCES

For Clients

Newsletter: The Cutting Edge, P.O. Box 20819, Cleveland OH 44124. *Workbook:* K. Trautmann & R. Conners (1994), *Understanding self-injury: A workbook for adults*, Pittsburgh Action Against Rape, 81 South 19th St., Pittsburgh, PA 15203.

Other Resources: Women and Self Injury Project, c/o ILCNS, 583 Chestnut St., Lynn, MA 01904, (617) 593-7500.

Voices In Action (specify interest in self-injury), P.O. Box 148309, Chicago, IL 60614.

For Treatment Providers

An information packet on self-injury is available from the Boston Women's Health Collective, 240 Elm St., Somerville, MA 02144. A small donation is requested.

Books by D. Miller (1994) and B. Walsh and P. Rosen (1988) specifically address treatment issues.

For treatment providers dealing with issues of vicarious traumatization: Cavalcade Productions, P.O. Box 2480, Nevada City, CA 95959, has available a set of two training videos. *Transforming the pain: A workbook on vicarious traumatization* by K. W. Saakvitne, L. A. Pearlman and the Staff of the Traumatic Stress Institute is available from Norton Professional Books, W.W. Norton & Co., 1609 Sherman Ave., Suite 304, Evanston, IL 60201; (800) 233-4830.

In Addition

Trautmann and Conners's 1994 workbook includes an annotated resource section for providers and self-injuring individuals. Some of the above listings are described more fully there. Also listed are resources in the areas of sexual abuse, dissociation, and ritual abuse.

An inpatient treatment program for people who self-injure operates through the Rock Creek Center in Alton, Illinois. This program is called S.A.F.E. (Self Abuse Finally Ends) Alternatives Program. The telephone number for the Rock Creek Center is (618) 465-7324.

Readers might want to check out internet web sites that address self-injury. One such site is at http://www.palace.net/ñlamma/psych/injury.html.

CHAPTER 12

THE EVALUATION AND MANAGEMENT OF ALCOHOL- AND DRUG-RELATED CRISES

GLENN R. TREZZA
SABRINA M. POPP

The purpose of this chapter is to describe the characteristics, assessment, and treatment options for the management of drug- and alcohol-related emergencies. Many psychiatric emergency situations may include substance use as a presenting complication, but three key situations may be defined as true alcohol- or drug-related crises: intoxication states, withdrawal states, and overdose. In the *Diagnostic and Statistical Manual of Mental Disorders,* fourth edition (DSM-IV; American Psychiatric Association, 1994), intoxication is defined as follows:

> The development of a reversible substance-specific syndrome due to the recent ingestion of (or exposure to) a substance. . . . Clinically significant maladaptive behavioral or psychological changes that are due to the effect of the substance on the central nervous system . . . and develop during or shortly after the use of the substance. (p. 184)

DSM-IV defines withdrawal as follows:

> The development of a substance-specific syndrome due to the cessation of (or reduction in) substance use that has been heavy and prolonged. . . .

The substance-specific syndrome causes clinically significant distress or impairment in social, occupational, or other important areas of functioning. (p. 185)

Unlike intoxication and withdrawal, overdose is not designated as a specific disorder; however, overdose may be defined as the ingestion of greater than usual quantities of a substance or substances that results in clinical signs of toxicity.

This chapter discusses each of these substance use situations as they relate to specific substances as well as provides an overview of polysubstance issues. It is important for the clinician to remember that substance use issues can present at any point in a patient's assessment, from a private practice session through an emergency room encounter. Recognition of these issues is an essential tool for the general clinician.

ALCOHOL AND DRUG INTOXICATION

A 45-year-old disheveled man presents in your community crisis center. Brought in by police, he was found ranting in a public park at 2 A.M. Currently, he is mumbling to himself, appears agitated, is pacing, and seems paranoid. His eyes dart nervously around the room, and he appears frightened of the emergency room team. He talks about hearing threatening voices. The patient's pulse is elevated, and the nurse tells you, "His eyes look wild." What should you consider?

If the clinician considered either amphetamine or cocaine intoxication in the differential diagnosis, he or she was correct. This case is an illustration of the often confusing initial presentation of intoxication states. In this particular case, the differential diagnosis could have also appropriately included bipolar disorder, manic phase; schizoaffective disorder; paranoid schizophrenia; and psychotic depression. However, failing to include intoxication or withdrawal could be a dangerous error, and such substance use diagnoses are often neglected under emergency conditions. Intoxication states often mimic psychiatric disorders and, without proper treatment, may put the patient and the clinician at risk of harm. In general, however, intoxication states are less likely to be problematic in the emergency room than are other substance use-related emergencies.

Amphetamine and Cocaine Intoxication

On initial presentation, cocaine and amphetamine intoxication greatly resemble each other, although symptoms of both are likely to vary based on amount consumed, route of administration, and previous experience with stimulants. Intravenous administration and/or smoking crack cocaine engender the most rapid effects, whereas ingestion or inhaling act more slowly. Prior experience with stimulant use makes these more pronounced effects of intoxication less likely to occur.

At low to moderate doses of stimulants, patients may present with increased energy, increased motor activity and rate of speech, symptoms of grandiosity, hypersexuality, and mood lability. Physiologically, patients may present with dilated pupils; diapharesis; increased respiration rate; mildly elevated temperature, pulse, and blood pressure; dry mouth; nasal/septal defects; and/or evidence of injection sites. At moderate to high doses, patients often experience paranoia; irritability with impulsive behavior; affective lability; hallucinations (including auditory, visual, tactile, or olfactory); delusional thinking; and possibly cardiac arrhythmias, seizures, and muscle weakness (Miller, Gold, & Millman, 1989; Tunving, 1989).

Violence is often associated with cocaine intoxication and has been associated with fatalities among cocaine users (Tardiff, Gross, Wu, Stajic, & Millman, 1989). As in the case illustration, these intoxication states often mimic major psychotic disorders or bipolar affective disorder (Tunving, 1989). Patient or collateral self-report may strongly implicate stimulants as the source of hypomanic or psychotic symptoms, but the only certain way to determine stimulants' etiological role is via toxic screen urinalysis, which should be obtained in the emergency room for maximal accuracy.

Management of these patients centers around providing safety for patients and staff alike, as well as supportive treatment for any medical complications, such as monitoring vital signs and treating symptoms of dehydration. In interactions with the patient, supportive, nonthreatening statements and actions are most helpful. At times, a destimulating environment is useful. It is important to remember that these patients often respond in a guarded, paranoid fashion and may be impulsive and threatening. The length of time required for the intoxicating effects of stimulants to wear off and for observing a patient varies depending on the patient and the amount of stimulant used. Occasionally, anxiolytics and/or antipsychotic agents may be useful in reducing agitation. At times, physical restraints may be necessary to maintain safety. Many pharmacological agents to combat the effects of cocaine have been researched, but none has conclusively proved to be an effective agent to manage cocaine intoxication, withdrawal, or overdose (Crosby, Halikas, & Carlson, 1991).

Alcohol Intoxication

Many emergency rooms must treat patients intoxicated with alcohol. Patients may arrive with alcohol intoxication as their stated problem or with alcohol intoxication as a comorbid complication of other psychiatric and/or medical conditions. Given its prevalence, alcohol intoxication is a syndrome with which the clinician should be thoroughly familiar. Symptoms of intoxication may not correlate with blood alcohol level. Patients with chronic excessive alcohol intake may have less intoxication symptomatology at higher blood levels than will patients with little experience of alcohol at lower blood levels. Levels of defined intoxication vary by state and may range from 80 to 150 mg/dL. Level of intoxication also varies with body size, metabolism, history of liver or kidney dysfunction, rate of consumption, and tolerance. Common symptoms of alcohol intoxication include slurred speech, unsteady gait, disinhibition with labile affect, flushing, nystagmus, smelling of alcohol, sedation, concentration/attention and memory difficulties, and gastrointestinal distress, while more severe intoxication states can also include respiratory depression and coma.

As with stimulant intoxication, management of alcohol intoxication involves mainly supportive measures. Intravenous hydration and nutritional supplements are often recommended because of poor nutritional status and dehydration, both of which occur frequently in alcohol abusers. Thiamine (100 mg) is especially important to prevent the development of Wernicke's encephalopathy. These patients also need to be monitored closely for symptoms of respiratory depression, and are at risk for aspiration. Ongoing staff monitoring of intoxicated patients is important, especially if patients begin to show early signs of alcohol withdrawal, and these patients should be observed regularly. Some intoxicated, disinhibited patients may report suicidal ideation and/or become belligerent with emergency room staff. These patients should be assessed carefully for lethality, keeping in mind that assurances of safety made while intoxicated may be of questionable validity. Moreover, patients may also require a destimulating environment, firm limit setting, physical restraints, and/or bedrest to help them retain appropriate self control.

Sedative Intoxication

Intoxication with sedatives (benzodiazepines, barbiturates, and sedative hypnotics) closely resembles alcohol intoxication's physiological and psychological symptoms. Slurred speech, unsteady gait, poor judgment, and somnolence are common. Treatment and management issues are essentially the same as for the alcohol-intoxicated patient. Diagnostic tools include urine and serum toxic screens in addition to patient and collateral self-report.

Heroin/Opiate Intoxication

Patients intoxicated from opiates, including heroin, opium, methadone, and narcotic analgesics (Percocet, Demerol, Dilaudid, Talwin, codeine, etc.) do not frequently present in emergency settings, unless they are experiencing medical complications from their opiate use or intoxication behavior. Symptoms of the opiate-intoxicated patient may include sedation; euphoria and/or apathy; inattention and memory problems; increased pain tolerance and risk taking; pinpoint pupils; pruritis; at times, decreased pulse, blood pressure, and respiratory rate; and occasional nausea or vomiting. Urine toxic screens, physical evidence such as injection sites, and obtainable history may help confirm the diagnosis. Unless more significant respiratory, blood pressure, or heart rate symptoms or excessive sedation develop, these patients often do not present to an emergency room. The need for treatment of opiate intoxication depends on level of sedation and/or complications, in particular respiratory depression. Treatment with opiate antagonists such as naloxone should be administered immediately in severe intoxication states, again with close monitoring of vital signs for acute changes in symptoms.

Hallucinogenics

Intoxication with hallucinogenics is an uncommon presenting diagnosis in the emergency room but, like stimulants, may cloud the presentation because intoxication symptoms often mimic symptoms of psychiatric disorders. Hallucinogenics include LSD, PCP, mescaline, psylocybin, peyote, "mushrooms," and a number of synthetic agents such as Ecstasy. Patients intoxicated from hallucinogenics may experience hallucinations, feelings of derealization and depersonalization, synesthesias, intensified perceptions, paranoid ideation, ideas of reference, fears of loss of control, and feelings of depression/anxiety (Brust, 1993). Treatment again includes destimulation, supportive measures, and close monitoring. Most emergency settings do not have effective screening mechanisms for confirmatory diagnosis of hallucinogen intoxication. PCP intoxication, which can also include symptoms of ataxia and dysarthria, is of particular concern because patients' severe disinhibition and greatly elevated pain tolerance may lead them to be more violent and unpredictable. These patients may require restraint to maintain safety of the patient and the emergency room staff.

Other Intoxication States

Although DSM-IV does include diagnoses of intoxication with inhalants, cannabinoids, and caffeine, these patients rarely, if ever, present to the emergency room unless other medical issues have arisen. Treatment of intoxication with these substances is once again primarily supportive. For completeness, the following is a review of these intoxication states.

Inhalants include amyl and butyl nitrate ("poppers"), nitrous oxide, and fumes from household products such as liquid paper, glue, aerosol cans, paint, and nail polish remover. Symptoms of inhalant intoxication include apathy, belligerence, euphoria, impaired judgment, dizziness, nystagmus, blurred vision, impaired gait and coordination, lethargy, and, in more severe cases, tremor, muscle weakness, stupor, and coma. Cases of permanent brain damage have been reported with abuse of these substances (Brust, 1993).

Common symptoms of intoxication with cannabinoids, which include marijuana, hashish, and THC, are dry mouth, increased appetite, euphoria, sensation of slowed time, poor motor coordination, anxiety, and impaired judgment.

Caffeine intoxication's symptoms include agitation, insomnia, flushing, diuresis, increased pulse, and gastrointestinal disturbance. Table 12.1 summarizes the common signs of and symptoms of intoxication for a variety of substances, as well as the signs and symptoms of withdrawal and overdose.

SUBSTANCE WITHDRAWAL

A 69-year-old female is brought to your clinic by concerned neighbors. On assessment, she complains of hearing noises on the ceiling and feels her neighbors are spying on her. According to one of the neighbors, the patient even called the police to report her suspicions on two occasions. Initially cooperative, the patient becomes more agitated during the exam, complaining that things in the room are bothering her. Left alone in the assessment room, staff members observe her talking aloud as if having a conversation and batting at the air. Her blood pressure and pulse are quite elevated and she appears flushed. What other information would you like to have to make a proper diagnosis?

In this case, the presentation appears to be consistent with an organic delirium; however, the important consideration is the cause. Despite the patient's age, unless the clinician included complicated alcohol withdrawal or delirium tremens (DTs) as a possible etiology, he or she may have made a serious error. In this example, a review of the woman's past medical history suggested significant alcohol abuse and a search of her belongings revealed an empty vodka bottle. The etiology of organic delirium can be broad, but alcohol or drug withdrawal should be a major consideration in making a diagnosis. Prompt treatment is essential to decrease the risk of further complications.

Alcohol and Sedative Withdrawal

We focus on alcohol withdrawal in our discussion because of the nearly identical symptomatology of and treatment for alcohol, benzodiazepine, barbiturate, and sedative hypnotic withdrawal. Different levels of alcohol withdrawal pose a variety of treatment considerations. Uncomplicated withdrawal can occur any time patients have any significant drop in their usual level of blood alcohol, most often within 24 hours of discontinuing alcohol intake. However, it is important to remember that alcohol withdrawal can occur while a patient is still

TABLE 12.1. Signs and Symptoms of Intoxication, Withdrawal, and Overdose

Alcohol

Intoxication	Withdrawal	Overdose
Slurred speech	*Uncomplicated:*	Alteration in mental status
Unsteady gait	Agitation	Respiratory depression
Disinhibition/labile affect	Anorexia	Central nervous system
Flushing	Mild tremor	depression
Nystagmus	Increased pulse and	
Odor of alcohol	blood pressure	
Sedation	Diaphoresis	
Concentration/attention/	Flushing	
memory difficulties	Fever	
Gastrointestinal distress	Sleep disturbances	
Decreased reaction time		
Severe symptoms:	*Complicated:*	
Respiratory depression	Seizures	
Coma	Hallucinations	
	Confusion	
	Disorientation	
	Delusional thinking	
	Combative behavior	
	Delirium tremens	

Sedatives

Intoxication	Withdrawal	Overdose
Similar to alcohol	*See Alcohol	*See Alcohol
Slurred speech		
Unsteady gait		
Poor judgment		
Somnolence		

Cannabinoid intoxification
Dry mouth
Increased appetite
Euphoria
Sensation of slowed time
Decreased motor coordi-
nation
Anxiety
Impaired judgment

Amphetamines/Cocaine

Intoxication	Withdrawal	Overdose
Low to moderate doses:	Craving	Hypertension
Increased energy	Fatigue	Increased heart rate
Increased motor activity	Vivid dreams	Seizures
Increased rate of speech	Sleep disturbances	Cardiac arrhythmias
Grandiosity	Increased appetite	
Hypersexual behavior		

(cont.)

TABLE 12.1. (cont.)

Labile mood	Agitation or sedation
Dilated pupils	Suicidal ideation
Diaphoresis	
Increased respiration rate	
Elevated temperature, pulse, blood pressure	
Dry mouth	

Moderate to high dose:

Paranoia
Irritability
Impulsivity
Labile affect
Hallucinations (auditory, visual, tactile, olfactory)
Delusions
Cardiac symptoms, including chest pains and arrhythmias
Seizures
Muscle weakness

Opiates

Intoxication	Withdrawal	Overdose
Sedation	*Early:*	Respiratory depression
Euphoria or apathy	Yawning	Central nervous system
Inattention or memory problems	Lacrimation	depression
Increased pain tolerance	Rhinorrhea	Hypotension
Impulsivity	Diaphoresis	Hypothermia
Pinpoint pupils		Coma
Pruritis	*Advanced:*	
Decreased pulse, blood pressure, respiratory rate	Increased intensity of early symptoms	
	Anorexia	
	Pupillary dilation	
	Piloerection	
	Restlessness	
	Irritability	
	Nausea/vomiting/abdominal cramps/diarrhea	
	Muscle spasms	
	Weakness	
	Increased heart rate and blood pressure	

Caffeine

Intoxication	Withdrawal
Agitation	Fatigue
Insomnia	Tremor
Flushing	Headache
Diuresis	Irritability
Increased pulse	
Gastrointestinal symptoms	

(cont.)

TABLE 12.1. (cont.)

Nicotine withdrawal

Dysphoric mood
Irritability
Anxiety
Decreased concentration
Restlessness
Insomnia
Daytime drowsiness
Increased appetite
Elevated blood pressure
Gastrointestinal disturbances

Hallucinogen intoxication

Hallucinations
Derealization
Depersonalization
Synethesias
Intensified perceptions
Paranoid ideation
Ideas of reference
Fears of loss of control
Depression
Anxiety
Insomnia
Loss of appetite
Pupillary dilation
Dizziness
Increased pulse, blood pressure, temperature

Inhalants

Intoxication	Overdose
Apathy	Cardiorespiratory complications
Belligerence	Permanent brain damage
Euphoria	
Impaired judgment	
Dizziness	
Nystagmus	
Blurred vision	
Impaired gait	
Impaired coordination	
Lethargy	

Severe:

Tremor
Muscle weakness
Stupor
Coma
Brain damage

intoxicated—if the level of intoxication is less than the patient typically exhibits. To ascertain whether withdrawal is occurring in such situations, it is important for the emergency room clinician to try to establish clearly the patient's recent pattern of alcohol consumption, the time of the last drink, and, if collateral report is available, usual level of intoxication.

Uncomplicated withdrawal may have a variety of symptoms, including agitation, anorexia, mild tremor, increased pulse and blood pressure, diapheresis, flushing, fever, and sleep disturbance. Treatment of this type of withdrawal consists of rehydration, nutritional support (especially thiamine replacement to avoid Wernicke's encephalopathy), and monitoring of vital signs. If indicated by progression of symptoms or history of previous withdrawal, including risk for seizures or DTs, medications such as benzodiazepines, which can be slowly tapered, can be used to alleviate withdrawal symptoms (Castaneda & Cushman, 1989). Regardless of pharmacological treatment recommended, however, the most important treatment of uncomplicated withdrawal is close monitoring to avoid progression of the withdrawal.

Complicated withdrawal is distinguished by the additional symptoms of seizures, hallucinations, confusion, disorientation, or delusional thinking. Typically, these symptoms start to occur between 48 and 96 hours after cessation of alcohol use. Complicated withdrawal is a medical emergency and should be treated on an inpatient medical or detoxification unit and occasionally requires monitoring in the intensive care unit. These complications of withdrawal indicate a need for close monitoring, more active treatment with benzodiazepines, and/or treatment for delirium. Longer-acting benzodiazepines, such as Valium (diazepam) and Librium (chlordiazepoxide), are often given in heavy "loading doses" to patients in severe withdrawal; the long half-life of these medications facilitates gradual pharmacological taper without need of many additional benzodiazepine doses. In patients with more pronounced liver disease, shorter-acting benzodiazepines such as Serax (oxazepam) and Ativan (lorazepam) may be required, as these medications do not require oxidation in the liver (Adinoff, 1994).

Patients in more severe alcohol or sedative withdrawal may also be agitated and quite combative and may require restraint. Delirium tremens is an extreme case of complicated withdrawal and carries risk of mortality without treatment. Treatment may include chemical or physical restraint, a destimulating environment, and pharmacological treatments, including benzodiazepines and antipsychotic medications. Seizures are also a real risk for more severely withdrawing patients, and an alcohol-induced seizure is often a terrifying experience for both patient and collaterals. However, careful monitoring and a thorough history can forestall seizure occurrence, and treatment with benzodiazepines greatly reduces any risk of withdrawal seizures. Anticonvulsant treatment, in fact, is seldom indicated unless the patient has a preexisting seizure disorder (Earnest, 1993).

Prediction models may also help the emergency room clinician correctly identify elevated risk for seizures. A recent empirical analysis indicated that alcohol withdrawal seizures are more likely to occur if the patient (1) has a prior history of seizures, (2) has used psychotropic medications in addition to alcohol, (3) has a history of head injury or trauma, (4) has a highly elevated pulse in the first 48 hours of withdrawal, (5) has a low serum sodium level at time of presentation, and (6) is not given magnesium at time of presentation (Morton, Laird, Crane, Partovi, & Frye, 1994). The age of the patient may also be a helpful predictor of potential severity of alcohol withdrawal. A retrospective chart review of older (mean age = 69) versus younger (mean age = 30) patients indicated that alcohol withdrawal is generally more severe in older patients, who tended to experience more withdrawal symptoms for longer periods and had more pronounced cognitive impairment, elevated blood pressure, weakness, and somnolence than did their younger counterparts (Brower, Mudd, Blow, Young, & Hill, 1994).

Heroin/Opiate Withdrawal

Unlike alcohol withdrawal, opiate withdrawal, although at times quite uncomfortable for the patient, is seldom, if ever, life-threatening. Opiate withdrawal can also present with several different levels of symptomatology. Early withdrawal symptoms include yawning, lacrimation, rhinorrhea, and diapheresis. As withdrawal progresses, there is an increase in severity of these symptoms, as well as symptoms of anorexia, pupillary dilation, piloerection, restlessness, irritability, nausea with vomiting and abdominal cramps, diarrhea, muscle spasms, and weakness. These patients may also experience an increase in heart rate and blood pressure, because they are prone to dehydration. In advanced opiate withdrawal, the patient is likely to report considerable distress. Medical complications are usually limited to the effects of the dehydration.

Treatment of withdrawal can consist of rehydration, monitoring of vital signs, and initiation of an opiate agonist such as methadone or other medications including clonidine. Other treatments, such as acupuncture and biofeedback, are suggested as useful in the reduction of withdrawal symptoms (Katin, Ng, & Lowison, 1992; Portenoy & Payne, 1992).

Stimulant Withdrawal

Far less likely to present in an emergency room setting, patients withdrawing from cocaine and amphetamines pose less medical but more psychiatric risks. The primary symptoms of stimulant withdrawal include fatigue, vivid dreams, sleep disturbance, increased appetite, and agitation or sedation (Lago & Kosten, 1994). Suicidal ideation is often a concomitant feature and must be carefully assessed in these patients. Definitive medical complications are not usually present. Symptoms of withdrawal can develop from a few hours to several days after discontinuing or reducing prolonged or heavy stimulant use. Behavioral interventions for cocaine withdrawal include providing a destimulating, supportive environment and bedrest.

Nicotine Withdrawal

Nicotine withdrawal is more likely to be a complicating presentation in a patient with other concerns in an emergency setting. Although not medically threatening, patients experiencing nicotine withdrawal can be agitated and irritable, making them more difficult to manage. Typically, these patients may be more uncooperative with behavioral and medical management, at times escalating to the point of attempting to leave the clinic or emergency room to smoke prior to completion of the evaluation. Symptoms of nicotine withdrawal include dysphoric mood, irritability, anxiety, difficulty with concentration, restlessness, insomnia and daytime drowsiness, and increased appetite. Physiological symptoms include elevated blood pressure. Generally, heavier smokers experience more pronounced effects of withdrawal. Nicotine withdrawal is sometimes worsened by concomitant caffeine toxicity, and the symptoms of the two may be confused by both the patient and the assessor (Swanson & Hopp, 1994). Some smokers do better with abrupt withdrawal, whereas others manage better with gradual nicotine cessation (Som-mese & Patterson, 1995). Interventions for withdrawal may include nicotine replacement treatments such as patches or gum (Cummings, Giovino, Jaen, & Emrich, 1985). Behavioral interventions may also be helpful. These include increased fluid intake; use of cigarette analogues such as carrot or celery sticks, toothpicks, or straws for oral and manual substitution; distraction techniques, including self-talk; avoidance of environmental and social smoking cues; review of motivations for smoking cessation; social support; and relaxation techniques.

OVERDOSE

> An ambulance brings a 15-year-old boy to the emergency room. He was found stuporous in a shopping mall men's room. On initial examination, the teen appears responsive to pain and to a loud noise but drifts off to sleep while answering questions. You leave the exam room to gather more information and a staff member runs to you, saying, "He's not breathing that well." What should you do next?

The answer to that question probably should be to get a medical doctor to evaluate the patient. Overdose should be considered a medical emergency and, in general, should not be treated by the mental health team. However, mental health staff are often the initial assessors of substance-related overdose, and prompt recognition of overdose symptoms is vital. This case is an illustration of heroin overdose, which can be treated by an opiate antagonist to block the effects of the heroin. Lack of appropriate treatment can lead to respiratory depression and death. Regardless of the patient's age and physical presentation, a patient with changes in consciousness should be considered to have possibly overdosed until this possibility is ruled out by medical staff.

Overdose is perhaps the most serious consequence of alcohol or drug abuse to be seen in an emergency setting. Studies have reported that between 0.4% and 2.0% of all emergency room visits are a direct result of drug overdose (Stern et al., 1991). Frequently, overdose presents as a mental health as well as a medical emergency; patients who have overdosed can be combative and difficult to manage, as well as severely medically compromised. Moreover, the most significant medical effect of overdose is often alterations in mental status (Stern et al., 1991). Although many of these patients are often not seen by mental health services in the emergency room because of the need for medical attention, the emergency room mental health team may be consulted regarding behavioral management or assessment of suicidality. Key assessment issues that may be presented to the mental health team include determining history of prior overdoses and history of amounts of substances typically used by the patient, ascertaining a purposeful versus an accidental overdose, and evaluating any primary psychiatric diagnoses, such as concomitant depression. The mental health team may also be asked to play a role in verbal management or physical restraint of an agitated patient and in interview of and support for the patient's family or friends who have accompanied the patient to the emergency room. A structured interview assessment may achieve more reliable data than an unstructured interview in the assessment of these overdose concerns (Burn, Edwards, & Machin, 1990).

In general, the full assessment of suicide intent and potential should be carried out after the patient is medically stabilized and no longer exhibits signs of intoxication. This may occur only after a period of inpatient treatment and observation. If an overdose is determined or strongly suspected to be purposeful, a patient may be stabilized in an intensive care unit or general medical ward under observation, then transferred to a psychiatric inpatient unit for more extensive evaluation, treatment, and establishment of safety for discharge. In general, there is a trend toward medical admission when patients are comatose and toward psychiatric admission when the patient is initially alert or agitated (Stern et al., 1991). In some epidemiological studies, overdose is found to be the most common means of attempted suicide (Bland, Newman, & Dyck, 1994; Stern et al., 1991), and suicidal intent in overdose should never be overlooked. A great many suicide attempts by college students, for instance, are associated with substance abuse, as are completed suicides by college students. The suicidal intent of an overdosed young person should be carefully considered during an emergency room presentation (Rivinus, 1990).

In the emergency room setting, the particular substance or substances on which a patient overdosed create different initial concerns for the emergency room clinician. For example, a patient who overdosed on benzodiazepines, barbiturates, or alcohol can present with respiratory or central nervous system depression, including coma. A patient who overdosed on heroin or other opiates may also arrive in the emergency room with these problems, particularly respiratory depression, but may also present with hypotension and hypothermia. Some cohort studies suggest that overdose is the largest single category of cause of death in heroin addicts (Oppenheimer, Tobutt, Taylor, & Andrew, 1994). Risk factors for heroin overdose include concomitant benzodiazepine use and use of heroin in an atypical setting (Gutierrez-Cebollada, de la Torre, Ortuno, Garces, & Cami, 1994).

Cocaine or amphetamine overdose produces hypertension, increased heart rate, seizures, and potentially fatal cardiac arrhythmias. The likelihood of overdose in cocaine use is influenced by delay of and duration of effects. Crack cocaine is less likely to cause a life-threatening overdose because of its rapid onset of action and brief length of action. Conversely, intravenous cocaine use is the most likely to result in overdose (Pottieger, Tressell, Inciardi, & Rosales, 1992).

The most serious outcomes of inhalant overdose can be cardiorespiratory complications and permanent brain damage. Perhaps most complicated to manage is polysubstance overdose, which can present a complicated mix of symptoms that may initially mask more serious complications. For example, in a cohort study of heroin addicts, 55% of fatal drug overdoses involved multiple substances (Oppenheimer et al., 1994). Moreover, the symptoms of any overdose may be present initially or may present over time as an overdose evolves, again necessitating early and aggressive medical interventions.

Medical management of overdose depends on the substances involved, the amounts consumed, the degree and severity of the presenting symptoms, and issues regarding suicidal intent. As noted earlier, many abusable substances can present with depressed respiratory function or coma. Monitoring vital signs, providing IV access for intravenous medications that may be needed, and possibly establishing or maintaining an adequate airway are often initial interventions that must be taken by the emergency room physician. Determining cause of overdose with urine or serum toxic screens may also be helpful in treating the patient, and general laboratory assessment, including kidney and liver function screens, can facilitate identification of confounding problems (Verebey, 1992). Examination of liver or kidney dysfunction may be important in determining the patient's ability to metabolize the overdosed substance and in treating the effects of the overdose (Chang & Kosten, 1992; Lipsky, 1984).

For an alcohol or a sedative overdose, monitoring and stabilization are the mainstays of treatment. Administration of thiamine is advisable to prevent the development of Wernicke's encephalopathy. In extreme overdose, hemodialysis should be considered, while gastric lavage may be considered with recent ingestion of benzodiazepines or barbiturates. The benzodiazepine antagonist Flumazenil was recently advocated as a possible treatment to reverse some of the sedative effects of benzodiazepine overdose. Flumazenil treatment, however, carries the risk of transient sedative withdrawal syndromes (Schauben,

1992). Overdose on stimulants, principally amphetamines and cocaine, may require intravenous diazepam for seizures and treatment for control of cardiac arrhythmias, often in an intensive care unit setting.

In cases of opiate overdose, intubation may be required if respiratory depression is severe. Hypotension is also frequently a significant problem in heroin/opiate overdose and often requires fluid replacement and, at times, medications such as pressor amines to maintain blood pressure. Opiate antagonists, such as naloxone (Narcan), can reverse symptoms of respiratory depression; however, the patient receiving these medications requires continued monitoring and often requires additional doses of naloxone to achieve stabilization. In a person already addicted to opiates who overdoses on these substances, the use of naloxone can be problematic, as naloxone may precipitate an acute withdrawal syndrome that may then require treatment. The protocol for this treatment is outlined earlier in the section on opiate withdrawal (Chang & Kosten, 1992).

In all cases of overdose, once the agents used are identified, treatment should be dictated by initial symptoms as well as predicted course. The patient should be observed continually for changes in symptomatology. As thorough a medical and psychiatric history as possible should be obtained from the patient, collaterals, and/or the medical record to predict possible sequelae of the overdose and to be ready with a range of possible medical interventions. Particular care with observation and history should be taken in cases of polydrug overdose.

POLYSUBSTANCE ABUSE ISSUES

After collapsing at a local dance club, a 26-year-old woman is brought into the emergency room. She is somnolent but when aroused becomes easily agitated and appears to be hallucinating. Her speech, even when agitated, is slurred, and her gait is unsteady. Friends who accompanied her to the emergency room state: "She was having a good time, you know, drinking a lot." Her vital signs are elevated, her skin is flushed, and she continues to be agitated at certain points but more somnolent again at other times. What other drugs might have caused this woman's difficulties?

If the clinician answered cocaine, hallucinogens, or inhalants, he or she is likely to be on the right track. Polysubstance abuse can present some of the most confusing pictures to the emergency room clinician. Multiple substances often mask some signs of intoxication while exaggerating others. Moreover, use of multiple substances can also make withdrawal from one substance less obvious until more severe withdrawal symptoms present. Often, reliable data about the kind and quality of drugs the polysubstance user consumed are unavailable. In addition, drugs that alone are relatively low risk in terms of fatality can become lethal in combination, as in the case of alcohol with either benzodiazepines or barbiturates. Benzodiazepine use, in fact, is often a marker of polysubstance use, as benzodiazepines are the most frequently used secondary drugs of abuse (Smith & Landry, 1990).

The patient in the previous case example has some signs of alcohol intoxication, such as somnolence, slurred speech, and unsteady gait, but her elevated vital signs contradict the diagnosis of intoxication solely with alcohol. Her agitation may be disinhibition from alcohol but is more likely to be from the other agents she had ingested (cocaine, inhalants, hallucinogens.) Her symptom presentation requires treatment for more than alcohol intoxication, and here difficulties for the emergency room clinician begin. Though polysubstance problems are becoming more and more common in substance use treatment settings (Chang & Kosten, 1992), little appears in the literature about assessment and treatment of polysubstance intoxication or withdrawal. This lack of formal attention may be because symptoms of polysubstance use are so varied, depending on the amounts and combinations of substances used. Moreover, polysubstance use is not explicitly treated in DSM-IV except for the diagnosis of polysubstance dependence. This lack of formal classification may also contribute to a lack of formal recommendations for managing intoxication, withdrawal, and overdose, the polysubstance use situations that may bring patients to the emergency room.

Intoxication states in the polysubstance user can be confusing at best. For example, alcohol may cover increased agitation from cocaine use or may hide the fact that benzodiazepines, barbiturates, or sedative hypnotics were also taken. In dual-diagnosis patients, the problems of substance use, and in particular polysubstance use, are extremely problematic, again masking symptoms and exaggerating others, increasing toxicity from the patient's usual medication regimen or increasing noncompliance with these medicines. Withdrawal from multiple substances can also heighten withdrawal risks and increase the patient's physical complaints and discomfort. Withdrawal from benzodiazepines, for instance, exacerbates the tremor and anxiety often seen in opiate withdrawal. Assessment of the intoxicated or withdrawing patient who is suspected of polysubstance ingestion should include a very thorough history, especially from outside sources, who may be more cooperative and coherent than the patient, and a detailed physical examination, which looks for contradictory signs and symptoms.

In overdose situations, it is important to remember that symptoms may continue to evolve as one substance wears off and another comes to the forefront. Typically, patients may have increasing or decreasing levels of sedation and may start withdrawing from one substance while still intoxicated from another. For example, a patient may have stopped drinking earlier in the evening, then started using cocaine. As the alcohol wears off, seizure risk from the cocaine can become more prominent. Additive effects of substances, such as additive sedation, are also of great importance and should be looked for in the patient suspected of multiple substance overdose.

Diagnosis of polysubstance ingestion, however, is often difficult at the time of initial presentation and is usually based on secondhand reports. Although toxic screens may be helpful in identifying multiple substances, such screens are limited in their usefulness because of the time they can take to be completed and because such screens often check for a finite number of substances (Verebey, 1992). The behavioral clinician may therefore be a key player in the polysubstance assessment in the emergency room as a careful history, review of the chart, and interview of collateral sources may provide as much key data as does the physical exam.

Treatment of polysubstance use crises should consist of treating the patient for the individual agents consumed and of being aware of the increased risks from the interaction of the particular drugs taken, such as heightened chances of seizure, respiratory depression, hallucinations, and/or other psychotic symptoms. Behavioral management again involves a supportive, destimulating environment along with careful monitoring.

SUMMARY

Substance abuse issues are common concerns of the mental health clinician. A thorough knowledge of intoxication, withdrawal, overdose, and polysubstance abuse issues can be an extremely helpful addition to the assessment tools used by the mental health practitioner working in the emergency room or elsewhere. Appropriate differential diagnosis can lead to more accurate and immediate treatment of the patient and increased safety for patients and staff alike.

REFERENCES

Adinoff, B. (1994). The alcohol withdrawal syndrome. *American Journal on Addictions, 3*, 277–288.

American Psychiatric Association. (1994). *Diagnostic and statistical manual of mental disorders* (4th ed.). Washington, DC: Author.

Bland, R. C., Newman, S. C., & Dyck, R. J. (1994). The epidemiology of parasuicide in Edmonton. *Canadian Journal of Psychiatry, 39*, 391–396.

Brower, K. J., Mudd, S., Blow, F. C., Young, J. P., & Hill, E. M. (1994). Severity and treatment of alcohol withdrawal in elderly versus younger patients. *Alcoholism: Clinical and Experimental Research, 18*, 196–201.

Brust, J. C. M. (1993). Other agents: Phencyclidine, marijuana, hallucinogens, inhalants, and anticholinergics. *Neurologic Clinics, 11*, 555–561.

Burn, W. K., Edwards, J. G., & Machin, D. (1990). Improving house physicians' assessments of self-poisoning. *British Journal of Psychiatry, 157*, 95–100.

Castaneda, R., & Cushman, P. (1989). Alcohol withdrawal: A review of clinical management. *Journal of Clinical Psychiatry, 50*, 278–284.

Chang, G., & Kosten, T. R. (1992). Emergency management of acute drug intoxication. In J. H. Lowinson, P. Ruiz, R. B. Millman, & J. G. Langrod (Eds.),

Substance abuse: A comprehensive textbook (pp. 437–446). Baltimore: Williams & Wilkins.

Crosby, R. D., Halikas, J. A., & Carlson, G. (1991). Pharmacotherapeutic interventions for cocaine abuse: Present practices and future directions. *Journal of Addictive Diseases, 10,* 13–30.

Cummings, K. M., Giovino, G., Jaen, C. R., & Emrich, L. J. (1985). Reports of smoking withdrawal symptoms over a 21 day period of abstinence. *Addictive Behaviors, 10,* 373–381.

Earnest, M. P. (1993). Seizures. *Neurologic Complications of Drug and Alcohol Abuse, 11,* 563–575.

Gutierrez-Cebollada, J., de la Torre, R., Ortuno, J., Garces, J. M., & Cami, J. (1994). Psychotropic drug consumption and other factors associated with heroin overdose. *Drug and Alcohol Dependence, 35,* 169–174.

Katin, J., Ng, L., & Lowison, J. H. (1992). Acupuncture and transcutaneous electrical nerve stimulation: Afferent nerve stimulation (ANS) in the treatment of addiction. In J. H. Lowinson, P. Ruiz, R. B. Millman, & J. G. Langrod (Eds.), *Substance abuse: A comprehensive textbook* (pp. 574–584). Baltimore: Williams & Wilkins.

Lago, J. A., & Kosten, T. R. (1994). Stimulant withdrawal. *Addiction, 89,* 1477–1481.

Lipsky, J. J. (1984). Poisoning, bites, and stings. In A. M. Harvey, R. J. Johns, V. A. McKusick, A. H. Owens, & R. S. Ross (Eds.), *The principles and practice of medicine* (pp. 1443–1449). Norwalk, CT: Appleton-Century-Crofts.

Miller, N. S., Gold, M. S., & Millman, R. B. (1989). Cocaine: General characteristics, abuse, and addiction. *New York State Journal of Medicine, 89,* 390–395.

Morton, W. A., Laird, L. K., Craine, D. F., Partovi, N., & Frye, L. H. (1994). A prediction model for identifying alcohol withdrawal seizures. *American Journal of Drug and Alcohol Abuse, 20,* 75–86.

Oppenheimer, E., Tobutt, C., Taylor, C., & Andrew, T. (1994). Death and survival in a cohort of heroin addicts from London clinics: a 22-year follow-up study. *Addiction, 89,* 1299–1308.

Portenoy, R., & Payne, R. (1992). Acute and chronic pain. In J. H. Lowinson, P. Ruiz, R. B. Millman, & J. G. Langrod (Eds.), *Substance abuse: A comprehensive textbook* (pp. 691–722). Baltimore: Williams & Wilkins.

Pottieger, A. E., Tressell, P. A., Inciardi, J. A., & Rosales, T. A. (1992). Cocaine use patterns and overdose. *Journal of Psychoactive Drugs, 24,* 399–410.

Rivinus, T. M. (1990). The deadly embrace: The suicidal impulse and substance use and abuse in the college student. *Journal of College Student Psychotherapy, 4,* 45–77.

Schauben, J. L. (1992). Flumazenil and precipitated benzodiazepine withdrawal reaction. *Current Therapeutic Research, 52,* 152–159.

Smith, D. E., & Landry, M. J. (1990). Benzodiazepine dependency discontinuation: Focus on the chemical dependency detoxification setting and benzodiazepine–polydrug abuse. *Journal of Psychiatric Research, 24,* 145–156.

Sommese, T., & Patterson, J. C. (1995). Acute effects of cigarette smoking withdrawal: A review of the literature. *Aviation, Space, and Environmental Medicine, 66,* 164–167.

Stern, T. A., Gross, P. L., Pollack, M. H., Browne, B. J., Mahoney, J. D., Alpert, H.

R., Reder, V., & Mulley, A. G. (1991). Drug overdoses seen in the emergency department: Assessment, disposition, and follow-up. *Annals of Clinical Psychiatry, 3,* 223–231.

Swanson, J. A., & Hopp, J. W. (1994). Caffeine and nicotine: A review of their joint use and possible interactive effects in tobacco withdrawal. *Addictive Behaviors, 19,* 229–256.

Tardiff, K., Gross, E., Wu, J., Stajic, M., & Millman, R. (1989). Analysis of cocaine-positive fatalities. *Journal of Forensic Sciences, 34,* 53–63.

Tunving, K. (1989). Cocaine abuse: Clinical aspects. *Nordisk Psykiatrisk Tidsskrift, 43,* 303–308.

Verebey, K. (1992). Diagnostic laboratory: Screening for drug abuse. In J. H. Lowinson, P. Ruiz, R. B. Millman, & J. G. Langrod (Eds.), *Substance abuse: A comprehensive textbook* (pp. 425–437). Baltimore: Williams & Wilkins.

PART V

MEDICAL CONDITIONS PRESENTING AS PSYCHOLOGICAL CRISES

CHAPTER 13

SIDE EFFECTS OF
AND REACTIONS TO
PSYCHOTROPIC MEDICATIONS

SABRINA M. POPP
GLENN R. TREZZA

This chapter provides an overview of commonly used psychiatric medications and their side effects. As the knowledge base about psychopharmacology increases, there is a much wider variety of medications from which to choose, all of which have different safety profiles and side effects. As the pharmacopeia grows, the range of disorders treated psychopharmacologically also expands to include such difficulties as premenstrual symptoms, dysthymia, posttraumatic stress disorder (PTSD), and "personality issues."

Today, many clients see a mental health clinician, who is their psychotherapist, and a psychiatrist, who manages their psychopharmacological treatment. With the increased prevalence of medications for emotional disorders, the psychotherapist needs an updated, working knowledge of current medication options and an ability to recognize their potential adverse reactions, especially as such reactions may influence overall treatment and, left untreated, may constitute significant medical and behavioral emergencies.

Medication side effects can significantly affect a course of treatment. Although a client's depression may have improved, the client may feel no better in terms of quality of life and daily functioning if he or she is experiencing constipation, insomnia, or sexual dysfunction. Side effects also affect medication compliance, psychotherapeutic alliances with treaters, and the willingness of a client's family or social network to support continued treatment. In more complex cases, drug interactions need to be considered and may complicate treatment for the client. It is important to remember that each individual client's experience of side effects may vary greatly in degree of severity. Moreover, proper education and preparation can often improve a client's willingness to continue medication or, if side effects prove difficult to manage, to choose with the clinician to follow a different treatment regimen.

To reduce the chances of unmanageable side effects, clinicians should consider several issues before initiating pharmacotherapy. Proper diagnosis and target symptoms are key criteria in selecting appropriate medications and assessing improvement. When the diagnosis is unclear, it can be particularly important to follow target symptoms to assess improvement or to assess the need to alter medication choices during a medication trial. Concomitant illnesses, medications, and disorders should be elucidated to help recognize potential difficulties or interactions while using psychiatric medications and to help recognize potential causes of side effects, unexpected responses, or poor responses. Patient education and involvement are essential not only to help with compliance but to help generate subjective monitors of improvement.

This chapter discusses the most commonly used psychiatric medications, as well as their side effects to provide the clinician with general guidelines for medication use and management. The chapter is divided into five major sections: antipsychotic medications, antidepressants, mood stabilizers, antianxiety medications, and special categories/potentiating agents, including agents to treat extrapyramidal symptoms (EPS) and sexual dysfunction.

ANTIPSYCHOTIC MEDICATIONS

General Considerations

The development and use of the first antipsychotic agents revolutionalized the treatment of mental illness in the 1950s by adding a new option to the treatment regimens available for psychotic disorders. Antipsychotic medications are also used as antiemetics, preanasthetics, and treatments for some movement disorders, but their mainstay of use is in the treatment of psychotic symptoms found in a range of disorders.

Antipsychotic medications can be loosely assigned to two main groups: the older or "typical" antipsychotics and the newer or "atypical" antipsychotics. These groups are separated by their actions on a subtype of dopamine receptor D2. In general, typical antipsychotics have their main affinity or action on the D2 receptors (Ellenbroek, 1993; Meltzer, Lee, & Ranjan, 1994). These antipsychotics include chlorpromazine (Thorazine), medonidazine (Serentil), thioridazine (Mellaril), fluphenazine (Prolixin), perphenazine (Trilafon), trifluoperazine (Stelazine), thiothixene (Navane), loxapine (Loxitane), properidol (Irapsine), haloperidol (Haldol), molindane (Moban), and pimozide (Orap). The atypical agents clozapine (Clozaril) and risperidone (Risperidol) either have little effect on D2 receptors or have effect on D2 receptors in combination with other receptors (Meltzer et al., 1994). Several agents in development also shifted focus from the D2 receptor to other possible sites of action (Lieberman, 1993). Although both typical and atypical medications demonstrate efficacy in treating positive symptoms of psychosis, including hallucinations, delusions, and disorganized thinking, the newer agents may have greater impact on negative symptoms, including social withdrawal, apathy, anhedonia, and anergia, and fewer EPS (Borison, 1995; Carpenter, 1995; Owens, 1994).

Typical Antipsychotics

The older antipsychotics all have similar profiles of action based on their relative potencies, despite different chemical structures. The potency of a drug is the amount required to achieve a desired effect. The high-potency antipsychotics include haloperidol, properidol, fluphenazine, and pimozide. The low-potency antipsychotics include chlorpromazine and thioridazine. The other typical antipsychotics have midrange potencies and, as a result, have a more mixed presentation of their main side effects.

The older antipsychotics also all have equal efficacy in their treatment of psychotic symptoms. Efficacy is the maximum therapeutic effect of a particular drug. The main differences in these classes of medications is in their predominant side effects, with low-potency medications more likely to be sedating, anticholinergic, and causing orthostatic hypotension and high-potency medications more likely to cause EPS (Hyman, Arana, & Rosenbaum, 1995).

When an older antipsychotic medication is being used for treatment, the rationale for the choice of agent should involve its side effect profile along with previous response to and side effects from prior medication trials. For example, if a client has a great deal of lethargy, a low-potency agent is likely to increase sedation. If the client had a previous trial on a high-potency agent and developed EPS or dystonia, reoccurrence is likely and an anti-Parkinsonian agent may be needed or a change to a low-potency antipsychotic may be required. Certain high-risk clients, such as the elderly or the actively suicidal, as well as certain medical conditions, such as cardiac disease, glaucoma, and benign prostatic hypertrophy, may also influence the choice of agent. Concomitant use of other psychiatric medications, such as carbamazepine (Tegretol) or the selective serotonin reuptake inhibitors (SSRIs) may alter plasma levels of antipsychotics, potentially increasing side effects, and may change dose ranges or choices of agent (Janicak, 1993). The route of administration (intravenous, intramuscular, or oral) may also affect the development of side effects and how a client feels in response to the medication (Hubbard et al., 1993).

The typical antipsychotics have a high level of safety in general use, but all have significant side effects that may complicate treatment. The following is a review of these side effects and their manifestations.

Side Effects

Neurological side effects are the most problematic caused by the older antipsychotics. Grouped under the rubric of EPS, these side effects include the acute reactions of dystonia, akathisia, and Parkinsonism, and the long-term effect of tardive dyskinesia or tardive dystonia.

Dystonias are sustained or intermittent muscle spasms that can lead to abnormal postures. The muscles most commonly involved are in the head, neck, tongue, and back. Dystonias occur very rapidly after the onset of treatment with antipsychotic medication, with approximately 50% of cases occurring within 48 hours and approximately 90% occurring within the first week of treatment. Younger age and previous history of dystonic reactions appear to be risk factors, and these reactions occur more commonly with high-potency medications, with an incidence of about 15% for any antispsychotic medication and an incidence as high as 51% for high-potency agents alone (Ellenbroek, 1993).

The most dangerous form of this side effect is laryngeal dystonia, which can lead to respiratory distress due to blockage of airways. The treatment of dystonia involves the administration of anticholinergic agents, such as benztropine (Cogentin), trihexyphenidyl (Artane), or diphenhydramine (Benadryl), either intravenously, intramuscularly, or orally, depending on the client's level of distress and symptomatology. These agents, as well as amantadine (Symmetrel), may be used concomitantly with the high-potency neuroleptics to help minimize the risk of these reactions; however, they add their own group of side effects and their use should be weighed against possible increases in other side effects (Hyman et al., 1995).

Akathisia is the client's subjective experience of restlessness, tension, or agitation, often with the presence of increased motoric activity. A frequent cause of noncompliance in patients, akathisia occurs in approximately 20% to 40% of clients taking the older antipsychotics. Akathisia seems most commonly caused by higher-potency antipsychotics and least likely to be caused by thioridazine. Treatment of choice for akathisia is reduction in dose of the antipsychotic, as well as change to a lower-potency agent; however, these changes may not be possible in certain circumstances. Beta-adrenergic blockers such as propranolol (Inderal), benzodiazepines, and some anticholinergic agents can also be useful in reducing akathisia.

Antipsychotic-induced Parkinsonism is another troubling form of EPS. Symptoms, which are consistent with primary Parkinson's disease, include shuffling gait, cogwheel rigidity, pillrolling tremor, masked face, and akinesia. Antipsychotic Parkinsonism is a common side effect, occurring in 20% to 40% of clients treated with older antipsychotics and often occurring within 1 to 4 weeks of treatment (Ellenbroek, 1993). Unlike other EPS symptoms, some tolerance to Parkinsonism side effects may develop but treatment is usually indicated. Treatment usually consists of either lowering medication dosage or adding anticholinergic agents or the anti-Parkinsonian agent amantadine. Traditional anti-

Parkinsonian agents such as L-Dopa are rarely used because of the likelihood that they would worsen psychotic symptoms.

Tardive dyskinesia is the most troubling EPS side effect because of its potential for permanence and the lack of any consistently successful treatment. Tardive dyskinesia is a syndrome consisting of involuntary, repetitive, often purposeless movements, most often involving facial and neck muscles but occasionally including the extremities and muscle groups involved with respiration and swallowing (Hyman et al., 1995). Reported prevalence rates have varied from 0.5 to 56.4%, with an average of 10% to 15% (Ellenbroek, 1993). The main body of evidence suggests that tardive dyskinesia rarely develops before at least several months of antipsychotic treatment, and the only clearly identified risk factor is advanced age. There have been suggestions that female gender and previous EPS may also increase vulnerability to tardive dyskinesia. No consistent treatment exists, although some patients have a reduction or discontinuation of symptoms with the removal of the antipsychotic medication. The main approach to tardive dyskinesia, therefore, is prevention, with regular monitoring for abnormal movements, as well as using lowest possible doses of medications for the least amount of time.

Other neurological complications of the older antipsychotics include neuroleptic malignant syndrome (NMS) and increased likelihood of seizures. Neuroleptic malignant syndrome is a poorly understood constellation of symptoms traditionally characterized by muscular rigidity, typically "lead pipe" rigidity; hyperthermia; altered consciousness; and autonomic dysfunction. Views differ on the identity of cardinal symptoms for diagnosis of NMS and on the significance of NMS syndromes (Reilly, Crowe, & Lloyd, 1991), but NMS can have a high mortality rate, approaching 20% of affected clients, who often succumb to respiratory failure. Treatment of NMS is often supportive and includes discontinuation of the antipsychotic medication; hydration; cooling; urinalysis monitoring for the presence of myoglobin, a protein that indicates skeletal muscle destruction; and use of the muscle relaxant dantrolene (Dantrium) (Dilsaver, 1993). The majority of case reports suggest that once a client has had NMS, there is a substantial risk of recurrence if antipsychotics are reinstituted.

Most typical antipsychotic agents can also lower seizure threshold, with chlorpromazine and other low-potency antipsychotic agents having the greatest risk of seizure. All antipsychotics need to be used with caution in clients with risk factors for seizure, such as history of head trauma or previous seizure disorder. Clients with a history of alcohol or drug dependence may also be at greater risk for seizures while detoxifying if they are being treated with antipsychotic agents.

Typical antipsychotic medications have several other side effects of concern besides EPS. Low-potency agents have more potential for orthostatic hypotension and possible fainting spells because of their greater activity with alpha-adrenergic receptors. The low-potency agents also generally have greater affinity for muscarinic receptors, which leads to such side effects as dry mouth, blurred vision, constipation, and urinary hesitancy. These effects can also precipitate narrow-angle glaucoma in predisposed individuals (Dilsaver, 1993).

Cardiac effects, although uncommon, can pose significant risk with some antipsychotic agents. Pimozide and thiordazine are most likely to cause these effects, and ECG monitoring is recommended when treatment with these agents is initiated or dosages are increased.

Another uncommon, though potentially life-threatening, side effect of antipsychotic agents is agranulocytosis, a decrease in white blood cells, particularly granulocytes, which puts the client at increased risk for infection. Clozapine, an atypical antipsychotic, is most likely to cause this effect; however, chlorpromazine and other older antipsychotics also cause agranulocytosis in rare cases.

Other side effects of the typical antipsychotics that were noted include significant weight gain, found with all antipsychotics with possible exception of molindane; sedation, more common in low-potency antipsychotics; ocular retinopathy, noted with low-potency antipsychotics, and pigmentary retinopathy, associated specifically with thioridazine in doses above 800mg/day; liver enzyme elevations with occasional development of cholestatic jaundice, especially with chlorpromazine; dermatological reactions, including dermatitis, rashes, and sun sensitivity, especially with chlorpromazine and thioridazine, at times leading to a blue-gray tinge to the skin after sun exposure; lupus erythmatous syndrome; and endocrine side effects, including increased prolactin levels, causing breast enlargement and, at times, galactorrhea, amenorrhea, decreased libido, impotence, and a rare syndrome of inappropriate antidiuretic hormone secretion. Some reports also state that the antipsychotics can contribute to a sense of slowed thinking or depressed emotional response, although these symptoms are difficult to separate from the symptoms of the treated disorders themselves (Dilsaver, 1993; Ellenbroek, 1993; Hyman et al., 1995).

Atypical Antipsychotics

The newer or atypical antipsychotics, clozapine (Clozaril) and risperidone (Risperidol), have unique side effects that may be related to their different activity on the D2 receptor in relation to their activity on other dopamine receptor subtypes, their effects on serotonin receptors; and their effects on other receptor sites.

Clozapine was the first atypical antipsychotic agent to come into regular use in this country. Initially synthesized around 1960, the drug was withdrawn from use because it appeared to cause agranulocytosis. Reinstituted since 1990, with strict guidelines for monitoring for early signs of agranulocytosis, clozapine has become an important medication for "treatment resistant" forms of psychosis. Although the exact mechanism of action is unclear, clozapine's greater efficacy in treatment-resistant schizophrenia and its greater impact on negative symptoms may be related to its higher affinity for the D4 dopamine receptor subtype and its effects on the serotonin receptors subtypes (Meltzer, 1994).

Clozapine is mainly utilized in treatment-resistant cases of psychosis because of the high risk of agranulocytosis. Approximately half these cases require at least 6 weeks of treatment to see effects, and some clients require as long as 6 months of treatment before response is noted. Clozapine is also indicated for clients whose severe EPS limits treatment options and for clients with both primary Parkinson's disease and psychosis (Meltzer et al., 1994). There may also be a role for clozapine in the management of other treatment refractory disorders, including schizoaffective and bipolar disorder (Hyman et al., 1995; Safferman, Lieberman, Kane, Szymanski, & Kinon, 1991).

Reviews suggest that more than 75% of clozapine-induced agranulocytosis cases develop in the first 18 weeks of treatment, with the greatest risk between weeks 4 and 18. The incidence rates of agranulocytosis vary but in general appear to be about 1% to 2% over time (Safferman et al., 1991). The risk of agranulocytosis may also be greater with advanced age or in women (Ellenbroek, 1993). Strict guidelines are required by the manufacturer of the drug to decrease potential mortality due to agranulocytosis. These guidelines include a weekly white blood cell (WBC) count or an immediate WBC count with any fever or sign of infection, especially if the fever or signs are within the first 18 weeks of treatment. A WBC count below 2,000 or a granulocyte count below 1,000 means clozapine must be discontinued. Clients who develop agranulocytosis should not be rechallenged with clozapine because they appear to redevelop agranulocytosis at lower doses and sooner than they did in their initial response. Since the institution of these monitoring guidelines, mortality rates secondary to agranulocytosis have dropped (Safferman et al., 1991).

Seizures occur more commonly with clozapine than with any other antipsychotic medication. Overall risk of seizure is thought to be about 3%, but seizure risk also appears to be dose-related, with doses up to 300 mg/day having a 1% risk, doses between 300 and 600 mg/day a 2.7% risk, and doses above 600 mg/day a 4.4% risk (Toth & Frankenburg, 1994). Strategies to lower seizure risk include using the lowest possible dose of clozapine and adding an anticonvulsant agent to minimize seizures. Valproate appears to be the most appropriate choice because of its lack of interaction with clozapine and no report of agranulocytosis with its use (Toth & Frankenburg, 1994).

Sedation and hypersalivation are both common side effects with clozapine treatment, occurring in almost one-third of patients who use the medication. Taking the majority of medication at night may decrease sedation, but hypersalivation appears worse at night and may be a persistent side effect during the use of clozapine.

Postural hypotension and increased heart rate appear to be the main cardiovascular side effects of clozapine, along with infrequent nonspecific ECG changes that are usually of no clinical significance. Tachycardia may be significant, with heart rate increases of up to 25 to 30 beats per minute, and may persist unless clozapine doses are reduced. At times, beta-adrenergic agents can be helpful in lowering heart rate (Safferman et al., 1991).

Additional side effects of clozapine can include nausea, constipation, liver function abnormalities and, rarely, cholestatic jaundice, urinary retention or incontinence, low-grade fever, sexual dysfunction, and weight gain. However, clozapine causes significantly less EPS than do more typical antipsychotics. To date, there have been no confirmed reports of clozapine's causing tardive dyskinesia or NMS when used as a sole agent. A few cases of NMS were reported when clozapine was used in combination with lithium, however (Safferman et al., 1991).

Risperidone, the newest atypical antipsychotic agent currently available, acts mainly on serotonin receptors and has some affinity for the dopamine D2 receptor. In comparison to haloperidol in a double-blind, placebo-controlled study, risperidone proved superior to haloperidol and produced significantly less EPS. Risperidone appeared to have quicker onset of action and showed greater improvement in both positive and negative symptoms of schizophrenia. In comparison with other typical antipsychotic medications, the results again suggested risperidone has greater efficacy in positive symptoms, although there was less evidence of improvement in negative symptoms (Borison, 1995).

Besides some possible increased benefit in the treatment of negative symptoms, the main advantage of treatment with risperidone appears to be less associated EPS (Owens, 1994). Two other significant advantages are no apparent risk of agranulocytosis and little or no anticholinergic side effects. However, risperidone can cause sedation or agitation with insomnia, orthostatic hypotension, weight gain, rhinitis, dizziness, headache, nausea, and sexual dysfunction, possibly secondary to risperidone's effects on prolactin levels (Hyman et al., 1995; Meltzer et al., 1994).

Several new compounds are about to be released or are in advanced prerelease trials. These include olanzapine (Zyprex), sertindole, quetiapine, and ziprasidone. These agents have varying potential mechanisms of action, often involving dopamine and serotonin receptors and other potential sites of activity.

Olanzapine shows promise as an agent with efficacy on both positive and negative symptoms of psychosis and with low EPS and no evidence of agranulocytosis. Major side effects appear to be liver enzyme elevations and anticholinergic side effects at higher doses (Borison, 1995), as well as sedation and dizziness (Ereshefsky, Overman, & Karp, 1996).

In a placebo-controlled comparison with haloperidol, EPS and akathisia caused by sertindole were comparable to placebo. Main side effects of sertindole appear to be rhinitis or nasal congestion, sedation, and abnormal ejaculation. Some ECG changes were also noted but were not felt to be clinically significant (Borison, 1995).

Both quetiapine and ziprasidone are in advanced clinical trials. Quetiapine appears to be similar to clozapine in its affinities to dopamine and serotonin receptors, suggesting similar efficacy. Moreover, quetiapine appears to have low EPS, minimal anticholinergic side effects, and little effect on prolactin, possibly minimizing sexual dysfunction. Principal side effects appear to be somnolence or agitation, weight gain, liver enzyme elevation, and orthostatic hypotension. Ziprasidone is still in early trials; however, it appears to have superior efficacy when compared with haloperidol. The main side effects of ziprasidone seem to be sedation, dizziness, nausea, orthostatic hypotension, and elevated prolactin levels, suggesting possible sexual dysfunction (Jibson & Tandon, 1996).

Many other agents are in the investigative phases of development as psychopharmacologists continue to explore advancing knowledge about receptors and their potential role in the treatment of psychosis. D1 antagonists, serotonin antagonists, mixed compounds, and sigma site and excitatory amino acid antagonists all may play future roles in medication treatment for psychosis (Lieberman, 1993). The roles of traditional antipsychotic medication are likely to change with growing information, and newer agents may further decrease unwanted side effects to improve compliance and client satisfaction.

ANTIDEPRESSANT MEDICATIONS

Antidepressants are some of the most widely prescribed medications in use today. They have an ever-broadening range of clinical applications, especially because of the increased safety and tolerability of the newer antidepressants. Moreover, newer antidepressants are being used to treat disorders that were not formerly treated with medication.

Choosing an antidepressant, however, has become a difficult task, as there are currently 19 different antidepressants, along with two agents approved for treatment of obsessive–compulsive disorder (OCD) that have likely antidepressant activity. In addition, several medications may be used in conjunction with a primary antidepressant to potentiate the antidepressant's effect. All currently available antidepressants have comparable efficacy in treating major depression, although some subtypes of depression may benefit from a specific class of medication. Individuals who respond minimally to one agent may respond with marked success to another. At times, patients may have to go through several trials of medication to find an antidepressant that is beneficial and without severe side effects. Studies indicate that premature cessation of antidepressant medication is often secondary to side effects. Patient education concerning use of medication and lower side effect profiles increases patient compliance (Lin et al., 1995).

There are also few clear guidelines about exact dosage and length of treatment with antidepressants. The recommendations that are available often depend on the disorder's being treated and the potential for chronic or recurrent symptoms, as well as the presence of risk factors for recurrence (Jefferson, 1995). The main indications for choosing a particular antidepressant are tolerability of side effects and previous medication responses by the patient or family members.

There are several different classes of antidepressants, as well as several agents that have unique structures and activity. These include tricyclic antidepressants (TCAs); monoamine oxidase inhibitors (MAOIs); selective serotonin reuptake inhibitors (SSRIs); and atypical agents, including bupropion (Wellbutrin), trazadone (Desyrel), venlafaxine (Effexor), and nefazodone (Serzone).

Tricyclic Antidepressants

The TCAs were the first medications found to have efficacy in the treatment of depression. Developed in the 1950s, these medications were long considered the "gold standard" of treatment until the more recently developed antidepressants, in particular the SSRIs, provided better side effect profiles and a higher therapeutic index. Although tricyclics are rarely considered first-line treatment choices at the current time, they are still widely prescribed by both primary care physicians and psychiatrists (Simon, VonKorff, Wagner, & Barlow, 1993). There are also instances in which TCAs would be considered a first-line agent. For example, a TCA would be preferred to treat a patient with a recurrent depression when the patient had had a favorable response to a TCA in the past or had a previous history of inability to tolerate the SSRIs or other newer agents. Cost is also a significant advantage of TCAs, as they are often much less expensive than their newer counterparts. Another potential advantage is the availability of therapeutic ranges for blood levels of several of the TCAs, in particular nortriptyline. These monitors can help guide the clinician in dosing and assessing response (Preskorn, 1993).

TCAs include imipramine (Tofranil), desipramine (Norpramin), amitriptyline (Elavil), nortriptyline (Pamelor), doxepin (Adapin, Sinequan), trimipramine (Surmantil), protriptyline (Vivactil), maprotiline (Ludiomil), and amoxapine (Asendin). Clomipramine (Anafranil) is not indicated for depression in the United States but is widely used in Europe for this purpose. In the United States it is indicated for the treatment of OCD. The TCAs have a wide array of indications, including major depression, panic disorder, attention-deficit/hyperactivity disorder, neuropathic pain syndromes, and other disorders.

The main difficulty with TCAs appears to be their wide range of side effects. The TCAs have affinity for histamine, muscarinic, and alpha-adrenergic receptors, as well as serotonin and norepinephrine receptors (Richelson, 1994). Unfortunately, this broad range of activity leads to a number of side effects for the patient and, compared to newer agents, an increased risk of lethality if taken in overdose.

Side effects of the TCAs are drug- and dose-dependent. Older compounds, or tertiary amines, such as imipramine, amitriptyline, and doxepin, often exhibit a higher degree of side effects compared to some of the secondary amines, such as desipramine and nortriptyline. The most commonly seen side effects include sedation, anticholinergic effects, orthostatic hypotension, weight gain, and sexual dysfunction. TCAs can also cause cardiotoxicity and lower seizure threshold to promote seizures in individuals at risk.

Sedation is a common side effect of the TCAs, especially amitriptyline, doxepin, and clomipramine. This effect can be advantageous if insomnia or anxiety are predominant clinical features with a patient, but daytime drowsiness can be a significant problem, causing difficulty with concentration and attention. TCAs with the lowest sedation include desipramine, nortriptyline, amoxipine, and protriptyline.

Anticholinergic side effects and orthostatic hypotension are again problematic, especially in vulnerable populations, such as the elderly. Dry mouth can lead to an increase in dental caries, decreased lacrimation can cause eye irritation and actual corneal damage to contact lens wearers, and constipation and urinary retention can lead to serious medical consequences, such as fecal impaction and urinary blockage. Anticholinergic side effects can also precipitate an attack of narrow angle glaucoma. Orthostatic hypotension can lead to syncope, falls, and fractures (Nierenberg, 1992). Amitriptyline, clomipramine, doxepin, and protriptyline have the greatest anticholinergic side effects, while desipramine, nortriptyline, maprotiline, and amoxipine have the least. Orthostatic hypotension is most significant with amitriptyline, clomipramine, desipramine, and imipramine. Nortriptyline has the lowest incidence of orthostatic symptoms among the TCAs (Hyman et al., 1995).

Sexual dysfunction can be a particularly problematic side effect, often resolving only when medication doses are decreased. With the exception of clomipramine, which has greater serontonergic activity, the TCAs may be one of the least likely classes of antidepressant to cause sexual dysfunction (Gitlin, 1994). In men, erectile dysfunction is the most common complaint, although both men and women have reported decreased sexual arousal and orgasmic impairment.

Weight gain is a common side effect with all TCAs and a common reason for discontinuing medication (Lin et al., 1995). Weight gain can be significant, at times more than a 10–20% increase in body weight.

Cardiac toxicity can limit the use of these medications in clients with pre-existing cardiac conditions and can be problematic in TCA overdose. Although cardiac complications from TCAs are rare in clients without pre-exisitng cardiac disease, nonspecific ECG changes may be noted. The toxicity of these drugs is a quinidine-like effect, causing a slowing of internal cardiac conduction; TCAs should therefore be avoided in clients with a history of bifascicular block, left bundle branch block, or prolonged QT interval at baseline. Clients may also experience a benign tachycardia. An ECG should be obtained prior to initiating a TCA for any patient with a history of cardiac disease or symptoms, and should be considered as a screening tool in patients over 40 (Hyman et al., 1995).

TCAs can also have neurological side effects. All TCAs can lower seizure threshold, especially for clients with predisposing factors for seizure. Maprotiline, in particular, has a high risk of seizures, even within therapeutic dose ranges, and should be used only when other choices have proven ineffective. Similarly, amoxapine has some dopamine activity similar to typical antipsychotics and can cause EPS and akathisia. Amoxapine, too, should be used only when other choices have proven ineffective. Tremor and myoclonal twitching have also been noted with TCAs.

Other side effects of TCAs include excessive diaphoresis, breast enlargement with occasional galactorrhea, nausea and gastrointestinal (GI) symptoms, liver enzyme elevations, alterations in blood glucose levels, and secretion of inappropriate antidiuretic hormone.

In addition to side effects, TCAs pose potential interactions with other medications, often mediated by TCAs' inhibition of a set of liver enzyme systems, called the cytochrome P450 enzyme systems. Several other medications also inhibit this system, and when these medications are given concomitantly with TCAs, plasma levels of both medications may increase. These medications include several antipsychotics, SSRIs, some arrhythmics, possibly some beta-adrenergic blockers, and other TCAs. Some medications, such as carbamazepine, phenobarbitol, and phenytoin, induce this enzyme system, and can therefore lower TCA concentrations (Preskorn, 1993). These interactions may require an adjustment in dose for both medications involved.

Selective Serotonin Reuptake Inhibitors

Since the approval and marketing in early 1988 of fluoxetine (Prozac), the SSRIs have revolutionized the pharmacotherapy of the treatment of depression, anxiety, and countless other disorders. Some of the most widely prescribed medications today, the SSRIs have become a cornerstone in our repetoire of psychopharmacologic agents. SSRIs are considered by most clinicians to be the first line of medication treatment in depression and many other disorders, surpassing TCAs because of their more favorable side effect profile and safety in overdose (Jefferson, 1995; Schatzberg, 1996). Three of the SSRIs, fluoxetine, sertraline (Zoloft), and paroxetine (Paxil), have indications for depressed clients and are used extensively in clients with other disorders. The SSRI fluoxamine (Luvox) was released with an indication for OCD but has efficacy in the treatment of major depression.

The SSRIs all work similarly well in treating depression and when compared to TCAs, although studies comparing one SSRI to another are relatively few. Side effect profiles of each SSRI are also similar, with the main differences being the degree of agitation or sedation each agent causes and the degree to which each agent causes one of the other main side effects. These main side effects are insomnia or hypersomnolence; GI symptoms, including nausea, vomiting, dyspepsia, diarrhea and/or constipation, or gas pain; dizziness; headache; sweating; and sexual dysfunction. In general, the SSRIs have minimal anticholinergic effects and are minimally cardiotoxic. Side effects are also usually dose-related. Often, lowering the dose can alleviate or reduce side effects (Leonard, 1993; Rickels & Schweizer, 1990).

In general, fluoxetine appears to be the most likely to cause side effects consistent with its activating profile, including tremor, anxiety, agitation, and insomnia. Paroxetine and fluoxamine are the most sedating SSRIs. Some individuals still experience a great deal of agitation for paroxetine, however, and a percentage of clients experience significant sedation and hypersomnia with fluoxetine.

leep disturbances and agitation/sedation often improve with time or by changing of dose time. Occasionally, a sedating antidepressant or benzodiazepine can be added at night to correct insomnia, but these agents can also increase side effects. Sleep disturbance can include more vivid or unusual dreams and, at times, nightmares that may be particularly problematic in clients with PTSD. SSRIs can also cause an akathisia-like syndrome in some clients.

GI symptomatology is fairly equivalent among the SSRIs, although sertraline may have a slightly higher incidence of nausea. Forty percent of clients treated with fluoxamine report GI symptoms, compared to 25–30% of clients treated with other SSRIs. Splitting doses, changing dosing times, or taking the medication with food can help decrease these symptoms, which often improve with time.

Headache is somewhat more common with fluoxetine than with other SSRIs, though fluoxetine has paradoxically shown some efficacy in the treatment of migraines. Headache caused by fluoxetine is often described as a tension headache on the top of the head and the back of the neck. Analgesics such as aspirin, acetomeniphen, or ibuprofen, are often useful in alleviating symptoms, and the headaches tend to lessen or resolve over time. Occasionally, a patient does not experience initial headaches but will develop them over the course of several weeks. These headaches often do not remit with continued treatment and may require a change in medication.

Perhaps one of the most difficult side effects of the SSRIs is sexual dysfunction, which can include decreased libido, decreased sexual response, delayed or absent orgasm, and erectile dysfunction. Rates of sexual dysfunction vary widely in the literature, probably secondary to variations in review of sexual side effects and lengths of treatment. Fluoxetine, for example, has ranges of sexual dysfunction from 8% to 75% (Gitlin, 1994). Most clinicians place the rate of sexual dysfunction for the SSRIs at approximately 20 to 30%, although officially reported rates are often listed as much lower. Unlike other side effects, sexual dysfunction is often quite persistent far into the course of treatment. Few courses of action have been helpful other than decreasing the medication or switching to other antidepressants. Several adjunct medications have been added to SSRI trials to counteract sexual side effects with limited success (Gitlin, 1994).

Other side effects are more infrequently seen, but several deserve mention. Both anticholinergic and postural hypotension are much more limited with the SSRIs than with the TCAs, but these symptoms can emerge, particularly at higher doses of SSRIs. Unlike both TCAs and MAOIs, increased appetite and weight gain are infrequent side effects of SSRIs; weight loss is actually more likely, particularly with fluoxetine, though all weight changes in response to SSRIs tend to be minimal. Allergic reactions or rash are possible with all SSRIs and should lead to discontinuing the medication. Rare reports of severe exfoliative dermatitis have been thought to be secondary to continuing SSRIs after the development of allergy or rash and have at times resulted in fatality. Increases and decreases in premenstrual and menstrual symptoms can also occur in women treated with SSRIs. More rarely, cardiac arrhythmias, liver enzyme elevations and hepatitis, seizures, and hematological abnormalities in response to SSRIs have been reported.

There have also been occasional reports of treatment-emergent suicidal ideation with these agents. However, in case review and research studies, no definite association has been made between use of SSRIs and suicidal ideation, and these rare reports may represent idiosyncratic responses to SSRIs (Tollefson, 1993).

The last concern regarding SSRIs is the potential for drug interactions, due to SSRIs' effects on liver enzyme systems and the potential inhibition of metabolism of other medications. The presence of an SSRI can lead to increased blood levels of certain other medications, including antipsychotics, TCAs, warfarin (Coumadin), carbamazepine, and a number of antihistamine, antimicrobial, antihypertensive, and cardiac medications. Increased levels of some of these medications can lead to potentially fatal cardiac arrhythmias, for example. For many clients, a main concern is increase in serum levels of TCAs and some antipsychotic agents, with resultant side effects, when SSRIs are coadministered. Levels of TCAs and antipsychotics can increase by one and a half to two times their usual level.

SSRIs may also potentiate side effects from many other medications and agents, including central nervous system (CNS) depressants such as alcohol. Whenever medications are coadministered, the clinician should review metabolism and other interactions that may occur between medications. In clinical practice, some of the enzyme system interactions may not have much bearing on clients' clinical symptomatology, but the clinician should be aware of these possibilities (Leonard, 1993; Nemeroff, Davane, & Pollack, 1995/1996; Tollefson, 1993). Despite these side effects, SSRIs remain a treatment of choice for depression and other disorders, and clinicians should familiarize themselves with their use and potential side effects.

Monoamine Oxidase Inhibitors

Although the frequency with which they are used has decreased since the introduction of newer antidepressants, MAOIs continue to be an important option for patients in whom other agents have failed. In general, however, the MAOIs are often used as a drug of last resort because of their side effect profile and dietary and medication restrictions. Two MAOIs are currently available for use in the United States: phenelzine (Nardil) and tranylcypromine (Parnate).

One of the major concerns with clients' starting an MAOI is the dietary and medication restrictions needed to avoid hyperadrenergic crisis, a potentially fatal side effect. Clients are required to follow a strict diet to avoid tyramine and to avoid sympathomimetic drugs and pressor amines, such as cold and allergy medications and many psychiatric medications, including other antidepressants. Clients considering treatment with an MAOI must therefore be clearly apprised of the symptoms of hyperadrenergic crisis, which include headache, sweating, blurred vision, high blood pressure, and neuromuscular excitation, and be advised to seek emergency treatment should any of these symptoms develop. Hyperadrenergic crisis is also a consideration in clients with significant suicidal ideation and may make MAOIs inappropriate when any question of client compliance exists. Other side effects of MAOIs include orthostatic hypotension, weight gain, anticholinergic side effects, sexual dysfunction, and, rarely, serious hepatotoxicity. Phenelzine is considered more sedating, while tranylcypromine may cause agitation and insomnia.

Atypical Antidepressants

This section covers five antidepressants whose structure and/or activity is unique to that agent. As many clinicians are less experienced with these agents, they are often used as second- or third-line treatment choices. All appear to have comparable efficacy in treating depression when compared with the TCAs and often offer favorable side effect profiles. These antidepressants include trazodone, bupropion, venlafaxine, nefazodone, and the most recently released, mirtazapine (Remeron).

Initially released in 1981, trazodone is the oldest of the atypical agents. Trazodone's main activity appears to be through the serotonin system, both through reuptake inhibition and serotonin 5-HT$_2$ antagonism. Trazodone also exhibits alpha-adrenergic activity but little anticholinergic activity. Indicated in the use of depression, trazodone's effectiveness, when compared with TCAs, MAOIs, and SSRIs, has been questioned. Trazodone is useful for treatment of concomitant anxiety symptoms and is frequently used in combination with the SSRIs for treatment of SSRI-induced insomnia. Trazodone's use has soared due its recent popularity as an anti-insomnia agent.

Problematic side effects of trazodone include sedation and orthostatic hypotension. Sedation is a particularly prominent side effect in dose ranges effective for the treatment of depression and may be one of the factors that has potentially lowered trazodone's usefulness in treating depression. Orthostatic hypotension is due to the alpha-adrenergic activity of trazodone and may be particularly problematic in the elderly. Trazodone's alpha-adrenergic effects may also cause dry mouth. GI disturbance, especially nausea, is common, and can be decreased by taking the medication with food. Weight gain is minimal and sexual dysfunction rare in clients taking trazodone. Cardiac side effects occur less often with trazodone than with TCAs or MAOIs, but occasional arrhthymias have been reported.

One significant, although rare, side effect of trazodone is priapism, especially early in treatment. Male clients should be alerted to report any prolonged or inappropriate erections to their doctor and the drug should be discontinued immediately as continued use could result in a need for surgical intervention and possible postoperative impotence.

Bupropion is perhaps one of the most energizing antidepressants currently available, in part because of its structural similarity to amphetamine. Bupropion appears to act on the norepinephrine and dopamine receptor systems, and its main clinical use is in treating depression or dysthymia. It may also be useful in the treatment of attention-deficit/hyperactivity disorder.

Bupropion's major side effects are related to its capacity to activate clients and include agitation, insomnia, and appetite suppression. Other side effects include headache, dry mouth, and GI disturbances, although GI problems are caused less often by bupropion than they are by SSRIs. An advantage of bupropion is a relative lack of anticholinergic, orthostatic, cardiac, or sexual functioning side effects.

The main concern when using bupropion is its potential to increase seizure risk when taken in too great a dose. In appropriate dose ranges, the seizure risk is approximately 0.4%, or four times greater than other antidepressants, but still in an acceptable range. In doses of 450 mg/day, the risk of seizure increases with dose, up to a maximal risk of 4%. Strict guidelines regarding dosage and dose changes exist because of these risks. These guidelines include the following: Total daily dose should not exceed 450 mg/day; each dose cannot exceed 150 mg; doses can be increased no sooner than 100 mg every 3 days; and doses should not be given closer than 4 hours, and preferably 6 hours, apart.

Bupropion is contraindicated in clients with seizure disorder or seizure disorder history and in patients with a current or prior diagnosis of anorexia or bulimia. Although not contraindicated, bupropion must be used with caution in clients with history of head trauma; CNS tumor or lesion; metabolic abnormalities that might predispose to seizure, such as low sodium, calcium, or magnesium; concurrent medications that may also lower seizure threshold; and recent withdrawal from alcohol or benzodiazepines.

Released in 1994, venlafaxine (Effexor) is a relatively new antidepressant that resembles the activity of TCAs and acts on norepinephrine and serotonin receptor systems. Venlafaxine lacks much interaction with histamine, alpha-adrenergic, or anticholinergic receptors, making its side effect profile much more tolerable than those of TCAs or MAOIs and similar to that of SSRIs. Some studies suggest that venlafaxine may be more effective than other antidepresant agents in more severely depressed or treatment resistant clients and may have a more rapid onset of action than other antidepressants. However, further comparison trials need to be done to verify this hypothesis (Ballenger, 1996; Clerc, Ruimy, & Verdeau-Pailles, 1994).

Venlafaxine has a range of doses that appears to be effective, with higher doses potentially the most effective in treating depression. However, side effects also increase with higher doses, so response must be weighed against side effects (Kelsey, 1996). The common side effects of venlafaxine include nausea, constipation and related GI side effects, anorexia, somnolence, nervousness, dry mouth, dizziness, asthenia, sweating, and sexual dysfunction. Nausea is most problematic, with an incidence of greater than 30% of clients treated with venlafaxine. In general, this nausea can be lessened by more gradual dosage increases and by ingestion of the agent with food. Dry mouth and constipation may be related to an adrenergic effect secondary to venlafaxine's norepinephrine activity. Weight gain or loss and headache do not appear to be significant side effects. Sexual dysfunction is reported in both sexes, although incidence may be less than with SSRIs.

More serious side effects with venlafaxine include increases in blood pressure, seizure, and elevations in liver enzymes. Blood pressure elevation appears dose-related, with little to no risk of blood pressure changes for doses less than 100mg/day and increases with dose to an incidence of up to 13% in doses above 300mg. Regular blood pressure monitoring is recommended through the course of treatment. Seizure risk appears to be the most significant side effect in overdose with venlafaxine, although venlafaxine is considered relatively safe in overdose. Overall seizure incidence is comparable to TCAs. Liver function tests have been elevated in a small percentage of clients treated with venlafaxine but appeared to return to normal ranges after drug discontinuation (Rudolph & Derivan, 1996).

Drug interactions for venlafaxine seem to be fairly minimal. This may be due in part to the minimal effect venlafaxine exhibits on the four major cytochrome P450 enzyme systems. Several studies looking at venlafaxine in combination with a variety of other medications found little drug interaction problems, with the possible exception of cimetidine (Tagamet). Interactions with cimetidine have not been considered clinically significant for most medically stable adults (Ereshefsky, 1996).

Nefazodone is an atypical agent released in 1995 that acts similarly to trazodone. Nefazodone has weak norepinephrine/serotonin blockage activity as well as weak alpha-adrenergic activity. Nor does it exhibit much anticholinergic activity. Nefazodone has been touted as more effective in anxious, more agitated depressions because of its sedating activity. Another significant benefit is its relative lack of effect on sexual functioning in most clients. In clinical trials, nefazodone has been comparable to imipramine in the treatment of depression and has been better tolerated by patients, although nefazodone appeared to require doses greater than 300 mg/day for good effect. Studies also have indicated that nefazodone has efficacy in treating depression-related anxiety (Schatzberg, 1996).

The most commonly observed side effects for nefazodone include somnolence, dry mouth, nausea, dizziness with orthostatic hypotension, constipation, asthenia, lightheadedness, blurred vision, and headache, although some patients experience a paradoxical increase in energy with possible agitation and insomnia. Of these side effects, somnolence and dry mouth are the most common complaints. GI symptoms, although present, are below rates for SSRIs or venlafaxine. These side effects can be lessened by lower starting doses and gradual increases in dosage.

Besides sedation, one of the more problematic aspects of using nefazodone is its potential for drug interaction. As a result, both ferfenadine and astemizole are contraindicated for concurrent use with nefazodone because increased levels of these medications can lead to potentially fatal cardiac arrhythmias. Other agents that need to be used with caution include alprazolam (Xanax), triazolam (Halcion), digoxin, ketoconazole, and erythromycin. Blood levels have been increased up to four times usual levels of alprazolam and triazolam with the coadministration of nefazodone. It is important to use caution when coadministering medications metabolized by the same enzyme systems as nefazodone. Dosages should be initially small and blood levels, when available, followed closely.

Mirtazapine is the most recently released antidepressant. Available for clinical use since August, 1996, there is to date minimal experience regarding the agent's clinical utility. Studies comparing mirtazapine to amitriptyline have shown that mirtazapine has comparable or greater efficacy in treating depression, with fewer anticholinergic and cardiovascular complaints (Bremner, 1995; Smith, Glaudin, Panagides, & Gilvary, 1990).

Currently, there are no studies comparing mirtazapine to the newer antidepressants, so comparative statements on efficacy and side effect profiles cannot yet be made. Mirtazapine is an alpha-2-adrenergic antagonist that enhances noradrenergic and serotonergic activity. Although it has little effect on anticholinergic or dopamine receptors, mirtazapine does exhibit high affinity for histamine receptors, possibly explaining its significant sedation (DeBoer, Ruigt, & Berendsen, 1995).

The most common side effects noted in prerelease trials were somnolence, increased appetite with weight gain, and dizziness. Somnolence was reported at rates of 40–60%, depending on the study, and may not remit over time, although more clinical experience with the drug will help ascertain this effect (Bremner, 1995; Smith et al., 1990). Another more serious potential side effect is a possible link to agranulocytosis. In premarketing trials, 2 of 2,796 patients developed agranulocytosis, and a third patient developed severe neutropenia. In all cases, the reaction was not clearly a result of treatment with mirtazapine, and no requirement of complete blood count monitoring was made, but clients who develop symptoms of agranulocytosis, such as sore throat, fever, flu-like symptoms, stomatitis, or low white blood count, should be monitored and the drug discontinued.

Other side effects include elevation of cholesterol/triglyceride levels and elevations in liver enzyme levels. Extensive experience in medically ill patients is currently lacking, so mirtazapine should be used with caution in these patients. Mirtazapine does not appear to have significant interaction with cytochrome P450 enzyme systems, making drug interactions less likely in laboratory studies, but risk of drug interaction with mirtazapine requires further clinical study (Ereshefsky et al., 1996).

MOOD STABILIZING AGENTS

Currently, three medications are commonly used for the treatment of bipolar affective disorder: lithium carbonate (Cibalith-S, Eskalith, Lithobid, Lithonate); valproic acid (Depakene, Depakote); and carbamazepine (Tegretol). Although carbamazepine does not have a Food and Drug Administration indication for bipolar disorder, it is one of the common treatment choices when clients are nonresponders to lithium. Valproic acid is also rising in popularity, in part because of its efficacy in more atypical presentations of bipolar disorder. Mood stabilizing compounds are also used to treat symptoms of impulsivity, aggression, and dementia and may have some indications in the treatment of PTSD and some substance abuse disorders (Jefferson, 1995; McElroy, Kosckow, Lott, & Keck, 1996; Brady, Malcolm, & Ballenger, 1996; Zajecka, 1995).

All three agents have significant side effect profiles, require regular blood level monitoring, and have significant drug interactions. These issues can complicate mood stabilizers' use and can increase client noncompliance; clinicians can foster effective treatment by familiarizing themselves with these problems and working to educate clients about the benefits and drawbacks of mood stabilizing medications.

Lithium

Lithium has long been the mainstay of treatment of bipolar disorder and continues to play a significant role despite its side effect profile and despite the recent surge in the use of anticonvulsants, especially valproic acid, to stabilize mood. Lithium is clearly efficacious in the treatment of acute mania, but several predictors may help delineate which clients are more likely to be lithium responders. Clients with pure mania or typical bipolar disorder, clients with infrequent episodes, previous lithium responders, and clients with a first-degree relative with bipolar disorder are more likely to respond positively to lithium (Bowden, 1995; Jefferson, 1995). Lithium therapy is often complicated, however, by a relatively high incidence of side effects in up to 75% of clients treated. Compared with all other psychiatric medications, lithium is reported to have the most day-to-day side effects (Keck, McElroy, Stanton, & Bennett, 1996). Lithium also has a low therapeutic index, and clients must be monitored regularly for signs of toxicity.

The most common side effects of lithium include GI symptoms including nausea, vomiting, and diarrhea; tremor; polyuria; polydipsia; acne and other dermatological reactions; hypothyroidism; and weight gain.

The neurological side effects of lithium are complex and, in some cases, not well understood. Clients often complain of feeling flattened and less creative and of having mild memory disturbances; however, the exact cause of these complaints is often difficult to discern. An essential tremor, which worsens with motion and can affect clients' handwriting, is the most common neurological effect of lithium and can be worsened by the presence of anxiety or caffeine. Beta blockers may reduce tremor symptoms. Benign intracranial hypertension (or pseudomotor cerebri) is rare but can occur at any point during lithium treatment. Primary symptoms are headache and increased intracranial pressure, at times with papilledema. Lithium should be discontinued if it is the suspected cause. Often, symptoms then resolve slowly over time, although surgical intervention may occasionally be necessary (Jefferson, 1995). Toxicity can lead to several neurological side effects, which are reviewed later in this chapter.

The GI side effects of lithium are usually dose-related. Nausea and diarrhea are common, as well as occasional vomiting, anorexia, and abdominal cramping. These symptoms often improve over time and can be minimized by changing the preparation of lithium or by taking lithium with food. Persistent GI side effects, or a return of symptoms, should alert the clinician to check for lithium toxicity.

Renal effects of lithium can include a decrease in renal concentrating ability, leading to polyuria. Dose reduction, if possible, often helps to manage this side effect. At times, a diuretic can be used cautiously to treat extreme polyuria or cases of nephrogenic diabetes insipidus where urinary output exceeds three liters per day. Polydipsia often results from polyuria, and clients often complain of significant thirst.

Lithium use may be associated with renal interstitial febrosis in rare cases. However, longitudinal studies have demonstrated no statistically significant difference in rates of renal interstitial febrosis among normal controls, those treated with lithium, and those affectively ill clients not treated with lithium, possibly implying that these renal effects may be related to mood disorder rather than lithium treatment (Morton, Sonne, & Lydiard, 1993). Occasionally, clients treated with lithium may develop an acute rise in serum creatinine, probably secondary to interstitial nephritis. If detected early, these changes are often reversible with discontinuation of lithium; routine monitoring of serum creatinine is recommended for all clients treated with lithium. Edema also occurs at times, although this remits spontaneously and may often be secondary to fluid intake.

Lithium treatment can sometimes lead to hypothyroidism, which can confound presenting symptoms, as clients may appear depressed. Thyroid stimulating hormone (TSH) levels are elevated in hypothyroidism, which should be treated with thyroid hormone replacement. Predisposing factors, such as history of thyroid disease in first-degree relatives or testing positive for antithyroid antibodies, may identify clients at greater risk for this side effect (Jefferson, 1995).

Cardiac side effects during lithium therapy are rare, but ECG changes and conduction disturbances have been noted. The most common ECG finding is T-wave inversion or flattening, a benign change. Lithium occasionally causes cardiac arrhthymias, although usually only in individuals with prior cardiac conduction defects. There have been case reports of sinoatrial ethode dysfunction, first-degree atrioventricular block, bradycardia, premature ventricular contractions, and ventricular tachycardia. Cardiomyopathy has also been reported in a few cases but may be an incidental finding (Morton et al., 1993).

Lithium can cause several dermatological problems and related conditions, including acne that can be quite severe, psoriasis, follicular keratosis, rash, and hair loss. All these side effects can contribute significantly to noncompliance, particularly in adolescent clients.

Blood monitoring of a number of indices is recommended during lithium therapy to check for toxicity. These indices include serum creatinine, thyroid function, and white blood count, the last of which can be increased to levels between 12,000 and 15,000 by lithium treatment.

The following are general recommendations for laboratory monitoring: Lithium levels should be drawn 5 to 7 days after dose increase and 12 hours after the last dose and should be drawn weekly for the first weeks of treatment. Thereafter, levels should be checked monthly for 3 months, then every 3 months or as indicated. A complete blood count (CBC) should be drawn prior to starting lithium treatment; CBC should then be followed as clinically indicated. Baseline blood chemistries, including creatinine, should be done at onset of treatment, then checked yearly or earlier if symptoms suggest renal dysfunction. An ECG is recommended for clients over age 45 or with preexisting cardiac disease and should be repeated every 12 months in clients with cardiac disease. Finally, thyroid function tests should be done prior to starting treatment and should be redone every 12 months (Ereshefsky et al., 1996).

Toxicity is perhaps the most dangerous side effect of lithium. Lithium because of its low therapeutic index, can begin to cause toxic side effects with minor dose changes or changes in environmental conditions, such as volume depletion because of gastroenteritis; the addition of medications such as diuretics, nonsteroidal anti-inflammatory agents, or tetracycline; or decreased sodium intake, often from dieting. Some individuals can experience toxicity even at therapeutic lithium levels (0.8–1.2 m Eq/liter). Side effects of toxicity include neurological symptoms, such as increasing confusion, slurred speech, ataxia, nystagmus, and increased tremor; severe nausea, vomiting, and diarrhea; and worsening of baseline polyuria or polydipsia. Lithium toxicity should be treated in an emergency room setting. Fluid replacement is one of the essential treatments, as well as gastric lavage in cases of acute overdose. In cases of severe toxicity, hemodialysis may be necessary (Okusa & Crystal, 1994).

Many medications can lower or increase lithium levels, potentially leading to disastrous effects. Many medications can elevate Lithium levels. These agents include diuretics; ACE inhibitors; nonsteroidal anti-inflammatory agents, such as indomethacin, ibuprofen, or naproxen; fluoxetine; metronidazole (Flagyl); and tetracycline. Drugs that can lower lithium levels include osmotic diuretics, theophylline, acetazolamide, and possibly caffeine. Antipsychotic medications, when used in combination with Lithium, may increase neurotoxic effects and may result in worse EPS (Ereshefsky et al., 1996; Morton et al., 1993). In general, the clinician should check for potential interactions whenever initiating treatment with lithium.

Valproic Acid

Valproic acid is rapidly becoming a primary treatment for atypical bipolar disorder. Although only recently officially approved for use in bipolar disorder, valproic acid was used empirically with success for years. Valproic acid seems particularly efficacious in the treatment of mixed mania states, secondary mania, rapid cycling bipolar illness, and bipolar illness in substance-abusing clients. The compound is also effective with more typical bipolar presentation (Bowden, 1995).

Besides its broader spectrum of action, valproic acid has other advantages over lithium, including the possibility of achieving therapeutic medication levels more rapidly using loading doses, possibly within 24 hours. Lithium, in contrast, may take several days to achieve similar effect. Though further study is needed, valproic acid also may have a role in treating several other psychiatric disorders, including aggression, PTSD, and panic states. Valproic acid has its disadvantages, though. The agent may be less useful in the treatment of bipolar depression. Moreover, it is unclear how well Valproic acid prevents future episodes of mania when used for maintenance treatment (Jefferson, 1995).

The side effects of valproic acid are generally mild and often lessen or abate with time. Among the most common side effects of valproic acid are GI effects, including nausea, vomiting, appetite suppression, diarrhea, and GI burning. Other common side effects include sedation, tremor, unsteady gait, weight gain, hair loss, diplopia, and thrombocytopenia. Neurological and GI side effects and sedation tend to abate, while hair loss is usually transient but can be quite extensive. Weight gain tends to happen initially then levels off. All these side effects tend to be dose-related, except for hair loss and thrombocytopenia. Sedation, experienced by more than half of clients initially, tends to be the most common side effect. Besides thrombocytopenia, other laboratory abnormalities include hyperammonemia, hyporatremia, hyperglycemia, and inappropriate antidiuretic hormone (ADH) secretion.

More serious side effects of valproic acid involve hematological, neurological, liver, pancreatic, and allergic reactions as well as drug interactions. There have been cases of hepatitis and hepatic failure resulting in death, so valproic acid must be used cautiously in clients with preexisting hepatic disease. Benign elevations in liver enzymes can also occur frequently and appear to be dose-related but do not necessarily indicate the development of more severe liver disease. More severe hematological side effects can include platelet dysfunction, increased propensity for bleeding, and, in rare cases, bone marrow suppression. Cases of acute pancreatitis can develop again, sometimes leading to fatality. Allergic and dermatological reactions are also possible and can lead to severe consequences, including erythema multiforme. Neurological side effects can include hallucinations, ataxia, encephalopathy, and coma in rare cases (*Physicians' Desk Reference, 1996*).

Initially, plasma levels of valproic acid should be followed closely to assess proper dose, then every 3 months, or as indicated clinically. A CBC and renal and liver function studies should be checked prior to initial therapy, then monitored every 6 months. Valproic acid interacts with many medications that are metabolized by the liver and may increase levels of SSRIs, TCAs, and phenobarbitol, causing significant CNS toxicity if not monitored. Phenytoin (Dilantin) levels initially increase, then decrease if valproic acid is used concomitantly. Anticoagulants and medications affecting platelet function, such as aspirin, should be used cautiously in clients taking valproic acid, as these patients may be more prone to bleeding or platelet dysfunction. Other medications that induce liver metabolism, such as carbamazepine, may decrease valproic acid levels. In general, potential drug interactions should be evaluated and blood levels monitored routinely if valproic acid is to be used in combination with other medications.

Carbamazepine

Carbamazepine is an anticonvulsant structurally related to the TCA imipramine that is used in bipolar disorder, particularly in the disorder's atypical and/or rapid cycling forms. Moreover, the agent is more effective than placebo for acute mania. Most studies of carbamazepine, however, were small or were case reports, so it remains unclear whether carbamazepine has utility in long-term prophylaxis of bipolar disorder or is as effective as lithium or valproic acid.

Carbamazepine is a treatment of choice for neuropathic pain syndromes and was suggested as efficacious in the treatment of secondary affective states, episodic dyscontrol syndromes, aggressive behaviors, and possibly withdrawal from alcohol and cocaine (Brady, Malcolm, & Ballenger, 1996; Hyman et al., 1995).

Fortunately, the several serious side effects of carbamazepine, including rash, hepatitis, aplastic anemia, and agranulocytosis, are quite rare. Most cases of aplastic anemia or agranulocytosis occur within 3 months of commencing treatment with carbamazepine; clients should be alerted to report any sudden febrile illness or unexplained bruising or bleeding (*Physicians' Desk Reference, 1996*).

Most common side effects of carbamazepine are dose-related and can be minimized by slow increases in dose or by lowering of dosage. Common side effects include nausea and GI upset, sedation, dizziness, clumsiness, ataxia, blurred vision or diplopia, and dysarthria. Minor decreases in WBC and mild elevations in liver function tests are common, while tremor, inappropriate secretion of antidiuretic hormone, cardiac complications, and memory difficulties or confusion, especially in the elderly, are more unusual. Occasionally, valproic acid can cause hyponatremia (because of sodium depletion) or hypothyroidism (because of undersecretion of thyroid hormones T3 and T4) (Potter & Ketter, 1993).

Several lab studies are recommended to monitor side effects and to assess for therapeutic level. Serum plasma levels should be checked 5 to 7 days after each dosage change, then every 3 months, or as indicated. A CBC, liver function tests, an ECG, and monitors of electrolytes, including sodium, should be done prior to initiation of treatment. A CBC should be done every 1 to 2 weeks for the first 1 or 2 months. Liver function tests should also be monitored regularly, although no specific recommendations are consistently suggested, and carbamazepine should be discontinued if a threefold increase in liver function tests is noted (Ereshefsky et al., 1996).

Carbamazepine increases its own metabolism and causes a reduction in its own plasma levels over time, which leads to needed dose increases to maintain same plasma level. In addition, carbamazepine can also increase metabolism of several other medications, including warfarin, phenytoin, theophylline, and doxycyline, lowering their plasma levels and possibly causing them to become subtherapeutic. Carbamazepine also decreases valproic acid and haloperidol levels and is itself decreased by phenytoin and phenobarbitol. Assessment of concomitant medications is key, therefore, when treating clients with carbamazepine.

ANTIANXIETY AGENTS/SEDATIVE HYPNOTICS

There are several classes of and individual medications in this category, including the benzodiazepines, zolpidem (Ambien), buspirone (Buspar), and beta blockers.

Benzodiazepines/Zolpidem

The benzodiazepines are a group of medications with a variety of indications, including anxiolytic, sedative hypnotic, muscle relaxant, anticonvulsant, and detoxification agents. These medications are also used in a number of ways in the treatment of agitated states, myoclonus, akathisia, and even catatonia and are often used as adjunct treatments with other medications, such as antipsychotics, antidepressants, and mood stabilizers (Pollack, 1993).

The benzodiazepines all have similar side effect profiles and all exhibit activity on gamma-aminobutyric acid (GABA), a neurotransmitter. The main consideration for choice of agent is the rate of onset of action, the duration of action, presence of active metabolites, and overall potency. Benzodiazepines usually considered anxiolytics include alprazolam, chlordiazepoxide (Librium), clonazepam (Klonopin), clorzepate (Tranxene), diazepam (Valium), lorazepam (Ativan), and oxazepam (Serax). Benzodiazepines usually considered sedative hypnotic agents include estazolam (Prosam), flurazepam (Dalmane), quazepam (Doral), temazepam (Restoril), triazolam, and midazolam (Versed).

The principal side effects of benzodiazepines are sedation and associated symptoms, memory impairment, blunting of affect, potential for dependence, and potentiation of other CNS depressants (Ashton, 1995). We discuss the intoxication, withdrawal, and overdose signs and symptoms of benzodiazepines more fully in Chapter 12 (this volume); however, a few more issues are important to review.

There are some differences in potential side effects when short-acting and long-acting benzodiazepines are compared. Compared with longer-acting agents, short-acting agents appear less likely to cause residual daytime sedation, may cause less respiratory depression, and may cause less cognitive impairment or falls, to which elderly clients taking benzodiazepines are particularly prone. Long-acting agency may be easier to discontinue, with less withdrawal, sleep anxiety, or rebound anxiety (Mendelson, 1992; Roth & Roehrs, 1991). All benzodiazepines are potentially addictive, and clients with histories of addiction, particularly with histories of sedative, alcohol, or polydrug abuse, may be at risk for misuse of and addiction to these medications (Roache & Meisch, 1995). In general, these medications are relatively safe, with minimal side effects if used properly.

Zolpidem is a nonbenzodiazepine that acts on a subset of receptors for the neurtransmitter GABA. It does not have significant anxiolytic or muscle relaxant effects and is used primarily as a sedative hypnotic. Zolpidem does exhibit additive effects with other CNS depressants, including alcohol and benzodiazepines, because of its effects on GABA receptors.

The main side effects of zolpidem include headache, dizziness, sedation, and GI problems. The medication did not produce withdrawal symptoms or rebound effects in a multicenter study (Scharf, Roth, Vogel, & Walsh, 1994). However, other trials report symptoms including fatigue, nausea and other GI symptoms, flushing, and lightheadedness after a 48-hour placebo substitution (*Physicians' Desk Reference,* 1996). To date, there is not enough clear data to assess dependency or overall safety in terms of abuse potential.

Buspirone

Buspirone is an anxiolytic agent that has no GABA activity and thus no cross-reactivity with benzodiazepines and does not exhibit the sedative, muscle relaxant, or dependence effects of the benzodiazepines. Instead, buspirone has activity on $5-HT_{1A}$ serotonin receptors (Taylor & Moon, 1991).

Buspirone has been shown to be effective in the treatment of anxiety and comparable to benzodiazepines except (1) in cases in which clients have been switched from benzodiazepines to buspirone in the treatment of benzodiazepine withdrawal and (2) in the treatment of panic attacks. Buspirone has been shown to be effective in treating generalized anxiety disorder; moreover, some evidence suggests that buspirone has antidepressant activity and may be used to augment the effects of other antidepressants. Other uses of buspirone include the treatment of aggressive behaviors in children with developmental disorders or conduct disorders and the possible treatment of several disorders, including OCD, PTSD, social phobia, and alcohol and drug abuse, including smoking cessation (Gelenberg, 1994).

Often, buspirone has a more favorable side effect profile than either the benzodiazepines or antidepressants used to treat anxiety. Buspirone's principal interactions are with MAOIs and clomipramine (increasing blood pressure), haloperidol (increasing haloperidol levels), disulfiram (causing mania), and cyclosporin A (increasing cyclosporin A levels). Buspirone also appears safer than benzodiazepines in use with the elderly as it causes less sedation, cognitive effects, or respiratory depression. In fact, buspirone appears to be a respiratory stimulant. Buspirone also does not exhibit any orthostatic hypotension effects or ataxia and does not have any additive effect on other CNS depressants. Perhaps most important, buspirone does not appear to cause any tolerance, dependence, or withdrawal syndrome and appears to be relatively safe in overdose (Gelenberg, 1994).

The side effects of buspirone tend to be dose-related and usually abate or decrease with time. Often, side effects can be treated by lowering dosages and then increasing dose more slowly. Common side effects include dizziness or lightheadedness, nausea, headache, nervousness or agitation, and excitement or insomnia. A disadvantage of buspirone is that it takes 1 to 2 weeks to have an initial effect and may take 4 weeks or longer to reach full effect. Buspirone is considered a very tolerable medication, however, and appears to have a widening application of use.

Beta Blockers

Beta adrenergic blockers are used primarily in the treatment of hypertension, angina pectoris, cardiac arrhythmias, and migraine but have been used in some cases in the treatment of several psychiatric disorders. These uses include treatment of medication-induced tremor from lithium or antipsychotic agents and performance anxiety and/or social phobias. Beta blockers are also used at times in the treatment of aggression and impulsive behaviors, particularly in clients with organic brain injuries or disorders or in clients whose aggression is not related to psychotic thinking (Corrigan, Yudofsky, & Silver, 1993). The usefulness of beta blockers in these disorders appears to be as a result of their blocking of sympathetic activity in the periphery, although other central mechanisms also play a role.

The most commonly used beta blocker is propranolol, although three others (atenolol [Tenormin], metaprolol [Lopressor], and nadolol) are also used to treat the previously named conditions. These medications differ in their selectivity, lipophilic properties, primary route of metabolism, and length of action. These differences help differentiate the degree of side effects and dosing frequency of these medications and often are used to choose a particular agent over another.

Primary side effects of beta blockers are hypotension; dizziness; bronchospasm, problematic to clients with history of asthma; hypoglycemia in diabetics treated with insulin or oral agents; blocking signs of hyperthyroidism; worsening of heart failure; GI side effects; sexual dysfunction; fatigue; insomnia and/ or vivid dreams; and development of or worsening of depression (*Physicians' Desk Reference*, 1996). The selective beta blockers metaprolol and atenolol are less likely to cause bronchospasm but still must be used with caution or not at all in clients with allergies or asthma. Vasospasm can also occur with these agents, which may be problematic for clients with peripheral circulation problems such as claudication or Raynaud's syndrome. Beta blockers may also interact with other medications, including increasing levels of theophylline and thyroxine, a thyroid medication, so caution should be exercised when these medications are used in conjunction with other medications or in medically ill clients.

New Agents

Research on the treatment of anxiety and related disorders by pharmacological agents continues to grow and provide new information. This work includes studies of medications that (1) work on GABA sites but may not have the sedative or addictive properties of benzodiazepines and (2) work on CCK-B and a variety of serotonergic sites (Mosconi, Chiamulera, & Recchia, 1993). The clinician can expect the options of the pharmacological management of anxiety disorders and sleep disorders to continue to expand and offer new treatment choices.

SPECIAL CATEGORIES

This section reviews several groups of medications that do not easily fit into the other categories discussed. These treatments are psychostimulants; clonidine (Catapres); thyroid hormone; verapimil (Calan); and medications used to treat side effects. Most of the medications in this section are, with the exception of psychostimulants, used less frequently and so are reviewed only briefly.

Psychostimulants

Four medications—methylphenidate (Ritalin), dextroamphetamine (Dexedrine), pemoline (Cylert), and the recently released Adderall (trade name; a medication that combines dextroamphetamine and amphetamine)—are used primarily in the treatment of attention-deficit/hyperactivity disorder. However, they have been used as primary antidepressants in medically ill or elderly clients as a means of potentiating narcotic analgesics, as adjunct treatment with other antidepressants to potentiate their effectiveness, and as treatments for narcolepsy. The use of these medications is limited by their potential for abuse.

Major side effects of the four psychostimulants are similar and secondary to CNS excitation. These side effects are insomnia, anxiety or agitation, paradoxical sedation or listlessness, dysphoria or euphoria, and occasional paranoid ideation or hallucinations. Dysphoria is more commonly reported in children than in adults. These medications also affect the cardiovascular system, causing elevated pulse and blood pressure, as well as tachyarrhythmias, and necessitating medical assessment of cardiovascular condition prior to initiating treatment. Other potential side effects are anorexia with weight loss, headache, GI symptoms, and development or worsening of vocal or motor tics. Children may also experience some growth suppression and weight loss, although this is generally mild and often returns to baseline when the medication is discontinued for a period of time. Pemoline can also affect liver function tests, at times leading to hepatitis and jaundice; therefore, liver function studies should be monitored when using pemoline and the medication should be discontinued if a threefold increase in liver function tests occurs. Moreover, pemoline should not be used in clients with preexisting liver disease.

A major concern for these medications is their potential for abuse; thus, psychostimulants should be used with caution in clients with a history of addiction. As the psychostimulants can also have a variety of drug interactions, coadministration with other medications should be reviewed for possible interactions prior to starting psychostimulant treatment.

Clonidine

Clonidine is used primarily as an antihypertensive agent but is used in several ways as a psychiatric medication. Most commonly, clonidine is used as a primary agent or in conjunction with a long-acting opiate such as methadone in opiate detoxification. Clonidine is also used in the treatment of Gilles de la Tourette syndrome, particularly when the client cannot tolerate antipsychotics. Other possible uses for clonidine include a role in the treatment of anxiety disorders and attention-deficit/hyperactivity disorder.

Clonidine's primary side effects include dry mouth, sedation, and postural hypotension. Other reported side effects are dry eyes, nausea, impotence, vivid dreams or nightmares, paradoxical agitation and insomnia, increased depression, and, rarely, visual or auditory hallucinations. Rare side effects include rash, hair loss, gynecomastia, and hyperglycemia. Drug interactions include possible increased sensitivity to alcohol and possible reduction in antihypertensive effect when used in combination with TCAs.

Thyroid Hormone and Verapimil

Thyroid hormone therapy, using the hormones T3 or T4, has been investigated as a treatment for depressive symptoms, while Verapimil, a calcium channel blocker used primarily in the treatment of cardiac arrhthymias, has been investigated as a treatment for mania, though research findings supporting these treatments have been mixed at best (Hyman et al., 1995). Thyroid hormones have myriad side effects consistent with hyperthyroidism and also interact with other drugs, causing, for example, increased response to anticoagulants. Verapimil's main side effects are postural hypotension, dizziness, headache, and constipation.

Medications Used to Treat Side Effects

The following section briefly reviews medications used to treat EPS, tremor, and sexual dysfunction side effects of psychiatric medications.

The four most commonly used agents for the treatment of antipsychotic-induced EPS are benztropine, trihexyphenidyl, diphenhydramine, and amantadine. Amantadine is a dopamine-releasing agent and may possibly exacerbate psychosis in some clients.

Benztropine, trihexyphenidyl, and diphenhydramine have similar side effect profiles because of their anticholinergic properties. These side effects include dry mouth, constipation, urinary retention, blurred vision, tachycardia, hypotension, and flushed skin. Of the three agents, trihexyphenidyl is the least sedating, but all have sedating properties and consequently can impair motor coordination. Diphenhydramine causes the greatest sedation due to its antihistaminic effects.

Amantadine has less sedation and no anticholinergic activity, so it may be useful in clients who cannot tolerate these effects. Amantadine is not as useful as anticholinergic agents in the treatment of acute dystonias (Kaplan & Sadock, 1991). Common side effects of amantadine include nausea, dizziness, and insomnia. Anxiety, irritability, ataxia, depression, headache, and orthostatic hypotension have also been reported.

Akathisia is less responsive to anticholinergic agents than are other forms of EPS. In general, akathisia is treated with beta-adrenergic blocking agents as a first-line agent and benzodiazepines and anticholinergic agents used as second-line treatments. Beta-adrenergic blockers and benzodiazepines can also be used to treat lithium-induced tremor.

Treatment of medication-induced sexual dysfunction can include several options: decreasing dose or changing the timing of a likely causative agent, waiting to see whether the dysfunction lessens over time, adding agents to counteract sexual dysfunction, or switching to an agent that causes less severe sexual dysfunction. Unfortunately, these options are often impractical in terms of treating psychpathology. In case reports, many agents have been reported to reduce medication-induced sexual dysfunction, but there have been questions as to rates of success (Gitlin, 1994). Medications reported to be helpful are bupropion, buspirone, cyproheptadine (Periactin), yohimbine (Yocon), amantadine, urecholine (Bethanechol), and bromocriptine (Parlodil).

Bupropion, buspirone, and amantadine were already reviewed. Of the remainder, cyproheptadine is used both daily and on an as-needed basis in both sexes as a treatment of anorgasmia; the main side effects are sedation, agitation, tremor, insomnia, and nausea. There have been some reports of cyproheptadine's capacity to decrease or reverse the positive effects of antidepressant treatment, which may limit its usefulness in some clients (Gitlin, 1994).

Yohimbine can be used as a treatment for impotence and has also been reported to be helpful for decreased desire and anorgasmia. The medication may increase blood flow to the genital region and decrease outflow via alpha-adrenergic blockade. The principal side effects of yohimbine are increased blood pressure and heart rate, tremor, irritability, agitation, dizziness, diaphoresis, headache, flushing, and GI symptoms.

Urecholine is a cholinergic agonist that has been reported to decrease sexual dysfunction with TCA and MAOI antidepressants, but its efficacy with newer antidepressants has yet to be established (Gitlin, 1994). Main side effects of urecholine are lethargy, GI side effects, increased salivation and tearing, hypotension with reflex tachycardia, flushing, headache, diaphoresis, and bronchial constriction.

Bromocriptine has been reported useful in the treatment of erectile dysfunction. Side effects, which are similar to those of other medications discussed in this section, are frequent and are often dose-dependent.

SUMMARY

This chapter reviewed the current main psychiatric agents and their side effects. As new medications are developed and become available, their side effects and interactions with other drugs will become important parameters in determining their efficacy and use.

REFERENCES

Ashton, H. (1995). Toxicity and adverse consequences of benzodiazepine use. *Psychiatric Annals, 25,* 158–165.

Ballenger, J. C. (1996). Clinical evaluation of venlafaxine. *Journal of Clinical Psychopharmacology, 16,* 29S–35S.

Borison, R. L. (1995). Clinical efficacy of serotonin-dopamine antagonists relative to classic neuroleptics. *Journal of Clinical Psychopharmacology, 15,* 24S–29S.

Bowden, C. L. (1995). Predictors of response to divalproex and lithium. *Journal of Clinical Psychiatry, 56,* 25–30.

Brady, K. T., Malcolm, R., & Ballenger, J. C. (1996). Anticonvulsants in substance use disorders. *Psychiatric Annals, 26,* S488–S491.

Bremner, J. D. (1995). A double-blind comparison of Org 3770, amitriptyline, and placebo in major depression. *Journal of Clinical Psychiatry, 56,* 519–525.

Carpenter, W. T. (1995). Serotonin-dopamine antagonists and treatment of negative symptoms. *Journal of Clinical Psychopharmacology, 15,* 30S–35S.

Clerc, G. E., Ruimy, P., & Verdeau-Pailles, J. (1994). A double-blind comparison of venlafaxine and fluoxetine in patients hospitalized for major depression and melancholia. *International Clinical Psychopharmacology, 9,* 139–143.

Corrigan, P. W., Yudofsky, S. C., & Silver, J. M. (1993). Pharmacological and behavioral treatments for aggressiveness psychiatric inpatients. *Hospital and Community Psychiatry, 44,* 125–133.

DeBoer, T., Ruigt, G. S. F., & Berendsen, H. H. G. (1995). The alpha2-selective adrenoceptor antagonist Org 3770 (mirtazapine, remeron) enhances noradrenergic and serotonergic transmission. *Human Psychopharmacology, 10,* S107–S118.

Dilsaver, S. C. (1993). Antipsychotic agents: A review. *American Family Physician, 47,* 199–204.

Ellenbroek, B. A. (1993). Treatment of schizophrenia: A clinical and preclinical evaluation of neuroleptic drugs. *Pharmacologic Therapies, 57,* 1–78.

Ereshefsky, L. (1996). Drug-drug interactions involving antidepressants: Focus on venlafaxine. *Journal of Clinical Psychopharmacology, 16,* 37S–50S.

Ereshefsky, L., Overman, G. P., & Karp, J. K. (1996). Current psychotropic dosing and monitoring guidelines. *Primary Psychiatry, 3,* 21–45.

Gelenberg, A. J. (1994). Buspirone: Seven-year update. *Journal of Clinical Psychiatry, 55,* 222–229.

Gitlin, M. J. (1994). Psychotropic medications and their effects on sexual function: Diagnosis, biology, and treatment approaches. *Journal of Clinical Psychiatry, 55,* 406–413.

Hubbard, J. W., Midha, K. K., Hawes, E. M., McKay, G., Marder, S. R., Aravagiri, M., & Korchinski, E. D. (1993). Metabolism of phenothiazine and butyrophenone antipsychotic drugs: A review of some recent research findings and clinical implications. *British Journal of Psychiatry, 163,* 19–24.

Hyman, S. E., Arana, G. W., & Rosenbaum, J. F. (1995). *Handbook of psychiatric drug therapy,* (3rd ed.). Boston: Little, Brown.

Janicak, P. G. (1993). The relevance of clinical pharmacokinetics and therapeutic drug monitoring: Anticonvulsant mood stabilizers and antipsychotics. *Journal of Clinical Psychiatry, 54,* 35–41.

Jefferson, J. W. (1995). Lithium: The present and the future. *Journal of Clinical Psychiatry, 56,* 41–48.

Jibson, M. D., & Tandon, R. (1996). A summary of research findings on the new antipsychotic drugs. *Psychiatry Forum, 16,* 1–7.

Kaplan, H. I., & Sadock, B. J. (1991). *Synopsis of psychiatry: Behavioral sciences clinical psychiatry* (6th ed.). Baltimore: Williams & Wilkins.

Keck, P. E., McElroy, S. L., Stanton, S. P., & Bennett, J. A. (1996). Pharmacoeconomic aspects of the treatment of bipolar disorder. *Psychiatric Annals, 26,* S449–S453.

Kelsey, J. E. (1996). Dose-response relationship with venlafaxine. *Journal of Clinical Psychopharmacology, 16,* 21S–26S.

Leonard, B. E. (1993). The comparative pharmacology of new antidepressants. *Journal of Clinical Psychiatry, 54,* 3–15.

Lieberman, J. A. (1993). Understanding the mechanism of action of atypical antipsychotic drugs. *British Journal of Psychiatry, 163,* 7–18.

Lin, E. H. B., Von Korff, M., Katon, W., Bush, T., Simon, G. E., Walker, E., & Robinson, P. (1995). The role of the primary care physician in patients' adherence to antidepressant therapy. *Medical Care, 33,* 67–74.

McElroy, S. L., Kasckow, J. W., Lott, A. D., & Keck, P. E. (1996). Valproate in the treatment of behavioral agitation of dementia. *Psychiatric Annals, 26,* S474–S479.

Meltzer, H. Y. (1994). An overview of the mechanism of action of clozapine. *Journal of Clinical Psychiatry, 55,* 47–52.

Meltzer, H. Y., Lee, M. A., & Ranjan, R. (1994). Recent advances in the pharmacotherapy of schizophrenia. *Acta Psychiatrica Scandinavica, 90,* 95–101.

Mendelson, W. B. (1992). Clinical distinctions between long- acting and short-acting benzodiazepines. *Journal of Clinical Psychiatry, 53,* 4–7.

Morton, W. A., Sonne, S. C., & Lydiard, R. B. (1993). Lithium side effects in the medically ill. *International Journal of Psychiatry in Medicine, 23,* 357–382.

Mosconi, M., Chiamulera, C., & Recchia, G. (1993). New anxiolytics in development. *Journal of Clinical Pharmacology Research, 13,* 331–344.

Nemeroff, C. B., Devane, C. L., & Pollack, B. G. (1995/1996). Summary and review of antidepressants and the cytochrome P450 system. *Progress Notes of the American Society of Clinical Psychopharmacology, 6,* 38–40.

Nierenberg, A. A. (1992). The medical consequences of the selection of an antidepressant. *Journal of Clinical Psychiatry, 53,* 19–24.

Okusa, M. D., & Crystal, L. J. T. (1994). Clinical manifestations and management of acute lithium intoxication. *American Journal of Medicine, 97,* 383–389.

Owens, D. G. C. (1994). Extrapyramidal side effects and tolerability of risperidone: A review. *Journal of Clinical Psychiatry, 55,* 29–35.

Physicians' Desk Reference (50th ed.). (1996). Montvale, NJ: Medical Economics.

Pollack, M. H. (1993). Innovative uses of benzodiazepines in psychiatry. *Canadian Journal of Psychiatry, 38,* S122–S126.

Potter, W. Z., & Ketter, T. A. (1993). Pharmacological issues in the treatment of bipolar disorder: Focus on mood-stabilizing compounds. *Canadian Journal of Psychiatry, 38,* S51–S56.

Preskorn, S. H. (1993). Pharmacokinetics of antidepressants: Why and how they are relevant to treatment. *Journal of Clinical Psychiatry, 54,* 14–34.

Reilly, J. J., Crowe, S. F., & Lloyd, J. H. (1991). Neuroleptic toxicity syndromes: A clinical spectrum. *Australian and New Zealand Journal of Psychiatry, 25,* 499–505.

Richelson, E. (1994). Pharmacology of antidepressants—Characteristics of the ideal drug. *Mayo Clinical Proceedings, 69,* 1069–1081.

Rickels, K., & Schweizer, E. (1990). Clinical overview of serotonin reuptake inhibitors. *Journal of Clinical Psychiatry, 51,* 9–12.

Roache, J. D., & Meisch, R. A. (1995). Findings from self- administration research on the addiction potential of benzodiazepines. *Psychiatric Annals, 25,* 153–157.

Roth, T., & Roehrs, T. A. (1991). A review of the safety profiles of benzodiazepine hypnotics. *Journal of Clinical Psychiatry, 52,* 38–41.

Rudolph, R. L., & Derivan, A. T. (1996). The safety and tolerability of venlafaxine hydrochloride: Analysis of the clinical trials database. *Journal of Clinical Psychopharmacology, 16,* 54S–59S.

Safferman, A., Lieberman, J. A., Kane, J. M., Szymanski, S., & Kinon, B. (1991). Update on the clinical efficacy and side effects of clozapine. *Schizophrenia Bulletin, 17,* 247–261.

Scharf, M. B., Roth, T., Vogel, G. W., & Walsh, J. K. (1994). A multicenter, placebo-controlled study evaluating zolpidem in the treatment of chronic insomnia. *Journal of Clinical Psychiatry, 55,* 192–199.

Schatzberg, A. F. (1996). Course of depression in adults: Treatment options. *Psychiatric Annals, 26,* 336–341.

Simon, G. E., VonKorff, M., Wagner, E. H., & Barlow, W. (1993). Patterns of antidepressant use in community practice. *General Hospital Psychiatry, 15,* 399–408.

Smith, W. T., Glaudin, V., Panagides, J., & Gilvary, E. (1990). Mirtazapine vs. amitriptyline vs. placebo in the treatment of major depressive disorder. *Psychopharmacology Bulletin, 26,* 191–196.

Taylor, D. P., & Moon, S. L. (1991). Buspirone and related compounds as alternative anxiolytics. *Neuropeptides, 19,* 15–19.

Tollefson, G. D. (1993). Adverse drug reactions/interactions in maintenance therapy. *Journal of Clinical Psychiatry, 54,* 48–58.

Toth, P., & Frankenburg, F. R. (1994). Clozapine and seizures. *Canadian Journal of Psychiatry, 39,* 236–238.

Zajecka, J. (1996). Panic disorder and posttraumatic stress disorder. *Psychiatric Annals, 26,* S480–S487.

CHAPTER 14

PSYCHOLOGICAL/BEHAVIORAL SYMPTOMS IN NEUROLOGICAL DISORDERS

ROBERTA F. WHITE
KAREN S. MARANS
MAXINE KRENGEL

The title of this chapter could be taken as implying a clear-cut, well-accepted distinction between "psychological" or "psychiatric" disorders and those that would be classified as "neurological." Increasingly, this dichotomy is untenable. Many disorders that fall under the purview of the psychiatrist are clearly shown to have a neurological basis. Schizophrenia, for example, clearly has neuropathologic correlates (Seidman, Cassens, Kremen, & Pepple, 1992) and disorders involving mood and affect such as major depression or posttraumatic stress disorder are shown to have associated neurotransmitter changes, at least in some patients (Charney, Deutch, Krystal, Southwick, & Davis, 1993; Post, 1992). Even in the case of Axis II diagnoses, such as obsessive–compulsive disorders, dysfunction is attributed to specific cerebral structures (Rauch et al., 1994; Saint-Cyr, Taylor, & Nicholson, 1995). Likewise, patients with such neurological disorders as traumatic brain injury or even primary progressive dementias often receive their treatment from psychiatrists. And there are a number of conditions—such as childhood and adult residual learning disabilities or attention-deficit disorders—that both camps claim.

However, for the purposes of this chapter we concentrate on the expression of symptoms that traditionally were considered to be psychiatric or psychological among patients who carry traditional neurological diagnoses. The kinds of *symptoms* we consider include hallucinations, delusions, paranoia, apathy, restlessness, agitation, sadness/depression, anxiety, denial, and regression. (It should be noted that these terms may have some what different referents in the case of primary neurological disease than they do in some of the psychological/psychotherapeutic literature. Ideally, the referent behaviors, which are concretely described, will clarify their meanings as they are discussed). The types of *disorders* we discuss include primary progressive dementias such as Alzheimer's disease and frontal lobe dementias, motor disorders such as Parkinson's disease and Huntington's disease, diseases involving multiple cerebral lesions such as cerebrovascular diseases and multiple sclerosis, and traumatic brain injury and epilepsy. We could not attempt an exhaustive review of all disorders (which would require a volume on to itself) but chose to focus on common conditions that present frequently in the context of psychological emergencies.

Because the neurological literature tends to focus on neuropathology and physical findings, the neuropsychological literature on cognitive deficits, and the psychiatric literature on disorders other than those we are discussing here, the literature on the occurrence of these symptoms is rather sparse and quite difficult to access. Our discussion here, therefore, largely emanates from our own extensive clinical experience. Because we were all trained in clinical psychology, with subsequent subspecialty training in neuropsychology, we are interested in the systematic expression of behavioral changes in neurological disease that go beyond the traditional cognitive deficits assessed in neuropsychology. Our observations are summarized in the following pages.

DEVELOPMENTAL, SOCIAL, AND MEDICAL INDICATORS OF POSSIBLE NEUROLOGICAL DISORDERS

When the patient presents in an emergency situation, the evaluation considers history (from the patient's chart and interview with the patient or significant others) as well as self-reported and observed behavioral symptoms. Developmental, social, and medical indicators of possible neurological disease that can be elicited on history are considered briefly here. Observation of these indicators can serve as a signal to consider neurological dysfunction as one possibility in the patient's evaluation. It should be noted that failure to observe any of the indicators listed here does not rule out the possibility that the patient suffers from a neurological disorder.

Developmental and Educational History

Patients who have experienced birth trauma, early head injuries or encephalitis/meningitis are at greater risk for neurological disorders such as epilepsy. In some patients with undiagnosed childhood epilepsy, there is a history of "day dreaming" or "blanking out" episodes in school or at home. Restlessness, hyperactivity or attentional problems in childhood can be seen inpatients with attention deficit disorder, and problems in school or limited schooling are common in patients diagnosed with learning disabilities or attentional deficit. Some of these same kinds of problems can be seen in patients with below average general intelligence, childhood or adolescent onset of a neurogenetic disorder (such as Huntington's disease), or childhood exposure to neurotoxicants. The latter (lead is especially common and special note should be taken if the patient has a history of childhood lead poisoning) can be associated later in life with behavioral and cognitive abnormalities.

Social/Occupational History

In a number of patients with primary neurological disorder, initial manifestation of the illness could be seen in the patient's social or occupational life. Undiagnosed brain tumors, strokes, primary progressive dementias or multiple sclerosis can result in deterioration of marriages and ability to retain a job. In some occupational histories, the patients' job status declines as their undiagnosed illness progresses. When these patients are questioned closely, it often becomes apparent that they lost jobs because of a decline in cognitive or motor capacity to carry out job demands. In other cases, the patient may have insufficient insight at the time of evaluation to note cause for job status changes. Other patients come to the attention of psychologists or other health care providers because of a social change noted in behavioral control. The patient may have suddenly or gradually become irritable and aggressive, paranoid, sexually disinhibited, unable to follow rules or obey the law or normal codes of behavior, apathetic, or consistently confused. These kinds of changes can be seen in patients with primary progressive dementias but can also occur in patients with slow-growing lesions such as brain tumors. A history of alcohol abuse puts the patient at risk for associated disorders such as withdrawal seizures, alcoholic dementia, or alcoholic Korsakoff's disease. Substance abuse histories can also be associated with disorders such as HIV infection (and AIDS-related dementia complex), seizures following overdoses and respiratory arrest, anoxic/hypoxic states from respiratory arrest, and primary brain changes (glue sniffing has, for example, been associated with changes in the white matter of the brain, [Filley, Heaton, & Rosenberg, 1990; Rosenberg et al., 1988]). Other occupational indicators of possible neurological disorder include history of exposure to neurotoxicants at work (e.g., dry cleaning or degreasing solvents, metals, and gases).

Medical History

A number of medical conditions predispose patients to the development of neurological disease. Chronic heart failure, hypertension, and diabetes are all associated with an increased risk for cerebrovascular disorders. Any patient with a history of stroke or transient ischemic attacks should be considered at risk for behavioral changes attributable to the vascular condition. Renal disease/dialysis is associated with metabolic encephalopathy. Some neurological disorders are strongly genetic (Huntington's disease, Alzheimer's disease, multiple sclerosis) and others seem to have a familial component (epilepsy, cerebrovascular disease, even Parkinson's disease in some cases). For this reason, family medical history should also be considered. Finally, medication status should be considered. Neuroleptics may be associated with tardive dyskinesia, certain medications affect memory and other cognitive and motor functions, and individual and combined medications can result in confusional states.

Physical Symptoms

Physical symptoms that can be seen in many neurological disorders include incontinence, fatigue, dizziness, and headaches. Visual disturbances (double vision, blindness) are common in multiple sclerosis and may wax and wane or even disappear completely for years. Sensitivity to heat is also seen in multiple sclerosis, at which time symptoms seem to worsen. Gait disturbance and tremors or abnormal movements may be seen in patients with Parkinson's disease, Huntington's disease or other disorders involving the brain's motor system (including strokes in motor areas). Weight loss in the year prior to diagnosis is also commonly reported in patients who develop primary progressive dementias, and these patients may also develop a sensitivity to cold (e.g., start wearing sweaters all of the time). Paresthesias (numb or tingly feelings in the skin) may also be seen with peripheral nervous system involvement (e.g., in alcoholic and toxicant-induced disorders).

PSYCHOLOGICAL/BEHAVIORAL SYMPTOMS

This section discusses a number of neurological disorders, beginning with a general description of the medical features of the disorder and proceeding to a summary of the types of psychological symptoms that can herald the onset of the disorder or feature prominently in a patient suffering from the disease who presents with a behavioral emergency.

Alzheimer's Disease

Alzheimer's disease (AD) is a neurodegenerative disorder that causes progressive cognitive decline, especially a striking memory impairment early in the process. The dementia associated with AD has an insidious onset and there is a progressive decline in almost all areas of cognitive functioning. Neuropathologically, AD is characterized by the development of neuritic plaques and neurofibrillary tangles throughout the brain. It is diagnosed presumptively and confirmed by autopsy or biopsy (see Moss & Albert, 1992, for a review of the neuropathology of the disease process and the neuropsychological consequences).

In addition to the deterioration in cognitive functioning that comprises the dementia associated with AD (impairments in memory, attention, executive system functioning, language, and visuospatial abilities), profound psychological sequelae and personality changes are associated with the disease process. In the early stages of the disease they often include loss of interest, apathy, lowered energy levels, and depressed mood (Hamdy, 1994). The "depression" associated with AD is qualitatively different than the clinical depression defined in the *Diagnostic and Statistical Manual of Mental Disorders,* fourth edition (DSM-IV; American Psychiatric Association, 1994). Patients are often described as appearing less interested and willing to engage in activities that they once found pleasurable. However, this change can be best described as reflecting apathy and passivity rather than feelings of sadness, worthlessness, or the anhedonia seen in depression. As the disease progresses common behavioral problems may include anxiety, agitation, extreme restlessness, and irritability. It is not uncommon for a patient with AD to present with delusions or hallucinations, which may occur in as many as 40% of patients with AD (Folstein & Bylsma, 1994). The hallucinations are most often visual or auditory but can be olfactory or tactile. Common delusions include the belief that people are stealing from the patient, that there are unwanted people living in their home, or that the house that they are living in is not their real home. Although wandering is commonly seen in AD, it may also occur in the context of a delusion in which the patient experiences the need to find his or her "real" house. The wandering coupled with the severe memory impairments may lead to patients becoming lost and being brought to the emergency room after being discovered by the police. The delusions dissipate as the dementia becomes more severe (Folstein & Bylsma, 1994).

Although mania may occur in patients with AD, it is rare. However, many AD patients have disturbances in their sleep–wake cycle. Therefore, it would be possible for a patient to have symptoms similar to those seen in mania, such as irritability, agitation, poor judgment, and sleep disturbances.

Word finding difficulties and impaired confrontational naming are hallmarks of the language disturbance in AD. These language disturbances are markedly different from the language disturbances seen in schizophrenia and its related disorders. Qualitatively, the language and speech problems observed in patients with AD often include circumlocutions that are reflective of naming problems. The loosening of associations and the speech disorder that is indicative of a thought disorder are not present. However, in the later stages of AD speech may become neologistic and incomprehensible. Such speech can resemble the word salad seen in schizophrenia. However, the AD patient at this stage is consistently incapable of intelligible speech.

Frontal Lobe Dementias

A few primary progressive dementing disorders affect the frontal lobes most extensively (see Moss, Albert, & Kemper, 1992, for a description of the typical pathological features of these disorders). Although these conditions are relatively rare, the initial presentations are quite frequently behavioral and the patients are often initially evaluated by psychologists or psychiatrists. The cardinal features of the change evident in these disorders are best summarized as a loss of behavioral control or monitoring. The patient may become irritable and aggressive, failing to inhibit words or aggressive acts that were previously inhibited. Similarly, behavior may become sexually disinhibited, with the patient approaching inappropriate persons, exhibiting an increased sexual drive, or talking about sexual activity inappropriately. Occasionally patients with no history of criminality or antisocial behavior begin to break the law, stealing objects or money or breaking into buildings. Faulty behavioral monitoring can also be observed as a lack of insight into behavioral changes in which the patient does not notice the inappropriateness of behaviors or even that he or she is acting differently than in the past. Finally, we see patients diagnosed with this type of dementia who appear to have lost the capacity for guilt, failing to ascribe any fault for behaviors considered antisocial. In one case, the patient came to medical attention because he had begun stealing tools from a coworker and was making sexual advances toward female family members besides his wife. He remembered and acknowledged these acts but said that he took advantage of the proximity of tools or women because they were convenient and he needed them. When asked if other people would consider these acts to be wrong, he also acknowledged that this was the case. However, he denied personal feelings of guilt.

Cerebrovascular Disease

"Cerebrovascular disease" is a term referring to the constellation of lesions occurring because of vascular pathology in the brain. It encompasses entities known as multi-infarct dementia (Hachinski, Lassen, & Marshall, 1974), leukoariosis (Hachinski, Potter, & Merskey, 1987), or Binswanger's disease (Binswanger, 1894). Patients with vascular disease may have experienced large clinical strokes, often with other small lesions identifiable by magnetic resonance imaging (MRI), or may have no clinically identified strokes despite showing evidence of lesions on MRI scans and exhibiting cognitive, behavioral, and neurological signs of such lesions. Patients may have a variety of lesions by the time of diagnosis that can involve cortical areas, subcortical white matter, basal ganglia, cerebellum, brain stem, or combinations of these areas. Patients with multiple lesions may show behavioral changes that are attributable to lesions occurring in specified brain regions or systems, and they may also show secondary or cumulative effects of having multiple subcortical lesions (Tatemichi, 1990).

The latter generally show up in group studies of these patients as "frontal system" dysfunction observable on neuropsychological tests of attention and executive functioning (Wolfe, Linn, Babikian, Knoefel, & Albert, 1990). Focal deficits are harder to establish in group studies of patients with cerebrovascular disease, presumably because the sites of these lesions vary among patients. Cerebrovascular disease is thought to occur rather commonly, perhaps accounting for 57% of dementia diagnoses (Tatemichi, 1990). From the perspective of psychological care it is an important disorder because behavioral (especially affective) changes are often the first symptoms bringing the patient in for diagnosis. In our experience, this diagnostic category is also common among geriatric patients receiving inpatient psychiatric evaluation and care (especially when the admission is the first psychiatric admission that they have experienced). We frequently find that history of strokes, abnormal MRI findings, and evidence of multifocal vascular disease are ignored etiologically in evaluation of thepatient's behavioral status.

Symptomatic changes that are behavioral in nature and that occur across the many types of presentations of multiple lesions in patients with cerebrovascular disease are often seen as a new presentation of agitation or agitated depression. The patient is frequently at a loss to explain any precipitants for periods or episodes of agitation or a sense of anxiety and may be quite debilitated because of it. The agitation may also be accompanied by easy tearfulness or irritability. Many of these patients are apathetic or amotivational when presented with cognitive tasks or life dilemmas, even when the agitation or anxiety is severe enough to produce akasthesia or pronounced restlessness. When patients are apathetic or lethargic, their behavioral changes may be interpreted by others as reflecting a depression when diagnosis for clinical depression would be inappropriate. Finally, patients with diffuse lesions may show evidence of behavioral changes attributable to frontal dysfunction and similar to those seen in frontal dementias (see previous section).

Patients with severe bilateral cerebrovascular disease may exhibit achronic or episodic confusional state. This state can be accompanied by a number of symptoms, including paranoid delusions. These delusions are often fixed in terms of their central theme (e.g., the belief that the patient's landlord is spying into the patient's home); however, the details of the patient's report about incidents that recently occurred in relation to the delusion are often highly variable from one report to another and the patient may completely forget having reported specific information related to the delusion. For example, the patient may report one afternoon that the landlord spied on him with a television camera and another that the spying occurred with a tape recorder; sometimes it may be the landlord who is the culprit; other times it is the next-door neighbor. In addition to delusions, "illusions" can also be observed in these patients. Often these illusions seem to be interpretations of sensory distortions caused by damage to the parietal or occipital lobes. One patient, for example, thought that a big black raven was sitting on his shoulder. This illusion was also vague and changeable, with the patient sometimes reporting that the bird was always there (other times it was not) and with the bird switching between the right and left shoulder. A similar phenomenon, known as reduplicative paramnesia, can occur in which the patient multiplies objects or people in the environment. Common manifestations include the patient's belief that he or she has two or more hospital rooms or homes. However, the belief can extend to the patient's body, so that the patient believes that he or she has many arms or legs. In the most dramatic case we have seen of this phenomenon, the patient believed that he had a double of himself who followed him around. Another behavioral anomaly that can be seen in patients with posterior damage is that of anosagnosia, in which the patient expresses a form of denial about medical status or physical functioning. In such cases, the patient may refuse to acknowledge having had a clinical stroke (either entirely or in a degraded fashion in which the patient acknowledges having been told that a stroke occurred) and may refuse to acknowledge hemiparesis, even when it is quite severe. This phenomenon does not seem to represent classic denial in the psychoanalytical sense but rather reflects the patient's altered perception of somatic functioning as a result of brain damage.

In addition to the above changes, patients may exhibit a wide variety of behavioral symptoms related to focal or lateralized brain damage. Patients with left hemisphere strokes may develop depressive symptoms on a delayed basis that are not entirely reactive in nature, and patients with right hemisphere strokes may show indifference or a lack of emotional comprehension in which emotional reactions are displayed but disconnected from the patient's perception of an affective reaction. For example, the patient may begin to cry whenever he hears his father mentioned; on questioning, the patient states that he was very upset about his father's death a year ago but that he did not "feel" sad when his father was mentioned and did not realize that he felt so until the crying began. Similarly, the patient may lose the ability to read the emotional states other people reveal in their facial expressions or body posture and may be surprised by statements others make about their feelings. Patients with right frontal lesions may develop paranoid delusions. Those with left temporal lesions may report auditory hallucinations while other patients with temporal lesions may become extremely religious. Occipital lesions may be associated with visual hallucinations (often of lights or colors or spots), and gustatory or olfactory hallucinations are seen in some patients with temporal lesions. Changes in sexual behavior are also sometimes evident.

Multiple Sclerosis

Multiple sclerosis (MS) is a neurological disorder in which the myelin sheaths of nerve fibers are damaged, producing lesions called demyelinating plaques. These lesions may occur throughout the central nervous system; therefore, there is wide variability in symptom presentation. Symptoms are transient in the early stages of the illness. There is often motor weakness, visual disturbance (partial or total loss of vision lasting up to days), numbness, vertigo, seizures, unformed auditory hallucinations, fatigue, and mood changes. The course of the illness may be rapidly progressive, relapsing and remitting, or chronic progressive, but the disease often persists for many years (Adams & Victor, 1985).

MS is sometimes confused with hysteria or somatoform disorder. This is because of the fleeting, evanescent nature of the physical symptoms of MS, preoccupation with physical functioning that occurs in some MS patients, and the tendency of MS patients to show profiles similar to those seen in patients with hysteria or somatoform disorders on personality tests.

Affective disorders are commonly seen in MS. In one study (Schiffer, Wineman, & Weitkamp, 1986), the rate of affective disorder was found to be twice as high as would be expected in the general population based on the individual occurrence rates of the two disorders. Patients are frequently described as euphoric. In fact, Cottrell and Wilson (1926) characterized the majority of their patients as "abnormally" optimistic. Manic episodes may occur with restlessness, grandiosity, reduced need for sleep, and in discriminant spending. We have seen patients whose depression appeared to be the most troubling of their symptoms. In some cases depression maybe the first sign of the disease (Goodstein & Farrell, 1977). White (1990) previously described some of her experiences with MS patients. For one of the patients, the initial MS symptom was probably suicidal ideation. Another's depression intensified as his MS progressed. As the disease progresses, it is not uncommon for patients to experience emotional lability. Patients may present to the emergency room with suicidal ideation, apathy, fatigue, irritability, and recent mood changes.

A smaller subgroup of patients present with delusions and hallucinations. Patients may have fixed persecutory delusions. They may also have symptoms consistent with frontal and temporal dysfunction (see discussion related to cerebrovascular disease) including hyperreligiosity (White, Nyenhuis, & Sax, 1992).

Parkinson's Disease

Idiopathic Parkinson's disease (PD) is characterized by motor symptoms such as tremor, rigidity, fatigue, slowness of movements, and an inability to initiate movement. Gait disturbance, slurred speech, and small and tremulous writing are also cardinal features of the disease. It is a progressive illness with patients in the early stages showing mild motor signs (beginning with unilateral involvement and moving to bilateral involvement) and patients later in the disease process showing more severe motor impairment. Cognitive deficitscan be seen at various stages, including visuospatial processing deficits, impaired retrieval of information, and attentional variability. Mood changes are also commonly seen in patients with PD. In addition, psychiatric symptoms such as hallucinations and paranoia are seen in patients with PD.

Depression is fairly common in patients with untreated PD, ranging from

40–60% (Santamaria, Tolosa, & Balles, 1986). There is some controversy about whether the mood changes are a result of organic changes or a reaction to having the illness. It is fairly well documented that the mood changes do not correlate reliably with the motor signs (Huber, Paulson, & Shuttleworth, 1988), age of onset, or duration of the motor symptoms (Celesia & Wanamaker, 1972). There is some indication that patients who are younger at disease onset are more likely to have depressive symptoms predating the motor symptoms. When motor symptoms are treated, the depression may initially improve slightly. However, this change in mood does not appear to hold over time even with continued improvement in motor symptoms.

In terms of hallucinations, patients with early PD may present with visual hallucinations. These most often involve fuzzy animals, hooded people, or indistinct people (White, Au, Durso, & Moss, 1992). Later in the course of the illness, patients may present with confusion and psychosis. The hallucinations may involve both auditory and visual modalities and are seen during confusional states (White et al., 1992). It is difficult to determine the extent to which these symptoms are related to medication side effects, although some patients complain of visual hallucinations even before they begin taking medications.

There is some indication that medication treatments for PD may cause vivid disturbing dreams (Moskovitz, Moses, & Klawans, 1978), visual hallucinations, and paranoid delusions (Celesia & Barr, 1970). Other treatment effects include confusional states with disorientation to time or place, anxiety, or mania. This is especially true for older patients (Saint-Cyr, Taylor,& Lang, 1993).

Visual hallucinations are the most common side effect of medication (Cummings, 1992), and the frequency of hallucinations ranges from 6% to 38% of patients treated with anti-Parkinsonian medications. Fully formed images of humans or animals are the most common. They are most often experienced at night and are recurrent nearly every night. Most patients report these as nonthreatening hallucinations. Patients who are older, taking anticholinergic drugs, and on medications longer are most likely to have visual hallucinations (Tanner, Bogel, Goetz, & Klawans, 1983).

Delusions are rare in untreated PD. However, they are found in conjunction with a variety of medication treatments (Crow, Johnstone, & McClelland, 1976), ranging from 3% to 30% of patients, and may represent emerging toxicity. Delusions from anti-Parkinsonian treatment tend to be persecutory in nature, involving fears of being harmed or tape-recorded (Moskovitz et al., 1978).

Mood elevation, which varies from euphoria to full-blown manic episodes, has also been reported in patients on anti-Parkinsonian medications. Again these episodes are related to amount of drug use and diminish with decreased drug use. Less common symptoms which have been found to relate to amount of drug use include increased anxiety, irritability, and insomnia.

Delirious states with fluctuating arousal, impaired attention, and incoherent verbal output have been observed in 5% to 25% of treated PD patients, most often later in the disease process after years of medication treatment (Cummings, 1992).

Overall, PD patient who are older, with dementia, on higher dosages of medication, and with a history of psychiatric illness predating the PD motor signs are described as being more likely to have psychiatric symptoms (Tanner et al., 1983).

Huntington's Disease

Huntington's disease (HD) is an autosomal dominant genetic disease with complete penetrance, meaning that the offspring of an affected individual has a 50% chance of being affected. It is characterized by a combination of symptoms that are described as an example of a subcortical triad (McHugh & Folstein, 1975; Peyser & Folstein, 1990). The triad includes uncontrollable involuntary movements (known as chorea), psychiatric disturbances, and a progressive dementia. McHugh (1989) described these cardinal features as a triad of Ds: dyskinesia, dementia, and depression. After the initial appearance of the symptoms there is a progressive decline in cognitive and motoric functioning.

Patients with HD show considerable variability in the onset of motor symptoms and in emotional and cognitive disturbances (Caine & Shoulson, 1983; Conneally, 1984; White, Vasterling, Koroshetz, & Myers, 1992).

The dyskinesias emerge as a result of the underlying neuropathology of the basal ganglia (McHugh, 1989; Monte, Vonsattel, & Richardson,1988). Among the neuropathological changes characteristic of HD is atrophy of the caudate and putamen, including cell loss and astrogliosis. The atrophy is more severe in the caudate than in the putamen. To a lesser extent, cell loss is also observed in the globus pallidus and the cerebral cortex (Dom, Malfroid, & Baro, 1976; Jernigan, Salmon, Butters, & Hesselink, 1991; Monte et al., 1988; Vonsattel et al., 1985). Alexander, DeLong, and Strick (1986) proposed five functionally segregated basal ganglia–thalamocortical circuits that link basal ganglia and cortex through a series of complex loops. Based on the neuroanatomy, they infer the involvement of the basal ganglia in cognitive and affective changes. These changes are consistent with the clinical syndrome associated with HD.

The characteristics of the behavioral and personality changes observed in HD share some features with other basal ganglia diseases. For example, depression and apathy are commonly seen in Parkinson's disease as well as in HD (Mayeux, Stern, Rosen, & Leventhal, 1981; McHugh, 1989; Sano, 1991). These mood state or affective changes are not typically a reaction to having a debilitating degenerative disease. Investigators found evidence of behavioral and mood changes occurring several years prior to the onset of the motor impairments (Bird, 1980; Folstein, Abbott, Chase, Jensen, & Folstein, 1983a; Hayden, 1981; Mayeux et al., 1981; Webb & Trzepacz, 1987). Other evidence suggesting the organic nature of the changes is the finding that HD patients experience manic episodes in addition to depression (Folstein, 1989; McHugh,

1989; Pflanz, Besson, Ebmeier, & Simpson, 1991). Peyser & Folstein (1983) reported that approximately 10% of their sample had manic episodes. Neither bipolar disorder nor mania is an expected functional reaction to living with this debilitating disease.

Presently, affective disorders (including depression, mania, and bipolar disorder) are reported as the most common psychiatric syndrome in HD. Up to 40% of HD patients sampled report major affective illness (Caine & Shoulson, 1983; Folstein & Folstein, 1983).

Some studies found that close to 60% of their HD samples were described as irritable (Pflanz et al., 1991; Burns, Folstein, Brandt, & Folstein, 1990). The irritability was at times severe enough to warrant the diagnosis of intermittent explosive disorder (Folstein, Franz, Jensen, Chase, & Folstein, 1983b; Webb & Trzepacz, 1987). Burns et al. (1990) found aggression in 59% of their HD sample. Folstein and Folstein (1983) hypothesized that the episodes of aggression observed in HD patients are an exacerbation of a premorbid personality trait. They proposed that as a result of the disease process, there may be a dysfunction in the normal regulatory (dampening) mechanisms and, therefore, there is heightened aggression.

HD patients may have difficulty inhibiting impulsive behavior (Caine, Hunt, Weingartner, & Ebert, 1978; Caine & Shoulson, 1983). There is a great deal of evidence of antisocial behavior associated with HD, ranging from criminal assaults and minor crimes to child abuse and neglect (Dewhurst, Oliver, & McKnight, 1970; Folstein et al., 1983b; Hayden, 1981; Oliver & Dewhurst, 1969). However, the relationships between (1) the development of these symptoms and the social effects of living in an HD family and (2) neuropathology of the disease are controversial (Folstein, 1989).

Some investigators believe that affected individuals often have a history of alcohol as well as substance abuse (e.g., Dewhurst et al., 1970; Folstein et al., 1983a; Folstein & Folstein, 1983). White, Vasterling et al. (1992) described a significant level of alcohol and drug abuse in some HD patients and in their families. They, as well as Webb and Trzepacz (1987), observed that the majority of alcohol use was in the earlier stages of the disease and tended to drop off as the disease progressed. They raised the possibility that for some, the use of alcohol and other recreational drugs may be a form of self-medication.

Disorders related to schizophrenia were reported to occur in between 5% and 10% of HD patients (Shoulson, 1990) with hallucinations and paranoid delusions frequently reported by HD patients (Caine & Shoulson, 1983; Folstein & Folstein, 1983; White, Vasterling et al., 1992).

White, Vasterling et al. (1992) pointed out that there are significant changes in mood state that do not reach the level of diagnosable affective disorders. Vegetative, biological signs of depression are common in HD, including psychomotor retardation as a result of the disease; insomnia (Shoulson, 1990; White, Vasterling et al., 1992) often resulting from the patient's chorea and restlessness (White, Vasterling et al., 1992); and anorexia (Hayden, 1981; White et al., 1992). White et al. (1992) noted that some HD patients reported diminished appetites and Hayden (1981) remarked on the unusual occurrence of dramatic weight loss observed even in patients who reported having excellent appetites. He suggested that the caloric expenditure exceeds what would be expected from the chorea and increase in movement alone and may, in some way, be related to the disease process itself.

The extraordinarily high suicide rate in this population (Dewhurst et al., 1970; Kessler & Block, 1989; Reed, Chandler, Hughes, & Davidson,1958; Schoenfeld et al., 1984) was noticed by Huntington and he remarked on it qualitatively in his seminal paper (Huntington, 1872). A quantitative study by Schoenfeld et al. (1984) found that, after statistically adjusting forage and sex, the suicide rate in a HD group was more than eight times that of the suicide rate in the Massachusetts population for individuals ages 50–69. Further, they concluded that because the preponderance of successful suicides were committed by individuals who had not yet been diagnosed, suicide may occur more frequently in the earlier stages of the disease. White, Vasterling et al. (1992) described patients who experienced command hallucinations regarding suicide, some who reported a compulsive urge to kill themselves, and some for whom suicidal ideation is secondary to their depression and demoralization related to the disease. Kessler (Kessler, 1987; Kessler & Block, 1989) made the provocative suggestion that passive encouragement on the part of the patient's family as well as the professional health care worker is a major factor underlying some of the suicides that occur.

Traumatic Brain Injury

There are two types of head injuries, open and closed. Open head injuries occur when the skull is penetrated and most often occur during war or civil commotions. Closed head injuries (CHIs) occur much more frequently. Motor vehicle accidents, falls, and sporting accidents resulting in head injuries aremost likely to be CHIs. Therefore, CHI is the subject of the following discussion.

Brain damage can result when a person is moving and strikes an obstacle (i.e., the brain accelerates and quickly decelerates) or when a person is struck by an object (i.e., creating pressure gradients from the skull distortion). Contusions and tissue shearing result and may cause losses in consciousness. The duration of the loss of consciousness (or length of coma) and the duration of the posttraumatic amnesia correlate with the severity of the head injury in terms of mortality and cognitive and emotional functioning (for detailed reviews of the neuropathological and neuropsychological consequences of CHIs, see Morse and Montgomery, 1992; Lezak, 1995).

Patients who suffer from these psychological and personality disturbances are remarkable in that they often appear completely healthy. It is often the case that no physical or neurological consequences of the CHI may remainand yet the behavior and personality changes that result from the injury may cause a significant degree of difficulty and stress. Lezak (1987) reported that for some patients the behavioral and emotional disturbances are more debilitating than the residual cognitive and physical disabilities. In later writings she pointed out that patients who survived severe head injuries are rarely able to resume their studies or return to their previous level of employment (Lezak, 1995).

The exact nature of the behavioral and cognitive disturbances associated with head injuries is directly dependent on the location of the primary as well as any secondary injuries. Readers are referred back to the discussion of the different psychological or psychiatric disturbances commonly associated with the dysfunction of specific areas of the brain in the section "Cerebrovascular Disease." In addition to the behavioral consequences related to the specific site of injury, there is often diffuse damage (i.e., small lesions and lacerations throughout the brain) that accompanies the injury. Even patients with mild injuries who were never admitted to a hospital, may not have gone to an emergency room at the time of their injury, and whose laboratory findings including computed tomography (CT), MRI, and electroencephalogram (EEG) are all normal may experience physical (pain nausea ,dizziness, etc.) and emotional symptoms (Morse & Montgomery, 1992).

Lezak (1978) suggested five categories of the kinds of alterations in the brain-injured patient's character that can cause the most amount of distress and problems in adjustment for the patients' families and loved ones:

1. *Impaired social perceptiveness, including an impaired awareness of one's self and surroundings.* Often patients lose the capacity to reflect and monitor their own behavior. They may lose their insight and empathy so that their understanding and feelings for others is diminished. They are sometimes seen as selfish.
2. *Impaired self control, including impulsivity, restlessness, and impatience.* At times this behavioral dyscontrol may lead to the patients' having legal problems, including committing criminal acts (Morse & Montgomery, 1992).
3. *Increased dependency due to lack of initiative, impaired judgmentand planning abilities.* In one study, Florian, Katz, and Labav (1989) found that several years post injury, dependency was characterized as the primary burden for the family of the head injured patient.
4. *Emotional change can include irritability, apathy, lability of mood, silliness or childishness and a change in sexual interest (most often hyposexuality).* Anxiety and depression can be prevalent even years after the injury (Lezak, 1987).
5. *An impaired capacity for social learning.* Even though the patients' ability to learn new information may be intact, they fail to learn from experience.

In addition to impulsivity and heightened emotional experiences, psychiatric assistance may also be sought by some patients who experience mania and paranoia (Lezak, 1995; Morse & Montgomery, 1992).

Idiopathic Temporal Lobe Epilepsy

Seizures are a common symptom of a wide range of neurological disorders and the hallmark symptom of epilepsy. A seizure results when an overactive group of neurons (the seizure focus) is released from its usual physiological control resulting in abnormal electrical rhythms in the brain. This transient disturbance is caused by an excessive discharge of cortical neurons. The excitation can spread and excite adjacent regions. Depending on the number of neurons affected, the excitation can lead to widespread electrical dysrhythmias. These generalized seizures are characterized by loss of consciousness and stereotyped motor activity including convulsions (Greenberg & Seidman,1992; Trimble & Thompson, 1986). (See Adams & Victor, 1985, for a more comprehensive review of the epilepsies; Trimble & Thompson, 1986, for a review of the neuropsychology of epilepsy).

Seizures can result from infections, head injuries, vascular malformations, strokes, tumors, toxic chemicals, high fevers, and other neurological disorders. Seizures of unknown etiology are referred to as idiopathic seizures. Idiopathic temporal lobe epilepsy (ITLE) has been of particular interest to neuropsychologists. Psychiatric/psychological problems are common in patients with ITLE. They often experience affective and behavior disturbances, hallucinations, psychosis, and personality changes.

During the seizure itself (ictus) patients can experience a wide variety of sensory, motoric, and emotional phenomena including autonomic sensations (fullness or "butterflies" in the stomach, blushing, etc.), cognitive disturbances including feelings of deja vu, hallucinations, alterations in mood (e.g., fear, panic, depression, and elation), illusions (i.e., misperception or misinterpretation of real external stimuli), and automatisms (e.g., lip smacking, grimacing, and automatic behavior) (Greenberg & Seidman, 1992).

ITLE is thought to be the type of epilepsy that is most frequently associated with the psychiatric changes known as the interictal behavioral syndrome (IBS). However, there is considerable controversy in neuropsychology regarding the specificity of this association (Osview, 1989). The personality disturbances most commonly described as part of the IBS include changes in sexual behavior (most often hyposexuality), viscosity (social clinging), religiosity, hypergraphia, and experiencing emotions more intensely (Blumer, 1975). Viscosity can be manifested in several different ways. Some patients find it difficult to end conversations. They can treat new acquaintances with the same degree of intimacy and candor that they would extend to a close friend and they seem to have difficulty ending conversations, even at the conclusion of professional appointments.

They can also show considerable changes in the manner of their interactions and conversations. Their speech is often circumstantial, weighted down with numerous unnecessary details, overly serious, and perhaps pedantic. An important difference between this type of circumstantial speech and the disordered (tangential) speech of schizophrenics is that although patients with ITLE if given enough time will reach their point, those patients with a thought disorder are pulled away from the point and are not able to return to it.

Patients with ITLE often have trouble controlling their anger. Irritable and impulsive behavior in the form of angry outbursts is very common, and on rare occasions violent or abusive behavior can be seen (Lezak, 1995). There is often a specific quality of moral indignation or a feeling that an injustice has occurred that accompanies that anger or aggressive outburst. For some patients the IBS can be more debilitating than the seizure disorder itself (Greenberg & Seidman, 1992).

Psychological and psychiatric attention is often required for patients who are experiencing not only anger and aggression more intensely but fear and depression as well. The depression of some patients is so severe that they are at risk for suicide. Less frequently seen than the personality and affective changes is interictal psychosis. In the latter stages of ITLE a paranoid psychosis can develop that resembles schizophrenia (Greenberg & Seidman,1992).

SUMMARY

Behavioral and psychological symptoms often seen in patients who have neurological conditions were presented. We provided examples of times at which affected patients may come to the attention of mental health care workers during psychological emergencies. We attempted to illustrate that thinking of disorders as either "psychiatric" or "neurological" imposes a false dichotomy and that in the context of what may appear to be a behavioral emergency, it may be beneficial to consider the patient's neurological status.

REFERENCES

Adams, R. D., & Victor, M. (1985). *Principles of neurology* (3rd ed.). New York: McGraw-Hill.

Alexander, G. E., DeLong, M. R., & Strick, P. L. (1986). Parallel organization of functionally segregated circuits linking basal ganglia and cortex. *Annual Reviewof Neuroscience, 9,* 357–381.

American Psychiatric Association. (1994). *Diagnostic and statistical manual of mental disorders* (4th ed.). Washington, DC: Author.

Binswanger, O. (1894). Die abgrenzung dids allgremeinen progressiven paralysie. *Berlinsk Klinisk Wochenschrift, 31,* 1103–1186.

Bird, E. D. (1980). Chemical pathology of Huntington's disease. *Annual Review of Pharmacology and Toxicology, 20,* 533–551.

Blumer, D. (1975). Temporal lobe epilepsy and its psychiatric significance. In D. Benson & D. Blumer (Eds.), *Psychiatric aspects of neurological disease* (pp.171–198). New York: Grune & Stratton.

Burns, A., Folstein, S., Brandt, J., & Folstein, M. (1990). Clinical assessment of irritability, aggression, and apathy in Huntington and Alzheimer disease. *Journal of Nervous and Mental Disease, 178*(1), 20–26.

Caine, E. D., Hunt, R. D., Weingartner, H., & Ebert, M. H. (1978). Huntington's dementia: Clinical and neuropsychological features. *Archives of General Psychiatry, 35,* 377–384.

Caine, E. D., & Shoulson, I. (1983). Psychiatric syndromes in Huntington's disease. *American Journal of Psychiatry, 140,* 728–733.

Celesia, G. G., & Barr, A. N. (1970). Psychosis and other psychiatric manifestations of levodopa therapy. *Archives of Neurology, 23,* 193–200.

Celesia, G. G., & Wanamaker, W. M. (1972). Psychiatric disturbances in Parkinson's disease. *Diseases of the Nervous System, 33,* 577–583.

Charney, D. S., Deutch, A. Y., Krystal, J. H., Southwick, S. M., & Davis, M. (1993). Psychobiologic mechanisms of posttraumatic stress disorder. *Archives of General Psychiatry, 50*(4), 295–305.

Conneally, P. M. (1984). Huntington disease: Genetics and epidemiology. *American Journal of Human Genetics, 36,* 506–526.

Cottrell, S. S., & Wilson, S. A. K. (1926). The affective symptomatology of disseminated sclerosis. *Journal of Neurology and Psychopathology, 7*(25), 1–30.

Crow, T. J., Johnstone, E. C., & McClelland, H. A. (1976). The coincidence of schizophrenia and Parkinsonism: Some neurochemical implications. *Psychology of Medicine, 6,* 227–233.

Cummings, J. L., (1992). Neuropsychiatric complications of drug treatment of Parkinson's disease. In S. J. Huber & J. L. Cummings (Eds.), *Parkinson's disease: Neurobehavioral aspects* (pp. 313–327). New York: Oxford University Press.

Dewhurst, K., Oliver, J. E., & McKnight, A. L. (1970). Socio-psychiatric consequences of Huntington's disease. *British Journal of Psychiatry, 116,* 255–258.

Dom, R., Malfroid, M., & Baro, F. (1976). Neuropathology of Huntington's chorea. *Neurology, 26,* 64–68.

Filley, C. M., Heaton, R. K., & Rosenberg, N. L. (1990). White matter dementiain chronic toluene abuse. *Neurology, 40,* 532–534.

Florian, V., Katz, S., & Labav, V. (1989). Impact of traumatic brain damage on family dynamics and functioning. *Brain Injury, 3,* 219–234.

Folstein, M. F., & Bylsma, F. W. (1994). Noncognitive symptoms of Alzheimer's disease. In R. D. Terry, R. Katzman, & K. L. Bick (Eds.), *Alzheimer's disease* (pp. 27–40). New York: Raven Press.

Folstein, S. E. (1989). *Huntington's disease: A disorder of families.* Baltimore: Johns Hopkins University Press.

Folstein, S. E., Abbott, M. H., Chase, G. A., Jensen, B. A., & Folstein, M. F. (1983a). The association of affective disorder with Huntington's disease in a case seriesand in families. *Psychology of Medicine, 13,* 537–542.

Folstein, S. E., & Folstein, M. F. (1983). Psychiatric features of Huntington's disease: Recent approaches and findings. *Psychological Development, 2,* 193–205.

Folstein, S. E., Franz, M. L., Jensen, B. A., Chase, G. A., & Folstein, M. F. (1983b). Conduct disorder and affective disorder among the offspring of patients with Huntington's disease. *Psychology of Medicine, 13,* 45–52.

Goodstein, R. K., & Farrell, R. B. (1977). Multiple sclerosis presenting as a depressive illness. *Disorders of the Nervous System, 38,* 127–131.

Greenberg, M. S., & Seidman, L. J. (1992). Temporal lobe epilepsy. In R. F. White (Ed.), *Clinical syndromes in adult neuropsychology: The practitioner's handbook* (pp. 345–379). Amsterdam: Elsevier.

Hachinski, V. C., Lassen, N. A., & Marshall, J. (1974). Multi-infarct dementia: A cause of mental deterioration in the elderly. *Lancet, 2,* 207–210.

Hachinski, V. C., Potter, P., & Merskey, H. (1987). Leukoaraiosis. *Archives of Neurology, 44,* 21–23.

Hamdy, R. C. (1994). Clinical presentation. In R. C. Hamdy, J. M. Turnbull, W. Clark, & M. M. Lancaster (Eds.), *Alzheimer's disease a handbook for caregivers* (2nd ed.). St. Louis: Mosby.

Harlow, J. (1868). Recovery after severe injury to the head. *Publication of the Massachusetts Medical Society, 2,* 327–346.

Hayden, M. R. (1981). *Huntington's chorea.* New York: Springer-Verlag.

Huber, S. J., Paulson, G. W., & Shuttleworth, E. C. (1988). Relationship of motor symptoms, intellectual impairment and depression on Parkinson's disease. *Journal of Neurology, Neurosurgery and Psychiatry, 5,* 855–858.

Huntington, G. W. (1872). On chorea. *Medical Surgical Report, 26,* 317–321.

Jernigan, T. L., Salmon, D. P., Butters, N., & Hesselink, J. R. (1991). Cerebral structure on MRI, Part II: Specific changes in Alzheimer's and Huntington's diseases. *Biological Psychiatry, 29,* 68–81.

Kessler, S. (1987). The dilemma of suicide and Huntington disease [Letter to the Editor]. *American Journal of Medical Genetics, 26,* 315–317.

Kessler, S., & Block, M. (1989). Social system responses to Huntington's disease. *Family Process, 28,* 59–68.

Lezak, M. D. (1978).Living with the characterologically altered brain injured patient. *Journal of Clinical Psychiatry, 39,* 592–598.

Lezak, M. D. (1987). Relationships between personality disorders, social disturbances and physical disability following traumatic brain injury. *Journal of Head Trauma Rehabilitation, 2*(1), 57–69.

Lezak, M. D. (1995). *Neuropsychological assessment* (3rd ed.). New York: Oxford University Press.

Mayeux, R., Stern, Y., Rosen, J., & Leventhal, J. (1981). Depression, intellectual impairment and Parkinson disease. *Neurology, 31,* 659–662.

McHugh, P. R. (1989). The neuropsychiatry of basal ganglia disorders: A triadic syndrome and its explanation. *Neuropsychiatry, Neuropsychology and Behavioral Neurology, 2*(4), 239–247.

McHugh, P. R., & Folstein, M. (1975). Psychiatric syndromes of Huntington's chorea: A clinical and phenomenological study. In D. Benson & D. Blumer (Eds.), *Psychiatric aspects of neurological disease* (pp. 267–286). New York: Grune & Stratton.

Monte, S. M. D. L., Vonsattel, J.-P., & Richardson, E. P. (1988). Morphometric demonstration of atrophic changes in the cerebral cortex, white matter, and neostriatum in Huntington's disease. *Journal of Neuropathology and Experimental Neurology, 47*(5), 516–525.

Morse, P. A., & Montgomery, C. E. (1992). Neuropsychological evaluation of traumatic brain injury. In R. F. White (Ed.), *Clinical syndromes in adult neuropsychology: The practitioner's handbook* (pp. 85–176). Amsterdam: Elsevier.

Moskovitz, C., Moses, H. III, & Klawans, H. L. (1978). Levodopa-induced psychosis: A kindling phenomenon. *American Journal of Psychiatry, 135,* 669–675.

Moss, M. B., & Albert, M. S. (1992). Neuropsychology of Alzheimer's disease. In R. F. White (Ed.), *Clinical syndromes in adult neuropsychology: The practitioner's handbook* (pp. 305–343). Amsterdam: Elsevier.

Moss, M. B., Albert, M. S., & Kemper, T. L. (1992). Neuropsychology of frontal lobe dementia. In R. F. White (Ed.), *Clinical syndromes in adult neuropsychology: The practitioner's handbook* (pp. 387–303). Amsterdam: Elsevier.

Oliver, J. E., & Dewhurst, K. E. (1969). Six generations of ill-used children in a Huntington's pedigree. *Postgraduate Medical Journal, 45*, 757–760.

Osview, F. (1989). Interictal behavior syndrome in temporal lobe epilepsy: The views of three experts. *Journal of Neuropsychiatry and Clinical Neuroscience, 1*, 308–318.

Peyser, C. E., & Folstein, S. E. (1990). Huntington's disease as a model for mood disorders, clues from neuropathology and neurochemistry. *Molecular and Chemical Neuropathology, 12*, 99–119.

Pflanz, S., Besson, J. A. O., Ebmeier, K. P., & Simpson, S. (1991). The clinical manifestation of mental disorder in Huntington's disease: a retrospective case record study of disease progression. *Acta Psychiatrica Scandinavica, 83*, 53–60.

Post, R. M. (1992). Transduction of psychosocial stress into the neurobiology of recurrent affective disorder. *American Journal of Psychiatry, 149*(8), 999–1010.

Rauch, S. L., Jenike, M. A., Alpert, N. M, Baer, L., Breiter, H. C., Savage, C. R., & Fischman, A. J. (1994). Regional cerebral blood flow measured during symptom provocation in obsessive–compulsive disorder using oxygen 15-labeled carbon dioxide and positron emission tomography. *Archives of General Psychiatry,51*(1), 62–70.

Reed, E., Chandler, J. H., Hughes, E. M., & Davidson, R. T. (1958). Huntington'schorea in Michigan, demography and genetics. American *Journal of Human Genetics, 10*, 210–225.

Rosenberg, N. L., Kleinschmidt-DeMasters, B. K., Davis, K. A., Dreisbach, J. N., Hormes, J. T., & Filley, C. M. (1988). Toluene abuse causes diffuse central nervous system white matter changes. *Annals of Neurology, 23*, 611–614.

Sano, M. (1991). Basal ganglia diseases and depression. Neuropsychiatry, *Neuropsychology and Behavioral Neurology, 4*(1), 41–48.

Santamaria, J., Tolosa, E., & Balles, A. (1986). Parkinson's disease with depression: A possible subgroup of idiopathic parkinsonism. *Neurology, 36*(8), 1130–1133.

Saint-Cyr, J. A., Taylor, A. E., & Lang, A. E. (1993). Neuropsychological and psychiatric side effects in the treatment of Parkinson's disease. *Neurology, 43*(12 Suppl. 6), 47–52.

Saint-Cyr, J. A., Taylor, A. E., & Nicholson, K. (1995). Behavior and the basal ganglia. *Advances in Neurology, 65*, 1–28.

Schiffer, R. B., Wineman, N. M., & Weitkamp, L. R. (1986). Association between bipolar affective disorder and multiple sclerosis. *American Journal of Psychiatry,143*, 94–95.

Schoenfeld, M., Myers, R. H., Cupples, L. A., Berkman, B., Sax, D. S., & Clark, E. (1984). Increased rate of suicide among patients with Huntington's disease. *Journal of Neurological Neurosurgery and Psychiatry, 47*, 1283–1287.

Seidman, L. J., Cassens, G. P., Kremen, W. S., & Pepple, J. R. (1992). Neuropsychology of schizophrenia. In R. F. White (Ed.), *Clinical syndromes in adult neuropsychology: The practitioner's handbook* (pp. 213–251). Amsterdam: Elsevier.

Shoulson, I. (1990). Huntington's disease: Cognitive and psychiatric features. *Neuropsychiatry, Neuropsychology and Behavioral Neurology, 3*(1), 15–22.

Tanner, C. M., Bogel, C., Goetz, C. G., & Klawans, H. L. (1983). Hallucinations in Parkinson's disease: A population study. *Annals of Neurology, 14,* 136.

Tatemichi, T. K. (1990). How acute brain failure becomes chronic: A view of the mechanisms of dementia related to stoke. *Neurology, 40,* 1652–1659.

Trimble, M. R., & Thompson, P. J. (1986). Neuropsychological aspects of epilepsy. In I. Grant & K. M. Adams (Eds.), *Neuropsychological assessment of neuropsychiatric disorders* (pp. 321–346). New York: Oxford University Press.

Vonsattel, J. P., Myers, R. H., Stevens, T. J., Ferrante, R. J., Bird, E. D., & Richardson, E. P. (1985). Neuropathological classification of Huntington's disease. *Journal of Neuropathology and Experimental Neurology, 44*(6), 559–577.

Webb, M., & Trzepacz, P. T. (1987). Huntington's disease: correlations of mental status with chorea. *Biological Psychiatry, 22,* 751–761.

White, R. F. (1990). Emotional and cognitive correlates of multiple sclerosis. *Journal of Neuropsychiatry, 2*(4), 422–428.

White, R. F., Au, R., Durso, R., & Moss, M. B. (1992). Neuropsychological function in Parkinson's disease. In R. F. White (Ed.), *Clinical syndromes in adult neuropsychology: The practitioner's handbook* (pp. 213–251). Amsterdam: Elsevier.

White, R. F., Nyenhuis, D. S., & Sax, D. S. (1992). Multiple sclerosis. In R. F. White (Ed.), *Clinical syndromes in adult neuropsychology: The practitioner's handbook* (pp. 177–212). Amsterdam: Elsevier.

White, R. F., Vasterling, J. J., Koroshetz, W., & Myers, R. (1992). Neuropsychology of Huntington's disease. In R. F. White (Ed.), *Clinical syndromes in adult neuropsychology: The practitioner's handbook* (pp. 213–251). Amsterdam: Elsevier.

Wolfe, N., Linn, R., Babikian, V. L., Knoefel, J. E., & Albert, M. E. (1990). Frontal systems impairment following multiple lacunar infarcts. *Archives of Neurology, 47,* 129–132.

CHAPTER 15

PSYCHOLOGICAL SYMPTOMS IN ENDOCRINE DISORDERS

JACQUELINE A. SAMSON
ROBERT M. LEVIN
GARY S. RICHARDSON

Rapid assessment and accurate diagnosis are essential for the effective management of psychological emergencies. For mental health practitioners, this means being aware not only of the psychiatric diagnoses that present as emergencies but also of medical disorders that can mimic psychological disorders. Of the many medical conditions that can present with psychological symptoms, endocrine disorders are among the most common and the most difficult to recognize. The primary reason for overlap in presentation is that hormones play an important role in the modulation of central nervous system (CNS) activity. Hormones have diverse direct and indirect effects on the brain, which means that endocrine imbalances can result in complex derangements of CNS systems that control mood as well as general arousal, attention, motor activity, and sleep–wake cycles. In this chapter, we review the specific nature of these interactions, and attempt to provide specific guidelines to aid in the differentiation of endocrine disorders from the psychiatric diagnoses they can mimic (see also Oakley, 1980; Goggins, 1986; Fava, Sonino, & Morphy, 1993; Rubinow & Schmidt, 1995; Stern & Prange, 1995).

GENERAL PRINCIPLES OF ENDOCRINOLOGY

The endocrine system consists of a number of discrete but overlapping functional units. The defining feature of each unit is that it uses a unique type of circulating hormone to achieve communication between the endocrine gland and specific target tissues. Communication between endocrine glands and target tissues depends on the unique structure of the hormone and its interaction with specific receptors at the site of action. These receptors then initiate cellular responses appropriate to the target tissue, as in the example of insulin regulation of metabolic activity in liver, muscle, and adipose tissue.

A second consistent feature of the endocrine system is autoregulation of hormone concentration. The concentration of a circulating hormone regulates the extent of its continued synthesis and secretion, acting through "feedback inhibition" of its trophic regulating hormone. Feedback inhibition can occur at the endocrine gland itself and/or at a separate site where stimulation of the gland originates. The endocrine system also shows a third consistent feature, that of hierarchical organization. For most hierarchically organized system units, secretion of the hormone from the endocrine gland is controlled by a separate, higher-order regulatory center (e.g., the pituitary gland), which secretes a number of tropic hormones.

NEUROENDOCRINOLOGY

In the case of the pituitary gland, hierarchical organization extends above the pituitary to the CNS. Pituitary gland secretion is itself regulated by stimulatory or inhibitory influences from a distinct area of the brain called the hypothalamus. Hypothalamic releasing factors are secreted in response to signals from the periphery, such as the concentration of the circulating hormones. Some endocrine glands, such as the parathyroid glands and the pancreatic islet cells, do not have a defined direct relationship with the brain hypothalamic–pituitary neuroendocrine axis but instead appear to accomplish sensing and regulatory roles within the gland itself. In most of these cases, however, the CNS is still important in the regulation of hormone secretion. For example, both parathyroid hormone and insulin secretion are modulated by the sympathetic nervous system. Regardless of the specific mechanism, the intimate ties between the endocrine system and the CNS may account for the similarities between psychiatric disorders and endocrine manifestations that are the focus of this chapter. These ties may also provide an explanation for the frequent observation of endocrine abnormalities in psychiatric disorders such as depression.

A second important area of overlap between the endocrine system and the CNS derives from the diverse effects of hormones on the brain itself. In some cases, hormone effects on the brain are indirect. For example, CNS function is potently affected by the serum calcium and blood sugar levels, which are controlled by insulin and by parathyroid hormone. In other cases, specific receptors for hormones such as estrogen, thyroxine, and cortisol exist within the brain, and trigger direct actions at the molecular, cellular, and behavioral levels. It is here that the overlap between psychiatric disorders and endocrine disorders becomes most complex in that abnormalities of hormonal regulation can clearly result in direct alterations of CNS function.

CHALLENGES FOR DIFFERENTIAL DIAGNOSIS

The bidirectional interactions between the endocrine system and the CNS create two important issues in the differential diagnosis of patients with psychological symptoms. First, the involvement of the CNS in the regulation of virtually all endocrine glands provides a functional basis for apparent endocrine disorders in patients with primary psychiatric disease. In some conditions, such as the hypercortisolemia of depression, the exclusion of a primary endocrine disorder (i.e., Cushing's syndrome) can be quite difficult. Conversely, the direct effects of some hormones on CNS function, and the indirect effects of others, can result in complex alterations in neuropsychiatric function in patients with primary endocrine disorders. In these patients, recognition of the true nature of the underlying pathology is essential to their accurate diagnosis and successful therapy.

Although most acute psychological disturbances are accompanied by transient changes in endocrine function, disturbances that are primarily psychological in origin do not generally require treatments targeted to endocrine functions. However, because many of the symptoms of endocrine imbalance are also characteristic of psychological disturbances, there is a need to become familiar with the signs and symptoms that differentiate the two. As a general principle, an endocrine work-up should be considered whenever there is a mental disturbance that has proven to be "treatment resistant" to the standard psychopharmacological interventions.

In the balance of this chapter, we examine the overlap between disorders of specific endocrine glands and neuropsychiatric symptoms. First, the endocrine disorders are organized by specific system to allow recognition of general patterns that might identify relevant CNS actions of specific hormones. Second, the psychiatric symptomatology is organized according to specific diagnostic criteria listed in the *Diagnostic and Statistical Manual of Mental Disorders,* fourth edition (DSM-IV; American Psychiatric Association, 1994) to facilitate identification of patients in whom consideration of an endocrine diagnosis is most appropriate and to identify features specific to either the endocrine or psychiatric patient that might aid in the differential diagnosis.

DISORDERS OF THE THYROID GLAND

The hypothalamic–pituitary–thyroid (HPT) axis includes the hypothalamus, the pituitary, and thyroid gland. The principal function of the HPT system is to regulate the body's metabolic rate.

In response to a variety of CNS signals (which may be triggered by environmental or physical stressors such as exposure to cold), thyroid releasing hormone (TRH) is secreted by the hypothalamus and stimulates the thyrotropic cells in the pituitary gland to release thyroid stimulating hormone (TSH) from the pituitary. TSH in turn stimulates the thyroid gland to release thyroxine (T4) and, to a lesser extent, triiodothyronine (T3). T3 is the more potent of the thyroid hormones. T4 is converted to T3 at multiple sites in the periphery including liver and kidney. T3 then acts by binding to specific thyroid hormone receptors in the body. The resulting effects of thyroid hormone at peripheral sites of action vary with the specific site, but a consistent aspect of thyroid hormone action is to potentiate metabolic activity. This is accomplished directly via effects on peripheral energy utilization and indirectly by stimulation of CNS centers that regulate metabolic activity.

Hyperthyroidism

Definition

Hyperthyroidism is caused by an excess of thyroid hormones and results in the increased metabolic activity of multiple organ systems. Most cases of hyperthyroidism occur in young adults and the most common cause is an autoimmune disorder called Graves' disease. In the elderly, toxic nodular goiter is a more common cause of hyperthyroidism. These two etiologies make up most of the cases of hyperthyroidism, but other etiologies may include:

- Subacute thyroiditis, which may present with clinical features of hyperthyroidism, may last from a few weeks to a few months and then spontaneously resolve.
- Factitious hyperthyroidism, which may be seen in obese individuals who consume large amounts of thyroid hormone in an effort to lose weight. These individuals are often nurses or other medical personnel who have access to samples of thyroid pills.
- Job–Basedow disease, which is a form of hyperthyroidism resulting from the ingestion of a large amount of iodide by a person with an underlying goiter. Hyperthyroidism may also follow the administration of an iodide-containing dye during contrast radiography.
- Less common causes include a pituitary tumor, which secretes an excessive amount of TSH (and secondary thyroid gland stimulation), and hydatidiform moles, which secrete large amounts of human chorionic gonadotropin (HCG), with TSH-like activity.

Prevalence

The prevalence of hyperthyroidism is 0.5–1.0% of the population. This disorder is primarily found in women (75% of the cases) and is more common in young adults.

Clinical Features

Clinical features of Graves' disease include an anterior neck mass (enlargement of the thyroid gland), weight loss despite a good appetite, weakness, palpitations, heat intolerance, sweating, shortness of breath, shakiness, hyperreflexia, menstrual abnormalities, insomnia, fatigue, and muscle wasting. A dramatic finding is bulging of the eyes caused by ocular muscle hypertrophy, increased proliferation of fibroblasts, and increased fluid in the retro-orbital space.

Laboratory Tests

A large number of thyroid function tests are available to the clinician, but only a few are needed to make a diagnosis of Graves' disease. These include the serum T4 or T3, serum TSH, and a 24-hour radioactive iodine uptake. In Graves' disease, the serum T4 and T3 are elevated, the TSH is suppressed, and the 24-hour radioactive iodine uptake is elevated.

Treatment

The treatment of hyperthyroidism is the administration of antithyroid drugs such as propylthiouracil or methimazole, surgical ablation of the thyroid, or the administration of an ablative dose of radioactive iodine. The choice of which of these modalities to use depends on the preference of the patient and her physician.

Psychological Symptoms

A number of psychiatric manifestations have been described in patients with hyperthyroidism. These include mood disturbances such as anxiety, irritability, and emotional lability as well as restlessness and hyperactivity. There may be problems with concentration and organizing thoughts. In about 10% of cases, psychosis (typically paranoid delusions) may develop (Ferrier, 1987). Elderly individuals with hyperthyroidism present somewhat differently than younger persons. They appear depressed, apathetic, and slowed down. They often have a poor appetite, and have lost considerable weight ("apathetic thyrotoxicosis").

Hypothyroidism

Definition

Hypothyroidism is a deficiency of circulating thyroid hormone and resultant slowing of the metabolic activity of most tissues in the body. A variety of conditions can produce this disorder such as previous thyroid ablation with either surgery or radioactive iodine during the treatment of hyperthyroidism. Additional causes are Hashimoto's disease (an autoimmune disorder which can result in a chronic inflammation of the thyroid), iodine deficiency, and less commonly, genetically linked deficiencies in thyroid hormone output.

Prevalence

Approximately 1–5% of the general population and 10–15% of the elderly demonstrate either clinical and/or biochemical evidence of hypothyroidism. Most of these individuals are women.

Clinical Features

The clinical features of hypothyroidism include cold intolerance; modest weight gain; brittle, dry hair; thickened cool skin; loss of the lateral third of the eyebrows; puffiness in the hands, face, and legs (myxedema); hoarseness; delayed relaxation phase of deep tendon reflexes; constipation; bradycardia; and excessive menstrual bleeding.

Laboratory Tests

The most important laboratory test to identify primary hypothyroidism is the serum TSH. Most patients have a decrease in the serum thyroid hormone levels (T4 and T3) and an increased serum TSH level. Subclinical hypothyroidism is characterized by normal serum thyroid hormone levels but slight elevation in the TSH level.

Treatment

The treatment of hypothyroidism is the administration of levothyroxine, a synthetic thyroid hormone preparation taken once daily.

Psychological Symptoms

The symptoms of hypothyroidism closely mimic those of depression. Patients may report sad mood and suicidal ideation, as well as apathy, fatigue, psychomotor retardation, and decreased libido. Cognitive functioning may be slowed with decreased concentration and deficits in short-term memory. In approximately 10% of patients, there may be paranoid delusions (Ferrier, 1987). A delirious state may occur ("myxedema madness") characterized by vivid visual hallucinations (Leigh & Kramer, 1984).

DISORDERS OF THE PARATHYROID GLANDS

The parathyroid glands are located on the posterior surface of the thyroid gland and secrete parathyroid hormone (PTH), which is essential in the regulation of calcium levels in the blood. PTH, in combination with vitamin D and calcitonin, maintains normal blood calcium levels by increasing gastrointestinal absorption of dietary calcium and stimulates bone resorption. Because calcium is important to the functioning of neuronal cell membranes, alterations in the serum level of this mineral can result in problems across a multitude of neurological and psychiatric systems.

Hyperparathyroidism

Definition

Primary hyperparathyroidism is characterized by excess levels of circulating PTH, low serum phosphate levels, and constant or intermittent hypercalcemia and hypercalciuria. It can occur as a result of excessive parathyroid production because of an adenoma or hyperplasia or, in rare cases, parathyroid carcinoma.

Prevalence

Primary hyperparathyroidism is present in about 1 out of every 1,000 individuals (0.1%). It is more commonly found in women over 40 years of age (Bauer, Droba, & Whybrow, 1987).

Clinical Features

Most patients with primary hyperparathyroidism are asymptomatic or may have an array of nonspecific neuropsychiatric symptoms (described below).

Since the introduction of the multichannel analyzer in the 1970s, hypercalcemia is now detected much earlier than in previous years when the diagnosis of primary hyperparathyroidism was made quite late in the course of the disorder. Previously, patients presented with kidney stones, bone pain, and/or peptic ulcer disease. However, now only 20% of patients with primary hyperparathyroidism give a history of kidney stones, and few have features of symptomatic bone disease. On the other hand, the patients may have vague neuropsychiatric symptoms such as lassitude, memory impairment, or a change in personality. Because these are quite nonspecific, it is important for a serum calcium level to be drawn in such patients to exclude hyperparathyroidism.

Laboratory Tests

The diagnosis of primary hyperparathyroidism is made by demonstrating an elevated serum calcium and elevated serum PTH level. It is important to note whether the patient is currently on a thiazide diuretic or lithium, either of which can increase the serum calcium level.

Treatment

The treatment of primary hyperparathyroidism is the surgical removal of the parathyroid adenoma, which is the cause in more than 80% of the cases. However, in a very elderly individual, who may have other serious underlying coexistent diseases, surgery may be too risky. Also, these patients may have few clinical manifestations of hyperparathyroidism.

Psychological Symptoms

Hyperparathyroid patients complain of sadness, anxiety, lassitude, lethargy, change in sleeping patterns, decreased concentration, and decreased memory for recent events. If hypomagnesemia is present, there may be auditory or visual hallucinations.

A number of reports, albeit each with a small number of patients, discuss the incidence of neuropsychiatric symptoms before and following surgery for primary hyperparathyroidism. Most of these studies have short follow-up periods (4 to 6 months) and describe little change in symptoms following surgery. A few reports indicate a striking improvement in neuropsychiatric symptoms in those who underwent successful removal of the parathyroid adenoma. Thus, the evidence is inconclusive that the neuropsychiatric manifestations of primary hyperparathyroidism clearly improve following surgery. This issue is discussed in detail by Kleerekoper (1994).

Hypoparathyroidism

Definition

Hypoparathyroidism is characterized by insufficient levels of circulating PTH. The most common cause of this condition is the inadvertent removal of the parathyroid glands during thyroid surgery for Graves' disease or following head and neck cancer surgery. Hypomagnesemia may cause reversible hypoparathyroidism due to impairment of the parathyroid gland function, a complication of alcoholism.

Clinical Features

Patients with hypoparathyroidism report symptoms such as tingling of the lips, fingers, and toes (which are manifestations of neuromuscular irritability); muscle cramps; hyperventilation; seizures; and extrapyramidal symptoms.

Laboratory Tests

The diagnosis of hypoparathyroidism is made by demonstrating a low serum calcium, an elevated serum phosphorous, and a low serum PTH level in a patient with normal renal function. One needs to exclude secondary causes of hypoparathyroidism such as hypomagnesemia.

Treatment

The treatment of primary hypoparathyroidism is calcium and vitamin D. These patients are controlled with 0.25–1.0 microgram of 1.25 (OH)$_2$ vitamin D daily. In addition, these patients are given an additional 1–2 grams of elemental calcium to supplement their diet. Patients are monitored initially with frequently performed serum and urinary calcium levels. Once serum calcium is normalized, serum calcium monitoring need only be done at 4- to 6-month intervals.

Psychological Symptoms

Patients with hypoparathyroidism may present with an array of nonspecific neuropsychiatric manifestations, such as irritability, fatigue, decreased concentration, confusion, and, rarely, psychotic symptoms.

DISORDERS OF THE ADRENAL GLANDS

The interrelationship between hormonal and neurotransmitter systems is seen most clearly during times of stress, when the adrenocortical system is activated to facilitate a "fight or flight" response. Activation of this system is characterized by production of corticotropin releasing factor (CRF) by the hypothalamus, which then stimulates the pituitary to release adrenocorticotropic hormone (ACTH) which stimulates the adrenal glands to secrete cortisol. This optimizes the physical state of the body for quick action. However, stimulation of the hypothalamus and production of CRF may also feed back on other systems, such as those that govern release of catecholamines (e.g., dopamine, epinephrine, and norepinephrine). Increased output of these neurotransmitters may then result in signs or symptoms such as an anxious mood, heightened arousal, hypervigilance to threatening stimuli, increased motor activity, decreased sleep, and, occasionally, hallucinations or delusional beliefs.

Hypercortisolism

Definition

Hypercortisolism refers to conditions characterized by elevated levels of circulating cortisol. The most common cause is the use of steroids (glucocorticoids) to treat certain autoimmune disorders. The second most common cause is Cushing's disease, or hypercortisolism associated with increased pituitary output of ACTH secondary to a pituitary tumor. Hypercortisolism may also be the result of adrenal tumors producing excess amounts of cortisol or ectopic tumors that secrete ACTH.

Prevalence

Of the hypercortisol conditions not associated with exogenous administration of steroids, about two-thirds are associated with pituitary tumors and increased secretion of ACTH. An additional 15% are associated with adrenal adenomas and, rarely, adrenal carcinoma (Morley & Krahn, 1987).

Clinical Features

The typical features of Cushing's disease include centripetal obesity, purple stretch marks on the abdomen, acne, rounded face, and muscle wasting. In women, hirsutism and amenorrhea are common. It is important to note that fewer than half of the cases of Cushing's syndrome present with these classical features, and these same features may be seen in the general population in the absence of disease (Reus, 1987; Reus & Berlant, 1986).

Laboratory Tests

The laboratory abnormalities include an elevated blood sugar, hypokalemia, and elevation of the 24-hour urinary-free cortisol. The dexamethasone suppression test (DST) is used to measure the capacity of feedback mechanisms involving the pituitary to regulate ACTH control of cortisol output. For the DST, the patient is asked to ingest a small amount (one milligram) of a synthetic steroid (dexamethasone), and a serum cortisol is obtained the following morning. In a normally functioning system, the morning serum cortisol level is very low or suppressed. In Cushing's disease, the serum cortisol will be normal or high after dexamethasone ingestion (called dexamethasone nonsuppression). Hyperglycemia and hypokalemia may also be seen.

Treatment

Treatment of hypercortisolism depends on its etiology. Tumors, benign or malignant, are treated by surgical removal. Exogenous administration of steroids should be reduced if possible.

Psychological Symptoms

Symptoms of hypercortisolism may resemble depression if the source of excess cortisol is endogenous (Cushing's syndrome with hypersecretion of ACTH or CRF. Depressive symptoms include a sad or anxious mood with suicidal ideation, decreased sleep, and memory deficits (see Dubrovsky, 1993). In 5% to 20% of patients there may be schizophreniform psychosis (Leigh & Kramer, 1984) and paranoid delusions. If the source of hypercortisolism is exogenous (e.g., following ingestion of large quantities of steroids), mood may be euphoric or irritable with pressured speech, hyperactivity, decreased sleep, intrusive thoughts, and decreased short-term memory. Psychotic episodes are seen in 5–15% of these patients, but schizophreniform presentations are uncommon.

Hypocortisolism

Definition

The underproduction of cortisol may result from damage to the adrenal cortex as a result of an autoimmune disorder (the most common is Addison's disease), infection (tuberculosis or sarcoidosis), or, less commonly, amyloidosis, hemochromatosis, or neoplastic infiltration. Alternatively, low levels of circulating cortisol (secondary adrenocortical insufficiency) may result from hypopituitarism. Low levels of cortisol may also result from the sudden withdrawal of glucocorticoids, which have been used to treat a chronic autoimmune disorder.

Clinical Features

The primary symptoms of Addison's disease include weight loss, weakness, fatigue, unexplained abdominal pain, and postural lightheadedness. Increases in ACTH may lead to darkening of the skin, especially around the knee, knuckles, and lips or in recent scars.

Laboratory Tests

Laboratory tests for assessment of cortisol output include 24-hour urinary-free cortisol levels and a cortrosyn stimulation test. Addison's patients may also show low blood sugar levels and decreased levels of mineralocorticoids, such as aldosterone. Decreased aldosterone is associated with low levels of sodium, a craving for salt, hypotensive hyperkalemia, and hyponatremia.

Treatment

Patients with adrenal insufficiency need to be replaced with a glucocorticoid preparation and, often, a mineralocorticoid. For example, most patients can be managed by taking 15–20 milligrams of hydrocortisone in the morning and 5–10 milligrams each afternoon. Occasionally, patients need an additional 0.5–1.0 milligrams of fluorocortisone acetate once daily.

Psychological Symptoms

Neuropsychiatric manifestations of adrenocortical deficiency include sad mood, apathy, anhedonia, and fatigue. There may be global impairments in cognitive functioning, including decreased concentration and poverty of thought. Psychotic symptoms are rare.

DIABETES MELLITUS

Maintenance of an adequate supply of glucose in the blood is essential for the proper functioning of neuronal cells. This task is accomplished by two hormones produced by the pancreas: insulin and glucagon. Insulin reduces blood glucose and fatty acids by facilitating entry of glucose into the cells of target tissues and helping to convert these substances for storage as glycogen, triglycerides, and protein. Glucagon works to preserve glucose and fatty acids from conversion and to increase glucose output by the liver. Insulin and glucagon (along with other hormones) balance the overall levels of glucose and fatty acids in the blood to maintain a steady state.

Dysfunction in glucose metabolism is generally the result of either deficiencies or excess in these hormones, as well as resistance to hormone action by target tissues. The inability to secrete adequate amounts of insulin is known as type I diabetes mellitus. This disorder is typically identified early in life and generally requires multiple daily injections of insulin to maintain blood glucose levels. Hence, type I diabetes is also known as insulin-dependent diabetes. Its etiology appears to involve a combination of genetic and autoimmune factors, resulting in destruction of the cells in the Islets of Langerhans in the pancreas that normally produce and secrete insulin. A second, more common form of diabetes shows onset later in life (typically over the age of 40) and is found in genetically vulnerable individuals. In these individuals, chronically high levels of blood glucose lead to increased insulin production and to the eventual desensitization of insulin receptors. This disorder is called type II diabetes or non-insulin-dependent diabetes. Type II diabetes is also associated with a defect in insulin secretion. Although the majority of patients with type II diabetes can be treated with diet and/or oral hypoglycemic agents, many patients require insulin injections.

For both types of diabetes, maintenance of a steady state of blood glucose is critical. Because regulation is not automatic, patients with diabetes must frequently monitor blood glucose levels and plan diet and exercise carefully. Foods and beverages high in sugar and fat should be avoided. Alcohol in large quantities can be associated with hypoglycemia. Proper control of blood glucose can slow the trajectory of the illness and delay the onset of the irreversible cardiovascular, renal, neural, and retinal complications associated with the disorder. These restrictions and the possibility of developing the severe complications are often demoralizing and frightening for the patient and may lead the patient to deny the illness or give up trying to maintain self-care regimens. Even when maintaining self-care regimens, blood glucose levels may fluctuate and precipitate medical crises in the form of hyperglycemic or hypoglycemic episodes.

Hyperglycemia

Definition

Hyperglycemia is the state of elevated levels of blood sugars that results from a deficiency in circulating levels of insulin.

Prevalence

According to estimates, diabetes mellitus affects 5% of the population in the United States, and an additional 5% have unrecognized diabetes. In a large community study, 15.6% of subjects with insulin-dependent diabetes and 22.1% with non-insulin-dependent diabetes reported having high urine or blood glucose levels always or most of the time (Cowie & Harris, 1995).

Clinical Features

Symptoms and signs include frequent urination, excessive thirst and increased fluid intake, increased food intake, nausea and vomiting, rapid weight loss, dry mouth, and dehydration. The patient may complain of blurred vision and fatigue. Severe hyperglycemia can lead to coma and can be associated with acidosis.

Laboratory Tests

Typical tests for hyperglycemia include blood glucose, serum electrolytes and urinary ketones.

Treatment

Hyperglycemic patients are treated with insulin, fluids (intravenous treatments in the case of severe hyperglycemia), and oral hyperglycemic agents such as sulfonylureas, metformin, and acarbose.

Psychological Symptoms

Symptoms of hyperglycemia can include sad mood, lethargy and fatigue, psychic retardation, and decreased concentration.

Hypoglycemia

Definition

Hypoglycemia is the state of low blood sugar that results from insufficient food intake, increased exercise, or an excessive concentration of insulin. This can be caused by injecting too much insulin or taking an excessive amount of certain oral hypoglycemic agents. Hypoglycemia can also be caused by ingestion of a large quantity of alcohol in insulin-dependent diabetes. Hypoglycemic states trigger the release of cortisol and epinephrine and stimulate the sympathetic nervous system, similar to the typical fight-or-flight reaction seen in response to psychosocial stressors.

Prevalence

Hypoglycemia accounts for approximately 0.45% of hospitalizations and 1.6% of all diabetic hospitalizations (Fishbein & Palumbo, 1995)

Clinical Features

Symptoms and signs are divided into two categories. Adrenergic symptoms occur early and include heart palpitations, sweating, tremulousness, and hunger. Neuroglycopenic symptoms occur later and include headache, confusion, and mental state changes. Patients with long-standing diabetes or tightly controlled diabetes may lose their adrenergic symptoms and have only neuroglycopenic symptoms over time.

Laboratory Tests

Blood glucose and urinary ketone levels are used to monitor the patient's course.

Treatment

Patients should learn to monitor the early warning signs of hypoglycemia and ingest foods high in simple sugar or carbohydrate content. Glucagon injection or intravenous glucose are indicated in more serious situations involving loss of consciousness.

Psychological Symptoms

Acute symptoms of hypoglycemia most closely resemble an anxiety reaction. They include anxious mood and physical signs such as sweating, palpitations, and dizziness. There may be an increase in specific fears and worries as well as feelings of depersonalization or unreality and perceptual disturbances such as blurred vision and tingling in the extremities. Concentration is impaired with signs of perseveration. Hypoglycemia can also mimic the focal neurological features of a stroke or a seizure.

Patients with chronic hypoglycemia may present with mild to moderate symptoms of depression including a sad mood, lethargy, and fatigue. Chronic hypoglycemia may also produce schizophreniform-like symptoms (Ettiggi & Brown, 1978).

PSYCHOLOGICAL SYMPTOMS
AND THE GONADAL STEROIDS

By and large, the effects of gonadal steroids on mental state are inferred from observations of patients with genetically based abnormalities (such as Kleinfelter's syndrome or Turner's syndrome), or from observations of changes in mood that occur throughout the menstrual cycle. Although there are no consistent data to show a direct causal relationship between imbalances in gonadal steroids and the emergence of a particular mental state, data from epidemiological studies of mental disorders suggest important links.

Community studies of lifetime prevalences of mental disorders consistently reveal that rates of depression and anxiety are twice as high in women as in men (see Kessler et al., 1994). These data lead to the speculation that imbalances in estrogen–progesterone cycling may be related to the appearance of certain affective disorders. It is common for depressive episodes in women to appear during times of major change in hormonal cycles such as the onset of puberty, after the birth of a child, and around the menopause (see Endicott, 1994; Robinson & Stewart, 1993; Sherwin, 1993). Moreover, many women report an increase in emotional lability and symptoms of irritability, sadness, decreased energy, and increased appetite during the late luteal phase of the menstrual cycle, when estrogen levels are low. Similar symptoms have also been reported by women during oral contraceptive use. At present, the literature does not support a connection between any specific imbalance and the appearance of depressive symptoms, or between any one type of hormone replacement therapy and alleviation of depressive symptoms. However, although not distinguishing depressed patients from nondepressed controls, lower serum estradiol levels are associated with greater severity of symptoms among depressed women (Baischer, Koinig, Hartman, Huber, & Langer, 1995). Recent studies suggest that estrogen inhibits dopamine receptors in the brain and, as such, acts similarly to neuroleptic medications. Indeed, patients with active symptoms of schizophrenia have been found to have decreased estrogen levels (Riecher-Rossler & Hafner, 1993). As estrogens may feed back on hypothalamic centers associated with regulating the output of catecholamines, it is clear that the links between psychiatric symptoms and gonadal hormonal abnormalities are complex.

Testosterone Levels
and Aggressive/Antisocial Behavior

It has long been recognized that aggressive behavior is reduced in male animals following removal of the testes, and that aggression is restored in castrated animals if testosterone is implanted in the hypothalamus (Donovan, 1988). However, in humans, the effects of castration on aggression seem to be limited to acts of sexual aggression, and hormone depletion studies require significant decreases (20–50%) in testosterone before behavioral changes are observed.

DIFFERENTIAL DIAGNOSIS

Depression

Endocrine disorders to consider during the evaluation of a patient with symptoms of depression include the following:

- Diabetes mellitus (hyperglycemia)
- Cushing's syndrome (endogenous hypercortisolism)
- Addison's disease (hypocortisolism)
- Hyperparathyroidism
- Hypothyroidism
- Hyperthyroidism in the elderly
- High progesterone–estrogen ratio contraceptives
- Late luteal phase low estrogen, low progesterone
- Menopause

Table 15.1 lists the symptoms used to diagnose a major depressive disorder in the DSM-IV and indicates which of the symptoms are reported to occur in the various endocrine disorders reviewed. The DSM criteria specify that the patient must show at least five of the symptom criteria (including the core symp-

TABLE 15.1. Symptoms of Major Depression Found in Endocrine Disorders

Symptom	Hyper-glycemia	Hyper-cortisolism	Hypo-cortisolism	Hyerpara-thyroidism	Hypo-thyroidism	Hyper-thyroidism—elderly
Core mood						
Sad mood	×	×	×	×	×	×
Anhedonia				×	×	
Associated						
symptoms						
Weight/ appetite change	×	×	×	×	×	×
Insomnia/ hypersomnia					×	
Psychomotor retardation				×	×	×
Fatigue/lost energy	×		×	×	×	
Guilt/ worthlessness						
Decreased concentration	×	×	×	×	×	
Suicidal thoughts		×		×		
DSM criteria met?	No	No	No	Yes	Yes	No

Note. Criteria specify that there must be five or more symptoms present during the same 2-week period with at least one of the symptoms being sad mood (six symptoms if mood is anhedonic).

tom of mood) and that the symptoms must be present most of the day, nearly every day for a period of at least 2 weeks. As is shown in Table 15.1, many of the symptoms of depression are shared by endocrine disturbances. However, only two disorders present with five or more of the DSM symptom criteria: hyperparathyroidism and hypothyroidism. Inspection of the items listed in Table 15.1 suggests the possibility that the depressive disorders may be distinguished from their endocrine mimics by the presence of negative thoughts such as guilt and worthlessness and the absence of humor. Thus, it is worth asking about these symptoms in detail when considering the diagnosis. If lowered self-esteem is present, it is important to determine whether it is primary to the depression or secondary to long periods of inactivity associated with chronic medical illness and inactivity (Tallis, 1993).

Reports suggest that subclinical hypothyroidism is present in 8–17% of depressed patients (Howland, 1993). The high prevalence of thyroid abnormalities in depressed patients suggests a special link between these two systems. Of particular importance to the mental health professional is the observation that antidepressant medications may be ineffective in patients with depression who are also hypothyroid. Such patients' depression may respond once thyroid therapy is begun. In patients on lithium carbonate, thyroid hormone levels may decline, and the patient's thyroid hormone replacement dose may have to be increased. There is no need to discontinue lithium under such circumstances.

Anxiety

Endocrine disorders to consider during the evaluation of a patient with symptoms of anxiety include the following:

- Diabetes mellitus (hypoglycemia)
- Hyperparathyroidism
- Hyperthyroidism
- Atypical hypothyroidism

In Table 15.2, the symptoms of these endocrine disorders are compared to the DSM-IV symptoms of a generalized anxiety disorder. The DSM criteria require that three or more of the six symptoms be present for the most recent 6-month period. Both hypoglycemia and hyperthyroid disorder may present with three or more of the listed symptoms. It would be uncommon for severe hypoglycemia to be present persistently over a 6-month period (the patient would more probably show a rapid decline and become comatose). However, persistent symptoms may be seen in hyperthyroidism or hypothyroidism in an elderly patient. What distinguishes disorders that are primarily psychological may be that anxiety symptoms remit in the presence of supportive others or with self-soothing activities. However, because somatic disorders may bring on secondary symptoms of anxiety, and anxiety may exacerbate the intensity of somatic

TABLE 15.2. Symptoms of Generalized Anxiety Found in Endocrine Disorders

Symptom	Hypoglycemia	Hyperparathyroidism	Hyperthyroidism
Restlessness; keyed up; on edge			×
Easily fatigued	×	×	×
Concentration problems; mind goes blank	×	×	×
Irritability	×	×	×
Increased muscle tension			
Sleep disturbances			×
	Yes	Yes	Yes

Note. Criteria specify that there must be three or more of the six symptom areas present more days than not for the past 6 months.

symptoms, some symptom remission may also be seen in primary endocrine disorders with social support.

Mania

Endocrine disorders to consider during evaluation of a patient with symptoms of mania include the following:

- Excessive testosterone
- Exogenous hypercortisolism
- Hyperthyroidism

As is shown in Table 15.3, both exogenous hypercortisolism (caused by steroid use) and hyperthyroidism can produce the core mood disturbance and three or more associated features that mimic manic states. It is unlikely, though, that these disturbances would result in the full-blown presentation of mania, and they are more likely to present with the less severe hypomanic presentation.

Psychosis

Endocrine disorders to consider during the evaluation of a patients with symptoms of psychosis include the following:

- Diabetes mellitus (hypoglycemia)
- Exogenous hypercortisolism
- Addison's disease (hypocortisolism)
- Hyperparathyroidism
- Hypoparathyroidism
- Hypothroidism

TABLE 15.3. Symptoms of Mania Found in Endocrine Disorders

Symptom	High testosterone	Exogenous hypercortisolism	Hyperthyroidism
Core mood	×	×	×
Elevated or expansive Irritable	×	×	×
Associated symptoms		×	
Inflated self-esteem			
Decreased need for sleep		×	
Pressured speech		×	×
Racing thoughts		×	×
Distractibility			×
Increased goal-directed activity/agitation		×	×
Poor judgment	×		
DSM criteria met?	No	Yes	Yes

Note. For mania, criteria specify that there must be a core mood distrubance plus three to four associated features with duration of at least 1 week. For hypomania, criteria specify that there must be a core mood disturbance plus three associated features for at least 4 days.

Throughout the endocrine literature, there are indications that psychotic-like symptoms can occur in most of the endocrine disorders. However, the frequency of occurrence is low. It appears that psychotic features tend to manifest as a function of the severity of the endocrine disorder, with less severe endocrinopathies manifesting with mood disturbance and vegetative signs. As the disorder becomes more severe, symptoms of cognitive clouding are common, then psychotic symptoms in the form of hallucinations, delusions, and delirium occur. Eventually, if untreated, coma and death ensue (see Brambilla, 1992). In reviewing this literature, it is difficult to determine whether the psychotic symptoms described are more typical of delirium or of a schizophrenia-like presentation. Table 15.4 presents the DSM-IV symptom criteria for schizophrenia. The criteria specify that the patient must show two or more of the above symptoms (or one if the symptom consists of bizarre delusions) for a significant portion of the day, and that signs of the illness must be present for a period of 6 months or more. The endocrine literature indicates that delusions may be present in at least three of the endocrine disorders: chronic hyperglycemia, hyperparathyroidism, and hypothyroidism. In cases in which the medical reports indicate "schizophrenia-like symptoms," it is not clear which symptoms are seen and whether the symptoms represent psychotic features or delirium.

According to DSM-IV, delirium is organic in origin and characterized by psychotic symptoms such as vivid hallucinations that are usually visual, delusions, changes in cognition such as memory deficits, disorientation or language disturbance, and agitation. The psychotic symptoms fluctuate, are fragmented and unsystematized, occur in the context of a reduced ability to shift and ap-

TABLE 15.4. Symptoms of Psychosis Found in Endocrine Disorders

Symptom	Hypo-glycemia	Chronic hyper-glycemia	Hypo-cortisolism	Exogenous hyper-cortisolism	Hyper-para-thyroidism	Hypo-thyroidism
Delusions		×			×	×
Hallucinations				×		
Disorganized speech						
Disorganized or catatonic behavior	×					
Negative symptoms (alogia, avolition, flat affect)						
DSM criteria met?	Possibly	Possibly	No	Possibly	Possibly	Possibly

Note. For schizophrenia, criteria specify that two or more of the above symptoms are present for a significant portion of time over a period of at least 6 months. For schizophreniform disorder, criteria specify that two or more of the above symptoms are clearly present for 1 to 6 months. For brief psychotic disorder, criteria specify that one or more symptoms are clearly present for 1 month or less. For delusional disorder, criteria specify persistent nonbizarre delusions for at least 1 month and no other of above symptoms. For delirium, criteria specify that the psychotic symptoms fluctuate, are fragmented and unsystematized, occur in the context of reduced ability to maintain and shift attention, and are usually accompanied by electroencephalogram impairment.

propriately maintain attention, and are usually accompanied by an abnormal electroencephalogram. There is a rapid onset of symptoms and symptoms show a fluctuating course during the day, often becoming worse in the evening (sometimes referred to as "sundowning").

What distinguishes the psychological disorders from the endocrine may be more difficult in the case of psychotic symptoms. Paranoid delusions appear to be the most common presentation reported in the endocrine literature, but this may be an artifact of what is noticed by the health care professionals in standard interactions with these patients. It would appear that the most useful material for a differential diagnosis would be careful attention to the onset, type, and course of symptoms. Presentations that are principally psychological are more likely to show a gradual onset (with the exception of a brief reactive psychosis which is an acute psychological response to an environmental stressor) and a more stable presentation. Delusions that are prominent and persistent and present with fixed themes are not likely to be the result of an organic delirium state. However, delusions of this type may be characteristic of thyroid or parathyroid disorder. If a patient presents with multiple delusions or the combination of a fixed delusion and persistent auditory hallucinations, it is likely that the disorder is in the schizophrenia family.

SUMMARY

Because of the important role that endocrine glands play in the modulation of CNS activity, clinicians need to be alert to the possibility of primary endocrine disorder whenever psychiatric symptoms occur. Screening should always include questions about recent medication use or comorbid medical conditions. If comorbid medical conditions exist, patients should also be questioned about their self-care practices and whether or not they are taking prescribed medications as indicated. If patients present with any of the clinical features characteristic of an endocrine disorder, they should be referred for endocrine evaluation. In patients with no identified comorbid medical condition but who show persistent symptoms that are resistant to the standard psychopharmacological and therapy interventions, a thorough work-up should be performed to rule out undiagnosed endocrine disturbance.

In the preceding pages, we outlined the areas of symptom overlap described in the literatures on endocrinology and psychiatric illness. It is important to note that the language used to describe symptoms is quite different across the endocrine and psychiatric literatures, so it can be difficult to ascertain whether the symptoms described truly represent the same or different phenomena. Moreover, the kinds of symptoms that are likely to be noticed by practitioners in each of the two disciplines differ as a function of the professional lens through which each has been trained to view his or her patients.

Despite these limitations, a number of interesting parallels emerge when reading across the endocrine and psychiatric literatures. First, the progression of symptoms from altered mood and lethargy to clouding of consciousness and final delirium described by Brambilla (1992) as characteristic of the progression of endocrine disorder is also characteristic of many forms of psychiatric illness (e.g., minor depression to major depression to depression with psychotic features). This raises the possibility that severe dysfunction that begins in any of these interrelated systems can lead to a more generalized impairment across multiple endocrine and neurotransmitter systems. Second, the observation that psychotic features triggered by endocrine abnormalities may not remit even after the endocrine abnormalities are corrected suggests that individuals may carry predispositions that determine the type and extent of psychiatric symptom development once an endocrine disorder occurs. More research that examines both endocrine and psychiatric processes is needed to address these possibilities.

ACKNOWLEDGMENTS

Preparation of this chapter was funded in part by grants from the Karen Tucker Fund and the Boston Mental Health Foundation.

We thank James Rosenzweig, MD, assistant professor of medicine at the Harvard Medical School and senior physician at the Joslin Diabetes Center, for assistance with material concerning clinical presentation of diabetes mellitus.

REFERENCES

American Psychiatric Association. (1994). *Diagnostic and statistical manual of mental disorders* (4th ed.). Washington, DC: Author.

Baischer, W., Koinig, G., Hartman, B., Huber, J., & Langer, G. (1995). Hypothalamic–pituitary–gonadal axis in depressed premenopausal women: Elevated blood testosterone concentrations compared to normal controls. *Psychoneuroendocrinology, 20*(5), 553–559.

Bauer, M. S., Droba, M., & Whybrow, P. C. (1987). Disorders of the thyroid and parathyroid. In C. B. Nemeroff & P. T. Loosen (Eds.), *Handbook of clinical psychoneuroendocrinology* (pp. 41–70). New York: Guilford Press.

Brambilla, F. (1992). Psychopathological aspects of neuroendocrine diseases: possible parallels with the psychoendocrine aspects of normal aging. *Psychoneuroendocrinology, 17*(4), 283–291.

Cowie, C. C., & Harris, M. I. (1995). Physical and metabolic characteristics of persons with diabetes. In *Diabetes in America* (2nd ed., NIH Publication No. 95-1468, pp. 117–133). Bethesda, MD: National Institute for Diabetes and Digestive and Kidney Diseases.

Donovan, B. T. (1988). *Humors, hormones and the mind, an approach to the understanding of behavior.* London: Macmillan Press.

Dubrovsky, B. (1993). Effects of adrenal cortex hormones on limbic structures: some experimental and clinical correlations related to depression. *Journal of Psychiatry and Neuroscience, 18*(1), 4–16.

Endicott, J. (1994). Differential diagnoses and comorbidity. In J. H. Gold & S. K. Severino (Eds.), *Premenstrual dysphorias, myths and realities* (pp. 3–17). Washington, DC: American Psychiatric Press.

Ettigi, P., & Brown, G. (1978). Brain disorders associated with endocrine dysfunction. *Psychiatric Clinics of North America, 1,* 117–136.

Fava, G. A., Sonino, N., & Morphy, M. A. (1993). Psychosomatic view of endocrine disorders. *Psychotherapy and Psychosomatics, 59,* 20–33.

Ferrier, I. N. (1987). Endocrinology and psychosis. *British Medical Bulletin, 43*(3), 672–678.

Fishbein, H., & Palumbo, P. J. (1995). Acute metabolic complications in diabetes. In *Diabetes in America* (2nd ed., NIH Publication No. 95-1468, pp. 283–291). Bethesda, MD: National Institute for Diabetes and Digestive and Kidney Diseases.

Goggins, F. C., Allen. R. M., & Gold, M. S. (1986). Primary hypothyroidism and its relationship to affective disorders. In I. Extein & M. Gold (Eds.), *Medical mimics of psychiatric disorders* (pp. 95–109). Washington, DC: American Psychiatric Press.

Howland, R. H. (1993). Thyroid dysfunction in refractory depression: Implications for pathophysiology and treatment. *Journal of Clinical Psychiatry, 54*(2), 47–54.

Kessler, R. C., McGonagle, K. A., Zhao, S., Nelson, C. B., Hughes, M., Eschleman, S., & Wittchen, H-U. (1994). Lifetime and 12-month prevalence of DSM-III-R psychiatric disorders in the United States. *Archives of General Psychiatry, 51,* 8–19.

Kleerekoper, M. (1994). Clinical course of primary hyperparathyroidism. In J. P. Belizikian (Ed.), *The parathyroids: Basic and clinical concepts* (pp. 471–483). New York: Raven Press.

Leigh, H., & Kramer, S. I. (1984). The psychiatric manifestations of endocrine diseases. In *Advances in internal medicine* (pp. 413–445). St. Louis, MO: Year Book Medical Publishers.

Morley, J. E., & Krahn, D. D. (1987). Endocrinology for the psychiatrist. In C. B. Nemeroff & P. T. Loosen (Eds.), *Handbook of clinical psychoneuro-endocrinology* (pp. 3–37). New York: Guilford Press.

Oakley, H. F. (1980). Psychiatric emergencies in endocrine and metabolic disease. *Clinics in Endocrinology and Metabolism, 9,* 615–624.

Reus, V. I. (1987). Disorders of the adrenal cortex and gonads. In C. B. Nemeroff & P. T. Loosen (Eds.), *Handbook of clinical psychoneuroendocrinology* (pp. 71–84). New York: Guilford Press.

Reus, V., & Berlant, J. R. (1986). Behavioral disturbances associated with disorders of the hypothalamic-pituitary-adrenal system. In I. Extein & M. Gold (Eds.), *Medical mimics of psychiatric disorders* (pp. 113–130). Washington, DC: American Psychiatric Press.

Riecher-Rossler, A., & Hafner, H. (1993). Schizophrenia and oestrogens: Is there an association? *European Archives of Psychiatry and Clinical Neuroscience, 242,* 323–328.

Robinson, G. E., & Stewart, D. E. (1993). Post-partum disorders. In D. E. Stewart & N. L. Stotland (Eds.), *Psychological aspects of women's health care, the interface between psychiatry and obstetrics and gynecology* (pp. 115–138). Washington, DC: American Psychiatric Press.

Rubinow, D. R., & Schmidt, P. J. (1995). Psychoneuroendocrinology. In H. I. Kaplan & B. J. Sadock (Eds.), *Comprehensive textbook of psychiatry* (Vol. 1, 6th ed., pp. 104–112). Baltimore: Williams & Wilkins.

Sherwin, B. B. (1993). Menopause, myths and realities. In D. E. Stewart & N. L. Stotland (Eds.), *Psychological aspects of women's health care, the interface between psychiatry and obstetrics and gynecology* (pp. 227–248). Washington, DC: American Psychiatric Press.

Stern, R., & Prange, A. J. (1995). Neuropsychiatric aspects of endocrine disorders. In H. I. Kaplan & B. J. Sadock (Eds.), (Vol. 1, 6th ed., pp. 241–251). Baltimore: Williams & Wilkins.

Tallis, F. (1993). Primary hypothyroidism: A case for vigilance in the psychological treatment of depression. *British Journal of Clinical Psychology, 32,* 261–270.

CHAPTER 16

PSYCHOLOGICAL FACTORS
IN CARDIAC DISEASE

MATTHEW M. CLARK
JUSTIN M. NASH
RONALD COHEN
CATHERINE CHASE
RAYMOND NIAURA

The goal of this chapter is to review the literature examining the role of psychological factors in cardiac disease and to provide suggestions for the practitioner based on these findings. To accomplish this task, this chapter reviews the biopsychosocial model and then examines the role of stress, anxiety, hostility, dementia, and depression in cardiac disease. Two case examples may help to highlight the complex issues involved in this population.

> Mr. Smith is a 55-year-old business executive who is seeing you for a stress management evaluation. He reports that work is very hectic and he is under a lot of pressure. He reports smoking more, overeating, and consuming three to four alcoholic beverages each night over the past month. He reports not being able to sleep and feeling "discomfort." After inquiry, he states he feels a heaviness in his chest. You inquire about pain and he says he has some but is vague. He states his belief that his symptoms are from being "stressed out." Mr. Smith has not seen a physician in 2 years. You wisely choose to have him call his physician from your office because he is advised to go directly to an emergency room where an electrocardiogram (ECG) reveals that he is having a silent myocardial infarction (MI).

Mr. Jones is a 35-year-old professional who is seeking "relaxation train-ing." Mr. Jones's father died of an MI at age 37. Mr. Jones read about "type A" and is certain he has cardiovascular disease and worries about dying from a heart attack. He experiences intense chest pain: a 12, on a 0 to 10 scale of increasing pain; his heart feels like it is pounding, racing, about to explode; he experiences shortness of breath and lightheadedness. These symptoms come on unexpectedly. Upon contacting his cardiologist, you learn that Mr. Jones has gone to the emergency room on numerous occasions and his ECGs are normal. He had a maximal exercise stress test, which was also normal. Mr. Jones probably is physically healthy but suf-fers from panic attacks.

Similar to these case examples, our clinical experience is that subjective report of symptoms is not always predictive of physiological versus psychologic etiology. Thus, focus on biopsychosocial factors is important in this popula-tion.

BIOPSYCHOSOCIAL MODEL

Biomedical models of illness traditionally assumed a clear delineation between the disorders of the mind and body. Each disease was thought to be caused by a unique pathology which, if identified, would lead to an effective therapy. Ef-forts to identify these specific causative agents led to major advances in medi-cine, as the bacterial, viral, or other factors underlying infection and damage to different tissue and organ systems were discovered. The biomedical model of illness has been the cornerstone of research and clinical efforts to alleviate car-diovascular diseases during most of this century. Yet, growing recognition of the limits of the biomedical model has emerged over the past two decades, particularly with respect to cardiovascular illness. Accordingly, there has been a shift toward a more comprehensive and integrated biopsychosocial approach to the study and treatment of cardiovascular disorders.

Several converging factors contributed to this shift in focus. Perhaps most important is the accumulation of data indicating that cardiovascular disease is not the byproduct of a single causal agent but rather of multiple factors. Dem-onstration of the importance of risk factors in the development of cardiovascu-lar disease is particularly important in this regard. It is now apparent that heart disease results from the interaction of multiple biological, environmental, psy-chological, and behavioral factors. Diet, "stress," smoking, depression, hostil-ity, exercise, activity level, and alcohol abuse are all identified risk factors for cardiovascular disease. Each of these risk factors reflects lifestyle considerations linked with human behavior.

Although the health and life span of Americans improved dramatically during the course of this century, cardiovascular disease continues to be one of the major health problems, particularly as the population ages. It is therefore imperative that practitioners be vigilant not only to the particular risk factors that might contribute to cardiovascular disease but also to the impact of cardiovascular disease on psychological state and the quality of life. It is not enough to keep a patient alive through the maintenance of cardiac function, especially if survival means existing in a state of complete misery, with poor quality of life, and with extreme costs to their loved ones and society. Cardiovascular disease needs to be conceptualized from the perspective of a *biopsychosocial model,* in which psychological, social, and cultural factors are considered in conjunction with biological and medical determinants.

In sum, there is now an abundance of evidence linking human behavior to the development of cardiovascular disease. Accordingly, cardiovascular health depends not only on effective treatments for reducing the symptoms of cardiac disease but also on the development of effective methods of prevention.

Psychobiological Foundations

The heart is both remarkably simple in its functional significance and extremely complex in its operation. Its role as a pump, supplying blood to all areas of the body, is so automatic that we take this function for granted in our daily activities. Yet, when startled, frightened, or angered, we may become acutely aware of changes in heart rate or rhythm. With the development of heart disease, people often become increasingly aware of the limits of their heart's pumping ability, as cardiac symptoms such as fatigue, chest pain, or shortness of breath indicate that the heart is laboring. Although the psychobiological foundations of cardiac function are often hidden under normal conditions, they become evident when humans are exposed to extreme situations.

The central task of the cardiovascular system, maintaining a constant supply of blood to all tissues of the body, depends on four key elements: (1) blood pressure, (2) heart rate, (3) heart rhythm, and (4) peripheral vasomotor responsivity. Under normal conditions, these responses occur within certain known limits, retaining a homeostatic balance. However, in patients with cardiovascular disease, one or more of these responses is altered, which ultimately leads to inefficient pump action and blood supply. Each of these responses is effected by a host of mechanical, biochemical, and physiological factors associated with the functioning of different peripheral organ systems. Furthermore, the central nervous system, including the brain, exerts direct influence on these responses as well (Figure 16.1).

Although it is beyond the scope of this chapter to review each of these responses in detail, it is essential that psychologists and other behavioral scientists be cognizant of the complexity of the interacting systems involved in normal cardiac regulation. We briefly review the major control systems underlying these responses. (For a more comprehensive review, see Braunwald, 1992; Cacioppo & Tassinary, 1990.)

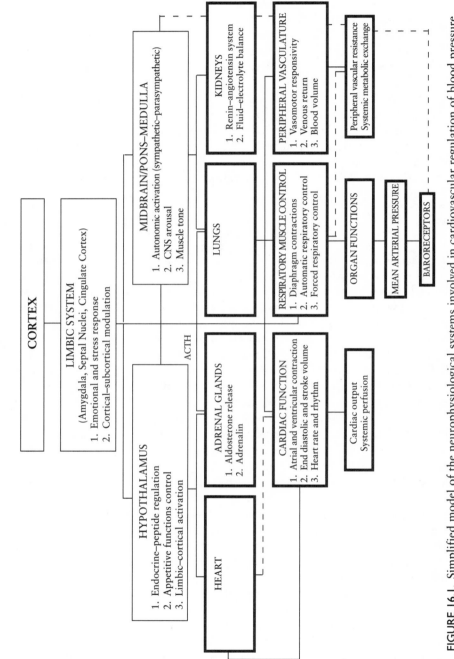

FIGURE 16.1. Simplified model of the neurophysiological systems involved in cardiovascular regulation of blood pressure.

358

Blood Pressure

For blood to reach all the vital organs of the body, a sufficient blood pressure is required. Blood pressure is a function of three mechanical factors: (1) force of the cardiac pump (stroke volume), (2) heart rate, and (3) peripheral resistance imposed by the amount of constriction of peripheral blood vessels. Pump force is a function of the health of the heart muscle. In young healthy people, the heart muscle is usually quite strong and capable of producing considerable force. However, the heart muscle becomes less elastic with age and pumping efficiency eventually declines. Following MI, cardiac aneurysm, and other forms of cardiopathology, the heart muscle becomes damaged, resulting in greatly diminished pumping efficiency.

Chronic high blood pressure leads to mechanical damage to blood vessels in much the same way that excessive water pressure in a hose eventually may cause rupture. Hypertension also may contribute to the development of atherosclerosis and other cardiovascular problems either by mechanical effect or by other physiological mechanisms. Chronic insufficiency of blood pressure leads to hypoperfusion and hypoxia to distal tissues of the body. Therefore, it is important the blood pressure remain relatively stable within a "normal" range.

Heart Rate and Rhythm

Perfusion of blood throughout the body depends not only on sustaining a basal pressure within the vascular system but also on the heart pumping at a rate reasonable enough to enable flow. The heart rate that determines this flow is controlled by pacing cells of the sinoatrial (S-A) node, which fire at a relatively constant rate and trigger muscle fibers of the heart to contract in a rhythmic manner.

Cardiac rhythm occurs as a function of the spread of electrical excitation across the heart muscle. Under normal conditions, coordination of the complex pumping action, involving a series of mechanical stages, is achieved by electrical impulses spreading in a particular sequence. After the S-A node fires, electrical activation in the auricles begins. This event causes contraction of the auricles and the movement of blood to the ventricles. The electrical spread across the auracle and associated contraction is reflected by the P-Q wave of the electrocardiogram (ECG). After crossing the auricles, the impulse activates a second pacemaker, the atrial–ventricular (A-V) node, which triggers a massive electrical polarization (Q-R-S wave), causing the ventricles to contract, pumping blood throughout the body and to the lungs for oxygenation. Subsequently, as blood flows throughout the body, blood pressure reaches its diastolic levels reflecting the peripheral resistance of the vasculature. Following the ventricular contraction, the heart also repolarizes, making itself ready for the next contraction. Heart damage from MI, stretching of the heart muscle, or other causes may produce major change in cardiac rhythm, as blockage of normal spread of electrical activation results in a failure of cardiac timing as well as problems in the force of the heart muscle.

Although cardiac pacemaker cells maintain rhythmicity without any other input, the firing rate and rhythm of the S-A and A-V nodes and electrical reactivity of other cardiac muscle cells are modifiable through autonomic nervous system stimulation. Heart rate is increased by sympathetic excitation and decreased by parasympathetic (vagal) inhibition. Numerous studies demonstrate that cognitive and behavioral factors influence autonomic reactivity. Accordingly, heart rate and rhythm fluctuate as a function of physical as well as cognitive, emotional, and behavioral demands. Conversely, heart arrhythmias may produce the sensation of palpitations, which contribute to anxiety or panic.

Electrolyte (e.g., sodium, potassium, and calcium), endocrine (e.g., thyroxine), and other peptide levels also have a direct influence on heart rate and rhythm. Therefore, it is essential that clinicians considering the possibility of anxiety disorder or panic disorder, based on the patient's report of perceived heart palpitations or tachycardia, first rule out the potential influence of these other biochemical factors.

DISTINGUISHING STRESS AND ANXIETY RESPONSES FROM CARDIOVASCULAR EVENTS

A patient presents with heart palpitations, breathlessness, chest pain, faintness, dizziness, parasthesias, weakness, trembling, shakiness, sweating, flushes, and dry mouth. Is it a stress response, panic attack, or MI? Whenever a patient enters a practitioner's office with these symptoms, questions arise about their psychological or cardiovascular origins. Many symptoms that occur during a stress response or panic attack overlap considerably with symptoms that occur during an MI or other cardiovascular event. This is a difficult differential diagnosis. False positives and false negatives are common. Individuals with cardiac disease may be misdiagnosed as being just "stressed" or "anxious" and individuals who are thought to be having a cardiac event are, in fact, in good health. As many as 30% of patients with chest pain who are referred for arteriography by their physician to determine the amount of arterial blockage are found to have normal coronary arteries (Lantinga et al., 1988). Therefore, being well informed about the overlapping presentation of cardiovascular events and stress and anxiety responses is important to every practitioner. Following is a brief discussion of clinical presentations of stress and anxiety responses.

The Human Stress Response

It was about a century ago when Harvard physiologist Walter B. Cannon first described the *fight-or-flight* response: the body's internal response to a threat to survival. Epinephrine and norepinephrine are released into the bloodstream stimulating sympathetic nervous system activity. This in turn triggers a series of other physiological events that prepare an individual to either run (flight) or fight as if survival is on the line. Foremost of these physiological events are an acceleration in heart rate, an increase in muscle tension, and a quickening in respiration rate. In addition, blood pressure increases as blood is shunted away from the periphery to the larger muscle groups that are required to handle the potential physical demands of an emergency. Organ systems that are not necessary for emergency responding, such as those involved in digestion, slow down.

Given the degree to which the body is mobilized during the fight-or-flight response, the individual's subjective experience can be quite dramatic. The individual often experiences heart racing or palpitations. Breathing becomes rapid and shallow, and even breathlessness can develop. As blood is redirected away from the periphery, coldness, numbness, and tingling can be experienced. With the brain experiencing some reduction in blood flow, dizziness, blurred vision, confusion, and a feeling of unreality can develop. With increased muscle tension, the individual can experience shaking, trembling, or even aches and pains. As the digestive system slows down, stomach heaviness and discomfort develop. When a compensatory cooling response is triggered, perspiration occurs.

The stress response does not have to be so all encompassing. When in less threatening situations or when under some level of enduring tension or stress, the cardiovascular response pattern can be essentially similar but of a lower magnitude. In these situations, only a portion of the physiological responses might be subjectively experienced. For example, an individual may experience recurrent bouts of breathlessness, heart palpitations, or chest pain.

Anxiety Responses

When a panic attack occurs, the symptoms experienced are similar to those observed during the fight-or-flight response. Conceptually, panic attacks can be thought of as a false alarm. Either cued or uncued, the fight-or-flight response is triggered. There is a sudden onset and quick surge that builds to a rapid peak. Palpitations, sweating, trembling, shaking, discomfort, abdominal distress, dizziness, lightheadedness, paresthesias, chills, or hot flashes can occur. In addition, a feeling of derealization or depersonalization, fear of dying, fear of losing control, or fear of having a stroke or heart attack can occur. After one or more attacks, individuals fear another attack and become excessively apprehensive and hypervigilant to somatic cues such as shortness of breath and chest pain, believing that these could be signals for another panic attack. These times of anxious apprehension can be accompanied by limited symptom anxiety attacks when fewer than four panic symptoms are present. In time, a panic disorder could develop, with the essential feature being recurrent, unexpected panic attacks followed by persistent concern about having another attack along with worry about the possible implications or consequences of panic attacks. Individuals can come to anticipate a catastrophic outcome (e.g., MI) from a mild physical symptom (palpitations, shortness of breath, chest discomfort).

PRESENTATIONS OF CARDIAC EVENTS AND STRESS REACTIONS

About 9% of the U.S. population has heart disease (Kannel & Thom, 1990). One out of every 3 men and 1 in 10 women will develop significant cardiovascular disease before age 60 (Gordon & Kannel, 1971). Coronary heart disease affects 6.9 million people with 800,000 new heart attacks and 450,000 recurrences per year (Kannel & Thom, 1990). Psychiatric illness is also a common occurrence. Therefore, by chance alone, the high prevalence of both cardiovascular and psychiatric disorders would produce frequent concurrence. However, psychiatric disorders occur in cardiac patients at a frequency greater than expected by chance association (Levenson, 1993), thus increasing the likelihood that psychiatric patients will also have cardiovascular illness. In addition, the onset of symptomatic cardiac disease is a potent provocation for anxiety and depressive symptoms and patients may present for assistance with management of these affective symptoms.

Classic presentation of angina involves substernal pressure that commonly begins with exertion and is relieved by rest. However, some patients experience angina in the absence of physical exertion or emotional stress, and not all chest pain that begins after exertion is angina (Hutter, 1995). As many as 30% of patients with chest pain who are referred for arteriography are found to have normal coronary arteries (Lantinga et al., 1988). Those with normal coronary arteries have a higher prevalence of atypical chest pain, are relatively young, mostly female, and have higher scores on depression and anxiety scales (Serlie, Erdman, Paschier, & Trijsburg, 1995). Medical conditions that account for noncoronary chest pain are typically musculoskeletal pain syndromes or esophageal disorders (Richter, 1992) but also could include conditions such as pleurisy, gallbladder pain, and hiatal hernias (Hutter, 1995). Psychological problems, especially panic disorder, can contribute to the development of chest pain and other cardiac like symptoms and are important in maintaining the symptoms over long periods (Potts & Bass, 1995). Panic disorder by itself accounts for one-third or more of chest pain patients with no or minimal coronary artery disease and may coexist with coronary artery disease (Fleet, Dupuis, Marchand, Burelle, & Beitman, 1994). (See Table 16.1.)

Recognizing a cardiovascular condition in a patient who presents with symptoms that could be predominantly psychological in nature relies on no singular formula but on an approach mindful of both cardiovascular and psychological manifestations. A variety of acute cardiovascular events, including arrhythmias, coronary ischemia (angina), acute valve dysfunction, and systemic and pulmo-

TABLE 16.1 Symptoms of Anxiety Attacks and Cardiovascular Disease

| | May occur from: | |
Symptoms	Anxiety source	Cardiovascular source
Abdominal discomfort/gastrointestinal upset	✓	✓
Arm pain		✓
Blurred vision	✓	
Chest pain/pressure	✓	✓
Confusion	✓	
Diaphoresis	✓	✓
Dizziness	✓	✓
Fatigue	✓	✓
Fears (of dying, losing control, having MI or stroke)	✓	✓
Feeling of unreality	✓	
Hyperventilation	✓	
Jaw pain		✓
Numbness/tingling	✓	
Palpitations	✓	
Presyncope/syncope	✓	
Shaking/trembling	✓	

nary embolism, may lead to acute sympathetic discharge, with a surge in circulating catecholamines, which may be experienced by the patient as generalized anxiety or a panic attack. Angina, arrhythmias, and mitral valve prolapse share many symptoms with panic attacks (dyspnea, fatigue, chest pain, palpitations, lightheadedness, and autonomic arousal). Hypotension can help to identify a cardiac source of symptomatology. Syncope, with actual loss of consciousness, is unusual in panic disorder but common with serious arrhythmias. Attacks of arrhythmia tend to be less stereotypical than panic attacks. Panic attacks last typically 5 to 10 minutes, whereas arrhythmias vary from seconds to days (Levenson, 1993). Heart failure can present with anxiety and subtle to profound cognitive impairment on the basis of decreased perfusion and its sequelae.

Because anxiety or an anxiety equivalent accompanies most cardiovascular phenomena in the elderly and in patients with known heart disease, the new abrupt onset of acute anxiety should lead the clinician to consider the possibility of an acute cardiac event and arrange timely medical evaluation.

HOSTILITY IN RELATION TO
CORONARY HEART DISEASE

Recent research on the type A behavioral pattern has focused on the central pathogenic role hostility plays in coronary heart disease (CHD) morbidity and mortality. Hostility is defined as a set of negative attitudes, beliefs, and apprais-als in which individuals are viewed as sources of mistreatment, frustration, and provocation and, therefore, are not to be trusted (Smith, 1992). Cynical hostil-ity, in particular, predicts mortality from all causes and, specifically, from CHD (Almada et al., 1991; Barefoot, Dodge, Peterson, Dahlstrom, & Williams, 1989). Components of hostility are typically assessed via structured interview (i.e., component scoring of the structured interview for type A behavioral pattern) (e.g., Dembroski & Costa, 1987; Hecker, Chesney, Black, & Frautschi, 1988) or through questionnaires, the most popular being the Cook–Medley Hostility Inventory (Cook & Medley, 1954) derived from the Minnesota Multiphasic Personality Inventory.

Hostility may exert its influence on CHD in numerous ways. It is associ-ated with lower education and socioeconomic status and poor health behav-iors, such as increased alcohol and tobacco consumption and increased ca-loric intake (Barefoot et al., 1991; Scherwitz et al., 1992). Hostility is also associated with metabolic disturbances such as insulin resistance and dyslipidemias, which contribute directly to CHD risk (Niaura et al., 1994; Siegler, Peterson, Barefoot, & Williams, 1992). Moreover, hostility may in-directly increase CHD risk by increasing sympathetic nervous system reactiv-ity to behavioral challenges, especially interpersonal provocation (Suarez & Williams, 1989), and by decreasing social support (Smith & Frohm, 1985). Finally, hostility often overlaps with other negative affective states, such as anxi-ety and depression, which are also linked to increased risk of CHD (Smith & Frohm, 1985).

More germane to this chapter are studies that suggest that hostile individu-als, probably because of their deeply held mistrust of others, are more likely to delay seeking treatment when they experience symptoms of CHD (Matthews, Siegel, Kuller, Thompson, & Varat, 1983; Robbins, 1988). In a recent study of patients hospitalized with CHD, hostility was found to be positively associated with delay in appraising CHD symptoms as a sign of illness. Moreover, hostil-ity was significantly associated with mistrust of physicians in general (Robbins, 1993).

From these studies we can tentatively extrapolate implications of hostility for individuals presenting for emergency treatment of coronary-related illness. Hostile individuals are more likely to be educationally and socioeconomically disadvantaged compared to less hostile individuals. This may interfere with delivery of care from the point of view of insurance and reimbursement, and it may also interfere with care because of difficulty communicating with staff and understanding the rationale for medical procedures, which, in turn, contributes to increased distress and discomfort.

Because hostility is associated with a confluence of other CHD risk fac-tors, and because hostile individuals are more likely to delay seeking treatment, they are likely to present with more advanced and complicated events which are more difficult to manage medically. This is likely to increase distress on the part of the patient, and the urgency with which medical procedures must be performed is likely to further contribute to lack of staff–patient communication. Mistrust of physicians further complicates approaches to treatment. Given that the core pathogenic feature of hostility is cognitive (i.e., cynical mistrust), hostility will not necessarily increase the likelihood of abusive or violent behavior on the part of the patient. Thus, management of the cynically hostile patient in an emergency context should focus on establishing clear communication concerning medical procedures and engendering trust in the medical staff, for example, by ensuring continuity of personnel who are delivering treatment.

Finally, because hostile individuals are more likely to be anxious and depressed, and because of their mistrust of physicians and the health care system, they are less likely to comply with recommended treatments. This, coupled with a lack of social support, will increase their chances of experiencing complications related to their CHD and subsequent rehospitalization. Thus, clinicians must ensure continuity of psychological care that extends beyond the emergency setting to reduce risk of future morbidity and mortality.

DEPRESSION

Depression is common in patients with CHD. Approximately 20% of post- MI patients have a major depression and 18% of patients with angiographically proven coronary artery disease meet criteria for depression (Carney, Freedland, Rich, & Jaffe, 1995). Symptoms of depression may be caused by a change in perceived health, inability to work, restriction of enjoyable activities, concern about the future, or a loss of self-esteem secondary to patient-role issues (Smith & Leon, 1992). Depression not only reduces the quality of an individual's life but also appears to have an effect on morbidity and mortality. For example, depression increases the risk of reinfarction and mortality following an MI, increases the risk of mortality in cardiac surgery patients, and doubles the risk of having a cardiac event in coronary angiography patients (Carney, Freedland, Eisen, Rich, & Jaffe, 1995).

To highlight the relationship between cardiovascular disease and depression, we describe a recent study next. Researchers recently investigated the role of depression in predicting cardiac events in an MI population. Two hundred twenty-two patients were followed for 12 months after having an MI. History of major depression (criteria according to the revised third edition of the *Diagnostic and Statistical Manual of Mental Disorders* [DSM-III-R; American Psychiatric Association, 1987]) and depressive symptoms (Beck Depression Inventory $\geq$ 10) had a significant and independent impact on reoccurrence of cardiac events (Frasure-Smith, Lesperance, & Talajic, 1995) and the risks associated with these psychological variables were as great as physiological variables (previous MI; prescription of angiotensin converting enzyne [ACE] inhibitors). Depression therefore appears to be an important risk factor in CHD.

Criteria for a major depressive disorder (DSM-IV; American Psychiatric Association, 1994) include an individual having over a 2-week period either a depressed mood for most of the day or markedly diminished interest or pleasure in almost all activities. Additional symptoms consist of significant change in weight or appetite, insomnia or hypersomnia, psychomotor agitation or retardation, fatigue, feelings of worthlessness or excessive guilt, diminished ability to concentrate, and recurrent thoughts of death. It is not always clear, however, when these symptoms are present whether the cause is from depression or other problems. Lack of enjoyable activities may be more reflective of health restrictions than a change in mood. Fatigue can be caused by physiological changes/damage caused by an MI or due to side effects of cardiac medications. Cardiac medications can cause changes in sexual functioning or may disrupt sleep (Smith & Leon, 1992). Therefore, careful evaluation of causal mechanisms is important. Collaboration with physicians about physiological changes and common side effects of the individual's medications is crucial in differentiating diagnoses.

ADDITIONAL PSYCHIATRIC COMORBIDITY ISSUES

It is well established that medical illnesses can cause psychiatric disorders, with cardiovascular and endocrine disorders the most frequent causes of psychiatric symptomatology (Hall, Popkin, De Vaul, Faillace, & Stickney, 1978). Review of studies by Herridge (1960), Davis (1965), and Johnson (1968) reveals a 5–42% incidence of medical illness causative of psychiatric symptoms, including such illnesses as infections, gastrointestinal and hematological disorders, pulmonary disease, central nervous system diseases, and malignancies. When a patient presents cardiovascular symptoms to the mental health clinician, in addition to consideration of primary medical causes (such as cardiac history and cardiac risk factors), it is useful to consider the inherent cardiovascular risks of a patient's Axis I disorder. Several substances of abuse, such as cocaine, alcohol, amphetamines, nicotine, caffeine, and inhalants (including over-the-counter decongestant nasal sprays) are cardiotoxic. Intravenous drug use carries the risk of subacute bacterial endocarditis which can present with cardiovascular symptoms. In addition, substance-abusing individuals are more prone to intercurrent infections, vitamin deficiencies, and electrolyte disturbances, all of which can cause cardiovascular damage and symptoms. Individuals with eating disorders, especially anorexia nervosa, are subject to these aforementioned cardiac effects as well as cardiomyopathy. Because these individuals are often young, the clinician may unwittingly ascribe cardiovascular symptoms to psychological disturbance. Similarly, real cardiovascular disease and symptoms can occur in our clinical population of somatoform-disordered patients; here the clinician has to be attendant to the possibility of an emergency in the face of the possible indifference of either or both the patient and the clinician. Confusing projections which are counterproductive to assessment may result.

In summary, a comprehensive approach to assessment of cardiovascular symptoms in a mental health setting includes an active "inventory" of possible cardiotoxic risk and sequelae in the patient with "cardiovascular comorbid" Axis I disorders.

HEART DISEASE AND NEUROBEHAVIORAL FUNCTIONING

The relationship between cardiovascular and cerebrovascular disease is now well recognized. Many of the risk factors are associated with the development of heart disease also are linked to the development of stroke and other cerebrovascular disorders (Fisher, 1965, 1982; Reivich & Waltz, 1980; Roman, 1991; Leys & Mounier-Vehier, 1996). Therefore, an assessment of risk factors is important not only for cardiovascular disease but also for identifying people at risk for stroke (Scheinberg, 1988; Caplan, 1993; Cohen & Kaplan, 1996).

Acute cardiac crises often result in cerebrovascular events as well. For example, cardioembolism accounts for between 15% and 20% of all cases of stroke (Caplan, 1993). Embolisms occur when plaque, fat, a clot, air bubble, or other foreign matter is dislodged in the blood vessel resulting in occlusion. Cardioembolisms can be caused by a variety of cardiac abnormalities but are particularly common secondary to certain arrhythmias, such as atrial fibrillation (Sherman, 1996). Atherosclerosis of the major coronary arteries, and especially the aorta, seems to be particularly associated with embolic stroke (Leys & Mounier-Vehier, 1996). Once a stroke develops, there tends to be a cascade of pathophysiological events that leads to cell death, infarction, and chronic brain damage (Tatemichi, 1990; Horn & Schote, 1992), which in turn results in severe focal cognitive disturbance, including dementia in a significant percentage of cases (Tatemichi, Desmond, Paik, et al., 1994; Tatemichi, Desmond, Stern, et al., 1994; Roman, 1991). Yet, vascular dementia secondary to cardiovascular disease tends to be underdiagnosed (Hachinski, Lassen, & Marshall, 1974; O'Brien, 1988).

Cardiovascular disease is also associated with other cerebrovascular disorders. For example, patients are increasingly being identified with evidence of subcortical white matter disease (leukoareosis), even though there is no evidence of an embolic event involving a major blood vessel of the brain (Fayad, Ransom, & Waxman, 1996). Although the pathophysiology of leukoareosis is not yet well understood, it appears that chronic hypoperfusion to the brain may be involved. Furthermore, patients who undergo cardiac arrest also often experience global ischemia, which frequently produces subcortical lesions of this type as well as diffuse cortical damage (Roine, 1996). Leukoareosis, global ischemia, and related cerebrovascular disorders are associated with the development of vascular dementia in patients without large cortical infarctions second-ary to major vessel stroke (Roman, 1991).

The relationship between cardiac and cerebrovascular disease has been rec-ognized for some time, but there are relatively few prospective studies follow-ing the development of stroke and other cerebrovascular disorders in the car-diac patient. In a recent study, we evaluated patients in a cardiac rehabilitation program on a screening battery of neuropsychological tasks. Even though these patients had no known prior history of neurological disease and were without current complaints of cognitive difficulties, a majority (72%) exhibited neuro-psychological dysfunction. Greatest impairments were found with respect to learning and memory and certain aspects of executive control (Cohen & Kaplan, 1996). This pattern of neuropsychological findings suggest that severe cardio-vascular disease may predispose patients to subtle frontal–subcortical dysfunc-tion, which may serve as a foundation for subsequent development of vascular dementia.

Other investigations are examining the neurobehavioral consequences of cardiac surgery. Patients undergoing coronary bypass surgery exhibit signifi-cant impairments immediately following their operation (Furlan, Sila, Chimowitz, & Jones, 1992). Although many of these impairments resolve over time, a significant number of patients continue to exhibit cognitive problems long after their surgery. Other procedures that require temporarily stopping heart function while repair is done also have associated risk of stroke.

Given the relationship between heart disease and stroke, practitioners assessing or working therapeutically with cardiovascular patients should make a habit of assessing the mental status of patients. At a minimum, a brief cognitive screening exam such as the Mini-Mental Status Examination should be conducted. However, because cardiac patients may exhibit pri-mary problems in the areas of executive control, including response persis-tence, particular emphasis should be placed on assessing frontal lobe and subcortical functions. Neuropsychological assessment is particularly help-ful in the assessment of patients with cerebrovascular disease (Finlayson, 1990). Such data may point to early cerebrovascular disease and may also predict functional outcome and aftercare needs following stroke (Galski, Bruno, Zorowitz, & Walker, 1993; see Lezak, 1995, for a review of neuro-psychological assessment procedures).

Besides having neurodiagnostic value, the cognitive status of patients with cardiovascular disease may ultimately prove useful in determining the thera-peutic approach that is likely to work in cardiac rehabilitation. Patients with memory problems are likely to have difficulty learning new information neces-sary for making gains in rehabilitation. For these patients, modified educational strategies may be required. On the other hand, patients with frontal–subcorti-cal dysfunction are likely to have difficulty with compliance as a result of their executive dyscontrol, inattention, and response impersistence. For such patients, coaching and other approaches aimed at cuing the patient to the task at hand may be critical.

The assessment of neurobehavioral status, including cognitive and functional capacity, may be extremely important within the context of the rapidly changing health care delivery system in the United States. There is a growing awareness that addressing the quality of life of patients is often as important as treating the symptoms of the cardiac patient. An essential determinant of the quality of life of patients with all forms of medical illness, but particularly cardiac problems, is mental status. Patients who recover physical capacity but remain cognitively and functionally incapacitated frequently require longer hospital stays and chronic care. They represent a major fiscal challenge for the health care industry. Because geriatric patients represent the largest cohort of individuals with cardiac problems, such consideration becomes increasingly important as the population ages. Therefore, the neurobehavioral assessment should be viewed as an essential part of any psychological assessment or intervention in cardiac patients.

COORDINATION OF CARE

Many patients with known cardiovascular disease are receiving active medical care at the time of presentation for mental health issues. However, about one-third of patients do not have a private physician and psychiatric patients are at a higher risk for concurrent medical illness than the general population. Comroe (1936) and Marshall (1949) demonstrated physical morbidity in psychiatric patients in the range of 24–44% and suggested that psychiatric and behavioral symptoms are often harbingers of an unrecognized physical illness. In a study of psychiatric clinic patients, Koranyi (1979) showed that almost half of the physical illnesses were undiagnosed by the referring source. Hall et al. (1978) demonstrated that although 70% of psychiatric outpatients surveyed reported having a private physician, about the same proportion reported not having had a physical examination in the previous year. Therefore, ensuring that mental health patients have had a recent and complete medical evaluation is essential.

The opposite imbalance is also true. Health providers frequently fail to diagnose mental health problems. About one-half of all persons who are receiving mental health services are seen only by providers of general medical care (Von Korff & Meyers, 1987). Thus, the primary care physician is the model provider of mental health services in the United States. A consensus of studies of representative groups of primary care physicians is that at least one-third of primary care patients with psychiatric disorders escape detection. Empirical explanations for these gaps in management are lacking, but a number of explanations are proposed: (1) patients with psychiatric disorders frequently present with physical complaints, and it is with this basic orientation that the physician feels more comfortable; (2) the physician is concerned about stigma associated with psychiatric diagnosis; (3) the physician is uncertain whether a psychiatric diagnosis is appropriate for inclusion in the medical record; (4) the physician may be pessimistic about the success of treatment outcomes in psychiatric cases;

and (5) there may seem to be too little time to spend evaluating a psychiatric complaint (Jones, Badger, Ficker, Leeper, & Anderson, 1987).

It seems clear that the mere presence of a physician of record, or a primary care physician following a patient, does not protect either the patient or the mental health clinician from the presence of an unrecognized cardiovascular disorder or ensure detection by the medical provider of a psychiatric disorder. The mental health clinician is faced with challenges of effectively communicating with the treating physician if one is identified, referring the mental health patient to a treating physician if one is not assigned, and following up on this, as well as developing a crisis plan for accessing appropriate clinical services. Fava, Wise, Molner, and Zielezny (1985) have proposed an integrated model of clinical psychosomatic medicine in which consultation psychiatry, liaison psychiatry, medical–psychiatric units, and psychosomatic outpatients were included. This model was based on data providing evidence that a medical–psychiatric unit may offer services to a subgroup of patients with combined physical and psychiatric illness who are qualitatively different from the patients encountered in consultation psychiatry or the standard psychiatric unit patients. Barsky and Brown (1982) looked at some of the difficulties encountered by primary care practitioners dealing with patients with comorbid medical and psychiatric illnesses. They found that mental health clinicians can be most helpful to their colleagues in primary care by developing close, informal relationships that allow the physician to obtain an informal psychological or psychiatric opinion without implying physician failure or incompetence. This model also tended to put the patient more at ease about the prospect of involvement of both their primary care physician and a mental health clinician.

With an integrated treatment approach, patients badly in need of a multidisciplinary approach to their cardiovascular disease and its psychological sequelae gain access to a more coherent treatment plan. Providers are identified and have communicated during the clinical course, ideally after initial evaluations are completed and periodically thereafter, and specifically if a substantial change occurs in any aspect of the biopsychological domains. Both medical and mental health providers can provide consistent education to patients about medical and psychological symptoms. This in turn facilitates the providers' and the patients' abilities alike in making rapid distinctions and decisions about emergencies that may arise. By relying on a predetermined algorithm that reduces confusion, anxiety and its detrimental effects on cardiovascular symptoms can be reduced in our patients.

ADHERENCE

Adherence rates to medical treatments in general are low, and the more complex the behavior, the lower the rate of adherence (Meichenbaum & Turk, 1987). Individuals with cardiovascular disease typically have a number of risk factors that they are asked to change. Many of these risk factors, however, require complex lifestyle changes. Individuals with coronary atherosclerosis can lower their rate of further narrowing of their coronary arteries by adopting a low-fat and low-cholesterol diet, exercising, losing weight, quitting smoking, and taking medications for lipoprotein profiles (Haskell et al., 1994). Post-MI patients can reduce their rate of reoccurrence by participation in a program that combines supervised on-site exercise, dietary intervention, information on drugs, surgical regimens, and cardiovascular pathophysiology and behavior therapy (progressive muscle relaxation and cognitive therapy) (Friedman et al., 1986). It is estimated that participation in a cardiac rehabilitation program lowers mortality by about 20%, improves rates of return to work (Ades, Huang, & Weaver, 1992), and improves psychological functioning (Denollet, 1993). However, up to 25% of cardiac rehabilitation patients drop out in the first 3 months and up to 50% drop out within 6 months (Oldridge, 1991).

Researchers propose numerous models to explain nonadherence. Examples include the health belief model, self-efficacy, and the transtheoretical model of behavior change. Another hypothesis is that psychiatric comorbidity may impact adherence and psychological factors are shown to have an effect on adherence. For example, depression, which was discussed earlier, appears to lower adherence rates. Aspirin is routinely prescribed to coronary artery disease patients for prevention of acute coronary events. Adherence to a twice-per-day regimen of aspirin was electronically monitored in a sample of 55 patients with coronary artery disease. The 10 subjects who met criteria for a current major depressive episode adhered to the regimen on 45% of the days over the 3-week study period. Nondepressed patients adhered on only 69% of the days (Carney, Freedland, Eisen, et al., 1995). Taking a medication twice a day is a simple behavioral change compared to lowering dietary fat or exercising. If adherence to this recommendation is only 50%, how low are adherence rates to more complex behaviors? Probably much lower. Not only does depression lower adherence, but the opposite also appears to be true in that positive outcome expectations increase adherence. Successful heart transplant recipients need to adhere to a lifelong complex regimen which includes a complex medication schedule, exercise, dietary changes, and daily monitor of blood pressure and for signs of infection. Pretransplant beliefs about the efficacy of treatment and chances for future health (positive expectations) were predictive of postoperative adherence rates and measures of postoperative physical health (Leedham, Meyerowitz, Muirhead, & Frist, 1995). Thus, optimism appears to increase adherence and improve health outcome.

Behavioral strategies are developed to enhance adherence. Recordkeeping or self-monitoring is usually a first step. Having patients complete food records or exercise diaries would be examples. Stimulus control procedures would include reminders to take medications, using pill monitors, removing high-fat foods from the home, or removing ashtrays and cigarettes. The patient–physician relationship is important, and therefore communication strategies are helpful. Having patients monitor and record their symptoms, make lists of questions for their physician, ask questions in an assertive manner, utilize social support (bring a spouse to the appointment), and ask for written information/ instruction can all facilitate communication and thereby improve the adherence (Meichenbaum & Turk, 1987).

SUMMARY

Psychiatric difficulties, such as depression or hostility, can cause cardiovascular disease. Cardiovascular disease can cause psychiatric difficulties. Symptoms of cardiovascular disease and psychiatric illness can be more similar than dissimilar. Therefore, careful assessment of physiological and psychological factors is important. For the mental health provider, close coordination of care with the primary care physician is essential in making a differential diagnosis and in providing ongoing treatment. Being aware of the contributing biopsychosocial factors and using a multidisciplinary approach should improve treatment interventions and thus enhance the quality of life of this patient population.

REFERENCES

Ades, P. A., Huang, D., & Weaver, S. O. (1992). Cardiac rehabilitation participation predicts lower rehospitalization costs. *American Heart Journal, 123,* 916–921.

Almada, S. J., Zonderman, A. B., Shekelle, R. B., Dyer, A. R., Daviglus, M. L., Costa, P. T., Jr., & Stamler, J. (1991). Neuroticism and cynicism and risk of death in middle-aged men: The Western Electric Study. *Psychosomatic Medicine, 53,* 165–175.

American Psychiatric Association. (1987). *Diagnostic and statistical manual of mental disorders* (3rd ed., rev.). Washington, DC: Author.

American Psychiatric Association. (1994). *Diagnostic and statistical manual of mental disorders* (4th ed.). Washington, DC: Author.

Barefoot, J. C., Dodge, K. A., Peterson, B. L., Dahlstrom, W. G., & Williams, R. B., Jr. (1989). The Cook–Medley Hostility Scale: Item content and ability to predict survival. *Psychosomatic Medicine, 51,* 46–57.

Barefoot, J. C., Peterson, B. L., Dahlstrom, W. G., Siegler, I. C., Anderson, N. B., & Williams, R. B., Jr. (1991). Hostility patterns and health implications: Correlates of Cook–Medley Hostility Scale scores in a national survey. *Health Psychology, 10,* 18–24.

Barsky, A. J., & Brown, H. N. (1982). Psychiatric teaching and consultation in a primary care clinic. *Psychosomatics, 23,* 908–921.

Beck, A. T., & Steer, R. A. (1987). *Beck Depression Inventory manual.* New York: The Psychological Corporation, Harcourt Brace Jovanovich.

Braunwald, E. (Ed). (1992). *Heart disease: A textbook of cardiovascular medicine* (4th ed.). Philadelphia: Saunders.

Cacioppo, J. T., & Tassinary, L. G. (1990). *Principles of psychophysiology.* New York: Cambridge University Press.

Caplan, L. R. (1993). *Stroke: A clinical approach* (2nd ed.). Boston: Butterworths.

Carney, R. M., Freedland, K. E., Eisen, S. A., Rich, M. W., & Jaffe, A. S. (1995). Major depression and medication adherence in elderly patients with coronary artery disease. *Health Psychology, 14*(1), 88–90.

Carney, R. M., Freedland, K. E., Rich, M. W., & Jaffe, A. S. (1995). Depression as a risk factor for cardiac events in established coronary heart disease: A review of possible mechanisms. *Annals of Behavioral Medicine, 17*(2), 142–149.

Cohen, R. A., & Kaplan, R. F. (1996). Neuropsychological aspects of cerebrovascular disease. In M. Fisher & J. Bogousslavsky (Eds.), *Current review of cerebrovascular disease* (2nd ed., pp. 59–68). Philadelphia: Current Medicine.

Comroe, B. I. (1936). Follow-up studies of one hundred patients diagnosed as neurotic. *Journal of Nervous Disease, 89,* 679–684.

Cook, W. W., & Medley, D. M. (1954). Proposed hostility and pharisaic-virtue scales for the MMPI. *Journal of Applied Psychology, 38,* 414–418.

Davis, D. W. (1965). Physical illness in psychiatric outpatients. *British Journal of Psychiatry, 111,* 27–33.

Dembroski, T. M., & Costa, P. T., Jr. (1987). Coronary-prone behavior: Components of the Type A pattern and hostility. *Journal of Personality, 55,* 211–235.

Denollet, J. (1993). Sensitivity of outcome assessment in cardiac rehabilitation. *Journal of Consulting and Clinical Psychology, 61*(4), 686–695.

Fava, G. A., Wise, T. N., Molner, G., & Zielezny, M. (1985). The medical–psychiatric unit. *Psychotherapy and Psychosomatics, 43,* 35–40.

Fayad, P. B., Ransom, B. R., & Waxman, S. G. (1996). Recent clinical and basic advances in white matter ischemia. In M. Fisher & J. Bogousslavsky (Eds.), *Current review of cerebrovascular disease* (2nd ed., pp. 59–68). Philadelphia: Current Medicine.

Finlayson, M. A. (1990). Neuropsychological assessment and treatment of stroke patients. An overview. *Stroke, 21,* 14–15.

Fisher, C. M. (1965). Lacunes: Small, deep cerebral infarcts. *Neurology, 15,* 774–784.

Fisher, C. M. (1982). Lacunar strokes and infarcts: A review. *Neurology, 32,* 871.

Fleet, R. P., Dupuis, G., Marchand, A., Burelle, D., & Beitman, B.D. (1994). Panic disorder, chest pain, and coronary artery disease: Literature review. *Canadian Journal of Cardiology, 10,* 827–834.

Frasure-Smith, N., Lesperance, F., & Talajic, M. (1995). The impact of negative emotions on prognosis following myocardial infarction: Is it more than depression? *Health Psychology, 14*(5), 388–398.

Friedman, M., Thoresen, C. E., Gill, J. J., Ulmer, D., Powell, L. H., Price, V. A., Brown, B., Thompson, L., Rabin, D. D., Breall, W. S., Bourg, E., Levy, R., & Dixon, T. (1986). Alteration of type A behavior and its effect on cardiac recurrences in post myocardial infarction patients: Summary results of the recurrent coronary prevention project. *American Heart Journal, 112*(4), 653–665.

Furlan, A. J., Sila, C. A., Chimowitz, M. I., & Jones, S. C. (1992). Neurological complications related to cardiac surgery. *Neurology Clinics, 10,* 145–166.

Galski, T., Bruno, R. L., Zorowitz, R., & Walker, J. (1993). Predicting length of stay, functional outcome, and aftercare in the rehabilitation of stroke patients. The dominant role of higher-order cognition. *Stroke, 24*(12), 1794–1800.

Gordon, T., & Kannel, W. B. (1971). Premature mortality from coronary heart disease: The Framingham Study. *Journal of the American Medical Association, 215,* 1617–1625.

Hachinski, V. C., Lassen, N. A., & Marshall, J. (1974). Multi-infarct dementia: A cause for mental deterioration in the elderly. *Lancet, 2,* 207–210.

Hall, R. C. W., Popkin, M. K., DeVaul, R., Faillace, L. A., & Stickney, S. K. (1978). Physical illness presenting as psychiatric disease. *Archives of General Psychiatry, 35,* 1315–1320.

Haskell, W. L., Alderman, E. L., Fair, J. M., Maron, D. J., Mackey, S. F., Superko, R., Williams, P. T., Johnstone, I. M., Champagne, M. A., Krauss, R. M., & Farquhar, J. W. (1994). Effects of intensive multiple risk factor reduction on coronary atherosclerosis and clinical cardiac events in men and women with coronary artery disease: The Stanford Coronary Risk Intervention Project (SCRIP). *Circulation, 89,* 975–990.

Hecker, M. H. L., Chesney, M. A., Black, G. W., & Frautschi, N. (1988). Coronary-prone behaviors in the Western Collaborative Group Study. *Psychosomatic Medicine, 50,* 153–164.

Herridge, C. F. (1960). Physical disorders in psychiatric illness: A study of 209 consecutive admissions. *Lancet, 2,* 949–951.

Horn, M., & Schote, W. (1992). Delayed neuronal death and delayed neuronal recovery in the human brain following global ischemia. *Acta Neuropathology, 85,* 79–87.

Hutter, A. M. (1995). Chest pain: How to distinguish between cardiac and noncardiac causes. *Geriatrics, 50,* 32–40.

Johnson, D. A. W. (1968). The evaluation of routine physical examination in psychiatric cases. *Practitioner, 200,* 686–691.

Jones, L. R., Badger, L. W., Ficker, R. P., Leeper, J. D., & Anderson, R. L. (1987). Inside the hidden mental health network: Examining mental health care delivery of primary care physicians. *General Hospital Psychiatry, 9,* 287–293.

Kannel, W. B., & Thom, T. J. (1990). Incidence, prevalence, and mortality of cardiovascular diseases. In J. W. Hurst, R. C. Schlant, C. E. Rackley, E. H. Sonnerblick, & N. K. Wenger (Eds.), *The heart, arteries, and veins* (7th ed., pp. 627–638). New York: McGraw-Hill.

Koranyi, E. K. (1979). Fatalities in 2070 psychiatric outpatients. *Archives of General Psychiatry, 34,* 1137–1142.

Lantinga, L. J., Sprafkin, R. P., McCroskery, J. H., Baker, M. T., Warner, R. A., & Hill, N. E. (1988). One-year psychosocial follow-up of patients with chest pain and angiographically normal coronary arteries. *American Journal of Cardiology, 62,* 209–213.

Leedham, B., Meyerowitz, B. E., Muirhead, J., & Frist, W. H. (1995). Positive expectations predict health after heart transplantation. *Health Psychology, 14*(1), 74–79.

Levenson, J. L. (1993). Cardiovascular disease. In A. Stoudemire & B. S. Fogel (Eds.), *Psychiatric care of the medical patient* (pp. 539–555). New York: Oxford University Press.

Leys, D., & Mounier-Vehier, F. (1996). Stroke prevention. In M. Fisher & J. Bogousslavsky (Eds.), *Current review of cerebrovascular disease* (2nd ed., pp. 13–26). Philadelphia: Current Medicine.

Lezak, M. (1995). *Neuropsychological assessment* (3rd ed.). New York: Oxford University Press.

Marshall, H. (1949). Incidence of physical disorders among psychiatric patients. *British Medical Journal, 2,* 468–470.

Matthews, K. A., Siegel, J. M., Kuller, L. H., Thompson, M., & Varat, M. (1983). Determinants of decisions to seek medical treatment by patients with acute myocardial infarction symptoms. *Journal of Personality and Social Psychology, 44,* 1144–1156.

Meichenbaum, D., & Turk, D. C. (1987). *Facilitating treatment adherence: A practitioner's guidebook.* New York: Plenum Press.

Molner, G., Fava, G. A., & Zielezny, M. A. (1985). Medical–psychiatric unit patients compared with patients in two other services. *Psychosomatics, 26,* 193–209.

Niaura, R., Stoney, C. M., Ward, K., Spiro, A., Aldwin, C. M., Landsberg, L., & Weiss, S. T. (1994, April). *Hostility and cardiovascular disease risk in older males: The Normative Aging Study.* Paper presented at the 52nd annual meeting of the American Psychosomatic Society, Boston.

O'Brien, M. D. (1988). Vascular dementia is underdiagnosed. *Archives of Neurology, 45,* 797–798.

Oldridge, N. B. (1991). Cardiac rehabilitation services: What are they and are they worth it? *Comprehensive Therapy, 17,* 59–66.

Potts, S. G., & Bass, C. M. (1995). Psychological morbidity in patients with chest pain and normal or near-normal coronary arteries: A long-term follow-up study. *Psychological Medicine, 25,* 339–347.

Reivich, M., & Waltz, A.G. (1980). Circulatory and metabolic factors in cerebrovascular disease. In *Cerebrovascular survey report* (pp. 55–134). Bethesda: NINCDS Monographs.

Richter, J. E. (1992). Overview of diagnostic testing for chest pain of unknown origin. *American Journal of Medicine, 92,* 41S–45S.

Robbins, M. L. (1988). *Delay in seeking treatment for suspected coronary artery disease: An evaluation of illness behavior, introspectiveness, and the Type A behavior pattern.* Unpublished master's thesis, Rutgers University, New Brunswick, NJ.

Robbins, M. L. (1993). *Hostility, illness cognition, and the process of coping with coronary heart disease.* Unpublished doctoral dissertation, Rutgers University, New Brunswick, NJ.

Roine, R. O. (1996). Global cerebral ischemia. In M. Fisher & J. Bogousslavsky (Eds.), *Current review of cerebrovascular disease* (2nd ed., pp. 159–174). Philadelphia: Current Medicine.

Roman, G. C. (1991). The epidemiology of vascular dementia. In A. Hartmann, W. Kuschinsky, & S. Hoyer (Eds.), *Cerebral ischemia and dementia* (pp. 9–15). Berlin: Springer-Verlag.

Scheinberg, P. (1988). Dementia due to vascular disease: A multifactorial disorder. *Stroke, 19,* 1291–1299.

Scherwitz, L. W., Perkins, L. L., Chesney, M. A., Hughes, G. H., Sidney, S., & Manolio, T. A. (1992). Hostility and health behaviors in young adults: The CARDIA study. *American Journal of Epidemiology, 136,* 136–145.

Serlie, A. W., Erdman, R. A., Paschier, J., & Trijsburg, R. W. (1995). Psychological aspects of non-cardiac chest pain. *Psychotherapy and Psychosomatics, 64,* 62–73.

Sherman, D. G. (1996). Atrial fibrillation and stroke. In M. Fisher & J. Bogousslavsky (Eds.), *Current review of cerebrovascular disease* (2nd ed., pp. 59–68). Philadelphia: Current Medicine.

Siegler, I. C., Peterson, B. L., Barefoot, J. C., & Williams, R. B. (1992). Hostility during late adolescence predicts coronary risk factors at mid-life. *American Journal of Epidemiology, 136,* 146–154.

Smith, T. W. (1992). Hostility and health: Current status of a psychosomatic hypothesis. *Health Psychology, 11,* 139–150.

Smith, T. W., & Frohm, K. D. (1985). What's so unhealthy about hostility? Construct validity and psychosocial correlates of the Cook and Medley Ho Scale. *Health Psychology, 4,* 503–520.

Smith, T. W., & Leon, A. S. (1992). *Coronary heart disease: A behavioral perspective.* Champaign, IL: Research Press.

Suarez, E. C., & Williams, R. B., Jr. (1989). Situational determinants of cardiovascular and emotional reactivity in high and low hostile men. *Psychosomatic Medicine, 51,* 404–418.

Tatemichi, T. K. (1990). How acute brain failure becomes chronic: A view of the mechanisms of dementia related to stroke. *Neurology, 40,* 1652–1659.

Tatemichi, T. K., Desmond, D. W., Paik, M., Figueroa, M., Gropen, T. I., Stern, Y., Sano, M., & Pemien, R. (1994). Clinical determinants of dementia related to stroke. *Annals of Neurology, 33*(6), 568–575.

Tatemichi, T. K., Desmond, D. W., Stern, Y., Paik, M., Sano, M., & Bagiellz, E. (1994). Cognitive impairments after stroke: Frequency, patterns, and relationship to functional ability. *Journal of Neurology, Neurosurgery and Psychiatry, 57*(2), 202–207.

Von Korff, M., & Myers, L. (1987). The primary care physician and psychiatric services. *General Hospital Psychiatry, 9,* 235–240.

PART VI

THE IMPACT
OF EMERGENCY SERVICE
ON THE CLINICIAN

CHAPTER 17

EMERGENCIES WITH SUICIDAL PATIENTS
The Impact on the Clinician

PHILLIP M. KLEESPIES
BARBARA L. NILES
DEANNA L. MORI
JAMES D. DELEPPO

You receive a call from the emergency service. The clinician asks if you are sitting down and then proceeds to say that the patient whom you evaluated and released yesterday stabbed himself in the chest last night. The question "Is he dead?" flashes through your mind. You feel shocked and a little sick and it's good that you are sitting down. The emergency room clinician goes on to say that the patient punctured a lung but at present seems to be stabilized medically. You breathe a sigh of relief and give the clinician information that might be helpful under these emergency conditions. Then other thoughts and feelings begin to occur: "There's no doubt that this was serious." "He didn't seem that depressed. His suicidal ideation seemed vague. Did I miss something?" "Why didn't I see this coming? Was I insensitive to his pain?" "Will I be blamed?" "I'm angry at him for doing this. He said he'd be safe." "It's sad that he felt so desperate." "Will there be a next time and will he be more successful then?"

Should one of your patients make a serious suicide attempt, these and a myriad of other reactions may possibly assail you.

Despite the distress that patient suicidal behavior can bring to clinicians and despite the worry and concern that they expend over the possibility that a patient/client might kill himself or herself, mental health clinicians seem to devote relatively little time to studying and attempting to understand suicidal phenomena and their aftermath. Thus, Bongar and Harmatz (1991, see also Introduction, this volume) conducted national surveys of the Council of University Directors of Clinical Psychology Programs and the National Council of Schools of Professional Psychology and found that only 40% of all graduate programs in clinical psychology offered any formal training in the study of suicide. In a similar vein, Kleespies, Penk, and Forsyth (1993) estimated that approximately 55% of the former psychology graduate students in their study received some formal suicide education in their graduate programs, but the educational efforts were quite minimal, usually consisting of one or two lectures.

There is a need to better understand the incidence of patient suicidal behavior in clinical practice and its impact on mental health practitioners at all levels. Much of the research in this area focuses on completed patient suicides, but we contend that there is a need to understand how clinicians might be better prepared to cope with the emotions aroused by a broader range of patient suicidal behavior (i.e., episodes of patient suicidal ideation and patient suicide attempts as well as patient suicide completions). As one former psychology intern in a study on the impact of patient suicidal behavior put it, "I was not prepared for the suicidality of the patients before my internship. It was an enormous difficulty that I hadn't bargained for... " (Kleespies et al., 1993).

THE INCIDENCE OF PATIENT SUICIDAL BEHAVIOR

The importance of understanding the impact of patient/client suicidal behavior on the clinician becomes apparent when we recognize how commonly clinicians are confronted with this high-stress scenario. In a recent survey conducted with mental health professionals, 97% of the respondents reported being afraid of losing a patient to suicide (Pope & Tabachnick, 1993). Tanney (1995) reported that between 3% and 7% of patients who come to the emergency room of a general hospital present with complaints related to self-destructive behavior. Chemtob, Bauer, Hamada, Pelowski, and Muraoka (1989), who studied the incidence of patient suicide, stated that "patient suicide is clearly an important occupational hazard for psychotherapists" (p. 294).

Several studies have been conducted in recent years that have helped to document the actual incidence of patient/client suicidal behavior, although, as noted previously, much of the research has been limited to the incidence of completed suicide. Brown (1987b) found that 33% of 55 graduates of a psychiatric residency program experienced the suicide of one of their patients during their training years. This rate is higher than that found in previous studies, which reported a 14–16% incidence rate of patient suicide for psychiatric residents in training (i.e., Kahne, 1968; Rosen, 1974; Schnur & Levin, 1985). The discrepancy may be accounted for by the fact that Brown's (1987b) study involved graduates of a residency program who were reporting retrospectively on their entire 4 years of training. The studies conducted previously used residents who were still in training and had completed less than 4 postgraduate years when surveyed. Brown (1987a), in another study, expanded the scope of his research by surveying 155 staff and trainees from various mental health disciplines. He found that social workers and psychologists both reported a 14% incidence rate of patient suicide during training years. Psychiatric residents, however, reported a 37% incidence rate, a rate slightly higher than that reported in Brown's original study.

Chemtob and his colleagues surveyed both psychologists and psychiatrists in their investigation of the incidence of patient suicide in clinical practice. These studies extended beyond the training years and included a national random sample of practitioners. Chemtob, Hamada, Bauer, Kinney, and Torigoe (1988) found that of their 259 psychiatrist respondents (46% response rate), 51% reported having had a patient commit suicide. In a parallel study with psychologists, Chemtob, Hamada, Bauer, Torigoe, and Kinney (1988) reported that of the 365 respondents (68% response rate), 22% reported having had a patient commit suicide. Also using psychologists, Pope and Tabachnick (1993) found that 28.8% of the clinicians in their study experienced the completed suicide of a patient. In their two studies, Chemtob et al. found a significant relationship between postgraduate training and patient suicide. In other words, clinicians with specialized postdoctoral training were less likely to have experienced a patient suicide. The authors also found that female clinicians reported fewer patient suicides than males.

To investigate the therapist variables that were associated with greater risk of patient suicide (e.g., gender and education), Chemtob et al. did a follow-up study with the respondents from both studies reported previously. They explored practice variables such as work setting and patient population treated (Chemtob et al., 1989). As the authors speculated, clinicians who spent a larger proportion of their professional time working in psychiatric hospitals or psychiatric wards or in outpatient mental health agencies were significantly more likely to experience a patient suicide than their colleagues who worked in private practice, academia, or research settings. Furthermore, clinicians were more likely to experience a patient suicide if their patients had organic, schizophrenic, affective, substance abuse, or other psychotic disorders. Conversely, clinicians who worked with patients with adjustment, anxiety, or personality disorders were less likely to experience a patient suicide. The authors also found that postgraduate training and gender of the therapist were related to patient suicide rates largely to the extent that they affect opportunities and choices regarding job decisions, patient populations served, and work settings. It should be noted, however, that the generalizability of these results is somewhat limited because the initial response rate was rather low (see above) and only 69% of the original respondents participated in the follow-up study.

Literature on the incidence of patient/client suicidal behaviors other than completed suicide has been largely overlooked even though there is evidence to suggest that these behaviors can have a major emotional impact on the clinician (Rodolfa, Kraft, & Reilley, 1988). Although there is little investigation on this topic, the research that exists clearly indicates that clinicians may encounter such behaviors with great frequency. For example, Kleespies, Smith, and Becker (1990) conducted a study with the 54 psychology interns who had completed a 1-year internship at the Boston Veterans Administration Medical Center during the years 1983–1988 (100% participation rate). Of these interns, 18.5% (10) reported having had a patient who made a suicide attempt during their training years and 16.7% (9) reported having had a patient commit suicide at some point during their training years. Kleespies et al. (1993) expanded on this study by using a larger sample and by investigating a broader spectrum of patient suicidal behaviors. Drawing from 11 psychology internship programs, 292 interns were located and contacted (out of a possible 307) and 100% agreed to participate. The investigators found that 96.9% of their respondents had had at least one patient with some form of suicidal behavior or ideation during their training years. Eighty-five (or 29.1%) reported having had a patient who made a suicide attempt and 33 (or 11.3%) reported having had a patient who actually committed suicide.

The incidence statistics reported here clearly highlight the fact that patient/client suicidal behavior is not rare in the experience of mental health clinicians. There is still much to be learned, however, and with the exception of the data reported in the two studies cited earlier, little is known about the incidence of suicidal behaviors other than completed suicide. Although many of the studies that are reported in this section have methodological limitations such as small and restricted samples and, in some cases, low response rates, the findings are compelling and clearly point to the need for further investigation.

THE IMPACT OF PATIENT SUICIDAL BEHAVIOR ON THE CLINICIAN

For therapists working in clinical settings, to a large extent, stress "is in the eye of the beholder." What some clinicians find stressful and difficult, others do not (Rodolfa et al., 1988). One important exception to this generality is patient/client suicidality. It is universal that therapists find patients' suicidal behavior to be highly stress inducing (Kleespies et al., 1993; Rodolfa et al., 1988). Rodolfa et al. (1988) found that patient suicide attempts were rated as second only to physical attack on the therapist as patient behaviors that were difficult for clinicians. Several studies by Chemtob and colleagues show that clients' completed suicides can have substantial negative effects on therapists in both personal and professional arenas (Chemtob et al., 1989; Chemtob, Hamada, Bauer, Kinney, et al., 1988; Chemtob, Hamada, Bauer, Torigoe, et al., 1988). Thus, it is commonly accepted that patients'/clients' suicidal behavior takes an emotional toll on clinicians. Recently, research has begun to accumulate to address the question, "Which suicidal behaviors are most stressful for whom?"

Behaviors

Among the various potential patient/client behaviors—suicide ideation, threats, attempts, and completions—the impact of suicide completion on the therapist has been most thoroughly examined. Chemtob et al. (1989) concluded that patient suicide appears to have a consistently strong impact on most mental health professionals. Kleespies et al. (1990) noted that even when they had been aware that they were working with high-risk patients, clinicians frequently used the term "shock" to describe their feelings on hearing about a patient suicide. Feelings of guilt or shame, denial or disbelief, incompetence, anger, depression, being blamed, relief, and fear in response to the suicide were significant emotional reactions reported by psychology interns in the Kleespies et al. (1990) study. In several studies, the Impact of Event Scale (IES; Horowitz, Wilner, & Alvarez, 1979) was used to evaluate the impact of patient suicidality on the therapist (Chemtob, Hamada, Bauer, Kinney, et al., 1988; Chemtob, Hamada, Bauer, Torigoe, et al., 1988; Chemtob et al., 1989; Kleespies et al., 1990, 1993). These studies indicated that patient suicide often results in intrusive symptoms of stress for the therapist that are comparable to posttrauma symptoms found in clinical groups (Zilberg, Weiss, & Horowitz, 1982). Kleespies et al. (1993) discussed the possibility that reactions of therapists to suicidal client behavior may be considered posttraumatic stress in some cases and concluded that more research into this area is needed to adequately explore this possibility. Kleespies et al. (1990) and Brown (1987b) illustrated that such intrusive symptoms diminish substantially over a period of weeks or months but that some longer-term emotional effects (e.g., heightened anxiety when evaluating suicidal patients or feeling humbled) remain for years for some clinicians.

Kleespies et al. (1993) examined a broader range of patient suicidal behaviors and their effects on psychology interns. They found a dose–response relationship between patient behavior and clinician reaction—that is, an increase in impact on the clinician associated with an increase in severity of patient suicidal behavior. Thus, more severe suicide behaviors (attempts and completions) were associated with more severe reactions on the part of clinicians (e.g., shock, disbelief, failure, sadness, self-blame, guilt, shame, and depression). By contrast, less severe behaviors (e.g., suicide ideation) were associated with more attenuated reactions.

Although the dose–response relationship rings true in many cases, there are important exceptions to this general rule. In some cases, patient suicide ideation can be extremely stressful for the clinician (Kleespies et al., 1993). As Tanney (1995) noted, "the impact of nonfatal suicidal behavior emotionally rivals that of completed suicide for some helpers" (p. 104). Rodolfa et al. (1988) found that clinicians rated patients' suicide attempts and suicidal statements as the second and third most stressful client behaviors they encountered; only physical attack on the therapist was rated as more stressful. In the case of a suicide attempt, the clinician may be required to work intensively with the patient following the attempt. This intensive contact may present additional stress to the clinician at a time when he or she may be struggling to manage his or her own reactions to the event.

Clinicians

Whether trainees are more vulnerable to negative reactions to clients' suicidal behaviors than professionals who completed their training is addressed in several investigations (e.g., Kleespies et al., 1990, 1993; Rodolfa et al., 1988; Brown, 1987b). One theory is that clinicians in training who have a patient commit suicide or make a serious suicide attempt have a "protective advantage" from any resulting negative emotional effects because they are under direct supervision and do not bear ultimate ethical or legal responsibility for the case (Brown, 1987a, 1987b). Others suggest that trainees are more likely to assume responsibility for "fixing the client" (Rodolfa et al., 1988, p. 47) and thus have stronger feelings of inadequacy when treatment interventions are unsuccessful. Empirical studies support the contention that mental health trainees are at least as vulnerable as those who completed their training. Kleespies et al. (1993) found that the impact of suicidal behavior on psychology interns/trainees as measured by the IES (Horowitz et al., 1979) was as high, if not higher, than that found in comparable studies of professional psychologists. Furthermore, Kleespies et al. (1993) found a negative relationship between intrusive thoughts and images and the year of training in which a patient suicide was experienced (i.e., the earlier in training the suicide occurred, the greater the perceived acute impact). Rodolfa et al. (1988) examined three levels of clinicians (professionals, interns, and practicum students) and found that patient suicidal statements and attempts were rated by all groups as highly stressful. Thus, even though trainees do not bear legal responsibility for their patients, patient suicidal behavior seems to affect them as much or more than it affects those at a staff level. This may be because trainees are less experienced, feel less prepared, feel less secure in their roles, and are more surprised or shocked by suicide threats, gestures, attempts, or completions than professionals.

Other Contributing Factors

Myriad other factors are thought to contribute to the impact of suicidal behavior on the therapist. Although no empirical studies have been conducted to investigate these potential factors, several have been suggested in the clinical literature. For example, Dunne, McIntosh, and Dunne-Maxim (1987) suggested that the nature of the relationship between the clinician and the patient (e.g., how long and how intensely the therapist has been associated with the patient) and the amount of anger or hostility involved in the relationship are two important influences on the therapist's reaction to patient suicide. Other factors that may influence the severity of the clinician's reaction are the level of perceived responsibility and whether the clinician was working alone with the patient or as part of a team. The degree of violence involved in the patient's suicide or suicide attempt as well as whether the clinician witnessed the act or the death scene might be other factors affecting clinician response. Thus, it is clear that more research in this area is needed to determine which factors are most salient in determining how a clinician responds to patient suicide behaviors. Nonetheless, it is safe to say that regardless of discipline or level of clinical training or practice, the work with the suicidal patient extracts a high emotional price from the clinician.

THE CLINICIAN'S ADAPTATION IN RESPONSE TO PATIENT SUICIDAL BEHAVIOR

The findings on the emotional impact of patient suicidal behavior lead to the question of whether the impact changes the thinking or perspective of the clinician in some important ways. In other words, how do mental health clinicians psychologically adapt to client suicidal behavior and what are the internal mechanisms that mediate this process? This section focuses on some theoretical speculations about the changes and adaptations that can occur in clinicians when confronted with patients or clients who are despairing and bent on self-destruction.

The Concept of Cognitive Schemas as Applied to Clinician Response

The concept of cognitive schemas and their development through the processes of assimilation and accommodation derives from the tradition of such cognitive developmental theorists as Piaget (1954). In more recent times, self-theorists such as Epstein (1991) have employed this concept to account for the effects of trauma, and other theorists (e.g., McCann & Pearlman, 1990) have extended its use to attempt to account for the psychological effects of working with trauma victims on the therapist. Horn (1994) proposed that a cognitive model of psychological adaptation to trauma (McCann, Sakheim, & Abrahamson, 1988) be applied toward an understanding of the relationship between a therapist's life experience and his or her experience of patient suicidal behavior. A therapist's core beliefs, assumptions, and expectations about self, others, and the world (cognitive schemas) are very important in clarifying the personal and professional reactions to self-destructive behavior. McCann and Pearlman (1990) and Epstein (1991) hold that these schemas or frames of reference are the cognitive manifestations of psychological needs; they are affect laden and derive from one's life experience. Janoff-Bulman (1992) contends that fundamental beliefs and assumptions do not change very easily. Change is slow and gradual when it occurs; however, extreme events (e.g., trauma or, for therapists, a patient suicide or attempted suicide) can challenge one's assumptive systems and lay the groundwork for change. As Brown (1987a) noted, the seriously suicidal patient can shockingly confront the clinician "with his or her limitations in achieving deeply held narcissistic aspirations" (p. 106). Thus, the therapist's schemas may be influenced by the client's suicidal behavior resulting in disruptions in schemas about oneself, others, and the world. Again, as Brown (1987a) stated, the suicidal client/patient may push the clinician toward concluding that either he or she (the therapist) is no good or that the client or patient is no good. Resultant changes in schemas may be apparent or subtle depending on the degree of accommodation needed to integrate the patient's suicidal behavior with the therapist's prevailing assumptions.

Epstein (1991) hypothesized that there are four basic assumptions that can be disrupted by trauma: the world is benign, the world is meaningful, the self is worthy, and people are trustworthy. These same schemas or beliefs can be influenced by a therapist's professional training, experience, and understanding of his or her role in a therapeutic relationship (Horn, 1994). For example, if a therapist has a strong belief that the world must be meaningful, orderly, and predictable, he or she is likely to have a need for power and control over the therapeutic relationship. The suicidal patient may challenge these schemas and the therapist may experience a sense of vulnerability and powerlessness. The therapist may have difficulty recognizing and containing the anxiety aroused by such a challenge to his or her sense of a meaningful and orderly world. Attempts by the therapist to reinstate control can be manifested in a variety of ways in the work with the suicidal patient. For example, the therapist may not attend to what the patient is saying about suicide and may take action prematurely to hospitalize rather than help the client arrive at an alternative to suicide. On the other hand, this same schema or belief in a meaningful or orderly world may be less entrenched in a different therapist. This therapist may be more tolerant in allowing a patient responsibility to make his or her own decisions and choices. In this case, the therapist may allow the patient to try to exercise control over the impulse to harm himself or herself. In both of these examples, the therapist's interventions or lack of interventions may be influenced by the therapist's specific cognitive schemas.

The effects of these schemas on managing suicidal behavior are influenced and shaped by the mental health professional's formal education and training. If the coursework and training do not provide adequate information and experience in the area of suicidality and/or are biased in ways not to challenge prevailing schemas, the result is that clinicians are unprepared to deal with the psychological impact of their patient's suicidal behavior. The schemas previously mentioned are but a few of many that clinicians may hold. Others might include that therapy is always under the control of the therapist and that there should always be a reason to be optimistic and positive.

McCann and Pearlman (1990) introduced the concept of "vicarious traumatization," which may result when a therapist is seriously affected by a patient's trauma and there is a disruption of the therapist's prevailing cognitive schemas. These authors state that regardless "of advanced degrees and training in the treatment of victims, they (i.e., therapists) are not immune to the painful images, thoughts, and feelings associated with exposure to their client's traumatic memories" (p. 132). We hypothesize that therapists who work with patient suicidal behavior, especially attempts and completions, can also experience a disruption of their prevailing assumptions that can affect both personal and professional aspects of their lives.

Epstein (1991), in applying his cognitive–experiential self theory to trauma, postulates that a threatening event can invalidate one's fundamental beliefs that the world is benevolent and meaningful and that the self is worthy. As in the McCann and Pearlman model (1990), Epstein (1991) argues that trauma can be disorganizing to the self-system which, in turn, can challenge the individual "with the task of accomplishing a significant reformulation of basic views about self and world" (p. 71). A dramatic illustration of both these models is offered by Foster (1987), who writes about her personal and professional reactions to the suicide of two of her patients within a period of 2½ years. She experienced feelings of worthlessness and incompetency as a therapist for a long period. She confesses to strong feelings of hate toward the two patients who suicided, as well as missing the hope she had for them and for herself. She writes about how she buried herself from the pain of the losses and avoided social interactions. Foster (1987) reports that she went through the process of healing which resulted in some modification of her understanding and thinking (schemas) relative to how she views "patient freedom" and "therapist power" (p. 202). She reconciled with that part of herself that previously would be "seductive" and "collude" with the patient to keep the patient alive. Foster appears to have reframed her experience with the two suicides and their aftermath as a phase of painful growth from which she "grew to respect her patient's freedom differently and to be aware of her limitations" (p. 204).

PREPARING CLINICIANS TO COPE WITH PATIENT SUICIDAL BEHAVIOR

Brown (1987a, 1987b) contends that there is a reluctance to explore the subject of patient suicide, at least on the part of training programs. This is probably the case, however, not only with training programs but also in settings that are more exclusively service oriented. It may be telling that there has been scant mention of the need for training to meet the demands of work with the suicidal patient by those who set the formal professional standards for psychologists (Bongar & Harmatz, 1991; see also Introduction, this volume). Such avoidance or inattention, however, is not warranted given the frequent expressions of shock from clinicians when there is a patient suicide attempt, let alone a completion (Kleespies et al., 1993), and given the acute as well as longer-term effects that patient suicidal behavior can have on clinicians. Rather, training programs and clinical sites need to be thinking of ways to reduce the stress and to assist in the constructive assimilation of such experiences into the clinician's frame of reference.

Educational preparation would seem to be one way to diminish shock and to help developing clinicians to make adjustments in their assumptions and beliefs about the occurrence of patient suicidal behavior and their ability to prevent it. Starting at the graduate or professional school level would seem to be one way to "institutionalize" such preparation. As Kleespies (1993) noted, graduate programs could make suicide education a more routine part of the training for clinical students. Issues related to suicide and suicidal behavior could be incorporated as a component of a psychopathology course and/or issues related to managing the suicidal patient could be made a component of a crisis intervention segment of a clinical methods course.

In the clinical setting, the need to be prepared cognitively and affectively for dealing with the impact of the suicidal patient is more immediate. Internship programs and supervisors would do well to develop creative ways to prepare interns and trainees. Likewise, professional settings should consider in-service or continuing education programs for their staff. Melchiode (1980) recognized the need to motivate medical students to become emotionally involved with the topic of the suicidal patient and developed a teaching technique that uses a simulated suicide call. One student is chosen to respond to the call, but the "patient" can be seen by all on a closed circuit television hook-up. The role of the patient can be portrayed in a variety of ways (e.g., depressed or provocative) and the outcome can also be varied. Immediately after the call, all students in the group are asked to explore the feelings evoked by the "patient's" behavior and to discuss the motives and intent of the "patient."

Another useful technique is to present clinicians with an actual case of patient suicidal behavior in which the therapist was an anonymous peer and ask them to put themselves in the place of the therapist. After the case presentation, the group can engage in a discussion of what they feel their reactions might be were they to experience such a situation.

Still another preparatory technique that can be utilized by students as well as by professional staff is to establish what Brown (1987a) referred to as a "patient at risk" rounds or what Kolodny, Binder, Bronstein, and Friend (1979) called an "impossible case" conference. This, in essence, is rounds or a conference where clinicians can present and discuss patients whom they consider at high risk for suicidal or other dangerous behavior. They can learn from each others cases and empathize with the feelings experienced by fellow clinicians. If led properly, the conference can be a source of support to the case presenter who may be working with a very difficult patient.

COPING WITH THE AFTERMATH OF PATIENT SUICIDAL BEHAVIOR

Clinicians

In Victoria Alexander's (1991) book, *Words I Never Thought to Speak,* a number of individuals who survived the suicide of a family member, a friend, or a patient related their experiences with the aftermath of suicide. In one of these vignettes, a social worker who had a patient who committed suicide remembered talking to a colleague at the time and gave the following description:

> I talked to the social worker at the hospital about Joe. We talked about what he was like, different aspects of his personality. She was one person I spoke to who knew him, maybe at a different level than I knew him, but knew what I was talking about and saw what I saw and liked him. That was helpful, to feel that there were other people out there who really could understand what I saw and knew of him. It's different from talking to somebody who doesn't know this person from a hole in the head and can empathize with you, may know what it feels like, but didn't know Joe. (p. 139)

Although clinicians are likely to differ on what they find helpful in coping with the aftermath of a patient suicide, the reaction of the social worker above does not seem atypical. It helped to talk to and to have her feelings understood by a colleague who also knew the patient. She seems somewhat dismissive of the support that can come from those who may not know the particular patient but have had similar experiences; however, this again may be an individual matter.

The previous example was of a clinician coping with a patient suicide. As emphasized throughout this chapter, however, patient suicide completions are not the only patient or client suicidal behaviors that are stressful and strain the coping abilities of the mental health clinician. One of the authors of this chapter (P.M.K.), for example, had a patient[1] who was distressed because her husband was seeking a divorce. She jumped from a seventh floor window in an apartment building and landed on her feet. The patient survived, but her life was profoundly and permanently changed. After a prolonged recovery from

---

[1]Certain details of the report of this case were changed to maintain the confidentiality of the patient. The report, however, is based on an actual experience.

her acute injuries, she required multiple surgeries and extensive physical therapy to repair her legs to the point where she could ambulate laboriously with braces and crutches. On a psychosocial level, she needed to be cared for by her parents and could never again work or live independently. The emotional impact of this nonfatal event on the clinician certainly seemed to rival that from a completed suicide (i.e., the clinician experienced acute feelings of shock, guilt, shame, inadequacy, anger, and so on, as well as longer-term thoughts and feelings about the limitations of a psychotherapist, the issues involved in suicide, and so on).

Other health professionals seem to expect that a certain number of failures or losses will inevitably occur in the process of providing patient care. Brown (1989) suggested that this objective attitude may be more difficult to adopt for the mental health clinician because he or she "brings more of herself or himself as a person to the clinical encounter" (p. 421). Of course, it can be said that the mental health clinician also gets to know more of the patient or client as a person as well. It is for these very reasons that authors such as Jones (1987) and Farberow (1993) noted that patient suicidal behavior can bring about both a personal crisis and a professional crisis for the clinician. On a personal level, the clinician comes to know the most intimate feelings of the patient and, so, may have reactions to the patient's suicidal behavior that are as intense as those of family members. On a professional level, however, the clinician may have concerns about responsibility, malpractice suits, censure from colleagues, damage to reputation, and so forth. The professional concerns often complicate and cloud the clinician's personal reactions, making it all the harder for him or her to cope. As Jones (1987) pointed out, these professional issues can lead the therapist to withdraw from colleagues and to become isolated from potential sources of support.

The treatment setting in which the clinician practices can also affect his or her efforts to cope. Both Horn (1994) and Valente (1994) noted how therapists in private practice and in some outpatient clinics can be relatively isolated and have limited access to support. Inpatient therapists, on the other hand, can feel overly scrutinized and pressured by administration to provide explanations quickly.

There have been a number of single case reports of what proved helpful to clinicians in coping with the aftermath of a patient suicide (e.g., Alexander, 1991; Berman, 1995). Other investigators have attempted to gather data from larger samples on this topic. Thus, Kleespies et al. (1990) asked former psychology interns who had had a patient suicide how they coped with such an event. Their responses could be classified under the following headings: use of support systems, contact with the patient's family, and postevent reviews. In a larger follow-up study (Kleespies et al., 1993), these categories were used in asking former psychology interns if they utilized these particular coping resources in the aftermath of a range of patient suicidal behaviors (i.e., an episode of suicidal ideation, a suicide attempt, or a suicide completion). In terms of support systems, the greatest percentage of subjects turned to their case supervisors for emotional support followed by seeking out peers, other staff members, and finally their own family or significant others. On a more cognitive level, individual postevent case reviews with supervisors were also well utilized and rated as helpful.

For the professional clinician, it seems to make intuitive sense that talking with a colleague who knows the client/patient or who has had a similar experience with a client can decrease isolation and provide support. This fact seems exemplified by a case reported by Berman (1995) in which a therapist had a patient suicide. The therapist spoke to her clinic director about the suicide and, in reference to the clinic director's remarks, she said:

> He then did the kindest thing. He told me of his own experience with patients who had committed suicide and what he had felt. I was so relieved to hear that someone I saw as my superior had not been able to avoid such a trauma. Somehow it helped relieve me somewhat of my self-reproach. Actually, in the ensuing days I was surprised to hear from a number of others who had had similar experiences. It was so generous of them and so healing for me. (p. 90)

Further supportive evidence can be found in the report of Kolodny et al. (1979), who noted how meaningful it was for four therapists to meet over the course of a year to discuss their reactions to patient suicides that each had recently experienced. Moreover, Jones (1987) described a successful self-help support group for therapist–survivors. The group provides a nonjudgmental atmosphere in which therapists can share their feelings and issues relatedto patient suicide, regardless of how recently or remotely the event ccurred.

As mentioned earlier, a postevent case review or, when there has been an actual suicide, a postmortem case conference can prove helpful in the coping process. Challenging though it may seem, such a meeting can assist the therapist in processing his or her feelings and in coming to a greater understanding of the case and of issues related to work with the suicidal patient. With patient suicides or with serious patient suicide attempts in which staff feelings can run high, clinical experience suggests that such reviews or conferences are best done some time (possibly 3–6 months) after the acute impact has receded. Given some distance from such an emotionally charged event, those involved can reexamine it with greater objectivity and benefit more from what is to be learned. Even with the lapse of time, however, the conference chairperson is well advised to be aware that sensitivities may still be heightened. In the vast majority of cases, the therapist and staff were engaged in good-faith efforts to help a very troubled individual, and their efforts need to be validated. It is best for all involved in such conferences to bear in mind that even those considered most expert in the field of mental health have yet to report any real success in predicting suicide or suicidal behavior.

Efforts made by the clinician to process his or her thoughts and feelings about a patient's suicidal behavior are likely to assist in his or her longer-term adaptation to therapeutic work, particularly with the suicidal patient. The surveys by Kleespies et al. (1990, 1993) provide data indicating that the experience of patient suicidal behavior in and of itself often leads therapists to reflect on and to change some of their existing schemas or assumptions. This is no more clearly illustrated than in the subjects' own words. Thus, for example, one of the survey participants[2] who had a patient with so-called lower-dose suicidal behavior (i.e., an episode of suicidal ideation) replied as follows to the question whether he experienced longer-lasting effects from the experience of this patient's suicidal episode:

> I learned a lot. One of the lessons was learning, or beginning to learn, to accept the power and limits of what we can do. Also (I learned) hearing from a supervisor that sometimes when we agree to work with someone like this, the patient may die. The other thing that stayed with me was a philosophical dilemma around trying to encourage people to stay alive and to ponder if for some people suicide isn't such a bad solution. I began to question my assumptions about life above everything. I became more empathic to the wish to die.

When this same question of longer-lasting effects was put to another survey subject[3] who had had an actual patient suicide, she responded:

> I think more than anything it cued me to issues of suicide with anybody whom I work with. I can't work with anyone without thinking back to his suicide. I was more sensitized by the emotional experience. The second thing I realized was a philosophical thing—people sometimes choose death. Sometimes people exercise the option not to go on living. I had known a psychiatrist. He talked about patients having a choice to live or die. At that point in my career, I was into making people feel better and I couldn't resonate with his point of view. With my patient's death, what this doctor said started to take on more meaning for me. Ultimately, people are going to make up their own minds. I had done everything that I knew to do. What started to arise for me out of this was a respect for that patient's choice. I had been with him on a long journey. He had been on a longer journey and had had many therapists. I was only one player in a larger drama. . .

Can this sort of deeper level processing be facilitated by talking with others who have had similar experiences or by reviewing the case? One would hope so, and the descriptions provided by authors such as Kolodny et al. (1979) strongly suggested it. If patient suicidal behavior provokes a crisis for the clinician, the outcome can be damaging or growth promoting and

[2]Certain details of this survey subject's report were changed to maintain confidentiality. The substance of the report, however, is accurate.
[3]Certain details of this survey subject's report were changed to maintain confidentiality. The substance of the report, however, is accurate.

maturing. Complicated reactions sometimes occur. As one of the subjects[4] in the surveys by Kleespies et al. (1990, 1993) said in reference to a patient suicide:

> I felt sad about the person. I can rationalize that this was the type of person who would eventually kill himself. I certainly don't like working with suicidal patients. I can't tell if I would have felt that anyway. I would rather avoid that responsibility entirely. I never really loved doing therapy as other people do. It's all intertwined with this event, and I can't sort it out.

To prevent damage, therapists often need to be reassured that a negative outcome to treatment does not necessarily make them a failure as a clinician (Brown, 1987a). Moreover, as Valente (1994) pointed out, they may need help in realizing that what in retrospect could have been done is not what would have been done by most clinicians or even should have been done given the circumstances at the time. Clearly, not all pain and distress that comes in the aftermath of a patient suicidal event can be or should be removed; however, processing the event in one of the ways suggested above can provide some relief and reassurance.

Clinical Sites

Although most clinical sites informally try to offer support to staff members who have a patient suicide or a serious patient suicidal event, it cannot be automatically assumed that this will be the case. Several respondents in the survey by Kleespies et al. (1993) indicated quite the opposite—that is, there was an effort to suppress discussion of the event. Rather, it would seem that clinical sites and training programs would do well to try to foster a more health-promotive environment in which clinicians feel supported in their efforts to work with and discuss difficult cases and clinical situations. Stokols (1992), taking a social ecological perspective, conceptualized such an environment as including organizational responsiveness and protective behavior. Brown (1987a, 1987b, 1989) and Kleespies (1993) called for and proposed means by which clinical training programs can be more responsive to clinicians in training who have a patient suicide. We recommend that not only training programs, but clinical sites more generally attempt to increase their responsiveness to clinicians who experience such events.

This responsiveness can take the form of a protocol for responding to clinicians who experience serious patient suicidal behaviors. Within 24 hours of a patient suicide or serious suicide attempt, the director of the service, clinic, or program (or someone whom he or she designates) should reach out and offer to

---

[4]Certain details of the report of this case were changed to maintain the confidentiality of the patient. The report, however, is based on an actual experience.

talk to the particular clinician. The therapist's style of coping should be respected and such a meeting should not be forced, but the therapist should know that support is available. Other clinicians who worked with the particular client or patient or who had similar experiences and are willing to share their thoughts and feelings can be encouraged to make contact with the therapist and vice versa. For those who have experienced a patient suicide, a group for therapist–survivors such as that facilitated by Jones (1987) would provide an ideal setting for processing feelings and gaining support.

In the event of a patient's suicide attempt, a meeting with the patient and his or her family or significant others can be helpful to all concerned and should be encouraged. Such a meeting may help to enlist the family in the patient's care if there is a likelihood of future risk. If there has been a client suicide, clinicians are often fearful about contacting the client's family. Brownstein (1992), however, found that most families of suicide victims wanted to be contacted by the treatment provider. If the suicide victim's family is receptive, the clinician may wish to attend the wake or funeral. Doing so may assist with the clinician's grief work. If the clinician is concerned about his or her own emotional reaction, perhaps the company of a supportive colleague might prove helpful. If the clinician encounters anger from some family members, it seems best to redirect this to a meeting at a later date and time. Whether the clinician attends the wake or funeral or not, it is often a good idea to invite family members to a meeting to discuss their loss. At such a meeting, the therapist can assess the need for postvention efforts with the family and can bring their attention to groups such as those sponsored by the Samaritans for family survivors of suicide. If family members are in need of psychotherapy, the clinician can make referrals.

Once the acute impact has subsided, the clinic or agency director should approach the therapist to discuss the possibility of a postevent or postmortem conference. As noted earlier, those who have been able to get beyond their anxiety and have participated in such conferences have found them helpful in processing further the issues raised by the case (Kleespies et al., 1993). It is important that the chairperson of such a conference have experience with this sort of review. Because of the heightened feeling around these cases, it is easy to be interpreted as being either too critical or too avoidant of analysis. As Brown (1989) stated, the chairperson needs to "steer a course between the twin dangers of participating in either a whitewash or a witchhunt" (p. 429). He also noted that this type of conference should address the following three objectives: (1) understanding why the suicide attempt or suicide occurred, (2) reviewing the quality of care provided, and (3) dealing with the impact of the event on the therapist and other involved staff. In the case of a suicide attempt, the conference might also address the future implications for treatment.

Finally, the director of the clinic or agency can offer to review the impact on the clinician 6 months or a year after the event. Such reviews can assist the clinician in monitoring for any longer-lasting negative effects such as undue anxiety or avoidance in working with suicidal patients. Kleespies et al. (1993)

found that the therapists in training in their study who had a patient suicide were more likely to experience anxiety when subsequently evaluating suicidal patients. More pathological reactions such as depression, extreme efforts at atonement, or persistent distortion were discussed by Maltsberger (1992). Should such reactions occur, the clinician should be encouraged to enter psychotherapy.

Fortunately, the more extreme reactions noted occur with relative infrequency. Rather, as both Brown (1987b) and Kleespies et al. (1990) indicated, most clinicians seem to resolve the crises associated with patient suicidal behavior in a growth-enhancing way, on both the personal and the professional level. With good academic and clinical preparation, and with a supportive and health-promoting work environment, those who deal with the suicidal patient can, as Foster (1987) maintains, look into the darkness, struggle with the feelings it evokes, and emerge as deeper and more thoughtful therapists.

ACKNOWLEDGMENT

We wish to thank Karen Krinsley, PhD, for her thoughtful review of this chapter.

REFERENCES

Alexander, V. (1991). *Words I never thought to speak: Stories of life in the wake of suicide.* New York: Lexington Books.

Berman, A. (1995). "To engrave herself on all our memories; to force her body into our lives": The impact of suicide on psychotherapists. In B. Mishara (Ed.), *The impact of suicide* (pp. 85–99). New York: Springer.

Bongar, B., & Harmatz, M. (1991). Clinical psychology graduate education in the study of suicide: Availability, resources, and importance. *Suicide and Life-Threatening Behavior, 21,* 231–244.

Brown, H. N. (1987a). The impact of suicide on therapist in training. *Comprehensive Psychiatry, 28,* 101–112.

Brown, H. N. (1987b). Patient suicide during residency training (1): Incidence, implications, and program response. *Journal of Psychiatric Education, 11,* 201–216.

Brown, H. (1989). Patient suicide and therapists in training. In D. Jacobs & H. Brown (Eds.), *Suicide: Understanding and responding* (pp. 415–434. Madison, CT: International Universities Press.

Brownstein, M. (1992). Contacting the family after a suicide. *Canadian Journal of Psychiatry, 37,* 208–212.

Chemtob, C., Bauer, G., Hamada, R., Pelowski, S., & Muraoka, M. (1989). Patient suicide: Occupational hazard for psychologists and psychiatrists. *Professional Psychology: Research and Practice, 20(5),* 294–300.

Chemtob, C., Hamada, R., Bauer, G., Kinney, B., & Torigoe, R. (1988). Patients' suicides: Frequency and impact on psychiatrists. *American Journal of Psychiatry, 145(2),* 224–228.

Chemtob, C., Hamada, R., Bauer, G., Torigoe, R., & Kinney, B. (1988). Patient suicide: Frequency and impact on psychologists. *Professional Psychology: Research and Practice, 19*(4), 416–420.

Dunne, E., McIntosh, J., & Dunne-Maxim, K. (Eds.). (1987). *Suicide and its aftermath: Understanding and counseling survivors.* New York: Norton.

Epstein, S. (1991). The self-concept, the traumatic neurosis, and the structure of personality. In D. Ozer, J. M. Healy, Jr., & A. J. Stewart (Eds.), *Perspectives in personality* (Vol. 3, Part A, pp. 63–98). London: Jessica Kingsley.

Farberow, N. (1993). Bereavement after suicide. In A. Leenaars, A. Berman, P. Cantor, R. Litman, & R. Maris (Eds.), *Suicidology: Essays in honor of Edwin S. Shneidman* (pp. 337–345). Northvale, NJ: Jason Aronson.

Foster, B. (1987). Suicide and the impact on the therapist. In D. Schwartz, J. Sacsteder, & Y. Akabane (Eds.), *Attachment and the therapeutic process* (pp. 197–204). Madison, CT: International Universities Press.

Horn, P. J. (1994). Therapists' psychological adaptation to client suicide. *Psychotherapy, 31*(1), 190–195.

Horowitz, M., Wilner, N., & Alvarez, W. (1979). Impact of Event Scale: A measure of subjective stress. *Psychosomatic Medicine, 41,* 209–218.

Janoff-Bulman, R. (1992). *Shattered assumptions.* New York: Free Press.

Jones, F. A. (1987). Therapists as survivors of client suicide. In E. Dunne, J. McIntosh, & K. Dunne-Maxim (Eds.), *Suicide and its aftermath: Understanding and counseling survivors* (pp. 126–141). New York: Norton.

Kahne, M. (1968). Suicide among patients in mental hospitals: A study of the psychiatrists who conducted their psychotherapy. *Psychiatry, 31,* 32–43.

Kleespies, P. (1993). The stress of patient suicidal behavior: Implications for interns and training programs in psychology. *Professional Psychology: Research and Practice, 24*(4), 477–482.

Kleespies, P., Penk, W., & Forsyth J. (1993). The stress of patient suicidal behavior during clinical training: Incidence, impact, and recovery. *Professional Psychology: Research and Practice, 24*(3), 293–303.

Kleespies, P., Smith, M., & Becker, B. (1990). Psychology interns as patient suicide survivors: Incidence, impact, and recovery. *Professional Psychology: Research and Practice, 21*(4), 257–263.

Kolodny, S., Binder, R., Bronstein, A., & Friend, R. (1979). The working through of patients' suicides by four therapists. *Suicide and Life-Threatening Behavior, 9,* 33–46.

Maltsberger, J. T. (1992). The implications of patient suicide for the surviving therapist. In D. Jacobs (Ed.), *Suicide and clinical practice* (pp. 169–182). Washington, DC: American Psychiatric Press.

McCann, L., & Pearlman, L. A. (1990). Vicarious traumatization: A framework for understanding the psychological effects of working with victims. *Journal of Traumatic Stress, 3*(1), 131–149.

McCann, I. L., Sakheim, D. K., & Abrahamson, D. J. (1988). Trauma and victimization: A model of psychological adaptation. *Counseling Psychologist, 16*(4), 531–594.

Melchiode, G. (1980). The suicide call—An affective learning experience. *The Journal of Psychiatric Education, 4,* 52–56.

Piaget, J. (1954). *The construction of reality in the child.* New York: Basic Books.

Pope, K., & Tabachnick, B. (1993). Therapists' anger, hate, fear, and sexual feelings: National survey of therapist responses, client characteristics, critical events, formal complaints, and training. *Professional Psychology: Research and Practice, 24*(2), 142–152.

Rodolfa, E., Kraft, W., & Reilley, R. (1988). Stressors of professionals and trainees at APA-approved counseling and VA medical center internship sites. *Professional Psychology: Research and Practice, 19*, 43–49.

Rosen, D. (1974). *Mental stresses in residency training and opportunities for prevention.* Paper presented at the 12th annual meeting of the American Psychiatric Association, Detroit.

Schnur, D., & Levin, E. (1985). The impact of successfully completed suicides on psychiatric residents. *Journal of Psychiatric Education, 9*, 127–136.

Stokols, D. (1992). Establishing and maintaining healthy environments: Towards a social ecology of Health promotion. *American Psychologist, 47*, 6–22.

Tanney, B. (1995). After a suicide: A helper's handbook. In B. Mishara (Ed.), *The impact of suicide* (pp. 100–120). New York: Springer.

Valente, S. (1994). Psychotherapist reaction to the suicide of a patient. *American Journal of Orthopsychiatry, 64*(4), 614–621.

Zilberg, N., Weiss, D., & Horowitz, M. (1982). Impact of Event Scale: A cross validation study and some empirical evidence supporting a conceptual model of stress response syndromes. *Journal of Consulting and Clinical Psychology, 50*, 407–414.

CHAPTER 18

THE STRESS OF VIOLENT BEHAVIOR FOR THE CLINICIAN

JAMES D. GUY
JOAN LAIDIG BRADY

Few challenges facing psychotherapists today are more upsetting and destabilizing than the possibility of patient attack. In recent years the media has documented several unfortunate episodes of violence directed at mental health professionals who were attacked by the very individuals that they were trying to help. It is hard to understand why these tragedies occur, and there is relatively little information available regarding the etiology, frequency, and outcomes of such events. Worse yet, there has been relatively little help available to those psychotherapists who were victims of patient violence. Most were left confused, frightened, and discouraged in the aftermath, surrounded by a sense of isolation, shame, and loneliness that made it difficult or impossible to discuss the episode with colleagues and friends.

Fortunately, increased interest in this topic led to new research regarding characteristics of the typical victim, assailant, cause, and consequences of patient attacks on psychotherapists. This chapter summarizes these findings and provides suggestions for addressing this issue during the training years and over the course of a career in clinical practice.

INCIDENCE AND IMPACT OF PATIENT ATTACK

Incidence

Because of the subjectivity involved in determining what actually constitutes a patient attack on a mental health professional, estimates of frequency vary widely.

398

Early studies suggested that attacks on psychologists, social workers, psychiatrists, and psychiatric nurses were relatively rare. For example, an early study of patient violence directed at the professional staff of Bellevue Psychiatric Hospital found that the number of attacks over a 5-year period ranged from 50 to 125 annually, a low frequency given the large number of patients who passed through the emergency units each day (Kalogerakis, 1971). Bernstein (1981) found that although 32% of the psychologists, social workers, psychiatrists, and marriage and family therapists surveyed had been threatened by patients, fewer than 10% were ever attacked.

More recent studies have suggested that the frequency of violence directed at clinicians is either greater than was once believed or is increasing. Tryon (1986) reported that 81% of those surveyed had experienced some sort of patient harassment, such as verbal abuse and threats. Although only 12% of those in private practice were ever attacked, more than 24% of those working in hospitals and clinics were victims of patient violence at some point in their careers. More alarming, Guy, Brown, and Poelstra (1990) found that 40% in a national sample of psychologists in clinical practice had been attacked at least once. In a more recent replication, 21% reported having been attacked by patients during their professional practice (Brown, Guy, Poelstra, & Clift, 1995). This is clearly not a rare occurrence. Instead, the frequency of violence directed at clinicians is high enough that every practitioner should be aware of its possibilities and implications.

Setting

It is commonly believed that the majority of assaultive incidents directed at clinicians occur during inpatient stays, when patients are likely to be most floridly psychotic and out of control. Indeed, the findings of Guy et al. (1990) were consistent with this expectation, with 41% of the reported attacks occurring in public psychiatric hospitals and 22% occurring in private inpatient settings. However, it is important to note that a surprising number of studies have found that clinicians in outpatient clinics and private practices are at greater risk than was once believed to be the case. Bernstein (1981) found that only 33% of the documented attacks occurred in inpatient settings, while 26% occurred in outpatient settings and 21% took place in private practice offices. Even more remarkable were the findings of Brown et al. (1995), who reported that only 28% of the attacks occurred in inpatient psychiatric settings, while the remaining 72% occurred in a variety of outpatient settings, the largest of which was private practice offices (41.6%). Given the pressure to keep inpatient stays infrequent and brief, it is logical to conclude that violence-prone patients may be confronted in any work setting. It is important that clinicians keep this possibility in mind, particularly when working alone in an isolated office.

Before moving on, it is interesting to note one curious finding recently reported. Brown et al. (1995) noted that 62% of reported attacks occurred in the afternoon, while morning hours accounted for 20% and evening hours comprised 18% of all attacks. This is counterintuitive because it is easier to picture violence occurring at night, at the end of a long day, under the cloak of darkness. Whether this finding is the result of a sampling error or indicative of the power of some intervening variable, such as might be related to scheduling or patient availability, is unknown.

Victim Characteristics

Who is most likely to get attacked? It is irresistible to attempt to bring logic and predictability to an act that is seemingly irrational and unexpected. At the outset, it must be said that anyone can become a victim of patient violence; that is the simple truth of the situation. There is a random, impulsive quality to many patient attacks that defy prediction and categorization. Yet, there are some patterns that permit a tentative description of those clinicians who are more likely to be attacked over the course of their professional careers, despite the sometimes contradictory nature of the data regarding the characteristics of both victim and perpetrator.

Although findings are mixed, it is generally believed that newer, less experienced clinicians are more likely to be attacked than veterans who have been practicing for a longer time. Madden, Lion, and Penna (1976) found that most assault incidences occurred during the training years, when clinicians had the least amount of professional experience. Guy et al. (1990) reported a similar pattern, finding that 46% of all attacks involved students and trainees, with the incidence of attack decreasing steadily as years of experience increased. A similar pattern was found by Carmel and Hunter (1991), who reported that less experienced psychiatrists were more likely to be attacked and injured by patients. Despite the fact that not everyone found a relationship between years of experience and the likelihood of patient attack (Farber, 1983), it is reasonable to conclude that the greatest risk of attack occurs during the training years. This could be a consequence of several factors. Perhaps students tolerate patient behaviors that veterans would find unacceptable, thereby setting fewer limits on clients and allowing more acting-out behaviors that result in an escalation of aggression leading to eventual violence. Students may also lack the experience necessary to anticipate, predict, and control patient behavior. It may be that students are more apt to receive their training in inpatient settings where they are assigned the most difficult, dangerous patients, increasing the possibility of becoming a victim of patient violence. It is reasonable to assume that more experienced, successful clinicians find ways to avoid working with patients who they suspect have greater potential for violence, thereby reducing their risk of patient attack.

Beyond the possible relationship between years of experience and the likelihood of patient attack, little can be said regarding the characteristics of the typical clinician who is attacked by a patient. For example, the gender of the practitioner does not appear to be an important factor. Several studies could find no difference between male and female clinicians regarding the incidence of patient violence (Guy et al., 1990; Tryon, 1986; Whitman, Armao, & Dent, 1976). However, it is interesting to note that Carmel and Hunter (1991) found that male psychiatrists were more likely to be injured by patient attacks than female psychiatrists. Langberg (1976) reported that male and female therapists were more likely to be threatened by same-sex patients than by those of their opposite sex, and both Brown et al. (1995) and Guy et al. (1990) found that male patients were more likely to attack male therapists than female therapists. Unfortunately, this does little to help us predict whether there is an overall relationship between the gender of the clinician and the likelihood of patient attack. It is also true that the age and theoretical orientation of the clinician were not reliable predictors of patient violence (Guy et al., 1990).

It must be concluded that aside from years of experience, there is as of yet no clear set of characteristics that describes the typical victim of patient violence. Any clinician is vulnerable to attack, and no demographic variable has been reliably identified as reducing the potential for becoming a victim. All practitioners must assume that they are at risk, regardless of their age, gender, theoretical orientation, or work site. Quite simply, it can happen to anyone.

Assailant Characteristics

As one would expect, there is a relationship between the severity of the mental disability and the likelihood of patient violence. Most agree that schizophrenics comprise the largest group of patient assailants. For example, Guy et al. (1990) found that 40% of those who attacked their psychologist were diagnosed as schizophrenic. Similarly, Brown et al. (1995) reported that schizophrenics constituted the largest group of patient assailants, with 31% falling into this diagnostic category. This finding was repeatedly replicated over the years (Hatti, Dubin, & Weiss, 1982; Jones, 1985; Karson & Bigelow, 1987) and can be assumed to be reliable. Patients with borderline or antisocial personality disorders were found to be the second most likely group to attack clinicians, with patients suffering from symptoms related to substance abuse, mood disorders, and organic mental disorders following close behind in likelihood of attack (Brown et al., 1995; Guy et al., 1990; Jones, 1985).

There is a strong consensus in the literature regarding the age of assailants. The majority were found to be young, between the ages of 20 and 40 years old (Annis & Baker, 1986; Brown et al., 1995; Guy et al., 1990; Karson & Bigelow, 1987). Many have speculated regarding the reasons for this well-documented pattern. Perhaps it is enough to simply state that younger patients are more likely to attack than older ones.

With the exception of one study (Edwards, Jones, Reid, & Chu, 1988), most researchers found that males are more likely to attack clinicians than are females (Brown et al., 1995; Guy et al., 1990; Hatti et al., 1982; Star, 1984; Tryon, 1986). In fact, Brown et al. (1995) reported that males comprised 72% of the identified assailants, while Guy et al. (1990) found that males represented 74% of the reported assailants. Regardless of whether there is a relationship between gender and the decision to seek inpatient or outpatient treatment, males are clearly more likely to direct violence at clinicians.

The findings regarding assailant characteristics lead us to conclude that although any patient has the potential to direct violence at a mental health professional, there is a greater likelihood for violence among those who are younger, male, and seriously emotionally disturbed—such as would be the case with a schizophrenic. Such individuals may be more likely to act out their aggression in an impulsive, unexpected manner, leading either intentionally or unintentionally to an actual physical attack on a mental health professional.

Weapons Used

When trying to imagine a patient attack on a clinician, it is not unusual for most people to picture a gun. Indeed, there certainly are documented cases involving the shooting of a psychotherapist by his or her client. Because of their dramatic nature, such unfortunate episodes quickly appear on television and in the printed media. In reality, such events are rare. Most attacks occur without involving any weapon or instrument whatsoever. Violent patients typically use their own bodies to hit, bite, kick, scratch, or choke the therapist (Bernstein, 1981; Guy et al., 1990; Hatti et al., 1982; Madden et al., 1976). When a physical object is used in the attack, it will most likely be something readily available in the consultation office, such as chairs, ashtrays, phones, bookends, books, and decorative accessories (Bernstein, 1981; Guy et al., 1990). This suggests that the acts of violence tend to be impulsive and spontaneous rather than premeditated and well planned. It is rare that an assailant will actually bring a weapon when meeting with a clinician. Although this would most obviously be the case in inpatient settings, it is also largely true in outpatient settings. However, when a patient does bring a weapon with the intent of attacking a clinician, it is most often a gun (24%) or a knife (11%) (Hatti et al., 1976). It goes without saying that a clinician should refuse to meet with a patient who is carrying a weapon. Moreover, these findings suggest that a psychotherapist should give consideration to avoiding objects that could become potential weapons when decorating his or her office.

Physical Harm

It is difficult to get an accurate picture of the severity of physical injury resulting from patient attacks on clinicians. Few studies do an adequate job of documenting the extent of harm that has been done. Certainly, there are cases in which a practitioner was murdered or badly injured by a current or former patient. Such tragedies are beyond comprehension or explanation. It is indeed fortunate that most attacks result in little or no physical injury for the psychotherapist. For example, Guy et al. (1990) found that only 30% of those attacked suffered any bodily injury whatsoever, and only 10% categorized their injury as "moderately" severe. No one reported a serious injury. There was no relationship between severity of injury and the gender of the clinician. A similar finding was reported by Brown et al. (1995). It would seem that few patients actually intend to hurt the clinician, and, as a result, few are actually injured. As mentioned previously, these acts of violence appear to be impulsive, spontaneous reactions that occur in the moment rather than premeditated, carefully planned conspiracies intended to accomplish a complicated outcome. As noted by Brown et al. (1995), clinicians who were victims of patient violence reported that most attacks were intended by the patient to either frighten the therapist (29%), release pent-up emotion (19%), get revenge after being upset with the therapist (17%), or manipulate the practitioner (13%). Only 17% of those attacked thought that the patient actually intended to cause injury, and only 2% believed that the client intended to kill them.

Emotional Distress

Far more problematic than physical injury is the emotional harm that may result from patient violence. The emotional consequences of a patient attack are quite complex and enduring. Frankly, the emotional distress that often results is more severe and harmful than the typical physical injury. The symptoms can involve an array of problems that undermine the stability and comfort of the clinician for months or even years.

Perhaps the most troubling emotional consequence is the assault that it represents on the practitioner's sense of safety. To come into such close contact with severe emotional distress and pain requires, at least at some level, the belief that the clinician will be invulnerable to the chaos and torment of the patient's inner world. Certainly, most would not expect to be physically attacked by the very person that he or she is trying to help! Perhaps there is a certain denial that allows psychotherapists to join their clients on such a perilous and intimate journey.

Whatever allows the practitioner to feel safe is shattered when a physical attack occurs, leaving the professional all too keenly aware of the true danger of the situation. Practitioners can be overwhelmed by an increased fear of future attacks and the risk of future physical harm to themselves or loved ones and damage to their home and personal property (Guy, Brown, & Poelstra, 1992). Indeed, this is the most frequently reported emotional consequence of being a victim of patient attack. Of those reporting one or more episodes of patient violence, Guy, Brown, and Poelstra (1991) found that 40% experienced a dramatically increased sense of vulnerability in the aftermath of an attack. The greater the extent of the resulting physical injury, the greater was the sense of fear and vulnerability that followed. It is as though such episodes prove that clinicians who work with dangerous patients are, in reality, doing so at some risk to their own health and safety. The unspoken social contract that protects the "helper" from harm is shattered in a moment of patient violence, and the clinician is left with an intense sense of vulnerability and fear.

Several other symptoms of emotional distress typically accompany this feeling of sensitivity and vulnerability. Guy et al. (1991) found that some victims reported a marked decrease in overall emotional well-being (16%) and sense of professional competency (14%), while others reported an increase in the concern of their loved ones for their safety (16%). Other consequences, reported less frequently, included marital and family discord, decreased motivation for work, and an increase in nightmares. Caldwell (1992) found that many of those who had been attacked or witnessed such an event suffered later from symptoms related to posttraumatic stress disorder, with a heightened sense of apprehension accompanied by a wide array of such emotional symptoms as fear, anxiety, paranoia, and depression and such physical symptoms as motor tension, autonomic hyperactivity, nightmares, flashbacks, and sleep disturbance.

One of the puzzling emotional consequences of patient attack is the resulting sense of personal responsibility reported by the victims. Despite the nearly unpredictable nature of patient violence, Guy et al. (1991) found that 39% of those clinicians who had been attacked reported that, in retrospect, the attack could have been predicted. Furthermore, 30% indicated that the violent episode could have been avoided and dealt with in a more helpful manner. This finding is consistent with previous research (Bernstein, 1981; Hatti et al., 1982). Clearly, such a belief serves to heighten the practitioner's feelings of guilt and regret. By placing too much confidence in their powers to predict and prevent such behaviors, these clinicians tend to attribute patient violence to therapeutic error or personal incompetence. The shame and sense of failure that result are a huge burden for the practitioner to carry, often alone without the support of others.

Interestingly, the heightened concern about professional competency has been found to be related to theoretical orientation. Guy et al. (1991) found that those who identified themselves as "behavioral" were most likely to doubt their professional competency following a patient attack, whereas humanistic psychologists were least likely to come to that conclusion. It appears that those who expect to be able to control the behavior of their patients conclude that acts of violence against themselves are ultimately a result of their own incompetence.

Because many of the victims of patient attacks are trainees or students, it is easy to imagine how such episodes increase the sense of incompetence and shame experienced by such individuals during these formative years. It is unfortunate that clinicians-in-training, who are already so vulnerable to self-doubt and self-criticism, should have to cope with the sense of failure and incompetence that seems to follow episodes of patient violence. When combined with the emotional turmoil inherent in being a graduate student, such as financial hardship, academic pressures, fear of the unknown, and loss of a prior support network, the emotional impact of a patient attack on the well-being of the trainee may be completely overwhelming and debilitating.

One cannot help but note another important emotional consequence of an act of violence directed at a mental health professional. Reviewing research results and clinical vignettes in the literature leaves one feeling that one of the most troublesome consequences may be denial. The tendency for clinician victims to minimize or ignore the impact of a patient attack may sometimes reach significant proportions. Such individuals may go to great lengths to reassure family and friends, as well as their patient assailant, that the attack was of little consequence and will soon be forgotten. They underestimate the seriousness of their physical injuries, emotional consequences, and general distress. It is also likely that they do not appreciate or understand the anguish that results for friends and family following the violent episode. Such individuals may return to work prematurely and take on even more difficult cases in an attempt to prove their clinical ability or exonerate themselves from blame for the past episode. Worse still, some will not discuss the attack with anyone, opting to cope with the impact of the event privately, even secretly. This silence is not motivated by the ethical constraints that prevent the disclosure of confidential material. It goes well beyond these limitations to include self-disclosure of the fear, pain, and regret that would normally accompany a traumatic event of this nature. The silence becomes complete, locking the victim in a world that denies the reality of what has occurred.

Denial of this magnitude may result from an inability to deal with the realization that their work is indeed dangerous, they have little control over patient behaviors, it is impossible to guarantee personal safety, and there is a limit to one's professional competence. Denial becomes a coping mechanism intended to help the clinician to continue unaffected by the trauma associated with the act of violence. It is also possible that this kind of denial belies a deeper, more subtle grandiosity that allows the clinician to believe that he or she is always "in control" of every clinical situation. Those trapped in maintaining this image of omnipotence will find it necessary to deny the true impact of a patient attack on their emotional well-being.

Other Clinician Responses

One researcher found that the most immediate reaction to a patient attack was typically to attempt to restrain the patient at the moment of attack (Guy et al., 1990). This natural self-protective response at times included actual physical violence on the part of the clinician, although this was rare and was limited in magnitude to a level necessary to protect the safety of the psychotherapist. For the most part, clinicians merely tried to end the patient attacks as quickly as possible. There was no report of physical retaliation. Although most clinicians handled the episode themselves, in private, occasionally it was necessary to summon the help of an office mate or a nearby colleague. Law enforcement officers were almost never contacted.

Once the immediate danger passed, most clinicians felt the need to discuss the episode with a supervisor or colleague (Guy et al., 1990). By talking over what happened, it seems that there was an opportunity for important reality testing, emotional catharsis, soliciting of support, and debriefing. Unfortunately, there was a tendency for some victims to be quite secretive about such events, causing them to avoid discussing the incidents with anyone else.

Because episodes of patient violence may require that the clinician use physical restraint or aggression in self-defense, it is not unusual for the practitioner to face weeks, months, or years of lingering fear concerning eventual litigation or malpractice claims (Guy et al., 1990). Because there is a natural tendency to feel responsible for the episode, it is easy to imagine that such individuals are concerned that they will have to take full responsibility for the entire affair, even if it were to involve a financial award to the patient or sanction by a licensing board or ethics committee. Although the reality is that few patients file complaints or lawsuits against clinicians who they have physically attacked, for all kinds of obvious reasons, it is nonetheless true that such fears are common among those who have been attacked.

As noted previously, some clinicians feel a decrease in their motivation to work following a patient attack, particularly those who were attacked on more than one occasion. It is logical to assume that the realization that continued practice involves ongoing risk to personal health and safety reduces the desire to work with patients. However, it is interesting to note that few psychotherapists reduced their workload following an episode of patient violence (Guy et al., 1991). It seems as though most continued to work as before, even while noting a decrease in motivation to do so.

Regardless of the tendency to maintain a consistent workload following an act of violence, it cannot actually be said that victims carried on "business as usual." Instead, those who were attacked coped with the common experience of an increased sense of vulnerability by taking steps to increase their sense of personal safety. First of all, 25% of those attacked reported that they immediately transferred the assailant to another clinician (Guy et al., 1990). If the patient refused to accept the referral, the practitioner terminated treatment at that point. The remaining victims who elected to continue treatment after the attack no doubt decided that the event was insignificant in importance or severity, or they were reassured that they would be able to predict and prevent such an occurrence in the future. Having said that, it is interesting to speculate whether a clinician electing to continue to treat an assailant might be tempted to become overly solicitous to client whims, wishes, and demands to prevent another attack in the future. This kind of "masochistic submission" response could subtly undermine the integrity of the treatment. Perhaps there would also be a tendency to use "chemical restraints" in an aggressive fashion, medicating the assailant into submission. Clearly, such reactions would occur at an unconscious level, if at all. Yet, they would certainly be understandable and worth noting.

The most common protective measure used by clinicians who were previously attacked was the refusal to accept certain patients who now presented themselves for treatment, particularly in the case of female practitioners (Guy et al., 1992; Tryon, 1986). This was especially true among those clinicians who believed that they could have predicted and/or prevented previous episodes of patient violence that they had experienced in years past; they apparently tried even harder to identify and avoid potentially violent patients who they saw at a later time. Victims seemed much more concerned about the potential of future violence when conducting intake evaluations. Rather than see potentially violent patients themselves, they were much more likely to refer such individuals to others. One can only hope that such referrals would not include trainees or students. Actually, such findings leave us wondering just who these clinicians selected to see patients who represented too great a risk for them to see themselves.

It must be noted that Tryon (1986) found that 60% of those who had been victims of patient aggression did not become more selective when evaluating future patients. Guy et al. (1992) report the same phenomenon, noting that 75% insisted that they did not become more selective of future clients following a patient attack. This puzzling finding suggests that either these individuals were satisfied with their predictive skills and regarded the previous attack as an anomaly not likely to reoccur or they were convinced that it is impossible to accurately identify future attackers—so why bother. Perhaps there is also some denial on the part of these practitioners who insist that the behavior of patients has so little impact on future clinical decisions and work.

As a result of the heightened sense of vulnerability and fear experienced by clinicians following a patient attack, it is not surprising to find an increased concern with overall safety of self and loved ones. Therapist victims were typically more aggressive about implementing protective measures to reduce personal risk following a patient attack (Guy et al., 1992). The greater the number of previous attacks, the more likely the clinician was to take specific steps to increase personal safety. For example, those attacked most often were also most likely to obtain special training for the management of assaultive patient behaviors. They were also more likely to discuss safety issues with their loved ones and develop a specific plan for protecting their safety. Victims were less likely to list their home address in the local telephone directory, and they set firmer boundaries to prevent patients from appearing at their private residence. As one would hope, clinicians who were previously attacked were more likely to formulate a contingency plan for obtaining assistance in the event of another attack in the future. Other safety measures used by victims of past patient violence included relocating to a "safer" building, specifying intolerable patient behaviors at the outset of treatment, avoiding working alone in the office, hiring a secretary, installing a home and/or office security alarm, and obtaining a weapon.

Understandably, as reflected in the protective measures mentioned in the previous paragraph, increased fear for the safety of loved ones can result from the aftermath of a patient attack (Guy et al., 1991). Not only must clinicians face the reality of their inability to guarantee personal safety, but they must now also deal with the fact that they cannot guarantee the safety of friends and family. This reality increases the fears of everyone involved. Family and friends become more concerned about the likelihood of a future attack on the clinician, and he or she becomes more concerned about protecting loved ones. This cycle results in a coordinated effort to take as many reasonable steps as possible to protect all concerned, and there is a often a general consensus on those safety measures that will help the most without creating unnecessary restrictions and inconveniences themselves (Guy et al., 1992).

Finally, some victims of patient violence obtain supervision or consultation from respected colleagues to work through the practice issues involved in dealing with the aftermath, prevent a reoccurrence, pursue their own personal psychotherapy to cope with the emotional consequences of the attack, and seek the advice and support of friends and close colleagues to address subtle doubts about professional competency and clinical skill (Guy et al., 1991). Such steps reflect a realization that initiative must be taken to ensure the well-being of the clinician to allow for a complete and satisfactory resolution of the trauma that is inherent in such a dramatic event.

Summary

Clinicians are attacked by patients with surprising frequency, regardless of work site, gender, age, or theoretical orientation. Although we have some information about the typical assailant, little can be said to identify a likely victim. Quite simply, any clinician can be attacked by a patient at any time. Although this seems obvious now, until recently this fact was relatively unknown. Some may want to conclude that there has actually been an increase in the frequency of attacks on mental health practitioners, as a result of de-institutionalization and decreased use of "chemical restraints." Others suggest that the higher reported incidence reflects better research on this issue in recent years, as well as greater openness among clinicians who are now more willing to admit their limitations and inability to control patient behaviors. Regardless of the conclusion, it must be said that every clinician must accept the possibility that he or she may be attacked at some point.

Although patient violence directed at mental health professionals can result in death or severe injury, most attacks do not seriously harm the clinician. In fact, if psychotherapist self-reports are to be believed, most attacks do not result in any physical injury whatsoever. On the other hand, it does appear that there are often serious consequences to the emotional health and well-being of the practitioner following a patient attack. There is an erosion of confidence, an increase in feelings of vulnerability and fear, and at times the onset of a profound sense of guilt and shame. Denial often complicates the process of recovery, and this makes it more difficult for the clinician to appreciate the full impact of the violent episode and invite the assistance of others in promoting healthy resolution of the trauma.

Despite a tendency to minimize the severity of the physical and emotional consequences of a patient attack, no practitioner cares to have a reoccurrence. As a result, many victims take specific measures to reduce the chance of future violence by transferring the assailant to someone else, becoming more selective when evaluating potential clients, developing specific plans for how to summon help or cope with potential attack in the future, and taking steps to make their office or work site generally more safe. This is especially true for those who have been attacked more than once. There seems to be a general realization that the possibility of physical violence is a reality that must be addressed rather than repeatedly denied. This realization often extends to a discussion with loved ones about their safety, as all concerned work together to reduce the possibility of patient violence directed at them in the future.

ADDRESSING VIOLENCE IN CLINICAL PRACTICE

The unique dynamics and relative infrequency of patient attacks on clinicians make it unnecessary to assume a posture of paranoia or fear. Instead, it seems most appropriate to develop a healthy respect for the possibility of patient violence in clinical work so that informed decisions can be made by the psychotherapists to effectively prevent, manage, and/or cope with physical aggression in everyday work.

Prevention

Let us begin by considering perhaps the most important means of addressing the likelihood of patient violence. All possible steps must be taken to prevent violence in the first place. For example, by heightening the awareness of clinicians in practice to the potential for patients to become violent, there is a greater possibility of effectively assessing the likelihood of violence before it occurs. Familiarizing themselves with the growing body of literature regarding the prediction of violent behavior will help practitioners to correctly identify relevant factors that increase the possibility of attack (e.g., episodes of previous violence, degree of social isolation, and level of current stress). This familiarity will also increase clinical and intuitive sensitivity to the warning signs of increased agitation, decreased frustration tolerance, increased hostility, and increased angry or threatening verbalizations. Training and experience make it easier for the clinician to understand inner conflicts and feelings of threat that promote violence, while enabling him or her to remain objective and protective of the client's self-esteem in a way that reduces the likelihood of aggressive acting out. Clinicians who know themselves at a deep level will be better able to stay in tune with their own inner reactions or countertransferences, thereby using their personal emotional reactions as a means of assessing potential danger in the clinical situation while enabling them to avoid inadvertently communicating something to their client that unintentionally increases the chance of violence.

Clinicians who are sensitive to the potential for patient violence will be less likely to tolerate aggressive, unacceptable behaviors and will set firmer limits intended to keep the patient from gaining momentum toward eventual violence. They will also be less likely to give out personal data such as home phone number and address, names and ages of family members, schedule of activities away from the office, and personal details regarding vacations and holiday festivities. Thoughtful clinicians will likely develop effective contingency plans for handling patient phone calls or appearances at their home or at places away from the office—in short, plans for how to handle "stalking" behavior will be formulated well in advance of their need. Although such steps will not prevent all acts of violence, they will help to reduce the likelihood of future patient attacks in some cases.

A number of steps can be taken at the office or work site to further reduce the possibility of patient violence. First, it may be wise to avoid conducting initial interviews or intake evaluations when alone in the office, suite, or building. Instead, the careful clinician may decide to schedule meetings with new patients at times of "high traffic" while taking steps to avoid seeing them in the evening, when few colleagues or tenants are nearby. When seeing an unknown patient, whenever possible it is helpful to contact the referral source and/or obtain psychological testing and records to evaluate for potential violence prior to the intake session or the start of treatment. This information enables the practitioner to get a reading on the present level of aggression, impulse control, and reality testing as well as reveals past episodes of violence. Some also suggest that creating a physical "buffer space" that allows both the patient and the clinician to exit the room easily is a helpful way to reduce the chance of a physical confrontation.

When working with an ongoing patient for whom there is some question of violence, it is best to avoid working alone in the office or building with this individual. It may be necessary to leave the door to the consultation room slightly ajar while placing the seats in a fashion that ensures an easy escape for both patient and clinician. It may be appropriate to remove potential weapons from sight, such as paperweights, letter openers, fountain pens, and so on. All sharp and heavy objects cannot be removed. However, a bit of reflection and forethought could eliminate objects that become simply too convenient to resist. If possible, it may be wise to work with a cotherapist or colleague present during the session. Using group therapy is another way to avoid being alone with a potentially violent patient. Obtaining supervision or seeking specialized consultation can be a great help and comfort while attempting to determine the appropriate diagnosis and formulate the most effective treatment plan to reduce the likelihood of violence and also to permit the most efficacious and least restrictive intervention possible.

Although expert assessment, correct identification, and effective containment go a long way to reduce the likelihood of patient violence, students and trainees continue to be at particular risk of becoming victims of attack. Not only are they least capable of adequate assessment, identification, and containment of physically aggressive patients, but they are often assigned the most disturbed patients who are inherently more likely to be dangerous. Perhaps one way to reduce the chance of patient violence would be to assign healthier clients to less experienced trainees while reserving the most disturbed and potentially dangerous individuals for senior clinicians. Although admittedly idealistic and unlikely to occur on some situations, following this recommendation would certainly help to protect our most vulnerable colleagues from potential harm. At the very least, it is imperative that supervisors of clinical trainees be cognizant of the possibility of patient attack, enabling them to anticipate the limitations of students in assessing, identifying, and containing those patients with the greatest potential for physical violence. By offering advice, support, and protection when necessary, such supervisors serve an essential function in the proper mentoring of future clinicians.

Management

Despite the best attempts to prevent acts of violence, it is nonetheless true that some patients will attack mental health professionals who are attempting to help them. Such attacks continue to be a reality, and responsible practitioners must take steps to effectively respond to such moments of potential danger. First, there must be some means available to "sound the alarm" when a patient becomes violent. Regardless of the work site or nature of the psychological evaluation or therapeutic intervention provided, a clinician must know how to summon immediate help. This is one of the most important means of effectively managing patient violence and mitigating the danger resulting from such an attack. Some may opt for expensive alarm systems; others may formulate a plan that involves a secret code word spoken over the phone or a tap on the wall that alerts others to the imminent danger. Such alarms put into motion a previously agreed upon plan for deescalating the violent situation and restraining the aggressive patient.

It is best that an intervention plan be made in advance of a crisis. It should be flexible enough to allow for the uniqueness of any given situation while clear enough to ensure quick action on the part of everyone involved. In some cases, it may involve the presentation of a weapon to be used for self-defense when an attack has begun, such as a can of mace or even a gun. More often, it may entail the use of specialized procedures obtained by receiving instruction in the management of assaultive patient behaviors or various forms of self-defense techniques. It may also include a preplanned speech intended to disarm or calm a violent patient. Although the type of plan used can vary widely from one clinician to another, a premeditated plan is essential for effectively handling this kind of emergency. Few clinicians have the ability to think clearly and act effectively at the time of attack if they have not given any advance thought to the matter.

Again, special attention must be given to enabling trainees to effectively and safely manage an episode of patient violence. Through the use of role play, dramatic reenactment, and detailed discussion, students can become familiar with the dynamics and patterns typical of these attacks. By taking away the mystery, shame, and fear that accompany consideration of this issue, trainees will be in a better position to successfully manage such a difficult episode when it occurs.

As mentioned in the "Prevention" section, it is important that steps be taken to help family and loved ones formulate a plan for managing patient violence should it touch their lives. Protecting home and family must be included in a thoughtful plan for dealing with physical attacks. Sound judgment and good conscience will guide the clinician who must consider a wide array of personal alarm and weapon systems. Perhaps it is sufficient to merely agree with a neighbor regarding a code word or signal that will prompt them to notify the police when a dangerous situation has developed.

Coping

Even after sincere attempts have been made to prevent or manage episodes of patient violence, the consequences of such an event can be truly devastating to the victim and his or her family. As discussed previously, genuine physical and emotional problems often result from a patient attack. These problems must be addressed openly and completely to ensure an uncomplicated process of recovery.

First, it is necessary for the clinician to admit to himself or herself that there has indeed been an attack. It may be appropriate to begin this process by presenting to a physician for an examination to determine the presence and extent of resultant injuries. A quick visit to the local hospital emergency room may be an appropriate way to immediately screen for possible injury following an attack.

Next, it is essential that the victim discuss the incident with an appropriate individual as soon as possible. Of course, the limits of confidentiality as outlined in both professional ethical codes and state regulations must be respected in this regard. It may mean that the victim is limited to talking through the attack with a supervisor, personal psychotherapist, appropriately recruited consultant, personal physician, or clergyperson. Discussions with family and loved ones are necessarily restricted to self-disclosures that do not in any way violate the assailant's rights to confidentiality. These limitations notwithstanding, there is a considerable amount of self-disclosure that must take place if the victim is to process the consequences and implications of the traumatic event with loved ones.

Some find it useful to seek supervision or consultation to obtain assistance with a host of practice-related concerns. A trusted colleague can help debrief regarding the clinical issues that led up to the attack, to enable the victim to sort through feelings of guilt or responsibility for the assailant's behavior. The supervisor/consultant can also assist in treatment planning for the future needs of the patient; for example, should he or she remain in treatment with the victim or should he or she be referred be made to someone else? Assistance can also be provided for addressing concerns regarding overall clinical competency, fears of future attacks, and effective management of ongoing work. The appropriate physician or psychiatrist may be contacted for help with sleep disturbance or nightmares. Consultations with a knowledgeable lawyer are helpful for evaluating legal issues regarding liability and responsibility for the attack and the management of the patient during and after the event. Visits with a personal pastor, priest, or rabbi may be helpful in addressing existential issues regarding the presence of suffering and injustice in the world. It is not unusual for clinicians to experience spiritual conflicts and questions following at patient attack, particularly when it involves harm to a loved one or family member. In short, one means of coping is for the victim to mobilize his or her personal team of experts and consultants in an effort to receive appropriate assistance and support.

As reported by Guy et al. (1991), it is not unusual for clinicians who were attacked by patients to enter or reenter personal psychotherapy following the incidence of violence. Psychological issues regarding personal vulnerability and safety are no doubt reactivated by the physical attack, making it advisable for the victim to obtain psychological help with resolving these issues in a healthy and effective manner. A talented and committed personal psychotherapist will assist the victim in understanding the issues and concerns that arise as a result of the attack, reducing the likelihood that there will be problematic "bleeding through" of these concerns into the clinician's own professional work. Furthermore, a personal therapist is perhaps in the best position to help the clinician evaluate whether the attack left him or her temporarily too impaired to carry on with his or her professional duties. In other words, it is important that the victim be evaluated to determine whether it is advisable to take a leave of absence from professional responsibilities for a time, allowing for sufficient recovery to occur before resuming the role of practitioner.

Few would deny that part of the coping with the impact of patient attack involves attending to the physical and emotional needs of family and friends. Even when they, themselves, were not involved in the actual episode of patient attack, the vicarious trauma can be quite debilitating. It is important that the clinician recognize that there are serious consequence for loved ones who have been affected by the act of violence in a more indirect but nonetheless significant way. Unless this issue is clearly addressed, loved ones may be hesitant to raise their own concerns, wishing not to divert attention from the clinician victim and to themselves. The spouse, children, family of origin, and close friends of the victim are especially vulnerable to physical symptoms of vicariously experienced posttraumatic stress disorder, such as sleep and appetite disturbance and emotional symptoms such as heightened anxiety, depression, and fear. Just as it is advisable for the clinician to seek the help and assistance of a cadre of experts in the aftermath of a patient attack, it is helpful for the victim to encourage family and close friends to do the same. Such efforts to assist loved ones inherently reduces the likelihood of the clinician withdrawing from such important sources of personal support. They also minimize the sense of abandonment experienced by those individuals who are significant in the life of the clinician, who may otherwise experience the clinician as withholding or distant. Given the tendency for the victim to minimize the impact of violent acts on family and friends (Guy et al., 1991), it is necessary to give special attention to their needs and concerns so that genuine distress is not overlooked.

The isolation and secrecy inherent in clinical practice make coping with violent acts a complex phenomenon. Physical injury plainly communicates to everyone that something frightful has occurred, regardless of how mysterious and unknown the work of the practitioner may be to loved ones and acquaintances. The evidence is there for all to see, and decisions regarding who and what to tell are an added burden in an already confusing situation. It is essential that the clinician not minimize the importance of these issues to avoid withdrawing from and denying the impact of the traumatic event. The emotional consequences, although perhaps not so obvious to others, nonetheless demonstrate to those who notice that the work of the mental health professional does include risks and hazards that at times are stressful. Despite the restrictions involved in maintaining confidentiality, the clinician victim must find appropriate and effective ways to deal with the emotional consequences of a patient attack. This requires overcoming the barriers of secrecy and mystery to reveal the vulnerability that is part of the work of the clinician. Victims of patient violence are forced to admit to others what they are hardly able to admit to themselves: Clinical practice involves risks that may lead to emotionally distressing situations with lasting negative consequences.

Summary

It is clear that mental health professionals must face the possibility of patient violence early in their careers, beginning with the training years. A number of practical steps intuitively seem likely to reduce the risk of attack, although their actual effectiveness has yet to be established by good research.

Yet, it is reassuring to believe that there are commonsense things that practitioners can do to reduce the likelihood of patient violence. This puts some control for a seemingly random act back in the hands of the clinician. At the very least, such preventive measures are worth the effort, even if they only reduce the chances of an attack by a modest amount.

It is unreasonable to hope that good preventive steps will eliminate the chances of patient violence altogether. Despite the best efforts and intentions, patients will continue to attack mental health practitioners with troubling frequency. As a result, it is important that those providing treatment to emotionally disturbed individuals formulate adequate plans for effectively managing patient attacks when they occur. Although this has yet to be established by widely known research, it is logical to believe that advance planning reduces the severity of some patient attacks, thereby reducing the lethality and extent of injury to the clinician. Certainly, effective means to summon assistance and disarm a violent patient can only help to mitigate the danger for all concerned.

Perhaps the least is known about the comparative effectiveness of the various means of coping used by most clinicians following a patient attack. Although few would argue that discussion with an appropriate colleague, supervisor, personal therapist, clergyperson, or confidant would be useful for dealing with the aftermath of a traumatic act of violence, restrictions of confidentiality and the isolation inherent in clinical work make this a complicated proposition. It is essential that the victim not be allowed to withdraw from his or her support network. A tendency to minimize the consequences of the attack must be directly and firmly confronted by a loved one or trusted friend as soon after the episode as possible. A team effort is the most effective way to help the clinician work through the array of consequences resulting from a physical attack. The more adequate the network of support, the more likely it would seem to be that the clinician victim will reach some kind of healthy closure and resolution.

CONCLUSION

Admittedly, this topic is one of the most uncomfortable and aversive imaginable. Clinicians seek to help those in distress. They make themselves emotionally and physically vulnerable to earn the trust and respect necessary to facilitate effective identification and treatment of emotional disorders. No one wants to be "on guard" when consulting with a patient. No one wants to be preoccupied with safety concerns when attempting to bring relief to someone in psychic distress. Frankly, few find it comfortable or helpful to focus on issues regarding their own health and safety when conducting intake or treatment interviews.

Devoting an entire chapter to this topic was a bold move on the part of the publisher, editor, and authors. Little has been published on this issue, and for good reason. This is an unpopular topic that makes everyone uncomfortable. Despite this fact, we have elected to include this chapter in a text on managing psychological emergencies. The reason for doing so is quite simple: Clinicians across the country are regularly attacked by patients. Given this reality, it is comforting to learn that clinicians can do specific things to reduce the likelihood of attack, manage the act of violence when it occurs, and deal effectively with the emotional and physical consequences in the aftermath.

Readers are invited to reflect on the recommendations contained in this chapter to improve their understanding and management of this issue. They are also encouraged to review this section from time to time, to refresh their memory regarding the dynamics of patient violence and useful steps for preventing, managing, and coping with physical attacks that do occur. It is our hope that doing so will reduce the likelihood of attack, at least to a limited extent, and assist the clinician victim with the recovery and resolution phases following such an unfortunate episode. It is with this goal that we have attempted to provide a comprehensive review of the literature and issues related to this topic.

REFERENCES

Annis, L. B., & Baker, C. A. (1986). A psychiatrist's murder in a mental hospital. *Hospital and Community Psychiatry, 37,* 505–506.

Bernstein, H. A. (1981). Survey of threats and assaults directed toward psychotherapists. *American Journal of Psychotherapy, 35,* 542–549.

Brown, K. B., Guy, J. D., Poelstra, P. L., & Clift, P. S. (1995). *Client assaults against therapists: Factors relating to therapist perception of assault and their relationship to subsequent impact.* Unpublished doctoral dissertation, Biola University, La Mirada, CA.

Caldwell, M. F. (1992). Incidence of PTSD among staff victims of patient violence. *Hospital and Community Psychiatry, 43,* 838–839.

Carmel, H., & Hunter, M. (1991). Psychiatrists injured by patient attack. *Bulletin of the American Academy of Psychiatry and the Law, 19,* 309–316.

Edwards, J. G., Jones, D., Reid, W. H., & Chu, C. (1988). Physical assaults in a psychiatric unit of a general hospital. *American Journal of Psychiatry, 145,* 1568–1571.

Farber, B. A. (1983). Psychotherapists' perceptions of stressful patient behavior. *Professional Psychology: Research and Practice, 14,* 697–705.

Guy, J. D., Brown, C. K., & Poelstra, P. L. (1990). Who gets attacked? A national survey of patient violence directed at psychologists in clinical practice. *Professional Psychology: Research and Practice, 21,* 493–495.

Guy, J. D., Brown, C. K., & Poelstra, P. L. (1991). Living with the aftermath: A national survey of the consequences of patient violence directed at psychotherapists. *Psychology in Private Practice, 9,* 35–44.

Guy, J. D., Brown, C. K., & Poelstra, P. L. (1992). Safety concerns and protective measures used by psychotherapists. *Professional Psychology: Research and Practice, 23,* 421–423.

Hatti, S., Dubin, W. R., & Weiss, K. J. (1982). A study of circumstances surrounding patient assaults on psychiatrists. *Hospital and Community Psychiatry, 33,* 660–661.

Jones, M. K. (1985). Patient violence: Report of 200 incidents. *Journal of Psychiatric Nursing and Mental Health Services, 23,* 12–17.

Kalogerakis, M. G. (1971). The assaultive psychiatric patient. *Psychiatric Quarterly, 45,* 372–381.

Karson, C., & Bigelow, L. B. (1987). Violent behavior in schizophrenic inpatients. *Journal of Nervous and Mental Disease, 175,* 161–164.

Langberg, R. E. (1976). Therapist avoidance of patient hostility during psychotherapy as a function of therapist and patient sex. *Dissertation Abstracts International, 36*(12), 6387B. (University Microfilms No. AAG76-12006)

Madden, D. J., Lion, J. R., & Penna, M. W. (1976). Assaults on psychiatrists by patients. *American Journal of Psychiatry, 133,* 422–425.

Star, B. (1984). Patient violence/Therapist safety. *Social Work 29,* 225–230.

Tryon, G. S. (1986). Abuse of therapist by patient: A national survey. *Professional Psychology: Research and Practice, 17,* 357–363.

Whitman, R. M., Armao, B. B., & Dent, O. B. (1976). Assault on the therapist. *American Journal of Psychiatry, 133,* 426–429.

CHAPTER 19

THE ECSTASY AND THE AGONY
The Impact of Disaster and Trauma Work on the Self of the Clinician

AMY EHRLICH CHARNEY
LAURIE ANNE PEARLMAN

Tragedy and suffering are inextricably woven into the fabric of human experience. Throughout the ages, the forces of nature wreak destruction in the forms of hurricane and flood, earthquake and fire, volcanic eruption and tornado, disease, famine, and drought. These forces bring terror to those who experience them, becoming the substance of myths and legends, superstitions, and religions as people try to integrate unfathomable events into their lives and cultures (Raphael, 1986).

Forces unique to humankind also contribute to the perils of existence—war, genocide, poverty, destruction, and pollution of the environment. In an ever more sophisticated technological society, the potential for destruction increases exponentially: There are seemingly endless possibilities for nuclear accident or industrial explosion; rail, sea, and air disasters; the collapse of structures; massive destruction by weapons of war; and the more personal tragedies arising from the widespread availability of firearms. The devastating impact of these types of events is compounded as they often affect people who may be far from home in unfamiliar places, reflect human failure or error, and occur suddenly and often without warning, taking away the illusion that we are masters of all we make (e.g., Hodgkinson & Stewart, 1991).

Finally, some losses are an inevitable aspect of the human condition—the personal pain and anguish that individuals suffer when confronted with unexpected loss, illness, violence, injury, or death. Regardless of the source, the overwhelming and often unavoidable nature of these experiences renders us temporarily helpless as control is taken out of our hands. Most often, this is the time when help is needed, before equilibrium can be restored.

In this chapter, we focus on the impact and unique challenges that disaster and trauma work impose on the self of the psychologist[1] and offer a theoretical framework for understanding how these effects, what we term "vicarious traumatization," can be transformed. Although our primary focus is on the aftermath of traumatic events such as disasters that have community impact, the concepts associated with vicarious traumatization are also applicable to clinicians who work with individual victims of violence (e.g., the victims of assault, rape, or other terrorizing behavior) (see, e.g., Pearlman & Saakvitne, 1995a).

WHAT IS A DISASTER?

Disasters, and the crises they give rise to, are traumatic events of overpowering force. They often strike with sudden swiftness and violence, affecting ordinary people who just happened to be in the wrong place at the wrong time (Hodgkinson & Stewart, 1991). All disasters, whether personal or large scale, contain the common elements of threat, urgency, and uncertainty, propelling people from the everyday routine of their lives into a world of emotional chaos and devastating loss. Perhaps the most profound loss occurs with regard to the shattering of assumptions about the predictability of life, our beliefs about safety and control that enable us to go about our daily routines in relative comfort (Janoff-Bulman, 1992). When extraordinary events occur that change the predictable sequence of our lives, it is hard to imagine that life could ever go on as before, that the pattern could be restored. When disaster strikes, lives are irrevocably altered, the fabric of everyday life torn.

Inherent in the definition of "disaster" is the notion that the forces giving rise to the event will be such that they will lead, at least temporarily, to a breach in the adaptational responses of the individual, the family, and the community, disrupting most areas of functioning as the individual tries to cope with the most basic issues of survival. Trauma is an inevitable component of disasters or crises, occurring simultaneously within the individual and the community. Erikson (1976) identifies *individual trauma* as a "blow to the psyche that breaks through one's defenses so suddenly and with such brutal force that one cannot react to it effectively"; *collective trauma* is "a blow to the basic tissues of social

---

[1]The term "psychologist" will be used throughout this chapter to denote any member of the helping profession who performs tasks in the area of disaster/crisis intervention. It is a reflection of our professional orientation, and is not meant to exclude any other discipline.

life that damages the bonds attaching people together and impairs the prevailing sense of community" (p. 110). We define psychological trauma as the experience of an event or chronic conditions, such as chronic neglect, abuse, war, or urban violence, that overwhelm the individual's ability to integrate affect and that create the experience of a threat to life or bodily integrity (Pearlman & Saakvitne, 1995a).

Disasters and crises tap into our deepest fears, setting in motion the struggle for survival and the pain and suffering that go along with it. For those who have not experienced a disaster, it is all but impossible to appreciate the enormity of the experience—the injury and/or loss of life, death of loved ones, loss of home, possessions, community, changes to the familiar environment, loss of identity and livelihood—that are too often the product of disasters. These events touch the mind, body, and soul of all who experience them. No one who participates in such an experience, including the helpers, can escape being affected by it (Hartsough & Myers, 1985; Hodgkinson & Stewart, 1991; Raphael, 1986).

ENTERING THE PHENOMENOLOGICAL WORLD OF THE SURVIVOR

It starts with a phone call or a distressing news item on television which heralds a crisis and the need to mobilize professional intervention. It may be a neighborhood fire, the accidental death of a child affecting the school community, or an employee who died of a heart attack while jogging. It may be brush fires engulfing an area, a plane crash, or the imminent landfall of a hurricane. No matter how it begins, or how large the event, it is hard not to experience a frisson of fearful anticipation—a knowing of what others must be suffering as they begin the process of survival in the wake of an event that inevitably alters their lives.

The task ahead is challenging and formidable. The goal is to restore people to adaptive functioning by helping them metabolize the flood of feelings, thoughts, fantasies, and realities that are the sequelae to disastrous events. The psychologist may help to avert long-term psychological distress by facilitating an understanding and integration of the terrible events into the fabric of their lives. There are many steps and many pitfalls that occur in this process, making the work challenging and demanding.

Disaster and crisis interventions are uniquely exhilarating and uniquely stressful for psychologists and other disaster workers. Talbot, Manton, and Dunn (1992), Hodgkinson and Stewart (1991), Raphael (1986), and others (e.g., Myers, 1994) provide detailed descriptions of the impact this work can have on professionals. We outline key concepts here.

The Urgency and Immediacy of Response

Disaster/crisis work often occurs under very stressful conditions. The psychologist may have little control over many aspects of the situation. Services must be provided in unfamiliar surroundings, often with little time for preparation and with few resources. Rapid but accurate assessments must be made to contain and stabilize the situation. Often, the sheer number of those in need and the intensity of affect they bring can be overwhelming.

Altruism and Arousal

There is an energy unique to disaster/crisis work. Although terrifying in its potential scope, danger is also thrilling. As described by Raphael (1986), the imminence of disaster/crisis generates arousal and special activities as traditional roles are relinquished and preparation for a period of intense activity begins. Psychologists and other helpers who approach this work often experience an adrenaline rush of excitement, leading to heightened arousal, sense of importance, increased alertness, potency, and impetus for action—the "ecstasy" of disaster work. Many examples of heroism, human resiliency, and human endurance are evident from survivors and workers alike in the aftermath of traumatic events.

Intensity of engagement and intimacy in relationships are products of the natural urge to help those in distress, and these special features of crisis intervention and disaster work often carry one through the intervention and beyond. The psychological energy generated by realized altruism and heightened arousal is gratifying and sustaining; the sense of oneself as powerful and even heroic can also create or enhance an energized grandiosity, often transcending the normal pace and dimensions of everyday life. These processes can also lead to overactivity and overinvolvement culminating in the responder working beyond his or her capacity ("counterdisaster syndrome" [Raphael, 1986]). Nevertheless, this energy can be hard to relinquish, and may, in fact, require special intervention to help the psychologist disengage from the work. Conversely, the postincident recognition that suffering and destruction were the occasion for this energy can lead to feelings of guilt (Raphael, 1986)—one aspect of the "agony" of this work.

The Ambiguity of the Psychologist's Role

Contrary to the therapy situation, where the client requests services from a professional, many survivors of disasters and crises are reluctant to ask for or receive help. Many believe that they should be able to "do it on their own" or are afraid of being labeled or pathologized by the "psychologist" (indeed, the literature warns against the use of titles such as "Dr." "psychologist," or "therapist," as these ways of identifying oneself often become barriers to the very support they are meant to give) (e.g., Myers, 1994). This can be frustrating, contributing to feelings of helplessness in the professional. Nevertheless, survivors need intervention of the most basic kind—the empathic connection with another human being who can bear witness and give comfort to their pain and sorrow. Within this uniquely intimate yet brief relationship, the responder must perform the tasks of normalizing the survivor's response, assessing the potential for long-term deleterious effects, and encouraging positive coping strategies. Important consideration must be given to the cultural norms of the affected individuals. Some cultures endorse "nobility through suffering." Others are vocal in their lament. The psychologist must be aware of the socially sanctioned norms for each group with which he or she works.

At times, the boundaries between the psychologist's role and those of the victims can become blurred. Victims are not always helpless or ineffectual. Psychologists are not always powerful and resourceful. In a local community disaster, the people who must treat others may themselves be survivors and victims as well. Those responding to traumatic events must be well grounded and prepared for the full range of potential responses, both from the victims and from themselves.

Countertransference Concerns

The feelings evoked in the midst of crisis are often intense and frightening. Death, injury, violence, destruction, pain, suffering and abandonment are realities for many survivors. The necessity of having to share in the survivor's experience with these realities can churn up unconscious and unresolved issues with similar themes in the psychologist's life—another aspect of the agony of disaster work. When these issues are not well metabolized, the feelings that are stirred can prompt nontherapeutic interventions such as avoidance of affectively charged material, attempts to contain or process one's own feelings through the survivor's exploration of feelings, withdrawal into more task-oriented behaviors, and increased symptomatology in the helper both during and after the intervention.

Everyone who experiences a crisis or participates in its aftermath is touched by it. One of our most valuable assets as responders is our willingness and our capacity to enter into the affective space of the victims—to join, and hold them in their loss in an effort to understand their experience and help them tolerate it. The psychologist-as-helper absorbs the emotional impact of the shattered assumptions of others as he or she empathically engages and identifies with survivors. Survivors have predictable but painful responses in the face of disaster. Those who intervene in crisis situations must both anticipate and hold these awarenesses to allow the survivors to find their way through the maze of responses that characterize the recovery process.

Preconceived ideas about how a person will navigate these dangerous waters may only inhibit or delay the exploration of feelings and thoughts that is a necessary aspect of recovery. Throughout this process of recovery work, it is easy to become overwhelmed by the magnitude of loss and one's inability to change it. Identification runs the risk of increased personal vulnerability. It is easy to feel assaulted by the awareness that the incident could have happened to oneself or a family member. All these feelings contribute to the agony of the work.

Every author writing in this field reminds us that all those who assist in disaster or crisis recovery work are human beings who have all the normal physical and psychological responses to the horror of human suffering (Hodgkinson & Stewart, 1991; Lane, 1993–1994; Mitchell, 1983; Myers, 1994; Raphael, 1986; Robinson & Mitchell, 1993; Talbot et al., 1992). A host of feelings, often paralleling the experiences of the victims, becomes possible for the treating psychologist. Anger and helplessness at the injustice of the situation and the extent of devastation, the awareness of danger to self or others, recognition that the incident could have been prevented or lessened in its severity, the pain and anguish of dealing with fatalities, the pain unique to the death of a child, and the concomitant loss of the belief that one can protect children from harm are inevitable reactions to disasters. There can be anger at the response of the media, sensationalizing the event and/or intruding on the grief of survivors. Particular increases in stress are associated with line-of-duty death of personnel, coping with multiple deaths of victims and disasters of long duration (Talbot et al., 1992), and injury to or death of children (Dyregov & Mitchell, 1992). Although the need to perform effectively may require that the psychologist hold the intense feelings associated with trauma and death in abeyance, ultimately, these feelings must be integrated into the psychologist's sense of himself or herself as a person and a professional. Failure to do so can result in disillusionment and loss of altruism as the reality of loss and permanent change sets in.

By processes of natural selection, by virtue of training, and as an adaptation to trauma, psychologists who offer their services to others in the face of disaster may be unaware of the psychological impact on them as they engage in disaster or crisis work. Rather, they may be prone to intellectualize their feelings, somewhat rigid in their thinking, and resistant to change (Talbot et al., 1992). Further, researchers find many behavioral correlates of stress among psychologists who engage in this type of work, including somatic complaints, sleep disturbance, increases in alcohol consumption, exhaustion, poor concentration, increased sensitivity to violence, experiencing family and friends as too demanding or not understanding, and expressing increased safety concerns. Talbot et al. (1992) caution that one does not "adjust" to the demands of trauma work over time; rather, one must develop ways of coping with it.

THE MANY FACES
OF THE PSYCHOLOGIST-AS-HELPER

A psychologist may serve in many capacities during a critical incident. Perhaps the most familiar role is that of *debriefer*. The debriefer's role is to normalize and educate, observe, and assess the behaviors, thoughts, and feelings that are evident among the many individuals who participate in the traumatic event. Good communication skills and knowledge of individual and group dynamics are essential for these interventions.

Debriefings may be applied to a range of individuals—groups of affected individuals, managers, emergency personnel, and/or members of the crisis team both during and after the incident. Regardless of the population, a debriefing provides a forum where people can process the myriad responses that arise throughout the hours and days following the incident and learn that their responses are normal, expectable reactions to the event.

During the debriefing process, there is an active review of all that has happened at each stage of the incident. People are asked to notice what their first thoughts, actions, and feelings were at the time of impact and immediate-ly following the event. Information is shared to clarify facts and clear up misconceptions. From this process, a sequence of events and a coherent "story" emerge. Hearing others talk about their reactions normalizes one's responses and helps define strategies for coping. This process, lasting from 1%1/2 hours to 4 hours, helps participants formulate their experience within a new cognitive framework, facilitating mastery. An especially important application of a critical incident stress debriefing is to support each crisis worker's disengagement from the survivors' experience by integrating "dissociated" emotion that has been "put on hold" (Robinson & Mitchell, 1993), that is, by providing a forum where the workers can talk about, feel, and make sense of their own experiences of helping. This process facilitates the workers' transition back into everyday functioning (Talbot et al., 1992) rather than leaving them stranded with images, stories, and feelings too painful or private to share.

In recent years, with research on the effects of such debriefings, questions were raised about their effects and effectiveness. Paton (1995) provides a thoughtful review of the literature and notes that it raises important questions about the timing and nature of debriefings as well as about who should perform this service. He points to the importance of assessing the needs of the victims and focusing attention on the unique features of each intervention, considerations that are only now arising in this work.

Participating directly in disaster interventions and serving as a debriefer during these events are the more "glamorous" roles for a psychologist, but there are numerous ways that the psychologist's skills can be utilized. These include, but are not limited to, (1) providing supervision to crisis team personnel; (2) acting as a behind-the-scenes coordinator; (3) consulting with managers, bosses, or leaders of an organization; (4) being a consultant to the emergency operations center; (5) being a consultant to community organizations involved in disaster awareness, prevention, counterdisaster, and management; (6) training emergency response teams; (7) providing aftercare groups, outreach, and follow-up; and (8) facilitating the dissemination of information to the community impacted by the crisis (Myers, 1994).

ATTRIBUTES OF THE HELPER—WHAT IS NEEDED

Crisis work often occurs under conditions of extreme difficulty. Frequently, roles and boundaries are blurred as the basic needs of survival are met. At times, it may not be clear who the leaders are or what is required. Sometimes, one hand does not know what the other hand is doing. Under these conditions, traditional beliefs and assumptions about the role of the psychologist or helper and the nature of therapy are of little use.

In crisis work, all the skills in the repertoire of the psychologist may be required to meet the numerous and varied emotional responses of the impacted individuals. Most important, we bring ourselves, oue essential humanity—an empathic, caring, and willing participant—to share in the sorrow, bear witness to the pain, shoulder the grief of those who need such help, and psychologically "carry" them until they can carry themselves. This work requires great finesse, as many survivors resist the need for interventions from others. The psychologist becomes a model from whom survivors may learn that it is possible to express feelings, to bear their vulnerability.

At times, "crisis intervention" means working under the same adverse conditions experienced by the survivors—working outdoors, in swiftly put-up shelters, in an area of devastation, under conditions of deprivation and danger, with few resources. At times, the psychologist may work alongside survivors as they dig through the rubble of their home. At times, it means accompanying individuals and families to identify their dead. At times, it means working with groups that have come through a shared disaster experience. Clearly, this work is not for everyone. Under certain circumstances, such as recent changes or bereavement in one's personal life, crisis work is contraindicated. It requires great personal resources as well as professional skills to maintain a therapeutic stance in the midst of an emotionally charged environment without becoming overinvolved, an unwitting "second victim," or without distancing from the survivors in an attempt to protect oneself from the enormity and immediacy of their pain.

Many traits are identified as being especially adaptive for crisis work. They include an essential altruism, maturity, high self-esteem, and self-control (Siporin, 1975). Raphael (1986) identifies spontaneity, an ability to tolerate ambiguity, confidence in the face of uncertainty, and the ability to adapt and move among many groups of people. Kobasa's (1979) term, "hardiness," is used (Myers, 1994) with reference to the necessary qualities for disaster responders, to indicate a strong sense of commitment, challenge, and control, with a strong and solid identity and sense of oneself as a helper. It includes a strong sense of resiliency and independence, good boundaries that allow for empathic connection, but not overidentification, with the survivor and the ability to respect the defenses of both workers and victims.

Not all those who need assistance are able to receive it. The natural response to disaster or crisis includes for many a period of shock and the resultant numbing of affect. The enormity of the situation is just too much to take in. However, survivors need to hear that reactions of shock, grief, pain, and terror are normal responses to extraordinary events. Although little emotion may be visible during the postimpact period of a crisis, many survivors need to address their feelings later on. The psychologist must be prepared, however, to tolerate rejection at times. The feelings of shame, embarrassment, helplessness, and anger can leave the psychologist feeling "deskilled" (a term Putnam, 1989, coined to refer to the experience of the therapist working with persons with dissociative identity disorder). These feelings may reflect a parallel process in the survivor. Too often, people do not seek out intervention until their symptoms have persisted many months after the event. The psychologist must be adept at offering services in a nonintrusive manner. It is flexibility in role and thought, the ability to drop professional barriers while maintaining boundaries, and the ability to assess and assist in both formal and informal situations that facilitate the acceptance of the help being offered.

TRAINING AND EXPERIENCE

The field of disaster work has grown dramatically in the past few decades, and has generated a growing literature with each crisis event. Each event becomes an opportunity for learning—what is needed to help whom, what we still need to know. It seems that there can never be enough training or experience to cover the infinite nuances of disaster and crisis work. Although there is no substitute for solid clinical training, it is nevertheless *not* sufficient *merely* to be a good clinician. The often extreme nature of these interventions demands that the psychologist have a firm theoretical grounding within a traumatology perspective and a solid understanding of grief, death, and dying issues. Those who lack the necessary background or whose altruism exceeds their psychological "preparedness" may find themselves unwitting participants in traumatizing further those they wish to help, as well as themselves.

Many important concepts are presented in the comprehensive books cited in this chapter, elaborating on the multitude of psychological and behavioral responses that are evident throughout the phases of recovery from a traumatic event. Each is replete with references to many other journal articles and books, with recommendations for disaster training. Content for training programs is listed in several publications by the National Institute of Mental Health (NIMH) (e.g., Myers, 1994; NIMH, 1978, 1987), and disaster training is offered periodically through the American Red Cross and other disaster response organizations. A specialized form of training—performing *critical incident stress debriefings*—is offered in workshop format from professionals performing these often-used interventions.

Finally, there are limitations to what can be learned from books and training. Hodgkinson and Stewart (1991) comment that training is only a "map with warning signs" and each crisis will be unique and fraught with uncertainty. Although it is harsh, "experience" is an invaluable teacher.

VICARIOUS TRAUMATIZATION IN DISASTER AND CRISIS WORK

If psychologists are to continue to function in healing capacities during times of crisis, they must heed the warnings of others: they must acknowledge the inevitability of the assault to the self and develop ways of coping with (e.g., Talbot et al., 1992) and integrating the experience. The concept of *vicarious traumatization* (VT), introduced by McCann and Pearlman (1990a) and further elaborated by Pearlman and Saakvitne (1995a, 1995b), provides a coherent and comprehensive theoretical framework for understanding the psychological impact of working with trauma survivors on the self of the psychologist. This concept is based in constructivist self development theory (CSDT; McCann & Pearlman, 1990b; Pearlman & Saakvitne, 1995a). It describes the transformation of the inner experience of the helper that comes about through empathic engagement with trauma survivors and their material, including graphic descriptions of traumatic experiences, witnessing intentional cruelty and random destruction, and both witnessing and participating in traumatic reenactments.

VT goes beyond enumerations of problems helpers may have in response to the work. The theoretical framework of CSDT guides the psychologist to areas of psychological disruption, which then in turn suggests specific interventions. The notion of VT allows for individual differences in what each helper finds problematic in the work, in the manifestations of the difficulties, and in the approaches to addressing it.

CSDT delineates areas of psychological (and thus intra- and interpersonal) functioning that can be affected by traumatic life experiences. In parallel, these same areas can be impacted, albeit less intensely, in the helper who enters empathically into the world the trauma survivor. Because they are transformations in the self, these changes are reflected in all of the trauma worker's relationships, both personal and professional. They can lead to less effective work relationships, to cynicism and withdrawal, and to numbing.

FRAME OF REFERENCE

Identity

The psychologist who is shifting roles from psychotherapist to critical incident responder is likely to experience shifts in identity. Particularly if the psychologist's professional identity is strongly built around his or her role as a therapist (or researcher or administrator), moving out of the office into the field will require a significant shift in identity. In the field, we have no diplomas on the wall, no waiting room, no aura of calm professionalism surrounding us. Rather than being respected because we bear the title of "Dr.," we may find our degrees more of a hindrance than an asset in connecting with people. This may present a unique challenge to the psychologist who must leave her or his degrees behind. How do we adjust to this new situation? How do we bring in our knowledge, our experience, and our dignity without the expectations that go hand in hand with the more formal trappings of the therapist's office?

Psychologists who are accustomed to bringing less of themselves into professional situations may find themselves at a loss doing crisis work in the field. Here our humanity is our strongest tool. (Although this may be true in the consultation room as well, our clients may feel less entitled to demand it of us.) In the field, the caring remark or warm handshake may be more significant than an informed interpretation. This is not to say we abandon our third ear upon entering the disaster site. On the contrary, crisis work requires us to retain all of our sensibilities and to respond in more immediate ways than we may be used to in our offices.

Psychologists who are accustomed to building therapeutic relationships over time, with great care and observation, may find themselves feeling less effective or less clear about how to be effective in the field. In addition, if relegated to a role of observing and debriefing the debriefers, the psychologist may find himself or herself in a strange no-person's land: without the invitation to interpret that is implicit in the therapy contract yet excluded from the immediate interaction with disaster victims that invites another kind of profound human connection. Whenever roles are shifting, ambiguous, or simply new, our identities may need to adjust.

Our training may have prepared us to believe we should be able to figure out any and all situations and to help whomever needs us, under whatever circumstances. If we can just step back far enough . . . but then, we run the risk of falling off the cliff—in this case a metaphor for losing touch with our own needs, feelings, and limitations. Disasters and emergencies challenge everyone, including responders. If we expect ourselves to be experts, to be able to work for endless hours without rest, to work without being deeply affected, we are setting ourselves up for vicarious traumatization.

World View

Participation as a helper in a disaster or crisis is invariably a major assault on one's world view. If we previously experienced the world as orderly and predictable, our schemas, or customary ways of understanding the world, may be profoundly shaken. Observing the physical chaos of a disaster site calls into question any previous illusions we may have held about controlling our surroundings. Loss, confusion, and grief may reign; everyone is an innocent victim, so "fairness" seems like a foreign concept. The inevitable shock that accompanies traumatic events must open the eyes of the psychologist (if his or her eyes were naively closed hitherto) to the possibility of some-thing disastrous happening in his or her own life or community. The loss of our own cherished views of causality (bad things do not happen to good people) can be psychologically stunning, again requiring a reorientation on our part.

Spirituality

The hallmark of psychological trauma, and, in parallel, of VT, is the disruption to spirituality. Our awareness of ephemeral aspects of experience, or our spirituality (Neumann & Pearlman, 1997), is extremely sensitive to the effects of trauma. Our personal sense of meaning and hope can and probably will be disrupted as we engage with people's despair and loss of that which they held meaningful and as we witness and connect with individuals struggling to recreate their lives.

Our sense of nonmaterial aspects of life may also be shaken as we encounter the destruction of life involved in any disaster or emergency. Many survivors and, in parallel, many responders, struggle with the question, "Where was God?" Our connection with something beyond ourselves may be deeply threatened or, for some, annihilated, by severe losses. In the face of such loss, can we feel connected to nature, to humanity, to time and timelessness?

Our spirituality may be narrowed as we are confronted with some of the most painful aspects of life. It becomes difficult, and can even feel disrespectful or absurd, to remain aware of beauty, loving relationships, and joy in the face of so much loss. Yet our awareness of all aspects of life is another aspect of our own spirituality. Does empathic responding require us to cut ourselves off from all feelings but pain? If we do, what are the consequences, for ourselves as individuals as well as for ourselves as professionals and helpers, and in turn, for our clients?

These spiritual disruptions then in turn have a recursive effect on our identities. Without our spirituality, who are we? Without our identities, we may feel cut adrift from all that is familiar, within ourselves and with others.

SELF CAPACITIES

Our self capacities are inner abilities that allow us to maintain a cohesive sense of self and self-worth over time. These include an inner sense of connection with benign others, the ability to tolerate strong affect, and the ability to maintain a positive sense of self-worth. Certainly these self capacities are compromised for disaster victims, and they can be compromised for us as responders.

The psychologist may feel disconnected from internalized mentors who surely would not understand the work he or she is now doing, disconnected from colleagues safely ensconced in their 50-minute hours back home, disconnected from family who mostly wonder when he or she will be back and why he or she has not called.

After working an intense 12-hour day, the psychologist may be numb internally, having disconnected from feelings to keep going. Or he or she may rage, driving back from the disaster site, rage at the loss, the destruction, the pain. Or, the psychologist may weep as he or she drifts into sleep, unable to hold the pain any longer.

Finally, the psychologist may find it hard to feel good about himself or herself. With so much need all around the psychologist, how much can he or she really offer? Although touched by the disaster, the psychologist has not suffered as much as the victims, which can give rise to some guilt and disconnection from those whom he or she would serve. And, can the psychologist really understand the depth of their loss?

PSYCHOLOGICAL NEEDS AND COGNITIVE SCHEMAS

CSDT identifies five central need areas that can be disrupted by psychological trauma in the survivor, and in parallel, in the trauma worker as a result of VT: safety, trust, esteem, intimacy, and control. It is only natural that, as a result of intervening in disasters and emergencies, the helper's beliefs about the safety of self and others, his or her ability to rely on others and on himself or herself, his or her esteem for self and for others, his or her sense of deep connection with self and others, and his or her sense of ability and the necessity to control his or her own and others' behaviors and rewards might shift. The loss of customary beliefs in these five areas is one we mourn as it occurs, and, at a meta-level, the disruption of familiar schemas introduces yet another assault to our identities.

ADDRESSING AND TRANSFORMING
VICARIOUS TRAUMATIZATION

VT is an inevitable aspect of trauma work that can nevertheless be transformed if we love what we do and if we are doing the work for some purpose beyond our own need for personal healing. There are many strategies for protecting ourselves from some of the effects of VT, or supporting ourselves in the work, and for transforming VT (Pearlman, 1995; Pearlman & Saakvitne, 1995a, 1995b; Saakvitne, Pearlman, & the Staff of the Traumatic Stress Institute, 1996). We present three types of strategies to address these three goals. Some of these approaches can be used during the intervention experience. Others are more appropriate or applicable afterwards.

Protecting Ourselves from Vicarious Traumatization

Work from a Theory

Working from some theoretical perspective helps protect us from the effects of VT because a theory provides guidance for effective treatment (and thus helps manage boundaries and protect against despair). Unlike lists of symptoms we might experience as a result of doing disaster interventions, a theoretical approach suggests ways we might do the work differently and support ourselves in it; it gives us hope both for our clients and for ourselves.

Don't Work Alone

It is essential to remain connected with others both during crisis and disaster work and after the intervention has passed. This may mean traveling with a colleague to and from the disaster area whenever possible and reconnecting frequently with colleagues (not only those for whom one has supervisory responsibility). It means participating in daily debriefings, getting supervision for the work, and, perhaps most often overlooked, forming a professional supportive connection for continuing to process the experience afterwards. This might mean bringing it to our usual psychotherapy supervision, talking with others who were at the site on a planned, regular basis for some time afterwards, and/ or talking about our experiences with colleagues at home to reconnect with our noncrisis identity. All these forums can facilitate the transition from intense engagement to disengagement from the trauma material.

Work within a Context

By "context" we mean a personal framework that enables us to find meaning in our lives. When we are grounded within a significant context, we are better able to integrate our experiences. A psychologically meaningful context might be the psychologist's entire professional life, his or her humanity, his or her connection with history, a connection with God or the gods, or his or her community. Context may include the awareness that many people survive disasters and create or recreate meaningful and rewarding lives.

When working with trauma, it is often helpful to bring to mind the thought that this work is one aspect of a broad professional life that includes many ways of contributing and helping others. Or, we may remind ourselves that pain and suffering are part of the human experience and bearing witness to it is an expansion of our humanity.

Addressing Vicarious Traumatization

Any activities that distract, soothe, support us, or help shore up our defenses and resources are important in addressing VT. This requires reflection on what we find interesting, distracting, or soothing. For some, it means activities like reading mysteries or listening to music. For others, it may mean engaging in craft activities as a means of distracting themselves from work, or soothing activities like lying under a tree remembering wonderful moments with loved ones. The activity is less important than the removal from the immediacy of loss, pain, and suffering.

Transforming Vicarious Traumatization

Activities that transform VT are those that address the psychological disruptions that take place as a result of the work. There are four approaches to transforming vicarious traumatization: creating meaning, challenging disrupted schemas, building community, and encouraging personal growth.

Create Meaning

Anything that allows us to discover what is meaningful in our lives and pursue it can be an antidote to VT. This may mean pursuing a spiritual path, considering how we spend our time and whether this is a true reflection of our values, or reordering priorities. It may mean infusing meaning into our usual activities. For example, the trip to work each day can be made in a dissociated fog of lists of things to do and reflections on regrets and disappointments. Or, it can be an opportunity to notice our surroundings, our physical sensations, the beauty of the morning, the strength and flexibility of our body. Mindful engagement in each moment can make the present delightfully meaningful.

Challenge Schemas

Before we can challenge disruptions to our schemas, we must first notice the cynicism, the lack of trust in our own judgment, the diminished esteem for others, or whatever toll the work has taken in each of the five need areas: safety, trust, esteem, intimacy, and control. Having done so, we can arrange modest life experiments intended to challenge these beliefs. For example, in one person, disaster work might create a self-protective need to be an expert, reflecting a disrupted self-esteem schema ("I must know what to do, when and how to do it"). A potentially transformative experiment would be to reflect on areas in our life where we are *not* an expert, and to consider that experience. In addition, the psychologist might want to create or enter a situation in which he or she is not an expert and attend to the feelings that emerge. So, for example, the psychologist might decide to take up golfing in order to have the opportunity to take lessons, learn, make mistakes, and to do something at which he or she cannot and need not attempt to excel. Finally, the psychologist might want to try acknowledging in the disaster situation that he or she does not have all the answers, that he or she is there to help the survivors reclaim their own expertise, and notice what follows, both interpersonally and intrapsychically.

Build Community

Connection with others is one of the strongest antidotes to the feelings of isolation and alienation that accompany VT. "Community" may mean family, friends, neighbors, the people who go to the gym at the same hour, or a group of professionals in our community who do trauma work. It means people who know and care about what happens to one another. Such a network can be a haven for the disaster responder, a place to go where he or she is not a psychologist (or not only a psychologist), but where he or she can be playful, spontaneous, outrageous, needy, cross, and inconsistent.

Encourage Personal Growth

A natural outcome of vicarious traumatization is the desire to shut down, to pull in and be safe. Activities that invite us to expand our self-awareness are marvelously healing. These include journal writing, yoga, creative endeavors such as drawing and painting, meditation, personal psychotherapy, and so forth. The specific nature of the activities we select or devise is far less important than an awareness of and commitment to their purpose. In fact, the same activity might be chosen by one person for escape and by another for growth. Our focus, for both psychologist and survivor alike, is primarily on meaning. By becoming and remaining aware, we can continue to do crisis intervention work effectively and with lessened negative impact on ourselves.

SUMMARY

Disaster work is compelling and demanding, often highlighting the *best* that we, as human beings, can offer one another. The resiliency of the human spirit that exists among survivors and crisis workers alike is sustaining, the feeling of esteem associated with powerfulness and intimate connections is exhilarating. The energy that propels us beyond the call of duty, the knowledge that we have helped many bear their terrible burden of pain is gratifying. The attention from the media and one's peers, family and friends can contribute to a feeling of "specialness" that is hard to relinquish (Raphael, 1986). This is the *ecstasy* of crisis work.

The reality of loss and suffering, the knowledge that lives have been irrevocably altered, and the awareness of our own limitations, that we can never undo what has been done, are painful. The long hours of work under stressful conditions and the fatigue and frustration in the face of at times insurmountable difficulties are exhausting. The images, memories, and encounters with death, reminding us of our own frailty, are haunting. The acceptance of shattered assumptions, the unpredictability of life, and the gratitude that it was not *I* or *mine* who suffered are humbling. This is the *agony* of crisis work.

ACKNOWLEDGMENT

We wish to thank John Clizbe, PhD, for comments on a draft of this chapter.

REFERENCES

Dyregov, A., & Mitchell, J. T. (1992). Work with traumatized children: Psychological effects and coping strategies. *Journal of Traumatic Stress, 5*(1), 5–17.

Erikson, K. T. (1976). *Everything in its path: Destruction of community in the Buffalo Creek Flood.* New York: Simon & Schuster.

Hartsough, D. M., & Myers, D. (1985). *Disaster work and mental health: Prevention and control of stress among workers.* Rockville, MD: National Institute of Mental Health.

Hodgkinson, P. E., & Stewart, M. (1991). *Coping with catastrophe.* New York: Routledge.

Janoff-Bulman, R. (1992). *Shattered assumptions: Towards a new psychology of trauma.* New York: Free Press.

Kobasa, S. C. (1979). Personality and resistance to illness. *American Journal of Community Psychology, 7,* 413–423.

Lane, P. (1993–1994). Critical incident stress debriefing for health care workers. *Omega, 28*(4), 301–315.

McCann, I. L., & Pearlman, L. A. (1990a). Vicarious traumatization: A contextual model for understanding the effects of trauma on helpers. *Journal of Traumatic Stress, 3*(1), 131–149.

McCann, I. L., & Pearlman, L. A. (1990b). *Psychological trauma and the adult survivor: Theory, therapy, and transformation.* New York: Brunner/Mazel.

Mitchell, J. T. (1983, March). When disaster strikes: The critical incident stress debriefing process. *Journal of Emergency Medical Services, 8,* 36–39.

Mitchell, J. T. (1988). Stress: Development and functions of a critical incident stress debriefing team. *Journal of Emergency Medical Services, 13,* 42–46.

Myers, D. (1994). *Disaster response and recovery: A handbook for mental health professionals.* Washington, DC: U.S. Department of Health and Human Services.

National Institute of Mental Health. (1978). *Field manual for human service workers in major disasters* (DHHS Publication No. ADM 90-537). Washington, DC: U.S. Government Printing Office.

National Institute of Mental Health. (1987). *Prevention and control of stress among emergency workers* (DHHS Publication No. ADM 88-1496). Washington, DC: U.S. Government Printing Office.

Neumann, D. A., & Pearlman, L. A. (1997). *Toward the development of a psychological language for spirituality.* Manuscript submitted for publication.

Paton, D. (1995). Debriefing and recovery from work-related trauma: The relationship between process, environment and counseling intervention. *Australian Counseling Psychologist, 11*(1), 39–44.

Pearlman, L. A. (1995). Self-care for trauma therapists: Ameliorating vicarious traumatization. In B. H. Stamm (Ed.), *Secondary traumatic stress: Self-care issues for clinicians, researchers, and educators* (pp. 51–64). Lutherville, MD: Sidran Press.

Pearlman, L. A., & Saakvitne, K. W. (1995a). *Trauma and the therapist: Countertransference and vicarious traumatization in psychotherapy with incest survivors.* New York: Norton.

Pearlman, L. A., & Saakvitne, K. W. (1995b). Treating traumatized therapists with vicarious traumatization and secondary traumatic stress disorders. In C. Figley

(Ed.), *Compassion fatigue: Coping with secondary traumatic stress disorder in those who treat the traumatized* (pp. 150–177). New York: Brunner/Mazel.

Putnam, F. W. (1989). *Diagnosis and treatment of multiple personality disorder.* New York: Guilford Press.

Raphael, B. (1986). *When disaster strikes: How individuals and communities cope.* New York: Basic Books.

Robinson, R.C., & Mitchell, J. T. (1993). Evaluation of psychological debriefings. *Journal of Traumatic Stress, 6*(3), 367–382.

Saakvitne, K. W., Pearlman, L. A., & the Staff of the Traumatic Stress Institute. (1996). *Vicarious traumatization: A workbook for professionals.* New York: Norton.

Siporin, M. (1975). *Introduction to social work practice.* New York: MacMillan.

Talbot, A., Manton, M., & Dunn, P. J. (1992). Debriefing the debriefers: An intervention strategy to assist psychologists after a crisis. *Journal of Traumatic Stress, 5*(1), 45–62.

INDEX